Peace Education Programme

ISLAMIC CURRICULUM ON PEACE AND COUNTER-TERRORISM

Further Essential Reading

Peace Education Programme

ISLAMIC CURRICULUM ON PEACE AND COUNTER-TERRORISM

Further Essential Reading

MINHAJ-UL-QURAN INTERNATIONAL

FARID-E-MILLAT RESEARCH INSTITUTE

Published by
Minhaj Publications India Forum
Umaj Road, At & Post : Karjan - 391240
Dist. Vadodara, Gujarat
India

All proceeds from the books, literature and audio-visual media (all multimedia) delivered by Dr Muhammad Tahir-ul-Qadri are entirely donated to Minhaj-ul-Quran International (MQI).

Team of Compilers
Dr. Raheeq Ahmed Abbasi, Muhammad Afzal Qadri, Dr. Faizullah Baghdadi and Ajmal Ali Mujaddidi

Acknowledgements
Shaykh Sohail Ahmad Siddiqui, Dr. Mayanaz Syeda-Miandadi, Jawed Iqbal Tahiri, Waqas Amin, Raffiq Patel and Mohammed Ramzan al-Madani

ISBN: 978–1–908229–40–3
www.minhaj.org | www.minhajuk.org | www.minhaj.in
www.minhajpublications.com | www.minhajproductions.in

First Published January 2016
Printed by -Minhaj Publications India Forum
Production Unit -1 :130/582, Bakarganj, Kanpur - 208023,U. P. India

Under the direct guidance and supervision of

SHAYKH-UL-ISLAM DR MUHAMMAD TAHIR-UL-QADRI

The Islamic Curriculum on Peace and Counter-Terrorism was compiled by a team of research scholars who benefitted from the Shaykh's comprehensive and historic *Fatwa on Terrorism and Suicide Bombings*, and other published and unpublished works, as well as orations and lectures.

بِسْمِ اللَّهِ الرَّحْمَٰنِ الرَّحِيمِ

In the name of God, Most Compassionate, Ever-Merciful

Saying of God تعالى

﴿مَن قَتَلَ نَفۡسَۢا بِغَيۡرِ نَفۡسٍ أَوۡ فَسَادٖ فِي ٱلۡأَرۡضِ فَكَأَنَّمَا قَتَلَ ٱلنَّاسَ جَمِيعٗا﴾

Whoever kills a person (unjustly), except as a punishment for murder or (as a prescribed punishment for spreading) disorder in the land, it is as if he killed all of humanity. [Qur'ān 5:32]

Saying of the Prophet ﷺ

عَنْ أَبِي بَكْرَةَ رضي الله عنه عَنِ النَّبِيِّ ﷺ أَنَّهُ قَالَ: «إِنَّ دِمَاءَكُمْ وَأَمْوَالَكُمْ وَأَعْرَاضَكُمْ عَلَيْكُمْ حَرَامٌ، كَحُرْمَةِ يَوْمِكُمْ هَذَا، فِي شَهْرِكُمْ هَذَا، فِي بَلَدِكُمْ هَذَا، إِلَى يَوْمِ تَلْقَوْنَ رَبَّكُمْ».

Abū Bakra رضي الله عنه reported that the Prophet ﷺ said, 'Indeed, your blood and your property and your honour are inviolable, like the inviolability of this day of yours and this month of yours and this land of yours until the day you meet your Lord'. [al-Bukhārī and Muslim]

Saying of God ﷻ

﴿يَهْدِى بِهِ ٱللَّهُ مَنِ ٱتَّبَعَ رِضْوَٰنَهُۥ سُبُلَ ٱلسَّلَٰمِ﴾

By this Allah guides those who seek His pleasure to the paths to peace (and security). [Qur'ān 5:16]

Saying of the Prophet ﷺ

«الْـمُؤْمِنُ مَنْ أَمِنَهُ النَّاسُ عَلَى أَنْفُسِهِمْ وَأَمْوَالِـهِمْ».

The true believer [*mu'min*] is he whom people trust with regard to their lives and their properties. [Aḥmad b. anbal and Ibn Mājah]

SHAYKH-UL-ISLAM DR MUHAMMAD TAHIR-UL-QADRI

Shaykh-ul-Islam Dr Muhammad Tahir-ul-Qadri was born in 1951 in the city of Jhang, Pakistan, hailing from a family of Islamic saints, scholars and teachers. His formal religious education was initiated in Medina at the age of 12 in *Madrasa al-ʿUlūm al-Sharʿiyya*, a traditional school situated in the blessed house of the Companion of the Prophet Muhammad ﷺ, Abū Ayyūb al-Anṣārī ؓ. He completed the traditional studies of classical and Arabic sciences under the tutelage of his father and other eminent scholars of the time. He continued to travel around the Islamic world in the pursuit of sacred knowledge, and studied under many famous scholars of Mecca, Medina, Syria, Baghdad, Lebanon, the Maghreb, India and Pakistan, and received around five hundred authorities and chains of transmission from them in hadith and classical Islamic and spiritual sciences. Amongst them is an unprecedented, unique and highly honoured chain of authority which connects him, through four teachers, to al-Shaykh ʿAbd al-Razzāq, the son of al-Shaykh ʿAbd al-Qādir al-Jīlānī al-Ḥasanī al-Ḥusaynī (of Baghdad), al-Shaykh al-Akbar Muḥyī al-Dīn b. ʿArabī [(the author of al-Futūḥāt al-Makkiyya) (Damascus)] and Imam Ibn Ḥajar al-ʿAsqalānī, the great hadith authority of Egypt. Through another chain he is linked to Imam Yūsuf b. Ismāʿīl al-Nabhānī directly via only one teacher. His chains of transmission are published in two of his *thabts* (detailed lists): *al-Jawāhir al-Bāhira fī al-Asānīd al-Ṭāhira* and *al-Subul al-Wahabiyya fī al-Asānīd al-Dhahabiyya*.

In the academic sphere, Dr Qadri received a First Class Honours Degree from the University of the Punjab in 1970. After earning his MA in Islamic studies with University Gold Medal in 1972 and achieving his LLB in 1974, Dr Qadri began to practise law in the district courts of Jhang. He moved to Lahore in 1978 and joined the University of the Punjab as a lecturer in law and completed his doctorate in Islamic Law. He was later appointed as a professor of Islamic Law and was head of the department of Islamic legislation for LLM.

Dr Qadri was also a jurist advisor to the Federal Shariat Court and Appellate Shariah Bench of the Supreme Court of Pakistan and advisor on the development of Islamic Curricula to the Federal Ministry of Education. Within a short span of time, Dr Qadri emerged as one of Pakistan's leading Islamic jurists and scholars and one of the world's most renowned and leading authorities on Islam. A prolific author, researcher and orator, Dr Qadri has written around one thousand books, of which more than four hundred and fifty have been published, and has delivered over six thousand lectures (in Urdu, English and Arabic) on a wide range of subjects.

In 2010, Shaykh-ul-Islam Dr Muhammad Tahir-ul-Qadri issued his historic and world-renowned fatwa on the critical matter of suicide bombings and terrorism carried out in the name of Islam. It has been regarded as a significant and historic step, the first time that such an explicit and unequivocal decree against the perpetrators of terror has been broadcast so widely. The original fatwa was written in Urdu, and amounts to 600 pages of research and references from the Qur᾿ān, hadith, the opinions of the Companions ﷺ, and the widely accepted classical texts of Islamic scholarship. This historic work has been published in English, Indonesian and Hindi, while translation into Arabic, Norwegian, Danish, Spanish, French and other major languages is also in process. The Islamic Research Academy of Jamia al-Azhar Egypt wrote a detailed description of the fatwa and verified its contents. It gained worldwide media attention and acclaim as an indispensable tool in the intellectual and ideological struggle against violent extremism.

Also Dr Qadri is the founder and head of Minhaj-ul-Quran International (MQI), an organisation with branches and centres in more than ninety countries around the globe; he is the chairman of the Board of Governors of Minhaj University Lahore, which is chartered by the Government of Pakistan; he is the founder of

Minhaj Education Society, which has established more than 600 schools and colleges in Pakistan; and he is the chairman of Minhaj Welfare Foundation, an organisation involved in humanitarian and social welfare activities globally.

Dr Qadri has spent his life, and especially the last decade, in an indefatigable effort to counter religious extremism and promote peace and harmony between communities. His painstaking research into the Qur'ān, hadith and classical Islamic authorities has resulted in landmark works, some published, and others soon to be published, demonstrating Islam as a religion that not only safeguards human rights, but promotes peace, tolerance and socioeconomic progress. He has travelled extensively to lecture at the invitation of government and non-government agencies, and has organised and took part in international conferences in order to promote peace. He has arrayed spiritual and educational training programmes across the Western world with a focus on addressing the roots of religious extremism. He is recognised for his commitment to interfaith dialogue, with over 12,000 people attending his Peace for Humanity Conference in 2011, probably the largest interfaith gathering ever held in the UK, and which announced the London Declaration, a charter for world peace, signed online by a quarter of a million people. He has been politically active in his native Pakistan, organising massive pro-democracy and anti-corruption demonstrations. When not travelling, he is based in Canada, busy in his research activities and producing vital works of Islamic scholarship relevant to Muslims in this day and age.

Formulaic Arabic Expressions

(*Subḥānahū wa taʿālā*) an invocation to describe the Glory of Almighty Allah: 'the Exalted and Sublime'

(*Ṣalla-llāhu ʿalayhi wa ālihī wa sallam*) an invocation of God's blessings and peace upon the Prophet Muhammad and his family: 'God's blessings and peace be upon him and his family'

(*ʿAlayhis-salām*) an invocation of God's blessings and peace upon a Prophet or an angel: 'May peace be upon him'

(*ʿAlayhas-salām*) an invocation of God's blessings and peace upon a Prophet's mother, wife, daughter and other pious woman: 'May peace be upon her'

(*ʿAlayhimus-salām*) an invocation of God's blessings and peace upon two Prophets or two angels: 'May peace be upon both of them'

(*ʿAlayhimus-salām*) an invocation of God's blessings and peace upon three or more Prophets: 'May peace be upon them'

(*Raḍiya-llāhu ʿanhu*) an invocation of God's pleasure with a male Companion of the Prophet: 'May God be pleased with him'

(*Raḍiya-llāhu ʿanhā*) an invocation of God's pleasure with a female Companion of the Prophet: 'May God be pleased with her'

(*Raḍiya-llāhu ʿanhumā*) an invocation of God's pleasure with two Companions of the Prophet: 'May God be pleased with both of them'

(*Raḍiya-llāhu ʿanhum*) an invocation of God's pleasure with more than two Companions of the Prophet: 'May God be pleased with them'

Transliteration Key

ا/آ/ى	ā	ظ	ẓ
ب	b	ع	ʿ
ت	t	غ	gh
ث	th	ف	f
ج	j	ق	q
ح	ḥ	ك	k
خ	kh	ل	l
د	d	م	m
ذ	dh	ن	n
ر	r	ه	h
ز	z	و	w/ū
س	s	ي	y/ī
ش	sh	ة	a
ص	ṣ	ء	ʾ
ض	ḍ	أ	a
ط	ṭ	إ	i

Contents

Preface 1

Curriculum Details 9

Section I

Relations of Muslims and Non-Muslims 11

1. To Murder a Human Being is to Commit One of the Worst of the Major Sins 11
2. The Protection of Life, Property and Honour of Non-Muslims is amongst the Supreme Duties of Islam 12
3. The Prohibition of Killing Women, Children, the Elderly and Priests 15
4. The Unlawfulness of Killing Diplomats, Farmers, Traders and non-Combatants 17
5. Freedom of Faith and Beliefs for Non-Muslims 18
6. Justice in all Judgments and Rulings for Non-Muslims 20
7. Treating Non-Muslims with Piety and Excellence 21
8. Non-Revengeful, Forbearing and Tolerant Behaviour towards Non-Muslims 23

9. Fulfilment of Agreements and Covenants with Non-Muslims 25
10. Financial Support for the Elderly, Infirm and Feeble amongst the Non-Muslims 26
11. Extracts from Ibn al-Qayyim's *A kām Ahl al-Dhimma* 27
11.1 Entrance of non-Muslims in the Sacred Mosque 27
11.1.1 First Report 27
11.1.2 Second Report 27
11.1.3 Third Report 28
11.2 Visiting the non-Muslims when They Are Sick 28
11.3 Attending the Funerals of non-Muslims 29
11.4 Giving Condolences to non-Muslims 30
11.5 The Slaughtered Animals of the People of the Book 30
11.5.1 Rulings about Meat are the same for the People of Treaty and People at War 31
11.5.2 Issues Pertaining to the Animals' Meat of the People of the Book 32
11.5.3 An Important Point 32
11.6 The Permissibility of Marrying a Woman from the People of the Book 33
12. Categories of the Abodes (Formulating International Law for Developing Peace) 34

12.1 The Abode of Islam (Dār al-Islām) 34
12.1.1 How Does an Abode of Islam Morph into an Abode of Disbelief and Abode of War? 35
12.1.2 The Stringent Conditions for the Abode of War 35
12.1.3 The Rationale for The Stringent Conditions Regarding the Abode of War 35
12.1.4 The Inaptness of Declaring an Abode of Islam an Abode of Disbelief due to Predominant Corruption 36
12.1.5 Absolute Power and Dominance are a Must for a Place to Be Judged as an Abode of War 36
12.1.6 The Viewpoint of al-Thānwī on the Abode of War 36
12.1.7 A Country Practicing Islamic Teachings and Signs cannot be Declared an Abode of War 36
12.1.8 No Land can be Declared an Abode of War Only Due to Disbelievers' Rule and Authority 37
12.2.1 The Difference between the Abode of Treaty and the Abode of Reconciliation 37
12.2.2 Instructions to Fulfil Agreements with the Abode of Reconciliation 38
12.2.3 Preference of Reconciliation and Compromise for the Establishment of Peace 38
12.3 The Abode of Treaty (*Dār al-ʿAhd*) 39

12.3.1 Qur'ānic Injunction to Fulfil Agreements with an Abode of Treaty 39
12.3.1.1 A Temporary or Long-Term Treaty 39
12.3.1.2 The General Treaty of Peace and Reconciliation 40
12.3.1.2.1 The Pact of Medina 40
12.3.1.2.2 Developing Political Unity to Stabilize the State and Establish Peace 40
12.3.1.2.3 Allah's Messenger ﷺ is the Founder of the Concept of Integration 41
12.3.1.2.3 The Pact of Najrān 41
12.4 The Abode of Peace (*Dār al-Amn*) 42
12.4.1 The Hanafī Stance on the Abode of Islam 42
12.5 The Abode of War (*Dār al- arb*) 43
12.5.1 The Islamic Ruling for the non-Combatants 43
12.5.2 The Qur'ānic Injunction on Excellent Morality with non-Combatants 43
12.5.3 The Affectionate Behaviour of Medina towards non-Combatants 44
12.5.4 The Stand of the Imams and Hadith-Scholars on non-Combatants 44
12.5.5 Why Medina was Chosen for Migration 45
12.5.6 The Difference of Pace and Number Between the Meccan and Medinan People in Accepting Islam 45

12.6 The Prophet ﷺ Integrated the Jews and the Muslims into a Collective Unity Through the Pact of Medina 45
12.6.1 The Prophetic Pronouncement: "The Jews Together with the Muslims are One Nation" 46
12.6.2 The Implications of "The Jews of Banū ʿAwf will be a Part of the Muslim Community" 46
12.6.2.1 Imam Ibn al-Athīr al-Jazarī 46
12.6.2.2 Interpretation by al-Zamakhsharī 47
12.6.2.3 Interpretation by Ibn Abī ʿUbayd al-Harawī 47
12.7 Five other Jewish Tribes were also Included in One Community along with Muslims 47
12.8 Abyssinia—The Model Abode of Peace 48
12.9 The Difference Between the Christian Rule of Abyssinia and the Meccan Rule 48
12.10 The Holy Prophet ﷺ Declared Abyssinia "The Land of Truth" 49
12.10.1 The Negus had yet to Know about the Final Messenger 49
12.10.2 The Companions' Praise for the Negus and his Rule 50
12.10.3 Allah's Excellent Reward for Negus's Excellent Conduct with the Muslims 50

12.10.4 The Prophet's Excellent Bestowal for Negus's Benevolence Towards the Companions 50
12.10.5 When did the Negus Embrace Islam Formally? 51
12.11 The Loyalty of the Muslim Abyssinian Refugees to Abyssinia and its Relevance to the Modern World 51
12.11.1 An Analysis of Human Rights in Western and some Muslim Countries (towards the Categories of Abodes) 51
12.11.2 The Message of Islam—the Establishment of a Global Human Society 51
12.12 Afterword 52

Section 2
Islam on Love and Non-Violence 53

1. Islam—A True Religion of Love 53
1.1 The Supremacy of Love on Allah's Attributes 53
1.2 Love and Forgiveness—the Divine Attributes 53
1.3 The Grace of Love is Sent from the Heavens 55
1.4 The Origin of Divinity is Also Love 55
1.5 Divine Address to the Sinful 56
1.6 Love is also Manifested in Reward and Favour 57

1.7 Love Stimulates Submission to Divine Injunctions 57
1.8 Love will Make up the Deficiency of Pious Deeds 58
1.9 The Injunction to Love the Beloved and the Chosen Ones 59
1.10 Raising the Prophets ﷺ is a Manifestation of Allah's love for His Creation 59
1.11 The Holy Prophet's ﷺ Attributes and Excellence Manifest Love 59
1.12 The Universality of the Prophet's ﷺ Mercy Permeates with the Message of Love 60
1.13 Love and Kindness for non-Muslims 60
1.14 If You Seek Mercy, then Love 60
1.15 Love as the Recompense of Preaching the Faith through Messengership 61
1.16 The Non-Specific, Specific and Grand Intercession are also a Manifestation of Love 62
1.17 The Non-Specific, Specific and Grand Intercession are also a Manifestation of Love 62
1.18 Founding Principles of Islamic Law are Based on Love and Mercy 62
1.18.1 The Prophet's ﷺ Liking for Gentleness and Easiness as a Sign of Love 63
1.18.2 Islam did not Spread by the Sword! 63
1.18.3 Love and Brotherhood—the Identity of Believers 63

1.18.4 Ambit of Love Encompasses non-Muslims 64
1.19 Afterword 64
2. Messenger ﷺ of Mercy: The Embodiment of Love 64
2.1 The Personality of the Prophet ﷺ is the Paragon of Mercy and Love 65
2.2 The Prophet's ﷺ Attributes of Mercy and Love in Earlier Scriptures 66
2.3 Islam Protects the Rights of the Elderly and children 66
2.4 Shortening Prayer for Mercy and Compassion to Minors 67
2.5 Islam is a Religion [*Dīn*] of Gentleness and Clemency 68
2.6 Appreciation of Deeds Rests on Gentleness and Politeness 68
2.7 Imams and Hadith Scholars of Early Times on Leniency and Clemency 69
2.8 Conduct based on Extremism is Contrary to Islamic Teachings 70
2.8.1 Injunctions to Abstain from Violence and Extremism 70
2.8.2 Prophet's ﷺ Admonition to Perpetrators of Extremism in Religion 70
2.8.3 Extremists are Promised Eradication 71
2.9 No Philosophy is Comparable to Islam's Altruistic Teachings 71
3. The Sanctity of Blood and Human Dignity 71

3.1 The Inviolability of a Believer Exceeds that of the *Ka'ba* 71
3.2 Killing a Human is A Grave Sin like Disbelief 71
3.3 Murder of a Human is the Greatest Wrong Like Polytheism 72
3.4 Bloodshed is the Greatest of all Crimes 72
3.5 Killing a Muslim is a Greater Sin than Destroying the World 73
3.6 The Veneration of the Dead is Imperative in Islam 74
3.7 The Sanctity of Human Graves is Indispensable 74
4. The Protection of Life and Property of Non-Muslims 74
4.1 Islam Guarantees Safety of the Whole of Humanity without Religious Discrimination 74
4.2 The Strict Prohibition of Killing Women even in the Battlefield 75
4.3 Strict Prohibition against Killing Children in Battlefield 75
4.3.1 Killing Women and Children is Strife, not Jihad 76
4.4 The Prohibition of Killing Foreign Delegates 76
4.5 The Prohibition of Killing Religious Leaders 77
4.6 The Unlawfulness of Killing non-Muslim Traders and Farmers 77

4.7 The Unlawfulness of Killing non-Muslim Service Personnel 77
4.8 The Unlawfulness of Killing non-Muslims who are non-Combatants 78
4.9 The Prohibition of Destroying the Cattle, Crops and Properties of the Enemy 78
4.10 Summary 79
5. The Messenger's ﷺ Mercy and Compassion on Animals 79
5.1 The Prohibition of Torturing Animals and Birds 79
5.2 No Place for Target Killing in the Teaching of Islam 80
5.4 The Prohibition of Torture to Animals When Slaughtering 82
6. The Killers of Humankind are Terrorists 83
6.1 The Prophet Clearly Indicated the emergence of terrorists 83
6.2 Terrorism is an Act of Disbelief 84
6.3 Inciting Religious Sentiments to Commit mass murder by Brainwashing is The Kharijites Method 85
6.4 The Blameworthy Religious Innovations of the Kharijites and their Extremist Sentiments 85
6.5 Massacring Muslims due to Ideological Difference is a General Sign of Kharijites 86
6.6 Salient Features and Signs of Terrorist Kharijites 86

7. The Stringent Prophetic Command to Eliminate Kharijites and Terrorists 89
7.1 The Prophetic Decree: The Tribulation of the Kharijites Must be Eliminated 89
7.1.1 Total Elimination of the Kharijites is Obligatory 89
7.1.2 Important Commentaries from the Imams of Hadith 90
7.2 Do not be Deceived by The Outward Religious Appearance of the Kharijites 90
7.3 The Kharijites are the Worst of Creation 91
7.3.1 A Noteworthy Point 91
7.4 Military Operations Against Kharijite Terrorists Bring Plenteous Reward 91
7.5 Glad Tidings of Great Reward for the Troops Fighting the Kharijites 92
7.6 Good News for the Killers of Terrorists and for those Martyred by Terrorists 92
7.7 Condemnation of the Supporters of Kharijites 93
8. Some Essential Measures for the Elimination of Kharijites Epilogue 93
8.1 No Place for Violence in Islam and in the Conduct of the Holy Prophet 93
8.2 Those who are Merciful to Others Deserve Mercy 93
8.3 Erasing Extremist Ideology is Inevitable 94

8.4 The Need for Changes in Academic Curricula 94
8.5 O Most Noble of the Messengers! It is A Moment to Supplicate! 94

Section 3

Islam On Serving Humanity 95

1. Human Dignity and Serving Humanity 95
1.1 The Sanctity of Human Blood, Property and Honour 95
1.2 Dignifying Human Beings 101
1.3 Assisting People in Welfare and Righteous Acts 103
1.4 Providing what is Desired for People 104
1.5 Feeding the Meals 106
1.6 Clothing the Destitute 107
1.7 Facilitating the Deprived and Waiving his Debt 107
2. Serving Mankind Through Excellent Social Morality 108
2.1 Brotherhood and Affection in Society 108
2.2 Supplications and Well Wishes For Brothers in their Absence 109
2.3 Excellent Fulfilment of Promises 109
2.4 Covering the Faults and Protecting the Secrets of Others 110
2.5 Forgiving, Overlooking and Hiding the Faults of Others 110
2.6 Generosity and Preference for Others 111

2.7 Visiting the Ailing 111
2.8 Protecting the Rights of People 112
3. Serving Humanity Through Charity 113
3.1 Excellence of Charity and its Rewards 113
3.2 Excellence of Undisclosed Charitable Donation 113
3.3 Glad Tidings for Charitable Donors 114
3.4 Charity enhances longevity and protects from Hellfire 115
3.5 Spending on Family 115
3.6 Charity to Relatives 116
3.7 Helping the Poor and Freeing the Captives 116
4. Helping Humanity Through Promoting Knowledge and Reform 117
4.1 The Best Charity is Acquiring Knowledge and Imparting to Others 117
4.2 Promoting Reconciliation amongst People 118
4.3 Well-Wishing of People 118
4.4 Excelling in Virtuous Deeds in Serving Humanity 119
5. Serving Humanity through Elevating Human Values 119
5.1 Excelling in Virtuous Deeds in Serving Humanity 119
5.2 Excellent Conduct, Piety and Kindness with Parents 120
5.3 Excellent Conduct, Piety and Kindness with Women 121

5.4 Excellent Conduct, Love and Kindness with the Wife 121
5.5 Excellent Conduct, Love and Compassion of the Holy Prophet ﷺ with His Wives 122
5.6 Compassion and Benevolence with Offspring 122
5.7 Compassion and Benevolence with Daughters 123
5.8 Compassion and Benevolence with Children 124
5.9 Excellent Conduct and Compassion with Neighbours 124
5.10 Excellent Conduct and Benevolence with other People 125
5.11 Excellent Conduct and Compassion with Widows and Orphans 126
5.12 Excellent Conduct and Compassion with the Weak and Indigent 126
5.13 Excellent Conduct and Compassion with Slaves and Workers 127
5.14 Excellent Conduct and Compassion with the Guilty and Sinners 128
5.15 Honouring the Funeral 128
6. Serving Humanity through the Modernity of Moral Excellence 129
6.1 Merits of Excellence of Moral Character and Manners 129
6.2 Cheerfulness and an Open Countenance 129
6.3 Pleasing and Polite Conversation 130
6.4 Protecting the Tongue from Backbiting 130

6.5 Truthfulness and Trust 131
6.6 Balance and Moderation 132
6.7 Leniency and Gentleness 132
6.8 Self-Control and Abstaining from Rage 133
6.9 Love and Kind Heartedness 133

Section 4
Islam on Mercy and Compassion 135

1. On the Infinite Mercy of Almighty Allah 135
1.1 Allah has Written Mercy upon Himself 135
1.2 Allah has Written Mercy upon Himself 135
1.3 Allah is the Owner of Mercy 136
1.4 Allah Shows Mercy to Whom He Wills 136
1.5 Allah is the All-Merciful, the Compassionate 136
1.6 Allah is the Most Merciful of Those Who Show Mercy 136
1.7 Allah's Mercy is Boundless and Encompasses All Things 137
2. Islam is the Religion of Mercy, Ease and Moderation 149
3. The Holy Qur'ān as Mercy and Cure 159
4. On the Precedence of Allah's Mercy over His Wrath 161
5. On the One Hundred Parts of Allah's Mercy, and that Ninety-nine of them are Reserved for the Day of Resurrection 163

6. Of the Seventy Thousand People of the Prophet's Umma to whom Allah shall Grant Paradise without reckoning, Every Thousand amongst them shall take another Seventy Thousand 165
7. On the Seventy Thousand People of the Prophet's Umma to whom Allah shall Grant Paradise without Reckoning, and Every Single Person among Them will be Granted Additional Seventy Thousand to Enter Paradise with Him without Reckoning 167
8. On the Increase of Allah's Mercy to His Servants in the Reward They Receive for Good Deeds, and the Pardoning of Passing Thoughts and Sins 168
9. On Allah's Descent to the Lower Heavens and His Calling Out to His Servants 170
10. On Allah's Mercy for the Dissolute and Sinful 172
11. On Allah's Mercy for Animals, Birds and Other Creatures 175

Section 5

The Supreme Jihad 179

1. Jihad and its Kinds 179
2. *Jihād bi'n-Nafs*—Struggle against Self [A Spiritual Dimension] 180
2.1 The Real Striver Strives against the Lower Self 180

3. *Jihād bi'l 'Ilm*—Striving for Knowledge [Intellectual Dimension] 182

4. *Jihād bi'l 'Amal*—Striving for Promotion of Morality and Human Values [The Social Dimension] 183

4.1 Striving against Oppression and Injustice is Jihad 183

4.2 Striving for Promotion of Moral Values is Jihad 184

4.3 Serving the Parents is Jihad 184

4.4 Striving for Allah's Remembrance and Worship is Jihad 185

5. *Jihād bi'l Māl*—Striving to Resolve the Economic Deadlock of the Indigent [Economic Dimension] 185

5.1 Striving for Altruism and Alleviation of Poverty is Superior to Military Option 186

5.2 Striving for Social Welfare and Altruism 186

6. The Reward of a Reviver of a Sunna is equal to that of 100 Martyrs 187

7. Pilgrimage to the House of Allah is Jihad 188

8. Allah's Remembrance Surpasses Fighting for the Cause of Allah 189

Section 6

Muhammad ﷺ: The Merciful 191

1. The Holy Prophet ﷺ is Mercy Incarnate 191

1.1 There is No Other Prophet That Comes Close to the Prophet ﷺ in Mercy 191
1.2 Allah Made the Prophet ﷺ Mercy for the Worlds 192
1.3 Allah Has Made Him ﷺ the Prophet of Mercy 193
1.4 Allah Sent the Prophet ﷺ as Mercy 193
1.5 Allah Made the Prophet ﷺ Mercy Gifted to the Worlds 193
1.6 The Prophet's Mercy is from Allah's Mercy 194
1.7 Allah Made the Prophet ﷺ Mercy for the Believers 194
1.8 Allah Made the Prophet ﷺ Clement and Compassionate to the Believers 194
1.9 The Prophet ﷺ is Nearer to the Believers than Their Own Selves 194
1.10 The Prophet ﷺ is Nearer to the Other Prophets Than They are to Their Respective Communities 195
1.11 The Prophet's Quality of Humility 196
1.12 The Prophet ﷺ was Neither Stern nor Harsh 196
1.13 The Prophet's Avidity for the Believers' Welfare 197
1.14 The Prophet a Lightened the Burden upon His Community 197
1.15 Allah Made the Prophet ﷺ a Source of Peace and Protection for Humanity 198

1.16 The Prophet's Continued Supplication for His People in His Worldly Life and After His Passing 198
1.17 The Fact That the Prophet ﷺ Was a Warner Implies Mercy 199
1.18 The Relationship between the Splitting Open of the Prophet's Chest and Mercy 199
1.19 The Relationship between Mercy and Sublime Character 200
1.20 It is a Mercy of Allah that He Took the Soul of His Prophet ﷺ before His People 200
1.21 The Prophet's Mercy toward the Jinn 200
1.22 The Prophet ﷺ did not Invoke Allah to Destroy the Confederates during the Battle of Trench 201
1.23 Important Point 202
2. The Holy Prophet ﷺ is Mercy to All The Worlds 202
2.1 Benefits Extracted from the Qur'ānic Verse 202
3. The Holy Prophet ﷺ is Mercy for Everyone in This World 203
4. The Holy Prophet ﷺ is Peace and Protection for Every Human Soul in this World 209
5. The Holy Prophet's Rank as Mercy to the Worlds and His Compassion for All the Creation 210

6. The Holy Prophet's Mercy and Kindness toward Women 216
7. The Holy Prophet's Mercy and Kindness toward Infants, Young Children and Youth 222
8. The Holy Prophet's Mercy and Kindness toward the Weak, the Poor and the Indigent 229
9. The Holy Prophet's Mercy and Kindness toward Widows and Orphans 233
10. The Holy Prophet's Mercy and Kindness toward Slaves and Servants 236
11. The Holy Prophet's Mercy and Kindness toward the Sick and the Deceased 238
12. The Holy Prophet's Mercy and Kindness toward the Bedouin Arabs, the Ignorant and the Beggars 247
13. The Holy Prophet's Mercy and Kindness toward Disobedient and Sinful 249
14. The Holy Prophet's Mercy and Kindness toward the Hypocrites 251
15. The Holy Prophet's Mercy and Kindness toward Enemies, Disbelievers and Idolaters 254
16. The Holy Prophet's Mercy and Kindness toward the Non-Muslim Citizens and Those under an Agreement of Protection 261
17. The Holy Prophet's Mercy and Kindness toward Animals and Birds 263
18. The Holy Prophet's Mercy and Kindness toward Plants and Inanimate Objects 272

Section 7

Muhammad ﷺ: The Peacemaker 277

1. The Prophet's ﷺ Universal Message of Peace and Harmony 277
1.1 Preliminary Statement 277
1.2 Faith in Allah and His Messenger ﷺ—The Foundation Stone of Peace and Security 278
1.3 Prophet Muhammad ﷺ—Conjunction of all Divine Faiths 278
1.3.1 The Prophet's ﷺ Stopover at Medina, Mount Sinai and Bethlehem during His Ascension Journey 278
1.3.2 The Prophet's ﷺ Address in *al-Aqṣā* Mosque, Jerusalem 279
1.3.3 Universality of the Prophetic Message 279
1.3.4 Declaration of the Moderate Character of Islamic Community 279
1.4 The Peace-Loving Nature of Islamic Faith 280
2. Peace Building Character of the Holy Prophet ﷺ 280
2.1 Preliminary Statement 281
2.2 Peacebuilding in the Holy Prophet's Young Life 281
2.3 Statement of Khadija ﷺ, his First Wife, on the Peace Loving Character of the Holy Prophet ﷺ 281

2.4 Statement of Jaʿfar in Abyssinian Royal Court on the Humanistic Character of the Holy Prophet ﷺ 281
2.5 The Prophet's Commandment of Peace to the Medinan Delegates at al-ʿAqaba 282
2.6 The Prophet's Message of Peace to Medinans at His Arrival in Medina 282
2.7 The Prophet's Instructions of Peace to the People of Khaybar 282
2.8 Declaration of Peace and Security for non-Muslim Inhabitants of Mecca at its Conquest 282
2.9 The Prophet's Address on Peace and Security at Tabūk 283
2.10 Proclamation of the Charter of Peace & Human Rights at his Last Hajj 283
2.11 General Policy Statements of the Holy Prophet ﷺ for Peacemaking 283
2.12 Continuity of Prophetic Policies for Peacemaking in the Caliphate Period 283
3. Seeking Inner and Outer Peace through Self Purification and Spiritual Transformation 284
3.1 Preliminary Statement 284
3.2 The Ideal of Allah's Pleasure Leads to Inner and Outer Peace 284
3.3 Each Act of the Believer is for Allah's Pleasure 284
3.4 The Ideal of Allah's Pleasure Leads to the Righteous Character 285

3.5 The Love of Faith: A Fountainhead of Peace and Tranquillity 285
3.6 The Anatomy of Divine Pursuit 286
3.7 The Genetics of Peaceful and Righteous Character 287
4. Establishing Peace through Mercy, Forgiveness and Moderation 287
4.1 Preliminary Statement 287
4.2 Islam Lightens the Burden of Obligations 287
4.3 Islam Teaches Easiness and does not Approve of Harshness 288
4.4 The Holy Prophet ﷺ Chose the Easier of the Two Options 289
4.5 The Best of Islamic Religion is the Middle Course and Moderation 289
4.6 Prohibition of Extremism and Commandment of Moderation 290
4.7 No Soul should be Burdened beyond its Ability 290
4.8 Things be Made Easy so that People may not Feel Aversion 291
4.9 Prescription of a Balanced and Moderate Way of Life 292
4.10 Extremism Destroys Communities 293
4.11 Recommendation of Lenience and Tolerance 294
4.12 Allah's Pleasure Lies in Helping and Forgiving Behaviour 295
4.13 Social and Economic Empowerment of the neglected segments of society 295

4.13.1 Providing what is Desired for People 296
4.13.2 Charity Encompasses the Whole of Society 296
4.13.3 Charity to Relatives 296
4.13.4 Helping the Poor and Freeing the Captives 296
4.13.5 Facilitating the Deprived 296
4.13.6 The Reward of Someone who Helps People in Difficulties 297
4.14 Everything is Permissible unless Expressly Prohibited 297
4.15 Legal Dispensations under Pressing Needs 298
4.16 Summary with Some Examples 298
4.16.1 Obligatory Prayer 299
4.16.2 Obligatory Fasting 299
4.16.3 Obligatory Charity 299
4.16.4 Performance of Hajj 299
4.16.5 Tenets of Faith 299
4.16.6 Acts of Worship 300
4.16.7 Manner of Invitation 300
4.16.8 Human Interactions 300
4.16.9 Marriage 300
4.16.10 Family Relations 300
4.16.11 International Relations 301
4.16.12 Sins and Punishments 301
5. Establishing Peace Through Human Rights 301
5.1 Preliminary Statement 301

5.2 The Right to Protection of Life 302
5.3 The Right to Freedom from Slavery 302
5.4 The Right to Liberty and Security of Person 302
5.5 The Right to Justice 303
5.6 The Right to Religious Freedom 304
5.7 The Right to Equality and Rule of Law 304
5.7.1 Ensuring Human Dignity and Equality 305
5.7.2 Sacredness of Human Life 305
5.8 The Right to be Heard 305
5.9 The Protection of the Rights of non-Muslims 305
5.10 The Protection of Women's Rights 306
5.10.1 The Prohibition of Domestic Violence and Forced Marriage 306
5.10.2 Integration of the Women into the Mainstream of Social Struggle 307
5.10.3 Integration of the Women into the Mainstream of Social Struggle 307
5.11 The Protection of the Rights of Parents 307
5.12 The Protection of the Rights of Children and Orphans 308
5.13 Protection of the Rights of Neighbours 310
5.14 Protection of the Rights of Birds and Animals 311
5.14.1 Saving a Dog's Life 312
5.14.2 The Sin of Taking a Cat's Life 312
6. Establishing Peace through Conflict Resolution 313

6.1 Peacemaking through Building Relationships and Resolving Conflicts 313
6.2 Collaborative Actions and Solidarity 313
6.3 Islamic Community (Ummah) 314
6.4 Inclusivity and Participatory Process 314
6.5 Right to people's participation in collective activities 314
7. Establishing Peace Through Charity, Altruism and Benevolence 314
7.1 Preliminary Statement 314
7.2 The Qur'ānic Approach to Charity and Righteousness 315
7.3 The Concepts of Ownership, Trust and Charity 315
7.4 The Benevolent Character of Allah's Beloved Servants 316
7.5 Whether Affluent or Poor, They Give to Charity 316
7.6 Act of Altruism and Charity Purifies the Self and Brings Peace 316
7.7 Charity and Benevolence Affirm the Faith 317
7.8 Miserliness is Declared as a Form of Hypocrisy 317
7.9 The Altruistic Character of the Companions of the Prophet Muhammad 317
7.9 The Altruistic Character of the Companions of the Prophet Muhammad 318

7.10 The Prophet ﷺ Established the Society of Benevolence 319
7.11 A Comparison of Justice and Benevolence 319
8. Establishing Peace through Fraternization and Integration 320
Fraternization 320
8.1 The Tribal Set-up of Medina 320
8.2 Integration of Meccan Immigrants in Medi-nan Society through Fraternization 320
8.3 Creating a Nation through the Constitution of Medina 320
Integration 321
8.4 The Prophet a Integrated the Jews and the Muslims into One Community 321
8.5 The Prophetic Pronouncement: "The Jews Together with the Muslims are One Nation" 321
8.6 The Implications of the Prophetic Statement "The Jews of Banū ʿAwf together with the Muslims are one Nation" 321
8.6.1 Interpretation by Ibn al-Athīr al-Jazarī 322
8.6.2 Interpretation by al-Zamakhsharī 322
8.6.3 Interpretation by Ibn Abī ʿUbayd al-Harawī 322
8.7 Five other Jewish Tribes were also Included in One Community along with Muslims 322
9. Establishing Peace through Education 323

9.1 Pre-Hijra Emphasis on Literacy, Knowledge and Education — 323
9.2 Formulation and Enforcement of Education System — 323
9.2.1 The Prophet ﷺ Himself would Manage Time to Educate the Illiterate Community — 324
9.2.1.1 POWs Appointed as Teachers — 324
9.2.1.2 Establishment of Boarding School—al-Ṣuffa—and Appointment of Teachers for Different Faculties of Knowledge — 324
9.2.1.3 Trained Teachers Dispatched as Trainers of Different Tribes — 324
9.2.1.4 The Prophetic Policy of Moving People Closer to Medina for Education — 325
9.2.1.5 70 Teachers Sent to Najd to Train Neigh-bouring Tribes — 325
9.2.1.6 Healthy Influx of Students — 325
9.2.1.7 Nine Mosque Schools in Medina — 325
9.2.1.8 The Study Circles and Worship Circles — 326
9.2.1.9 The Prophet's Supervision and Control — 326
9.2.1.10 Sudden Increase in the Literacy Rate — 326
9.2.2.1 The Qur'ānic Commandment for Written Record of Trade Transactions — 326
9.2.2.2 Expansion of the Scope of Written Work — 327
9.2.2.3 Prophetic Letters and Traditions — 327
9.2.2.4 Introduction of Seals and Stamps — 327

9.2.2.5 Commencement of Specialization and Research Work 327
9.2.2.6 Teachers Disallowed to Accept Gifts from Pupils 328
9.2.2.7 Promotion of Foreign Languages and Their Experts 328
9.2.2.8 The Curricula and Syllabi Development 328
9.2.2.9 Emphasis on Women Education 328
10. Establishing Intercommunal Peace through Tolerant and Compassionate Behaviour 329
10.1 Preliminary Statement 329
10.2 Freedom of Faith and Beliefs for Non-Muslims 329
10.3 Absolute Justice for Non-Muslims 330
10.4 Treating Non-Muslims with Piety and Excellence 332
10.5 Non-Revengeful, Forbearing and Tolerant Behaviour towards Non-Muslims 332
10.6 The Fulfilment of Agreements and Covenants with Non-Muslims 332
10.7 Financial Support for the Elderly, Infirm and Feeble amongst the Non-Muslims 332
11. Prophetic Reconciliatory Efforts and Peace Treaties with Different Nations, Tribes and Communities 333
11.1 Peace Treaty with the People of Ḍamra (Sa-far 2 ah) 333

11.2 Peace Treaty with the People of Zurʿa and Rabʿa 333

11.3 Peace Treaty of Hudaybia (6 ah) 333

11.3.1 The Terms of the Hudaybia Treaty 334

11.3.2 Allah Declared the Treaty of Hudaybia 'A Clear Victory' 334

11.4 Peace Treaty of St. Catherine (Sinai, Egypt) 334

11.5 Peace Treaty with the Jews of Khaybar (7 ah) 334

11.6 Peace Treaty with the People of Ṭāʾif and Thaqīf (8—9 ah) 335

11.7 Peace Treaty with the Christians of Najran (8 ah) 335

11.8 The Prophet's Letter to the Christians of Najran (8 ah) 335

11.9 Peace Treaty with the Jews of Tayma (9 ah) 335

11.10 Peace Treaties with the Peoples of Banu Janba, Hayna, Maqnaʿ, Ayla, Jarbā and Adhruh (9 ah) 336

11.11 Peace Treaty with the Jews of South and East of Arabia (9 ah) 336

11.12 The Prophet's Letters to the Different Tribes Granting them Peace and Security 336

11.12.1 Letter to Banū al-Khashkhāsh 336

11.12.2 Letter to the People of Jabl Ti āma 337

11.12.3 Letter to Different Tribes of the Jews 337

11.13 Peace Treaty with the People of Ghifār (2 ah) 337
12. *Al-Qitāl* (Defensive Warfare) and Qur'ānic Peacemaking Mechanism 337
12.1 Peacemaking Struggle in Meccan Period 337
12.2 Permission of Defensive War for Maintain-ing Peace during the Medinan Period 338
12.3 The Prophet a Preferred Diplomacy over War for the Sake of Peace 338
12.4 Historical Background of the Permission for Defensive War 338
12.5 The Prophet a Imposed further Conditions and Limits on a Lawful War in Repulsion of Ag-gression and Prevention of Tyranny 338
Recommended Books for Further Study and Teaching 339
Recommended Lectures for Further Study and Teaching 345
Bibliography 377

Preface

THE WORLD IS FACING A GREAT DILEMMA DUE TO DESPICABLE, inhumane and barbaric acts of terrorism, indiscriminate killings, warfare, anarchy and disorder, and suicide bombings over the past two decades. This is an international phenomenon which is being sponsored by many elements to further their clandestine motives. It is not only destroying the peace of any specific region, group or country but is destroying world peace. Besides many Muslim countries, youth living in the U.K., Canada, U.S., and other western countries, who do not have conceptual clarity regarding Islam, are wrongly considering terrorism and indiscriminate killing to be Jihad and are being drawn towards it.

The second disturbing issue with regards to this is that the terrorists declare their evil goals to be part and parcel of the Islamic concept of Jihad. Furthermore they speak of enforcing the Islamic Shariah according to their extremist and terrorist ideology. They use the slogan of '*Iʿlāʾ Kalima aqq*' (raising the banner for the truth); they also call for the re-establishment of the Caliphate as part of their ideology; and they use the Islamic terminologies and concepts of Fiqh (Islamic Jurisprudence) to legally justify their claims. By quoting the Qurʾān, hadith and texts from the books of Fiqh out of context, they influence common Muslims who are not acquainted with the true teachings of Islam, especially youngsters.

No part of the world is safe from the brutal atrocities carried out by terrorists in the name of Islam. At the international level, the sanctity of life has been violated in Iraq, Syria, Yemen, Afghanistan, Sudan, Nigeria and Somalia etc.; people are being indiscriminately shot and killed, and videos of beheadings are being made in order to spread terror and fear among people. Pakistan is also not safe from this evil; in one instance, football is being played using the heads of fallen soldiers, then on the other, barbaric acts of indiscriminate killing of innocent children take place in Peshawar. This issue is not confined to a single country but is of international importance.

Be it the 9/11 attacks on the U.S. or 7/7 in the U.K., the Mumbai attack or the Charlie Hebdo assault in France; the indiscriminate killing of students in a university in Kenya or the wicked atrocities carried out by terrorist groups in Iraq, Syria, Libya and Yemen; the two decade war in Afghanistan or the attacks on markets, mosques, army institutions and schools in Pakistan; there is one point in common with regards to the groups that perpetrate such attacks, that they consider these to be Jihad and that they legitimise them using self-concocted interpretations of Islamic concepts and ideologies.

In view of this, it is a need of the time to prepare every segment of society, conceptually, at the international level against the terrorist ideology and extremist concepts in the light of Islamic teachings and universal truths. There is a need for practical steps to be taken in order to eliminate extremism from society so that those who give ideological and conceptual support and backing to the terrorists can also be eliminated once and for all. Furthermore, there is a need to provide authentic, comprehensive material against extremism to all people, from every walk of life, according to their needs, so that fanaticism and extremism, the conceptual and ideological supporters of terrorism, can be eliminated.

Shaykh-ul-Islam Dr Muhammad Tahir-ul-Qadri has comprehensively struggled against extremism, conservatism, sectarianism and terrorism at the ideological front for the last 34 years. His historic Fatwa against terrorism and extremism comprising of irrefutable evidences was published in 2010 in book form and has since been available in several countries. This comprehensive Fatwa was published in Urdu, English, Hindī and Indonesian, and is in the process of being published in Arabic, Norwegian, Danish, French, German and Spanish. Dozens of books by Shaykh-ul-Islam that are against extremist ideology and are based upon the Islamic teachings of love, mercy, peace, mutual harmony and non-violence are widely available, some of which are given below:

1. Fatwa on Terrorism and Suicide Bombings
2. Islam on Mercy and Compassion
3. Muhammad ﷺ: The Merciful

4. Muhammad ﷺ: The Peacemaker
5. Relations of Muslims and non-Muslims
6. Islam on Serving Humanity
7. Islam on Love & Non-Violence
8. The Supreme Jihad
9. Islamic Means of Peace
10. Peace, Integration and Human Rights
11. Teachings of Islam Series: Peace and Submission
12. Teachings of Islam Series: Faith
13. Teachings of Islam Series: Spiritual & Moral Excellence
14. Islamic Spirituality & Modern Science (The Scientific Basis of Sufism)
15. Fatwa: Dehshat Gardī aur Fitna-e Khawārij (comprehensive historic fatwa)
16. Islām aur Ahl-e Kitāb (Taʿlīmāt-e Qurʾān o Sunnat aur Taṣrīḥāt-e Aʾimma)
17. al-Jihād al-Akbar
18. Islām mein Maḥabbat awr ʿAdm-e Tashaddud
19. al-Bayān fī Raḥma al-Mannān (Raḥmat-e Ilāhī par Īmān Afroz Aḥādīth kā Majmūʿa)
20. al-Wafā fī Raḥma al-Nabī al-Muṣṭafā ﷺ (Jamīʿ Khalq par Ḥazūr Nabī Akram ﷺ kī Raḥmat aur Shafaqat)
21. Silsila Arbaʿīnāt: al-ʿAṭāʾ al-ʿAmīm fī Raḥma al-Nabī al-ʿAẓīm ﷺ
22. al-Aḥkām al-Sharʿiyya fī Kawn al-Islām Dīn li Khidma al-Insāniyya (Islām aur Khidmat-e Insāniyyat)

The need of the time was to take it a step further, and in light of these academic resources, prepare courses of varied duration for people of different walks of life, so that through them every individual in society can be made practically firm; so that not only themselves but the ideologies of people at every level is safeguarded from the extremist version. They can then propagate the true Islamic teachings and conduct that are based upon peace, love and tolerance in their perspective circles of influence.

Currently the most important issue for mankind is the restoration of peace. No single institution, state or university has come forward to achieve the urgent and pressing need to introduce 'establishing peace, and countering terrorism and extremism' as a subject and curriculum. Shaykh-ul-Islam Dr Muhammad Tahir-ul-Qadri has comprehended this urgent and immediate need and has decided that Minhāj-ul-Qur'ān International, according to its constructive and academic customs, will fulfil this responsibility. In order to achieve this, the research institute of Minhāj-ul-Qur'ān International, the Farid-e-Millat Research Institute (FMRi) has compiled the 'Islamic Curriculum on Peace and Counter-Terrorism' under the direct instructions and supervision of Shaykh-ul-Islam. It has been prepared for five different segments of society. He not only monitored every stage of every curriculum but also examined the final compendiums. In this way the credit of completing this important project also goes to Minhāj-ul-Qur'ān International. This is a unique gift from Minhāj-ul-Qur'ān International not only for the Muslim community, but for the whole of humanity. God willing, this curriculum will prove to be a great step in restoring peace with regards to the ideological and conceptual training of various sections of society.

This particular curriculum has been compiled for students of colleges, universities and other educational institutions and youngsters; so that instead of being influenced by extremist ideologies they can get acquainted with the Islamic concept of peace and harmony and become responsible and productive members of society.

A specific methodology has been used in this curriculum in order to increase its content with a reduction in its length. Main headings are followed by the subheading 'Additional Readings for Teachers and Students', which is followed by complete references from the Holy Qur'ān, hadith and other books and resources where material regarding the subject in hand can be found. Quoting the text of all the references would have rendered the syllabus to be increasingly voluminous. However, text giving various explanations have been included in some parts where needed.

Similarly, at the end of the 'Additional Readings for Teachers and Students' sections, references from the books of Shaykh-ul-Islam Dr Muhammad Tahir-ul-Qadri have been provided which give the text, translation and explanations of the main references under the particular subject. In order to fully benefit from this curriculum, it is vital to refer to the relevant books authored by Shaykh-ul-Islam.

It is to be noted that a detailed list of all relevant books and English lectures by Shaykh-ul-Islam has been included at the end of the curriculum as an aid for instructors and teachers of this curriculum. Furthermore a complete bibliography of all references used in the curriculum is included at the end.

The National Peace Education Curriculum (NPEC) compiled under the instructions and guidance of Shaykh-ul-Islam Dr Muhammad Tahir-ul-Qadri is immensely comprehensive. If those in power fully adopt this national curriculum in order to promote moderate ideology and arrange these courses for the relevant segments of society, then we can guarantee that the evils of conservatism, fanaticism and extremism will be totally eradicated from society—God willing. It will no longer become possible for extremist ideology to be provided to terrorists by extremist preachers. God willing, society will become an embodiment of peace, security, tolerance, moderation and mutual cooperation according to the true teachings of Islam.

Dr Raheeq Ahmad Abbasi
Farid-e-Millat Research Institute (FMRi)

Curriculum Details

SECTION I

Relations of Muslims and Non-Muslims

1. To Murder a Human Being is to Commit One of the Worst of the Major Sins

Essential Reading:

1. Dr Tahir-ul-Qadri, Relations of Muslims and Non-Muslims, Ch:1, pp.7-15.

Additional Readings for Teachers and Students:

1. al-Bukhārī in *al-Ṣaḥīḥ*: *Kitāb al-Ḥajj* [The Book of Pilgrimage], chapter: "The sermon during the days of Mina," 2:620 §1654.
2. Muslim in *al-Ṣaḥīḥ*: *Kitāb al-qasāma wa al-muḥāribīn wa al-qiṣāṣ wa al-diyāt* [The Book of Apportioning Wealth, Warmongers, Legal Retribution and Bloodwit], chapter: "The inviolability of a believer's blood, honour and property," 3:1305–1306 §1679.
3. al-Bukhārī in *al-Ṣaḥīḥ*: *Kitāb al-diyāt* [The Book of Blood Money], chapter: "Whoever Kills a Believer Intentionally, His Recompense is Hell," 6:2517 §6470.
4. al-Bayhaqī in *al-Sunan al-kubrā*, 8:21 §15637.
5. al-Bukhārī in *al-Ṣaḥīḥ*: *Kitāb al-diyāt* [The Book of Blood Money], chapter: "Whoever Kills a Believer intentionally," 6:2517 §6471.
6. Muslim in *al-Ṣaḥīḥ*: *Kitāb al-qasāma wa al-muḥāribīn wa al-qiṣāṣ wa al-diyāt* [The Book of Taking an Oath, Warmongers, Legal Retribution

and Bloodwit], chapter: "The (cases of) Bloodshed would be Decided first of all on the Day of Resurrection," 3:1304 §1678.

7. Aḥmad b. Ḥanbal in *al-Musnad*, 1:442 §4213.
8. al-Tirmidhī in *al-Sunan: Kitāb al-diyāt* [The Book of Blood Money], chapter: "The Legal Ruling Concerning Blood," 4:17 §1397.
9. al-Nasā'ī in *al-Sunan*: *Kitāb taḥrīm al-dam* [The Book on the Prohibition of Bloodshed], chapter: "The Sanctity of Blood," 7:83 §3994.
10. Ibn Mājah in *al-Sunan: Kitāb al-Diyāt* [The Book of Blood Money], chapter: "The Gravity of unjustly Killing a Muslim," 2:873 §2615.
11. Ibn Ḥibbān in *al-Ṣaḥīḥ*, 16:339 §7344.
12. Abū Ya'lā in *al-Musnad*, 9:35 §5099.
13. Ibn al-Mubārak in *al-Musnad*, 1:59 §97.
14. Ibn Abī al-Dunyā in *al-Ahwāl*, p. 190 §183.
15. Ibn Abī 'Āṣim in *al-Diyāt*, p. 2 §2.
16. al-Bayhaqī in *Shu'ab al-īmān*, 4:345 §5344.
17. Ibn Abī al-Dunyā in *al-Ahwāl*, p. 190 §183.
18. Ibn Abī 'Āṣim in *al-Diyāt*, p. 2 §2.
19. al-Bayhaqī in *Shu'ab al-īmān*, 4:345 §5344.
20. Abū Manṣūr al-Māturīdī, *Ta'wilāt Ahl al-Sunna*, 3:501.
21. Abū afṣ al- anbalī, *al-Lubāb fī 'ulūm al-Kitāb*, 7:301.
22. Qur'ān 4:93.
23. Qur'ān 25:68.
24. Qur'ān 6:151.
25. Ibn Kathīr, *Tafsīr al-Qur'ān al-'Aẓīm*, 1:535.

2. The Protection of Life, Property and Honour of Non-Muslims is amongst the Supreme Duties of Islam

Essential Reading:

1. Dr Tahir-ul-Qadri, Relations of Muslims and Non-Muslims, Ch:2, pp.15-35.

Additional Readings for Teachers and Students:

1. Qur'ān 2:179.
2. Qur'ān 2:188.
3. Qur'ān 5:45.
4. Qur'ān 7:165.
5. Qur'ān 17:33.
6. al-Bukhārī in *al-Ṣaḥīḥ*: *Kitāb al-jizya* [The Book of Annual Security Tax for Non-Muslims Living in an Islamic State], chapter: "The Sin of Someone Who Kills a Non-Muslim Citizen without his having Committed a Crime," 3:1155 §2995; and in *Kitāb al-Diyāt* [The Book of Blood Money], chapter: "The Sin Of Someone Who Kills a Soul Without His Having Committed A Crime," 6:2533 §6516.
7. Ibn Mājah in *al-Sunan*: *Kitāb al-diyāt* [The Book of Blood Money], chapter:"Someone Who Kills a Non-Muslim Citizen," 2:896 §2686.
8. al-Bazzār in *al-Musnad*, 6:368 §2383.
9. al-Nasā'ī in *al-Sunan*: *Kitāb al-qasāma* [The Book of Taking an Oath], chapter: "The Gravity of Killing a Non-Muslim Citizen," 8:25 §4750; and in *al-Sunan al-Kubrā*, 4:221 §6952.
10. Aḥmad b. Ḥanbal in *al-Musnad*, 2:186§6745.
11. al-Bazzār in *al-Musnad*, 6:361 §3273.
12. al-Ḥākim in *al-Mustadrak*, 2:137 §2580.
13. Ibn al-Jārūd in *al-Muntaqā*, 1:212 §834.
14. al-Tirmidhī in *al-Sunan*: *Kitāb al-diyāt* [The Book of Blood Money], chapter: "What has Come to us Concerning Someone Who Kills a Non-Muslim Citizen," 4:20 §1403.
15. Ibn Mājah in *al-Sunan*: *Kitāb al-diyāt* [The Book of Blood Money], chapter: "Someone Who Kills a Non-Muslim Citizen," 2:896 §2687.
16. Abū Ya'lā in *al-Musnad*, 11:335 §6452.
17. al- ākim in *al-Mustadrak*, 2:138 §2581. 18. al-Bayhaqī in *al-Sunan al-kubrā*, 9:205 §18511.
18. Aḥmad b. anbal in *al-Musnad*, 4:237, 5:369 §§18097, 23177.
19. al-Nasā'ī in *al-Sunan*: *Kitāb al-qasāma* [The Book of Taking an Oath], chapter: "The Enormity of Murdering a Non-Muslim Citizen," 8:25 §4749; and in *al-Sunan al-kubrā*, 4:221 §6951.
20. al-Mundhirī in *al-Targhīb wa al-Tarhīb*, 3:204 §3695.
21. al-Nasā'ī in *al-Sunan*: *Kitāb al-qasāma* [The Book of Taking an Oath], chapter: "The Enormity of Murdering a Non-Muslim Citizen," 8:25 §4748; and in *al-Sunan al-kubrā*, 4:221 §6950.
22. 'Abd al-Razzāq in *al-Muṣannaf*, 10:102 §18521.
23. Ibn ibbān in *al-Ṣaḥīḥ*, 16:391 §8382.

24. al-Bazzār in *al-Musnad*, 9:138 §3696.
25. al-Ṭabarānī in *al-Muʿjam al-awsaṭ*, 1:207 §663.
26. al- ākim in *al-Mustadrak ʿalā al-Ṣaḥīḥayn*, 1:105 §133.
27. al- ākim in *al-Mustadrak ʿalā al-Ṣaḥīḥayn*, 1:105 §134.
28. Ibn Abī Shayba in *al-Muṣannaf*, 5:457 §27944.
29. Aḥmad b. Ḥanbal in *al-Musnad*, 5:36–38 §§20393, 20419.
30. Abū Dāwūd in *al-Sunan*: *Kitāb al-jihād* [The Book of Struggle], chapter: "Fulfilling the Contract of a Non-Muslim Citizen and the Sanctity of His Contract," 3:83 §2760.
31. al-Nasāʾī in *al-Sunan*: *Kitāb al-qasāma* [The Book of Taking an Oath], chapter: "The Gravity of Killing a Non-Muslim Citizens," 8:24 §4747; and in *al-Sunan al-kubrā*, 4:221, §6949.
32. al-Dārimī in *al-Sunan*, 2:308 §2504.
33. al-Bazzār in *al-Musnad*, 9:129 §3679.
34. Ibn Abī Shayba in *al-Muṣannaf*, 5:457 §27946.
35. al-Ḥākim in *al-Mustadrak*, 2:154 §2631.
37. al-Ṭabarānī in *al-Muʿjam al-awsaṭ*, 8:76 §8011.
38. Ibn al-Jārūd in *al-Muntaqā*, 1:213 §835.
39. al-Ṭayālisī in *al-Musnad*, 1:118 §879.
40. al-Bayhaqī in *al-Sunan al-kubrā*, 9:231 §18629.
41. Aḥmad b. anbal in *al-Musnad*, 5:36 §20399.
42. al- ākim in *al-Mustadrak ʿalā al-Ṣaḥīḥayn*, 1:105 §135.
43. Anwar Shāh Kāshmīrī, *Fayḍ al-Bārī ʿalā Ṣaḥīḥ al-Bukhārī*, 4:288.
44. Aḥmad b. Ḥanbal in *al-Musnad*, 4:89 §16862.
45. Abū Dāwūd in *al-Sunan*: *Kitāb al-aṭʿima* [The Book of Foodstuffs], chapter: "The Unlawfulness of Eating Beasts of Prey," 3:356 §3806.
46. al-Shaybānī in *al-Āḥād wa al-mathānī*, 2:29 §703.
47. Ibn Zanjawayh in *Kitāb al-amwāl*, p. 379 §618.
48. al-Ṭabarānī in *al-Muʿjam al-kabīr*, 4:111 §3828.
49. Ibn Zanjawayh in *Kitāb al-amwāl*, p. 380 §619.
51. al-Dāraquṭnī in *al-Sunan*, 4:287 §63.
52. Abū Dāwūd in *al-Sunan*: *Kitāb al-jihād* [The Book of Jihad], 3:66 §2705.
53. al-Bayhaqī in *al-Sunan al-kubrā*, 9:61 §17789.
54. Mālik in *al-Muwaṭṭā*, 2:447 §965.
55. Mālik in *al-Muwaṭṭā*, 2:448 §966.
56. ʿAbd al-Razzāq in *al-Muṣannaf*, 5:199.
57. al-Bayhaqī in *al-Sunan al-kubrā*, 9:85.
58. al-Hindī in *Kanz al-ʿummāl*, 1:296.
59. Ibn Qudāma in *al-Mughnī*, 8:451–452, 477 §17904.
60. al-Hindī in *Kanz al-ʿummāl*, 4:474 §11409.
61. Ibid., 4:475 §11411.
62. al-Tirmidhī in *al-Sunan*: *Kitāb al-siyar* [The Book of Military

Expeditions], 4:122 §1552.
63. Abū Yūsuf in *al-Kharāj*, p. 141.
64. Ibn Qudāma in *al-Mughnī*, 9:181.
65. al-Zaylaʿī in *Naṣb al-rāya*, 3:381.
66. Al-Nawawī, *Sharḥ Ṣaḥīḥ Muslim*, 12:7.
67. Ibn Qudāma, *al-Mughnī*, 9:112.
68. Ibn Rushd al-Mālikī, *Bidāyat al-mujtahid*, 2:299.
69. Al-Ḥaṣkafī, *al-Durr al-mukhtār*, 2:223.
70. Ibn ʿĀbidīn al-Shāmī, *Radd al-muḥtār*, 3:273.
71. al-Qurāfī, *al-Furūq*, 3:29.
72. al-Qurāfī, *al-Furūq*, 3:29.
73. Ibn Abī Shayba in *al-Muṣannaf*, 6:483 §33121.
74. al-Bayhaqī in *al-Sunan al-kubrā*, 8:133 §16260.

3. The Prohibition of Killing Women, Children, the Elderly and Priests

Essential Reading:

1. Dr Tahir-ul-Qadri, Relations of Muslims and Non-Muslims, Ch:3, pp.37-48.

Additional Readings for Teachers and Students:

1. Muslim in *al-Ṣaḥīḥ: Kitāb al-jihād wa al-siyar* [The Book of Jihad and Battles], chapter: "Women participants in jihid to be given a prize but not a regular share in the booty, and prohibition to kill children of the enemy," 3:1444 §1812.
2. Aḥmad b. Ḥanbal in *al-Musnad*, 3:488 §16035.
3. Abū Dāwūd in *al-Sunan*: *Kitāb al-jihād* [The Book of Jihad], chapter: "The Killing of Women," 3:53 §2669.
4. Ibn Mājah in *al-Sunan*: *Kitāb al-jihād* [The Book of Jihad], chapter: "Making a sudden raid at night and the killing women and children," 2:948 §2842.
5. al-Nasāʾī in *al-Sunan al-kubrā*, 5:186–187 §§8625, 8627.
6. Ibn ibbān in *al-Ṣaḥīḥ*, 11:110 §4789.
7. Ibn Abī Shayba in *al-Muṣannaf*, 6:482 §33117.

8. Abū Yaʿlā in *al-Musnad*, 3:115–116 §1546.
9. al-Ḥākim in *al-Mustadrak*, 2:133 §2565.
10. al-Ṭabarānī in *al-Muʿjam al-kabīr*, 4:10 §3489.
11. al-Bayhaqī in *al-Sunan al-kubrā*, 9:82 §17883.
12. al-Bukhārī in *al-Ṣaḥīḥ*: *Kitāb al-jihād wa al-siyar* [The Book of Struggle and Military Expeditions], chapter: "The Prophet's summons to Islam and Prophethood," 3:1077 §2784.
13. Aḥmad b. anbal in *al-Musnad*, 3:159 §12639.
14. Abū Yaʿlā in *al-Musnad*, 6:431 §3804.
15. Ibn ibbān in *al-Ṣaḥīḥ*, 11:49 §4745.
16. al-Bukhārī in *al-Ṣaḥīḥ*: *Kitāb al-jihād wa al-siyar* [The Book of Struggle and Military Expeditions], chapter: "The Prophet ﷺ calling people to Islam and Prophethood," 3:1077 §2785.
17. al-Tirmidhī in *al-Sunan*: *Kitāb al-siyar* [The Military Expeditions], chapter: "Waging night offences and indiscriminate nocturnal attacks," p. 335," 4:121 §1550.
18. al-Nasāʾī in *al-Sunan al-kubrā*, 5:178 §8598.
19. Ibn ibbān in *al-Ṣaḥīḥ*, 11:51 §4746.
20. Aḥmad b. Ḥanbal in *al-Musnad*, 3:435 §15626-15627 and in 4:24 §16342.
21. al-Nasāʾī in *al-Sunan al-kubrā*: *Kitāb al-siyar* [The Book of Military Expeditions], chapter: "The Prohibition of Killing the Children of the Pagans," 5:184 §8616.
22. al-Dārimī in *al-Sunan*, 2:294 §2463.
23. Ibn Abī Shayba in *al-Muṣannaf*, 6:484 §33131.
24. Ibn ibbān in *al-Ṣaḥīḥ*, 1:341 §132.
25. al- ākīm in *al-Mustadrak*, 2:133–134 §2566–2567.
26. al-Ṭabarānī in *al-Muʿjam al-kabīr*, 1:284 §829.
27. al-Shaybānī in *al-Āḥād wa al-Mathānī*, 2:375 §1160.
28. Abū Nuʿaym in *Ḥilya al-Awliyāʾ*, 8:263.
29. al-Bayhaqī in *al-Sunan al-kubrā*, 9:77 §17868.
30. al-Haythamī in *Majmaʿ al-zawāʾid*, 5:316.
31. Aḥmad b. anbal in *al-Musnad*, 3:435 §15626–15627.
32. al-Bayhaqī in *al-Sunan al-kubrā*, 9:77 §17868.
33. Aḥmad b. anbal in *al-Musnad*, 1:300 §2728.
34. Ibn Abī Shayba in *al-Muṣannaf*, 6:484 §33132.
35. Abū Yaʿlā in *al-Musnad*, 4:422 §2549.
36. Ibn Rushd in *Bidāya al-mujtahid*, 1:281.
37. Ibn Abī Shayba in *al-Mussannaf*, 6:484 §33132.
38. Abū Yaʿlā in *al-Musnad*, 5:59 §2650.
39. al-Ṭaḥāwī in *Sharḥ maʿānī al-āthār*, 3:225.
40. al-Daylamī in *Musnad al-firdaws*, 5:45 §7410.
41. al-Bayhaqī in *al-Sunan al-kubrā*, 9:90 §17934.

42. al-Hindī in *Kanz al-ʿummāl*, 4:205 §11425.
43. Abū Dāwūd in *al-Sunan*: *Kitāb al-jihād* [The Book of Jihad], 3:37 §2614.
44. Ibn Abī Shayba in *al-Muṣannaf*, 6:483 §33118.
45. al-Bayhaqī in *al-Sunan al-kubrā*, 9:90 §17932.
46. Ibn Abī Shayba in *al-Muṣannaf*, 6:483 §33135.
47. ʿAbd al-Razzāq in *al-Muṣannaf*, 5:202 §9385.
48. al-Shāfiʿī in *al-Musnad*, p. 238.
49. al-Ṭaḥāwī in *Sharḥ maʿānī al-āthār*, 3:221.
50. al-Bayhaqī in *al-Sunan al-kubrā*, 9:77 §17865.
51. Ibn Ḥibbān in *al-Ṣaḥīḥ*: *Kitāb al-siyar* [The Book of Military Expeditions], chapter: "An assertive act of resistance against the head of the state and the method of jihad," 11:109 §4788.
52. ʿAbd al-Razzāq in *al-Muṣannaf*, 10:179 §18742.
53. al-Ṭabarānī in *al-Muʿjam al-kabīr*, 17:164 §434.
54. al-Bayhaqī in *al-Sunan al-kubrā*, 6:166 §11098.
55. al-Ṭabarānī in *al-Muʿjam al-awsaṭ*, 7:113 §7011.
56. Qurʾān 40:25.

4. The Unlawfulness of Killing Diplomats, Farmers, Traders and non-Combatants

Essential Reading:

1. Dr Tahir-ul-Qadri, Relations of Muslims and Non-Muslims, Ch:4, pp.49-58.

Additional Readings for Teachers and Students:

1. Aḥmad b. anbal in *al-Musnad*, 3:487 §16032.
2. Abū Dāwūd in *al-Sunan*, chapter: "On Envoys," 3:83 §2761.
3. al- ākim in *al-Mustadrak ʿalā al-Ṣaḥīḥayn*, 2:155 §2632 and 3:54 §4377.
4. Aḥmad b. anbal in *al-Musnad*, 1:390 §3708 and 1:404 §3837.
5. al-Nasāʾī in *al-Sunan al-kubrā*, 5:205 §8675.
6. al-Dārimī in *al-Sunan*, 2:307 §2503.
7. Abū Yaʿlā in *al-Musnad*, 9:31 §5097.
8. Aḥmad in *al-Musnad*, 1:396 §3761.

9. al-Ṭayālisī in *al-Musnad*, 1:34 §251.
10. Ibn al-Qayyim in *Zād al-maʿād*, 3:611.
11. Ibn Abī Shayba in *al-Muṣannaf*, 6:484 §33129.
12. al-Bayhaqī in *al-Sunan al-kubrā*, 9:91 §17939.
13. Ibn Ādam al-Qurashī in *Kitāb al-Kharāj*, 1:52 §133.
14. Ibn Abī Shayba in *al-Muṣannaf*, 6:483 §33120.
15. Ibn Ādam al-Qurashī in *Kitāb al-Kharāj*, 1:52 §132.
16. al-Bayhaqī in *al-Sunan al-kubrā*, 9:91 §17938.
17. Ibn Abī Shayba in *al-Muṣannaf*, 6:484 §33132.
18. Abū Yaʿlā in *al-Musnad*, 5:59 §2650.
19. al-Ṭaḥāwī in *Sharḥ maʿānī al-āthār*, 3:225.
20. al-Daylamī in *Musnad al-firdaws*, 5:45 §7410.
21. Ibn Abī Shayba in *al-Muṣannaf*, 6:483 §33127.
22. al-Bayhaqī in *al-Sunan al-kubrā*, 9:85 §17904.
23. al-Ṭaḥāwī in *Sharḥ Mushkil al-āthār*, 3:144.
24. Ibn ʿAsākir in *Tārīkh Madīna Dimashq*, 2:75.
25. al-Hindī in *Kanz al-ʿummāl*, 4:203 §11408.
26. al-Bayhaqī in *al-Sunan al-kubrā*, 9:90 §17929.
27. ʿAbd al-Razzāq in *al-Muṣannaf*, 10:123 §18590.
28. ʿAbd al-Razzāq in *al-Muṣannaf*, 10:124 §18591.
29. Ibn al-Qayyim in *Aḥkām ahl al-dhimma*, 1:165.
30. Ibn Qudāma al-Maqdisī, *al-Mughnī*, 9:251.
31. Ibn al-Qayyim, *Aḥkām ahl al-dhimma*, 1:165.
32. Ibid., 1:172.

5. Freedom of Faith and Beliefs for Non-Muslims

Essential Reading:

1. Dr Tahir-ul-Qadri, Relations of Muslims and Non-Muslims, Ch:5, pp.59-70.

Additional Readings for Teachers and Students:

1. Qurʾān 6:108.
2. Ibid., 3:64.
3. Ibid., 6:164.
4. Ibid., 10:99.

5. Ibid., 18:29.
6. Ibid., 22:40.
7. Ibid., 88:21–22.
8. Ibid., 109:6.
9. Abū Dāwūd in *al-Sunan*: *Kitāb al-kharāj wa al-imāra wa al-fay*ʾ [The Book on the Land Tax, Leadership and Spoils Acquired without Fighting], chapter: "Taking One Tenth from Non- Muslim Citizens When They Do Business," 3:170 §3052.
10. al-Bayhaqī in *al-Sunan al-kubrā*, 9:205 §18511.
11. al-Mundhirī in *al-Targhīb wa al-tarhīb*, 4:7 §4558.
12. al-ʿAjlūnī in *Kashf al-khafā*ʾ, 2:342.
13. al-Bayhaqī in *Dalāʾil al-Nubuwwa*, 5:382.
14. Ibn Saʿd in *al-Ṭabaqāt al-kubrā*, 1:357.
15. Ibn Hishām in *al-Sīra al-Nabawiyya*, 2:239–240.
16. Ibn Kathīr in *al-Sīra*, 4:108.
17. Ibn Qayyim in *Zād al-maʿād*, 3:629.
18. al-Bayhaqī in *Dalāʾil al-Nubuwwa*, 5:359, 389.
19. Ibn Saʿd in *al-Ṭabaqāt al-kubrā*, 1:288, 358.
20. Abū Yūsuf in *Kitāb al-kharāj*, p. 78.
21. Abū ʿUbayd al-Qāsim b. Sallām in *Kitāb al-amwāl*, pp. 244–245 §503.
22. Ibn Zanjawayh in *Kitāb al-amwāl*, pp. 449–450 §732.
23. al-Bayhaqī in *al-Sunan al-kubrā*, 9:85 §17904.
24. al-Ṭaḥāwī in *Sharḥ Mushkil al-āthār*, 3:144.
25. Ibn ʿAsākir in *Tārīkh Madina Dimashq*, 2:75.
26. al-Hindī in *Kanz al-ʿummāl*, 4:203 §11408.
27. Al-Ṭabarī, *Tārīkh al-umam wa al-mulūk*, 2:449.
28. Ibn Abī Shayba in *al-Muṣannaf*, 6:467 §32982.
29. al-Bayhaqī in *al-Sunan al-kubrā*, 9:202 §18496.
30. Ibn Zanjawayh in *Kitāb al-amwāl*, p. 328.
31. Ibn Qudāma in *al-Mughnī*, 9:283.
32. al-Maqdisī in *al-Furūʿ*, 6:250.
33. Ibn al-Qayyim in *Aḥkām ahl al-dhimma*, 3:1181, 1195, 1235.
34. Ibn Ḍawyān in *Manār al-sabīl*, 1:283.
35. Al-Balādhurī, *Futūḥ al-buldān*, p. 132.
36. Qurʾān 2:256.
37. Ibn Kathīr, *Tafsīr al-Qurʾān al-ʿAẓīm*, 1:310.
38. Qurʾān 22:40.
39. Abū Bakr al-Jaṣṣāṣ, *Aḥkām al-Qurʾān*, 5:83.
40. Ibn al-Qayyim, *Aḥkām ahl al-dhimma*, 3:1169.
41. Abū Bakr al-Jaṣṣāṣ, *Aḥkām al-Qurʾān*, 5:83.
42. Ibn al-Qayyim, *Aḥkām ahl al-dhimma*, 3:1169.
43. Abū Bakr al-Jaṣṣāṣ, *Aḥkām al-Qurʾān*, 5:83.

6. Justice in all Judgments and Rulings for Non-Muslims

Essential Reading:

1. Dr Tahir-ul-Qadri, Relations of Muslims and Non-Muslims, Ch:6, pp.71-82.

Additional Readings for Teachers and Students:

1. Qur'ān 5:8.
2. Qur'ān 6:164.
3. Qur'ān 57:25.
4. Qur'ān 60:8.
5. al-Shāfiʿī in *al-Musnad,* p. 343 and in *al-Umm*, 7:320.
6. Abū Nuʿaym in *Musnad Abī Ḥanīfa*, p. 104.
7. al-Bayhaqī in *al-Sunan al-kubrā*, 8:30 §15696.
8. al-Shaybānī in *al-Mabsūṭ*, 4:488 and in *al- ujja*, 4:342-344.
9. al-Qurashī in *al-Kharāj*, p. 82 §238.
10. al-Bayhaqī in *al-Sunan al-kubrā*, 8:30 §15697 and in *Maʿrifa al-sunan wa al-āthār*, 6:149 §4814.
11. al-Daraquṭunī in *al-Sunan*, 3:135 §167.
12. al-Shāfiʿī in *al-Musnad*, 1:443.
13. Qur'ān 2:178.
14. Abū Dāwūd in *al-Sunan*: *Kitāb al-diyāt* [The Book of Blood Money], chapter: "The Leader Should Urge Forgiveness in the Matter of Shedding Blood," 4:169 §4496.
15. ʿAbd al-Razzāq in *al-Muṣannaf*, 10:86 §18454.
16. al-Shāfiʿī in *al-Umm*, 7:320.
17. al-Shaybānī in *Kitāb al-ḥujja ʿalā ahl al-Madīna*, 4:347.
18. Ibn Abī Shayba in *al-Muṣannaf*, 5:406 §27444.
19. Ibid., §27445.
20. Ibid., §27446.
21. ʿAbd al-Razzāq in *al-Muṣannaf*, 10:97 §18494.
22. al-Tirmidhī in *al-Sunan*: *Kitāb al-diyāt* [The Book of Blood Money], chapter: "What Has Come To Us Concerning The Blood Money Of Non-Muslims," 4:25 §1413.

23. ʿAbd al-Razzāq in *al-Muṣannaf*, 10:95 §18491.
24. al-Shāfiʿī in *al-Umm*, 7:321.
25. al-Shaybānī in *al-Ḥujja*, 4:351.
26. al-Bukhārī in *al-Ṣaḥīḥ*: *Kitāb al-ʿilm* [The Book of Knowledge], chapter: "On Writing Down Knowledge," 1:53 §111.
27. al-Shāfiʿī in *al-Umm*, 7:321.
28. al-Bayhaqī in *al-Sunan al-kubrā*, 8:32 §15706.
29. al-Shaybānī in *al- ujja*, 4:335.
30. al-Zaylaʿī in *Naṣb al-rāya*, 4:337.
31. al-Shāfiʿī in *al-Musnad* p. 344.
32. Abū Yūsuf in *Kitāb al-kharāj*, p. 187.
33. al-Bayhaqī in *al-Sunan al-kubrā*, 8:34 §15712.
34. al-ʿAsqalānī in *al-Dirāya fī takhrīj aḥādīth al-Hidāya*, 2:263.
35. al-Zaylaʿī in *Naṣb al-rāya*, 4:336.
36. Ibn ʿAbd al- akam in *Futūḥ Miṣr wa akhbaru-hā*, p. 114–115.
37. al-Hindī in *Kanz al-ʿummāl*, 12:294 §36010.

7. Treating Non-Muslims with Piety and Excellence

Essential Reading:

1. Dr Tahir-ul-Qadri, Relations of Muslims and Non-Muslims, Ch:7, pp.83-92.

Additional Readings for Teachers and Students:

1. Qurʾān 29:46.
2. al-Bukhārī in *al-Ṣaḥīḥ*: *Kitāb al-hiba wa faḍlu-hā* [The Book of Gifts and their Excellence], chapter: "Gifts to idolaters," 2:924 §2477 and in *Kitāb al-Jizya* [The Book of Annual Security Tax for non-Muslims], chapter: The sin committed by someone who promises and then betrays, 3:1162 §3012.
3. Muslim in *al-Ṣaḥīḥ*: *Kitāb al-Zakāt* [The book of the Alms-due], chapter: "The excellence of spending on and giving alms to relatives, to spouse, to children, and parents even if they are polytheists," 2:696 §1003.
4. Aḥmad b. anbal in *al-Musnad*, 6:347 §26985.

5. Abū Dāwūd in *al-Sunan*: *Kitāb al-Zakāt* [The book of the Alms-due], chapter: "Bestowing charity upon the non-Muslim citizens of a Muslim country," 2:127 §1668.
6. al-Ṭabarānī in *al-Muʿjam al-kabīr*, 24:78 §203.
7. ʿAbd al-Razzāq in *al-Muṣannaf*, 6:38 §9932.
8. al-Bukhārī in *al-Ṣaḥīḥ*: *Kitāb al-Janāʾiz* [The Book of Funeral Ceremonies], chapter: "Someone standing up for a Jewish funeral procession," 1:441 §1249.
9. Muslim in *al-Ṣaḥīḥ*: *Kitāb al-Janāʾiz* [The Book of Funeral Ceremonies], chapter: "Someone standing up for a funeral procession," 2:660 §960.
10. al-Nasāʾī in *al-Sunan*: *Kitāb al-Janāʾiz* [The Book of Funeral Ceremonies], chapter: "Someone standing up for the funeral procession of the people who associate partners with Allah," 4:45 §1922 and in *al-Sunan al-kubrā*, 1:626 §2049.
11. al-Bukhārī in *al-Ṣaḥīḥ*: *Kitāb al-Janāʾiz* [The Book of Funeral Ceremonies], chapter: "Someone standing up for a Jewish funeral procession," 1:441 §1250.
12. Muslim in *al-Ṣaḥīḥ*: *Kitāb al-Janāʾiz* [The Book of Funeral Ceremonies], chapter: "Someone getting to his feet for a funeral procession," 2:661 §961.
13. Aḥmad b. Ḥanbal in *al-Musnad*, 6:6 §23893.
14. al-Nasāʾī in *al-Sunan*: *Kitāb al-Janāʾiz* [The Book of Funeral Ceremonies], chapter: "Someone standing up for the funeral procession of the people who associate partners with Allah," 4:45 §1921 and in *al-Sunan al-Kubrā*, 1:626 §2048.
15. Ibn Abī Shayba in *al-Muṣannaf*, 3:39 §11918.
16. Ibn al-Jaʿd in *al-Musnad*, p. 27 §70.
17. al-Ṭabarānī in *al-Muʿjam al-Kabīr*, 6:90 §5606.
18. al-Bayhaqī in *al-Sunan al-Kubrā*, 4:27 §6672.
19. Muslim in *al-Ṣaḥīḥ*: *Kitāb al-birr wa al-ṣila wa al-ādāb* [The Book of Piety, Filial Duty and Good Manners], chapter: "The Severe Divine Threat to the One Who Punishes People Unjustly," 4:2018 § 2613.
20. Aḥmad b. Ḥanbal in *al-Musnad*, 3:403, 404, 468.
21. Abū Dāwūd in *al-Sunan*: *Kitāb al-kharāj* [The Book of Land Taxation], chapter: "On Being Harsh," 3:106 §3045.
22. al-Nasāʾī in *al-Sunan al-kubrā*, 5:236 §8771.
23. Muslim in *al-Ṣaḥīḥ*: *Kitāb al-birr wa al-ṣila wa al-ādāb* [The Book of Piety, Filial Duty and Good Manners], chapter: "The Severe Divine Threat for Someone Who Punishes People Unjustly," 4:2018 §2613.
24. Aḥmad b. Ḥanbal in *al-Musnad*, 3:404 §5612.
25. Abū Dāwūd in *al-Sunan*: *al-Kharāj wa al-Imāra wa al-Fay*ʾ [The Book of the Land Tax, Imperial Authority and the Bestowal of Booty], chapter: "Recovering the Capitation Tax Forcibly," 3:169 §3045.

26. al-Nasāʾī in *al-Sunan al-Kubrā*, 5:236 §8771.
27. al-Bayhaqī in *Shuʿab al-īmān*, 6:518 §9125 and in *Dalāʾil al-Nubuwwa*, 2:307.
28. al-Ṣaydāwī in *Muʿjam al-shūyūkh*, 1:97.
29. al- alabī in *al-Sīra al- alabiyya*, 2:758.
30. Ibn Kathīr in *al-Sīra*, 2:31.
31. Abū ʿUbayd al-Qāsim b. Sallām in *Kitāb al-amwāl*, p. 54 §114.
32. Ibn Qudāma in *al-Mughnī*, 9:290.
33. al-Ḥaṣkafī, *al-Durr al-mukhtār*, 2:223.
34. Ibn ʿĀbidīn al-Shāmī, *Radd al-muḥtār*, 3:273–274.
35. al-Qurāfī, *al-Furūq*, 3:14.
36. Ibn ʿĀbidīn al-Shāmī, *Radd al-muḥtār*, 3:273–274.
37. al-Kāsānī, *Badāʾiʿ al-ṣanāʾiʿ*, 7:111.
38. Aḥmad b. anbal in *al-Musnad*, 3:319 §14467.

8. Non-Revengeful, Forbearing and Tolerant Behaviour towards Non-Muslims

Essential Reading:

1. Dr Tahir-ul-Qadri, Relations of Muslims and Non-Muslims, Ch:8, pp.93-103.

Additional Readings for Teachers and Students:

1. al-Bukhārī in *al-Ṣaḥīḥ*: *Kitāb badʾu al-khalq* [The Beginning of Creation], chapter: "When one of you says, "Amen," as do the angels in the heaven, and they coincide with one another, he will be forgiven his past wrong actions," 3:1180 §3059.
2. Muslim in *al-Ṣaḥīḥ*: *Kitāb al-jihād wa al-siyar* [The Book of Jihad and Military Expeditions], chapter: "On the Harm Experienced by the Prophet ﷺ at the Hands of the Pagans and Hypocrites," 3:1420 §1795.
3. al-Nasāʾī in *al-Sunan al-kubrā*, 4:405 §7706.
4. al-Ṭabarānī in *al-Muʿjam al-awsaṭ*, 8:370 §8902.

5. al-Bukhārī in *al-Ṣaḥīḥ*: *Kitāb al-hiba wa faḍlu-hā* [The Book of Gifts and their Excellence], chapter: "Accepting a gift from the idolaters," 2:923 §2474.
6. Muslim in *al-Ṣaḥīḥ*: *Kitāb al-salām* [The salutation of peace], chapter: "On Poison," 4:1721 §2190.
7. Aḥmad b. anbal in *al-Musnad*, 3:218 §13309.
8. Abū Dāwūd in *al-Sunan*: *Kitāb al-jihād wa al-siyar* [The Book of Struggle and Military Expeditions], chapter: "Someone hanging his sword on a tree in a journey at midday," 4:173 §4508.
9. al-Ṭabarānī in *al-Muʿjam al-awsaṭ*, 3:43 §2417.
10. al-Bayhaqī in *al-Sunan al-kubrā*, 10:11 §19500.
11. al-Bukhārī in *al-Ṣaḥīḥ: Kitāb al-jihād wa al-siyar* [The Book of Struggle and Military Expeditions], chapter: "Someone hanging his sword on a tree in a journey at midday," 3:1065–1066 §2753–2756 and in *Kitāb al-Maghāzī* [The Book of Military Expeditions], chapter: "The expedition of Dhāt al-Riqāʿ," 4:515 §3905.
12. Muslim in *al-Ṣaḥīḥ: Kitāb al-Faḍāʾil* [The Book of Excellent Merits], chapter: "The reliance of the Prophet on Allah, exalted is He, and how Allah protected the Messenger from the people," 4:1786 §843.
13. Aḥmad b. Ḥanbal in *al-Musnad*, 3:311 §14374.
14. al-Nasāʾī in *al-Sunan al-Kubrā*, 5:236, 267 §8772, 8852.
15. al-Bayhaqī in *al-Sunan al-Kubrā*, 6:319 §12613.
16. al-Ṭabarānī in *Musnad al-Shāmiyyīn*, 3:66 §1815.
17. al-Bukhārī in *al-Ṣaḥīḥ*: *Kitāb istitāba al-murtaddīn wa al-muʿānidīn wa qitālihim* [The Book on Demanding the Repentance of the Apostates and Reprobates, and Fighting Them], chapter: "What is to be Done When a Non-Muslim Citizen or Anyone Else Presents Himself," 6:2539 §6528.
18. Muslim in *al-Ṣaḥīḥ*: *Kitāb al-birr wa al-ṣila wa al-ādāb* [The Book of Piety, Filial Duty and Good Manners], chapter: "The Virtue of Gentleness," 4:2003 §2593.
19. Abū Dāwūd in *al-Sunan*: *Kitāb al-adab* [The Book of Good Manners], chapter: "On Gentleness," 4:254 §4807.
20. Ibn Mājah in *al-Sunan*: *Kitāb al-adab* [The Book of Good Manners], chapter: "On Gentleness," 2:1216 §3688.
21. al-Bukhārī in *al-Ṣaḥīḥ*: *Kitāb istitāba al-murtaddīn wa al-muʿānidīn wa qitālihim* [The Book on Demanding the Repentance of the Apostates and Reprobates, and Fighting Them], chapter: "What is to be Done When a Non-Muslim Citizen or Anyone Else Presents Himself," 6:2538 §6527.
22. Muslim in *al-Ṣaḥīḥ*: *Kitāb al-salām* [The salutation of peace], chapter: "The Prohibition of the People of the Scripture [Jews and Christians] from beginning with the salutation of peace, and how to respond to them," 4:1705 §2163.
23. Aḥmd b. anbal in *al-Musnad*, 3:218 §13308.

24. Abū Yaʿlā in *al-Musnad*, 5:445 §3153.
25. Qurʾān 48:24.
26. Muslim in *al-Ṣaḥīḥ*, 3:1442 §1808.
27. Aḥmad b. anbal in *al-Musnad*, 3:124, 290 §12276, 14122.
28. Abū Dāwūd in *al-Sunan*: *Kitāb al-jihād* [The Book of Striving], chapter: "Freeing Captives without Ransom," 3:61 §2688.
29. al-Tirmidhī in *al-Sunan*: *Kitāb al-Tafsīr* [The Book of Interpretation], "From Sūra al-Fatḥ," 5:386 §3264.
30. al-Nasāʾī in *al-Sunan al-kubrā*, 5:202, 6:464 §§8667, 11510.
31. Ibn Abī Shayba in *al-Muṣannaf*, 7:405 §36916.
32. Abū ʿAwāna in *al-Musnad*, 4:291 §6782–6783.
33. ʿAbd b. umayd in *al-Musnad*, 1:363 §1208.
34. Muslim in *al-Ṣaḥīḥ*: *Kitāb al-birr wa al-ṣila wa al-ādāb* [The Book of Piety, Filial Duty and Good Manners], chapter: "The Prohibition of Invoking Curses on Creatures and Other Things," 4:2006 §2599.
35. al-Bukhārī in *al-Adab al-mufrad*, p. 119 §321.
36. Abū Yaʿlā in *al-Musnad*, 11:35 §6174.
37. al- usaynī in *al-Bayān wa al-taʿrīf*, 1:283 §754.
38. Ibn Kathīr in *Tafsīr al-Qurʾān al-ʿAẓīm*, 3:202.
39. al-Bayhaqī in *Shuʿab al-īmān*, 2:144 §1403.
40. Ibn ʿAsākir in *Tārīkh Madīna Dimashq*, 4:92.
41. Abū Nuʿaym in *Dalāʾil al-Nubuwwa*, 1:40 §2.
42. Ibn ibbān in *al-Ṣaḥīḥ*, 3:254 §973.
43. Ibn ʿĀṣim in *al-Āḥād wa al-mathānī*, 4:123 §2096.
44. al-Ṭabarānī in *al-Muʿjam al-kabīr*, 6:120 §5694.
45. al-Bayhaqī in *Shuʿab al-īmān*, 2:164 §1448.
46. al-Daylamī in *Musnad al-firdaws*, 1:500 §2042.
47. al-Haythamī in *Majmaʿ al-zawāʾid*, 6:117.
48. al-Shāfiʿī in *al-Umm*, 7:361.
49. Ibn ibbān in *al-Thiqāt*, 2:56.
50. al-Rabīʿ in *al-Musnad*, p. 170 §419.
51. al-Bayhaqī in *al-Sunan al-kubrā*, 9:118 §18055.
52. Aḥmad b. anbal in *al-Musnad*, 1:112 §902.

9. Fulfilment of Agreements and Covenants with Non-Muslims

Essential Reading:

1. Dr Tahir-ul-Qadri, Relations of Muslims and Non-Muslims, Ch:9, pp.105-108.

Additional Readings for Teachers and Students:

1. Aḥmad b. anbal in *al-Musnad*, 4:111 §17056.
2. al-Tirmidhī in *al-Sunan*, 4:143 §1580.
3. al-Ṭayalisī in *al-Musnad*, 1:157 §1155.

10. Financial Support for the Elderly, Infirm and Feeble amongst the Non-Muslims

Essential Reading:

1. Dr Tahir-ul-Qadri, Relations of Muslims and Non-Muslims, Ch:10, pp.109-114.

Additional Readings for Teachers and Students:

1. Abū ʿUbayd al-Qāsim b. Sallām in *Kitāb al-amwāl*, p. 57 §119.
2. Qurʾān 9:60.
3. Abū Yūsuf in *Kitāb al-kharāj*, p. 136.
4. Mālik in *al-Muwaṭṭā*ʾ, 2:280.
5. Ibn al-Qayyim, *Aḥkām ahl al-Dhimma*, 1:172. This tradition is considered as *marfū*ʿ but the same is proved from the authority of Ibn ʿUmar ﷺ.
6. Ibn al-Qayyim in *Aḥkām ahl al-Dhimma*, 1:172.
7. ʿAbd al-Razzāq in *al-Muṣannaf*, 6:85 §10090.
8. al-Bayhaqī in *al-Sunan al-kubrā*, 9:195 §18463.

11. Extracts from Ibn al-Qayyim's *A kām Ahl al-Dhimma*

11.1 Entrance of non-Muslims in the Sacred Mosque

11.1.1 First Report

Essential Reading:

1. Dr Tahir-ul-Qadri, Relations of Muslims and Non-Muslims, Ch:11, pp.117-119.

Additional Readings for Teachers and Students:

1. Aḥmad b. anbal in *al-Musnad*, 4:218 §17942.
2. Abū Dāwūd in *al-Sunan*, *Kitāb al-kharāj wa al-imāra wa al-fay'* [The Book of Land Tax, Leadership, and War Spoils Captured without Fighting], chapter: "What has been Reported about Ṭā'if," 3:163 §3026.
3. al-Ṭabarānī in *al-Muʿjam al-Kabīr*, 9:54 §8372.
4. al-Bayhaqī in *al-Sunan al-kubrā*, 2:444 §4131.
5. Ibn Khuzayma in *al-Ṣaḥīḥ*, 2:285 §1328. The narrators of the above hadith are authentic.
6. ʿAbd al-Razzāq in *al-Muṣannaf*, 1:414 §1622.
7. al-Bayhaqī in *Dalā'il al-Nubuwwa*, 5:382.
8. Ibn Saʿd in *al-Ṭabaqāt al-kubrā*, 1:357.
9. Ibn al-Qayyim in *Zād al-maʿād*, 3:629.
10. al-Dhahabī in *Tārīkh al-Islām*, 2:695.
11. Ibn al-Qayyim, *Aḥkām ahl al-dhimma*, 2:822.

11.1.2 Second Report

Essential Reading:

1. Dr Tahir-ul-Qadri, Relations of Muslims and Non-Muslims, Ch:11, pp.119-120.

Additional Readings for Teachers and Students:

1. Ibn Hishām, *al-Sīra al-Nabawiyya*, 5:49–51.
2. Ibn Kathīr, *al-Bidāya wa al-nihāya*, 4:280.
3. al- alabī, *al-Sīra al- alabiyya*, 3:6–8.

11.1.3 Third Report

Essential Reading:

1. Dr Tahir-ul-Qadri, Relations of Muslims and Non-Muslims, Ch:11, pp.120-121.

Additional Readings for Teachers and Students:

1. al-Ṭabarānī in *al-Muʿjam al-kabīr*, 17:58 §118.
2. Ibn al-Athīr in *al-Kāmil fī al-tārīkh*, 2:30–31.
3. Ibn Kathīr in *al-Bidāya wa al-nihāya*, 3:313–314.
4. al-Haythamī in *Majmaʿ al-zawāʾid*, 8:284–285.
5. al-Ṭabarānī in *al-Muʿjam al-kabīr*, 17:58 §118.
6. Ibn Kathīr in *al-Bidāya wa al-nihāya*, 3:313–314.
7. Ibn al-Athīr in *al-Kāmil fī al-tārīkh*, 2:30–31.
8. al-Haythamī in *Majmaʿ al-zawāʾid*, 8:284–285.

11.2 Visiting the non-Muslims when They Are Sick

ESSENTIAL READING:

1. Dr Tahir-ul-Qadri, Relations of Muslims and Non-Muslims, Ch:11, pp.121-124.

ADDITIONAL READINGS FOR TEACHERS AND STUDENTS:

1. al-Khallāl in *Aḥkām ahl al-milal*, p. 212 §597.
2. Ibn al-Qayyim in *Aḥkām ahl al-dhimma*, 1:427.
3. al-Khallāl in *Aḥkām ahl al-milal*, p. 212 §598.
4. Ibn al-Qayyim in *Aḥkām ahl al-dhimma*, 1:427.
5. Ibn al-Qayyim, *Aḥkām ahl al-dhimma*, 1:430.
6. al-Bukhārī in *al-Ṣaḥīḥ*: *Kitāb al-janāza* [The Book of the Funeral Prayer], chapter: "When a Young Boy Embraces Islam and Dies, should He be Prayed over, and should He be Invited to Islam?" 1:455 §1290, and also in *al-Adab al-mufrad*, 1:185 §524.
7. Abū Yaʿlā in *al-Musnad*, 6:93 §3350.
8. al-Bayhaqī in *al-Sunan al-kubrā*, 3:383 §6389.
9. Aḥmad b. anbal in *al-Musnad*, 3:280 §§14009,14010.
10. Abū Dāwūd in *al-Sunan*: *Kitāb al-janāʾiz* [The Book of Funeral Rites], chapter: "On Visiting a Non-Muslim Citizen," 3:185 §3095.
11. Aḥmad b. anbal in *al-Musnad*, 5:201 §21806.
12. Abū Dāwūd in *al-Sunan*: *Kitāb al-janāʾiz* [The Book of Funeral Rites], chapter: "On Visiting the Sick," 3:184 §3094.
13. al- ākim in *al-Mustadrak*, 1:491 §1262.
14. al-Ṭabarānī in *al-Muʿjam al-kabīr*, 1:163 §390.
15. al-Maqdisī in *al-Aḥādīth al-mukhtāra*, 4:117 §1328. The narrators of this chain of transmission are all reliable.

11.3 ATTENDING THE FUNERALS OF NON-MUSLIMS

ESSENTIAL READING:

1. Dr Tahir-ul-Qadri, Relations of Muslims and Non-Muslims, Ch:11, pp.124-127.

Additional Readings for Teachers and Students:

1. al-Khallāl in *Aḥkām ahl al-milal*, p. 218 §620.
2. Ibn al-Qayyim in *Aḥkām ahl al-dhimma*, 1:432.
3. al-Khallāl in *Aḥkām ahl al-milal*, p. 218 §621.
4. Ibn al-Qayyim in *Aḥkām ahl al-dhimma*, 1:433.
5. al-Khallāl in *Aḥkām ahl al-milal*, p. 218 §622.
6. Ibn al-Qayyim in *Aḥkām ahl al-dhimma*, 1:433.
7. al-Khallāl in *Aḥkām ahl al-milal*, p. 219 §623.
8. al-Dāraquṭnī in *al-Sunan*: *Kitāb al-janāʾiz* [The Book of Funeral Rites], chapter: "On Placing the Right Hand over the Left Hand and Raising the Hands During the Opening *Takbīr*," 2:75 §6.
9. al-Zaylaʿī in *Naṣb al-rāya*, 2:292.
10. Ibn al-Qayyim in *Aḥkām ahl al-dhimma*, 1:434.
11. al-Khallāl in *Aḥkām ahl al-milal*, p. 219 §624.
12. Ibn al-Qayyim in *Aḥkām ahl al-dhimma*, 1:435.
13. al-Khallāl in *Aḥkām ahl al-milal*, p. 219 §624.
14. Ibn al-Qayyim in *Aḥkām ahl al-dhimma*, 1:436.
15. al-Khallāl in *Aḥkām ahl al-milal*, p. 220 §628.
16. Ibn al-Qayyim, in*Aḥkām ahl al-dhimma*, 1:437.

11.4 Giving Condolences to non-Muslims

Essential Reading:

1. Dr Tahir-ul-Qadri, Relations of Muslims and Non-Muslims, Ch:11, pp.127.

Additional Readings for Teachers and Students:

1. al-Khallāl in *Aḥkām ahl al-milal*, p.224 §638.
2. Ibn al-Qayyim in *Aḥkām ahl al-dhimma*, 1:439.

11.5 The Slaughtered Animals of the People of the Book

ESSENTIAL READING:

1. Dr Tahir-ul-Qadri, Relations of Muslims and Non-Muslims, Ch:11, pp.128-131.

ADDITIONAL READINGS FOR TEACHERS AND STUDENTS:

1. Ibn al-Qayyim, *Aḥkām ahl al-dhimma*, 1:502.
2. al-Bukhārī in *al-Ṣaḥīḥ, Kitāb al-dhabā'iḥ wa al-ṣayd* [The Book of Slaughtered Animals and Hunting], chapter: "The Slaughtered Animals and Fat of the People of the Book and the People of War, and Others," 5:2097.
3. al-Bayhaqī in *al-Sunan al-kubrā*, 9:282 §18934.
4. Ibn al-Qayyim in *Aḥkām ahl al-dhimma*, 1:502.
5. Ibn al-Qayyim, *Aḥkām ahl al-dhimma*, 1:502.
6. Ibid., 1:503.
7. al-Khallāl in *Aḥkām ahl al-milal*, p. 362 §1007.
8. Ibn al-Qayyim in *Aḥkām ahl al-dhimma*, 1:503–504.
9. al-Khallāl in *Aḥkām ahl al-milal*, p. 362 §1008.
10. Ibn al-Qayyim in *Aḥkām ahl al-dhimma*, 1: 504.
11. Qur'ān 6:121.
12. al-Khallāl in *Aḥkām ahl al-milal*, pp. 362–363 §1009.
13. Ibn al-Qayyim in *Aḥkām ahl al-dhimma*, 1:504–505.
14. al-Khallāl in *Aḥkām ahl al-milal*, pp. 364 §1016.
15. Ibn al-Qayyim in *Aḥkām ahl al-dhimma*, 1:505.
16. al-Khallāl in *Aḥkām ahl al-milal*, pp. 365–366 §1018.
17. Ibn al-Qayyim in *Aḥkām ahl al-dhimma*, 1:505.
18. Ibn al-Qayyim, *Aḥkām ahl al-dhimma*, 1:505.
19. Ibid., 1:510.

11.5.1 RULINGS ABOUT MEAT ARE THE SAME FOR THE PEOPLE OF TREATY AND PEOPLE AT WAR

ESSENTIAL READING:

1. Dr Tahir-ul-Qadri, Relations of Muslims and Non-Muslims, Ch:11, pp.131.

11.5.2 Issues Pertaining to the Animals' Meat of the People of the Book

Essential Reading:

1. Dr Tahir-ul-Qadri, Relations of Muslims and Non-Muslims, Ch:11, pp.131-137.

Additional Readings for Teachers and Students:

1. al-Khallāl in *Aḥkām ahl al-milal*, p. 367 §1028.
2. Ibn al-Qayyim in *Aḥkām ahl al-dhimma*, 1:515.
3. al-Khallāl in *Aḥkām ahl al-milal*, p. 367 §1029.
4. Ibn al-Qayyim in *Aḥkām ahl al-dhimma*, 1:515–516.
5. Ibn al-Qayyim, *Aḥkām ahl al-dhimma*, 1:516
6. al-Khallāl in *Aḥkām ahl al-milal*, pp. 363–364 §1009.
7. Ibn al-Qayyim in *Aḥkām ahl al-dhimma*, 1:516.
8. Ibn Taymiyya, *al-Muḥarrar fī al-fiqh ʿalā madhab al-Imām Aḥmad b. anbal*, 2:192.
9. Ibn al-Qayyim, *Aḥkām ahl al-dhimma*, 1:516.
10. Ibn al-Qayyim, *Aḥkām ahl al-dhimma*, 1:517.
11. Ibn ʿAbd al-Barr, *al-Istidhkār*, 5:258.
12. Ibn al-Qayyim, *Aḥkām ahl al-dhimma*, 1:517. The chain of this narration is rigorously authentic and its narrators are all reliable.
13. al-Bukhārī in *al-Tārīkh al-kabīr*, 2:214 §2236.
14. Ibn ʿAbd al-Barr in *al-Istidhkār*, 5:258.
15. Ibn al-Qayyim in *Aḥkām ahl al-dhimma*, 1:519.
16. Ibn al-Qayyim, *Aḥkām ahl al-dhimma*, 1:517.
17. al-Shāṭibī, *al-Muwāfaqāt*, 1:173–174.
18. al-Qurāfī in *al-Furūq*, 1:304. The narrators in this chain of transmission are all reliable.

11.5.3 An Important Point

Essential Reading:

1. Dr Tahir-ul-Qadri, Relations of Muslims and Non-Muslims, Ch:11, pp.137-142.

Additional Readings for Teachers and Students:

1. Ibn ʿAbd al-Barr in *al-Istidhkār*, 5:258.
2. al-Kāsānī, *Badāʾiʿ al-ṣanāʾiʿ fī tartīb al-sharāʾiʿ*, 6:230.
3. Ibn al-Qayyim, *Aḥkām ahl al-dhimma*, 1:520.
4. Ibn ʿAbd al-Barr, *al-Istidhkār*, 5:258. The chain of this narration is rigorously authentic and its narrators are all reliable.

5. Ibn al-Qayyim, *Aḥkām ahl al-dhimma*, 1:521.
6. Ibid.
7. Ibid. The narrators of this chain are all reliable.
8. Ibid.
9. Ibid., 1:523
10. Ibn ʿAbd al-Barr, *al-Istidhkār*, 5:259.
11. Ibn al-Qayyim, *Aḥkām ahl al-dhimma*, 1:523–524.
12. Ibn al-Qayyim, *Aḥkām ahl al-dhimma*, 1:525.
13. Ibn ʿAbd al-Barr, *al-Istidhkār*, 5:259.
14. Ibn al-Qayyim, *Aḥkām ahl al-dhimma*, 1:526.
15. Ibid.
16. Ibid.

11.6 The Permissibility of Marrying a Woman from the People of the Book

Essential Reading:

1. Dr Tahir-ul-Qadri, Relations of Muslims and Non-Muslims, Ch:11, pp.142-147.

Additional Readings for Teachers and Students:

1. al-Khallāl in *Aḥkām ahl al-milal*, p. 159 §448.
2. Ibn al-Qayyim in *Aḥkām ahl al-dhimma*, 1:795.
3. Qur'ān 5:5.
4. Qur'ān 2:221
5. Qur'ān 60:10.
6. Qur'ān 98:1.
7. Qur'ān 22:17.
8. Ibn al-Qayyim, *Aḥkām ahl al-dhimma*, 1:797
9. Qur'ān 2:221.
10. al-Khallāl in *Aḥkām ahl al-milal*, pp. 164–165 §467.
11. Ibn al-Qayyim in *Aḥkām ahl al-Dhimma*, 1:797.

12. Categories of the Abodes (Formulating International Law for Developing Peace)

12.1 The Abode of Islam (Dār al-Islām)

Essential Reading:

1. Dr Tahir-ul-Qadri, Relations of Muslims and Non-Muslims, Ch:12, pp.151-155.

Additional Readings for Teachers and Students:

1. Ibn al-Mufliḥ, *al-Ādāb al-sharʿiyya*, 1:211.
2. al-Shawkānī, *al-Sayl al-jarār*, 4:575.
3. Abū Zuhra, *al-ʿAlāqāt al-duwaliyya fī al-Islām*, p. 56.

12.1.1 How Does an Abode of Islam Morph into an Abode of Disbelief and Abode of War?

Essential Reading:

1. Dr Tahir-ul-Qadri, Relations of Muslims and Non-Muslims, Ch:12, pp.155-159.

Additional Readings for Teachers and Students:

1. al-Kāsānī, *Badāʾiʿ al-ṣanāʾiʿ*, 8:130.
2. al- aṣkafī, *al-Durr al-mukhtār*, 4:174–175.
3. Ibn Qudāma, *al-Mughnī fī fiqh al-Imām Aḥmad b. anbal*, 9:25–26.
4. al-Dasūqī, *āshiya ʿalā al-Sharḥ al-kabīr*, 2:188.
5. al-Shawkānī, *al-Sayl al-jarār*, 4:575.

12.1.2 The Stringent Conditions for the Abode of War

Essential Reading:

1. Dr Tahir-ul-Qadri, Relations of Muslims and Non-Muslims, Ch:12, pp.159-160.

12.1.3 The Rationale for The Stringent Conditions Regarding the Abode of War

Essential Reading:

1. Dr Tahir-ul-Qadri, Relations of Muslims and Non-Muslims, Ch:12, pp.160-162.

12.1.4 The Inaptness of Declaring an Abode of Islam an Abode of Disbelief due to Predominant Corruption

Essential Reading:

1. Dr Tahir-ul-Qadri, Relations of Muslims and Non-Muslims, Ch:12, pp.162.

12.1.5 Absolute Power and Dominance are a Must for a Place to Be Judged as an Abode of War

Essential Reading:

1. Dr Tahir-ul-Qadri, Relations of Muslims and Non-Muslims, Ch:12, pp.162-163.

12.1.6 The Viewpoint of al-Thānwī on the Abode of War

Essential Reading:

1. Dr Tahir-ul-Qadri, Relations of Muslims and Non-Muslims, Ch:12, pp.163-164.

12.1.7 A Country Practicing Islamic Teachings and Signs cannot be Declared an Abode of War

Essential Reading:

1. Dr Tahir-ul-Qadri, Relations of Muslims and Non-Muslims, Ch:12, pp.164-165.

Additional Readings for Teachers and Students:

. al-Dusūqī, āshiya ʿalā al-Sharḥ al-kabīr ʿalā Mukhtaṣar Khalīl li al-Dardīr, 2:188.

12.1.8 No Land can be Declared an Abode of War Only Due to Disbelievers' Rule and Authority

Essential Reading:

1. Dr Tahir-ul-Qadri, Relations of Muslims and Non-Muslims, Ch:12, pp.165-166.

Additional Readings for Teachers and Students:

1. Ibn Taimiyya, *Majmūʿ al-Fatāwā*, 28:354.
2. Ibn al-Qayyim, *Aḥkām ahl al-dhimma*, 2:728.

12.2.1 The Difference between the Abode of Treaty and the Abode of Reconciliation

Essential Reading:

1. Dr Tahir-ul-Qadri, Relations of Muslims and Non-Muslims, Ch:12, pp.166-167.

Additional Readings for Teachers and Students:

1. al-Shāfiʿī, *al-Umm*, 4:184.
2. al-Urūsī, *Fiqh al-jihād wa al-ʿalaqāt al-duwaliyya fī al-Islām*, p. 333.

12.2.2 Instructions to Fulfil Agreements with the Abode of Reconciliation

Essential Reading:

1. Dr Tahir-ul-Qadri, Relations of Muslims and Non-Muslims, Ch:12, pp.167-171.

Additional Readings for Teachers and Students:

1. Qurʾān 4:91.
2. al-Rāzī, *al-Tafṣīr al-kabīr*, 1:179.
3. Qurʾān 9:12.
4. Ibid., 9:13.
5. al-Baghawī, *Maʿālim al-tanzīl*, 2:273.
6. al-Qurṭubī, *al-Jāmiʿ li aḥkām al-Qurʾān*, 8:55.
7. Ibn ayyān, *al-Baḥr al-muḥīṭ*, 5:17.
8. Ibn Kathīr, *Tafsīr al-Qurʾān al-ʿAẓīm*; 4:60.
9. al-Shawkānī, *Fatḥ al-qadīr*, 2:343.
10. al-Wāḥidī, *al-Wasīṭ fī tafsīr al-Qurʾān al-Majīd*, 2:481
11. Ibn Kathīr, *Tafsīr al-Qurʾān al-Aẓīm*, 2:340.
12. al-Jaṣṣāṣ, *Aḥkām al-Qurʾān*, 5:83.

12.2.3 Preference of Reconciliation and Compromise for the Establishment of Peace

Essential Reading:

1. Dr Tahir-ul-Qadri, Relations of Muslims and Non-Muslims, Ch:12, pp.171-172.

Additional Readings for Teachers and Students:

1. Qur'ān 8:58.
2. Qur'ān 9:6.

12.3 The Abode of Treaty (*Dār al-ʿAhd*)

Essential Reading:

1. Dr Tahir-ul-Qadri, Relations of Muslims and Non-Muslims, Ch:12, pp.172-173.

12.3.1 Qur'ānic Injunction to Fulfil Agreements with an Abode of Treaty

Essential Reading:

1. Dr Tahir-ul-Qadri, Relations of Muslims and Non-Muslims, Ch:12, pp.173-175.

Additional Readings for Teachers and Students:

1. Qur'ān 9:7.

12.3.1.1 A Temporary or Long-Term Treaty

Essential Reading:

1. Dr Tahir-ul-Qadri, Relations of Muslims and Non-Muslims, Ch:12, pp.175-177.

Additional Readings for Teachers and Students:

1. Abū Dāwūd, *al-Sunan*, 3:86 §2766
2. Ibn Hishām, *al-Sīra al-Nabawiyya*, 5:48.
3. al-Wāḥidī, *al-Wasīṭ fī tafsīr al-Kitāb al-ʿAzīz*, 1:454–455.

12.3.1.2 The General Treaty of Peace and Reconciliation

12.3.1.2.1 The Pact of Medina

Essential Reading:

1. Dr Tahir-ul-Qadri, Relations of Muslims and Non-Muslims, Ch:12, pp.177-179.

Additional Readings for Teachers and Students:

1. Ibn Hishām, *al-Sīra al-Nabawiyya*, 3:33.
2. Ibn Kathīr, *al-Bidāya wa al-nihāya*, 3:225.
3. Ibn Hishām, *al-Sīra al-Nabawiyya*, 3:33.
4. Ibn Kathīr, *al-Bidāya wa al-nihāya*, 3:225.
5. Ibn Hishām, *al-Sīra al-Nabawiyya*, 3:34.
6. Ibn Kathīr, *al-Bidāya wa al-nihāya*, 3:225.

12.3.1.2.2 Developing Political Unity to Stabilize the State and Establish Peace

Essential Reading:

1. Dr Tahir-ul-Qadri, Relations of Muslims and Non-Muslims, Ch:12, pp.179.

Additional Readings for Teachers and Students:

1. Ibn Hishām in *al-Sīra al-Nabawiyya*, 2:501.
2. al-Bayhaqī in *al-Sunan al-kubrā*, 8:106 §16147–16148.
3. Ibn Kathīr in *al-Bidāya wa al-nihāya*, 3:224.
4. Dr Hamīd Ullāh in *al-Wathā'iq al-siyasīyya*, p. 41.

12.3.1.2.3 Allah's Messenger ﷺ is the Founder of the Concept of Integration

Essential Reading:

1. Dr Tahir-ul-Qadri, Relations of Muslims and Non-Muslims, Ch:12, pp.180.

Additional Readings for Teachers and Students:

1. Ibn Hishām in *al-Sīra al-Nabawiyya*, 2:501.
2. al-Bayhaqī in *al-Sunan al-kubrā*, 8:106 §16147–16148.
3. Ibn Kathīr in *al-Bidāya wa al-nihāya*, 3:224.
4. Dr Hamīd Ullāh in *al-Wathā'iq al-siyasīyya*, p. 41.

12.3.1.2.3 The Pact of Najrān

Essential Reading:

1. Dr Tahir-ul-Qadri, Relations of Muslims and Non-Muslims, Ch:12, pp.180-182.

Additional Readings for Teachers and Students:

1. Ibn Sa'd in *al-Ṭabaqāt al-kubrā*, 1:288, 358.
2. Abū Yūsuf in *al-Kharāj*, 78.
3. Abū 'Ubayd al-Qāsim b. Sallām in *Kitāb al-amwāl*, p. 244–245 §503.

4. Ibn Zanjawayh in *Kitāb al-amwāl,* pp. 449–450 §732.
5. al-Balādhurī in *Futūḥ al-buldān*, p. 90.
6. Ibn Zanjaways in *Kitāb al-amwāl*, pp. 450–451 §732.
7. Muslim in *al-Ṣaḥīḥ*: *Kitāb al-imāra* [The Book of Leadership], chapter: "The Obligation to Stick to the Main Body of the Muslims in the Time of Trials," 3:1476–1477 §1848.
8. Aḥmad b. Ḥanbal in *al-Musnad*, 2:296, 488.
9. al-Nasāʾī in *al-Sunan*: *Kitāb taḥrīm al-dam* [The Book on the Prohibition of Bloodshed], 7:123 §4114.

12.4 The Abode of Peace (*Dār al-Amn*)

Essential Reading:

1. Dr Tahir-ul-Qadri, Relations of Muslims and Non-Muslims, Ch:12, pp.182.

Additional Readings for Teachers and Students:

1. Ibn Saʿd in *al-Ṭabaqāt al-kubrā*, 1:288, 358.
2. Abū Yūsuf in *al-Kharāj*, 78.
3. Abū ʿUbayd al-Qāsim b. Sallām in *Kitāb al-amwāl,* p. 244–245 §503.
4. Ibn Zanjawayh in *Kitāb al-amwāl,* pp. 449–450 §732.
5. al-Balādhurī in *Futūḥ al-buldān*, p. 90.
6. Ibn Zanjaways in *Kitāb al-amwāl*, pp. 450–451 §732.
7. Muslim in *al-Ṣaḥīḥ*: *Kitāb al-imāra* [The Book of Leadership], chapter: "The Obligation to Stick to the Main Body of the Muslims in the Time of Trials," 3:1476–1477 §1848.
8. Aḥmad b. Ḥanbal in *al-Musnad*, 2:296, 488.
9. al-Nasāʾī in *al-Sunan*: *Kitāb taḥrīm al-dam* [The Book on the Prohibition of Bloodshed], 7:123 §4114.

12.4.1 The Hanafī Stance on the Abode of Islam

Essential Reading:

1. Dr Tahir-ul-Qadri, Relations of Muslims and Non-Muslims, Ch:12, pp.182-187.

Additional Readings for Teachers and Students:

1. Al-Kāsānī, *Badā'iʿ al-ṣanā'iʿ*, 7:131.
2. ibid.
3. Abū Zuhra, *al-ʿAlāqāt al-duwaliyya fī al-Islām*, p. 60.
4. Qur'ān 9:4.

12.5 The Abode of War (*Dār al- arb*)

Essential Reading:

1. Dr Tahir-ul-Qadri, Relations of Muslims and Non-Muslims, Ch:12, pp.187.

12.5.1 The Islamic Ruling for the non-Combatants

Essential Reading:

1. Dr Tahir-ul-Qadri, Relations of Muslims and Non-Muslims, Ch:12, pp.187.

12.5.2 The Qur'ānic Injunction on Excellent Morality with non-Combatants

Essential Reading:

1. Dr Tahir-ul-Qadri, Relations of Muslims and Non-Muslims, Ch:12, pp.188-189.

Additional Readings for Teachers and Students:

1. Ibn al-Jawzī, *Zād al-masīr*, 8:237.
2. al-Qurṭubī, *al-Jāmiʿ li aḥkām al-Qurʾān*, 18:59.
3. Ibn Kathīr, *Tafsīr al-Qurʾān al-Aẓīm*, 4:350.

12.5.3 The Affectionate Behaviour of Medina towards non-Combatants

Essential Reading:

1. Dr Tahir-ul-Qadri, Relations of Muslims and Non-Muslims, Ch:12, pp.189-190.

Additional Readings for Teachers and Students:

1. al-Sarakhsī, *Sharḥ Kitāb al-siyar al-kabīr*, 1:70.

12.5.4 The Stand of the Imams and Hadith-Scholars on non-Combatants

Essential Reading:

1. Dr Tahir-ul-Qadri, Relations of Muslims and Non-Muslims, Ch:12, pp.190-192.

Additional Readings for Teachers and Students:

1. Ibn al-Qayyim, *Aḥkām ahl al-dhimma*, 1:172–173.
2. Ibn Qudāma, *al-Mughnī*, 9:251.
3. Ibn al-Qayyim, *Aḥkām ahl al-dhimma*, 1:165.

4. Ibn Qudāma al-Maqdisī, *al-Mughnī*, 9:251.
5. al-Bayhaqī in *al-Sunan al-kubrā*, 9:91 §1738.

12.5.5 Why Medina was Chosen for Migration

Essential Reading:

1. Dr Tahir-ul-Qadri, Relations of Muslims and Non-Muslims, Ch:12, pp.192-193.

12.5.6 The Difference of Pace and Number Between the Meccan and Medinan People in Accepting Islam

Essential Reading:

1. Dr Tahir-ul-Qadri, Relations of Muslims and Non-Muslims, Ch:12, pp.193-194.

12.6 The Prophet ﷺ Integrated the Jews and the Muslims into a Collective Unity Through the Pact of Medina

Essential Reading:

1. Dr Tahir-ul-Qadri, Relations of Muslims and Non-Muslims, Ch:12, p.194.

Additional Readings for Teachers and Students:

1. Ḥumayd b. Zanjawayh in *Kitāb al-Amwāl,* 1:393.
2. Abū ʿUbayd al-Qāsim b. Sallām in *Kitāb al-Amwāl,* 1:393.
3. Ibn Hishām in *al-Sīra al-Nabawiyya*, 2:497.
4. Ibn Kathīr in *al-Bidāya wa al-nihāya*, 3:224.
5. Ibn Hishām in *al-Sīra al-Nabawiyya*, 2:497.
6. al-Bayhaqī in *al-Sunan al-kubrā*, 8:106.
7. Ibn Kathīr in *al-Bidāya wa al-nihāya*, 3:224.
8. Ḥumayd b. Zanjawayh in *Kitāb al-amwāl,* 1:394.
9. Abū ʿUbayd al-Qāsim b. Sallām in *Kitāb al-amwāl,* 1:394.
10. Ibn Hishām in *al-Sīra al-Nabawiyya*, 2:497–498.
11. al-Bayhaqī in *al-Sunan al-kubrā*, 8:106.
12. Ibn Kathīr in *al-Bidāya wa al-nihāya*, 3:224–225.

12.6.1 The Prophetic Pronouncement: "The Jews Together with the Muslims are One Nation"

Essential Reading:

1. Dr Tahir-ul-Qadri, Relations of Muslims and Non-Muslims, Ch:12, p.194-200.

Additional Readings for Teachers and Students:

1. Abū ʿUbayd al-Qāsim b. Sallām in *Kitāb al-amwāl*, p. 263.
2. Maḥmūd b. ʿUmar al-Zamakhsharī in *al-Fāʾiq fī gharīb al-ḥadīth wa al-āthār,* 2:25.

12.6.2 The Implications of "The Jews of Banū ʿAwf will be a Part of the Muslim Community"

12.6.2.1 Imam Ibn al-Athīr al-Jazarī

Essential Reading:

1. Dr Tahir-ul-Qadri, Relations of Muslims and Non-Muslims, Ch:12, p.200-202.

Additional Readings for Teachers and Students:

1. Ibn al-Athīr, *Manāl al-ṭālib fī Sharḥ Ṭiwāl al-gharā'ib ḥadīth*, the book of Quraysh and al-Anṣār, 1:183.

12.6.2.2 Interpretation by al-Zamakhsharī

Essential Reading:

1. Dr Tahir-ul-Qadri, Relations of Muslims and Non-Muslims, Ch:12, p.202-203.

12.6.2.3 Interpretation by Ibn Abī ʿUbayd al-Harawī

Essential Reading:

1. Dr Tahir-ul-Qadri, Relations of Muslims and Non-Muslims, Ch:12, p.203.

12.7 Five other Jewish Tribes were also Included in One Community along with Muslims

Essential Reading:

1. Dr Ṭahir-ul-Qadri, Relations of Muslims and Non-Muslims, Ch:12, p.203-206.

Additional Readings for Teachers and Students:

1. Ḥumayd b. Zanjawayh in *Kitāb al-amwāl,* 1:395.
2. Ibn Hishām in *al-Sīra al-Nabawiyya*, 1:331, 2:499–500.
3. Abū ʿUbayd al-Qāsim b. Sallām in *Kitāb al-amwāl,* 1:224.
4. al-Ṭabarī, *Tārīkh al-umam wa al-mulūk*, 1:547.
5. al-Zamakhsharī in *al-Fāʾiq fī gharīb al-ḥadīth wa al-āthār,* 2:25.
6. al-Dhahabī, *Tārīkh al-Islām*, 1:184.
7. Ibn Kathīr, *al-Bidāya wa al-nihāya*, 3:66.
8. al-ʿAynī, *ʿUmda al-qārī*, 7:268.

12.8 Abyssinia—The Model Abode of Peace

Essential Reading:

1. Dr Tahir-ul-Qadri, Relations of Muslims and Non-Muslims, Ch:12, p.206-207.

12.9 The Difference Between the Christian Rule of Abyssinia and the Meccan Rule

Essential Reading:

1. Dr Tahir-ul-Qadri, Relations of Muslims and Non-Muslims, Ch:12, p.207-211.

Additional Readings for Teachers and Students:

1. Qurʾān 3:199.

2. Qur'ān 5:82
3. Qur'ān 16:41.
4. al-Qurṭubī, *al-Jāmiʿ li aḥkām al-Qur'ān*, 10:107.
5. Ibn Abī Ḥātim al-Rāzī, *Tafsīr al-Qur'ān al-ʿAẓīm*, 7:2284 §21518.
6. al-Ṭabarī, *Jāmiʿ al-Bayān fī Tafsīr al-Qur'ān*, 14:107.
7. Makkī b. Abī Ṭālib al-Muqrī, *al-Hidāya ilā bulūgh al-nihāya*, 6:3996.
8. Ibn ʿAṭiyya, *al-Muḥarrar al-wajīz fī tafsīr al-kitāb al-ʿazīz*, 3:394.
9. Abū ayān, *al-Baḥr al-muḥīṭ*, 5:492.
10. Qur'ān 29:56.
11. Ibn Kathīr, *Tafsīr al-Qur'ān al-ʿAẓīm*, 6:290.

12.10 The Holy Prophet ﷺ Declared Abyssinia "The Land of Truth"

Essential Reading:

1. Dr Tahir-ul-Qadri, Relations of Muslims and Non-Muslims, Ch:12, p.211-213.

Additional Readings for Teachers and Students:

1. al-Ṭabarī, *Tārīkh al-umam wa al-mulūk*, 1:547.

12.10.1 The Negus had yet to Know about the Final Messenger

Essential Reading:

1. Dr Tahir-ul-Qadri, Relations of Muslims and Non-Muslims, Ch:12, p.213-214.

Additional Readings for Teachers and Students:

1. Yūsuf al-Ṣāliḥī, *Subul al-hudā wa al-rishād fī sīra khayr al-ʿibād*, Ch:13 2:391.

12.10.2 The Companions' Praise for the Negus and his Rule

Essential Reading:

1. Dr Tahir-ul-Qadri, Relations of Muslims and Non-Muslims, Ch:12, p.214-215.

12.10.3 Allah's Excellent Reward for Negus's Excellent Conduct with the Muslims

Essential Reading:

1. Dr Tahir-ul-Qadri, Relations of Muslims and Non-Muslims, Ch:12, p.215-216.

12.10.4 The Prophet's Excellent Bestowal for Negus's Benevolence Towards the Companions

Essential Reading:

1. Dr Tahir-ul-Qadri, Relations of Muslims and Non-Muslims, Ch:12, p.216-217.

12.10.5 When did the Negus Embrace Islam Formally?

Essential Reading:

1. Dr Tahir-ul-Qadri, Relations of Muslims and Non-Muslims, Ch:12, p.216.

12.11 The Loyalty of the Muslim Abyssinian Refugees to Abyssinia and its Relevance to the Modern World

Essential Reading:

1. Dr Tahir-ul-Qadri, Relations of Muslims and Non-Muslims, Ch:12, p.217-218.

12.11.1 An Analysis of Human Rights in Western and some Muslim Countries (towards the Categories of Abodes)

Essential Reading:

1. Dr Tahir-ul-Qadri, Relations of Muslims and Non-Muslims, Ch:12, p.218.

12.11.2 The Message of Islam—the Establishment of a Global Human Society

Essential Reading:

1. Dr Tahir-ul-Qadri, Relations of Muslims and Non-Muslims, Ch:12, p.219.

12.12 Afterword

Essential Reading:

1. Dr Tahir-ul-Qadri, Relations of Muslims and Non-Muslims, Ch:12, p.219-220.

SECTION II

Islam on Love and Non-Violence

1. Islam—A True Religion of Love

Essential Reading:

1. Dr Tahir-ul-Qadri, Islam on Love and Non-Violence, Ch:1, p.5.

1.1 The Supremacy of Love on Allah's Attributes

Essential Reading:

1. Dr Tahir-ul-Qadri, Islam on Love and Non-Violence, Ch:1, p.8.

1.2 Love and Forgiveness—the Divine Attributes

Essential Reading:

1. Dr Tahir-ul-Qadri, Islam on Love and Non-Violence, Ch:1, p.8-16.

Additional Readings for Teachers and Students:

1. Abū Nuʿaym, *ilya al-awliyāʾ*, 9:351.
2. al- ākim in *al-Mustadrak*, 1:111 §51.
3. Ibn Rāshid in *al-Jāmiʿ*, 11:143 §20150.
4. al-Ṭabarānī in *al-Muʿjam al-Kabīr*, 3:131 §151.
5. al-Bayhaqī in *al-Sunan al-Kubrā*, 10:191 §20570.
6. Qurʾān, 3:134.
7. Qurʾān, 2:165.
8. Qurʾān, 5:54.
9. Aḥmad b. anbal in *al-Zuhd*, p. 197.
10. al-Bukhārī in *al-Ṣaḥīḥ*, *Kitāb al-tawḥīd* [The Book of Divine Unity], chapter: "What has been reported about the Prophet, may Allah bless him and grant him peace, calling his community to proclaim the oneness of Allah Almighty," 6:2686 §6940.
11. Muslim in *al-Ṣaḥīḥ*, *Kitāb Ṣalāt al-Musāfirīn wa Qaṣru-hā* [The Book of Ritual Prayer of the Travellers and its Curtailment], chapter, "The excellent merit of reciting the Qurʾānic chapter 'Say: He is God the One,'" 1:557 §813.
12. al-Nasāʾī in *al-Sunan*, *Kitāb al-Iftitāḥ* [The Book of the Commencement], chapter, "The excellent merit of reciting the Qurʾānic chapter 'Say: He is God the One,'" 2:170 §993.
13. al-Bukhārī in *al-Ṣaḥīḥ*, *Kitāb al-tawḥīd* [The Book of Divine Unity], chapter: "The words of Allah Almighty, 'They desire to alter Allah's words...,'" (Qurʾān 48:15), 6:2725 §7065.
14. Aḥmad b. anbal in *al-Musnad*, 2:418 §9400.
15. al-Nasāʾī in *al-Sunan*, *Kitāb al-janāʾiz* [The Book of Funeral Rites], chapter, "Concerning someone who loves meeting Allah," 4:10 §1835.
16. Mālik in *al-Muwaṭṭāʾ*, 1:240 §569.
17. Ibn ibbān in *al-Ṣaḥīḥ*, 2:84 §363.
18. al-Daylamī in *Musnad al-Firdaws*, 3:172 §4460.
19. Muslim in *al-Ṣaḥīḥ*: *Kitāb al-dhikr wa al-duʿāʾ wa al-tawba wa al-istighfār* [The Book of Remembrance, Supplication, Repentance and Seeking Forgiveness], chapter, "He who loves to meet Allāh, Allāh loves to meet him, and he who dislikes to meet Allāh, Allāh abhors to meet him," 4:2065 §2684.
20. Mundhirī in *al-Targhīb wa al-Tarhīb*, 4:171 §5297.
21. Qurʾān, 5:54.
22. Muslim in *al-Ṣaḥīḥ*: *Kitāb al-dhikr wa al-duʿāʾ wa al-tawba wa al-istighfār* [The Book of Remembrance, Supplication, Repentance and Seeking Forgiveness], chapter, "Urging on the recollection of Allah Most High," 4:2061 §2675.
23. Aḥmad b. anbal in *al-Musnad*, 2:316 §8178 & 3:283 §14045.
24. Aḥmad b. anbal in *al-Musnad*, 5:238 §22125.

25. Ṭabarānī in *al-Muʿjam al-Kabīr*, 20:125 §251.

1.3 The Grace of Love is Sent from the Heavens

Essential Reading:

1. Dr Tahir-ul-Qadri, Islam on Love and Non-Violence, Ch:1, p.16-17.

Additional Readings for Teachers and Students:

1. Aḥmad b. anbal in *al-Musnad*, 5:279 §22454.
2. al-Ṭabarānī in *al-Muʿjam al-Awsaṭ*, 2:57 §1240.

1.4 The Origin of Divinity is Also Love

Essential Reading:

1. Dr Tahir-ul-Qadri, Islam on Love and Non-Violence, Ch:1, p.17-20.

Additional Readings for Teachers and Students:

1. Muslim in *al-Ṣaḥīḥ: Kitāb al-Tawba* [The Book of Repentance], chapter: ""The Vastness of Allah's Mercy and That His Mercy Precedes His Wrath," 4:2108 §2752.
2. Aḥmad b. Ḥanbal in *al-Musnad*, 2:434 §9607.
3. al-Tirmidhī in *al-Sunan: Kitāb al-Daʿawāt ʿan Rasūl Allāh* ﷺ [The Book of Invocations from Allāh's Messenger a], chapter: "Allāh Created One Hundred Mercies," 5:549 §3541.
4. Ibn Mājah in *al-Sunan: Kitāb al-Zuhd* [The Book of the Renunciation], chapter: ""Hope for Allāh's Mercy on the Day of Resurrection," 2:1435 §4293.
5. Abū Yaʿlā in *al-Musnad*, 11:258; 328 §6372; 6445.

1.5 Divine Address to the Sinful

Essential Reading:

1. Dr Tahir-ul-Qadri, Islam on Love and Non-Violence, Ch:1, p.20-24.

Additional Readings for Teachers and Students:

1. al-Bukhārī in *al-Ṣaḥīḥ*: *Kitāb al-Daʿawāt* [The Book of Supplications], chapter: "Repentance," 5:2324 §5949.
2. Muslim in *al-Ṣaḥīḥ*: *Kitāb al-tawba* [The Book of Penitence], chapter: "Exhorting to be penitent and extreme delight over it," 4:2104 §2747.
3. Aḥmad b. anbal in *al-Musnad*, 4:283 §18515.
4. Abū Yaʿlā in *al-Musnad*, 3:257 §1704.
5. Muslim in *al-Ṣaḥīḥ*: *Kitāb Ṣalāt al-Musāfirīn wa Qaṣru-hā* [The Book of Ritual Prayer of the Travellers and its Curtailment], chapter, "Exhortation to supplicate and pray," 1:523 §758.
6. Aḥmad b. anbal in *al-Musnad*, 3:34 §11313.
7. al-Nasāʾī in *al-Sunan al-kubrā*, 6:124 §10315.
8. ʿAbd b. umayd in *al-Musnad*, 1:272 §861.
9. Ibn Abī Shayba in *al-Muṣannaf*, 6:72 §29556. ʿAbd al-Razzāq in *al-Muṣannaf*, 10:444 §19654.
10. al-Ṭabarānī in *al-Muʿjam al-Kabīr*, 22:370 §927.
11. al-Tirmidhī in *al-Sunan*: *Kitāb al-Daʿawāt ʿan Rasūl Allāh* ﷺ [The Book of Invocations from Allāh's Messenger ﷺ], chapter: "The excellent merit of repentance and seeking forgiveness, and what has been mentioned about Allah's Mercy for His servants," 5:548 §3540.
12. al-Dārimī in *al-Sunan*, 2:414 §2788.
13. Aḥmad b. Ḥanbal in *al-Musnad*, 5:167 §21510–21544.
14. al-Ṭabarānī, on the authority of Ibn ʿAbbās k, in *al-Muʿjam al-Kabīr*, 12:19 §12346, & in *al-Muʿjam al-Awsaṭ*, 5:337 §5483, & in *al-Muʿjam al-Ṣaghīr*, 2:82 §820.
15. al-Bayhaqī, on the authority of Abū Dharr ؓ, in *Shuʿab al-Īmān*, 2:17 §1042.
16. al-Haithamī in *Majmaʿ al-Zawāʾid*, 10/216.
17. al-Qushayrī in *al-Risāla*, p. 332.

1.6 LOVE IS ALSO MANIFESTED IN REWARD AND FAVOUR

ESSENTIAL READING:

1. Dr Tahir-ul-Qadri, Islam on Love and Non-Violence, Ch:1, p.24-26.

ADDITIONAL READINGS FOR TEACHERS AND STUDENTS:

1. Qur'ān 42:19.
2. al-Ṭabarānī in *Musnad al-Shāmiyyīn*, 2:93 §974–975.
3. al-Bayhaqī in *Shuʿab al-Īmān*, 4:134 §4563.
4. al-Daylamī in *Musnad al-Firdaws*, 3:166 §4439.

1.7 LOVE STIMULATES SUBMISSION TO DIVINE INJUNCTIONS

ESSENTIAL READING:

1. Dr Tahir-ul-Qadri, Islam on Love and Non-Violence, Ch:1, p.26-28.

ADDITIONAL READINGS FOR TEACHERS AND STUDENTS:

1. Qur'ān, 76:8.
2. al-Bukhārī in *al-Ṣaḥīḥ: Kitāb al-Īmān* [The Book of Faith], chapter: "Sweetness of Faith *[ḥalāwat al-Īmān]*," 1:14 §16 & in *Kitāb al-Īmān* [The Book of Faith], chapter: "Someone who detests the prospect of reverting to unbelief, just as he detests the prospect of being thrown into the Fire of Hell from faith," 1:16 §21.
3. Muslim in *al-Ṣaḥīḥ: Kitāb al-Īmān* [The Book of Faith], chapter: "Explanation of the qualities by which someone who is characterized by them discovers the sweetness of faith," 1:66 §43.
4. al-Tirmidhī in *al-Sunan: Kitāb al-Īmān* [The Book of Faith] according to Allah's Messenger a, chapter: "(10), 5:15 §2624.

5. al-Nasāʾī in *al-Sunan: Kitāb al-Īmān wa Sharāʾiʿu-h* [The Book of Faith and its laws], Ch: The taste of faith, 8:94 §4987.

1.8 Love will Make up the Deficiency of Pious Deeds

Essential Reading:

1. Dr Tahir-ul-Qadri, Islam on Love and Non-Violence, Ch:1, p.28-32.

Additional Readings for Teachers and Students:

1. al- Bukhārī in *al-Ṣaḥīḥ*: *Kitāb al-Adab* [Proper Conduct], chapter: "The sign of love for the sake of Allah, 3:1349 §3485.
2. Muslim in *al-Ṣaḥīḥ*: *Kitāb al-Birr wa al-Ṣila wa al-Ādāb* [Piety, Affinity and Good Manners], chapter: "The man is together with the one he loves, 4:2032 §2639.
3. al-Tirmidhī in *al-Sunan*: *al-Zuhd* [Abstinence] according to Allah's Messenger a, chapter: "What has come to inform us that the man is together with the one he loves, 4:595 §2385.
4. Aḥmad b. Ḥanbal in *al-Musnad*, 5:166 § 21501.
5. Abū Dāwūd in *al-Sunan*, *Kitāb al-Adab* [Proper Conduct], chapter: "The man's informing the man of his love for him," 4:333 §5126.
6. al-Dārimī in *al-Sunan*, 2:414 §2787.
7. al-Bazzār in *al-Musnad*, 9:373 §395.
8. Ibn Ḥibbān in *al-Ṣaḥīḥ*, 2:315 §556.
9. al-Bukhārī in *al-Adab al-Mufrad*, 1:128 §351.
10. al-Bukhārī in *al-Ṣaḥīḥ: Kitāb al-   udūd* [The Prescribed Punishments], chapter: ""The Offensiveness of Cursing the One Who Drinks Alcohol, and Establishing that He is Not outside the Fold of the Religion," 6:2489 §6398.

1.9 The Injunction to Love the Beloved and the Chosen Ones

Essential Reading:

1. Dr Tahir-ul-Qadri, Islam on Love and Non-Violence, Ch:1, p.32-35.

Additional Readings for Teachers and Students:

1. Ibn al-Jawzī in *Ṣifat al-Ṣafwa*, 4:112.
2. Ibn al-Mullaqan in *adāʾiq al-Awliyāʾ*, p. 202.
3. al-Rifāʿī in *āla ahl al-ḥaqīqa maʿa Allāh*, p. 127.
4. Aḥmad b. anbal in *al-Musnad*, 4:337 §18992.
5. Ibn Mājah in *al-Sunan*, *Kitāb al-janāʾiz* [The Book of Funeral Rites], chapter, "What has come to us regarding digging the grave," 1:497 §1559.
6. Ibn Abī ʿĀṣim in *al-Āḥād wa al-Mathānī*, 4:348 §2382.
7. Ibn ibbān in *al-Thiqāt*, 2:99.
8. al-Ṭabarānī in *al-Muʿjam al-Awsaṭ*, 9:52 §9111.
9. al-Bayhaqī in *Shuʿab al-Īmān*, 1:417 §583.

1.10 Raising the Prophets ﷺ is a Manifestation of Allah's love for His Creation

Essential Reading:

1. Dr Tahir-ul-Qadri, Islam on Love and Non-Violence, Ch:1, p.35-36.

1.11 The Holy Prophet's ﷺ Attributes and Excellence Manifest Love

Essential Reading:

1. Dr Tahir-ul-Qadri, Islam on Love and Non-Violence, Ch:1, p.36-37.

Additional Readings for Teachers and Students:

1. Qur'ān 33:6.

1.12 The Universality of the Prophet's ﷺ Mercy Permeates with the Message of Love

Essential Reading:

1. Dr Tahir-ul-Qadri, Islam on Love and Non-Violence, Ch:1, p.37-38.

1.13 Love and Kindness for non-Muslims

Essential Reading:

1. Dr Tahir-ul-Qadri, Islam on Love and Non-Violence, Ch:1, p.38-39.

Additional Readings for Teachers and Students:

1. al-Shāfiʿī in *Tārīkh Madīna Damishq*, 23:454.
2. ʿAbd al-Barr in *al-Istīʿāb*, 2:597.
3. al-Shawkānī in *Nayl al-Awṭār*, 8:168.

1.14 If You Seek Mercy, then Love

Essential Reading:

1. Dr Tahir-ul-Qadri, Islam on Love and Non-Violence, Ch:1, p.39-43.

Additional Readings for Teachers and Students:

1. Qur'ān 9:24.
2. al-Bukhārī in *al-Ṣaḥīḥ: Kitāb al-Īmān* [The Book of Faith], chapter: "Love of the Messenger ﷺ is a part of faith," 1:14 §15.
3. Muslim in *al-Ṣaḥīḥ*: *Kitāb al-Īmān* [The Book of Faith], chapter: "The necessity of loving Allah's Messenger a more than the family, the children, the parents and people altogether," 1:67 §44.* Set forth by
4. al-Bukhārī in *al-Ṣaḥīḥ*: *Kitāb al-Īmān* [The Book of Faith], chapter: "Love of the Messenger a is a part of faith; 1:14 §14.
5. Muslim in *al-Ṣaḥīḥ*: *Kitāb al-Imāra* [The Book of Imperial Authority], chapter: "The excellent merit of the just imam, the chastisement of the despot, the urging of kind treatment of the subjects, and the prohibition of inflicting hardship upon them," 3/1458 §1828.

1.15 Love as the Recompense of Preaching the Faith through Messengership

Essential Reading:

1. Dr Tahir-ul-Qadri, Islam on Love and Non-Violence, Ch:1, p.43-45.

Additional Readings for Teachers and Students:

1. Qur'ān, 19:96.
2. al-Tirmidhī in *al-Sunan*: *Kitāb al-Manāqib* [The Book of Virtues] according to Allah's Messenger a, chapter: "The excellent merits of the household of the Prophet," 5:664 §3789.
3. al- ākim in *al-Mustadrak*, 3:162 §4716.
4. al-Ṭabarānī in *al-Muʿjam al-Kabīr*, 3:46 §2639 & 10:281 §10664.
5. al-Bayhaqī in *Shuʿab al-Īmān*, 1:366 §408.
6. Qur'ān, 19:96.

7. al-Tirmidhī in *al-Sunan*: *Kitāb al-Tafsīr* [The Book of Interpretation], chapter: "From the *Sūra* of Maryam," 5:317 §3161.

1.16 The Non-Specific, Specific and Grand Intercession are also a Manifestation of Love

Essential Reading:

1. Dr Tahir-ul-Qadri, Islam on Love and Non-Violence, Ch:1, p.46-47.

1.17 The Non-Specific, Specific and Grand Intercession are also a Manifestation of Love

Essential Reading:

1. Dr Tahir-ul-Qadri, Islam on Love and Non-Violence, Ch:1, p.47-48.

Additional Readings for Teachers and Students:

1. al-Tirmidhī in *al-Sunan*: *Kitāb al-Daʿawāt* [The Book of Supplications], chapter (73), 5:522 §3490.
2. al- ākim in *al-Mustadrak*, 2:470 §3621.
3. al-Daylamī in *Musnad al-Firdaws*, 3:271 §4810.

1.18 Founding Principles of Islamic Law are Based on Love and Mercy

Essential Reading:

1. Dr Tahir-ul-Qadri, Islam on Love and Non-Violence, Ch:1, p.48.

1.18.1 The Prophet's ﷺ Liking for Gentleness and Easiness as a Sign of Love

Essential Reading:

1. Dr Tahir-ul-Qadri, Islam on Love and Non-Violence, Ch:1, p.49-51.

Additional Readings for Teachers and Students:

1. al-Bukhārī in *al-Ṣaḥīḥ: Kitāb al-ʿIlm* [The Book of Knowledge], chapter: "On the Prophet a Being Careful about Giving People Admonition and Knowledge Lest They Feel Aversion to It," 1:38 §69.
2. Muslim in *al-Ṣaḥīḥ: Kitāb al-Jihād wa al-siyar* [The Book of the Striving and Military Expeditions], chapter: "The Command to Make Things Easy and Not Making Others Feel Aversion," 3:1359 §1734.

1.18.2 Islam did not Spread by the Sword!

Essential Reading:

1. Dr Tahir-ul-Qadri, Islam on Love and Non-Violence, Ch:1, p.51-52.

1.18.3 Love and Brotherhood—the Identity of Believers

Essential Reading:

1. Dr Tahir-ul-Qadri, Islam on Love and Non-Violence, Ch:1, p.52-53.

Additional Readings for Teachers and Students:

1. Qur'ān, 49:10.

1.18.4 Ambit of Love Encompasses non-Muslims

Essential Reading:

1. Dr Tahir-ul-Qadri, Islam on Love and Non-Violence, Ch:1, p.54.

1.19 Afterword

Essential Reading:

1. Dr Tahir-ul-Qadri, Islam on Love and Non-Violence, Ch:1, p.54-55.

2. Messenger ﷺ of Mercy: The Embodiment of Love

Essential Reading:

1. Dr Tahir-ul-Qadri, Islam on Love and Non-Violence, Ch:2, p.57-61.

Additional Readings for Teachers and Students:

1. Muslim in *al-Ṣaḥīḥ: Kitāb al-birr wa ṣila wa al-adab* [On Piety, Filial Duty, and Good Manners], chapter: "The Prohibition of Invoking Curses Against Creatures and Other Things," 4:2006 §2599.
2. al-Bukhārī in *al-Adab al-mufrad*, 119 §321.
3. Abū Yaʿlā in *al-Musnad*, 11:35 §6174.

4. Abū Nuʿaym in *Dalāʾil al-nubuwwa*, 1:40 §2.
5. al-Bayhaqī in *Shuʿab al-īmān*, 2:144 §1403.
6. Ibn ʿAsākir in *Tārīkh Dimashq*, 4:92.
7. al- usaynī in *al-Bayān wa al-taʿrīf*, 1:283 §754.
8. Ibn Kathīr in *Tafsīr al-Qurʾān al-ʿAẓīm*, 3:202.
9. al-Bayhaqi, Shub al-Iman, 2:144, §1403.
10. Ibn Asakar, Tarikh Madina Damishq, 4:92
11. Aḥmad b. anbal in *al-Musnad*, 5:268, 437 §§22361, 23757.
12. Abū Dāwūd in *al-Sūnan: Kitāb al-sunna* [The Book of the Sunna], chapter: "The Prohibition of Maligning the Companions of the Messenger of Allāh ﷺ," 4:215 §4659.
13. al-Ṭabarānī in *al-Muʿjam al-kabīr*, 8:196 §7803.
14. Abū Nuʿaym in *Dalāʾil al-nubuwwa*, 1:4 §1.
15. al-Mundhirī in *al-Targhīb wa al-tarhīb*, 3:181 §3583.
16. Ibn Rajab in *Jāmiʿ al-ʿulūm wa al-ḥikam*, 1:415.
17. al-Haythamī in *Majmaʿ al-zawāʾid*, 5:69.
18. al-Suyūṭī in *al-Durr al-manthūr*, 5:688.

2.1 The Personality of the Prophet ﷺ is the Paragon of Mercy and Love

Essential Reading:

1. Dr Tahir-ul-Qadri, Islam on Love and Non-Violence, Ch:2, p.61-63.

Additional Readings for Teachers and Students:

1. Ahmed b. Hanbal in *al-Musnad*, 5:257, 268, 437 §22272, 22361, 23757.
2. Abu Nuʿaym in *Dalāil al-Nubuwah*, 1:4 §1.
3. Mundhiri, *al-Targhib wa al-Tarhib*, 3-181 §3583

2.2 THE PROPHET'S ﷺ ATTRIBUTES OF MERCY AND LOVE IN EARLIER SCRIPTURES

ESSENTIAL READING:

1. Dr Tahir-ul-Qadri, Islam on Love and Non-Violence, Ch:2, p.63-64.

2.3 ISLAM PROTECTS THE RIGHTS OF THE ELDERLY AND CHILDREN

ESSENTIAL READING:

1. Dr Tahir-ul-Qadri, Islam on Love and Non-Violence, Ch:2, p.64-66.

ADDITIONAL READINGS FOR TEACHERS AND STUDENTS:

1. Aḥmad b. Ḥanbal in *al-Musnad*, 1:257 §2329.
2. al-Tirmidhī in *al-Sunan*, *Kitāb al-birr wa al-ṣila* [The Book of Piety and the Filial Duty], chapter: "On what has been Reported Concerning Mercy Toward Young Children," 4:322 §1921.
3. Ibn Ḥībbān in *al-Ṣaḥīḥ*, 2:203 §458.
4. al-Bazzār in *al-Musnad*, 7:158 §2718.
5. al-Ṭabarānī in *al-Muʿjam al-awsaṭ*, 5:107 §4812 and in *al-Muʿjam al-kabīr*, 11:449 §12276.

2.4 SHORTENING PRAYER FOR MERCY AND COMPASSION TO MINORS

ESSENTIAL READING:

1. Dr Tahir-ul-Qadri, Islam on Love and Non-Violence, Ch:2, p.66-68.

ADDITIONAL READINGS FOR TEACHERS AND STUDENTS:

1. al-Bukhārī in *al-Ṣaḥīḥ: Kitāb al-adhān* [The Book on the Azan], chapter: "Concerning He Who Complains about His Imam When the Latter Lengthens the Prayer for Too Long," 1:249 §672.
2. Muslim in *al-Ṣaḥīḥ: Kitāb al-ṣalāh* [The Book of Prayer], chapter: "On Commanding the Imams to Lighten the Prayer," 1:340 §466.
3. al-Bukhārī in *al-Ṣaḥīḥ, Kitāb al-adhān* [The Book of the Azan], chapter: "When One Prays Alone Let Him Lengthen it for as Long as He Likes," 1:248 §671.
4. Muslim in *al-Ṣaḥīḥ, Kitāb al-ṣalāh* [The Book of Prayer], chapter: "On Commanding the Imams to Lighten the Prayer," 1:341 §467.
5. Aḥmad b. Ḥanbal in *al-Musnad*, 2:486 §10311.
6. Abū Dāwūd in *al-Sunan, Kitāb al-ṣalāh* [The Book of Prayer], chapter: "On Lightening the Prayer," 1:211 §794.
7. al-Tirmidhī in *al-Sunan, Kitāb al-ṣalāh* [The Book of Prayer], chapter: "On What has been Reported Regarding the Statement that if One of You Leads the People in Prayer, that He Should Lighten It," 1:461 §236.
8. al-Nasā'ī in *al-Sunan, Kitāb al-imāma* [The Book on the Imamate], chapter: "On the Duty of the Imam to Lighten [the Prayer]," 2:94 §823.
9. Mālik in *al-Muwaṭṭa', Kitāb ṣalāt al-jamā'a* [The Book on the Congregational Prayer], chapter: "What is Done in the Congregational Prayer," 1:134 §301.
10. Ibn Ḥibbān in *al-Ṣaḥīḥ*, 5:56 § 1760.
11. al-Bayhaqī in *al-Sunan al-kubrā*, 3:117 §5058.

2.5 Islam is a Religion [*Dīn*] of Gentleness and Clemency

Essential Reading:

1. Dr Tahir-ul-Qadri, Islam on Love and Non-Violence, Ch:2, p.69-70.

Additional Readings for Teachers and Students:

1. Aḥmad b. Ḥanbal, *al-Musnad*, 6:116, 233.
2. al-Ḥumaydī, *al-Musnad*, 1:123 §254.
3. Ibn Ḥajar, *Fatḥ al-bārī*, 2:444.
4. ibid., Bk.: *Mawāqīt al-ṣalāt* [The Timing of the Prayers], Ch.: "On the Missed Prayers that Can Be Prayed After the ʿAṣr Prayer," 1:213 §565.
5. ibid., Bk.: *al-Manāqib* [The Exemplary Virtues], Ch.: "The Qualities of the Prophet ﷺ," 3:1306 §3367.
6. Muslim in *al-Ṣaḥīḥ:* Bk.: *al-Faḍāʾil* [Virtues], Ch.: "The Prophet's Distance Away from Sins," 4:1813 §2327.
7. al-Bukhari, al-Sahih, Bk: Friday, Ch: Brushing teeth on Fridays, 1:303, §847

2.6 Appreciation of Deeds Rests on Gentleness and Politeness

Essential Reading:

1. Dr Tahir-ul-Qadri, Islam on Love and Non-Violence, Ch:2, p.70-73.

Additional Readings for Teachers and Students:

1. Muslim in *al-Ṣaḥīḥ*: *Kitāb al-birr wa al-ṣila wa al-ādāb* [The Book of

Piety, Filial Duty and Good Manners], Ch.: 'The Virtue of Gentleness', 4:2003 §2593.
2. Abū Dāwūd in *al-Sunan*: *Kitāb al-adab* [The Book of Good Manners], Ch.: 'On Gentleness', 4:254 §4807.
3. Aḥmad b. Ḥanbal in *al-Musnad*, 1:112 §902.
4. Muslim in *al-Ṣaḥīḥ:* Bk.: *al-Birr wa al-ṣila wa al-ādāb* [Piety, Keeping Family Ties and Good Manners], Ch.: "The Virtue of Gentleness," 4:2003 §2592.
5. Abū Dāwūd in *al-Sunan:* Bk.: *al-Adab* [Good Manners], Ch.: "Gentleness," 4:255 §4809.
6. Aḥmad b. Ḥanbal in *al-Musnad*, 4:362.
7. Ibn Mājah in *al-Sunan:* Bk.: *al-Adab* [Good Manners], Ch.: "Gentleness," 21:1216 §3687.
8. Ibn Ḥibbān in *al-Ṣaḥīḥ*, 2:308 §598.
9. Muslim, al-Sahih, Bk: Piety and recompense of propriety, chapter: Gentleness, 4:2004, §2594.
10. Abu Dawud, al-Sunan, Bk: jihad, chapter: What has come to us about emigration and peace, 3:3, §2478

2.7 Imams and Hadith Scholars of Early Times on Leniency and Clemency

Essential Reading:

1. Dr Tahir-ul-Qadri, Islam on Love and Non-Violence, Ch:2, p.73-75.

Additional Readings for Teachers and Students:

1. Qur'ān, 2:256.
2. Aḥmad b. Ḥanbal in *al-Musnad*, 3:479.
3. al-Haythamī in *Majmaʿ al-zawāʾid*, 1:61.
4. Ibn Ḥajar in *Fatḥ al-Bārī*, 1:94; while al-Ṭabarānī in *al-Muʿjam al-kabīr*, 18:230 §573.
5. Ibn Abī ʿĀṣim in *al-Āḥād wa al-mathānī*, 4:349 §2383; al-Quḍāʿī in *Musnad al-Shihāb*, 2:219–220 §§1224–1225; and al-Maqdisī in *al-Aḥādīth al-mukhtāra* (7:132 §2565).

2.8 Conduct based on Extremism is Contrary to Islamic Teachings

Essential Reading:

1. Dr Tahir-ul-Qadri, Islam on Love and Non-Violence, Ch:2, p.75-76.

2.8.1 Injunctions to Abstain from Violence and Extremism

Essential Reading:

1. Dr Tahir-ul-Qadri, Islam on Love and Non-Violence, Ch:2, p.76-77.

Additional Readings for Teachers and Students:

1. Qur'ān, 3:103.
2. al-Nasā'ī, *al-Sunan*, 5:268 §3058.
3. Ibn Mājah, *al-Sunan*, 2:1008 §3029.
4. Ibn Ḥibbān, *al-Ṣaḥīḥ*, 9:183–184 §3871.
5. Abū Yaʿlā, *al-Musnad*, 4:316 §2427.
6. al-Ṭabarānī, *al-Muʿjam al-kabīr*, 12:156 §12747.
7. al-Bayhaqī, *al-Sunan al-kubrā*, 5:127.

2.8.2 Prophet's ﷺ Admonition to Perpetrators of Extremism in Religion

Essential Reading:

1. Dr Tahir-ul-Qadri, Islam on Love and Non-Violence, Ch:2, p.77-79.

2.8.3 Extremists are Promised Eradication

Essential Reading:

1. Dr Tahir-ul-Qadri, Islam on Love and Non-Violence, Ch:2, p.80.

2.9 No Philosophy is Comparable to Islam's Altruistic Teachings

Essential Reading:

1. Dr Tahir-ul-Qadri, Islam on Love and Non-Violence, Ch:2, p.80-81.

3. The Sanctity of Blood and Human Dignity

3.1 The Inviolability of a Believer Exceeds that of the *Ka'ba*

Essential Reading:

1. Dr Tahir-ul-Qadri, Islam on Love and Non-Violence, Ch:3, p.83-85.

3.2 Killing a Human is A Grave Sin like Disbelief

Essential Reading:

1. Dr Tahir-ul-Qadri, Islam on Love and Non-Violence, Ch:3, p.86-90.

Additional Readings for Teachers and Students:

1. Abū Manṣūr al-Māturīdī, *Ta'wilāt Ahl al-Sunna,* 3:501.
2. Qur'ān 5:32.
3. Qur'ān 5:33–34.
4. usayn al-Baghawī, *Ma'ālim al-Tanzīl,* 2:33.
5. al-Rāzī, *al-Tafsīr al-kabīr,* 11:196.
6. Abū Ḥafṣ al-Ḥanbalī, *al-Lubāb fī 'ulūm al-Kitāb*, 7:301.
7. Qur'ān 4:93.

3.3 Murder of a Human is the Greatest Wrong Like Polytheism

Essential Reading:

1. Dr Tahir-ul-Qadri, Islam on Love and Non-Violence, Ch:3, p.90-93.

Additional Readings for Teachers and Students:

1. Qur'ān 25:68.
2. Ibn Kathīr, *Tafsīr al-Qur'ān al-'Aẓīm,* 1:535.
3. al-Bukhārī in *al-Ṣaḥīḥ*: *Kitāb al-Ḥajj* [The Book of Pilgrimage], 2:620 §1654,
4. ibid., *Kitāb al-'ilm* [The Book of Knowledge], chapter: "The Saying of the Prophet ﷺ, 'Many a Person to Whom Something is Conveyed Retains it Better than the One Who Heard It"', 1:37 §67.
5. Muslim in *al-Ṣaḥīḥ*, 3:1305– 1306 §1679.
6. al-Tirmidhī in *al-Sunan*: *Kitāb al-diyāt* [The Book of Blood Money], chapter: "The Legal Ruling Concerning Blood", 4:17 §1398.
7. al-Rabī' in *al-Musnad*, 1:292 §757.
8. al-Daylamī in *Musnad al-firdaws*, 3:361 §5089.

3.4 Bloodshed is the Greatest of all Crimes

Essential Reading:

1. Dr Tahir-ul-Qadri, Islam on Love and Non-Violence, Ch:3, p.93-94.

Additional Readings for Teachers and Students:

1. al-Bukhārī in *al-Ṣaḥīḥ*: *Kitāb al-diyāt* [The Book of Blood Money], chapter: "Whoever Kills a Believer Intentionally", 6:2517 §6470.
2. al-Bayhaqī in *al-Sunan al-kubrā*, 8:21 §15637.
3. al-Bukhārī in *al-Ṣaḥīḥ*: *Kitāb al-fitan* [The Book of Tribulation], chapter: "The Emergence of Tribulations", 6:2590 §6652.
4. Muslim in *al-Ṣaḥīḥ*: *Kitāb al-fitan wa ashrāṭ al-sāʿa* [The Book of Tribulations and the Portents of the Final Hour], chapter: "When Two Muslims Confront Each Other with Their Swords", 4:2215.
5. Abū Dāwūd in *al-Sunan: Kitāb al-fitan wa al-malāḥim* [The Book of Tribulations and Battles], chapter: "Mention of Tribulations", 4:94 §4242.

3.5 Killing a Muslim is a Greater Sin than Destroying the World

Essential Reading:

1. Dr Tahir-ul-Qadri, Islam on Love and Non-Violence, Ch:3, p.94-96.

Additional Readings for Teachers and Students:

1. al-Nasāʾī in *al-Sunan*: *Kitāb taḥrīm al-dam* [The Book on the Prohibition of Bloodshed], chapter: "The Sanctity of Blood", 7:82–83 §3988–3990.
2. al-Ṭabarānī in *al-Muʿjam al-ṣaghīr*, 1:355 §594.
3. al-Bayhaqī in *al-Sunan al-kubrā*, 8:22 §15647.
4. Ibn Abī al-Dunyā in *al-Ahwāl*, p. 190 §183.
5. Ibn Abī ʿĀṣim in *al-Diyāt*, p. 2 §2.

6. al-Bayhaqī in *Shuʿab al-Īmān*, 4:345 §5344.

3.6 The Veneration of the Dead is Imperative in Islam

Essential Reading:

1. Dr Tahir-ul-Qadri, Islam on Love and Non-Violence, Ch:3, p.96-97.

Additional Readings for Teachers and Students:

1. al-Bukhārī in *al-Ṣaḥīḥ*, *al-Janāʾiz* [Funerals], Ch.: Someone standing up for a Jewish funeral procession, 1:441 §1250.
2. Muslim in *al-Ṣaḥīḥ*, *al-Janāʾiz* [Funerals], Ch.: Standing up for a funeral procession, 2:661 §961.
3. Aḥmad b. Ḥanbal in *al-Musnad*, 6:6 §23893.
4. al-Nasāʾī in *al-Sunan*, *al-Janāʾiz* [Funerals], Ch.: Standing up for the funerals of polytheists, 4:45 §1921.

3.7 The Sanctity of Human Graves is Indispensable

Essential Reading:

1. Dr Tahir-ul-Qadri, Islam on Love and Non-Violence, Ch:3, p.97-98.

4. The Protection of Life and Property of Non-Muslims

4.1 Islam Guarantees Safety of the Whole of Humanity without Religious Discrimination

Essential Reading:

1. Dr Tahir-ul-Qadri, Islam on Love and Non-Violence, Ch:4, p.98-102.

Additional Readings for Teachers and Students:

1. Aḥmad b. anbal in *al-Musnad*, 2:186 §6745.
2. al-Nasā'ī in *al-Sunan*, 8:25 §4750 & in *al-Sunan al-Kubrā*, 4:221 §6952.
3. al-Bazzār in *al-Musnad*, 6:361 §2373.
4. al- ākim in *al-Mustadrak ʿala al-Ṣaḥīḥayn*, 2:137 §2580.
5. Ibn al-Jārūd in *al-Muntaqā*, 1:212 §834.
6. al-Bayhaqī in *al-Sunan al-kubrā*, 8:133 §16260.
7. al-Mundhirī in *al-Targhīb wa al-tarhīb*, 3:204 §3693.

4.2 The Strict Prohibition of Killing Women even in the Battlefield

Essential Reading:

1. Dr Tahir-ul-Qadri, Islam on Love and Non-Violence, Ch:4, p.102-103.

4.3 Strict Prohibition against Killing Children in Battlefield

Essential Reading:

1. Dr Tahir-ul-Qadri, Islam on Love and Non-Violence, Ch:4, p.103-107.

Additional Readings for Teachers and Students:

1. al-Nasā'ī in *al-Sunan al-kubrā*: *Kitāb al-siyar* [The Book of Military Expeditions], chapter: "The Prohibition of Killing the Children of the

Pagans," 5:184 §8616.

2. al-Dārimī in *al-Sunan*, 2:294 §2463.
3. al-Ḥākim in *al-Mustadrak*, 2:133–134 §§2566–2567.
4. al-Ṭabarānī in *al-Muʿjam al-kabīr*, 1:284.
5. Aḥmad b. Ḥanbal in *al-Musnad*, 3:435 §§15626–15627.
6. al-Nasʾī in *al-Sunan al-kubrā*, 5:184 §8616.
7. al-Dārimī in *al-Sunan*, 2:294 §2463.
8. Ibn Abī Shayba in *al-Muṣannaf*, 6:484 §33131.
9. Ibn ibbān in *al-Ṣaḥīḥ*, 1:341 §132.
10. al- ākīm in *al-Ṣaḥīḥ*, 2:133–134, §2566–2567.
11. al-Bayhaqī in *al-Sunan al-kubrā*, 9:77 §17868.
12. al-Haythamī in *Majmaʿ al-zawāʾid*, 5:316.
13. Qurʾān 40:25.
14. al-Sarakhsī,*al-Mabsūṭ*, 10:5–6.

4.3.1 Killing Women and Children is Strife, not Jihad

Essential Reading:

1. Dr Tahir-ul-Qadri, Islam on Love and Non-Violence, Ch:4, p.108.

4.4 The Prohibition of Killing Foreign Delegates

Essential Reading:

1. Dr Tahir-ul-Qadri, Islam on Love and Non-Violence, Ch:4, p.108-110.

Additional Readings for Teachers and Students:

1. Aḥmad b. Ḥanbal in *al-Musnad*, 1:390, 396 §3708, 3761.
2. ʿAbd al-Razzāq in *al-Muṣannaf*, 10:196 §18708.
3. Aḥmad b. Ḥanbal in *al-Musnad*, 1:390 §3708.

4.5 The Prohibition of Killing Religious Leaders

Essential Reading:

1. Dr Tahir-ul-Qadri, Islam on Love and Non-Violence, Ch:4, p.110-111.

Additional Readings for Teachers and Students:

1. Aḥmad b. Ḥanbal in *al-Musnad*, 1:390, 396 §3708, 3761.
2. ʿAbd al-Razzāq in *al-Muṣannaf*, 10:196 §18708.
3. Aḥmad b. Ḥanbal in *al-Musnad*, 1:390 §3708.

4.6 The Unlawfulness of Killing non-Muslim Traders and Farmers

Essential Reading:

1. Dr Tahir-ul-Qadri, Islam on Love and Non-Violence, Ch:4, p.111-112.

Additional Readings for Teachers and Students:

1. Ibn Abī Shayba in *al-Muṣannaf*, 6:483 §33120.
2. Ibn Ādam al-Qurashī in *Kitāb al-Kharāj*, 1:52 §132.
3. al-Bayhaqī in *al-Sunan al-kubrā*, 9:91 §17938.
4. Ibn al-Qayyim, *Aḥkām ahl al-dhimma*, 1:165.
5. Ibn Qudāma al-Maqdisī, *al-Mughnī*, 9:251.

4.7 The Unlawfulness of Killing non-Muslim Service Personnel

Essential Reading:

1. Dr Tahir-ul-Qadri, Islam on Love and Non-Violence, Ch:4, p.112-114.

Additional Readings for Teachers and Students:

1. Ibn Qayyim al-Jawziyya, *Aḥkām ahl al-dhimma*, 1:172.

4.8 The Unlawfulness of Killing non-Muslims who are non-Combatants

Essential Reading:

1. Dr Tahir-ul-Qadri, Islam on Love and Non-Violence, Ch:4, p.114-115.

Additional Readings for Teachers and Students:

1. ʿAbd al-Razzāq in *al-Muṣannaf*, 10:123-124 §18590-18591.

4.9 The Prohibition of Destroying the Cattle, Crops and Properties of the Enemy

Essential Reading:

1. Dr Tahir-ul-Qadri, Islam on Love and Non-Violence, Ch:4, p.115-118.

Additional Readings for Teachers and Students:

1. Mālik in *al-Muwaṭṭa*: *Kitāb al-jihād* [The Book of Jihad], chapter: "The Unlawfulness of Killing Women and Children During Military Expeditions", 2:447 §965.
2. ʿAbd al-Razzāq in *al-Muṣannaf*, 5:199 §9375.
3. Ibn Abī Shayba in *al-Muṣannaf*, 6:483 §33121.
4. al-Bayhaqī in *al-Sunan al-kubrā*, 9:89–90 §§17927, 17929.
5. al-Marwazī in *Musnad Abī Bakr*, pp. 69–72 §21.
6. Ibn Abī Shayba in *al-Muṣannaf*, 6:483 §33122.
7. al-Marwazī in *Musnad Abī Bakr*, pp. 69–72 §21.
8. Abū Dāwūd in *al-Sunan*: *Kitāb al-jihād* [The Book of Jihad], 3:66 §2705.
9. al-Bayhaqī in *al-Sunan al-kubrā*, 9:61 §17789.

4.10 Summary

Essential Reading:

1. Dr Tahir-ul-Qadri, Islam on Love and Non-Violence, Ch:4, p.118.

5. The Messenger's ﷺ Mercy and Compassion on Animals

Essential Reading:

1. Dr Tahir-ul-Qadri, Islam on Love and Non-Violence, Ch:5, p.119-121.

5.1 The Prohibition of Torturing Animals and Birds

Essential Reading:

1. Dr Tahir-ul-Qadri, Islam on Love and Non-Violence, Ch:5, p.121-126.

Additional Readings for Teachers and Students:

1. Qur'ān, 38:26.
2. al-Bukhārī in *al-Ṣaḥīḥ*, *Kitāb al-musāqāt* [The Book of Watering], chapter, "The Virtue of Providing Water," 2:833 §2234, and in *Kitāb al-maẓālim wa al-ghaṣb* [On Oppression and Wrongful Seizure of Land], chapter, "Allowing Wells on Pathways as long as They Do not Cause Inconveniance," 2:870 §2334.
3. Muslim in *al-Ṣaḥīḥ*, *Kitāb al-salām* [The Book of Salutations], chapter, "On Giving Food and Water to Honoured Animals," 4:1761 §2244.
4. Aḥmad b. Ḥanbal in *al-Musnad*, 2:517 §1071.
5. Abū Dāwūd in *al-Sunan*, *Kitāb al-jihād* [The Book of Jihad], chapter,

"The Commands Pertaining to the Riding of Animals and Beasts of Burden," 3:24 §255

6. Mālik in *al-Muwaṭṭā'*, 2:929 §1661.
7. Aḥmad b. anbal in *al-Musnad*, 2:92, 115 §5661, 5956.
8. Ibn al-Jaʿd in *al-Musnad*, p. 330 §2264.
9. Ibn Rajab al- anbalī in *Jāmiʿ al-ʿulūm wa al-ḥikam*, 1:153.
10. al-Mundhirī in *al-Targhīb wa al-tarhīb*, 2:102 §1676.
11. al-Haythamī in *Majmaʿ al-zawā'id*, 4:32.
12. Ibn ajar al-ʿAsqalānī in *Fatḥ al-bārī*, 9:644.
13. Aḥmad b. anbal in *al-Musnad*, 4:389 §19844.
14. al-Nasā'ī in *al-Sunan*: *Kitāb al-Ḍaḥāyā* [The Book of Sacrificial Animals], chapter: "Killing a Sparrow Without Right," 4:239 §4446 & in *al-Sunan al-kubrā*, 3:73 §4535.
15. Ibn ibbān in *al-Ṣaḥīḥ*, 13:214 §5894.
16. al-Ṭabarānī in *al-Muʿjam al-kabīr*, 7:317 §7245.
17. al-Nasā'ī in *al-Sunan*: *Kitāb al-Ṣayd wa al-Dhabāʿiḥ*7:206 §4349 & in *al-Sunan al-kubrā*, 3:163 §4860.
18. al-Shāfiʿī in *al-Sunan al-ma'thūra*, p. 413 §606.
19. al- ākim in *al-Mustadrak*, 4:261 §7574.
20. al-Ṭayālisī in *al-Musnad*, p. 301 §2279.
21. al- ākim in *al-Mustadrak*, 4:267 §7599.
22. al-Bayhaqī in *Dalā'il al-nubuwwa*, 1:321
23. al-Hunād in *al-Zuhd*, 2:620 §1337.

5.2 No Place for Target Killing in the Teaching of Islam

Essential Reading:

1. Dr Tahir-ul-Qadri, Islam on Love and Non-Violence, Ch:5, p.126-128.

Additional Readings for Teachers and Students:

1. Muslim in *al-Ṣaḥīḥ*: *Kitāb al-ṣayd wa al-dhabā'iḥ wa mā yu'kal min al-ḥayawān* [The Book of Game and Slaughtered Animals and Edible Animals], chapter: "The Prohibition of Seizing Animals for Targeting," 3:1550 §1958.

2. al Tirmidhī in *al-Sunan*, *Kitāb al-ṣayd* [The Book of Game], chapter: "The Offensiveness of Eating an Animal That Has Died through Being Seized and Targeted," 4:72 §1475.
3. al-Nasāʾī in *al-Sunan*, *Kitāb al-ḍaḥāyā* [The Book of Sacrificial Animals], chapter: "The Prohibition of Seizing Animals for Targeting," 7:239 §4444.
4. Ibn Mājah in *al-Sunan*, *Kitāb al-dhabāʾiḥ* [The Book of Slaughtered Animals], chapter: "The Prohibition of Seizing Animals for Targeting and Cutting Parts of Living Animals," 2:63 §3187.
5. Muslim in *al-Ṣaḥīḥ*, *Kitāb al-ṣayd wa al-dhabāʾiḥ* [The Book of Game and Slaughtered Animals], chapter: "The Prohibition of Seizing Animals for Targeting," 3:1549 §1957.
6. Aḥmad b. Ḥanbal in *al-Musnad*, 1:280, 285, 340 §§§2532, 2586, 3155.
7. al-Tirmidhī in *al-Sunan*, *Kitāb al-ṣayd* [The Book of Game], chapter: "The Offensiveness of Eating an Animal That Has Died through Being Seized and Targeted," 4:72 §1475.
8. al-Nasāʾī in *al-Sunan*, *Kitāb al-ḍaḥāyā* [The Book of Sacrificial Animals], chapter: "The Prohibition of Seizing Animals for Targeting," 7:238 §4443;
9. Ibn Mājah in *al-Sunan*, *Kitāb al-dhabāʾiḥ* [The Book of Slaughtered Animals], chapter: "The Prohibition of Seizing Animals for Targeting and Cutting Parts of Living Animals," 2:1063 §3187.
10. Ibn Ḥibbān in *al-Ṣaḥīḥ*, 12:422 §5608.
11. Abū ʿAwāna in *al-Musnad*, 5:52 §7759.
12. al-Ṭaḥāwī in *Sharḥ maʿānī al-āthār*, 3:181.

5.3 The Prohibition of Burning and Branding the Animals

Essential Reading:

1. Dr Tahir-ul-Qadri, Islam on Love and Non-Violence, Ch:5, p.128-132.

Additional Readings for Teachers and Students:

1. Muslim in *al-Ṣaḥīḥ*, *Kitāb al-libās wa al-zīna* [The Book of Clothing and Adornment], chapter: "The Prohibition of Striking and Branding the Faces of Animals," 3:1673 §2117.

2. Aḥmad b. Ḥanbal in *al-Musnad*, 3:323 §14499.
3. ʿAbd al-Razzāq in *al-Musnad*, 9:444 §17949.
4. Ibn Ḥibbān in *al-Ṣaḥīḥ*, 12:432 §5627.
5. Abū Yaʿlā in *al-Musnad*, 4:76 §2099.
6. al-Bukhārī in *al-Adab al-mufrad*, 72 §175.
7. al-Bayhaqī in *al-Sunan al-kubrā*, 7:35 §13037.
8. al-Mundhirī in *al-Targhīb wa al-tarhīb*, 3:153 §3464.
9. al-Nawawī in *Riyāḍ al-ṣāliḥīn*, 367.
10. al-ʿAynī in *ʿUmdat al-Qārī*, 21:139.
11. Muslim in *al-Ṣaḥīḥ*, *Kitāb al-libās wa al-zīna* [The Book of Clothing and Adornment], chapter: "The Prohibition of Striking and Branding the Faces of Animals," 4:1673 §2118.
12. Ibn Ḥibbān in *al-Ṣaḥīḥ*, 12:441 §5624.
13. al-Ṭabarānī in *al-Muʿjam al-kabīr*, 10:332 §10822.
14. al-Nawawī in *Riyāḍ al-ṣāliḥīn*, 367.
15. al-Zaylaʿī in *Takhrīj al-ahādīth wa al-āthār*, 4:78.
16. Aḥmad b. Ḥanbal in *al-Musnad*, 3:323 §14499.
17. ʿAbd al-Razzāq in *al-Muṣannaf*, 9:444 §17949.
18. al-Bukhārī in *al-Adab al-mufrad*, 72 §175.
19. Ibn Ḥibbān in *al-Ṣaḥīḥ*, 12:432 §5627.
20. Abū Yaʿlā in *al-Musnad*, 4:76 §2099.
21. Ibn Ḥibbān in *al-Ṣaḥīḥ*, 12:440 §5623.
22. al-Bayhaqī in *al-Sunan al-kubrā*, 7:36 §13041.
23. al-Zaylaʿī in *Takhrīj al-ahādīth wa al-āthār*, 4:78.

5.4 The Prohibition of Torture to Animals When Slaughtering

Essential Reading:

1. Dr Tahir-ul-Qadri, Islam on Love and Non-Violence, Ch:5, p.132-134.

Additional Readings for Teachers and Students:

1. Aḥmad b. Ḥanbal in *al-Musnad*, 2:108 §5864.
2. Ibn Mājah in *al-Sunan*, *Kitāb al-dhabāʾiḥ* [The Book of Slaughtered Animals], chapter: "When You Slaughter, Slaughter Well," 2:1059

§3172.

3. al-Bayhaqī in *al-Sunan al-kubrā*, 9:280 §18920, and in *Shuʿab al-īmān*, 7:483 §11074.
4. al-Mundhirī in *al-Targhīb wa al-tarhīb*, 2:101 §1671.
5. al-Ṭabarānī in *al-Muʿjam al-kabīr*, 8:234 §7915.
6. al-Bukhārī in *al-Adab al-mufrad*, p. 138 §181.
7. al-Bayhaqī in *Shuʿab al-īmān*, 7:482 §1107.
8. al-Haythamī in *Majmaʿ al-zawāʾid*, 4:33.

6. The Killers of Humankind are Terrorists

Essential Reading:

1. Dr Tahir-ul-Qadri, Islam on Love and Non-Violence, Ch:6, p.135-138.

6.1 The Prophet Clearly Indicated the emergence of terrorists

Essential Reading:

1. Dr Tahir-ul-Qadri, Islam on Love and Non-Violence, Ch:6, p.138-141.

Additional Readings for Teachers and Students:

1. Aḥmad b. Ḥanbal in *al-Musnad*, 2:198 §6871.
2. al-Ḥākim in *al-Mustadrak*, 4:533 §8497.
3. Nuʿaym b. Ḥammād in *al-Fitan*, 2:532.
4. Ibn Rāshid in *al-Jāmiʿ*, 11:377.
5. al-Ājurrī in *al-Sharīʿa*, p. 113 §260.
6. Ibn Mājah in *al-Sunan*: 'Introduction', section, 'Mention of the Kharijites', 1:61 §1

6.2 Terrorism is an Act of Disbelief

Essential Reading:

1. Dr Tahir-ul-Qadri, Islam on Love and Non-Violence, Ch:6, p.141-146.

Additional Readings for Teachers and Students:

1. Aḥmad b. Ḥanbal in *al-Musnad*, 5:36–38 §20393, 20419.
2. Abū Dāwūd in *al-Sunan*: *Kitāb al-jihād* [The Book of Jihad], chapter: "Fulfilling the Contract of a Non-Muslim Citizen and the Sanctity of His Contract," 3:83 §2760.
3. al-Nasā'ī in *al-Sunan*: *Kitāb al-qasāma* [The Book of Apportioning Wealth], chapter: "The Gravity of Killing Non-Muslim Citizens," 8:24 §4747, and in *al-Sunan al-kubrā*, 4:221, §6949.
4. al-Dārimī in *al-Sunan*, 2:308 §2504.
5. al-Bazzār in *al-Musnad*, 9:129 §3679.
6. Ibn Abī Shayba in *al-Muṣannaf*, 5:457 §27946.
7. al-Ḥākim in *al-Mustadrak*, 2:154 §2631.
8. al-Munāwī, *Fatḥ al-Qadīr,* 6:153
9. Aḥmad b. anbal in *al-Musnad*, 5:36 §20399.
10. al- ākim in *al-Mustadrak ʿala al-Ṣaḥīḥayn*, 1:105 §135.
11. Anwar Shāh Kāshmīrī in *Fayḍ al-Bārī ʿalā Ṣaḥīḥ al-Bukhārī*, 4:288.
12. al-Bukhārī in *al-Ṣaḥīḥ*: *Kitāb al-jizya* [The Book of Annual Security Tax for Non-Muslims Living in an Islamic State], chapter: "The Sin of Someone Who Kills a Non-Muslim Citizen without His Having Committed a Crime," 3:1155 §2995.
13. Ibn Mājah in *al-Sunan*: *Kitāb al-diyāt* [The Book of Blood Money], chapter: "Someone Who Kills a Non-Muslim Citizen," 2:896 §2686.
14. al-Bazzār in *al-Musnad*, 6:368 §2383.
15. al-Tirmidhī in *al-Sunan*, 4:20 §1403.
16. Ibn Mājah in *al-Sunan*, 2:896 §2687.
17. Abū Yaʿlā in *al-Musnad*, 11:335 §6452.
18. al- ākim in *al-Mustadrak*, 2:138 §2581.
19. al-Bayhaqī in *al-Sunan al-kubrā*, 9:205 §18511.
20. al-Nasā'ī in *al-Sunan*, 8:25 §4748,
21. ibid., *al-Sunan al-kubrā*, 4:221 §6950.
22. ʿAbd al-Razzāq in *al-Muṣannaf*, 10:102 §18521.
23. Ibn ibbān in *al-Ṣaḥīḥ*, 16:391 §8382.
24. al-Bazzār in *al-Musnad*, 9:138 §3696.

25. al-Ṭabarānī in *al-Muʿjam al-awsaṭ*, 1:207 §663.

6.3 Inciting Religious Sentiments to Commit mass murder by Brainwashing is The Kharijites Method

Essential Reading:

1. Dr Tahir-ul-Qadri, Islam on Love and Non-Violence, Ch:6, p.146-150.

Additional Readings for Teachers and Students:

1. Ibn Kathīr, *al-Bidāya wa al-nihāya*, 7:288.
2. Ibn al-Athīr, *al-Kāmil fī al-tārīkh*, 3:218.
3. Ibn Kathīr, *al-Bidāya wa al-nihāya*, 7:288.

6.4 The Blameworthy Religious Innovations of the Kharijites and their Extremist Sentiments

Essential Reading:

1. Dr Tahir-ul-Qadri, Islam on Love and Non-Violence, Ch:6, p.150-151.

Additional Readings for Teachers and Students:

1. al-Ḥākim in *al-Mustadrak*, 2:166 §2657.
2. Abū Yaʿlā in *al-Musnad*, 1:90 §90.
3. ʿAbd al-Qāhir al-Baghdādī, *al-Farq bayn al-firaq*, p. 73.
4. Ibn Taymiyya, *Majmūʿa al-fatāwā*, 13:31.
5. al-Shahrastānī, *al-Milal wa al-niḥal*, 1:118.
6. Ibid., 1:121.

6.5 MASSACRING MUSLIMS DUE TO IDEOLOGICAL DIFFERENCE IS A GENERAL SIGN OF KHARIJITES

ESSENTIAL READING:

1. Dr Tahir-ul-Qadri, Islam on Love and Non-Violence, Ch:6, p.151-154.

ADDITIONAL READINGS FOR TEACHERS AND STUDENTS:

1. Ibn Ḥajar al-ʿAsqalānī, *Fatḥ al-Bārī*, 8:69.
2. Shabbīr Aḥmad ʿUthmānī, *Fatḥ al-Mulhim*, 5:151.
3. al-Bukhārī in *al-Ṣaḥīḥ*: *Kitāb istitāba al-murtaddīn wa al-muʿānidīn wa qitālihim* [The Book on Demanding the Repentance of the Apostates and Reprobates, and Fighting Them], chapter: "On Fighting the Kharijites and the Heretics after Establishing the Evidence against Them", 6:2539 §6531.
4. Muslim in *al-Ṣaḥīḥ*: *Kitāb al-Zakāt* [The Book of Zakat], chapter: "The Encouragement to Kill the Kharijites", 2:746 §1066.
5. Aḥmad b. Ḥanbal in *al-Musnad*, 1:81, 113, 131 §§§616, 912, 1086.
6. al-Nasāʾī in *al-Sunan*: *Kitāb taḥrīm al-dam* [The Book on the Prohibition of Bloodshed], chapter: "Regarding the One Who Unsheathes His Sword and Wields it amongst People", 7:119 §4102.
7. Ibn Mājah in *al-Sunan*: "Introduction", section: "Mention of the Kharijites", 1:59 §168.
8. Ibn Ḥajar al-ʿAsqalānī, *Fatḥ al-Bārī*, 2:377.

6.6 SALIENT FEATURES AND SIGNS OF TERRORIST KHARIJITES

ESSENTIAL READING:

1. Dr Tahir-ul-Qadri, Islam on Love and Non-Violence, Ch:6, p.154-161.

Additional Readings for Teachers and Students:

1. al-Bukhārī in *al-Ṣaḥīḥ*: *Kitāb istitāba al-murtaddīn wa al-muʿānidīn wa qitālihim* [The Book on Demanding the Repentance of the Apostates and Reprobates, and Fighting Them], chapter: "On Fighting the Kharijites and the Heretics after Establishing the Evidence against Them", 6:2539 §6531.
2. Muslim in *al-Ṣaḥīḥ*: *Kitāb al-Zakāt* [The Book of Zakat], chapter: "The Encouragement to Kill the Kharijites", 2:746 §1066.
3. al-Bukhārī in *al-Ṣaḥīḥ*: *Kitāb al-maghāzī* [The Book of Military Expeditions], chapter: "The Dispatch of ʿAlī b. Abī Ṭālib and Khālid b. al-Walīd to Yemen before the Farewell Pilgrimage", 4:1581 §4094.
4. Muslim in *al-Ṣaḥīḥ*: *Kitāb al-Zakāt* [The Book of Zakat], chapter: "On the Kharijites and their Qualities", 2:742 §1064.
5. Ibid.
6. al-Bukhārī in *al-Ṣaḥīḥ*: *Kitāb al-tawḥīd* [The Book of Divine Unity], chapter: "The Recitation, Articulation and Reading of the Reprobate and Hypocrite [Reading the Qurʾān] Does Not Pass Beyond Their Throats", 6:2748 §7123.
7. al-Nasāʾī in *al-Sunan*: *Kitāb taḥrīm al-dam* [The Book on the Prohibition of Bloodshed], chapter: "Regarding the One Who Unsheathes His Sword and Wields it amongst People", 7:119 §4103.
8. al-Bukhārī in *al-Ṣaḥīḥ*: *Kitāb istitāba al-murtaddīn wa al-muʿānidīn wa qitālihim* [The Book on Demanding the Repentance of the Apostates and Reprobates, and Fighting Them], chapter: "On Killing the Kharijites and the Heretics after Establishing the Evidence against Them", 6:2539 §6531.
9. Muslim in *al-Ṣaḥīḥ*: *Kitāb al-Zakāt* [The Book of Zakat], chapter: "The Encouragement to Kill the Kharijites", 2:746 §1066.
10. Abū Yaʿlā in *al-Musnad*, 1:90 §90.
11. ʿAbd al-Razzāq in *al-Muṣannaf*, 10:155 §18673.
12. al-Bukhārī in *al-Ṣaḥīḥ*: *Kitāb al-adab* [The Book of Good Manners], chapter: "What Has Come to Us About Someone Saying, 'Woe to you!'", 5:2281 §5811, and *Kitāb istitāba al-murtaddīn wa al-muʿānidīn wa qitālihim* [The Book on Demanding the Repentance of the Apostates and Reprobates, and Fighting Them], chapter: "On the One Who Refrains from Fighting the Kharijites for the Sake of Drawing Hearts Near and so People Will Not Flee", 6:2540 §6534.
13. Muslim in *al-Ṣaḥīḥ*: *Kitāb al-Zakāt* [The Book of Zakat], chapter: "On the Kharijites and Their Qualities", 2:744 §1064.
14. Muslim in *al-Ṣaḥīḥ*: *Kitāb al-Zakāt* [The Book of Zakat], chapter: "The Encouragement to Kill the Kharijites", 2:748 §1066.

15. Ibid.
16. al-Bukhārī in *al-Ṣaḥīḥ*: *Kitāb istitāba al-murtaddīn wa al-muʿānidīn wa qitālihim* [The Book on Demanding the Repentance of the Apostates and Reprobates, and Fighting Them], chapter: "On Killing the Kharijites and Heretics after Establishing the Evidence against Them", 6:2540 §6532.
17. Muslim in *al-Ṣaḥīḥ: Kitāb al-Zakāt* [The Book of Zakat], chapter: "On the Kharijites and Their Qualities", 2:743 §1064.
18. Muslim in *al-Ṣaḥīḥ*: *Kitāb al-Zakāt* [The Book of Zakat], chapter: "The Encouragement to Kill the Kharijites", 2:748 §1066.
19. Abū Dāwūd in *al-Sunan*: *Kitāb al-Sunna* [The Book of the Sunna], chapter: "On Fighting the Kharijites", 4:243 §4765.
20. al-Bukhārī in *al-Ṣaḥīḥ*: *Kitāb istitāba al-murtaddīn wa al-muʿānidīn wa qitālihim* [The Book on Demanding the Repentance of the Apostates and Reprobates, and Fighting Them], chapter: "On Fighting the Kharijites and the Heretics after Establishing the Evidence against Them", 6:2539 §6531.
21. Muslim in *al-Ṣaḥīḥ*: *Kitāb al-Zakāt* [The Book of Zakat], chapter: "The Encouragement to Kill the Kharijites", 2:746 §1066.
22. al-Ṭabarānī in *al-Muʿjam al-awsaṭ*, 6:186 §6142.
23. Abū Dāwūd in *al-Sunan*: *Kitāb al-Sunna* [The Book of the Sunna], chapter: "On Killing the Kharijites", 4:243 §4765.
24. Muslim in *al-Ṣaḥīḥ: Kitāb al-Zakāt* [The Book of Zakat], chapter: "The Kharijites Are the Most Evil of Creation", 2:750 §1067.
25. Ibn Abū ʿĀṣim in *al-Sunna*, 2:455 §934;
26. al-Haythamī in *Majmaʿ al-Zawāʾid*, 6:228. And he said that its transmitters are those of a sound tradition.
27. al-Bukhārī in *al-Ṣaḥīḥ: Kitāb al-Manāqib* [The Book of Virtues], chapter: "The Signs of Prophethood in Islam", 3:1321 §3414.
28. Muslim in *al-Ṣaḥīḥ*: *al-Zakāt* [The Alms-due], chapter: Discussion of the Kharijites and their Qualities, 2:744 §1064.
29. al-Ḥākim in *al-Mustadrak*, 2:166 §2657.
30. al-Ṭabarī in *Jāmiʿ al-Bayān fī Tafsīr al-Qurʾān*, 3:181;
31. al-ʿAsqalānī, *Fatḥ al-Bārī*, 12:300.
32. al-Tirmidhī in *al-Sunan*: *Kitāb tafsīr al-Qurʾān* [The Book of Qurʾānic Exegesis], chapter: "From *Sūra Āl ʿImrān*", 5:226 §3000.
33. ʿAbd al-Qāhir al-Baghdādī, *al-Farq bayn al-firaq*, p. 73.
34. Ibn Taymiyya, *Majmūʿa al-fatāwā*, 13:31.

7. The Stringent Prophetic Command to Eliminate Kharijites and Terrorists

7.1 The Prophetic Decree: The Tribulation of the Kharijites Must be Eliminated

Essential Reading:

1. Dr Tahir-ul-Qadri, Islam on Love and Non-Violence, Ch:7, p.163.

7.1.1 Total Elimination of the Kharijites is Obligatory

Essential Reading:

1. Dr Tahir-ul-Qadri, Islam on Love and Non-Violence, Ch:7, p.165-169.

Additional Readings for Teachers and Students:

1. al-Bukhārī in *al-Ṣaḥīḥ*: *Kitāb al-maghāzī* [The Book of Military Expeditions], chapter: "The Dispatch of ʿAlī b. Abī Ṭālib and Khālid b. al-Walīd to Yemen before the Farewell Pilgrimage", 4:1581 §4094.
2. Muslim in *al-Ṣaḥīḥ*: *Kitāb al-Zakāt* [The Book of Zakat], chapter: "On the Kharijites and their Qualities", 2:742, 743 §1064.
3. Aḥmad b. Ḥanbal in *al-Musnad*, 3:4 §11021.
4. Ibn Khuzayma in *al-Ṣaḥīḥ*, 4:71 §2373.
5. Ibn Ḥibbān in *al-Ṣaḥīḥ*, 1:205 §25.
6. Abū Yaʿlā in *al-Musnad*, 2:390 §1163.
7. Abū Dāwūd in *al-Sunan*: *Kitāb al-Sunna* [The Book of the Sunna], chapter: "On Fighting the Kharijites", 4:243 §4765.
8. Aḥmad b. Ḥanbal in *al-Musnad*, 3:224 §13362.
9. Ibn Mājah in *al-Sunan*: 'Introduction', section: 'Discussion of the Kharijites', 1:60 §169.
10. al-Ḥākim in *al-Mustadrak*, 2:161 §2649.
11. al-Bayhaqī in *al-Sunan al-kubrā*, 8:171.

12. al-Maqdisī in *al-Aḥādīth al-mukhtāra*, 7:15 §2391–2392 (and he declared its chain of transmission sound).
13. Abū Yaʿlā in *al-Musnad*, 5:426 §3117.
14. Aḥmad b. Ḥanbal in *al-Musnad*, 3:15 §11133.
15. al-Haythamī in *Majmaʿ al-zawāʾid*, 6:225.
16. al-ʿAsqalānī in *Fatḥ al-Bārī*, 12:229.
17. Ibn ʿAbd al-Barr, *al-Tamhīd*, 23:338–339.

7.1.2 Important Commentaries from the Imams of Hadith

Essential Reading:

1. Dr Tahir-ul-Qadri, Islam on Love and Non-Violence, Ch:7, p.169-172.

Additional Readings for Teachers and Students:

1. Yaḥyā al-Nawawī, *Sharḥ Ṣaḥīḥ Muslim*, 7:170.
2. Shabbīr Aḥmad ʿUthmānī, *Fatḥ al-Mulhim*, 5:166–167.

7.2 Do not be Deceived by The Outward Religious Appearance of the Kharijites

Essential Reading:

1. Dr Tahir-ul-Qadri, Islam on Love and Non-Violence, Ch:7, p.172-174..

Additional Readings for Teachers and Students:

1. al-Ḥākim in *al-Mustadrak*, 2:164 §2656.
2. al-Nasāʾī in *al-Sunan al-kubrā*, 5:165 §8575.
3. ʿAbd al-Razzāq in *al-Muṣannaf*, 10:146.
4. al-Ṭabarānī in *al-Muʿjam al-kabīr*, 10:257 §10598.
5. al-Bayhaqī in *al-Sunan al-kubrā*, 8:179.

6. al-Ṭabarānī in *al-Muʿjam al-awsaṭ*, 4:227 §4051.
7. al-Haythamī in *Majmaʿ al-zawāʾid*, 4:227.
8. Ibn Ḥajar al-ʿAsqalānī in *Fatḥ al-Bārī*, 12:296.
9. al-Shawkānī in *Nayl al-awṭār*, 7:349.

7.3 The Kharijites are the Worst of Creation

Essential Reading:

1. Dr Tahir-ul-Qadri, Islam on Love and Non-Violence, Ch:7, p.174-178.

Additional Readings for Teachers and Students:

1. Ibn Ḥibbān in *al-Ṣaḥīḥ*, 1:282 §81.
2. al-Bazzār in *al-Musnad*, 7:220 §2793.

7.3.1 A Noteworthy Point

Essential Reading:

1. Dr Tahir-ul-Qadri, Islam on Love and Non-Violence, Ch:7, p.178.

Additional Readings for Teachers and Students:

1. al-Khalāl, *al-Sunna*, p. 145 §110.

7.4 Military Operations Against Kharijite Terrorists Bring Plenteous Reward

Essential Reading:

1. Dr Tahir-ul-Qadri, Islam on Love and Non-Violence, Ch:7, p.179-182.

Additional Readings for Teachers and Students:

1. al-Bukhārī in *al-Ṣaḥīḥ*: *Kitāb istitāba al-murtaddīn wa al-muʿānidīn wa qitālihim* [The Book on Demanding the Repentance of the Apostates and Reprobates, and Fighting Them], chapter: "On Fighting the Kharijites and the Heretics after Establishing the Evidence against Them", 6:2539 §6531.
2. Muslim in *al-Ṣaḥīḥ*: *Kitāb al-Zakāt* [The Book of Zakat], chapter: "The Encouragement to Kill the Kharijites", 2:746 §1066.
3. al-Bukhārī in *al-Ṣaḥīḥ*: *Kitāb al-maghāzī* [The Book of Military Expeditions], chapter: "The Dispatch of ʿAlī b. Abī Ṭālib and Khālid b. al-Walīd to Yemen before the Farewell Pilgrimage", 4:1581 §4094.
4. Muslim in *al-Ṣaḥīḥ*: *Kitāb al-Zakāt* [The Book of Zakat], chapter: "On the Kharijites and their Qualities", 2:742, 743 §1064.
5. Aḥmad b. Ḥanbal in *al-Musnad*, 3:4 §11021.
6. Ibn Khuzayma in *al-Ṣaḥīḥ*, 4:71 §2373.
7. Ibn Ḥibbān in *al-Ṣaḥīḥ*, 1:205 §25.
8. Abū Yaʿlā in *al-Musnad*, 2:390 §1163.
9. Aḥmad b. Ḥanbal in *al-Musnad*, 4:421 §19798.
10. al-Nasāʾī in *al-Sunan*: *Kitāb taḥrīm al-dam* [The Book on the Prohibition of Bloodshed], chapter: "Regarding the One Who Unsheathes His Sword and Wields it amongst People", 7:119 §4103.
11. al-Ḥākim in *al-Mustadrak*, 2:160 §2647.

7.5 Glad Tidings of Great Reward for the Troops Fighting the Kharijites

Essential Reading:

1. Dr Tahir-ul-Qadri, Islam on Love and Non-Violence, Ch:7, p.182-184.

7.6 Good News for the Killers of Terrorists and for those Martyred by Terrorists

Essential Reading:

1. Dr Tahir-ul-Qadri, Islam on Love and Non-Violence, Ch:7, p.184-186.

7.7 Condemnation of the Supporters of Kharijites

Essential Reading:

1. Dr Tahir-ul-Qadri, Islam on Love and Non-Violence, Ch:7, p.187-190.

Additional Readings for Teachers and Students:

1. Ibn Ḥajar al-ʿAsqalānī, *Fatḥ al-Bārī*, 1:432.
2. ibid., *Tahdhīb al-tahdhīb*, 8:114.

8. Some Essential Measures for the Elimination of Kharijites Epilogue

8.1 No Place for Violence in Islam and in the Conduct of the Holy Prophet

Essential Reading:

1. Dr Tahir-ul-Qadri, Islam on Love and Non-Violence, Ch:8, p.191.

8.2 Those who are Merciful to Others Deserve Mercy

Essential Reading:

1. Dr Tahir-ul-Qadri, Islam on Love and Non-Violence, Ch:8, p.193-195.

Additional Readings for Teachers and Students:

1. Muslim in *al-Ṣaḥīḥ, [Kitāb al-faḍā'il]* Bk.: Virtue, Ch.: "Mercy Toward Children and Family Members," 4:1809 §2319.
2. al-Bukhārī in *al-Adab al-Mufrad*, 1:48 §96.
3. Ibn Abī Shayba in *al-Muṣannaf*, 5:214 §25356.
4. al-Quḍāʿī in *Musnad al-shihāb*, 2:66 §894.
5. al-Bayhaqī in *al-Sunan al-kubrā*, 9:41 §17682.

8.3 Erasing Extremist Ideology is Inevitable

Essential Reading:

1. Dr Tahir-ul-Qadri, Islam on Love and Non-Violence, Ch:8, p.195-196.

8.4 The Need for Changes in Academic Curricula

Essential Reading:

1. Dr Tahir-ul-Qadri, Islam on Love and Non-Violence, Ch:8, p.196-197.

8.5 O Most Noble of the Messengers! It is A Moment to Supplicate!

Essential Reading:

1. Dr Tahir-ul-Qadri, Islam on Love and Non-Violence, Ch:8, p.197.

SECTION III

Islam On Serving Humanity

1. Human Dignity and Serving Humanity

1.1 The Sanctity of Human Blood, Property and Honour

Essential Reading:

1. Dr Tahir-ul-Qadri, Islam on Serving Humanity, Ch:1, p.5-46.

Additional Readings for Teachers and Students:

1. Qur'ān 4:29–30.
2. Ibid., 4:92–93.
3. Ibid., 5:32.
4. al-Baghawī, *Maʿālim al-tanzīl,* 2:33.
5. al-Rāzī, *al-Tafsīr al-kabīr,* 11:196.
6. Qur'ān, 5:45.
7. Ibid., 17:33.
8. Ibid., 25:68.
9. Ibid., 85:10.
10. al-Suyūṭī, *Tafsīr al-Jalalayn*, p. 801.
11. al-Qurṭubī, *al-Jāmiʿ li aḥkām al-Qur'ān*, 19:295.

12. Abū afṣ al- anbalī, *al-Lubāb fī ʿulūm al-Kitāb*, 20:253.
13. al-Bukhārī in *al-Ṣaḥīḥ: Kitāb al-Īmān* [The Book of Faith], chapter: "The Muslim is He from Whose Tongue and Hand the Muslims Are Safe", 1:13 §10.
14. Muslim in *al-Ṣaḥīḥ: Kitāb al-Īmān* [The Book of Faith], chapter: "Explaining the Ranks of Virtue within Islam and which of its Affairs are Most Virtuous", 1:65 §41.
15. Aḥmad b. Ḥanbal in *al-Musnad*, 2:163 §6515.
16. Abū Dāwūd in *al-Sunan*: *Kitāb al-Jihād* [The Book of Jihad], chapter: "Has migration ended?", 3:4 §2481.
17. al-Nasāʾī in *al-Sunan*: *Kitāb al-Īmān wa Sharāʾiʿuhū* [The Book of Faith and its Branches], chapter: "Description of the Muslim", 8:105 §4996.
18. al-Bukhārī in *al-Ṣaḥīḥ: Kitāb al-Īmān* [The Book of Faith], chapter: "On whose Islam is best", 1:13 §11.
19. Muslim in *al-Ṣaḥīḥ: Kitāb al-Īmān* [The Book of Faith], chapter: "Explaining the Ranks of Virtue within Islam and which of its Affairs are Most Virtuous", 1:66 §42.
20. Aḥmad b. Ḥanbal in *al-Musnad*, 3:372 §15037.
21. al-Nasāʾī in *al-Sunan*: *Kitāb al-Īmān wa sharāʾiʿuhū* [The Book of Faith and its Branches], chapter: "Whose Islam is most virtuous?", 8:106 §4999.
22. al-Bukhārī in *al-Ṣaḥīḥ: Kitāb al-Riqāq* [The Book of Mercy in the Heart], chapter: "Ceasing acts of disobedience", 5:2379 §6119.
23. Muslim in *al-Ṣaḥīḥ: Kitāb al-Īmān* [The Book of Faith], chapter: "Clarifying the superiority of Islam, and what part of it is best", 1:65 §40.
24. Aḥmad b. Ḥanbal in *al-Musnad*, 2:379 §8918.
25. al-Tirmidhī in *al-Sunan: Kitāb al-Īmān* [The Book of Faith], chapter: "What has been related [about] 'The Muslim is the one from (the harm) whose tongue and hand (other) Muslims are safe'", 5:17 §2627.
26. al-Nasāʾī in *al-Sunan: Kitāb al-Īmān wa sharāʾiʿuhu* [The Book of Faith and its Revealed Laws], chapter: "The Quality of the True Believer", 8:104 §4995.
27. Ibn ibbān in *al-Ṣaḥīḥ*, 1:406 §180.
28. Aḥmad b. Ḥanbal in *al-Musnad*, 6:21 §24004.
29. al- ākim in *al-Mustadrak*, 1:54 §24.
30. Ibn ibbān in *al-Ṣaḥīḥ*, 11:203–204 §4862.
31. Ibn al-Mubārak in *al-Musnad*, 1:16 §29.
32. al-Ṭabarānī in *al-Muʿjam al-kabīr*, 18:309 §796.
33. al-Bayhaqī in *Shuʿab al-īmān*, 7:499 §11123.
34. Ibn Mājah in *al-Sunan: Kitāb al-fitan* [The Book of Tribulations], chapter: 'The Inviolability of a Believer's Blood and Property', 2:1298 §3934.

35. Ibn Manẓūr al-Afrīqī in *Lisān al-ʿArab*, 13:24.
36. al-Bukhārī in *al-Ṣaḥīḥ: Kitāb al- ajj* [The Book of Pilgrimage], chapter: "The sermon during the days of Minā", 2:620 §1654; & in *Kitāb al-ʿIlm* [The Book of Knowledge], chapter: "On the words of the Prophet ﷺ, 'Many a person to whom something is conveyed may retain it better than the one who actually heard it'", 1:37 §67.
37. Muslim in *al-Ṣaḥīḥ*: *Kitāb al-Qiṣāṣ wa al-Muḥāribīn wa al-Diyāt* [The Book of Pertaining to Oath, for Establishing the Responsibility of Murders Fighting, Requital and Blood Money], chapter: "Blood shed, the honour and wealth are thickly forbidden", 3:1305–1306 §1679.
38. al-Bukhārī in *al-Ṣaḥīḥ: Kitāb al-Fitan* [The Book of Turmoils], chapter: "The words of the Prophet ﷺ, 'Do not revert to being unbelievers after me, striking the necks of one another'", 6:2594 §6668.
39. al-Ṭabarānī in *al-Muʿjam al-awsaṭ*, 4:269 §4162.
40. al-Bukhārī in *al-Ṣaḥīḥ*: *Kitāb al- ajj* [The Book of Pilgrimage], chapter: "The sermon during the days of Minā", 2:620 §1655; & in *Kitāb al-Adab* [The Book of Good Manners], chapter: "On the words of Almighty Allah: ﴾*O believers! Let no community ridicule another community*﴿ [Q.49:11], 5:2247 §5696.
41. al-Tirmidhī in *al-Sunan*, 3:467 §1163.
42. Ibn Mājah in *al-Sunan*, 1:594 §1851.
43. al-Nasāʾī in *al-Sunan al-Kubrā*, 5:372 §9169.
44. al-Bukhārī in *al-Ṣaḥīḥ: Kitāb al-diyāt* [The Book of Blood Money], chapter: "Whoever Kills a Believer Intentionally, His Recompense Is Hell," 6:2517 §6470.
45. al-Bayhaqī in *al-Sunan al-kubrā*, 8:21 §15637.
46. Ibn Mājah in *al-Sunan: Kitāb al-fitan* [The Book of Tribulations], chapter: "The Inviolability of a Believer's Blood and Property", 2:1297 §3932.
47. al-Ṭabarānī in *Musnad al-Shāmiyyīn*, 2:396 §1568.
48. al-Mundhīrī in *al-Targhīb wa al-tarhīb*, 3:201 §3679.
49. al-Tirmidhī in *al-Sunan*: *Kitāb al-birr wa al-ṣila* [The Book of
50. Righteousness and Maintaining Good Relations with Relatives], chapter: "What has been related about honouring the believer", 4:378 §2032.
51. Muslim in *al-Ṣaḥīḥ*: *Kitāb al-birr wa al-ṣila wa al-ādāb* [Piety, affinity and good manners], chapter: "The prohibition of wronging the Muslim, deserting him, and despising him, his goods, his blood and his wealth", 4:1986 §2564.
52. Aḥmad b. Ḥanbal in *al-Musnad*, 2:277 §7713.
53. ʿAbd b. Ḥumayd in *al-Musnad*, 1:420 §1442.
54. al-Bayhaqī in *al-Sunan al-kubrā*, 6:92 §11276, & in *Shuʿab al-īmān*, 5:280 §6660.
55. al-Daylamī in *Musnad al-Firdaws*, 2:470 §4002.

56. Ibn Rajab in *Jāmiʿ al-ʿulūm wa al-ḥikam*, 1:326.
57. Ibn Ḥajar al-ʿAsqalānī in *Fatḥ al-bārī*, 10:483.
58. Aḥmad b. anbal in *al-Musnad*, 4:168 §17570.
59. al-Tirmidhī in *al-Sunan: Kitāb al-birr wa al-ṣila* [The Book of Piety and Affinity], chapter: "What has come to us concerning the Muslim's compassion for the Muslim", 4:325 §1927.
60. Ibn Rajab in *Jāmiʿ al-ʿulūm wa al-ḥikam*, 1:326.
61. al-Nawawī in *al-Adhkār*, p. 268 §1038, & in *Riyāḍ al-ṣāliḥīn*, p. 60 §234.
62. al-Bukhārī in *al-Ṣaḥīḥ: Kitāb al-maghāzī* [The Book of Military Expeditions], chapter: "On the Angels Being Present at the Battle of Badr", 4:1474 §3794.
63. Muslim in *al-Ṣaḥīḥ: Kitāb al-īmān* [The Book of Faith], chapter: "On the Prohibition of Killing a Disbeliever He says, 'There is no god but God'", 1:95 §95.
64. Abū Dawūd in *al-Sunan: Kitāb al-jihād* [The Book of Jihad], chapter: "On which basis polytheists should be fought", 3:45 §2644.
65. al-Bukhārī in *al-Ṣaḥīḥ: Kitāb al-maghāzī* [The Book of Military Expeditions], chapter: "The Blessed Prophet's Sending of Usāma b. Zayd to the Campsites of the Juhayna Tribe", 4:1555 §4021, & *Kitāb al-diyāt* [The Book of Blood Money], chapter: "Regarding the Saying of God Most High, 'And Whoever Saves the Life of One Person. . .'" [Qurʾān 5:32], 6:2519 §6478.
66. Muslim in *al-Ṣaḥīḥ*: *Kitāb al-Īmān* [The Book of Faith], chapter: "Prohibition of killing of an infidel after he says: 'There is no god but God'", 1:97 §94–97.
67. Ibn Ḥibbān in *al-Ṣaḥīḥ*, 11:56 §4751.
68. al-Bukhārī in *al-Ṣaḥīḥ*: *Kitāb al-fitan* [The Book of Tribulations], chapter: "The words of the Prophet ﷺ, 'Whoever bears arms against us is not one of us'", 6:2592 §6664.
69. Muslim in al *al-Ṣaḥīḥ*: *Kitāb al-birr wa al-ṣila wa al-ādāb* [The Book of Virtue, Good Manners and Joining of the Ties of Relationship], chapter: "He who goes in the mosque or in the bazaar or a place of gathering like it with a weapon would see that the spearhead does not harm anyone", 4:2019 §2615.
70. Abū Dāwūd in *al-Sunan*: *Kitāb al-jihād* [The Book of Jihad], 3:31 §2587. Ibn Mājah in *al-Sunan*: *Kitāb al-adab* [The Book of Good Manners], 2:1241 §3778.
71. Ibn Khuzayma in *al-Ṣaḥīḥ*, 2:280 §1318.
72. Abū Yaʿlā in *al-Musnad*, 13:276 §7291.
73. Muslim in *al-Ṣaḥīḥ: Kitāb al-birr wa al-ṣila wa al-ādāb* [The Book of Piety, Filial Duty and Good Manners], chapter: "On the Prohibition of Pointing a Weapon at Someone Else", 4:2020 §2616.

74. al-Tirmidhī in *al-Sunan: Kitāb al-fitan* [The Book of Tribulations], chapter: "What has Come to Us Regarding the Muslim who Points a Weapon at His Brother", 4:463 §2162.
75. al-Ḥākim in *al-Mustadrak*, 2:171 §2669.
76. Ibn Ḥibbān in *al-Ṣaḥīḥ*, 13:272 §5944.
77. al-Bayhaqī in *al-Sunan al-kubrā*, 8:23 §15649.
78. Muslim in *al-Ṣaḥīḥ: Kitāb al-birr wa al-ṣila wa al-ādāb* [The Book of Piety, Filial Duty and Good Manners], chapter: "On the Prohibition of Pointing a Weapon at Someone Else", 4:2020 §2617.
79. al-Ḥākim in *al-Mustadrak*, 3:587 §6176.
80. al-Bayhaqī in *al-Sunan al-kubrā*, 8:23 §2617.
81. Abū Dāwūd in *al-Sunan: Kitāb al-jihād* [The Book of Jihad], chapter: "What has Come to Us Regarding the Prohibition of Handing Someone an Unsheathed Sword", 3:31 §2588.
82. al-Tirmidhī in *al-Sunan: Kitāb al-fitan* [The Book of Tribulation], chapter: "What has Come to Us Regarding the Prohibition of Handing Someone an Unsheathed Sword", 4:464 §2163.
83. al-Ḥākim in *al-Mustadrak*, 4:322 §7785.
84. Ibn Ḥibbān in *al-Ṣaḥīḥ*, 13:275 §5946.
85. al-Tirmidhī in *al-Sunan*: *Kitāb al-diyāt* [The Book of Blood Money], chapter: "The Legal Ruling Concerning Blood", 4:17 §1398.
86. al-Rabīʿ in *al-Musnad*, 1:292 §757.
87. al-Daylamī in *Musnad al-firdaws*, 3:361 §5089.
88. Ibn Mājah in *al-Sunan*: *Kitāb al-Diyāt* [The Book of Blood Money], chapter: The Gravity of unjustly Killing a Muslim, 2:874 §2620.
89. al-Bayhaqī in *al-Sunan al-kubrā*, 8:22 §15646.
90. al-Rabīʿ in *al-Musnad*, 1:368 §960.
91. al-Tirmidhī in *al-Sunan*: *Kitāb al-diyāt* [The Book of Blood Money], chapter: "What has Come to Us Concerning the Gravity of Killing a Believer", 4:16 §1395. al-Nasāʾī in *al-Sunan*: *Kitāb taḥrīm al-dam* [The Book on the Prohibition of Bloodshed], chapter: "The Sanctity of Blood", 7:82 §3987.
92. Ibn Mājah in *al-Sunan*: *Kitāb al-diyāt* [The Book of Blood Money], chapter: "The Gravity of Killing a Muslim unjustly", 2:874 §2619.
93. al-Nasāʾī in *al-Sunan*: *Kitāb taḥrīm al-dam* [The Book on the Prohibition of Bloodshed], chapter: "The Sanctity of Blood", 7:82–83 §§3988–3990.
94. al-Ṭabarānī in *al-Muʿjam al-ṣaghīr*, 1:355 §594.
95. al-Bayhaqī in *al-Sunan al-kubrā*, 8:22 §15647.
96. Muslim in *al-Ṣaḥīḥ*: *Kitāb al-birr wa al-ṣila wa al-ādāb* [The Book of Piety, Filial Duty and Good Manners], chapter: "The Severe Divine Threat for Someone Who Punishes People unjustly," 4:2018 §2613.
97. Abū Dāwūd in *al-Sunan*: *Kitāb al-fitan wa al-malāḥim* [The Book of

Tribulations and Battles], chapter: 'The Gravity of Killing a Believer', 4:103 §4270.

98. al-Ṭabarānī in *Musnad al-Shāmiyyīn*, 2:266 §1311.
99. al-Mundhirī in *al-Targhīb wa al-tarhīb*, 3:203 §3691.
100. al-ʿAsqalānī in *al-Dirāya*, 2:259.
101. al-Shawkānī in *Nayl al-awṭār*, 7:197.
102. al-Bukhārī in *al-Ṣaḥīḥ*: *Kitāb al-jizya* [The Book of Taxation for Non-Muslims Living in an Islamic State], chapter: "The Sin of Someone Who Kills a Non-Muslim Citizen Without His Having Committed a Crime", 3:1155 §2995.
103. Ibn Mājah in *al-Sunan*: *Kitāb al-diyāt* [The Book of Blood Money], chapter: "Someone Who Kills a Non-Muslim Citizen", 2:896 §2686.
104. al-Bazzār in *al-Musnad*, 6:368 §2383.
105. Anwar Shāh Kāshmīrī, *Fayḍ al-Bārī ʿalā Ṣaḥīḥ al-Bukhārī*, 4:288.
106. al-Nasāʾī in *al-Sunan*: *Kitāb al-qasāma* [The Book of Taking an Oath], chapter: "The Gravity of Killing A Non-Muslim Citizen," 8:25 §4750; and in *al-Sunan al-Kubrā*, 4:221 §6952.
107. Aḥmad b. Ḥanbal in *al-Musnad*, 2:186§6745.
108. al-Bazzār in *al-Musnad*, 6:361 §3273.
109. al-Ḥākim in *al-Mustadrak*, 2:137 §2580.
110. Ibn al-Jārūd in *al-Muntaqā*, 1:212 §834.
111. al-Bayhaqī in *al-Sunan al-kubrā*, 8:133 §16260.
112. Aḥmad b. anbal in *al-Musnad*, 4:237, 5:369 §§18097, 23177.
113. al-Nasāʾī in *al-Sunan*: *Kitāb al-qasāma* [The Book of Taking an Oath], chapter: "The Enormity of Murdering A Non-Muslim Citizen," 8:25 §4749; and in *al-Sunan al-kubrā*, 4:221 §6951.
114. al-Mundhirī in *al-Targhīb wa al-Tarhīb*, 3:204 §3695.
115. al-Nasāʾī in *al-Sunan*: *Kitāb al-qasāma* [The Book of Taking an Oath], chapter: "The Enormity of Murdering A Non-Muslim Citizen," 8:25 §4748; and in *al-Sunan al-kubrā*, 4:221 §6950.
116. ʿAbd al-Razzāq in *al-Muṣannaf*, 10:102 §18521.
117. Ibn ibbān in *al-Ṣaḥīḥ*, 16:391 §8382.
118. al-Bazzār in *al-Musnad*, 9:138 §3696.
119. al-Ṭabarānī in *al-Muʿjam al-awsaṭ*, 1:207 §663.
120. al- ākim in *al-Mustadrak ʿalā al-Ṣaḥīḥayn*, 1:105 §134.
121. Ibn Abī Shayba in *al-Muṣannaf*, 5:457 §27944.
122. al- ākim in *al-Mustadrak ʿalā al-Ṣaḥīḥayn*, 1:105 §133.
123. Aḥmad b. Ḥanbal in *al-Musnad*, 4:89 §16862.
124. Abū Dāwūd in *al-Sunan*: *Kitāb al-aṭʿima* [The Book of Foodstuffs], chapter: "The Unlawfulness of Eating Beasts of Prey," 3:356 §3806.
125. al-Shaybānī in *al-Āḥād wa al-mathānī*, 2:29 §703.
126. Ibn Zanjawayh in *Kitāb al-amwāl*, p. 379 §618.
127. al-Ṭabarānī in *al-Muʿjam al-kabīr*, 4:111 §3828.

128. Ibn Zanjawayh in *Kitāb al-amwāl*, p. 380 §619.
129. al-Dāraquṭnī in *al-Sunan*, 4:287 §63.
130. Abū Dāwūd in *al-Sunan*: *Kitāb al-jihād* [The Book of Jihad], 3:66 §2705.
131. al-Bayhaqī in *al-Sunan al-kubrā*, 9:61 §17789.
132. Abū Dāwūd in *al-Sunan*: *Kitāb al-kharāj wa al-imāra wa al-fay'* [The Book of Land Tax, Leadership and the Spoils Acquired without Fighting], 3:170 §3050.
133. al-Bayhaqī in *al-Sunan al-kubrā*, 9:204 §18508.
134. Ibn ʿAbd al-Barr in *al-Tamhīd*, 1:149.
135. Mālik in *al-Muwaṭṭā*, 2:447 §965.
136. Ibn Abī Shayba in *al-Muṣannaf*, 6:483 §33121.
137. Mālik in *al-Muwaṭṭā*, 2:448 §966.
138. ʿAbd al-Razzāq in *al-Muṣannaf*, 5:199.
139. al-Bayhaqī in *al-Sunan al-kubrā*, 9:85.
140. al-Hindī in *Kanz al-ʿummāl*, 1:296.
141. Ibn Qudāma in *al-Mughnī*, 8:451–452, 477 §17904.
142. al-Hindī in *Kanz al-ʿummāl*, 4:474 §11409.
143. Ibid., 4:475 §11411.
144. al-Tirmidhī in *al-Sunan*: *Kitāb al-siyar* [The Book of Military Expeditions], 4:122 §1552.
145. Abū Yūsuf in *al-Kharāj*, p. 141.
146. Ibn Qudāma in *al-Mughnī*, 9:181.
147. al-Zaylaʿī in *Naṣb al-rāya*, 3:381.
148. Al-Nawawī, *Sharḥ Ṣaḥīḥ Muslim*, 12:7.
149. Ibn Qudāma, *al-Mughnī*, 9:112.
150. Ibn Ḥazm, *al-Muḥallā*, 10:351.
151. Ibn Rushd al-Mālikī, *Bidāyat al-mujtahid*, 2:299.
152. Al-Ḥaṣkafī, *al-Durr al-mukhtār*, 2:223.
153. Ibn ʿĀbidīn al-Shāmī, *Radd al-muḥtār*, 3:273.
154. al-Qurāfī, *al-Furūq*, 3:29.

1.2 Dignifying Human Beings

Essential Reading:

1. Dr Tahir-ul-Qadri, Islam on Serving Humanity, Ch:1, p.47-56.

Additional Readings for Teachers and Students:

1. Qur'ān, 5:32.
2. Ibid., 6:151.
3. Ibid., 4:86.
4. Ibid., 89:15–20.
5. Ibid., 95:1–4.
6. al-Bukhārī in *al-Ṣaḥīḥ*, 1:20 §30.
7. Muslim in *al-Ṣaḥīḥ*, 3:1283 §1661.
8. Aḥmad b. anbal in *al-Musnad*, 5:161 §21469.
9. Aḥmad b. anbal in *al-Musnad*, 3:432 §15597.
10. al-Mundhirī in *al-Targhīb wa al-Tarhīb*, 3:253 §3917.
11. al-Bukhārī in *al-Ṣaḥīḥ*, 3:1155 §2995.
12. Ibn Mājah in *al-Sunan*, 2:896 §2686.
13. al-Bazzār in *al-Musnad*, 6:368 §2383.
14. Aḥmad b. anbal in *al-Musnad*, 5:36, 38 §20393, 20419.
15. Abū Dāwūd in *al-Sunan*, 3:83 §2760.
16. al-Nasā'ī in *al-Sunan*, 8:24 §4747.
17. al-Darimī in *al-Sunan*, 2:308 §2504.
18. al-Bazzār in *al-Musnad*, 9:129 §3679.
19. Muslim in *al-Ṣaḥīḥ*, 4:2018 §2613.
20. Aḥmad b. anbal in *al-Musnad*, 3:404 §15372.
21. Abū Dāwūd in *al-Sunan*, 3:169 §3045.
22. Aḥmad b. anbal in *al-Musnad*, 4:444 §20010.
23. Abū Dāwūd in *al-Sunan*, 3:53 §2667.
24. ʿAbd al-Razzāq in *al-Muṣannaf*, 8:436 §15819.
25. Aḥmad b. anbal in *al-Musnad*, 6:58 §24353.
26. Abū Dāwūd in *al-Sunan*, 3:212 §3207.
27. Ibn Mājah in *al-Sunan*, 1:516 §1616.
28. Mālik in *al-Muwaṭṭa'*, 1:238 §563.
29. ʿAbd al-Razzāq in *al-Muṣannaf*, 3:444 §6256–6257.
30. al-Bayhaqī in *Shuʿab al-Īmān*, 1:174 §152.
31. Abū ʿAbd al-Raḥmān al-Sulamī in his *Tafsīrah*, 1:429.
32. Jaʿfar b. iyyān in *al-Tawbīkh wa al-Tanbīh*, 1:74.
33. Abū ʿAbd al-Raḥmān al-Sulamī in his *Tafsīrah*, 1:271.
34. al-ʿAsqalānī in *Fatḥ al-Bārī bī Sharḥ Ṣaḥīḥ al-Bukhārī*, 9:113.

1.3 ASSISTING PEOPLE IN WELFARE AND RIGHTEOUS ACTS

ESSENTIAL READING:

1. Dr Tahir-ul-Qadri, Islam on Serving Humanity, Ch:1, p.57-66.

ADDITIONAL READINGS FOR TEACHERS AND STUDENTS:

1. Qurʾān, 9:71.
2. Ibid., 90:11–18.
3. Ibid., 107:1–7.
4. Muslim in *al-Ṣaḥīḥ*, 4:2074 §2699.
5. Aḥmad b. anbal in *al-Musnad*, 2:252 §7421.
6. al-Tirmidhī in *al-Sunan*, 4:34 §1425, 1930, 2945.
7. Abū Dāwūd in *al-Sunan*, 4:287 §4946.
8. Ibn Mājah in *al-Sunan*, 1:82 §225.
9. al-Bukhārī in *al-Ṣaḥīḥ*, 2:880 §2354.
10. Muslim in *al-Ṣaḥīḥ*, 4:1944 §2500.
11. al-Nasāʾī in *al-Sunan al-Kubrā*, 5:247 §8798.
12. Abū Yaʿlā in *al-Musnad*, 13:293 §7309.
13. al-Bayhaqī in *al-Sunan al-Kubrā*, 10:132 §20223.
14. Abū Nuʿaym in *Musnad Abī anīfa*, p. 151.
15. Abū Yaʿlā, on the authority of Anas b. Mālik, in *al-Musnad*, 7:275 §4296.
16. Tamām al-Rāzī in *al-Fawāʾid*, 2:65 §1157.
17. al-Ṣaydāwī in *Muʿjam al-Shuyūkh*, p. 184.
18. al-ʿAsqalānī in *al-Maṭālib al-ʿĀliya*, 5:709 §981, & in *Fatḥ al-Bārī*, 11:12.
19. Abū Yaʿlā in *al-Musnad*, 7:255 §4266.
20. al-Bayhaqī in *Shuʿab al-Īmān*, 6:120 §7670.
21. Ibn Abī al-Dunā in *Qaḍāʾ al- awāʾij*, p. 41 §29.
22. Ibn ʿAsākir in *Tārīkh Madīna Damishq*, 19:138.
23. Muslim in *al-Ṣaḥīḥ*, 3:1354 §1728.
24. Aḥmad b. anbal in *al-Musnad*, 3:34 §11311.
25. Abū Dāwūd in *al-Sunan*, 2:125 §1663.
26. Ibn ibbān in *al-Ṣaḥīḥ*, 12:238 §5419.
27. Abū Yaʿlā in *al-Musnad*, 2:326 §1064.
28. al-Bayhaqī in *al-Sunan al-Kubrā*, 3:182 §7571.

29. al-Bukhārī in *al-Ṣaḥīḥ*, 1:216 §577; 3:1312 §3388; 5:2274 §5789; 5:2274 §5790.
30. Muslim in *al-Ṣaḥīḥ*, 3:1627 §2057.
31. Aḥmad b. anbal in *al-Musnad*, 1:197 §1702, 1712.
32. al-Bazzār in *al-Musnad*, 6:228 §2263.
33. Abū ʿAwāna in *al-Musnad*, 5:204 §8398.
34. Aḥmad b. anbal in *al-Musnad*, 5:75 §20742.
35. Abū Dāwūd in *al-Sunan*, 3:100 §2813.
36. al-Dārimī in *al-Sunan*, 2:108 §1958.
37. al-Bayhaqī in *al-Sunan al-Kubrā*, 9:292 §19001.
38. al-Bukhārī in *al-Adab al-Mufrad*, p. 198 §562.
39. al-Numayrī in *Akhbār al-Madīna*, p. 392 §1238.
40. al-Tamīmī in *al-Jarḥ wa al-Taʿdīl*, 1:192.
42. Abū Nuʿaym in *ilyat al-Awliyāʾ*, 5:198.
43. al-Ghazālī in *Iḥyāʾ ʿUlūm al-Dīn*, 2:176.
44. Ibn Abī al-Dunyā in *al-Ikhwān*, p. 99 §49.
45. Ibn Qudāma in *al-Mutaḥābbīn fī Allah*, p. 78 §104.
46. al-Māwardī in *Adab al-Dunyā wa al-Dīn*, p. 216.

1.4 Providing what is Desired for People

Essential Reading:

1. Dr Tahir-ul-Qadri, Islam on Serving Humanity, Ch:1, p.67-80.

Additional Readings for Teachers and Students:

1. Qurʾān, 51:19.
2. Ibid., 59:7–9.
3. al-Bukhārī in *al-Ṣaḥīḥ*, 2:862 §2310.
4. Muslim in *al-Ṣaḥīḥ*, 4:1996 §2580.
5. Aḥmad b. anbal in *al-Musnad*, 2:91 §5646.
6. al-Tirmidhī in *al-Sunan*, 4:34 §1426.
7. Abū Dāwūd in *al-Sunan*, 4:273 §4893.
8. al-Nasāʾī in *al-Sunan al-Kubrā*, 4:308 §7286.
9. Ibn ibbān in *al-Ṣaḥīḥ*, 2:291 §533.

10. al-Ṭabarānī in *al-Muʿjam al-Kabīr*, 5:118 §4802.
11. al-Haythamī in *Majmaʿ al-Zawāʾid*, 8:193.
12. al-ʿAsqalānī in *al-Maṭālib al-ʿĀlīya*, 5:715.
13. Aḥmad b. anbal in *al-Musnad*, 6:450 §27583.
14. al-Tirmidhī in *al-Sunan*, 4:327 §1931.
15. al-Bayhaqī in *al-Sunan al-Kubrā*, 8:168 §16461.
16. Abū Yaʿlā in *al-Musnad*, 5:175 §2789.
17. Ibn ajar al-ʿAsqalanī in *al-Maṭālib al-ʿĀlīya*, 5:703 §978.
18. al-Haythamī in *Majmaʿ al-Zawāʾid*, 8:190.
19. Ibn ibbān in *al-Ṣaḥīḥ*, 2:287 §530.
20. al-Ṭabarānī in *Musnad al-Shāmiyyīn*, 1:307 §537.
21. al-Quḍāʿī in *Musnad al-Shihāb*, 1:316 §532.
22. al-Bayhaqī in *al-Sunan al-Kubrā*, 8:167 §16457.
23. al-Haythamī in *Mawārid al-Ẓamān*, 1:505 §2069.
24. al-Ṭabarānī in *al-Muʿjam al-Awsaṭ*, 7:221 §7326.
25. al-Bayhaqī in *Shuʿab al-Īmān*, 3:424 §3965.
26. al-Haythamī in *Majmaʿ al-Zawāʾid*, 8:192.
27. al-Mundhirī in *al-Targhīb wa al-Tarhīb*, 3:263 §3971.
28. al-Ṭabarānī in *al-Muʿjam al-Kabīr*, 2:358 §13334.
29. al-Quḍāʿī in *Musnad al-Shihāb*, 2:117 §1007–1008.
30. al-Mundhirī in *al-Targhīb wa al-Tarhīb*, 3:262 §3966.
31. al-Haythamī in *Majmaʿ al-Zawāʾid*, 8:192.
32. al-Ṭabarānī in *al-Muʿjam al-Awsaṭ*, 5:228 §5162.
33. al-Bayhaqī in *Shuʿab al-Īmān*, 6:117 §7662.
34. al-Ṭabarānī in *al-Muʿjam al-Awsaṭ*, 8:186 §8350.
35. al-Haythamī in *Majmaʿ al-Zawāʾid*, 8:192.
36. al-Ṭabarānī in *al-Muʿjam al-Awsaṭ*, 8:153 §8245, & in *al-Muʿjam al-Kabīr*, 3:85 §2738.
37. al-Quḍāʿī in *Musnad al-Shihāb*, 2:179 §1139.
38. Abū Nuʿaym in *ilyat al-Awliyāʾ*, 7:90.
39. al-Mundhirī in *al-Targhīb wa al-Tarhīb*, 3:265 §3981.
40. al-Ṭabarānī in *al-Muʿjam al-Awsaṭ*, 7:289 §7519, & in *al-Muʿjam al-Ṣaghīr*, 2:132 §910.
41. al-Haythamī in *Majmaʿ al-Zawāʾid*, 8:193.
42. al-Mundhirī in *al-Targhīb wa al-Tarhīb*, 3:265 §3984.
43. al-Ṭabarānī in *al-Muʿjam al-Kabīr*, 11:71 §11079, & in *al-Muʿjam al-Awsaṭ*, 8:45 §7911.
44. al-Haythamī in *Majmaʿ al-Zawāʾid*, 8:193.
45. al-Mundhirī in *al-Targhīb wa al-Tarhīb*, 3:265 §3983.
46. Ibn Abī al-Dunyā in *Qaḍāʾ al- awāʾij*, p. 97 §115.
47. al-Hindī in *Kanz al-ʿUmmāl*, 6:184 §16409.
48. al-Ṭabarānī in *al-Muʿjam al-Kabīr*, 12:453 §13646, & in *Muʿjam al-Awsaṭ*, 6:139 §6026.

49. al-Mundhirī in *al-Targhīb wa al-Tarhīb*, 3:265 §3985.
50. al-Haythamī in *Majmaʿ al-Zawāʾid*, 8:191.
51. al-Ṭabarānī in *Musnad al-Shāmiyyīn*, 3:196 §2068.
52. al-Bukhārī in *al-Tārīkh al-Kabīr*, 8:43 §2089.
53. al-Khaṭīb al-Baghdādī in *Tārīkh Baghdād*, 3:114 §1124.
54. Ibn Abī al-Dunyā in *Qaḍāʾ al- awāʾij*, p. 54 §46.
55. Ibn Abī al-Dunyā in *Qaḍāʾ al- awāʾij*, p. 89 §103.
56. Ibn Rajab al- anbalī in *Jāmiʿ al-ʿUlūm wa al- ikam*, 1:341.
57. Ibn Abī al-Dunyā in *Qaḍāʾ al- awāʾij*, p. 60 §59.
58. Ibn Abī al-Dunyā in *Qaḍāʾ al- awāʾij*, p. 61 §61.
59. Ibn Abī al-Dunyā in *Qaḍāʾ al- awāʾij*, p. 64 §67.
60. Ibn Abī al-Dunyā in *al-Ikhwān*, p. 191 §138.

1.5 Feeding the Meals

Essential Reading:

1. Dr Tahir-ul-Qadri, Islam on Serving Humanity, Ch:1, p.81-85.

Additional Readings for Teachers and Students:

1. Qurʾān, 22:36.
2. Ibid., 58:4.
3. Ibid., 76:8–9.
4. Ibid., 90:11–16.
5. al-Bukhārī in *al-Ṣaḥīḥ*, 1:13 §12.
6. Muslim in *al-Ṣaḥīḥ*, 1:65 §39.
7. Abū Dāwūd in *al-Sunan*, 4:350 §5194.
8. al-Nasāʾī in *al-Sunan*, 6:107 §5000.
9. Ibn Mājah in *al-Sunan*, 2:1083 §3253.
10. Ibn ibbān in *al-Ṣaḥīḥ*, 2:258 §505.
11. al-Bukhārī in *al-Ṣaḥīḥ*, 2:817 §2195.
12. Muslim in *al-Ṣaḥīḥ*, 3:1189 §1553.
13. Muslim in *al-Ṣaḥīḥ*, 3:1188 §1552.
14. al-Tirmidhī in *al-Sunan*, 4:287 §1855.
15. ʿAbd b. umayd in *al-Musnad*, 1:139 §355.

1.6 Clothing the Destitute

Essential Reading:

1. Dr Tahir-ul-Qadri, Islam on Serving Humanity, Ch:1, p.86-88.

Additional Readings for Teachers and Students:

1. Abū Dāwūd in *al-Sunan*, 2:130 §1682.
2. al-Tirmidhī in *al-Sunan*, Ch.: (8), 4:633 §2449.
3. al-Tirmidhī in *al-Sunan*, Ch.: (41), 4:651 §2484.
4. al-Ṭabarānī in *al-Muʿjam al-Kabīr*, 12:97 §12591.
5. al-Ṭabarānī in *al-Muʿjam al-Awsaṭ*, 5:202 §5081.

1.7 Facilitating the Deprived and Waiving his Debt

Essential Reading:

1. Dr Tahir-ul-Qadri, Islam on Serving Humanity, Ch:1, p.89-93.

Additional Readings for Teachers and Students:

1. al-Bukhārī in *al-Ṣaḥīḥ*, 2:731 §1971.
2. Muslim in *al-Ṣaḥīḥ*, 3:1194 §1560.
3. Muslim in *al-Ṣaḥīḥ*, 4:2074 §2699.
4. Aḥmad b. anbal in *al-Musnad*, 2:252 §7421.
5. Abū Dāwūd in *al-Sunan*, 4:287 §4946.
6. al-Tirmidhī in *al-Sunan*, 5:195 §2945.
7. Ibn Mājah in *al-Sunan*, 1:82 §225.
8. Aḥmad b. anbal in *al-Musnad*, 2:359 §8696.
9. al-Tirmidhī in *al-Sunan*, 3:599 §1306.

10. al-Quḍāʿī in *Musnad al-Shihāb*, 1:281 §459.
11. Aḥmad b. anbal in *al-Musnad*, 2:23 §4749.
12. ʿAbd b. umayd in *al-Musnad*, 1:262 §826.
13. Aḥmad b. anbal in *al-Musnad*, 1:327 §3017.
14. Ibn Mājah in *al-Sunan*, 2:808 §2419.
15. al-Ṭabarānī in *al-Muʿjam al-Kabīr*, 19:167 §376.
16. al-Bayhaqī in *al-Sunan al-Kubrā*, 6:27 §10917.
17. Ibn Mājah in *al-Sunan*, 2:812 §2430.
18. Ibn Mājah in *al-Sunan*, 2:812 §2431.
19. al-Ṭabarānī in *al-Muʿjam al-Awsaṭ*, 7:16 §6719.

2. Serving Mankind Through Excellent Social Morality

2.1 Brotherhood and Affection in Society

Essential Reading:

1. Dr Tahir-ul-Qadri, Islam on Serving Humanity, Ch:2, p.89-102.

Additional Readings for Teachers and Students:

1. Qurʾān, 3:159.
2. Ibid., 41:34–35.
3. Ibid., 49:10.
4. al-Bukhārī in *al-Ṣaḥīḥ*, 2:862 §2310.
5. Muslim in *al-Ṣaḥīḥ*, 4:1996 §2580.
6. Aḥmad b. anbal in *al-Musnad*, 2:91 §5646.
7. al-Tirmidhī in *al-Sunan*, 4:34 §1426.
8. Abū Dāwūd in *al-Sunan*, 4:273 §4893.
9. al-Nasāʾī in *al-Sunan al-Kubrā*, 4:308 §7286.
10. Ibn ibbān in *al-Ṣaḥīḥ*, 2:291 §533.
11. al-Bayhaqī in *al-Sunan al-Kubrā*, 6:94 §11292.

2.2 Supplications and Well Wishes For Brothers in their Absence

Essential Reading:

1. Dr Tahir-ul-Qadri, Islam on Serving Humanity, Ch:2, p.103-107.

Additional Readings for Teachers and Students:

1. Qur'ān 40:7.
2. Ibid., 59:10.
3. Muslim in *al-Ṣaḥīḥ*, 4:2094 §2732.
4. Ibn ibbān in *al-Ṣaḥīḥ*, 3:268 §989.
5. Ibn ʿAsākir in *Tārīkh Madīna Damishq*, 25:126.
6. al-Nawawī in *al-Adhkār*, 1:319 §1211.

2.3 Excellent Fulfilment of Promises

Essential Reading:

1. Dr Tahir-ul-Qadri, Islam on Serving Humanity, Ch:2, p.108-112.

Additional Readings for Teachers and Students:

1. Qur'ān, 16:91.
2. Ibid., 17:34.
3. al-Bukhārī in *al-Ṣaḥīḥ*, 1:21 §34.
4. Muslim in *al-Ṣaḥīḥ*, 1:78 §58.
5. Aḥmad b. anbal in *al-Musnad*, 2:189 §6768.
6. Abū Dāwūd in *al-Sunan*, 4:221 §4688.
7. al-Tirmidhī in *al-Sunan*, 5:19 §2632.

8. al-Nasā'ī in *al-Sunan*, 8:16 §5020.

2.4 Covering the Faults and Protecting the Secrets of Others

Essential Reading:

1. Dr Tahir-ul-Qadri, Islam on Serving Humanity, Ch:2, p.113-117.

Additional Readings for Teachers and Students:

1. Qur'ān, 24:16.
2. Ibid., 66:3.
3. Ibid., 49:12.
4. Ibid., 104:1.
5. al-Bukhārī in al-Ṣaḥīḥ, 2:862 §2310.
6. Muslim in al-Ṣaḥīḥ, 4:1996 §2580.
7. Abū Dāwūd in al-Sunan, 4:273 §4893.
8. al-Tirmidhī in al-Sunan, 4:34 §1435.

2.5 Forgiving, Overlooking and Hiding the Faults of Others

Essential Reading:

1. Dr Tahir-ul-Qadri, Islam on Serving Humanity, Ch:2, p.118-125.

Additional Readings for Teachers and Students:

1. Qur'ān, 7:199.
2. Ibid., 15:85.
3. Ibid., 42:40.
4. al-Bukhārī in *al-Ṣaḥīḥ*, 3:1282 §3290.
5. Muslim in *al-Ṣaḥīḥ*, 3:1417 §1792.
6. Aḥmad b. anbal in *al-Musnad*, 1:453 §4331.
7. Ibn Mājah in *al-Sunan*, 2:1335 §4025.
8. Abū Yaʿlā in *al-Musnad*, 9:131 §5205.
9. al-Bazzār in *al-Musnad*, 5:106–107 §1686.

2.6 Generosity and Preference for Others

Essential Reading:

1. Dr Tahir-ul-Qadri, Islam on Serving Humanity, Ch:2, p.125-139.

Additional Readings for Teachers and Students:

1. Qur'ān, 3:92.
2. Ibid., 59:9.
3. Ibid., 59:9.
4. al-Bukhārī in *al-Ṣaḥīḥ*, 1:6 §6.
5. Muslim in *al-Ṣaḥīḥ*, 4:1803 §2308.
6. Aḥmad b. anbal in *al-Musnad*, 1:288 §2616.
7. al-Nasā'ī in *al-Sunan*, 4:125 §2095.

2.7 Visiting the Ailing

Essential Reading:

1. Dr Tahir-ul-Qadri, Islam on Serving Humanity, Ch:2, p.140-151.

Additional Readings for Teachers and Students:

1. al-Bukhārī in *al-Ṣaḥīḥ*, 5:2055 §5058; 5:2139 §5325.
2. Aḥmad b. anbal in *al-Musnad*, 4:394 §19535.
3. ʿAbd al-Razzāq in *al-Muṣannaf*, 3:593 §6763.
4. Ibn ibbān in *al-Ṣaḥīḥ*, 8:116 §3324.
5. Aḥmad b. anbal in *al-Musnad*, 6:126 §24990.
6. Abū Yaʿlā in *al-Musnad*, 7:436 §4459.
7. al-Ṭabarānī in *al-Duʿāʾ*, 336 §1102.
8. al-Ṭayālisī in *al-Musnad*, 1:200 §1404.
9. Ibn al-Sunnī in *ʿAmal al-Yawm wa al-Layla*, p. 503 §551.
10. Aḥmad b. anbal in *al-Musnad*, 5:259 §22290.
11. al-Tirmidhī in *al-Sunan*, 5:76 §2731.
12. al-Ṭabarānī in *al-Muʿjam al-Kabīr*, 8:211 §7854.
13. al-Ruyānī in *al-Musnad*, 2:287 §1217.
14. al-Bayhaqī in *Shuʿab al-Īmān*, 6:472 §8948.

2.8 Protecting the Rights of People

Essential Reading:

1. Dr Tahir-ul-Qadri, Islam on Serving Humanity, Ch:2, p.151-155.

Additional Readings for Teachers and Students:

1. Qurʾān, 4:29.
2. Ibid., 5:2.
3. al-Bukhārī in *al-Ṣaḥīḥ*, 1:94 §236.
4. Muslim in *al-Ṣaḥīḥ*, 1:235 §282.
5. Ibn Mājah in *al-Sunan*, 1:124 §344.

3. Serving Humanity Through Charity

3.1 Excellence of Charity and its Rewards

Essential Reading:

1. Dr Tahir-ul-Qadri, Islam on Serving Humanity, Ch:3, p.159-167.

Additional Readings for Teachers and Students:

1. Qur'ān, 2:245.
2. Ibid., 2:177.
3. Ibid., 2:276.
4. Ibid., 5:12.
5. Ibid., 34:39.
6. Ibid., 57:18.
7. Ibid., 107:1–7.
8. al-Bukhārī in *al-Ṣaḥīḥ*, 5:2241 §5676.
9. Muslim in *al-Ṣaḥīḥ*, 2:699 §1008.
10. Aḥmad b. anbal in *al-Musnad*, 4:395 §19549.
11. al-Nasā'ī in *al-Sunan*, 5:64 §2538.

3.2 Excellence of Undisclosed Charitable Donation

Essential Reading:

1. Dr Tahir-ul-Qadri, Islam on Serving Humanity, Ch:3, p.167-171.

Additional Readings for Teachers and Students:

1. Qur'ān, 2:274.
2. al-Bukhārī in *al-Ṣaḥīḥ*, 1:234 §629.
3. Muslim in *al-Ṣaḥīḥ*, 2:715 §1031.
4. Aḥmad b. anbal in *al-Musnad*, 2:439 §9663.
5. al-Tirmidhī in *al-Sunan*, 4:598 §2391.
6. al-Nasā'ī in *al-Sunan*, 8:222 §5380.
7. Mālik in *al-Muwaṭṭā'*, 2:952 §1709.
8. Aḥmad b. anbal in *al-Musnad*, 3:124 §12275.

3.3 Glad Tidings for Charitable Donors

Essential Reading:

1. Dr Tahir-ul-Qadri, Islam on Serving Humanity, Ch:3, p.172-179.

Additional Readings for Teachers and Students:

1. Qur'ān, 2:267.
2. Ibid., 2:272–274.
3. Ibid., 13:22–24.
4. Ibid., 34:39.
5. Ibid., 35:29–30.
6. al-Bukhārī in *al-Ṣaḥīḥ*, 4:1724 §4407.
7. Muslim in *al-Ṣaḥīḥ*, 2:690 §993.
8. Aḥmad b. anbal in *al-Musnad*, 2:313, 500 §8125, 10507.
9. Ibn Mājah in *al-Sunan*, 1:71 §197.

3.4 CHARITY ENHANCES LONGEVITY AND PROTECTS FROM HELLFIRE

ESSENTIAL READING:

1. Dr Tahir-ul-Qadri, Islam on Serving Humanity, Ch:3, p.179-183.

ADDITIONAL READINGS FOR TEACHERS AND STUDENTS:

1. Qurʾān, 5:12.
2. Ibid., 9:99.
3. al-Tirmidhī in *al-Sunan*, 3:52 §664.
4. Ibn ibbān in *al-Ṣaḥīḥ*, 8:103 §3309.
5. al-Bayhaqī in *Shuʿab al-Īmān*, 3:213 §3351.
6. al-Maqdisī in *al-Aḥādīth al-Mukhtāra*, 5:218 §1897.
7. al-Haythamī in *Mawārid al-Ẓamʾān*, 1:209 §816.
8. Ibn Rajab al- anbalī in *Jāmiʿ al-ʿUlūm wa al- akam*, 1:272.
9. al-Ṭabarānī in *al-Muʿjam al-Kabīr*, 17:22 §31.
10. al-Ṭabarānī in *al-Muʿjam al-Kabīr*, 25:35 §3449.
11. al-Ṭabarānī in *al-Muʿjam al-Kabīr*, 4:274 §4402.
12. al-Ṭabarānī in *al-Muʿjam al-Kabīr*, 17:286 §787.

3.5 SPENDING ON FAMILY

ESSENTIAL READING:

1. Dr Tahir-ul-Qadri, Islam on Serving Humanity, Ch:3, p.183-186.

ADDITIONAL READINGS FOR TEACHERS AND STUDENTS:

1. Aḥmad b. anbal in *al-Musnad*, 2:358 §8687.
2. Abū Dāwūd in *al-Sunan*, 2:129 §1677.
3. al- ākim in *al-Mustadrak*, 1:574 §1509.
4. Ibn ibbān in *al-Ṣaḥīḥ*, 8:134 §3346.

5. Ibn Khuzayma in *al-Ṣaḥīḥ*, 4:102 §2451

3.6 Charity to Relatives

Essential Reading:

1. Dr Tahir-ul-Qadri, Islam on Serving Humanity, Ch:3, p.186-191.

Additional Readings for Teachers and Students:

1. Qur'ān, 2:180.
2. Ibid., 2:215.
3. Ibid., 8:41.
4. Ibid., 17:26.
5. al-Tirmidhī in *al-Sunan*, 5:92 §2582.
6. Ibn Mājah in *al-Sunan*, 1:591 §1844.
7. al- ākim in *al-Mustadrak*, 1:564 §1476.
8. Ibn Khuzayma in *al-Ṣaḥīḥ*, 8:132 §3344.
9. al-Bukhārī in *al-Ṣaḥīḥ*, 2:530 §1392.
10. Muslim in *al-Ṣaḥīḥ*, 2:693 §998.

3.7 Helping the Poor and Freeing the Captives

Essential Reading:

1. Dr Tahir-ul-Qadri, Islam on Serving Humanity, Ch:3, p.192-196.

Additional Readings for Teachers and Students:

1. Qur'ān, 9:60.

. Ibid., 76:8–12.
. Ibid., 93:10.
. al-Bayhaqī in *Shuʿab al-Īmān*, 3:311 §3629.
. Ibn ʿAsākir in *Tārīkh Madīna Damishq*, 4:25.
. al-Haythamī in *Majmaʿ al-Zawāʾid*, 3:150.
. al-Shaʿrānī in *al-Ṭabqāt al-Kubrā*, 1:377.
. al-Suyūṭī in *al-Shamāʾil al-Sharīfa*, 1:142.

4. Helping Humanity Through Promoting Knowledge and Reform

4.1 The Best Charity is Acquiring Knowledge and Imparting to Others

Essential Reading:

. Dr Tahir-ul-Qadri, Islam on Serving Humanity, Ch:4, p.199-206.

Additional Readings for Teachers and Students:

1. Qurʾān, 9:122.
2. Ibid., 16:43.
3. Muslim in *al-Ṣaḥīḥ*, 3/1255 §1631.
4. Abū Dāwūd in *al-Sunan*, 3/117 §2880.
5. al-Tirmidhī in *al-Sunan*, 3:660 §1376.
6. al-Nisāʾī in *al-Sunan*, 6:251 §3651, & in *al-Sunnan al-Kubrā*, 4:109 §6478.
7. Aḥmad b. anbal in *al-Musnad*, 2:372 §8831.
8. Ibn Khuzayma in *al-Ṣaḥīḥ*, 4:122 §2494.
9. Ibn ibban in *al-Ṣaḥīḥ*, 1:295 §93; 7:286 §3016.

4.2 Promoting Reconciliation amongst People

Essential Reading:

1. Dr Tahir-ul-Qadri, Islam on Serving Humanity, Ch:4, p.207-213.

Additional Readings for Teachers and Students:

1. Qurʾān, 2:224.
2. Ibid., 4:114.
3. Ibid., 49:9–10.
4. al-Bukhārī in *al-Ṣaḥīḥ*, 3:1090 §2827.
5. Muslim in *al-Ṣaḥīḥ*, 2:699 §1009.
6. Aḥmad b. anbal in *al-Musnad*, 2:316 §8168.

4.3 Well-Wishing of People

Essential Reading:

1. Dr Tahir-ul-Qadri, Islam on Serving Humanity, Ch:4, p.214-222.

Additional Readings for Teachers and Students:

1. Qurʾān, 7:92–93.
2. Ibid., 11:33–34.
3. al-Bukhārī in *al-Ṣaḥīḥ*, 1:30.
4. Muslim in *al-Ṣaḥīḥ*, 1:74 §55.
5. Aḥmad b. anbal in *al-Musnad*, 4:102 §16983.
6. Abū Dāwūd in *al-Sunan*, 4:286 §4944.
7. al-Tirmidhī in *al-Sunan*, 4:324 §1926.
8. al-Nasāʾī in *al-Sunan*, 7:156 §4197.

4.4 Excelling in Virtuous Deeds in Serving Humanity

Essential Reading:

1. Dr Tahir-ul-Qadri, Islam on Serving Humanity, Ch:4, p.222-225.

Additional Readings for Teachers and Students:

1. Qur'ān, 21:90.
2. al-Bukhārī in *al-Ṣaḥīḥ*, 2:515 §1353.
3. Muslim in *al-Ṣaḥīḥ*, 2:716 §1032.
4. Aḥmad b. anbal in *al-Musnad*, 2:231 §7159.
5. al-Nasā'ī in *al-Sunan*, 6:237 §3611.
6. Muslim in *al-Ṣaḥīḥ*, 1:110 §118.
7. Aḥmad b. anbal in *al-Musnad*, 2:303 §8017.
8. al-Tirmidhī in *al-Sunan*, 4:487 §2195.
9. Ibn ibbān in *al-Ṣaḥīḥ*, 15:96 §6704.
10. Abū Yaʿlā in *al-Musnad*, 11:396 §6515. al-Ṭabarānī in *al-Muʿjam al-Awsaṭ*, 3:156 §2774.
11. al-Tirmidhī in *al-Sunan*, 2306.
12. al-Bayhaqī in *Shuʿab al-Īmān*, 7:357 §10572.

5. Serving Humanity through Elevating Human Values

5.1 Excelling in Virtuous Deeds in Serving Humanity

Essential Reading:

1. Dr Tahir-ul-Qadri, Islam on Serving Humanity, Ch:5, p.229-237.

ADDITIONAL READINGS FOR TEACHERS AND STUDENTS:

1. Qur'ān, 2:201–202.
2. Ibid., 3:134.
3. Ibid., 5:93.
4. Ibid., 7:56.
5. Ibid., 9:91.
6. Ibid., 16:90.
7. Ibid., 55:60.
8. Muslim in *al-Ṣaḥīḥ: Kitāb al-Birr wa al-Ṣila wal-Ādāb* [The Book of Virtue, Good Manners and Joining of the Ties of Relationship], chapter: "Joining the Tie of Relationship and Prohibition to Break it", 4:1982 §2558.
9. Aḥmad b. Ḥanbal in *al-Musnad*, 2:300 §7979.
10. Ibn ibbān in in *al-Ṣaḥīḥ*, 2:195 §450.
11. al-Ṭabarānī in *al-Muʿjam al-awsaṭ*, 3:157–158 §2786.

5.2 EXCELLENT CONDUCT, PIETY AND KINDNESS WITH PARENTS

ESSENTIAL READING:

1. Dr Tahir-ul-Qadri, Islam on Serving Humanity, Ch:5, p.238-244.

ADDITIONAL READINGS FOR TEACHERS AND STUDENTS:

1. al-Bukhārī in *al-Ṣaḥīḥ*, 5:227 §5625, & 1:197 §504.
2. Muslim in *al-Ṣaḥīḥ*, 1:89 §85.
3. al-Bukhārī in *al-Ṣaḥīḥ*, 5:2227 §5627.

4. Muslim in *al-Ṣaḥīḥ*, 4:1975 §2549. 54. Abū Dāwūd in *al-Sunan*, 3:17 §2528–2529.
5. al-Nasāʾī in *al-Sunan*, 7:143 §4163.

5.3 Excellent Conduct, Piety and Kindness with Women

Essential Reading:

1. Dr Tahir-ul-Qadri, Islam on Serving Humanity, Ch:5, p.245-248.

Additional Readings for Teachers and Students:

1. Qurʾān, 4:127.
2. Ibid., 28:23–24.
3. al-Bukhārī in *al-Ṣaḥīḥ*, 3:1096 §2849.
4. Ibn Abī Shayba in *al-Muṣannaf*, 3:118 §12635.
5. Abū ʿAwāna in *al-Musnad*, 1:103 §68.

5.4 Excellent Conduct, Love and Kindness with the Wife

Essential Reading:

1. Dr Tahir-ul-Qadri, Islam on Serving Humanity, Ch:5, p.249-258.

Additional Readings for Teachers and Students:

1. Qurʾān, 2:233.

2. Ibid., 4:19–20.
3. Ibid., 4:128–129.
4. Ibid., 65:1–2.
5. Ibid., 65:6–7.
6. al-Tirmidhī in *al-Sunan*, 3:467 §1163.
7. Ibn Mājah in *al-Sunan*, 1:594 §1851.
8. al-Nasā'ī in *al-Sunan al-Kubrā*, 5:372 §9169.
9. Aḥmad b. Ḥanbal in *al-Musnad*, 4:447, 5:3 §20027, 20036.

5.5 Excellent Conduct, Love and Compassion of the Holy Prophet ﷺ with His Wives

Essential Reading:

1. Dr Tahir-ul-Qadri, Islam on Serving Humanity, Ch:5, p.259-264.

Additional Readings for Teachers and Students:

1. al-Bukhārī in *al-Ṣaḥīḥ*, 5:1988 §4894, & 5:2006 §4938.
2. Muslim in *al-Ṣaḥīḥ*, 2:609 §892.
3. al-Nasā'ī in *al-Sunan*, 3:195 §1595.

5.6 Compassion and Benevolence with Offspring

Essential Reading:

1. Dr Tahir-ul-Qadri, Islam on Serving Humanity, Ch:5, p.265-272.

Additional Readings for Teachers and Students:

1. Qur'ān, 2:233.
2. Ibid., 4:11.
3. Ibid., 6:140.
4. Ibid., 6:151.
5. Ibid., 17:31.
6. Muslim in *al-Ṣaḥīḥ*, 3:1691 §2147.
7. Abū Dāwūd in *al-Sunan*, 4:328 §5106.
8. Abū ʿAwāna in *al-Musnad*, 1:172 §518.
9. Ibn Abī Shayba in *al-Muṣannaf*, 5:219 §25415.
10. Ibn al-Sarrī in *al-Zuhad*, 2:486 §995.
11. Ibn Abī al-Dunyā in *al-ʿAyāl*, 1:306 §150.
12. al-Sulamī in *Ādāb al-Ṣuḥba wa usn al-ʿAshra*, 97 §137.
13. al-Ṭabarānī in *al-Muʿjam al-Awsaṭ*, 4:237 §4076.
14. al-Hindī in *Kanz al-ʿUmmāl*, 16:190 §45419.
15. ʿAbd al- Raʾūf al-Manāwī in *Fayḍ al-Qadīr*, 2:13.
16. Aḥmad b. anbal in *al-Musnad*, 4:78 §16763.

5.7 Compassion and Benevolence with Daughters

Essential Reading:

1. Dr Tahir-ul-Qadri, Islam on Serving Humanity, Ch:5, p.273-279.

Additional Readings for Teachers and Students:

1. Qur'ān, 28:25–26.
2. Ibid., 81:8–9.
3. al-Bukhārī in *al-Ṣaḥīḥ*, 5:2234 §5649.
4. Muslim in *al-Ṣaḥīḥ*, 4:2027 §2629.
5. Muslim in *al-Ṣaḥīḥ*, 4:2027 §2630.
6. Aḥmab b. anbal in *al-Musnad*, 6:92 §24655.
7. Ibn ibbān in *al-Ṣaḥīḥ*, 2:193 §448.
8. Aḥmad b. Ḥanbal in *al-Musnad*, 3:97 §11943.

5.8 Compassion and Benevolence with Children

Essential Reading:

1. Dr Tahir-ul-Qadri, Islam on Serving Humanity, Ch:5, p.280-286.

Additional Readings for Teachers and Students:

1. Qur'ān, 18:82.
2. al-Bukhārī in *al-Ṣaḥīḥ*, 5:2235 §5652, & in *al-Adab al-Mufrad*, 48 §98.
3. Muslim in *al-Ṣaḥīḥ*, 4:1808 §2317.
4. Aḥmad b. anbal in *al-Musnad*, 6:56 §24336.
5. Ibn Mājah in *al-Sunan*, 2:1209 §3665.
6. al-Bayhaqī in *Shuʿab al-Īmān*, 7:466 §11013.

5.9 Excellent Conduct and Compassion with Neighbours

Essential Reading:

1. Dr Tahir-ul-Qadri, Islam on Serving Humanity, Ch:5, p.287-298.

Additional Readings for Teachers and Students:

1. al-Bukhārī in *al-Ṣaḥīḥ*: *Kitāb al-adab* [The Book of Good Manners], chapter: 'If Someone Believes in God and the Last Day, He Must Not Harm His Neighbour', 5:2240 §5672, and *Kitāb al-adab* [The Book of Good Manners], chapter: 'Honouring the Guest and Serving Him Personally', 5:2273 §5785, and *Kitāb al-riqāq* [The Book of Heart-softening Narrations], chapter: 'Safeguarding the Tongue', 5:2376 §6110.

2. Muslim in *al-Ṣaḥīḥ*: *Kitāb al-Īmān* [The Book of Faith], chapter: 'Urging Piety for the Neighbour and the Guest, and the Necessity of Maintaining Silence Except when Having Something Good to Say', 1:6968 §§47–48.
3. al-Tirmidhī in *al-Sunan*: *Kitāb al-adab* [The Book of Manners], chapter 50, 4:659 §2500; Abū Dāwūd in *al-Sunan*: *Kitāb al-Adab* [The Book of Good Manners], chapter: 'The Rightful Due to the Neighbour', 4:339 §5154.
4. Ibn Mājah in *al-Sunan*: *Kitāb al-adab* [The Book of Good Manners], chapter: 'The Right Due to the Neighbour', 2:1211 §3672.

5.10 Excellent Conduct and Benevolence with other People

Essential Reading:

1. Dr Tahir-ul-Qadri, Islam on Serving Humanity, Ch:5, p.299-308.

Additional Readings for Teachers and Students:

1. Qur'ān, 9:71.
2. Ibid., 49:10.
3. al-Bukhārī in *al-Ṣaḥīḥ*, 1:418 §1183.
4. Muslim in *al-Ṣaḥīḥ*, 4:1704 §2162.
5. Aḥmad b. Ḥanbal in *al-Musnad*, 2:540 §10979.
6. Ibn Mājah in *al-Sunan*, 1:461 §6435.
7. Ibn Ḥibbān in *al-Ṣaḥīḥ*, 1:476 §241.
8. al-Ḥākim in *al-Mustadrak*, 1:550 §1292.
9. al-Nasā'ī in *al-Sunan al-Kubrā*, 6:64 §10049

5.11 Excellent Conduct and Compassion with Widows and Orphans

Essential Reading:

1. Dr Tahir-ul-Qadri, Islam on Serving Humanity, Ch:5, p.299-318.

Additional Readings for Teachers and Students:

1. Qur'ān 2:215.
2. Ibid., 76:8–9.
3. Ibid., 90:11–18.
4. Ibid., 93:6–11.
5. al-Bukhārī in *al-Ṣaḥīḥ*, 5:2047 §5038, & 5:2237 §5660.
6. Muslim in *al-Ṣaḥīḥ*, 4:2286 §2982.
7. Aḥmad b. Ḥanbal in *al-Musnad*, 2:361 §8717.
8. al-Tirmidhī in *al-Sunan*, 4:346 §1969.
9. al-Nasā'ī in *al-Sunan*, 5:86 §2577.
10. Ibn Mājah in *al-Sunan*, 2:724.

5.12 Excellent Conduct and Compassion with the Weak and Indigent

Essential Reading:

1. Dr Tahir-ul-Qadri, Islam on Serving Humanity, Ch:5, p.319-323.

Additional Readings for Teachers and Students:

1. Qur'ān, 9:60.
2. Ibid., 107:1–3.

3. al-Bukhārī in *al-Ṣaḥīḥ*, 1:248 §671.
4. Muslim in *al-Ṣaḥīḥ*, 1:341 §467.
5. Aḥmad b. anbal in *al-Musnad*, 2:486 §10311.
6. al-Tirmidhī in *al-Sunan*, 1:461 §236.
7. al-Nasāʾī in *al-Sunan*, 2:94 §823.
8. Abū Dāwūd in *al-Sunan*, 1:211 §794.
9. Mālik in *al-Muwaṭṭāʾ*, 1:134 §301.

5.13 EXCELLENT CONDUCT AND COMPASSION WITH SLAVES AND WORKERS

ESSENTIAL READING:

1. Dr Tahir-ul-Qadri, Islam on Serving Humanity, Ch:5, p.324-334.

ADDITIONAL READINGS FOR TEACHERS AND STUDENTS:

1. Qurʾān, 9:60.
2. Ibid., 22:36.
3. al-Bukhārī in *al-Ṣaḥīḥ*, 5:2245 §5691.
4. Muslim in *al-Ṣaḥīḥ*, 4:1804 §2309.
5. Aḥmad b. anbal in *al-Musnad*, 3:265.
6. al-Tirmidhī in *al-Sunan*, 4:368 §2015.
7. Ibn ibbān in *al-Ṣaḥīḥ*, 7:152 §2893.
8. Abū Yaʿlā in *al-Musnad*, 6:104 §3367.
9. anbal in *al-Musnad*, 3:231 §13442.
10. Ibn Abī ʿĀṣim in *al-Sunna*, 1:157 §355.
11. Ibn ʿAsākir in *Tārīkh Madīna Damishq*, 50:65.

5.14 Excellent Conduct and Compassion with the Guilty and Sinners

Essential Reading:

1. Dr Tahir-ul-Qadri, Islam on Serving Humanity, Ch:5, p.335-339.

Additional Readings for Teachers and Students:

1. Qur'ān, 3:159.
2. al-Bukhārī in *al-Ṣaḥīḥ*, 2:684 §1834.
3. Muslim in *al-Ṣaḥīḥ*, 2:781 §111.
4. Aḥmad b. anbal in *al-Musnad*, 2:241 §7288 & 6:276 §26402.
5. al-Tirmidhī in *al-Sunan*, 3:102 §724.
6. Abū Dāwūd in *al-Sunan*, 2:313 §2390.
7. Ibn Mājah in *al-Sunan*, 1:534 §1671.
8. al-Nasā'ī in *al-Sunan al-Kubrā*, 2:212 §3117.

5.15 Honouring the Funeral

Essential Reading:

1. Dr Tahir-ul-Qadri, Islam on Serving Humanity, Ch:5, p.340-342.

Additional Readings for Teachers and Students:

1. al-Bukhārī in *al-Ṣaḥīḥ*, 1:441 §1246.
2. Muslim in *al-Ṣaḥīḥ*, 2:660 §958.
3. al-Ṭabarānī in *al-Mu'jam al-Awsaṭ*, 1:123 §391.

6. Serving Humanity through the Modernity of Moral Excellence

6.1 Merits of Excellence of Moral Character and Manners

Essential Reading:

1. Dr Tahir-ul-Qadri, Islam on Serving Humanity, Ch:6, p.345-358.

Additional Readings for Teachers and Students:

1. Qur'ān, 29:69.
2. Ibid., 31:22.
3. Ibid., 33:21.
4. Ibid., 39:10.
5. Ibid., 41:34.
6. Ibid., 68:4.
7. al-Bukhārī in *al-Ṣaḥīḥ*, 3:1305 §3366.
8. Muslim in *al-Ṣaḥīḥ*, 4:1810 §2321.
9. Aḥmad b. anbal in *al-Musnad*, 2:161 §6504.
10. al-Tirmidhī in *al-Sunan*, 4:349 §1975.

6.2 Cheerfulness and an Open Countenance

Essential Reading:

1. Dr Tahir-ul-Qadri, Islam on Serving Humanity, Ch:6, p.359-364.

Additional Readings for Teachers and Students:

1. Qur᾿ān, 31:18.
2. Ibid., 83:24.
3. Ibid., 84:13.
4. al-Bukhārī in *al-Ṣaḥīḥ*, 3:1305 §3363.
5. Muslim in *al-Ṣaḥīḥ*, 4:2127 §2769.
6. Aḥmad b. anbal in *al-Musnad*, 3:458 §15827.
7. al-Nasā᾿ī in *al-Sunan al-Kubrā*, 6:359 §11232

6.3 Pleasing and Polite Conversation

Essential Reading:

1. Dr Tahir-ul-Qadri, Islam on Serving Humanity, Ch:6, p.365-370.

Additional Readings for Teachers and Students:

1. Qur᾿ān, 2:263.
2. Ibid., 17:53.
3. Ibid., 22:24.
4. al-Bukhārī in *al-Ṣaḥīḥ*, 5:2241 §5677.
5. Muslim in *al-Ṣaḥīḥ*, 2:704 §1016.
6. Aḥmad b. anbal in *al-Musnad*, 4:256 §18279.
7. al-Nasā᾿ī in *al-Sunan*, 5:75 §2553.

6.4 Protecting the Tongue from Backbiting

Essential Reading:

1. Dr Tahir-ul-Qadri, Islam on Serving Humanity, Ch:6, p.371-379.

Additional Readings for Teachers and Students:

1. Qur'ān, 16:62.
2. Ibid., 24:23–24.
3. Ibid., 33:58.
4. Ibid., 33:70.
5. Ibid., 49:12.
6. Ibid., 50:18.
7. al-Bukhārī in *al-Ṣaḥīḥ*, 1:13 §10.
8. Muslim in *al-Ṣaḥīḥ*, 1:66 §42.
9. al-Tirmidhī in *al-Sunan*, Ch.: (52), 4:661 §2504.
10. al-Nasā'ī in *al-Sunan*, 8:106 §4999.

6.5 Truthfulness and Trust

Essential Reading:

1. Dr Tahir-ul-Qadri, Islam on Serving Humanity, Ch:6, p.380-388.

Additional Readings for Teachers and Students:

1. Qur'ān, 3:16–17.
2. Ibid., 5:119.
3. Ibid., 9:119.
4. Ibid., 17:80.
5. Ibid., 23:8.
6. al-Bukhārī in *al-Ṣaḥīḥ*, 5:2261 §5743.
7. Muslim in *al-Ṣaḥīḥ*, 4:2013 §2607.
8. Aḥmad b. anbal in *al-Musnad*, 1:432 §4108.
9. Abū Dāwūd in *al-Sunan*, 4:297 §4989.
10. al-Tirmidhī in *al-Sunan*, 4:347 §1971.
11. Aḥmad b. Ḥanbal in *al-Musnad*, 2/176 §6641.

6.6 Balance and Moderation

Essential Reading:

1. Dr Tahir-ul-Qadri, Islam on Serving Humanity, Ch:6, p.389-393.

Additional Readings for Teachers and Students:

1. Qur'ān, 17:29.
2. Ibid., 25:67.
3. al-Bukhārī in *al-Ṣaḥīḥ*, 5:2373 §6099.
4. Muslim in *al-Ṣaḥīḥ*, 4:2171 §2818.
5. Aḥmad b. anbal in *al-Musnad*, 6:273 §26386.

6.7 Leniency and Gentleness

Essential Reading:

1. Dr Tahir-ul-Qadri, Islam on Serving Humanity, Ch:6, p.394-401.

Additional Readings for Teachers and Students:

1. Qur'ān, 2:263, 3:159.
2. ibid., 25:63.
3. Muslim in *al-Ṣaḥīḥ*, 1:48 §17.
4. al-Tirmidhī in *al-Sunan*, 4:366 §2011.
5. Abū Ya'lā in *al-Musnad*, 12:242 §4868.
6. al-Ṭabarānī in *al-Mu'jam al-Awsaṭ*, 3:30 §2374
7. ibid., *al-Mu'jam al-Ṣaghīr*, 2:67 §792
8. ibid., *al-Mu'jam al-Kabīr*, 12:230 §12969.
9. al-Bayhaqī in *al-Sunan al-Kubrā*, 10:104 §20060.

10. ibid., *Shuʿab al-Īmān*, 6:141 §7729.

6.8 Self-Control and Abstaining from Rage

Essential Reading:

1. Dr Tahir-ul-Qadri, Islam on Serving Humanity, Ch:6, p.402-409

Additional Readings for Teachers and Students:

1. Qurʾān, 3:159.
2. Ibid., 42:37.
3. al-Bukhārī in *al-Ṣaḥīḥ*, 5:2267 §5763.
4. Muslim in *al-Ṣaḥīḥ*, 4:2014 §2609.
5. Aḥmad b. anbal in *al-Musnad*, 2:268 §7628.
6. al-Nasāʾī in *al-Sunan al-Kubrā*, 6:105 §10226.

6.9 Love and Kind Heartedness

Essential Reading:

1. Dr Tahir-ul-Qadri, Islam on Serving Humanity, Ch:6, p.410-419.

Additional Readings for Teachers and Students:

1. Qurʾān, 8:63.
2. Ibid., 17:24.
3. Ibid., 21:107.
4. al-Bukhārī in *al-Ṣaḥīḥ*, 6:2686 §6941.
5. Muslim in *al-Ṣaḥīḥ*, 4:1809 §2319.

6. Aḥmad b. anbal in *al-Musnad*, 4:358 §19189.
7. al-Tirmidhī in *al-Sunan*, 4:323 §1922.

SECTION IV

Islam on Mercy and Compassion

1. On the Infinite Mercy of Almighty Allah

1.1 Allah has Written Mercy upon Himself

Essential Reading:

1. Dr Tahir-ul-Qadri, Islam on Mercy and Compassion, Ch:1, p.5.

Additional Readings for Teachers and Students:

1. Qur'ān 6:54.

1.2 Allah has Written Mercy upon Himself

Essential Reading:

1. Dr Tahir-ul-Qadri, Islam on Mercy and Compassion, Ch:1, p.6.

Additional Readings for Teachers and Students:

1. Qur'ān 18:58.

1.3 Allah is the Owner of Mercy

Essential Reading:

1. Dr Tahir-ul-Qadri, Islam on Mercy and Compassion, Ch:1, p.6-7.

Additional Readings for Teachers and Students:

1. Qurʾān 2:105.
2. Qurʾān 35:2.

1.4 Allah Shows Mercy to Whom He Wills

Essential Reading:

1. Dr Tahir-ul-Qadri, Islam on Mercy and Compassion, Ch:1, p.7-8.

Additional Readings for Teachers and Students:

1. Qurʾān 29:21.

1.5 Allah is the All-Merciful, the Compassionate

Essential Reading:

1. Dr Tahir-ul-Qadri, Islam on Mercy and Compassion, Ch:1, p.8-9.

1.6 Allah is the Most Merciful of Those Who Show Mercy

Essential Reading:

1. Dr Tahir-ul-Qadri, Islam on Mercy and Compassion, Ch:1, p.9-11.

Additional Readings for Teachers and Students:

1. Qur'ān 12:64.
2. ibid., 21:83.
3. Muslim in *al-Ṣaḥīḥ:* Bk.: *al-Īmān* [The Faith], Ch.: "Knowing the Routes of Transmission," 1:170 §302.
4. al-Bukhārī in *al-Ṣaḥīḥ:* Bk.: *al-Adab* [The Manners], Ch.: "On Showing Mercy to a Child and Kissing and Hugging Him," 5:2235 §5653.
5. Muslim in *al-Ṣaḥīḥ:* Bk.: *al-Tawba*, [The Repentance], Ch.: "On Allah's Vast Mercy, and That is Precedes His Wrath," 4:2109 §2754.

1.7 Allah's Mercy is Boundless and Encompasses All Things

Essential Reading:

1. Dr Tahir-ul-Qadri, Islam on Mercy and Compassion, Ch:1, p.11-12.

Additional Readings for Teachers and Students:

1. Qur'ān 40:7.

1.8 Allah's Multiplied Mercy for the Believers

Essential Reading:

1. Dr Tahir-ul-Qadri, Islam on Mercy and Compassion, Ch:1, p.12.

1.9 The Prophets Supplicate Allah to Envelop Them in Mercy

Essential Reading:

1. Dr Tahir-ul-Qadri, Islam on Mercy and Compassion, Ch:1, p.13-14.

Additional Readings for Teachers and Students:

1. Qur'ān 21:83.
2. Qur'ān 27:19.
3. Qur'ān 21:86.

1.10 The Recipients of Mercy

Essential Reading:

1. Dr Tahir-ul-Qadri, Islam on Mercy and Compassion, Ch:1, p.14-16.

Additional Readings for Teachers and Students:

1. al-Bukhārī in *al-Ṣāḥīḥ*: Bk.: *al-Tawḥīd*, [Divine Unity], Ch.: "On Allah's Saying, ﴾*Say, 'Call upon Allah or call upon the All-Merciful; whichever you call to Him belong the beautiful names.'*﴿, 6:2686 §6941.
2. Muslim in *al-Ṣaḥīḥ*: Bk.: *al-Faḍā'il* [The Exemplary Virtues], Ch.: "On the Prophet's Mercy toward Children and Dependents," §66.
3. al-Bukhārī in *al-Ṣaḥīḥ:* Bk.: *al-Adab* [The Proper Conduct], Ch.: Kind treatment of the child, kissing him and hugging him, 5:2235 §5651.
4. Muslim in *al-Ṣaḥīḥ:* Bk.: *al-Faḍā'il* [The Virtues and Merits], Ch.: "Kind treatment of the family and humility is to your credit", 4:1808 §2315
5. Aḥmad b. Ḥanbal in *al-Musnad*, 2:241 §7287.
6. Ibn Ḥibbān in *al-Ṣaḥīḥ*, 2:202 §457.
7. al-Bukhārī in *al-Adab al-Mufrad*, 1:46 §91, 99.
8. al-Bayhaqī in *al-Sunan al-Kubrā*, 7:100 §13354.
9. Aḥmad b. Ḥanbal, *al-Musnad* (2:160).
10. ibid., 21:83.
11. al-Tirmidhī, *al-Sunan:* Bk.: *al-Birr wa al-ṣila* [Piety and Familial Integration], Ch.: "What Has been Reported Regarding Mercy toward Muslims," §1924.
12. Ibn Abī Shayba, *al-Muṣannaf* (8:526).
13. al-Ḥumaydī, *al-Musnad* (2:269 §591).
14. al-Khaṭīb al-Baghdādī, *Tārīkh Baghdad* (3:260).
15. al-Bayhaqī, *al-Sunan al-kubrā* (9:41) and *al-Asmā' wa al-ṣifāt* (423).
16. Ibn Ḥajar al-ʿAsqalānī in *Fatḥ al-Bārī* (13:359). This hadith is known as *al-Musalsal bi al-awwaliyya* (the first hadith traditionally transmitted from teacher to student).

1.11 Those Who Shall Triumph with Allah's Mercy

Essential Reading:

1. Dr Tahir-ul-Qadri, Islam on Mercy and Compassion, Ch:1, p.16-18.

Additional Readings for Teachers and Students:

1. Qur'ān 11:43.
2. Qur'ān 11:118–119.
3. Qur'ān 12:53.
4. Qur'ān 6:15–16.

1.12 Taking Delight in Allah's Mercy

Essential Reading:

1. Dr Tahir-ul-Qadri, Islam on Mercy and Compassion, Ch:1, p.18.

1.13 Those Whom Mercy Shall Encompass

Essential Reading:

1. Dr Tahir-ul-Qadri, Islam on Mercy and Compassion, Ch:1, p.18.

1.14 The People who Possess Firm Faith

Essential Reading:

1. Dr Tahir-ul-Qadri, Islam on Mercy and Compassion, Ch:1, p.18-19.

1.15 The People who Obey Allah ﷻ and His Noble Prophet ﷺ

Essential Reading:

1. Dr Tahir-ul-Qadri, Islam on Mercy and Compassion, Ch:1, p.19.

1.16 The People who Follow the Qur'ān and Fear Allah

Essential Reading:

1. Dr Tahir-ul-Qadri, Islam on Mercy and Compassion, Ch:1, p.19.

1.17 The People who are Committed to Spiritual Excellence

Essential Reading:

1. Dr Tahir-ul-Qadri, Islam on Mercy and Compassion, Ch:1, p.20.

1.18 The Believers Who Hold Fast to Allah

Allah ﷻ said,

Essential Reading:

1. Dr Tahir-ul-Qadri, Islam on Mercy and Compassion, Ch:1, p.20.

1.19 The People Who Consider What They Spend will Draw Them Near to Allah and Who Seek the Supplication of Allah's Messenger ﷺ

Essential Reading:

1. Dr Tahir-ul-Qadri, Islam on Mercy and Compassion, Ch:1, pp.20-21.

1.20 The People Who Pray, Pay Zakat and Obey Allah's Messenger

Essential Reading:

1. Dr Tahir-ul-Qadri, Islam on Mercy and Compassion, Ch:1, p.21.

1.21 The People Who Exercise Piety for Fear of Torment

Essential Reading:

1. Dr Tahir-ul-Qadri, Islam on Mercy and Compassion, Ch:1, p.21.

1.22 The Believers Who Do Righteous Works

Essential Reading:

1. Dr Tahir-ul-Qadri, Islam on Mercy and Compassion, Ch:1, pp.21-22.

1.23 The People Who Listen to the Qur'ān with Extreme Respect

Essential Reading:

1. Dr Tahir-ul-Qadri, Islam on Mercy and Compassion, Ch:1, p.22.

1.24 The People Who Seek Allah's Forgiveness

Essential Reading:

1. Dr Tahir-ul-Qadri, Islam on Mercy and Compassion, Ch:1, p.22.

1.25 The Believers Who Migrate and Strive Hard in the Cause of Allah

Essential Reading:

1. Dr Tahir-ul-Qadri, Islam on Mercy and Compassion, Ch:1, pp.22-23.

1.26 The People Who are Martyred in the Path of Allah

Essential Reading:

1. Dr Tahir-ul-Qadri, Islam on Mercy and Compassion, Ch:1, p.23.

1.27 The People Who Are Well Endowed with Knowledge

Essential Reading:

1. Dr Tahir-ul-Qadri, Islam on Mercy and Compassion, Ch:1, p.23.

1.28 The People Who Bring Peace between the Brothers

Essential Reading:

1. Dr Tahir-ul-Qadri, Islam on Mercy and Compassion, Ch:1, p.24.

1.29 The People Who are Patient During Afflictions

Essential Reading:

1. Dr Tahir-ul-Qadri, Islam on Mercy and Compassion, Ch:1, p.24.

1.30 The People Whose Faces would be Brightened because of Good Deeds

Essential Reading:

1. Dr Tahir-ul-Qadri, Islam on Mercy and Compassion, Ch:1, p.24.

1.31 The Believers Who Practise Good Moral and Spiritual Values

Essential Reading:

1. Dr Tahir-ul-Qadri, Islam on Mercy and Compassion, Ch:1, p.25.

1.32 What Brings Mercy to Fruition?

Essential Reading:

1. Dr Tahir-ul-Qadri, Islam on Mercy and Compassion, Ch:1, pp.25-27.

Additional Readings for Teachers and Students:

1. Qur'ān 7:63.
2. Qur'ān 24:56.
3. Qur'ān 27:46.
4. Qur'ān 36:45.
5. Qur'ān 49:10.

1.33 The Loser is the One Who Does Not Gain Allah's Mercy

Essential Reading:

1. Dr Tahir-ul-Qadri, Islam on Mercy and Compassion, Ch:1, pp.27-28.

Additional Readings for Teachers and Students:

1. Qur'ān 11:47.
2. Qur'ān 2:64.
3. Qur'ān 24:14.

1.34 Allah's Mercy is the Source of Salvation

Essential Reading:

1. Dr Tahir-ul-Qadri, Islam on Mercy and Compassion, Ch:1, pp.28-30.

Additional Readings for Teachers and Students:

1. Qur'ān 6:16.
2. Qur'ān 11:43.
3. Qur'ān 11:118–119.
4. Qur'ān 40:9.

1.35 The Believers' Prayer for Mercy

Essential Reading:

1. Dr Tahir-ul-Qadri, Islam on Mercy and Compassion, Ch:1, pp.30-31.

Additional Readings for Teachers and Students:

1. Qur'ān 2:286.
2. Qur'ān 23:118.

1.36 Who Despairs and Loses Hope of Allah's Mercy?

Essential Reading:

1. Dr Tahir-ul-Qadri, Islam on Mercy and Compassion, Ch:1, pp.31-32.

Additional Readings for Teachers and Students:

1. Qur'ān 29:23.
2. Qur'ān 39:53.

1.37 The Disbeliever Does Not Merit Allah's Mercy

Essential Reading:

1. Dr Tahir-ul-Qadri, Islam on Mercy and Compassion, Ch:1, pp.32-33.

Additional Readings for Teachers and Students:

1. Qur'ān 10:21.

1.38 Various Manifestations of Allah's Vast Mercy

1.38.1 Allah Conditioned the Punishment and Torment with the Sending of Messengers

Essential Reading:

1. Dr Tahir-ul-Qadri, Islam on Mercy and Compassion, Ch:1, p.33.

Additional Readings for Teachers and Students:

1. Qur'ān 28:59.

1.39 Allah Has Not Burdened a Soul with More Than it can Bear, and He Has Pardoned Them for What They are Unable to Do

Essential Reading:

1. Dr Tahir-ul-Qadri, Islam on Mercy and Compassion, Ch:1, pp.34-36.

Additional Readings for Teachers and Students:

1. Qur'ān 24:61.
2. Qur'ān 2:173.
3. Qur'ān 5:6.
4. Qur'ān 39:53.
5. Qur'ān 4:48.

1.40 Allah Forgives who Repents of His Error

Essential Reading:

1. Dr Tahir-ul-Qadri, Islam on Mercy and Compassion, Ch:1, pp.36-38.

Additional Readings for Teachers and Students:

1. Muslim in *al-Ṣaḥīḥ:* Bk.: *al-dhikr wa al-duʿā* [The Remembrance and Supplication], Ch.: "The Recommendation to Seek Forgiveness," 4:2076 §2703.
2. Aḥmad in *al-Musnad*, 2:395, 427, 495, 506.
3. Muslim in *al-Ṣaḥīḥ:* Bk.: *al-dhikr wa al-duʿā* [The Remembrance and Supplication], Ch.: "The Recommendation to Seek Forgiveness," 4:2113 §2759.
4. Aḥmad in *al-Musnad*, 4:395.
5. al-Bukhārī in *al-Ṣaḥīḥ:* Bk.: *al-Tawḥīd* [Divine Unity], Ch.: "*And His Throne Was on Water, and He is the Lord of the Mighty Throne*," 6:2700 §6986.
6. Muslim in *al-Ṣaḥīḥ:* Bk.: *al-Tawba* [Repentance], Ch.: "The Vastness of Allah's Mercy and That His Mercy Precedes His Wrath," §2751.
7. al-Nasāʾī in *al-Sunan al-kubrā*, 4:418 §7757.

1.41 How are Good and Bad Deeds Dealt with?

Essential Reading:

1. Dr Tahir-ul-Qadri, Islam on Mercy and Compassion, Ch:1, pp.40-46.

Additional Readings for Teachers and Students:

1. al-Bukhārī in his *al-Ṣaḥīḥ:* Bk.: *al-daʿawāt* [The Supplications], Ch.: "On Repentance," 5:2324 §5949.
2. Muslim in *al-Ṣaḥīḥ:* Bk.: *al-tawba* [The Repentance], Ch.: "The Encouragement to Repent," 4:2103–2103 §§§2744, 2746–2747.
3. al-Bukhārī in *al-Ṣaḥīḥ:* Bk.: *al-Adab* [Good Manners], Ch.: "Allāh Made Mercy One Hundred Parts," 5:2236 §5654.
4. Muslim in *al-Ṣaḥīḥ:* Bk.: *al-Tawba* [Repentance], Ch: "The Vastness of

Allāh's Mercy and That His Mercy Precedes His Wrath," 4:2108 §2752.

5. al-Dārimī in *al-Sunan*, 2:413 §2785.
6. Ibn Ḥibbān in *al-Ṣaḥīḥ*, 14:16 §6148.
7. al-Ṭabarānī in *al-Muʿjam al-awsaṭ*, 1:297 §991.
8. al-Bayhaqī in *Shuʿab al-īmān*, 7:457 §10975.
9. Muslim in *al-Ṣaḥīḥ:* Bk.: *al-Tawba* [Repentance], Ch.: "The Vastness of Allah's Mercy and That His Mercy Precedes His Wrath," 4:2108 §2752.
10. Aḥmad b. Ḥanbal in *al-Musnad*, 2:434 §9607.
11. al-Tirmidhī in *al-Sunan:* Bk.: *al-Daʿawāt ʿan Rasūl Allāh* ﷺ [The Invocations from Allāh's Messenger ﷺ], Ch.: "Allāh Created One Hundred Mercies," 5:549 §3541.
12. Ibn Mājah in *al-Sunan:* Bk.: *al-Zuhd* [The Renunciation], Ch.: "Hope for Allāh's Mercy on the Day of Resurrection," 2:1435 §4293.
13. Ibn Ḥibbān in *al-Ṣaḥīḥ*, 14:15 §6147.
14. Ibn al-Mubārak in *al-Musnad*, 1:20 §35.
15. Abū Yaʿlā in *al-Musnad*, 11:328 §6445.
16. Qur'ān 6:160.
17. Qur'ān 11:114.
18. Qur'ān 25:70.
19. Qur'ān 25:70.
20. Qur'ān 27:76–77.
21. Qur'ān 31:1–3.
22. Qur'ān 7:52.
23. Qur'ān 16:89.
24. Qur'ān 17:82.
25. Qur'ān 6:154.
26. al-Bukhārī in *al-Ṣaḥīḥ:* Bk.: *al-Marḍā* [The Patients], Ch.: "On the Sick Person Wishing for Death," 5:2147 §5349.
27. Muslim in *al-Ṣaḥīḥ:* Bk.: *Ṣifāt al-munāfiqīn* [On the Traits of the Hypocrites], Ch.: "No One Shall Enter Paradise by Virtue of His Deeds; It is Only by Allah's Mercy," 4:2064 §2680.
28. Muslim in *al-Ṣaḥīḥ:* Bk.: *al-Birr wa al-ṣila* [The Piety and Familial Integration], Ch.: "The Glad Tidings for the One Whose Faults Allah Conceals in the World That His Fault Will Be Concealed in the Hereafter," 4:2002 §2590.
29. al-Bukhārī in *al-Ṣaḥīḥ:* Bk.: *al-Adab* [Manners], Ch.: "A believer concealing himself", 5:2254 §5721.
30. Muslim in *al-Ṣaḥīḥ:* Bk.: *al-Birr wa al-ṣila* [Piety and Familial Integration], Ch.: "The Glad Tidings for the One Whose Faults Allah Conceals in the World That His Fault Will Be Concealed in the Hereafter," 4:2291 §2990.

2. Islam is the Religion of Mercy, Ease and Moderation

Essential Reading:

1. Dr Tahir-ul-Qadri, Islam on Mercy and Compassion, Ch:2, p.49.

Additional Readings for Teachers and Students:

1. Qur'ān 3:85.

2.1 Islam Desires Ease and Removal of Hardships

Essential Reading:

1. Dr Tahir-ul-Qadri, Islam on Mercy and Compassion, Ch:2, pp.49-51.

Additional Readings for Teachers and Students:

1. Qur'ān 22:78.
2. Qur'ān 5:6.

2.2 Islam Lightens the Burden of Obligations

Essential Reading:

1. Dr Tahir-ul-Qadri, Islam on Mercy and Compassion, Ch::2, pp.51-54.

Additional Readings for Teachers and Students:

1. Qur'ān 8:66.
2. Qur'ān 3:159.
3. Qur'ān 33:45.
4. al-Bukhārī in *al-Ṣaḥīḥ:* Bk.: *al-Buyūʿ* [Transactions], Ch.: "The Prohibition of Being Loud and Boisterous in the Marketplace," 2:747 §2018.
5. Qur'ān 9:61.
6. Qur'ān 21:107.
7. Qur'ān 9:128.
8. Qur'ān 7:157.

2.3 Islam Teaches Easiness and Does not Approve of Harshness

Essential Reading:

1. Dr Tahir-ul-Qadri, Islam on Mercy and Compassion, Ch:2, pp.54-55.

Additional Readings for Teachers and Students:

1. al-Bukhārī in *al-Ṣaḥīḥ:* Bk.: *al-ʿAmal fī al-ṣalāt* [On Extraneous Actions Performed in the Prayer], Ch.: "When One's Animal Runs Away During the Prayer," 1:405 §1153.
2. ibid., Bk.: *Mawāqīt al-ṣalāt* [The Timing of the Prayers], Ch.: "On the Missed Prayers that Can Be Prayed After the ʿAṣr Prayer," 1:213 §565.

2.4 The Holy Prophet ﷺ Chose the Easier of the Two Options

Essential Reading:

1. Dr Tahir-ul-Qadri, Islam on Mercy and Compassion, Ch:2, p.55-56.

2.5 The Best of Your Religion is the Middle Course

Essential Reading:

1. Dr Tahir-ul-Qadri, Islam on Mercy and Compassion, Ch:2, pp.56-57.

Additional Readings for Teachers and Students:

1. Aḥmad b. Ḥanbal in *al-Musnad*, 3:479.
2. al-Haythamī in *Majmaʿ al-zawāʾid*, 1:61.
3. Ibn Ḥajar in *Fatḥ al-Bārī*, 1:94; while al-Ṭabarānī in *al-Muʿjam al-kabīr*, 18:230 §573.
4. Ibn Abī ʿĀṣim in *al-Āḥād wa al-mathānī*, 4:349 §2383; al-Quḍāʿī in *Musnad al-Shihāb*, 2:219–220 §1224–1225; and al-Maqdisī in *al-Aḥādīth al-mukhtāra* (7:132 §2565).
5. Aḥmad b. Ḥanbal in *al-Musnad*, 5:69.
6. al-Bukhārī in *al-Tārīkh al-kabīr*, 7:30–31 §135.
7. Ibn Abī ʿĀṣim in *al-Āḥād wa al-mathānī*, 2:397 §1190.
8. Abū Yaʿlā in *al-Musnad*, 12:274 §6863.
9. Ibn al-Qāniʿ in *Muʿjam al-Ṣaḥāba*, 2:262 §780.
10. al-Haythamī in *Majmaʿ al-zawāʾid*, 1:61–62.

2.6 Prohibition of Extremism and Commandment of Moderation

Essential Reading:

1. Dr Tahir-ul-Qadri, Islam on Mercy and Compassion, Ch:2, pp.58-59.

Additional Readings for Teachers and Students:

1. Aḥmad b. Ḥanbal, *al-Musnad*, 5:350, 361.
2. al-Ṭayālisī, *al-Musnad*, p. 109 §809.
3. Ibn Abī ʿĀṣim, *al-Sunna*, 1:46 §95.
4. Ibn Khuzayma, *al-Ṣaḥīḥ*, 2:199 §1179.
5. al-Ḥākim, *al-Mustadrak*, 1:457 §1176.
6. al-Bayhaqī, *al-Sunan al-kubrā*, 3:18.
7. Aḥmad b. Ḥanbal, *al-Musnad*, 1:236.
8. ʿAbd b. Ḥumayd, *al-Musnad*, p. 199 §569.
9. al-Bukhārī, *al-Adab al-mufrad*, p. 108 §287.
10. Aḥmad b. Ḥanbal, *al-Musnad*, 6:116, 233.
11. al-Ḥumaydī, *al-Musnad*, 1:123 §254.
12. Ibn Ḥajar, *Fatḥ al-bārī*, 2:444.
13. al-Bukhārī, *al-Ṣaḥīḥ*, 1:173 §443 and 3:1063 §2745.
14. Muslim, *al-Ṣaḥīḥ*, 2:608–610 §892–893.

2.7 No Soul should be Burdened beyond its Ability

Essential Reading:

1. Dr Tahir-ul-Qadri, Islam on Mercy and Compassion, Ch:2, pp.59-62.

Additional Readings for Teachers and Students:

1. Qurʾān 2:286.
2. Qurʾān 94:5–6.
3. al-Bukhārī in *al-Ṣaḥīḥ:* Bk.: *al-Iʿtiṣām* [The Holding Fast to the Qurʾān and Sunna], Ch.: "Emulating the Sunnas of Allah's Messenger ﷺ," 6:2658 §6858.
4. Muslim in *al-Ṣaḥīḥ:* Bk.: *al-Faḍāʾil* [The Virtues], Ch.: "Respect for the Prophet ﷺ and Avoiding Frequent Questions Posed to Him as Long as There is No Harm," 4:1832 §2359.

5. Ibid., Bk.: *al-Aḥkām* [The Legal Rulings], Ch.: "How the Imam is to Take the Pledge of Fealty from the People," 6:2633 §6776.
6. Muslim in *al-Ṣaḥīḥ:* Bk.: *al-Imāra* [The Leadership], Ch.: "Swearing fealty for listening to and obeying the orders of the leader as far as possible," 3:1490 §1867.
7. Ibid., 6:2633 §6778;
8. Muslim in *al-Ṣaḥīḥ:* Bk.: *al-Īmān* [The Faith], Ch.: "Explanation that the Religion is Sincere Counsel," 1:75 §56.
9. Aḥmad b. Ḥanbal in *al-Musnad*, 6:357, 365;
10. Mālik in *al-Muwaṭṭa*ʾ, 2:982 §1775.
11. al-Bukhārī in *al-Ṣaḥīḥ:* Bk.: *al-ʿIlm* [Knowledge], Ch.: "On the Prophet ﷺ Being Careful about Giving People Admonition and Knowledge Lest They Feel Aversion to It," 1:38 §69.
12. Muslim in *al-Ṣaḥīḥ:* Bk.: *al-Jihād wa al-siyar* [The Striving and Military Expeditions], Ch.: "The Command to Make Things Easy and Not Making Others Feel Aversion," 3:1359 §1734.

2.8 Things be Made Easy so that People may not Feel Aversion

Essential Reading:

1. Dr Tahir-ul-Qadri, Islam on Mercy and Compassion, Ch:2, pp.62-64.

Additional Readings for Teachers and Students:

1. al-Bukhārī in *al-Ṣaḥīḥ:*, Bk.: *al-Maghāzī* [The Expeditions], Ch.: "Abū Mūsā al-Ashʿarī and Muʿādh's Mission to Yemen before the Farewell Pilgrimage," 3:1104 §2873.
2. Muslim in *al-Ṣaḥīḥ*, ibid., 3:1359 §1733.
3. Muslim in *al-Ṣaḥīḥ*, ibid., 3:1358 §173.
4. Abū Dāwūd in *al-Sunan*, 4:260 §4835.
5. al-Bukhārī in *al-Ṣaḥīḥ:* Bk.: *al-Wuḍū*ʾ [The Ablution], Ch.: "Pouring Water Over Urine in the Mosque," 1:89 §217.
6. Muslim in *al-Ṣaḥīḥ:* Bk.: *al-Ṭahāra* [The Purification], Ch.: "The Obligation to Wash Away Urine and Other Impurities," 1:236 §§284–285.

7. Muslim in *al-Ṣaḥīḥ:* Bk.: *al-Dhikr wa al-duʿā* [The Remembrance and Supplication], Ch.: "The Virtue of Congregating to Recite the Qurʾān and Invoke,' 4:1996 §2580.

2.9 Prescription of a Balanced and Moderate Way of Life

Essential Reading:

1. Dr Tahir-ul-Qadri, Islam on Mercy and Compassion, Ch:2, pp.64-68.

Additional Readings for Teachers and Students:

1. al-Bukhārī in *al-Ṣaḥīḥ:* Bk.: *al-Ṣawm* [The Fasting], Ch.: "The Body's Right When Fasting," 2:697 §1874.
2. Muslim in *al-Ṣaḥīḥ:* Bk.: *al-Ṣiyām* [The Fasting], Ch.: "The Prohibition of Perpetual Fasts for Those Who are Harmed by Them," 2:812–817 §1159.
3. al-Bukhārī in *al-Ṣaḥīḥ:* Bk.: *al-Nikāḥ* [Marriage], Ch.: "The Prohibition celibacy and castration," 5:1952 §4786.
4. Muslim in *al-Ṣaḥīḥ:* Bk.: *al-Nikāḥ* [Marriage], Ch.: "Fasting of that who is unable to support and marry," 2:1020 §1402.
5. Ibid., Bk.: *al-Nikāḥ* [The Marriage], Ch.: "The Encouragement to Marry," 5:1949 §4776.
6. Muslim in *al-Ṣaḥīḥ:* Bk.: *al-Nikāḥ* [Marriage], Ch.: "The Recommendation of Marriage for Those who are Able," 2:1020 §1401.
7. Ibid., Bk.: *Jazāʾ al-ṣayd* [The Penalty for Hunting During Hajj], Ch.: "Concerning the One Who Vows to Walk to the Kaʿba," 2:659 §1766;
8. Muslim in *al-Ṣaḥīḥ:* Bk.: *al-Nadhr* [Vows], Ch.: Concerning the One Who Vows to Walk to the Kaʿba," 3:1263 1642.
9. Muslim in *al-Ṣaḥīḥ:* Bk.: *Ṣalāt al-musāfirīn* [The Travelers' Prayer], Ch.: "The Command for the One who is Drowsy while Praying, or Who Mixes up The Qurʾān or Remembrance, to Take Rest," 1:541 §784.
10. Aḥmad b. anbal in *al-Musnad*, 3:101.

2.10 Extremism Destroys Communities

Essential Reading:

1. Dr Tahir-ul-Qadri, Islam on Mercy and Compassion, Ch:2, pp.68-71.

Additional Readings for Teachers and Students:

1. al-Bukhārī in *al-Ṣaḥīḥ:* Bk.: *al-Wuḍū'* [The Ablution], Ch.: "On Performing Ablution after Sleep," 1:87 §209.
2. Muslim in *al-Ṣaḥīḥ:* Bk.: *Ṣalāt al-musāfirīn* [The Travelers' Prayer], Ch.: "The Command for the One who is Drowsy while Praying, or Who Mixes up The Qur'ān or Remembrance, to Take Rest," 1:542 §786.
3. Muslim in *al-Ṣaḥīḥ:* Bk.: *al-ʿIlm* [The Knowledge], Ch.: "The Extremists Have Perished," 4:2055 §2670.
4. al-Bukhārī in *al-Ṣaḥīḥ:* Bk.: *al-ʿIlm* [The Knowledge], Ch.: "Delivering Fatwas While Stationary upon an Animal," 1:43 §83.
5. Muslim in *al-Ṣaḥīḥ:* Bk.: *al-Ḥajj* [The Hajj], Ch.: "Regarding the One Who Shaves His Head before Sacrificing or Sacrifices before Casting Stones," 2:948 §1306.
6. Muslim in *al-Ṣaḥīḥ:* Bk.: *Ṣalāt al-musāfirīn* [The Travelers' Prayer], Ch.: "On Combining between Two Prayers while Resident," 1:489 §705.

2.11 Recommendation of Lenience and Tolerance

Essential Reading:

1. Dr Tahir-ul-Qadri, Islam on Mercy and Compassion, Ch:2, pp.71-73.

Additional Readings for Teachers and Students:

1. Muslim in *al-Ṣaḥīḥ:* Bk.: Bk.: *al-Istiqrāḍ* [The Loans], Ch.: "Easyness in

Sale and Purchase," 2:730 §1970.
2. Ibid., Bk.: *al-Istiqrāḍ* [The Loans], Ch.: "Seeking Loans for Camels," 2:842 §2260.
3. Muslim in *al-Ṣaḥīḥ:* Bk.: *al-Musāqāt* [The Sharecropping], Ch.: "On the One Whose Property is Damaged and Receives Something Better than It," 3:1225 §1601.
4. Muslim in *al-Ṣaḥīḥ:* Bk.: *al-Zuhd* [Renunciation], Ch.: "The Long Hadith of Jābir and the Story of Abū al-Yasar," 4:2302 §3006.

2.12 ALLAH'S PLEASURE LIES IN HELPING AND FORGIVING BEHAVIOUR

ESSENTIAL READING:

1. Dr Tahir-ul-Qadri, Islam on Mercy and Compassion, Ch:2, pp.73, 74.

ADDITIONAL READINGS FOR TEACHERS AND STUDENTS:

1. Aḥmad b. Ḥanbal in *al-Musnad*, 2:361 §8715.
2. al-Nasāʾī in *al-Sunan:* Bk.: *al-Buyūʿ* [The Sales], Ch.: "On Dealing with Others Well and Being Kind in Seeking Repayment of Loans," 7:381 §3696.
3. Ibn Ḥibbān in *al-Ṣaḥīḥ*, 11:422 §5403.
4. al-Ḥākim in *al-Mustadrak*, 2:33 §2223.

2.13 EVERYTHING IS PERMISSIBLE UNLESS EXPRESSLY PROHIBITED

ESSENTIAL READING:

1. Dr Tahir-ul-Qadri, Islam on Mercy and Compassion, Ch:2, pp.74-80.

ADDITIONAL READINGS FOR TEACHERS AND STUDENTS:

1. al-Ṭabarī, *Jāmiʿ al-bayān fī tafsīr al-Qurʾān*, 1:149.
2. al-Nasafī, *Madārik al-tanzīl*, 1:35.
3. al-Zamakhsharī, *al-Kashshāf ʿan ḥaqāʾiq ghawāmiḍ al-tanzīl*, 1:152.
4. Qurʾān 7:32.
5. al-Ṭabarī, *Jāmiʿ al-bayān fī tafsīr al-Qurʾān*, 8:163.
6. Abū al-Saʿūd, *Irshād al-ʿaql al-salīm ilā mazāyā al-Qurʾān al-karīm*, 3:224.
7. Qurʾān 7:31.
8. al-Ṭabarī, *Jāmiʿ al-bayān fī tafsīr al-Qurʾān*, 8:159.
9. Qurʾān 4:24.
10. Qurʾān 5:3.
11. Qurʾān 6:119.
12. Qurʾān 5:101.
13. Qurʾān 7:31.
14. al-Ṭabarī, *Jāmiʿ al-bayān fī tafsīr al-Qurʾān*, 8:159.
15. Qurʾān 4:24.
16. Qurʾān 5:3.
17. Qurʾān 6:119.
18. Qurʾān 5:101.
19. Qurʾān 16:116.
20. Qurʾān 10:59.
21. al-Tirmidhī in *al-Sunan: Bk.: al-Libās* [The Dresses], Ch.: "What is said about furry clothes?" 4:220 §1726; and Ibn Mājah in *al-Sunan:* Bk.: *al-Aṭʿima* [The Foods], Ch.: "Eating of ghee and cheese," 2:1117 §3367.
22. al-Bukhārī in *al-Ṣaḥīḥ:* Bk.: *al-Iʿtiṣām bi al-Kitāb wa al-Sunna* [Holding Fast to the Book and the Sunna], Ch.: "What is disliked of asking too many questions and burdening oneself with that which does not concern one," 6:2658 §6859.
23. Muslim in *al-Ṣaḥīḥ:* Bk.: *al-Faḍāʾil* [The Virtues and Merits], Ch.: "The Prophet's veneration and leaving aside the questions which are not required," 4:1831 §2358.
24. Ibn ajar al-ʿAsqalānī, *Fatḥ al-bārī*, 13:268.
25. al-Sarakhsī in *al-Mabṣūṭ*, 24:77.
26. al-Suyūṭī in *al-Ashbāh wa al-naẓāʾir*, p. 60.

2.14 Legal Dispensations under Pressing Needs

Essential Reading:

1. Dr Tahir-ul-Qadri, Islam on Mercy and Compassion, Ch:2, pp.80-86.

Additional Readings for Teachers and Students:

1. Qur'ān 5:3.
2. Qur'ān 16:115.
3. Qur'ān 4:43.
4. Qur'ān 5:6.
5. al-Bukhārī in *al-Ṣaḥīḥ*: Bk.: *al-Jihād wa al-siyar* [Jihad and Military Expeditions], Ch.: "Silk during war," 3:169 §2763.
6. Aḥmad b. anbal in *al-Musnad*, 5:218 §§21948, 21951; and al-Bayhaqī in *al-Sunan al-kubrā*, 9:356.
7. al-Sarakhsī in *al-Mabṣūṭ*, 10:154.
8. al-Shāṭibī in *al-Muwāfaqāt*, 4:145–146.

2.15 Summary

2.15.1 Obligatory Prayer

2.15.2 Obligatory Fasting

2.15.3 Obligatory Charity [Zakat]

2.15.4 Performance of Hajj

2.15.5 Tenets of Faith

2.15.6 Acts of Worship

2.15.7 Manner of Invitation [*Daʿwa*]

2.15.8 *Muʿāmalāt* [Interactions]

2.15.9 Marriage

2.15.10 Family Relations

2.15.11 International Relations

2.15.12 Sins and Punishments

Essential Reading:

1. Dr Tahir-ul-Qadri, Islam on Mercy and Compassion, Ch:2, pp.86-90.

3. The Holy Qurʾān as Mercy and Cure

Essential Reading:

1. Dr Tahir-ul-Qadri, Islam on Mercy and Compassion, Ch:3, pp. pp.91-101.

Additional Readings for Teachers and Students:

1. Qur'ān 16:64.
2. Qur'ān
3. Qur'ān 31:2–3.
4. Qur'ān 44:6.
5. Qur'ān 45:20.
6. Qur'ān 16:64.

7. Qur'ān 6:155.
8. Qur'ān 10:57.
9. Qur'ān 17:82.
10. Qur'ān 41:44.
11. al-Bukhārī in *al-Ṣaḥīḥ:* Bk.: *al-Ṭibb* [The Medicine], Ch.: "Using Incantations and the Refuge *Sūrās* of the Qur'ān," 5:2165 §5403 & in Ch.: "A Woman Doing an Incantation for a Man," 5:2170 §5419.
12. Muslim in *al-Ṣaḥīḥ:* Bk.: *al-Salām* [The Well-being], Ch.: "Doing an Incantation for a Patient," 4:1723 §2192.
13. Aḥmad b. Ḥanbal in *al-Musnad*, 6:114 §24875, 24971, 26306.
14. Ibn Mājah in *al-Sunan:* Bk.: *al-Ṭibb* [The Medicine], Ch.: "What Should be Recited When One Goes to the Bed," 2:1275 §3875.
15. al-Nasā'ī in *al-Sunan al-Kubrā*, 4:255 §7086.
16. Mālik in *al-Muwaṭṭa'*, 2:942 §1687.
17. Ibn Ḥibbān in *al-Ṣaḥīḥ*, 7:230 §2963.
18. ʿAbd b. Ḥumayd in *al-Musnad*, 1:429 §1474.
19. al-Bukhārī in *al-Ṣaḥīḥ:* Bk.: *Faḍā'il al-Qur'ān* [The Excellent Merits of the Qur'ān], Ch.: "The Excellent Merits of the *Muʿawwidhāt* (the Last Two Chapters of the Qur'ān)," 4:1916 §4728.
20. Muslim in *al-Ṣaḥīḥ:* Bk.: *al-Salām* [The Well-being], Ch.: "Doing an Incantation for a Patient with the *Muʿawwidhāt* (the Last Two Chapters of the Qur'ān) and Blowing," 4:1723 §2192.
21. Abū Dāwūd in *al-Sunan:* Bk.: *al-Ṭibb* [The Medicine], Ch.: "How to Perform the Incantation," 4:15 §3902.
22. Ibn Mājah in *al-Sunan:* Bk.: *al-Ṭibb* [The Medicine], Ch.: "Blowing in the Course of Performimg Incantation," 2:1166 §3529.
23. al-Nasā'ī in *al-Sunan al-Kubrā*, 6:250 §10847.
24. al-Bukhārī in *al-Ṣaḥīḥ:* Bk.: *al-Ṭibb* [The Medicine], Ch.: "Blowing in the Course of Performimg Incantation," 5:2169 §5416.
25. Aḥmad b. Ḥanbal in *al-Musnad*, 6:154 §25249.
26. Ibn Ḥibbān in *al-Ṣaḥīḥ*, 12:352 §5543.
27. al-Ḥakīm al-Tirmidhī in *Nawādir al-Uṣūl*, 3:213.
28. Abū Dāwūd in *al-Sunan:* Bk.: *al-Adhān* [The Call to Prayer], Ch.: "On the Two *Sūrās* of Refuge (*Sūra al-Falaq* and *Sūra al-Nās*)," 2:73 §1463.
29. al-Bayhaqī in *al-Sunan al-kubrā*, 2:294 §3856
30. al-Bayhaqī, *Shuʿab al-īmān*, 2:511, 517 §2563, 2573.
31. al-Mundharī in *al-Targhīb wa al-tarhīb*, 2:251 §2283.
32. Ibn Mājah in *al-Sunan* on the authority of ʿĀ'isha ﵂, Bk.: *Iqāmat al-Ṣalāt wa al-Sunna fi-hā* [The Performance of the Ritual Prayer and the Sunna therein], Ch.: "What Has Come to us Concerning Killing the Scorpion and the Snake in the Course of Ritual Prayer," 1:395 §1246.
33. Ibn Abī Shayba in *al-Muṣannaf*, 5:44 §23553.
34. al-Daylamī in *al-Firdaws bi-ma'thūr al-khiṭāb*, 3:465 §5442.

35. al-Bayhaqī in *Shuʿab al-īmān*, 2:518 §2575.
36. al-Ṭabarānī in *al-Muʿjam al-awsaṭ*, 6:91 §5890 & in *al-Muʿjam al-ṣaghīr*, 2:87 §830.
37. al-Daylamī in *al-Firdaws bi-ma'thūr al-khiṭāb*, 3:465 §5442. Accordning to al-Haythamī: "Its chain of transmission is excellent."
38. al-Ḥākim in *al-Mustadrak*, 4:223 §7437.
39. Ibn Abī Shayba in *al-Muṣannaf*, 5:60 §23689 & in 6:126 §30019.
40. al-Ṭabarānī in *al-Muʿjam al-kabīr*, 9:222 §9076.
41. al-Bayhaqī in *Shuʿab al-īmān*, 2:519 §2581.
42. al-Bayhaqī in *al-Sunan al-kubrā*, 9:345.
43. al-Bayhaqī in *Shuʿab al-īmān*, 2:519 §2580.
44. al-Bayhaqī in *Shuʿab al-īmān*, 2:518 §2579.
45. al-Daylamī in *al-Firdaws bi-ma'thūr al-khiṭāb*, 2:197 §2980.

4. On the Precedence of Allah's Mercy over His Wrath

Essential Reading:

1. Dr Tahir-ul-Qadri, Islam on Mercy and Compassion, Ch:4, pp.106-120.

Additional Readings for Teachers and Students:

1. al-Bukhārī in *al-Ṣaḥīḥ*: Bk.: *al-Tawḥīd*, [Divine Unity], Ch.: "﴾*And His Throne Was on Water, and He is the Lord of the Mighty Throne*﴿," 6:2700 §6986.
2. al-Nasā'ī in *al-Sunan al-kubrā*, 4:418 §7757.
3. al-Ṭabarānī in *Musnad al-Shāmiyyīn*, 4:275 §3270.
4. Aḥmad b. Ḥanbal in *al-Musnad*, 2:433 §9595.
5. al-Tirmidhī in *al-Sunan*: Bk.: *al-Daʿwāt ʿan Rasūl Allāh* ﷺ [The Invocations from Allah's Messenger ﷺ], Ch.: "Allāh Created One Hundred Mercies," 5:549 §3543.
6. al-Nasā'ī in *al-Sunan al-kubrā*, 4:417 §7751.
7. Ibn Abī Shayba in *al-Muṣannaf*, 7:60 §34199.
8. Muslim in *al-Ṣaḥīḥ*: Bk.: *al-Birr wa al-ṣila wa al-ādāb* [Piety, Familial Integration and Manners], Ch.: "The Prohibition of Oppression," 4:1944 §2577.
9. al-Tirmidhī in *al-Sunan*: Bk.: *Ṣifat al-qiyāma wa al-raqā'iq wa al-waraʿ*

ʿan Rasūl Allāh [Description of the Resurrection, Heart Softeners and THE SCRUPULOUSNESS OF ALL¥H’S MESSENGER A], 4:656 §2495.

10. IBN ABĪ SHAYBA IN AL-MU|ANNAF, 6:72 §29557.
11. ʿAbd al-Aʿlā b. Mashar in *Nuskhat Abī Mashar*, 1:23 §1.
12. al-Bukhārī in *al-Ṣaḥīḥ:* Bk.: *al-Tawḥīd* [Divine Unity], Ch.: “The Words of Allāh, Most High: ﴾*They want to replace the speech of Allāh*﴿, 6:2725 §7068.
13. Aḥmad b. Ḥanbal in *al-Musnad*, 2:405 §9245.
14. al-Ḥākim in *al-Mustadrak*, 4:270 §7608 (who said, “This is a rigorously authentic narration that fulfills the conditions of al-Bukhārī and Muslim.”).
15. al-Bayhaqī in *al-Sunan al-kubrā*, 10:188 §20553, *al-Arbaʿūn al-ṣughrā*, 1:30 §9.
16. Muslim in *al-Ṣaḥīḥ:* Bk.: *al-Tawba* [The Repentance], Ch.: “The Acceptance of Repenting from Sins,” 4:2112 §2758.
17. Aḥmad b. Ḥanbal in *al-Musnad*, 2:492 §10384.
18. Ibn Ḥibbān in *al-Ṣaḥīḥ*, 2:392 §625.
19. Abū Yaʿlā in *al-Musnad*, 11:408 §6534.
20. al-Ḥākim in *al-Mustadrak*, 4:270 §7608 (who said, “This is an authentic tradition conforming to the stipulation of the two Shaykhs [i.e., al-Bukhārī and Muslim])
21. al-Tirmidhī in *al-Sunan:* Bk.: *Ṣifat jahannam ʿan Rasūl Allāh* [The Description of *Jahannam* as Told by Allāh’s Messenger], 4:714 §2599.
22. Ibn al-Mubārak in *al-Musnad*, 1:68 §111.
23. Aḥmad b. Ḥanbal in *al-Musnad*, 5:154 §21405.
24. al-Tirmidhī in *al-Sunan:* Bk.: *Ṣifat al-qiyāma wa al-raqāʾiq wa al-waraʿ ʿan Rasūl Allāh* [The Description of the Resurrection, Heart Softeners and the Scrupulousness of Allāh’s Messenger], 4:656 §2495.
25. Ibn Mājah in *al-Sunan:* Bk.: *al-Zuhd* [The Asceticism], Ch.: “Repentance,” 2:1422 §4257.
26. al-Tirmidhī in *al-Sunan:* Bk.: *al-Daʿawāt ʿan Rasūl Allāh*, [Invocation from Allāh’s Messenger], Ch.: “The Virtue of Repentance and Seeking Forgiveness,” 5:548 §3540.
27. al-Ṭabarānī in *al-Muʿjam al-awsaṭ*, 4:315 §4305.
28. Abū Nuʿaym in *Ḥilyat al-Awliyāʾ*, 2:231.
29. al-Bukhārī in *al-Ṣaḥīḥ:* Bk.: *al-Anbiyāʾ* [The Prophets], Ch.: “What Has Been Mentioned About the Children of Israel,” 3:1272 §3266, and in Bk.: *al-Buyūʿ* [Trade], Ch.: “Giving Time to Someone who is Able to Pay His Debt,” 2:731 §1971.
30. al-Bukhārī in *al-Ṣaḥīḥ:* Bk.: *al-Anbiyāʾ* [The Prophets], Ch.: “The Narration of the Cave,” 3:1282 §3291, and in Bk.: *al-Riqāq* [Heart Softeners], Ch.: “Fearing Allāh,” 5:2378 §6116.

31. Aḥmad b. Ḥanbal in *al-Musnad*, 3:69 §§11682,11753.
32. Ibn Ḥibbān in *al-Ṣaḥīḥ*, 2:417 §649.
33. Abū Yaʿlā in *al-Musnad*, 2:314 §1047.
34. al-Ṭabarānī in *al-Muʿjam al-kabīr*, 19:423 §1026.
35. al-Bukhārī in *al-Ṣaḥīḥ:* Bk.: *al-Anbiyāʾ* [The Prophets ﷺ], Ch.: "The Narration of the Cave," 3:1283 §3292.
36. al-Bazzār in *al-Musnad*, 7:244 §2822.
37. al-Bayhaqī in *Shuʿab al-īmān*, 5:430 §7160.
38. Ibn ajar in *Fatḥ al-Bārī*, 6:522 §3294.
39. al-ʿAynī in *ʿUmdat al-qārī*, 16:62 §9743.
40. Ibn Kathīr in *Tafsīr al-Qurʾān al-Aẓīm*, 3:583.
41. al-Bukhārī in *al-Ṣaḥīḥ:* Bk.: *al-Tawḥīd* [Divine Oneness], Ch.: "The Words of Allāh, Most High: ﴾*They want to replace the speech of Allāh*﴿," 6:2725 §7067.
42. Muslim in *al-Ṣaḥīḥ:* Bk.: *al-Tawba* [The Repentance], Ch.: "The Vastness of Allah's Mercy and That His Mercy Precedes His Anger," 4:2109 §2756.
43. Mālik in *al-Muwaṭṭaʾ*, 1:240 §570.
44. Muslim in *al-Ṣaḥīḥ:* Bk.: *al-Tawba* [The Repentance], Ch.: "The Vastness of Allah's Mercy and That His Mercy Precedes His Wrath," 4:2110 §2756.
45. Aḥmad b. Ḥanbal in *al-Musnad*, 2:269 §7635.
46. Ibn Mājah in *al-Sunan:* Bk.: *al-Zuhd* [The Renunciation], Ch.: "Repentance," 2:1421 §4255.
46. ʿAbd al-Razzāq in *al-Muṣannaf*, 11:283 §20548.
47. Muslim in *al-Ṣaḥīḥ:* Bk.: *al-Tawba* [The Repentance], Ch.: "The Vastness of Allah's Mercy and That His Mercy Precedes His Wrath," 4:2109 §2755.
48. Aḥmad b. Ḥanbal in *al-Musnad*, 2:334 §8396.
49. al-Tirmidhī in *al-Sunan:* Bk.: *al-Daʿawāt ʿan Rasūl Allāh* ﷺ [Invocations from Allāh's Messenger ﷺ], Ch.: "Allāh Created One Hundred Mercies," 5:549 §3542.
50. Abū Yaʿlā in *al-Musnad*, 11:392 §6507.
51. al-Daylamī in *Musnad al-firdaws*, 3:349 §5056.
52. al-Qurashī in *Ḥusn al-ẓann billāh*, 1:29 §19.

5. On the One Hundred Parts of Allah's Mercy, and that Ninety-nine of them are Reserved for the Day of Resurrection

Essential Reading:

1. Dr Tahir-ul-Qadri, Islam on Mercy and Compassion, Ch:5, pp.121-130.

Additional Readings for Teachers and Students:

1. al-Bukhārī in *al-Ṣaḥīḥ:* Bk.: *al-Adab* [Good Manners], Ch.: "Allāh Made Mercy One Hundred Parts," 5:2236 §5654.
2. Muslim in *al-Ṣaḥīḥ:* Bk.: *al-Tawba* [The Repentance], Ch.: "The Vastness of Allāh's Mercy and That His Mercy Precedes His Wrath," 4:2108 §2752.
3. al-Dārimī in *al-Sunan*, 2:413 §2785.
4. Ibn Ḥibbān in *al-Ṣaḥīḥ*, 14:16 §6148.
5. al-Ṭabarānī in *al-Muʿjam al-awsaṭ*, 1:297 §991.
6. al-Bayhaqī in *Shuʿab al-īmān*, 7:457 §10975.
7. Muslim in *al-Ṣaḥīḥ:* Bk.: *al-Tawba* [Repentance], Ch.: "The Vastness of Allah's Mercy and That His Mercy Precedes His Wrath," 4:2108 §2752.
8. Aḥmad b. Ḥanbal in *al-Musnad*, 2:434 §9607.
9. al-Tirmidhī in *al-Sunan:* Bk.: *al-Daʿawāt ʿan Rasūl Allāh* ﷺ [Invocations from Allāh's Messenger ﷺ], Ch.: "Allāh Created One Hundred Mercies," 5:549 §3541.
10. Ibn Mājah in *al-Sunan:* Bk.: *al-Zuhd* [The Renunciation], Ch.: "Hope for Allāh's Mercy on the Day of Resurrection," 2:1435 §4293.
11. Ibn Ḥibbān in *al-Ṣaḥīḥ*, 14:15 §6147.
12. Ibn al-Mubārak in *al-Musnad*, 1:20 §35.
13. Abū Yaʿlā in *al-Musnad*, 11:328 §6445.
14. Aḥmad b. Ḥanbal in *al-Musnad*, 4:312 §18821.
15. Abū Dāwūd in *al-Sunan:* Bk.: *al-Adab* [Good Manners], Ch.: "Whom the Ruling of Backbiting Does Not Concern," 4:271 §4885.
16. al-Ruwayānī in *al-Musnad*, 2:140 §957.
17. al-Ḥākim in *al-Mustadrak*, 1:124 §187, and 4:276 §7630.
18. al-Ṭabarānī in *al-Muʿjam al-kabīr*, 2:161 §1667.
19. al-Haythamī in *Majmaʿ al-zawāʾid*, 10:213.
20. Aḥmad b. Ḥanbal in *al-Musnad*, 5:439 §23771.
21. al-Ṭabarānī in *al-Muʿjam al-kabīr*, 6:250 §6126.
22. al-Bayhaqī in *Shuʿab al-īmān*, 2:15 §1038.
23. al-Ṭabarānī in *al-Muʿjam al-kabīr*, 11:374 §12047.
24. al-Haythamī in *Majmaʿ al-zawāʾid*, 10:214,385.
25. Aḥmad b. Ḥanbal in *al-Musnad*, 2:514 §10681.
26. al-Ḥākim in *al-Mustadrak*, 1:123 §185.
27. al-Haythamī in *Majmaʿ al-zawāʾid*, 10:385.

28. al-Albānī in *Silsilat al-aḥādīth al-ṣaḥīḥa*, 4:176 §1634.
29. al-Ṭabarānī in *al-Muʿjam al-kabīr*, 19:417 §1006.
30. Tamām al-Rāzī in *al-Fawāʾid*, 1:248 §606.
31. Ibn ʿAsākir in *Tārīkh Dimashq*, 8:259.
32. al-Haythamī in *Majmaʿ al-zawāʾid*, 10:385.
33. Aḥmad b. Ḥanbal in *al-Musnad*, 2:514 §10680.
34. al-Ḥākim in *al-Mustadrak*, 4:276 §7629.
35. al-Haythamī in *Majmaʿ al-zawāʾid*, 10:214,385.
36. al-Albānī in *Silsilat al-aḥādīth al-ṣaḥīḥa*, 4:176 §1634.
37. Aḥmad b. Ḥanbal in *al-Musnad*, 2:484 §10285.
38. al-Tirmidhī in *al-Sunan:* Bk.: *al-Daʿawāt ʿan Rasūl Allāh* ﷺ [Invocations from Allāh's Messenger ﷺ], Ch.: "Allāh Created One Hundred Mercies," 5:549 §3541.
39. Ibn Kathīr in *Tafsīr al-Qurʾān al-ʿAẓīm*, 2:201.
40. al-Haythamī in *Majmaʿ al-zawāʾid*, 10:385.
41. al-Hindī in *Kanz al-ʿummāl*, 4:439 §10406.

6. Of the Seventy Thousand People of the Prophet's Umma to whom Allah shall Grant Paradise without reckoning, Every Thousand amongst them shall take another Seventy Thousand

Essential Reading:

1. Dr Tahir-ul-Qadri, Islam on Mercy and Compassion, Ch:6, pp.131-141.

Additional Readings for Teachers and Students:

1. al-Bukhārī in *al-Ṣaḥīḥ:* Bk.: *al-Riqāq* [Heart Softeners], Ch.: "Seventy Thousand Shall Enter Paradise Without Reckoning," 5:2396 §6176, and in Bk.: *al-Libās* [Clothing], Ch.: "The Cloak and Over garment," 5:2189 §5474.
2. Muslim in *al-Ṣaḥīḥ:* Bk.: *al-Īmān* [The Faith], Ch.: "The Proof That Some Groups of Muslims Shall Enter Paradise without Reckoning or Punishment," 1:197 §216.
3. Aḥmad b. Ḥanbal in *al-Musnad*, 2:400 §9202.

4. Ibn Manda in *al-Īmān*, 2:892 §970 (with an authentic chain of transmission).
5. Ibn Kathīr in *Tafsīr al-Qurʾān al-ʿAẓīm*, 1:394.
6. al-Bukhārī in *al-Ṣaḥīḥ:* Bk.: *al-Riqāq* [Heart Softeners], Ch.: "Seventy Thousand Shall Enter Paradise Without Reckoning," 5:2396 §6175.
7. Muslim in *al-Ṣaḥīḥ:* Bk.: *al-Īmān* [The Faith], Ch.: "The Proof That Some Groups of Muslims Shall Enter Paradise without Reckoning or Punishment," 1:197 §216.
8. Aḥmad b. Ḥanbal in *al-Musnad*, 2:302 §8016.
9. Ibn Rāhawayh in *al-Musnad*, 1:143 §76.
10. Ibn Manda in *al-Īmān*, 2:894 §974.
11. Muslim in *al-Ṣaḥīḥ:* Bk.: *al-Īmān* [The Faith], Ch.: "Those on the Lowest Level of Paradise," 1:177 §191.
12. Aḥmad b. Ḥanbal in *al-Musnad*, 3:345 §14721 (and the narration is fully connected to the Prophet ﷺ).
13. ʿAbd Allāh b. Aḥmad b. Ḥanbal in *al-Sunna*, 1:248 §457.
14. Ibn Manda in *al-Īmān*, 2:825 §851 (with an authentic chain of transmission).
15. Ibn Kathīr in *Tafsīr al-Qurʾān al-ʿAẓīm*, 1:394–395.
16. Aḥmad b. Ḥanbal in *al-Musnad*, 2:359 §8707.
17. Ibn Manda in *al-Īmān*, 2:895 §976 (with a rigorously authentic chain of transmission similar to those of Muslim).
18. al-Haythamī in *Majmaʿ al-zawāʾid*, 10:404 (who said: "Its men are those of rigorously authentic chains of transmission.").
19. Ibn ajar in *Fatḥ al-Bārī*, 11:410 (who said: "It has a good chain").
20. Aḥmad b. Ḥanbal in *al-Musnad*, 5:393 §23336.
21. Ibn Kathīr in *Tafsīr al-Qurʾān al-ʿAẓīm*, 2:122.
22. al-Haythamī in *Majmaʿ al-zawāʾid*, 10:68.
23. al-Tirmidhī in *al-Sunan:* Bk.: *Ṣifat al-qiyāma wa al-raqāʾiq wa al-waraʿ* [The Description of the Resurrection, Heart Softeners and Scrupulousness], Ch.: "Intercession," 4:626 §2437.
24. Aḥmad b. Ḥanbal in *al-Musnad*, 5:268 §22303 (with an authentic chain of transmission).
25. Ibn Mājah in *al-Sunan:* Bk.: *al-Zuhd* [The Renunciation], Ch.: "The Description of Muhammad ﷺ," 2:1433 §4286.
26. Ibn Abī Shayba in *al-Muṣannaf*, 6:315 §31714.
27. Ibn Abī ʿĀṣim in *al-Sunna*, 1:260,261 §§588,589.
28. Ibn Kathīr in *Tafsīr al-Qurʾān al-ʿAẓīm*, 1:295.
29. Ibn ajar in *al-Iṣāba*, 6:646 §9233 (with an an authentic chain of transmission).
30. Ibn Ḥibbān in *al-Ṣaḥīḥ*, 16:232 §7247.
31. al-Ṭabarānī in *al-Muʿjam al-kabīr*, 17:127 §312.
32. *al-Muʿjam al-awsaṭ*, 1:127 §402.

33. Ibn Kathīr in *Tafsīr al-Qur'ān al-ʿAẓīm*, 1:395.
34. al-Haythamī in *Majmaʿ al-zawā'id*, 10:409,414.
35. Ibn Abī Shayba in *al-Muṣannaf*, 6:318 §31739.
36. Hannād b. al-Sirrī in *al-Zuhd*, 1:135 §178.
37. al-Daylamī in *Musnad al-firdaws*, 2:311 §3407.

7. On the Seventy Thousand People of the Prophet's Umma to whom Allah shall Grant Paradise without Reckoning, and Every Single Person among Them will be Granted Additional Seventy Thousand to Enter Paradise with Him without Reckoning

Essential Reading:

1. Dr Tahir-ul-Qadri, Islam on Mercy and Compassion, Ch:7, pp.142-149.

Additional Readings for Teachers and Students:

1. Aḥmad b. Ḥanbal in *al-Musnad*, 1:197 §1706.
2. al-Bazzār in *al-Musnad*, 6:234 §2268.
3. al-Haythamī in *Majmaʿ al-zawā'id*, 10:410.
4. Ibn Kathīr in *Tafsīr al-Qur'ān al-ʿAẓīm*, 1:393.
5. Abū Yaʿlā in *al-Musnad*, 6:417 §3783.
6. al-Maqdisī in *al-Aḥādīth al-mukhtāra*, 6:54 §2028.
7. Ibn Kathīr in *Tafsīr al-Qur'ān al-ʿAẓīm*, 1:395 (who said, "It is an authentic tradition with reliable sources) ʿAbd al-Qādir b. al-Sirrī. When asked about him, Ibn Maʿīn said, 'A pious man.'").
8. al-Haythamī in *Majmaʿ al-zawā'id*, 10:404 (who said: "Its chain is authentic.").
9. al-Bayhaqī in *Shuʿab al-īmān*, 1:252 §268.
10. Aḥmad b. Ḥanbal in *al-Musnad*, 5:257 §22215.
11. al-Ṭabarānī in *al-Muʿjam al-kabīr*, 8:143 §7638.
12. *Musnad al-Shāmiyyīn*, 2:147 §1079.
13. al-Haythamī in *Majmaʿ al-zawā'id*, 10:381.
14. Ibn Kathīr in *Tafsīr al-Qur'ān al-ʿAẓīm*, 4:248.
14\. Aḥmad b. Ḥanbal in *al-Musnad*, 5:312.
15\. Ibn Mājah in *al-Sunan:* Bk.: *al-Zuhd* [The Renunciation], Ch.: "The

Description of Hell," 2:1446 §4323.
16. Ibn Abī Shayba in *al-Muṣannaf*, 6:313 §31702.
17. Abū Yaʿlā in *al-Musnad*, 3:154 §1581.
18. al-Ḥākim in *al-Mustadrak ʿalā al-Ṣaḥīḥayn*, 1:242 §238.
19. Ibn Abī ʿĀṣim in *al-Āḥād wa al-mathānī*, 2:294 §1056.

8. On the Increase of Allah's Mercy to His Servants in the Reward They Receive for Good Deeds, and the Pardoning of Passing Thoughts and Sins

Essential Reading:

1. Dr Tahir-ul-Qadri, Islam on Mercy and Compassion, Ch:8, pp.151-157.

Additional Readings for Teachers and Students:

1. al-Bukhārī in *al-Ṣaḥīḥ:* Bk.: *al-Riqāq* [Heart Softeners], Ch.: "Thinking to Do Something Good or Bad," 5:2380 §6126.
2. Muslim in *al-Ṣaḥīḥ:* Bk.: *al-Īmān* [The Faith], Ch.: "When a Person Plans to Do a Righteous Deed It Is Written Down But When He Plans to Do an Evil Deed It Is Not Written Down," 1:118 §131.
3. Aḥmad b. Ḥanbal in *al-Musnad*, 1:310 §2828.
4. Ibn Manda in *al-Īmān*, 1:494 §380.
5. al-Mundhirī in *al-Targhīb wa al-tarhīb*, 1:27 §21.
6. al-Bukhārī in *al-Ṣaḥīḥ:* Bk.: *al-Tawḥīd* [Divine Unity], Ch.: "The Words of Allāh, Most High: ﴾*They want to replace the speech of Allāh*﴿, 6:2724 §7062.
7. Ibn Ḥibbān in *al-Ṣaḥīḥ*, 2:105 §382.
8. al-Bayhaqī in *Shuʿab al-īmān*, 1:300 §336.
9. al-Ṭabarānī in *Musnad al-Shāmiyyīn*, 1:87 §123.
10. al-Daylamī in *Musnad al-firdaws*, 5:246 §8087.
11. al-Qazwīnī in *al-Tadwīn*, 1:489.
12. Abū Nuʿaym in *Tārīkh Aṣbahān*, 2:74 §1130.
13. Ibn Rajab in *Jāmiʿ al-ʿulūm wa al-ḥikam*, 1:349.

14. Muslim in *al-Ṣaḥīḥ:* Bk.: *al-Īmān* [The Faith], Ch.: "When a Person Plans to Do a Righteous Deed It Is Written Down But When He Plans to Do an Evil Deed It Is Not Written Down," 1:117 §128.
15. Aḥmad b. Ḥanbal in *al-Musnad*, 2:242 §7294.
16. al-Nasāʾī in *al-Sunan al-kubrā*, 6:344 §11181.
17. ʿAbd al-Razzāq in *al-Muṣannaf*, 11:287 §20557.
18. Ibn Manda in *al-Īmān*, 1:491 §375.
19. Abū Yaʿlā in *al-Musnad*, 11:171 §6282.
20. Muslim in *al-Ṣaḥīḥ:* Bk.: *al-Īmān* [The Faith], Ch.: "When a Person Plans to Do a Righteous Deed It Is Written Down But When He Plans to Do an Evil Deed It Is Not Written Down," 1:117 §128.
21. al-Ḥākim in *al-Mustadrak*, 4:275 §7624 (who said: "This tradition has an authentic chain of transmission").
22. Ibn Manda in *al-Īmān*, 1:493 §378.
23. al-Daylamī in *Musnad al-firdaws*, 3:173 §4463.
24. Zayn al-Dīn in *al-Ittiḥāfāt al-saniyya*, 1:18 §21.
25. Muslim in *al-Ṣaḥīḥ:* Bk.: *al-Īmān* [The Faith], Ch.: "When a Person Plans to Do a Righteous Deed It Is Written Down But When He Plans to Do an Evil Deed It Is Not Written Down," 1:117 §129.
26. Aḥmad b. Ḥanbal in *al-Musnad*, 2:315 §8151.
27. Hammām b. Munabbih al-Ṣanʿānī in *al-Ṣaḥīfa*, 1:41 §53.
28. Abū ʿAwāna in *al-Musnad*, 1:81 §240.
29. Ibn Ḥibbān in *al-Ṣaḥīḥ*, 2:103 §379.
30. al-Bayhaqī in *Shuʿab al-īmān*, 5:389 §7045.
31. Abū Nuʿaym in *Musnad al-mustakhraj*, 1:198 §335.
32. Ibn Ḥazm in *al-Muḥallā*, 1:18.
33. Muslim in *al-Ṣaḥīḥ:* Bk.: *al-Dhikr wa al-duʿā wa al-tawba wa al-istighfār* [Remembrance, Invocation, Repentance, and Seeking Forgiveness], Ch.: "The Virtue of Remembrance, Invocation and Seeking Nearness to Allāh, Most High," 4:2068 §2687.
34. Aḥmad b. Ḥanbal in *al-Musnad*, 5:153 §21398.
35. Ibn Mājah in *al-Sunan:* Bk.: *al-Adab* [Good Manners], Ch.: "The Virtue of Deeds," 2:1255 §3821.
36. al-Bazzār in *al-Musnad*, 9:399 §3991.
37. Abū Nuʿaym in *Ḥilyat al-awliyāʾ*, 5:56.
38. Ibn al-Mubārak in *al-Zuhd*, 1:366 §1035.
39. al-Nawawī in *Riyāḍ al-ṣāliḥīn*, 1:124 §124.

9. On Allah's Descent to the Lower Heavens and His Calling Out to His Servants

Essential Reading:

1. Dr Tahir-ul-Qadri, Islam on Mercy and Compassion, Ch:9, pp.159-168.

Additional Readings for Teachers and Students:

1. al-Bukhārī in *al-Ṣaḥīḥ*: Bk.: *al-Jumuʿa* [Friday], Ch.: "Supplication in Prayer During the Last Part of the Night," 1:384 §1094.
2. al-Tirmidhī in *al-Sunan*: Bk.: *al-Daʿawāt ʿan Rasūl Allāh* ﷺ [Invocations from Allāh's Messenger ﷺ], 5:526 §3498 (al-Tirmidhī said: "This is a fine authentic tradition").
3. Abū Dāwūd in *al-Sunan*: Bk.: *al-Sunna* [The Sunna], Ch.: "Replying to the Jahmites," 4:234 §4733.
4. al-Dārimī in *al-Sunan*, 1:413 §1479.
5. al-Rabīʿ in *al-Musnad*, 1:202 §501.
6. Muslim in *al-Ṣaḥīḥ*: Bk.: *Ṣalāt al-musāfirīn wa qaṣruhā* [The Traveler's Prayer and Shortening It], Ch.: "The Encouragement to Supplicate at the Last Part of the Night and How Supplications Are Answered During This Time," 1:522 §758.
7. Aḥmad b. Ḥanbal in *al-Musnad*, 2:419 §9426.
8. al-Tirmidhī in *al-Sunan*: Bk.: *al-Ṣalāh* [The Prayer], Ch.: "The Lord's Descending to the Lowest Heaven Every Night," 2:307 §446 (al-Tirmidhī said: "The narration of Abū Hurayra ؓ is *ḥasan-ṣaḥīḥ*"). al-Maqdisī in *al-Targhīb fī al-duʿāʾ*, 1:69 §30.
9. Muslim in *al-Ṣaḥīḥ*: Bk.: *Ṣalāt al-musāfirīn wa qaṣruhā* [The Traveler's Prayer and Shortening It], Ch.: "The Encouragement to Supplicate and Recite Words of Remembrance," 1:522 §758.
10. al-Nasāʾī in *al-Sunan al-kubrā*, 6:123 §10312.
11. *ʿAmal al-yawm wa al-layla*, 1:339 §478.
12. al-Ṭabarānī in *al-Duʿāʾ*, 1:63 §146.
13. al-Bayhaqī in *Faḍāʾil al-awqāt*, 1:168 §51.
14. Muslim in *al-Ṣaḥīḥ*: Bk.: *Ṣalāt al-musāfirīn wa qaṣruhā* [The Traveler's Prayer and Shortening It], Ch.: "The Encouragement to Supplicate and Recite Words of Remembrance," 1:522 §758.

15. al-Bayhaqī in *al-Sunan al-kubrā*, 3:2 §4428.
16. Abū ʿAwāna in *al-Musnad*, 1:127 §§377,378.
17. al-Mizzī in *Tahdhīb al-kamāl*, 27:261.
18. Muslim in *al-Ṣaḥīḥ:* Bk.: *Ṣalāt al-musāfirīn wa qaṣruhā* [The Traveler's Prayer and Shortening It], Ch.: "The Encouragement to Supplicate and Recite Words of Remembrance," 1:522 §758.
19. Muslim in *al-Ṣaḥīḥ:* Bk.: *Ṣalāt al-musāfirīn wa qaṣruhā* [The Traveler's Prayer and Shortening It], Ch.: "The Encouragement to Supplicate and Recite Words of Remembrance," 1:523 §758.
20. Aḥmad b. Ḥanbal in *al-Musnad*, 3:34 §11313.
22. al-Nasāʾī in *al-Sunan al-kubrā*, 6:124 §10315.
23. ʿAbd b. Ḥumayd in *al-Musnad*, 1:272 §861.
24. Ibn Abī Shayba in *al-Muṣannaf*, 6:72 §29556.
25. ʿAbd al-Razzāq in *al-Muṣannaf*, 10:444 §19654.
26. al-Ṭabarānī in *al-Muʿjam al-kabīr*, 22:370 §927.
27. Ibn ʿAbd al-Barr in *al-Istidhkār*, 2:68.
28. al-Tirmidhī in *al-Sunan:* Bk.: *al-Ṣalāh* [The Prayer], Ch.: "The Lord's Descending to the Lowest Heaven Every Night," 2:307 §446.
29. Ibn Ḥibbān in *al-Ṣaḥīḥ*, 3:201 §921.
30. al-Nasāʾī in *al-Sunan al-kubrā*, 6:125 §10319.
31. al-Lālikāʾī in *Iʿtiqād ahl al-Sunna*, 3:440 §752.
32. al-Tirmidhī in *al-Sunan:* Bk.: *al-Ṣawm* [Fasts], Ch.: "The Night of Fifteenth of Shaʿbān," 3:116 §739.
33. Ibn Mājah in *al-Sunan:* Bk.: *Iqāmat al-ṣalāh wa al-sunna fīhā* [Establishing the Prayer and the Sunna Therein], Ch.: "The Night of Fifteenth of Shaʿbān," 1:444 §1389.
34. ʿAbd b. Ḥumayd in *al-Musnad*, 1:437 §1509.
35. al-Bayhaqī in *Shuʿab al-īmān*, 3:379 §3825, and in •*Faḍāʾil al-awqāt*, 1:130 §28.
36. al-Ḥusaynī in *al-Bayān wa al-taʿrīf*, 1:193 §505.
37. Ibn Mājah in *al-Sunan:* Bk.: *Iqāmat al-ṣalāh wa al-sunna fīhā* [Establishing the Prayer and the Sunna Therein], Ch.: "The Night of the Fifteenth of Shaʿbān," 1:444 §1388.
38. al-Bayhaqī in *Shuʿab al-īmān*, 3:378 §3822, and in *Faḍāʾil al-awqāt*, 1:122 §24.
39. al-Fākihī in *Akhbār Makka*, 3:84 §1837.
40. al-Daylamī in *Musnad al-firdaws*, 1:259 §1007.
41. al-Mundhirī in *al-Targhīb wa al-tarhīb*, 2:74 §1550.
42. Aḥmad b. Ḥanbal in *al-Musnad*, 6:238 §26060.
43. Ibn Mājah in *al-Sunan* : Bk.: *Iqāmat al-ṣalāh wa al-sunna fīhā* [Establishing the Prayer and the Sunna Therein], Ch.: "The Night of the Fifteenth of Shaʿbān," 1:444 §1389.
44. Ibn Rāhawayh in *al-Musnad*, 2:326 §850.

45. ʿAbd b. Ḥumayd in *al-Musnad*, 1:437 §1509.
46. al-Ḥusaynī in *al-Bayān wa al-taʿrīf*, 1:193 §505.
47. al-Suyūṭī in *al-Durr al-manthūr*, 7:402.
48. Ibn Mājah in *al-Sunan* : Bk.: *Iqāmat al-ṣalāh wa al-sunna fīhā* [Establishing the Prayer and the Sunna Therein], Ch.: "The Night of the Fifteenth of Shaʿbān," 1:445 §1390.
49. Ibn Ḥibbān in *al-Ṣaḥīḥ*, 12:481 §5665.
50. al-Ṭabarānī in *al-Muʿjam al-awsaṭ*, 7:36 §6776.
51. Ibn Abī ʿĀṣim in *al-Sunna*, 1:224 §512.
52. al-Bayhaqī in *Shuʿab al-īmān*, 5:272 §6628.
53. Ibn ʿAsākir in *Tārīkh Dimashq*, 38:235.

10. On Allah's Mercy for the Dissolute and Sinful

Essential Reading:

1. Dr Tahir-ul-Qadri, Islam on Mercy and Compassion, Ch:10, pp.169-180.

Additional Readings for Teachers and Students:

1. al-Bukhārī in *al-Ṣaḥīḥ:* Bk.: *al-Adab* [Good Manners], Ch.: "Being Merciful Toward One's Children and Kissing and Hugging Them," 5:2235 §5651.
2. Aḥmad b. Ḥanbal in *al-Musnad*, 2:241 §7287.
3. Abū Dāwūd in *al-Sunan:* Bk.: *al-Adab* [Good Manners], Ch.: "A Man Kissing His Child," 4:355 §5218.
4. Ibn Ḥibbān in *al-Ṣaḥīḥ*, 2:202 §457.
5. al-Bayhaqī in *al-Sunan al-kubrā*, 7:100 §13354.
6. al-Bukhārī in *al-Adab al-mufrad*, 1:46 §91.
7. al-Bukhārī in *al-Ṣaḥīḥ:* Bk.: *al-Tawḥīd* [Divine Unity], Ch.: "The Word of Allāh: ﴾*Say: "Call Allāh or call the Most Merciful."*﴿, 6:2686 §6941, and in *al-Adab al-mufrad*, 1:48 §96.
8. Ibn Abī Shayba in *al-Muṣannaf*, 5:214 §25356.
9. al-Quḍāʿī in *Musnad al-shihāb*, 2:66 §894.
10. al-Bayhaqī in *al-Sunan al-kubrā*, 9:41 §17682.

11. Muslim in *al-Ṣaḥīḥ:* Bk.: *al-Faḍā'il* [Virtues], Ch.: "Mercy Toward Children and Family Members," 4:1809 §2319.
12. al-Bukhārī in *al-Adab al-Mufrad*, 1:48 §96.
13. Ibn Abī Shayba in *al-Muṣannaf*, 5:214 §25356.
14. al-Quḍā'ī in *Musnad al-shihāb*, 2:66 §894.
15. al-Bayhaqī in *al-Sunan al-kubrā*, 9:41 §17682.
16. al-Bukhārī in *al-Ṣaḥīḥ:* Bk.: *al-Adab* [Good Manners], Ch.: "There Should Be Gentleness in Everything," 5:2242 §5678, and in Bk.: *al-Isti'dhān* [Asking for Permission to Enter], Ch.: "How to Return the Greeting of Non-Muslim Citizens," 5:2308 §5901, and in Bk.: *al-Da'awāt* [Supplications], Ch.: "Supplicate to Allāh Against the Polytheists," 5:2349 §6032.
17. Muslim in *al-Ṣaḥīḥ:* Bk.: *al-Salām* [Salutations], Ch.: "The Prohibition of Greeting the People of the Book First and How to Return Their Greetings,"4:1706 §2165.
18. Aḥmad b. Ḥanbal in *al-Musnad*, 6:37 §24136.
19. al-Tirmidhī in *al-Sunan:* Bk.: *al-Isti'dhān 'an Rasūl Allāh* ﷺ [How Allāh's Messenger ﷺ Taught Us to Ask for Permission Before Entering], Ch.: "How to Greet Non-Muslim Citizens," 5:60 §2701.
20. al-Nasā'ī in *al-Sunan al-kubrā*, 6:102 §10213.
21. 'Abd al-Razzāq in *al-Muṣannaf*, 6:11 §9839.
22. al-Bukhārī in *al-Adab al-mufrad*, 1:164 §462.
23. al-Mundhirī in *al-Targhīb wa al-tarhīb*, 3:278 §4047.
24. al-Bukhārī in *al-Ṣaḥīḥ:* Bk.: *Istitāba al-murtaddīn wa al-mu'ānidīn wa qitālihim* [Asking Apostates and Rebels to Repent and Fighting Them], Ch.: "When a Non-Muslim Citizen or Someone Else Slanders the Prophet ﷺ Indirectly Without Being Explicit Such as Saying: '*al-sām 'alaykum*,'" 6:2539 §6528.
25. Muslim in *al-Ṣaḥīḥ:* Bk.: *al-Birr wa al-ṣila wa al-ādāb* [Piety, Keeping Family Ties and Good Manners], Ch.: "The Virtue of Gentleness," 4:2003 §2593; •Aḥmad b. Ḥanbal in *al-Musnad*, 1:112 §902.
26. Abū Dāwūd in *al-Sunan:* Bk.: *al-Adab* [Good Manners], Ch.: "Gentleness," 4:254 §4807.
27. Ibn Mājah in *al-Sunan:* Bk.: *al-Adab* [Good Manners], Ch.: "Gentleness," 2:1216 §3688.
28. Mālik in *al-Muwaṭṭa'*, 2:979 §1767.
29. al-Bukhārī in *al-Ṣaḥīḥ:* Bk.: *Istitāba al-murtaddīn wa al-mu'ānidīn wa qitālihim* [Asking Apostates and Rebels to Repent and Fighting Them], Ch.: "When a Non-Muslim Citizen or Someone Else Slanders the Prophet ﷺ Indirectly Without Being Explicit Such as Saying: '*al-sām 'alaykum*,'" 6:2539 §6528.
30. Muslim in *al-Ṣaḥīḥ:* Bk.: *al-Birr wa al-ṣila wa al-ādāb* [Piety, Keeping Family Ties and Good Manners], Ch.: "The Virtue of Gentleness,"

4:2003 §2593.
31. Aḥmad b. Ḥanbal in *al-Musnad*, 1:112 §902.
32. Abū Dāwūd in *al-Sunan:* Bk.: *al-Adab* [Good Manners], Ch.: "Gentleness," 4:254 §4807.
33. Ibn Mājah in *al-Sunan:* Bk.: *al-Adab* [Good Manners], Ch.: "Gentleness," 2:1216 §3688.
34. Mālik in *al-Muwaṭṭa'*, 2:979 §1767.
35. Muslim in *al-Ṣaḥīḥ:* Bk.: *al-Birr wa al-ṣila wa al-ādāb* [Piety, Keeping Family Ties and Good Manners], Ch.: "The Virtue of Gentleness," 4:2003 §2592.
36. Abū Dāwūd in *al-Sunan:* Bk.: *al-Adab* [Good Manners], Ch.: "Gentleness," 4:255 §4809.
37. Aḥmad b. Ḥanbal in *al-Musnad*, 4:362.
38. Ibn Mājah in *al-Sunan:* Bk.: *al-Adab* [Good Manners], Ch.: "Gentleness," 21:1216 §3687. Ibn Ḥibbān in *al-Ṣaḥīḥ*, 2:308 §598.
39. Aḥmad b. Ḥanbal in *al-Musnad*, 2:160 §6494; •al-Tirmidhī in *al-Sunan:* Bk.: *al-Birr wa al-ṣila ʿan Rasūl Allāh* ﷺ [Piety and Keeping of Family Ties as Taught by Allāh's Messenger ﷺ], Ch.: "Having Mercy Towards People," 4:323 §1924.
40. Ibn Abī Shayba in *al-Muṣannaf*, 5:214 §25355.
41. al-Ḥākim in *al-Mustadrak*, 4:175 §7274.
42. Abū Dāwūd in *al-Sunan:* Bk.: *al-Adab* [Good Manners], Ch.: "Mercy," 4:285 §4941.
43. Ibn Abī Shayba in *al-Muṣannaf*, 5:214 §25355.
44. al-Bayhaqī in *al-Sunan al-kubrā*, 9:41 §17683, and in *Shuʿab al-īmān*, 7:476 §11048.
45. Ibn Qudāma in *Ithbāt ṣifat al-ʿuluww*, 1:45.
46. al-Daylamī in *Musnad al-Firdaws*, 2:288 §3328.
47. al-Mundhirī in *al-Targhīb wa al-tarhīb*, 3:140 §3412.
48. Muslim in *al-Ṣaḥīḥ:* Bk.: *al-Musāqa* [Watering], Ch.: "The Virtue of Giving Time for Someone Who Is Unable to Pay His Debt," 3:1194 §1560.
49. Aḥmad b. Ḥanbal in *al-Musnad*, 2:361 §8715.
50. al-Nasā'ī in *al-Sunan:* Bk.: *al-Buyūʿ* [Trade], Ch.: "Fair Dealings With People and Gentleness in Asking for One's Rights," 7:318 §4694, and in *al-Sunan al-kubrā*, 4:60 §6293.
51. al-Dārimī in *al-Sunan*, 2:324 §2546.
52. Aḥmad b. Ḥanbal in *al-Musnad*, 2:286 §7834.
53. Abū Dāwūd in *al-Sunan:* Bk.: *al-Adab* [Good Manners], Ch.: "Removing Harmful Things from the Pathway," 4:362 §5245.
54. Ibn Ḥibbān in *al-Ṣaḥīḥ*, 2:297 §540.
55. al-Ṭabarānī in *al-Muʿjam al-awsaṭ*, 3:276 §3133.

56. al-Daylamī in *Musnad al-Firdaws*, 3:99 §4276.
57. al-Bukhārī in *al-Ṣaḥīḥ:* Bk.: *al-Dhabā'iḥ wa al-ṣayd* [The Slaughtered Animals and Game], Ch.: "The Offensiveness of Cutting Parts of Living Animals or Seizing Them for Targeting," 5:2100 §5197.
58. Aḥmad b. Ḥanbal in *al-Musnad*, 4:307 §§18762, 18764.
59. Ibn Abī Shayba in *al-Muṣannaf*, 4:481 §22321.
60. Ibn al-Ja'd in *al-Musnad*, 1:85 §476.
61. Ibn Abī 'Āṣim in *al-Āḥād wa al-mathānī*, 4:137 §2117.
62. al-Ṭabarānī in *al-Mu'jam al-kabīr*, 4:124 §3872.
63. Muslim in *al-Ṣaḥīḥ:* Bk.: *al- udūd* [Prescribed Punishments], Ch.: "Concerning the One Who Confesses to Adultery," 3:1321–1322 §1690.
64. al-Nasā'ī in *al-Sunan al-kubrā*, 4:286 §7163.
65. al-Dāraquṭnī in *al-Sunan*, 3:91 §49.
66. Abū 'Awāna in *al-Musnad*, 4:134–135 §6292.
67. al-Ṭabarānī in *al-Mu'jam al-awsaṭ*, 5:118 §4843.
68. al-Bayhaqī in *al-Sunan al-kubrā*, 6:83 §11231.
69. Muslim in *al-Ṣaḥīḥ:* Bk.: *al- udūd* [Prescribed Punishments], Ch.: "Confessing One's Adultery," 3:1324 §1696.
70. al-Dārimī in *al-Sunan*, 2:235§2325.
71. al-Ṭabarānī in *al-Mu'jam al-awsaṭ*, 5:117 §4843.
72. al-Mizzī in *Tahdhīb al-kamāl*, 34:325 §7654.
73. al-Shawkānī in *Nayl al-awṭār*, 7:280.
74. Ibn Ḥazm in *al-Muḥallā*, 11:127.

11. On Allah's Mercy for Animals, Birds and Other Creatures

Essential Reading:

1. Dr Tahir-ul-Qadri, Islam on Mercy and Compassion, Ch:11, pp.181-192.

Additional Readings for Teachers and Students:

1. al-Bukhārī in *al-Ṣaḥīḥ*: Bk.: *Bad'u al-khalq* [On the Beginning of Creation], Ch.: "There are Five Injurious Animals that may be Killed in the Sacred Precint," 2:1205 §3140.

2. Ibn Mājah in *al-Sunan:* Bk.: *al-Zuhd* [The Renunciation], Ch.: "On Repentance," 2:1421 §4256.
3. ʿAbd al-Razzāq in *al-Muṣannaf*, 11:284 §20549.
4. Muslim in *al-Ṣaḥīḥ:* Bk.: *al-Birr wa al-ṣila wa al-Adab* [Piety, Familial Integration and Good Manners], Ch.: "The Unlawfulness of Tormenting Cats and other Non-injurious Animals," 4:2110 §2619.
5. al-Bukhārī in *al-Ṣaḥīḥ:* Bk.: *al-Musāqāt* [The Watering], chapter, "The Virtue of Providing Water," 2:833 §2234, and in Bk.: *al-Maẓālim wa al-ghaṣb* [On Oppression and Wrongful Seizure of Land], chapter, "Allowing Wells on Pathways as long as They Do not Cause Inconveniance," 2:870 §2334.
6. Abū Dāwūd in *al-Sunan:* Bk.: *al-Jihād* [The Striving], chapter, "The Commands Pertaining to the Riding of Animals and Beasts of Burden," 2:28 §2550.
7. Mālik in *al-Muwaṭṭā*ʾ, 2:929 §1661.
8. Muslim in *al-Ṣaḥīḥ:* Bk.: *al-Salām* [The Salutations], chapter, "On Giving Food and Water to Honoured Animals," 4:1761 §2244.
9. Aḥmad b. Ḥanbal in *al-Musnad*, 2:375, 517, 521 §§§8861, 10710, 10762.
10. Abū Dāwūd in *al-Sunan:* Bk.: *al-Jihād* [The Striving], chapter, "The Commands Pertaining to the Riding of Animals and Beasts of Burden," 2:28 §2550.
11. Ibn ibbān in *al-Ṣaḥīḥ*, 4:185 §7595.
12. al-Nawawī in *Sharḥ Ṣaḥīḥ Muslim*, 14:242.
13. Muslim in *al-Ṣaḥīḥ:* Bk.: *al-Salām* [The Salutations], chapter, "On Giving Food and Water to Honoured Animals," 4:1761 §2245.
14. Aḥmad b. Ḥanbal in *al-Musnad*, 2:507 §10591.
15. Abū Yaʿlā in *al-Musnad*, 10:423 §6035.
16. Ibn ibbān in *al-Ṣaḥīḥ*, 2:110 §386.
17. al-Ṭabarānī in *al-Muʿjam al-kabīr*, 8:234 §7915.
18. al-Bayhaqī in *Shuʿab al-īmān*, 7:482 §11070.
19. al-Bukhārī in *al-Adab al-mufrad*, 1:138 §181.
20. al-Bukhārī in *al-Ṣaḥīḥ:* Bk.: *al-Dhabāʾiḥ wa al-Ṣayd* [Slaughtering and Hunting], chapter, "The prohibition of mutilation of live animals," 5:2100 §5196.
21. al-Nasāʾī in *al-Sunan:* Bk.: *al-Ḍaḥāyā* [Slaughtering], chapter, "The prohibition setting up animals in a cage as a target," 7:238 §4442.
22. al-Dārimī in *al-Sunan*, 2:113 §1973.
23. Ibn ibbān in *al-Ṣaḥīḥ*, 12:434 §5617.
24. Aḥmad b. Ḥanbal in *al-Musnad*, 2:13 §4622.
25. al-Dārimī in *al-Sunan*, 2:113 §1973.
26. al- ākim in *al-Mustadrak*, 4:261 §7575.
27. Abū Nuʿaym in *ilya al-Awliyā*ʾ, 4:296.
28. al-Bukhārī in *al-Ṣaḥīḥ:* Bk.: *al-Dhabāʾiḥ wa al-ṣayd* [Sacrificial Animals

and Game], Ch.: "The Offensiveness of Cutting Parts of Living Animals or Seizing Them for Targeting," 5:2100 §5194.

29. Aḥmad b. Ḥanbal in *al-Musnad*, 3:171 §12769.
30. Abū Dāwūd in *al-Sunan:* Bk.: *al-Ḍaḥāyā* [Sacrificial Animals], Ch.: "The Prohibition of Seizing Animals for Targeting and the Order to Slaughter Gently," 3:100 §2816.
31. al-Bayhaqī in *al-Sunan al-kubrā*, 9:86 §17908.
32. al-Bukhārī in *al-Ṣaḥīḥ:* Bk.: *al-Dhabā'iḥ wa al-ṣayd* [Slaughtered Animals and Game], Ch.: "The Offensiveness of Cutting Parts of Living Animals and Seizing Animals for Targeting," 5:2100 §5195.
33. Aḥmad b. Ḥanbal in *al-Musnad*, 2:94 §5682.
34. Abū ʿAwāna in *al-Musnad*, 5:53 §7765.
35. al-Bayhaqī in *al-Sunan al-kubrā*, 9:334 §19268.
36. al-Bukhārī in *al-Ṣaḥīḥ:* Bk.: *al-Dhabā'iḥ wa al-ṣayd* [The Slaughtered Animals and Game], Ch.: "The Offensiveness of Cutting Parts of Living Animals or Seizing Animals for Targeting," 5:2100 §5196.
37. Ibn al-Sarāyā in *Silāḥ al-mu'min fī al-duʿā'*, 1:229 §412.
38. al-Ḥusaynī in *al-Bayān wa al-taʿrīf*, 2:162 §1367.
39. al-ʿAsqalānī in *al-Wuqūf ʿalā al-mawqūf*, 1:105 §134.
40. Muslim in *al-Ṣaḥīḥ:* Bk.: *al-Ṣayd wa al-dhabā'iḥ wa mā yu'kalu min al-ḥayawān* [The Hunting, Slaughter and what may be Eaten of the Animals], Ch.: "The Forbiddance of Tying the Animal and Making it a Target of Arrows," 3:1550 §1958.
41. al-Tirmidhī in *al-Sunan:* Bk.: *al-Ṣayd* [The Hunting], Ch.: "What has Come to Us about the Offensiveness of Eating the Animal Killed after Trapping," 4:72 §1475.
42. al-Nasā'ī in *al-Sunan*: Bk.: *al-Ḍaḥāyā* [The Sacrifices], Ch.: "The Prohibition of Eating the Animal Used as a Target," 7:239 §4444.
43. Abū Dāwūd in *al-Sunan:* Bk.: *al-Jihād* [Striving], Ch.: " The Offensiveness of Burning the Enemy with Fire," 3:55 §2675, and in Bk.: *al-Adab* [Good Manners], Ch.: "Killing Small Ants," 4:367 §5268.
44. al-Dhahabī in *al-Kabā'ir*, 1:206.
45. al-Zaylaʿī in *Naṣb al-rāya*, 3:407.
46. al-Nawawī in *Riyāḍ al-ṣāliḥīn*, 367 §367.
47. al-Ḥākim in *al-Mustadrak:* Bk.: *al-Dhabā'iḥ* [Slaughtered Animals], Ch.: "4:267 §7599.
48. al-Bayhaqī in *Dalā'il al-nubuwwa*, 1:321.
49. al-Hannād in *al-Zuhd*, 2:620 §1337.
50. al-Jazarī in *al-Nihāya*, 4:121.
51. Aḥmad b. Ḥanbal in *al-Musnad*, 1:396 §3763.
52. al-Ṭayālisī in *al-Musnad*, 1:46 §345.
53. al-Fākihī in *Akhbār Makka*, 5:141.
54. al-Haythamī in *Majmaʿ al-zawā'id*, 4:41.

SECTION V

The Supreme Jihad

(Peacemaking through the Supreme Jihad)

1. Jihad and its Kinds

Essential Reading:

1. Dr Tahir-ul-Qadri, The Supreme Jihad, Ch:1, pp.6-19.

Additional Readings for Teachers and Students:

1. al-Samʿānī, *al-Tafsīr al-Qurʾān*, 3:457.
2. Ibn al-Jawzī, *Zād al-masīr*, 3:443.
3. al-Rāzī, *al-Tafsīr al-kabīr*, 11:9.
4. Aḥmad b. Ghunaym al-Nafrāwī (d. 1126 AH), *al-Fawākih al-Dawānī*, 2:879.
5. Ibn al- ājj al-Mālikī, *al-Madkhal*, 3:2.
6. ibid., 3:66–67.
7. al-Dhahabī, *al-Muntaqā min minhāj al-iʿtidāl*, 1:512.
8. Ibn al-Qayyim, *Zād al-maʿād*, 3:571.
9. Ibn ajar al-ʿAsqalānī, *Fatḥ al-Bārī*, 6:3.

2. *Jihād bi'n-Nafs*—Struggle against Self [A Spiritual Dimension]

Essential Reading:

1. Dr Tahir-ul-Qadri, The Supreme Jihad, Ch:2, pp.21.

2.1 The Real Striver Strives against the Lower Self

Essential Reading:

1. Dr Tahir-ul-Qadri, The Supreme Jihad, Ch:2, pp.21-35.

Additional Readings for Teachers and Students:

1. Aḥmad b. anbal in *al-Musnad*, 6:20 §23996.
2. al-Tirmidhī in *al-Sunan*, 4:165 §1621.
3. al-Bazzār in *al-Musnad*, 2:156 §3753.
4. al- ākim in *al-Mustadrak*, 2:156 §2637.
5. Ibn ibbān in *al-Ṣaḥīḥ*, 10:484 §4624.
6. al-Ṭabarānī in *al-Muʿjam al-kabīr*, 18:256 §641.
7. Abū ʿAwāna in *al-Musnad*, 4:496 §7463.
8. al-Bayhaqī in *al-Zuhd al-kabīr*, p. 163 §369.
9. Ibn Rajab al- anbalī in *Jāmiʿ al-ʿulūm wa al-ḥikam*, p. 196.
10. Ibn Baṭṭāl, *Sharḥ Ṣaḥīḥ al-Bukhārī*, 10:210–211.
11. al-Ṭayālisī in *al-Musnad*, p. 300 §2277.
12. al-Bayhaqī in *al-Zuhd al-kabīr*, 162–163 §368.
13. Ibn Rajab al- anbalī in *Jāmiʿ al-ʿulūm wa al-ḥikam*, p. 196, and also in *Sharḥ ḥadīth Labbayk*, p. 128.
14. al-Mizzī in *Tahdhīb al-kamāl*, 7:426.
15. Ibn ajar al-ʿAsqalānī in *al-Maṭālib al-ʿālīya*, 9:238 §1928.
16. Ibn Baṭṭāl, *Sharḥ Ṣaḥīḥ al-Bukhārī*, 10:210.

17. al-Ghazālī in *Iḥyāʾ ʿulūm al-Dīn*, 3:66.
18. Ibn Rajab al- anbalī in *Jāmiʿ al-ʿulūm wa al-ḥikam*, p. 196.
19. al-Rāghib al-Aṣfahānī in *Muḥāḍarāt al-udabāʾ wa muḥāwarāt al-shuʿarāʾ wa al-bulaghāʾ*, 1:613.
20. Ibn Baṭṭāl, *Sharḥ Ṣaḥīḥ al-Bukhārī*, 10:210.
21. al-ʿAynī, *ʿUmda al-qārī sharḥ Ṣaḥīḥ al-Bukhārī*, 23:87.
22. Ibn ajar al-ʿAsqalānī, *Fatḥ al-Bārī*, 11:338.
23. al-Bukhārī in *al-Ṣaḥīḥ*, 5:2267 §5763.
24. Muslim in *al-Ṣaḥīḥ*, 4:2014 §2609.
25. Aḥmad b. anbal in *al-Musnad*, 1:382 §3626.
26. Abū Dāwūd in *al-Sunan*, 4:248 §4779.
27. Ibn ibbān in *al-Ṣaḥīḥ*, 7:214 §2950.
28. Ibn Abī Shayba in *al-Muṣannaf*, 5:216 §25378.
29. Abū Yaʿlā in *al-Musnad*, 9:96 §5162.
30. al-Bayhaqī in *al-Sunan al-kubrā*, 4:68 §6937 & 10:235 §20874.
31. al-Bukhārī in *al-Ṣaḥīḥ*, 5:2267 §5763.
32. Aḥmad b. anbal in *al-Musnad*, 2:236, 268, 517 §7218, 7628, 10713.
33. al-Nasāʾī in *al-Sunan al-kubrā*, 6:105 §10226, 10228.
34. Mālik in *al-Muwaṭṭā*, 2:906 §1613.
35. ʿAbd al-Razzāq in *al-Muṣannaf*, 11:188 §20287.
36. al-Bayhaqī in *al-Sunan al-kubra*, 10:241 §20915.
37. al-Ṭabarānī in *Musnad al-shāmiyyīn*, 3:25 §1730, 4:184 §3066.
38. Abū Nuʿaym in *Ḥilya al-awliyāʾ wa ṭabaqāt al-aṣfiyāʾ*, 2:249.
39. al-Qazwīnī in *al-Tadwīn fī akhbār Qazwīn*, 3:133.
40. Ibn ʿAsākir in *Tārīkh Dimashq al-kabīr*, 48:429.
41. al-Suyūṭī in *Jamʿ al-jawāmiʿ* generally known as *al-Jāmiʿ al-kabīr*, 1:745 §137, 3807.
42. al-Hindī in *Kanz al-ʿummāl fī Sunan al-aqwāl wa al-afʿāl*, 4:185 §11265.
43. al-Albānī graded it sound in *Silsila al-aḥādīth al-ṣaḥīḥa*, 3:483 §1496.
44. Ibn al-Najjār as said by al-Suyūṭī in *Jāmiʿ al-aḥādīth*, 2:13–14 §3501.
45. al-Munāwī in *Fayḍ al-qadīr*, 2:31.
46. al-Albānī graded it sound in *Silsila al-aḥādīth al-ṣaḥīḥa*, 3:483 §1496.
47. al-Mullā ʿAlī al-Qārī, *Sharḥ Musnad Abī anīfa*, p. 371.
48. al- akīm al-Tirmidhī in *Nawādir al-uṣūl fī aḥādith al-rasūl* ﷺ, 2:234.
49. al-Marwazī in *Taʿẓīm qadr al-ṣalā*, 2:596 §634.
50. al-Ṭabarānī as said by al-Hindī in *Kanz al-ʿummāl*, 15:363 §43427.
51. al-Munāwī in *Fayḍ al-qadīr*, 2:49, and *al-Taysīr bi sharḥ al-Jāmiʿ al-ṣaghīr*, 1:188.
52. al-Baghawī, *Maʿālim al-tanzīl*, 3:475.
53. al-Samʿānī in *Tafsīr al-Qurʾān*, 4:194.
54. Ibn al-Jawzī, *Dhamm al-hawā*, p. 48 §50.
55. al-Daynawarī, *Mujālasa wa jawāhir al-ʿulūm*, p. 335 §1963.

56. Abū Nuʿaym in *Ḥilya al-awliyāʾ wa ṭabaqāt al-aṣfiyāʾ*, 9:283.
57. Ibn al-Jawzī in *Ṣifa al-ṣafwa*, 4:278.
58. Ibn ʿAsākir in *Tārīkh Dimashq al-kabīr*, 48:429.
59. Ibn al-Qayyim in *Zād al-maʿād*, 3:6
60. al-Ālūsī, *Rūḥ al-maʿānī fī Tafsīr al-Qurʾān al-ʿaẓīm wa al-sabʿ al-mathānī*, 17:209.

3. *Jihād bi'l ʿIlm*—Striving for Knowledge [Intellectual Dimension]

Essential Reading:

1. Dr Tahir-ul-Qadri, The Supreme Jihad, Ch:3, pp.37-42.

Additional Readings for Teachers and Students:

1. Ibn ʿAbd al-Barr in *Jāmiʿ bayān al-ʿilm wa faḍlihī*, 1:115 §202.
2. al-Daylamī in *Musnad al-firdaws*, 2:41 §2237.
3. al-Rabīʿ in *al-Musnad*, 1:30 §22.
4. al-Mundhirī in *al-Targhīb wa al-tarhīb*, 1:52 §107.
5. al- ājī al-Khalīfa in *Kashf al-ẓunūn*, 1:18.
6. al-Qanūjī in *Abjad al-ʿulūm*, 1:92.
7. Ibn Rajab al- anbalī in *Jāmiʿ al-ʿulūm wa al-ḥikam*, p. 235.
8. Ibn Saʿd in *al-Ṭabaqāt al-kubrā*, 2:22.
9. al-Qurṭubī, *al-Jāmiʿ li aḥkām al-Qurʾān*, 8:296.
10. Ibn Abī Yaʿla, *Ṭabqāt al- anābila*, 2:225.
11. al-Baghawī, *Maʿālim al-tanzīl*, 3:475.
12. Muhammad Aḥmad Ismāʿīl al-Muqaddam, *Tafsīr al-Qurʾān al-karīm*, 1:2.

4. *JIHĀD BIʾL ʿAMAL*—STRIVING FOR PROMOTION OF MORALITY AND HUMAN VALUES [THE SOCIAL DIMENSION]

4.1 STRIVING AGAINST OPPRESSION AND INJUSTICE IS JIHAD

ESSENTIAL READING:

1. Dr Tahir-ul-Qadri, The Supreme Jihad, Ch:4, pp.43-49.

ADDITIONAL READINGS FOR TEACHERS AND STUDENTS:

1. Aḥmad b. anbal in *al-Musnad*, 4:315 §18850.
2. Abū Dāwūd in *al-Sunan*, 4:123 §4344.
3. al-Tirmidhī in *al-Sunan*, 4:471 §2174.
4. al-Nasāʾī in *al-Sunan*, 7:161 §4209.
5. Ibn Mājah in *al-Sunan*, 2:1329 §4011.
6. Aḥmad b. anbal in *al-Musnad*, 4:314 §18848.
7. al-Nasāʾī in *al-Sunan*, 7:161 §4209 and also in *al-Sunan al-kubra*, 4:435 §7834.
8. Ibn al-Jaʿd in *al-Musnad*, p. 480 §3326.
9. Ibn Mājah in *al-Sunan*, 2:1330 §4012.
10. al-Rūyānī in *al-Musnad*, 2:271 §1179.
11. al-Quḍāʿī in *Musnad al-Shihāb*, 2:248 §1288.
12. al-Ṭabarānī in *al-Muʿjam al-kabīr*, 8:282 §8081, and also in *al-Muʿjam al-awsaṭ*, 7:52 §6824.
13. al-Daylamī in *Musnad al-firdaws*, 1:357 §1438.
14. al-Khaṭīb al-Baghdādī in *al-Muttafaq wa al-muftaraq*, 3:1653 §1139.
15. al-Suyūṭī in *Jāmiʿ al-aḥādīth*, 2:14 §3504.
16. Ibn ʿAbd al-Barr in *al-Tamhīd limā fī al-Muwaṭṭāʾ min al-maʿānī wa al-asānīd*, 8:390.

4.2 Striving for Promotion of Moral Values is Jihad

Essential Reading:

1. Dr Tahir-ul-Qadri, The Supreme Jihad, Ch:4, pp.49-50.

Additional Readings for Teachers and Students:

1. al-Thaʿlabī in *al-Kashf wa al-bayān ʿan tafsīr al-Qurʾān*, 3:123.
2. al-Rāzī in *al-Tafsīr al-kabīr*, 8:147.
3. Abū Saʿūd in *Irshād al-ʿaql al-salīm ilā mazāyā al-Qurʾān al-karīm*, 2:68.
4. al-Nasafī in *Madārik al-tanzīl wa ḥaqāʾiq al-taʾwīl*, 1:171.
5. al-Zamakhsharī in *al-Kashshāf ʿan ḥaqāʾiq ghawāmiḍ al-tanzīl*, 1:425.
6. al-Rifāʿī in *al-Burhān al-muʾayyid*, 1:103.

4.3 Serving the Parents is Jihad

Essential Reading:

1. Dr Tahir-ul-Qadri, The Supreme Jihad, Ch:4, pp.50-52.

Additional Readings for Teachers and Students:

1. al-Bukhārī in *al-Ṣaḥīḥ*, 5:2227 §5627.
2. Muslim in *al-Ṣaḥīḥ*, 4:1975 §2549.
3. Abū Dāwūd in *al-Sunan*, 3:17 §2528–2529.
4. al-Nasāʾī in *al-Sunan*, 7:143 §4163.
5. al-Nasāʾī in *al-Sunan*, 6:11 §3104.
6. al-Ṭabarānī in *al-Muʿjam al-kabīr*, 2:289 §2202.
7. al-Mundhirī in *al-Targhīb wa al-Tarhīb*, 3:216 §3750.
8. al-Haythamī in *Majmaʿ al-zawāʾid*, 8:138.

4.4 Striving for Allah's Remembrance and Worship is Jihad

Essential Reading:

1. Dr Tahir-ul-Qadri, The Supreme Jihad, Ch:4, pp.52-54.

Additional Readings for Teachers and Students:

1. al-Ṭabarānī in *Muʿjam al-kabīr*, 25:129 §313, and *al-Muʿjam al-awsaṭ*, 7:21 §6735.
2. Ibn Shāhīn in *al-Targhīb fī faḍāʾil al-aʿmāl wa thawāb dhālika*, 1:194 §163.
3. al-Mundhirī in *al-Targhīb wa al-tarhīb*, 2:257 §2311.
4. al-Haythamī in *Majmaʿ al-zawāʾid*, 4:217–218, & 10:75.
5. al-Baghawī in *Maʿālim al-tanzīl*, 3:475.
6. Ibn ʿAsākir in *Tārīkh Dimashq al-kabīr*, 48:429.

5. *Jihād biʾl Māl*—Striving to Resolve the Economic Deadlock of the Indigent [Economic Dimension]

Essential Reading:

1. Dr Tahir-ul-Qadri, The Supreme Jihad, Ch:5, pp.55-58.

Additional Readings for Teachers and Students:

1. Qurʾān 92:8–10.
2. Qurʾān 90:13–16.

5.1 Striving for Altruism and Alleviation of Poverty is Superior to Military Option

Essential Reading:

1. Dr Tahir-ul-Qadri, The Supreme Jihad, Ch:5, pp.58-60.

Additional Readings for Teachers and Students:

1. Qurʾān 9:41.
2. Qurʾān 49:15.
3. Qurʾān 4:95.
4. Qurʾān 61:11.
5. Muslim in *al-Ṣaḥīḥ*, 3:1503 §1888.
6. Aḥmad b. anbal in *al-Musnad*, 3:16 §11141.
7. Ibn ibbān in *al-Ṣaḥīḥ*, 2:369 §606.
8. al-Ṭabarānī in *Musnad al-shāmiyyīn*, 3:54 §1793.

5.2 Striving for Social Welfare and Altruism

Essential Reading:

1. Dr Tahir-ul-Qadri, The Supreme Jihad, Ch:5, pp.60-64.

Additional Readings for Teachers and Students:

1. al-Bukhārī in *al-Ṣaḥīḥ*, 5:2047 §5038, & 5:2237 §5660.
2. Muslim in *al-Ṣaḥīḥ*, 4:2286 §2982.
3. Aḥmad b. Ḥanbal in *al-Musnad*, 2:361 §8717.
4. al-Tirmidhī in *al-Sunan*, 4:346 §1969.
5. al-Nasāʾī in *al-Sunan*, 5:86 §2577.
6. Ibn Mājah in *al-Sunan*, 2:724.

7. Ibn Mājah in *al-Sunan*, 2:1213 §3680.
8. al-Daylamī in *Musnad al-firdaws*, 3:489 §5520.
9. al-Mundhirī in *al-Targhīb wa al-tarhīb*, 3:235 §3834.
10. al-Tirmidhī in *al-Sunan*, 4:339 §1956.
11. al-Bazzār in *al-Musnad*, 9:457 §4070.
12. Ibn ibbān in *al-Ṣaḥīḥ*, 2:286 §529.
13. al-Bukhārī in *al-Adab al-mufrad*, 1:307 §891.
14. al-Ṭabarānī in *al-Muʿjam al-awsaṭ*, 8:183 §8342.
15. Ibn Rajab al- anbalī in *Jāmiʿ al-ʿulūm wa al-ḥikam*, 1:235.
16. Aḥmad b. anbal in *al Musnad*, 5:168 §21522.
17. al-Nasāʾī in *al-Sunan al-kubra*, 5:325 §9027.
18. Ibn ibbān in *al-Ṣaḥīḥ*, 8:171 §3377.
19. al-Bayhaqī in *Shuʿab al-īmān*, 6:106 §7618.
20. al-Mundhirī in *al-Targhīb wa al-tarhīb*, 3:377 §4503.
21. al-Haythamī in *Mawārid al-ẓamʾān*, 1:219 §862.
22. al-Daylamī in *Musnad al-firdaws*, 2:124 §2646.
23. al-Suyūṭī in *Jamʿ al-jawāmiʿ* generally known as *al-Jāmiʿ al-kabīr*, 3:615 §21:10424.
24. al-Hindī in *Kanz al-ʿummāl fī sunan al-aqwāl wa al-afʿāl*, 6:200 §16585.
25. Ismāʿīl al- aqqī in *Tafsīr rūḥ al-bayān*, 1:173.

6. The Reward of a Reviver of a Sunna is equal to that of 100 Martyrs

Essential Reading:

1. Dr Tahir-ul-Qadri, The Supreme Jihad, Ch:6, pp.65-69.

Additional Readings for Teachers and Students:

1. Abū Nuʿaym in *ilya al-awliyāʾ*, 8:200.
2. al-Suyūṭī in *Miftāḥ al-janna*, 1:13.
3. Abū Nuʿaym in *ilya al-awliyāʾ*, 8:200.
4. al-Bayhaqī in *al-Zuhd al-kabīr*, 2:118 §207.
5. al-Daylamī in *Musnad al-firdaws*, 4:198 §6608.
6. al-Mundhirī in *al-Targhīb wa al-tarhīb*, 1:41 §65.

7. al-Mizzī in *Tahdhīb al-kamāl*, 24:364.
8. Ibn ʿAdī on the authority of Ibn ʿAbbās ﷺ in *al-Kāmil*, 2:327 §460.
9. al-Dhahabī in *Mīzān al-iʿtidāl*, 2:270.
10. al-Baghawī in *Maʿālim al-tanzīl*, 3:375.

7. Pilgrimage to the House of Allah is Jihad

Essential Reading:

1. Dr Tahir-ul-Qadri, The Supreme Jihad, Ch:7, pp.69-75.

Additional Readings for Teachers and Students:

1. al-Bukhārī in *al-Ṣaḥīḥ*, 2:553 §1448, & 3:1026 §2632.
2. Abū Yaʿlā in *al-Musnad*, 8:166 §4717.
3. al-Bayhaqī in *al-Sunan al-kubrā*, 9:21 §17583.
4. Aḥmad b. anbal in *al-Musnad*, 6:294, 303, 314 §26563, 26627, 26716.
5. Ibn Mājah in *al-Sunan*, 2:968 §2902.
6. Ibn Abī Shayba in *al-Muṣannaf*, 3:122 §12656.
7. Abū Yaʿlā in *al-Musnad*, 12:347, 458 §6916, 7029.
8. Ibn al-Jaʿd in *al-Musnad*, p. 486 §3380.
9. al-Ṭabarānī in *al-Muʿjam al-kabīr*, 23:292 §647.
10. Ibn Mājah in *al-Sunan*, 2:995 §2989.
11. al-Ṭabarānī in *al-Muʿjam al-awsaṭ*, 7:171 §6723.
12. al-Nasāʾī in *al-Sunan*, 5:113 §2626.
13. al-Maqdisī in *al-Furūʿ*, 1:417.
14. Abū ʿAbd Allāh al-Maghribī in *Mawāhib al-jalīl*, 2:480.
15. al-Haythamī in *Majmaʿ al-zawāʾid*, 3:206.
16. al-ʿAynī in *ʿUmda al-qārī*, 9:134.
17. al-Suyūṭī in *Jāmiʿ al-aḥādīth*, 4:200 §11069.
18. al-Hindī in *Kanz al-ʿummāl fī sunan al-aqwāl wa al-afʿāl*, 5:7 §11845.

8. ALLAH'S REMEMBRANCE SURPASSES FIGHTING FOR THE CAUSE OF ALLAH

ESSENTIAL READING:

1. Dr Tahir-ul-Qadri, The Supreme Jihad, Ch:8, pp.77.

ADDITIONAL READINGS FOR TEACHERS AND STUDENTS:

1. Aḥmad b. anbal in *al-Musnad*, 3:438 §15699.
2. al-Ṭabarānī in *al-Muʿjam al-kabīr*, 20:186 §407.
3. al-Mundhirī in *al-Targhīb wa al-tarhīb*, 2:257 §2309.
4. al-Haythamī in *Majmaʿ al-zawāʾid*, 1:74.
5. Ibn Abī Shayba in *al-Muṣannaf*, 6:57 §29452, & 7:169 §35046.
6. ʿAbd b. umayd in *al-Musnad*, 1:73 §127.
7. Ibn ʿAbd al-Barr in *al-Tamhīd*, 6:57.
8. al-Bayhaqī in *Shuʿab al-īmān*, 1:396 §522.
9. al-Mundhirī in *al-Targhīb wa al-tarhīb*, 2:254 §2295.
10. Ibn al-Qayyim in *al-Wabil al-ṣayyib*, 1:60.
11. al-Munāwī in *Fayḍ al-qadīr*, 2:511.
12. al-Bayhaqī in *Shuʿab al-īmān*, 1:395 §521.
13. Ibn Abī Shayba in *al-Muṣannaf*, 6:58 §29456, & 7:170 §35047.
14. Ibn al-Mubārak in *al-Zuhd*, 1:394 §1116.
15. Ibn ʿAbd al-Barr in *al-Tamhīd*, 6:59.
16. al-Daylamī in *Musnad al-firdaws*, 3:454 §5402.
17. Ibn Abī Shayba in *al-Muṣannaf*, 6:58 §29462, & 7:170 §35056.
18. al-Suyūṭī in *al-Durr al-manthūr fī tafsīr bi al-māthūr*, 1:150.
19. Ibn Abī ʿĀṣim in *al-Zuhd*, 1:184.
20. Abū Nuʿaym in *ilya al-awliyāʾ wa ṭabaqāt al-aṣfiyāʾ*, 1:235.
21. Ibn ʿAbd al-Barr in *al-Tamhīd*, 6:57.
22. al-Dhahabī in *Siyar aʿlām al-nubalāʾ*, 1:455.
23. Ibn Abī Shayba in *al-Muṣannaf*, 6:134 §30089.

SECTION VI

MUHAMMAD ﷺ: THE MERCIFUL

1. THE HOLY PROPHET ﷺ IS MERCY INCARNATE

1.1 THERE IS NO OTHER PROPHET THAT COMES CLOSE TO THE PROPHET ﷺ IN MERCY

ESSENTIAL READING:

1. Dr Tahir-ul-Qadri, Muhammad ﷺ: The Merciful, Ch:1, p.5-15.

ADDITIONAL READINGS FOR TEACHERS AND STUDENTS:

1. al-Bukhārī in *al-Ṣaḥīḥ:* Bk.: *Bada' al-khalq* [The Beginning of Creation], Ch.: "When One of You Says *Āmīn* along with the Angels, and the Two Coincide, His Past Sins Are Forgiven," 3:1180 §3059.
2. Muslim in *al-Ṣaḥīḥ:* Bk.: *al-Jihād* [The Striving], Ch.: "On the Harm That the Prophet ﷺ Experienced from the Pagans and Hypocrites," 3:1420 §1795.
3. Qur'ān 9:114.
4. al-Bukhārī in *al-Ṣaḥīḥ:* Bk.: *Aḥādīth al-anbiyā'* [The Traditions of the Prophets], Ch.: "On Allah's Statement, ﴾*And Allah took Ibrāhīm as an intimate friend*﴿," 3:1223 §3172.
5. Qur'ān 2:126.
6. Ibid., 5:25–26.

7. al-Bukhārī in *al-Ṣaḥīḥ:* Bk.: *al-Janā'iz* [The Funerals], Ch.: "The Offensiveness of Prayers and Supplications of Forgiveness for the Hypocrites," 1:459 §1300.
8. Qur'ān 5:116–117.
9. Ibid., 5:78.
10. Ibid., 14:36.
11. Ibid., 5:118.
12. Muslim in *al-Ṣaḥīḥ:* Bk.: *al-Īmān* [The Faith], Ch.: "On the Prophet's Supplication for His Nation ﷺ," 1:191 §202.
13. Muslim in *al-Ṣaḥīḥ:* Bk.: *al-Birr wa ṣila wa al-adab* [On Piety, Familial Integration, and Good Manners], Ch.: "The Prohibition of Invoking Curses Against Creatures and Other Things," 4:2006 §2599.
14. al-Bukhārī in *al-Adab al-mufrad*, 119 §321.
15. Abū Ya'lā in *al-Musnad*, 11:35 §6174.
16. Abū Nu'aym in *Dalā'il al-nubuwwa*, 1:40 §2.
17. al-Bayhaqī in *Shu'ab al-īmān*, 2:144 §1403.
18. Ibn 'Asākir in *Tārīkh Dimashq*, 4:92.
19. Ibn Kathīr in *Tafsīr al-Qur'ān al-'Aẓīm*, 3:202.
20. al-Bukhārī in *al-Ṣaḥīḥ:* Bk.: *al-Anbiyā'* [On the Prophets], Ch.: "The Hadith About the Cave," 3:1282 §3290.
21. Muslim in *al-Ṣaḥīḥ:* Bk.: *al-Jihād wa al-siyar* [The Striving and Military Expeditions], Ch.: "On the Battle of Uḥud," 3:1417 §1792.
22. Aḥmad b. anbal in *al-Musnad*, 1:453 §4331.
23. Ibn Mājah in *al-Sunan:* Bk.: *al-Fitan* [On Tribulations], Ch.: "Patience with Affliction," 2:1335 §4025.
24. Abū Ya'lā in *al-Musnad*, 9:131 §5205.
25. al-Bazzār in *al-Musnad*, 5:106–107 §1686.
26. Ibid., Bk.: *al-Tafsīr* [The Qur'ānic Exegesis], Ch.: "On Sūrat al-Isrā': *﴿The progeny of those carried with Nūḥ﴾*," 4:1745–1746 §4435.
27. Muslim in *al-Ṣaḥīḥ:* Bk.: *al-Īmān* [The Faith], Ch.: "The Inhabitant of Paradise with the Lowest Rank," 1:180–185 §§193–194.
28. Ibid., Bk.: *al-Tawḥīd* [The Divine Unity], Ch.: "Allah's Speech to the Prophets and Others on the Day of Judgment," 6:2727 §7072.
29. Muslim in *al-Ṣaḥīḥ:* Bk.: *al-Īmān* [The Faith], Ch.: "," 1:183 §193.

1.2 ALLAH MADE THE PROPHET ﷺ MERCY FOR THE WORLDS

ESSENTIAL READING:

1. Dr Tahir-ul-Qadri, Muhammad ﷺ: The Merciful, Ch:1, p.15-16.

1.3 ALLAH HAS MADE HIM ﷺ THE PROPHET OF MERCY

ESSENTIAL READING:

1. Dr Tahir-ul-Qadri, Muhammad ﷺ: The Merciful, Ch:1, p.16.

1.4 ALLAH SENT THE PROPHET ﷺ AS MERCY

ESSENTIAL READING:

1. Dr Tahir-ul-Qadri, Muhammad ﷺ: The Merciful, Ch:1, p.16-17.

ADDITIONAL READINGS FOR TEACHERS AND STUDENTS:

1. Aḥmad b. anbal in *al-Musnad*, 5:268, 437 §22361, 23757.
2. Abū Dāwūd in *al-Sunan:* Bk.: *al-Sunna* [The Sunna], Ch.: "The Prohibition of Maligning the Companions of the Messenger of Allāh ﷺ," 4:215 §4659.
3. al-Ṭabarānī in *al-Muʿjam al-kabīr*, 8:196 §7803.
4. Abū Nuʿaym in *Dalāʾil al-nubuwwa*, 1:4 §1.
5. al-Mundhirī in *al-Targhīb wa al-tarhīb*, 3:181 §3583.
6. Ibn Rajab in *Jāmiʿ al-ʿulūm wa al-ḥikam*, 1:415.
7. al-Haythamī in *Majmaʿ al-zawāʾid*, 5:69.
8. al-Suyūṭī in *al-Durr al-manthūr*, 5:688.

1.5 ALLAH MADE THE PROPHET ﷺ MERCY GIFTED TO THE WORLDS

ESSENTIAL READING:

1. Dr Tahir-ul-Qadri, Muhammad ﷺ: The Merciful, Ch:1, p.17-18.

1.6 The Prophet's Mercy is from Allah's Mercy

Essential Reading:

1. Dr Tahir-ul-Qadri, Muhammad ﷺ: The Merciful, Ch:1, p.18.

1.7 Allah Made the Prophet ﷺ Mercy for the Believers

Essential Reading:

1. Dr Tahir-ul-Qadri, Muhammad ﷺ: The Merciful, Ch:1, p.18-19.

1.8 Allah Made the Prophet ﷺ Clement and Compassionate to the Believers

Essential Reading:

1. Dr Tahir-ul-Qadri, Muhammad ﷺ: The Merciful, Ch:1, p.19-20.

Additional Readings for Teachers and Students:

1. al-Bukhārī in *al-Ṣaḥīḥ:* Bk.: *al-Adhān* [The *Adhān*], Ch.: "On the *Adhān* for the Traveler if There is a Congregation," 1:226 §605.
2. Muslim in *al-Ṣaḥīḥ:* Bk.: *al-Masājid* [The Mosques], Ch.: "Who has More Right to the Imamate," 1:564 §674.

1.9 The Prophet ﷺ is Nearer to the Believers than Their Own Selves

Essential Reading:

1. Dr Tahir-ul-Qadri, Muhammad ﷺ: The Merciful, Ch:1, p.20-21.

Additional Readings for Teachers and Students:

1. Muslim in *al-Ṣaḥīḥ:* Bk.: *al-Jumuʿa* [The Friday Prayer], Ch." "Shortening the Prayer and the Sermon," 2:592 §867.
2. Aḥmad b. anbal in *al-Musnad*, 3:310 §14373.
3. al-Nasāʾī in *al-Sunan:* Bk.: *Ṣalā al-ʿīdayn* [The Two Eid Prayers], Ch.: "On How the Sermon is Given," 3:188 §1578, also in *al-Sunan al-kubrā*, 1:550 §1786.
4. Ibn Mājah in the introduction to *al-Sunan*, Section, "Abstinence from Blameworthy Innovation and Argumentation," 1:17 §45.
5. Ibn ibbān in *al-Ṣaḥīḥ,* 1:186 §10.
6. al-Ṭabarānī in *al-Muʿjam al-awsaṭ*, 3:160 §9418, and in *al-Muʿjam al-kabīr*, 3:100 §8531.
7. Abū Yaʿlā in *al-Musnad*, 4:85, 90 §§2111, 2119.
8. al-Bayhaqī in *al-Sunan al-kubrā*, 3:206 §5544.
9. al-Bukhārī in *al-Ṣaḥīḥ:* Bk.: *al-Istiqrāḍ wa adāʾ al-duyūn wa al-ḥijr wa al-taflīs* [The Loans, Repayment of Debts, Rent, and Bankruptcy], Ch.: "Prayer Over One Who Leaves a Debt Behind," 2:845 §2269, and in Bk.: *al-Tafsīr* [The Qurʾānic Exegesis], Ch.: "﴿*The Prophet is closer to the believers than their own selves*﴾," 4:1795 §4503.
10. Muslim in *al-Ṣaḥīḥ:* Bk.: *al-Farāʾiḍ* [The Inheritance], Ch.: "Whoever Leaves Behind Wealth Then it is For His Heirs," 3:1238 §1619.
11. Aḥmad b. anbal in *al-Musnad*, 2:334 §8399.
12. ʿAbd al-Razzāq in *al-Muṣannaf*, 8:291 §15261.
13. Abū ʿAwāna in *al-Musnad*, 3:445 §5630.
14. al-Bayhaqī in *al-Sunan al-kubrā*, 6:238 §12148.
15. Ibn Kathīr in *Tafsīr al-Qurʾan al-ʿAẓīm*, 3:469.

1.10 The Prophet ﷺ is Nearer to the Other Prophets Than They are to Their Respective Communities

Essential Reading:

1. Dr Tahir-ul-Qadri, Muhammad ﷺ: The Merciful, Ch:1, p.22-23.

Additional Readings for Teachers and Students:

1. al-Bukhārī in *al-Ṣaḥīḥ:* Bk.: *Manāqib al-anṣār* [On the Exemplary Virtues of the Anṣār], Ch.: "The Jews' Visit to the Prophet ﷺ When He Arrived in Medina," 3:1244 §3215.
2. Muslim in *al-Ṣaḥīḥ:* Bk.: *al-Ṣiyām* [The Fasting], Ch.: "Fasting on the Day of ʿĀshūrāʾ," 2:795 §§1130.
3. ibid., Bk.: *Aḥādīth al-anbiyāʾ* [The Narrations of the Prophets], Ch.: "On Allah's Statement, ﴾*Mention in the Book, Maryam when she withdrew from her family*﴿," 3:1270 §3259.
4. Muslim in *al-Ṣaḥīḥ:* Bk.: *al-Faḍāʾil* [The Virtues], Ch.: "The Virtues of ʿĪsā b. Maryam ﷺ," 4:1837 §2365.

1.11 The Prophet's Quality of Humility

Essential Reading:

1. Dr Tahir-ul-Qadri, Muhammad ﷺ: The Merciful, Ch:1, p.23-24.

Additional Readings for Teachers and Students:

1. Qurʾān 26:214–215.

1.12 The Prophet ﷺ was Neither Stern nor Harsh

Essential Reading:

1. Dr Tahir-ul-Qadri, Muhammad ﷺ: The Merciful, Ch:1, p.23-24.

Additional Readings for Teachers and Students:

1. al-Bukhārī in *al-Ṣaḥīḥ:* Bk.: *al-Buyūʿ* [The Transactions], Ch.: "The Prohibition of Being Loud and Boisterous in the Marketplace," 2:747 §2018.
2. ibid, Bk.: *al-Tafsīr* [The Qurʾānic Exegesis], Ch.: "On the Verse ﴾*Certainly We have sent you as a witness, a giver of glad tidings, and a warner*﴿," 4:1831 §4558, and in *al-Adab al-mufrad*, 95 §246.
3. Aḥmad b. anbal in *al-Musnad*, 2:174 §6622.
4. al-Dārimī in *al-Sunan*, 1:16 §6.
5. Abū Nuʿaym in *ilya al-Awliyāʾ*, 5:387.
6. Ibn Saʿd in *al-Ṭabaqāt al-Kubrā*, 1:360–362.
7. al-Bayhaqī in *al-Sunan al-kubrā*, 7:45 §13079,
8. ibid., *Shuʿab al-īmān*, 2:137 §1410,
9. ibid., *al-Iʿtiqād*, 1:256.
10. al-Maqdisī in *al-Aḥādīth al-mukhtāra*, 9:460 §435.
11. al-Ṭabarī in *Jāmiʿ al-bayān*, 9:83.
12. Ibn Kathīr in *Tafsīr al-Qurʾān al-ʿAẓīm*, 2:254.

1.13 The Prophet's Avidity for the Believers' Welfare

Essential Reading:

1. Dr Tahir-ul-Qadri, Muhammad ﷺ: The Merciful, Ch:1, p.24-27.

Additional Readings for Teachers and Students:

1. Qurʾān 18:6.
2. Qurʾān 35:8.
3. Qurʾān 27:70.
4. Qurʾān 7:157.

1.14 The Prophet a Lightened the Burden upon His Community

Essential Reading:

1. Dr Tahir-ul-Qadri, Muhammad ﷺ: The Merciful, Ch:1, p.27-28.

Additional Readings for Teachers and Students:

1. Qur'ān 7:157.

1.15 Allah Made the Prophet ﷺ a Source of Peace and Protection for Humanity

Essential Reading:

1. Dr Tahir-ul-Qadri, Muhammad ﷺ: The Merciful, Ch:1, p.28-29.

Additional Readings for Teachers and Students:

1. Qur'ān 8:32.

1.16 The Prophet's Continued Supplication for His People in His Worldly Life and After His Passing

Essential Reading:

1. Dr Tahir-ul-Qadri, Muhammad ﷺ: The Merciful, Ch:1, p.30-31.

Additional Readings for Teachers and Students:

1. Muslim in *al-Ṣaḥīḥ*: Bk.: *al-Birr wa ṣila wa al-adab* [On Piety, Familial

Integration, and Good Manners], Ch.: "The Prohibition of Invoking Curses Against Creatures and Other Things," 4:2006 §2599.
2. al-Bukhārī in *al-Adab al-mufrad*, 119 §321.
3. Abū Yaʿlā in *al-Musnad*, 11:35 §6174.
4. Abū Nuʿaym in *Dalāʾil al-nubuwwa*, 1:40 §2.
5. al-Bayhaqī in *Shuʿab al-īmān*, 2:144 §1403.
6. Ibn ʿAsākir in *Tārīkh Dimashq*, 4:92.
7. Ibn Kathīr in *Tafsīr al-Qurʾān al-ʿAẓīm*, 3:202.
8. al-Bukhārī in *al-Ṣaḥīḥ:* Bk.: *al-Jihād wa al-siyar* [The Striving and Military Expeditions], Ch.: "On Praying for the Guidance of the Idolaters in order to Reconcile Their Hearts," 3:1073 §2779.
9. Muslim in *al-Ṣaḥīḥ*: Bk.: *Faḍāʾil al-ṣaḥāba* [The Virtues of the Companions], Ch.: "From the Virtues of Ghifār, Aslam, Juhayna, Ashjaʿ, Muzina, Daws, and Ṭayʾ," 4:1957 §2524.
10. al-Ṭabarānī in *al-Muʿjam al-kabīr*, 8:326 §8219; and in *Musnad al-Shāmiyyīn*, 4:296 §3352.

1.17 THE FACT THAT THE PROPHET ﷺ WAS A WARNER IMPLIES MERCY

ESSENTIAL READING:

1. Dr Tahir-ul-Qadri, Muhammad ﷺ: The Merciful, Ch:1, p.31-34.

ADDITIONAL READINGS FOR TEACHERS AND STUDENTS:

1. Qurʾān 5:19.
2. Qurʾān 33:45–46.
3. al-Bukhārī in *al-Ṣaḥīḥ:* Bk.: *al-Riqāq* [The Heart Softening Narrations], Ch.: "Eschewing Disobedience," 5:2379 §6118.
4. Muslim in *al-Ṣaḥīḥ:* Bk.: *al-Faḍāʾil* [The Exemplary Virtues], Ch.: "The Prophet's Kindness toward His *Umma*," 4:1788 §§2283.

1.18 THE RELATIONSHIP BETWEEN THE SPLITTING OPEN OF THE PROPHET'S CHEST AND MERCY

Essential Reading:

1. Dr Tahir-ul-Qadri, Muhammad ﷺ: The Merciful, Ch:1, p.34.

1.19 The Relationship between Mercy and Sublime Character

Essential Reading:

1. Dr Tahir-ul-Qadri, Muhammad ﷺ: The Merciful, Ch:1, p.34.

1.20 It is a Mercy of Allah that He Took the Soul of His Prophet ﷺ before His People

Essential Reading:

1. Dr Tahir-ul-Qadri, Muhammad ﷺ: The Merciful, Ch:1, p.35.

Additional Readings for Teachers and Students:

1. Qur'ān 5:19.
2. Qur'ān 33:45–46.

1.21 The Prophet's Mercy toward the Jinn

Essential Reading:

1. Dr Tahir-ul-Qadri, Muhammad ﷺ: The Merciful, Ch:1, p.35-40.

ADDITIONAL READINGS FOR TEACHERS AND STUDENTS:

1. Muslim in *al-Ṣaḥīḥ:* Bk.: *al-Ṣalāt* [The Prayer], Ch.: "Audible Recitation in the Morning Prayer and Recitation to the Jinn," 1:332 §450.
2. Muslim in *al-Ṣaḥīḥ:* Bk.: *al-Salām* [The Peace], Ch.: "On Killing Snakes," 4:1756 §2236.
3. Muslim in *al-Ṣaḥīḥ:* Bk.: *al-Salām* [The Peace], Ch.: "On Killing Snakes," 4:1756 §2236.
4. Muslim in *al-Ṣaḥīḥ:* Bk.: *al-Salām* [The Peace], Ch.: "On Killing Snakes," 4:1752 §2233.
5. al-Bukhārī in *al-Ṣaḥīḥ:* Bk.: *Badʾ al-khalq* [The Beginning of Creation], Ch.: "On Allah's Statement, ﴾*And spread among them every beast*﴿," 3:1201 §3123.
6. Muslim in *al-Ṣaḥīḥ*, 4:1752 §2223.
7. Qurʾān 2:255
8. al-Bukhārī in *al-Ṣaḥīḥ:* Bk.: *al-Wakāla* [The Authorization], Ch.: "If Someone Authorizes Another and the Authorized Person Hands Over Something Which the Authorizer Allows, it is Permissible," 2:812 §2187.

1.22 THE PROPHET ﷺ DID NOT INVOKE ALLAH TO DESTROY THE CONFEDERATES DURING THE BATTLE OF TRENCH

ESSENTIAL READING:

1. Dr Tahir-ul-Qadri, Muhammad ﷺ: The Merciful, Ch:1, p.40-41.

ADDITIONAL READINGS FOR TEACHERS AND STUDENTS:

1. Qurʾān 2:521.
2. al-Bayhaqī, *Dalāʾil al-nubuwwa* (3:459, 462–463, 465),
3. Ibn Kathīr, *al-Sīra* (3:273–277),
4. al-Qurṭubī, *al-Jāmiʿ li aḥkām al-Qurʾān*, 18:58.
5. Ibn Ḥajar al-ʿAsqalānī, *Fatḥ al-bārī*, 2:521.

1.23 Important Point

Essential Reading:

1. Dr Tahir-ul-Qadri, Muhammad ﷺ: The Merciful, Ch:1, p.41-42.

2. The Holy Prophet ﷺ is Mercy to All The Worlds

2.1 Benefits Extracted from the Qur'ānic Verse

Essential Reading:

1. Dr Tahir-ul-Qadri, Muhammad ﷺ: The Merciful, Ch:2, p.45-55.

Additional Readings for Teachers and Students:

1. Qur'ān 3:159.
2. Ibn Abī Ḥātim Rāzī, *Tafsīr Qur'ān al-ʿaẓīm*, 3:800.
3. Ibn Kathīr, *Tafsīr al-Qur'ān al-ʿaẓīm*, 2:148.
4. Fakhr al-Dīn al-Rāzī, *Mafātīḥ al-ghayb*, 22:199–200.
5. al-Māwardī, *al-Nukat wa al-ʿuyūn*, 3:475–476.
6. Ibn Jarīr al-Ṭabarī, *Jāmiʿ al-bayān fī tafsīr al-Qur'ān*, 17:106.
7. al-Baghawī, *Maʿālim al-tanzīl*, 3:271–272.
8. al-Biqāʿī, *Naẓam al-durar fī tanāsub al-āyāt wa al-suwar*, 5: 508–509.
9. Jalāl al-Dīn al-Suyūṭī, *al-Durr al-manthūr*, 5:687.
10. Ibn Jarīr al-Ṭabarī, *Jāmiʿ al-bayān*, 17:106.
11. al-Biqāʿī, *Naẓam al-Durar fī Tanāsub al-Āyāt wa al-Suwar*, 5:508–509.
12. Ibn Kathīr, *Tafsīr al-Qur'ān al-ʿaẓīm*, 3:201.
14. al-Nuḥās, *Iʿrāb al-Qur'ān al-karīm*, 2:386.
15. Qur'ān 42:16–24.
16. Ibn Hishām, *Awḍaḥ al-masālik ilā Alfiya Ibn Mālik* (3:29–40) for further details on the meanings of the *lām* and *bā'* governing particles.

He explains that each of them have twelve meanings.
17. *al-Mustadrak* (1:91 §100) who declared it authentic.
18. al-Fayrūzabādī, *Baṣāʾir dhawī al-tamyīz fī laṭāʾif al-kitāb al-ʿazīz*, 4:95
19. Qurʾān 3:159.
20. ibid., 21:108.
21. al-Bukhārī in *al-Ṣaḥīḥ:* Bk.: *al-ʿIlm* [The Knowledge], Ch.: "Whomever Allah Wishes Good For, He Gives Him Deep Knowledge of the Religion," 3:1134 §2948.
22. ibid., 3:1134 §2949.

3. The Holy Prophet ﷺ is Mercy for Everyone in This World

Essential Reading:

1. Dr Tahir-ul-Qadri, Muhammad ﷺ: The Merciful, Ch:3, p.57-94..

Additional Readings for Teachers and Students:

1. Qurʾān 9:128.
2. Muslim in *al-Ṣaḥīḥ, Kitab al-Fitan* [The Tribulations], Ch.: "The Internecine Warfare That Will Destroy This Nation," 4:2215 §2889.
3. ibid., 4:2216 §2890.
4. Muslim in *al-Ṣaḥīḥ:* Bk.: *Ṣalāt al-musāfirīn* [The Travelers' Prayer], Ch.: "The Qurʾān Was Revealed in Seven Modes," 1:561 §820.
5. al-Bukhārī in *al-Ṣaḥīḥ:* Bk.: *al-Daʿawāt* [The Supplications], Ch.: "Every Prophet had an Accepted Supplication," 5:2323 §5945.
6. Muslim in *al-Ṣaḥīḥ:* Bk.: *al-Daʿawāt* [The Supplications], Ch.: "The Prophet's Supplication for Intercession Saved for His Nation," 1:189 §199.
7. Muslim in *al-Ṣaḥīḥ:* Bk.: *al-Birr wa al-ṣila* [The Piety and Familial Integration], Ch.: "On Those Whom the Prophet ﷺ Spoke Ill of or Prayed against," 4:2008–2009 §2601.
8. Aḥmad in *al-Musnad*, 5:437.
9. Abū Dāwūd in *al-Sunan:* Bk.: *al-Sunna* [The Sunna], Ch.: "The Prohibition of Insulting the Companions of Allah's Messenger ﷺ," 2:626

§4659.

10. al-Ṭabarānī in *al-Muʿjam al-kabīr*, 6:259 §6156. See al-Nawawī, *Sharḥ Ṣaḥīḥ Muslim* (16:150–153) for a detailed commentary on the meaning of this hadith.
11. ibid., 9:128.
12. al-Bukhārī in *al-Ṣaḥīḥ:* Bk.: *al-Riqāq* [The Heart Softening Narrations], Ch.: "Eschewing Disobedience," 5:2379 §6118.
13. Muslim in *al-Ṣaḥīḥ:* Bk.: *al-Faḍāʾil* [The Exemplary Virtues], Ch.: "The Prophet's Kindness toward His *Umma*," 4:1789 §2284.
14. Qurʾān 7:157.
15. Muslim in *al-Ṣaḥīḥ:* Bk.: *al-Ṭahāra* [The Purification], Ch.: "On Cleaning One's Self," 1:223 §262.
16. Aḥmad b. Ḥanbal in *al-Musnad*, 5:153, 162.
17. Ibn Ḥibbān in *al-Ṣaḥīḥ*, 1:267 §65.
18. al-Ṭabarānī in *al-Muʿjam al-kabīr*, 2:155 §1647.
19. al-Ṭayālisī in *al-Musnad*, 65 §479.
20. Haythamī, *Kashf al-Astār ʿan Zawāʾid al-Bazzār*, 1:88 §147.
21. Abū Yaʿlā in *al-Musnad*, 9:46 §5109.
22. Haythamī, *al-Maqṣad al-ʿalī fī zawāʾid Abī Yaʿlā al-Mūṣilī*, 1:150–151.
23. Ibn Ḥajar al-ʿAsqalānī in *al-Maṭālib al-ʿāliya*, 15:630 §3846.
24. al-Haythamī in *Majmaʿ al-zawāʾid*, 8:263–264.
25. Aḥmad b. Ḥanbal in *al-Musnad*, 4:126, Ibn Mājah in *al-Sunan*, Introduction, 1:16 §43.
26. al-Ḥākim in *al-Mustadrak*, 1:175–176 §§331–332.
27. Qurʾān 33:6.
28. al-Bukhārī in *al-Ṣaḥīḥ:* Bk.: *al-Kafāla* [The Guarantees], Ch.: "On Debt," 2:805 §2176.
29. Muslim in *al-Ṣaḥīḥ:* Bk.: *al-Farāʾiḍ* [The Estate Division], Ch.: "Whoever Leaves Behind Wealth then it is For His Heirs," 3:1237 §1619.
30. al-Bukhārī in *al-Ṣaḥīḥ:* Bk.: *al-Istiqrāḍ* [The Loans], Ch.: "Prayer over a Person Who has Left Behind Debt,"2:845 §2269.
31. ibid., Bk.: *al-Jumuʿa* [The Friday Prayer], Ch.: "Using the Tooth Stick on Friday," 1:303 §847.
32. Muslim in *al-Ṣaḥīḥ:* Bk.: *al-Ṭahāra* [The Purification], Ch.: "On the Tooth Stick," 1:220 §252.
33. Muslim in *al-Ṣaḥīḥ:* Bk.: *al-Imāra* [The Leadership], Ch.: "The Virtue of Jihad and Expeditions in the Path of Allah," 3:1497 §1876.
34. al-Bukhārī in *al-Ṣaḥīḥ:* Bk.: *al-Adhān* [The *Adhān*], Ch.: "When There is a Wall or a Barrier between the Imam and the Congregation," 1:313 §882.
35. Muslim in *al-Ṣaḥīḥ:* Bk.: *Ṣalāt al-musāfirīn* [The Travelers' Prayer], Ch.: "The Encouragement to Pray During the Nights of Ramaḍān," 1:524 §761.

36. Muslim in *al-Ṣaḥīḥ:* Bk.: *al-Hajj* [The Hajj], Ch.: "The Obligation of Hajj Once in One's Life," 2:975 §1337.
37. Ibid., Bk.: *al-Imāra* [The Leadership], Ch.: "The Virtue of the Just Imam and the Punishment of the Oppressive Leader," 3:1458 §1828.
38. al-Bukhārī in *al-Ṣaḥīḥ:* Bk.: *al-Adhān* [The *Adhān*], Ch.: "Concerning He Who Complains about His Imam When the Latter Lengthens the Prayer for Too Long," 1:249 §672.
39. Muslim in *al-Ṣaḥīḥ:* Bk.: *al-Ṣalāh* [The Prayer], Ch.: "On Commanding the Imams to Lighten the Prayer," 1:340 §466.
40. al-Bukhārī in *al-Ṣaḥīḥ:* Bk.: *al-Adhān* [The *Adhān*], Ch.: "On the One who Lightens his Prayer when Young Children Cry," 1:250 §677.
41. Muslim in *al-Ṣaḥīḥ:* Bk.: *al-Ṣalāh* [The Prayer], Ch.: "Commanding the Imams to Lighten the Prayer," 1:342 §470.
42. Muslim in *al-Ṣaḥīḥ:* Bk.: *al-Birr wa al-ṣila wa al-adab* [On Piety, Familial Integration, and Good Manners], Ch.: "The Prohibition of Invoking Curses Against Creatures and Other Things," 4:2006 §2599.
43. al-Bukhārī in *al-Adab al-mufrad*, 119 §321.
44. Abū Yaʿlā in *al-Musnad*, 11:35 §6174.
45. Abū Nuʿaym in *Dalāʾil al-nubuwwa*, 1:40 §2.
46. al-Bayhaqī in *Shuʿab al-Īmān*, 2:144 §1403.
47. Ibn ʿAsākir in *Tārīkh Dimashq*, 4:92.
48. al- usaynī in *al-Bayān wa al-Taʿrīf*, 1:283 §754.
49. Ibn Kathīr in *Tafsīr al-Qurʾān al-ʿAẓīm*, 3:202.
50. al-Bukhārī in *al-Ṣaḥīḥ:* Bk.: *al-Jihād wa al-siyar* [The Striving and Military Expeditions], Ch.: "On Praying for the Guidance of the Idolaters in order to Reconcile Their Hearts," 3:1073 §2779.
51. Muslim in *al-Ṣaḥīḥ:* Bk.: *Faḍāʾil al-ṣaḥāba* [The Virtues of the Companions], Ch.: "From the Virtues of Ghifār, Aslam, Juhayna, Ashjaʿ, Muzina, Daws, and Ṭayʾ," 4:1957 §2524.
52. al-Ṭabarānī in *al-Muʿjam al-kabīr*, 8:326 §8219, and in *Musnad al-Shāmiyyīn*, 4:296 §3352.
53. Ibid., Bk.: *al-Īmān* [The Faith], Ch.: "The Most Beloved Element of the Religion in the Sight of Allah is the Most Consistent of It," 1:24 §43.
54. Muslim in *al-Ṣaḥīḥ:* Bk.: *Ṣalāt al-musāfirīn* [The Travelers' Prayer], Ch.: "The Virtue of Consistent Actions Such as Night Vigil Prayer and the Like,' 1:540 §782.
55. al-Nasāʾī in *al-Sunan:* Bk.: *al-Sahw* [The Mistake], Ch.: "Sendings salutations on to the Prophet ﷺ," 3:43 §1282.
56. al-Dārimī, *al-Sunan*, 2:409 §2774.
57. Ibn · ibbān, *al-Ṣaḥīḥ*, 3:195 §914.
58. Ibn Abī Shayba, *al-Muṣannaf*, 2:253 §8705.
59. ʿAbd al-Razzāq, *al-Muṣannaf*, 2:215 §3116.
60. al-Ḥākim, *al-Mustadrak*, 2:456 §3576.

61. al-Bazzār, *al-Baḥr al-Zakkhār*, 5:307 §1924.
62. Abū Yaʿlā, *al-Musnad*, 9:137 §5213.
63. al-Ṭabarānī, *al-Muʿjam al-kabīr*, 10:219 §§§10528–10530.
64. al-Bayhaqī, *Shuʿab al-īmān*, 2:217 §1582.
65. al-Shāshī in *al-Musnad*, 2:252 §825–826.
66. al-Bazzār in *al-Baḥr al-zakkhār*, 5:308–309 §1925.
67. Al- akīm al-Tirmidhī, *Nawādir al-uṣūl*, 4:176.
68. al-Daylamī in *al-Firdaws* (1:183 §686) on the authority of Abu Hurayra ؓ.
69. al-Qaḍī ʿIyāḍ, *al-Shifā*, 1:19.
70. Ibn Kathīr in *al-Bidāya wa al-nihāya*, 4:257.
71. Qurʾān 93:5.
72. Qurʾān 14:36.
73. Qurʾān 5:118.
74. Muslim in *al-Ṣaḥīḥ:* Bk.: *al-Īmān* [The Faith], Ch.: "On the Prophet's ﷺ Supplication for His Nation," 1:191 §202.
75. Ibn Ḥajar al-ʿAsqalānī, *Fatḥ al-bārī*, 11:428–429.
76. Muslim in *al-Ṣaḥīḥ:* Bk.: *al-Fitan* [The Tribulations], Ch.: "Mention of the Anti-Christ, His Qualities and What is with Him," 4:2251 §2937.
77. al-Bukhārī in *al-Ṣaḥīḥ:* Bk.: *Kitāb al-Riqāq* [The Heart Softening Narrations], Ch.: "What is to Be Warned against of the Ornaments of the World and Competition Therein," 5:2361 §6061.
78. Muslim in *al-Ṣaḥīḥ:* Bk.: *al-Zuhd* [The Renunciation], 4:2273 §2961.
79. Muslim in *al-Ṣaḥīḥ:* Bk.: *al-Faḍāʾil* [The Exemplary Virtues], Ch.: "Affirmation of the Prophet's Basin (*Ḥawḍ*) and its Qualities," 4:1795 §2296.
80. Ibid., Bk.: *al-Zakāt* [The Zakat], Ch.: "What is Taken Out from the Ornaments of the World," 1:728 §1052.
81. Qurʾān 2:143.
82. al-Bukhārī in *al-Ṣaḥīḥ:* Bk.: *al-Janāʾiz* [The Funeral Prayers], Ch.: "Prayer upon the Martyr," 1:450 §1278.
83. Ibid., 1:451 §1279;
84. Muslim in *al-Ṣaḥīḥ:* Bk.: *al-Faḍāʾil* [The Exemplary Virtues], Ch.: "Affirmation of the Prophet's Basin and its Qualities," 4:1795 §2296.
85. Aḥmad b. Ḥanbal in *al-Musnad*, 4:388 §19470.
86. al-Nasāʾī in *al-Sunan:* Bk.: *al-Janāʾiz* [The Funeral Prayers], Ch.: "On Praying Over a Grave," 4:84 §2022.
87. Ibn Mājah in *al-Sunan:* Bk.: *al-Janāʾiz* [The Funerals], Ch.: "On What has been Reported Regarding Prayer Over Graves," 1:489 §1528.
88. Ibn Abī Shayba in *al-Muṣannaf*, 2:475 §11217.
89. al-Ṭabarānī in *al-Muʿjam al-kabīr*, 22:240 §628.
90. Ibn Abī ʿĀṣim in *al-Āḥād wa al-Mathānī*, 4:27 §1970.
91. al-Bayhaqī in *al-Sunan al-kubrā*, 4:48 §6809.

92. al-Bukhārī *al-Ṣaḥīḥ:* Bk.: *al-Ṣalāh* [The Prayer], Ch.: "On Sweeping the Mosque," 1:175–176 §§446, 448, and in Bk.: *al-Janā'iz* [The Funerals], Ch.: "Praying Over the Grave After [the Deceased] is Buried," 1:448 §2172.
93. Muslim in *al-Ṣaḥīḥ:* Bk.: *al-Janā'iz* [The Funerals], Ch.: "Praying Over a Grave," 2:659 §956.
94. Aḥmad b. Ḥanbal in *al-Musnad*, 2:388 §9025.
95. Abū Dāwūd in *al-Sunan:* Bk.: *al-Janā'iz* [The Funerals], Ch.: "Praying Over a Grave," 3:211 §3203.
96. Ibn Mājah in *al-Sunan:* Bk.: *Mā jā' fī al-Janā'iz* [What has been Reported Regarding the Funeral Prayers], Ch.: "On What has been Reported Regarding Prayers Over the Graves," 1:489 §1527–1529.
97. al-Nasā'ī in *al-Sunan al-kubrā*, 1:651 §2149.
98. Ibn Ḥibbān in *al-Ṣaḥīḥ*, 7:355 §3086.
99. al-Bayhaqī in *al-Sunan al-kubrā*, 4:46–47 §§6802, 6806.
100. Qur'ān 9:128.
101. al-Bukhārī in *al-Ṣaḥīḥ*: *al-Adab* [Proper Conduct], Ch.: "Kind Treatment of the child, kissing him and hugging him," 5:2235 §5651.
102. Muslim in *al-Ṣaḥīḥ:* Bk.: *Faḍā'il* [Excellent Qualities], Ch.: "Kind treatment of the family and humility is to your credit," 4:1808 §2315.
103. Aḥmad b. Ḥanbal in *al-Musnad*, 2:241 §7287.
104. Ibn Ḥibbān in *al-Ṣaḥīḥ*, 2:202 §457.
105. al-Bukhārī in *al-Adab al-mufrad*, 1:46 §91, 99.
106. al-Bayhaqī in *al-Sunan al-kubrā*, 7:100 §13354.
107. Aḥmad b. Ḥanbal, *al-Musnad*, 2:160.
108. Abū Dāwūd, *al-Sunan:* Bk.: *al-Adab* [The Etiquette], Ch.: "On Mercy," 2:703 §4951.
109. al-Tirmidhī, *al-Sunan:* Bk.: *al-Birr wa al-ṣila* [The Piety and Familial Integration], Ch.: "What Has been Reported Regarding Mercy toward Muslims," 4:323 §1924.
110. Ibn Abī Shayba, *al-Muṣannaf*, 5:214 §25355.
111. al-Ḥumaydī, *al-Musnad*, 2:269 §591.
112. al-Khaṭīb al-Baghdādī, *Tārīkh Baghdad*, 3:260.
113. al-Bayhaqī, *al-Sunan al-kubrā*, 9:41.
114. Ibn Ḥajar al-ʿAsqalānī, Fatḥ al-Bārī, 13:359.
115. Muslim in al-Ṣaḥīḥ: Bk.: al-Faḍā'il [The Exemplary Virtues], Ch.: "When Allah Intends Mercy for an Umma He Takes its Prophet's Soul before It," 4:1791 §2288.
116. Aḥmad b. Ḥanbal, *al-Musnad*, 6:137.
117. Ibn Rahawayh, *al-Musnad*, 3:652 §1241.
118. al-Tirmidhī, *al-Sunan*, 3:223 §873.
119. Ibn Mājah, *al-Sunan*, 2:1018 §3064.
120. Ibn Khuzayma, *al-Ṣaḥīḥ*, 4:333 §3041

121. al-Ḥākim, *al-Mustadrak*, 1:653 §1752.
122. al-Bayhaqī, *al-Sunan al-kubrā*, 5:159.
123. al-Bukhārī in *al-Ṣaḥīḥ:* Bk.: *al-Ḥajj* [The Hajj], Ch.: "Providing Water for the Pilgrims," 2:589 §1554.
124. Muslim in *al-Ṣaḥīḥ:* Bk.: *al-Ḥajj* [The Hajj], Ch.: "The Description of the Prophet's Pilgrimage," 2:891 §1218.
125. al-Bukhārī in *al-Ṣaḥīḥ:* Bk.: *al-Shahādāt* [The Testimony], Ch.: "On the Praise that is Deemed Offensive, and the Order to Say What One Knows," 2:947 §2520.
126. Muslim in *al-Ṣaḥīḥ:* Bk.: *al-Zuhd* [The Renunciation], Ch.: "The Prohibition of Praising Others if it is Excessive and there is Fear of Tribulation for the Recipient," 4:2297 §3001.
127. Muslim in *al-Ṣaḥīḥ*, ibid. 4:2297 §3002.
128. Muslim in *al-Ṣaḥīḥ:* Bk.: *al-Birr* [The Piety], Ch.: "When a Righteous Person is Praised it is a Glad Tidings and Will Not Harm Him," 4:2034 §2642.
129. al-Bukhārī in *al-Ṣaḥīḥ:* Bk.: *al-Jihād* [The Striving], Ch.: "On Wearing Silken Garments in Battle and on Other Occasions," 3:1069 §§§2762–2764.
130. Muslim in *al-Ṣaḥīḥ:* Bk.: *al-Libās* [The Clothing], Ch.: "The Permissibility of a Man Wearing Silk if He Suffers from a Skin Condition and the Like," 3:1646 §2076.
131. Aḥmad b. Ḥanbal, *al-Musnad*, 6:444.
132. al-Tirmidhī, *al-Sunan* 4:663 §2509.
133. al-Bukhārī, *al-Adab al-mufrad*, 141–142 §391.
134. Hannād, *al-Zuhd*, 2:611 §1310.
135. Ibn Ḥibbān, *al-Ṣaḥīḥ*, 11:489 §5092.
136. Abū Dāwūd in *al-Sunan:* Bk.: *al-Ṭalāq* [Divorce], Ch.: "Those who trot woman against her husband," 2:254 §2175.
137. al-Ḥākim in *al-Mustadrak*, 2:214 §2795.
138. ʿAbd al-Razzāq in *al-Muṣannaf*, 11:456 §20994.
139. Abū Yaʿlā in *al-Musnad*, 4:303 §2413.
140. Muslim in *al-Ṣaḥīḥ:* Bk.: *al-Birr wa al-ṣila wa al-ādāb* [Piety, affinity and good manners], Ch.: "The prohibition of wronging the Muslim, deserting him, and despising him, his goods, his blood and his wealth," 4:1986 §2564.
141. Aḥmad b. Ḥanbal, *al-Musnad*, 2:277 §7713.
142. al-Bayhaqī, *al-Sunan al-kubrā*, 6:92 §11276, & in *Shuʿab al-īmān*, 5:280 §6660;
143. al-Daylamī, *al-Firdaws bi-maʾthūr al-khiṭāb*, 2:470 §4002.
144. Ibn Rajab, *Jāmiʿ al-ʿUlūm wa al-Ḥikam*, 1:326.
145. ʿAbd b. Ḥumayd, *al-Musnad*, 1:420 §1442.
146. Ibn Ḥajar al-ʿAsqalānī in *Fatḥ al-Bārī*, 10:483.

147. al-Bukhārī in *al-Ṣaḥīḥ:* Bk.: *al-Adab* [The Manners], Ch.: "On Migration," 5:2253 §5719.
148. Muslim in *al-Ṣaḥīḥ:* Bk.: *al-Birr wa al-ṣila* [The Piety and Familial Integration], Ch.: "The Prohibition of Nursing Mutual Envy, Hatred, and Enmity," 4:1983 §2559.
149. Muslim in *al-Ṣaḥīḥ:* Bk.: *al-Imāra* [The Leadership], Ch.: "The Obligation to Stick to the Main Body of the Muslims in the Time of Trials", 3:1476, 1477 §1848.
150. al-Nasā'ī in *al-Sunan:* Bk.: *Taḥrīm al-dam* [The Prohibition of Bloodshed], 7:123 §4114.
151. Aḥmad b. Ḥanbal in *al-Musnad*, 2:296 §488.
152. Ibid., 3:1478 §1851.
153. Ibid., Bk.: *al-Imāra* [The Leadership], Ch.: "The Ruling on the One Who Causes Disunity among the Muslims when They Are United," 3:1480 §1852.
154. Ibid., Ch.: "On the Best and the Worst of the Leaders," 3:1481 §1855.
155. al-Bukhārī in *al-Ṣaḥīḥ:* Bk.: *al-Fitan* [The Tribulations], Ch.: "The Saying of the Prophet ﷺ 'After My Departure, You Will Observe Things that You Will Dislike,'" 6:2588 §6647.
156. Muslim in *al-Ṣaḥīḥ:* Bk.: *al-Imāra* [The Leadership], Ch.: "The Obligation to Obey the Rulers in that which Does not Entail Disobedience, and the Prohibition of Disobeying Their Orders," 3:1470 §1709.

4. The Holy Prophet ﷺ is Peace and Protection for Every Human Soul in this World

Essential Reading:

1. Dr Tahir-ul-Qadri, Muhammad ﷺ: The Merciful, Ch:4, p.95-108.

Additional Readings for Teachers and Students:

1. Qur'ān 26:117–120.138.
2. Ibid., 26:117–120.
3. Ibid., 29:14–15.

4. Ibid., 46:21–25.
5. Ibid., 11:58.
6. Ibid., 11:66–67.
7. Ibid., 11:94–95.
8. Ibid., 26:170–173.
9. Ibid., 11:82–83.
10. Ibid., 10:88–90.
11. Ibid., 5:24–26.
12. Ibid., 2:65.
13. Ibid., 29:40.
14. Muslim in *al-Ṣaḥīḥ:* Bk.: *al-Faḍā'il* [The Exemplary Virtues], Ch.: "When Allah Intends Mercy for an *Umma* He Takes its Prophet's Soul before It," 4:1791 §2288.
15. Qur'ān 8:33.
16. Muslim in *al-Ṣaḥīḥ:* Bk.: *Faḍā'il al-ṣaḥāba* [The Virtues of the Companions], Ch.: "That the Presence of the Prophet ﷺ is a Security for the Companions, and that the Presence of the Companions is a Security for the *Umma*," 4:1961 §2531.
17. Aḥmad b. Ḥanbal in *al-Musnad*, 4:398.
18. Abū Ya'lā in *al-Musnad*, 13:260 §7276.
19. Ibid., 14:36.
20. Ibid., 5:118.
21. Muslim in *al-Ṣaḥīḥ:* Bk.: *al-Īmān* [The Faith], Ch.: "On the Prophet's Supplication for His Nation ﷺ," 1:191 §202.

5. The Holy Prophet's Rank as Mercy to the Worlds and His Compassion for All the Creation

Essential Reading:

1. Dr Tahir-ul-Qadri, Muhammad ﷺ: The Merciful, Ch:5, p.113-136.

Additional Readings for Teachers and Students:

1. al-Bukhārī in *al-Ṣaḥīḥ:* Bk.: *al-Anbiyā'* [On the Prophets], Ch.: "The Hadith About the Cave," 3:1282 §3290.

2. Muslim in *al-Ṣaḥīḥ:* Bk.: *al-Jihād wa al-siyar* [The Striving and Military Expeditions], Ch.: "On the Battle of Uḥud," 3:1417 §1792.
3. Aḥmad b. anbal in *al-Musnad*, 1:453 §4331.
4. Ibn Mājah in *al-Sunan:* Bk.: *al-Fitan* [On Tribulations], Ch.: "Patience with Affliction," 2:1335 §4025.
5. Abū Yaʿlā in *al-Musnad*, 9:131 §5205.
6. al-Bazzār in *al-Musnad*, 5:106–107 §1686.
7. Muslim in *al-Ṣaḥīḥ:* Bk.: *al-Birr wa ṣila wa al-adab* [On Piety, Familial Integration, and Good Manners], Ch.: "The Prohibition of Invoking Curses Against Creatures and Other Things," 4:2006 §2599.
8. al-Bukhārī in *al-Adab al-mufrad*, 119 §321;.
9. Abū Yaʿlā in *al-Musnad*, 11:35 §6174.
10. Abū Nuʿaym in *Dalāʾil al-nubuwwa*, 1:40 §2.
11. al-Bayhaqī in *Shuʿab al-īmān*, 2:144 §1403.
12. Ibn ʿAsākir in *Tārīkh Dimashq*, 4:92.
13. al- usaynī in *al-Bayān wa al-taʿrīf*, 1:283 §754.
14. Ibn Kathīr in *Tafsīr al-Qurʾān al-ʿAẓīm*, 3:202.
15. Aḥmad b. anbal in *al-Musnad*, 5:437 §23757.
16. Abū Dāwūd in *al-Sunan:* Bk.: *al-Sunna* [The Sunna], Ch.: "The Prohibition of Maligning the Companions of Allah's Messenger ﷺ," 4:215 §4659.
17. Aḥmad b. anbal in *al-Musnad*, 5:268 §22361.
18. al-Ṭabarānī in *al-Muʿjam al-Kabīr*, 8:196 §7803.
19. al-Mundhirī in *al-Targhīb wa al-Tarhīb*, 3:181 §3583.
20. Ibn Rajab in *Jāmiʿ al-ʿulūm wa al-ḥikam*, 1:415.
21. al-Haythamī in *Majmaʿ al-Zawāʾid*, 5:69.
22. al-Suyūṭī in *al-Durr al-Manthūr*, 5:688.
23. al-Dārimī in the introduction of *al-Sunan*, section, "How the Prophet's Affair Was in the Beginning ﷺ," 1:21 §10.
24. Ibn Abī Shayba in *al-Muṣannaf*, 6:325 §31782.
25. al- ākim in *al-Mustadrak*, 1:91 §100.
26. al-Quḍāʿī in *Musnad al-Shihāb*, 2:189–190 §1160–1161.
27. al-Ṭabarānī in *al-Muʿjam al-Awsaṭ*, 3:223 §2981 and in *al-Muʿjam al-Ṣaghīr*, 1:168 §264.
28. al-Bayhaqī in *Shuʿab al-Īmān*, 2:143–144 §§§1402, 1404, 1445.
29. al-Haythamī in *Majmaʿ al-Zawāʾid*, 8:257.
30. Muslim in *al-Ṣaḥīḥ:* Bk.: *al-Faḍāʾil* [The Virtues], Ch.: "Regarding His Names ﷺ," 4:1828 §2355.
31. Aḥmad b. anbal in *al-Musnad*, 4:395 §§404, 407.
32. Ibn Abī Shayba in *al-Muṣannaf*, 6:311 §31692–31693.
33. al- ākim in *al-Mustadrak*, 2:659 §4185–4186.
34. al-Ṭabarānī in *al-Muʿjam al-Awsaṭ*, 4:327 §§4338, 4417.
35. Ibn Jaʿd in *al-Musnad*, 1:479 §3322.

36. al-Bukhārī in *al-Ṣaḥīḥ:* Bk.: *al-Buyūʿ* [The Transactions], Ch.: "The Prohibition of Being Loud and Boisterous in the Marketplace," 2:747 §2018, and in Bk.: *al-Tafsīr* [The Qurʾānic Exegesis], Ch.: "On the Verse ﴾*Certainly We have sent you as a witness, a giver of glad tidings, and a warner*﴿," 4:1831 §4558, and in •*al-Adab al-Mufrad*, 95 §246.
37. Aḥmad b. anbal in *al-Musnad*, 2:174 §6622.
38. al-Dārimī in *al-Sunan*, 1:16 §6.
39. Abū Nuʿaym in *ilya al-Awliyāʾ*, 5:387.
40. Ibn Saʿd in *al-Ṭabaqāt al-Kubrā*, 1:360–362.
41. al-Bayhaqī in *al-Sunan al-Kubrā*, 7:45 §13079, and
42. ibid., •*Shuʿab al-Īmān*, 2:137 §1410, and in •*al-Iʿtiqād*, 1:256.
43. al-Maqdisī in *al-Aḥādīth al-Mukhtāra*, 9:460 §435.
44. al-Ṭabarī in *Jāmiʿ al-Bayān*, 9:83.
45. Ibn Kathīr in *Tafsīr al-Qurʾān al-ʿAẓīm*, 2:254.
46. Muslim in *al-Ṣaḥīḥ:* Bk.: *al-Masājid wa mawāḍiʿ al-ṣalāh* [The Mosques and Places of Prayer], Ch.: "On Who Has More Right to the Imamate," 1:465 §674.
47. al-Dāraquṭnī in *al-Sunan*, 1:272 §1.
48. al-Ṭabarānī in *al-Muʿjam al-Kabīr*, 19:288 §637.
49. al-Bayhaqī in *al-Sunan al-Kubrā*, 1:385 §1678, 2:17 §2102, and 3:120 §5076.
50. al-Tirmidhī in *al-Sunan:* Bk.: *al-Daʿawāt* [The Supplications], Ch.: "Regarding the Supplication of a Weak Person," 5:569 §3578; •Aḥmad b. anbal in *al-Musnad*, 4:138 §17240–17242.
51. Ibn Mājah in *al-Sunan:* Bk.: *Iqāmat al-ṣalāh wa al-sunna fīhā* [The Establishing the Prayer and the Sunna Therein], Ch.: "On What Has Been Reported Regarding the Prayer of Need," 1:441 §1385.
52. al-Nasāʾī in *al-Sunan al-Kubrā*, 6:168 §10495, 10494.
53. Ibn Khuzayma in *al-Ṣaḥīḥ*, 2:225 §1219.
54. al- ākim in *al-Mustadrak*, 1:458, 700, and 707 §§§1180, 1909, 1929.
55. al-Ṭabarānī in *al-Muʿjam al-Ṣaghīr*, 1:306 §508, and in •*al-Muʿjam al-Kabīr*, 9:30 §8311.
56. ʿAbd b. umayd in *al-Musnad*, 1:147 §379.
57. al-Mundhirī in *al-Targhīb wa al-Tarhīb*, 1:272 §1018.
58. al-Haythamī in *Majmaʿ al-Zawāʾid*, 2:279.
59. al-Tirmidhī in *al-Sunan*, *Kitab al-Manāqib* [The Exemplary Qualities], Ch.: "On What Has Been Reported About the Prophet's Prophethood ﷺ," 5:590 §3620.
60. Ibn Abī Shayba in *al-Muṣannaf*, 6:317 §§31733, 36541.
61. Ibn ibbān in *al-Thiqāt*, 1:42.
62. Abū Nuʿaym in *Dalāʾil al-Nubuwwa*, 1:45 §19.
63. al-Ṭabarī in *Tārīkh al-Umam wa al-Mulūk*, 1:519.
64. Ibn Mājah in *al-Sunan:* Bk.: *Iqāmat al-ṣalāh wa al-sunna fīhā* [The

Establishing the Prayer and the Sunna Therein], Ch.: "On Sending Prayers Upon the Prophet ﷺ," 1:293 §906.

65. Abū Yaʿlā in *al-Musnad*, 9:175 §5267.
66. al-Ṭabarānī in *al-Muʿjam al-Kabīr*, 8:115 §8594.
67. al-Bayhaqī in *Shuʿab al-Īmān*, 2:208 §1550.
68. al-Shāshī in *al-Musnad*, 2:89 §611.
69. al-Maḥāmilī in *al-Amālī*, 1:287–288 §294.
70. al-Mundhirī in *al-Targhīb wa al-Tarhīb*, 2:329 §2588.
71. al-Ṭabarānī in *al-Muʿjam al-Kabīr*, 100:89 §10046.
72. al-Daylamī in *Musnad al-Firdaws*, 2:400 §3779.
73. al-Haythamī in *Majmaʿ al-Zawāʾid*, 8:271.
74. Ibn ʿAsākir in *Tārīkh Dimashq*, 3:32.
75. al-Qurṭubī in *al-Jāmiʿ li Aḥkām al-Qurʾān*, 18:84.
76. al-Dhahabī in *Mīzān al-Iʿtidāl*, 1:336.
77. al-ʿAsqalānī in *Lisān al-Mīzān*, 1:354 §1096.
78. al-Nawawī in *Tahdhīb al-Asmāʾ*, 1:49.
79. al-Suyūṭī in *al-Khaṣāʾiṣ al-Kubrā*, 1:133.
80. al-Bukhārī in *al-Ṣaḥīḥ:* Bk.: *al-Istiqrāḍ wa adāʾ al-duyūn wa al-ḥijr wa al-taflīs* [The Loans, Repayment of Debts, Rent, and Bankruptcy], Ch.: "Prayer Over One Who Leaves a Debt Behind," 2:845 §2269, and in Bk.: *al-Tafsīr* [The Qurʾānic Exegesis], Ch.: "﴾*The Prophet is closer to the believers than their own selves*﴿," 4:1795 §4503.
81. Muslim in *al-Ṣaḥīḥ:* Bk.: *al-Farāʾiḍ* [The Inheritance], Ch.: "Whoever Leaves Behind Wealth Then it is For His Heirs," 3:1238 §1619.
82. Aḥmad b. anbal in *al-Musnad*, 2:334 §8399.
83. ʿAbd al-Razzāq in *al-Muṣannaf*, 8:291 §15261.
84. Abū ʿAwāna in *al-Musnad*, 3:445 §5630.
85. al-Bayhaqī in *al-Sunan al-Kubrā*, 6:238 §12148.
86. Ibn Kathīr in *Tafsīr al-Qurʾan al-ʿAẓīm*, 3:469.
87. Muslim in *al-Ṣaḥīḥ:* Bk.: *al-Jumuʿa* [The the Friday Prayer], chapter" "Shortening the Prayer and the Sermon," 2:592 §867.
88. Aḥmad b. anbal in *al-Musnad*, 3:310 §14373.
89. al-Nasāʾī in *al-Sunan* in *Kitāb Ṣalāh al-ʿīdayn* [The Two Eid Prayers], Ch.: "On How the Sermon is Given," 3:188 §1578, also in *al-Sunan al-Kubrā*, 1:550 §1786.
90. Ibn Mājah in the introduction to *al-Sunan*, section, "Abstinence from Blameworthy Innovation and Argumentation," 1:17 §45.
91. Ibn ibbān in *al-Ṣaḥīḥ*, 1:186 §10
92. al-Ṭabarānī in *al-Muʿjam al-Awsaṭ*, 3:160 §9418, and in •*al-Muʿjam al-Kabīr*, 3:100 §8531.
93. Abū Yaʿlā in *al-Musnad*, 4:85, 90 §§2111, 2119.
94. al-Bayhaqī in *al-Sunan al-Kubrā*, 3:206 §5544.

95. al-Bukhārī in *al-Ṣaḥīḥ:* Bk.: *al-Ḥudūd* [The Prescribed Punishments], Ch.: "Striking With Palm Branches and Shoes," 6:2488 §6395, also in the Ch.: "What is Detested of Curses Uttered Against Those who Consume Alcohol and Evidence that the Drinker is Not Expelled From the Religion," 6:2489 §6399.
96. Aḥmad b. anbal in *al-Musnad*, 2:299 § 7973.
97. Abū Dāwūd in *al-Sunan:* Bk.: *al-Ḥudūd* [The Prescribed Punishments], Ch.: "The Prescribed Punishment for Drinking Alcohol," 4:162 §4477.
98. Muslim in *al-Ṣaḥīḥ:* Bk.: *Faḍā'il al-ṣaḥāba* [The Virtues of the Companions], Ch.: "That the Presence of the Prophet ﷺ is a Security for the Companions, and that the Presence of the Companions is a Security for the *Umma*," 4:1961 §2531.
99. Aḥmad b. Ḥanbal in *al-Musnad*, 4:398.
100. Abū Ya'lā in *al-Musnad*, 13:260 §7276.
101. Muslim in *al-Ṣaḥīḥ:* Bk.: *Ṣalāt al-musāfir wa qaṣruhā* [The Traveler's Prayer and its Shortening], Ch.: "That the Qur'ān Has Seven Modes of Recitation, and What that Means," 1:562 §821.
102. al-Nasā'ī in *al-Sunan al-kubrā:* Bk.: *al-Iftitāḥ* [The what is Said in the Beginning of the Prayer], Ch.: "A Compendium of what is Mentioned About the Qur'ān," 2:152 §939.
103. al-Bukhārī *al-Ṣaḥīḥ:* Bk.: *al-Ṣalāh* [The Prayer], Ch.: "On Sweeping the Mosque," 1:175–176 §§446, 448, and in Bk.: *al-Janā'iz* [The Funerals], Ch.: "Praying Over the Grave After [the Deceased] is Buried," 1:448 §2172.
104. Muslim in *al-Ṣaḥīḥ:* Bk.: *al-Janā'iz* [The Funerals], Ch.: "Praying Over a Grave," 2:659 §956.
105. Aḥmad b. Ḥanbal in *al-Musnad*, 2:388 §9025.
106. Abū Dāwūd in *al-Sunan:* Bk.: *al-Janā'iz* [The Funerals], Ch.: "Praying Over a Grave," 3:211 §3203.
107. Ibn Mājah in *al-Sunan:* Bk.: *Mā jā' fī al-Janā'iz* [What has been Reported Regarding the Funeral Prayers], Ch.: "On What has been Reported Regarding Prayers Over the Graves," 1:489 §1527–1529.
108. al-Nasā'ī in *al-Sunan al-Kubrā*, 1:651 §2149.
109. Ibn Ḥibbān in *al-Ṣaḥīḥ*, 7:355 §3086.
110. al-Bayhaqī in *al-Sunan al-Kubrā*, 4:46–47 §§§6802, 6806.
111. al-Bukhārī in *al-Ṣaḥīḥ:* Bk.: *al-Adhān* [The *Adhān*], Ch.: "Concerning He Who Complains About His Imam When the Latter Lengthens the Prayer for Too Long," 1:249 §672.
112. Muslim in *al-Ṣaḥīḥ:* Bk.: *al-Ṣalāh* [The Prayer], Ch.: "On Commanding the Imams to Lighten the Prayer," 1:240 §466. Aḥmad b. Ḥanbal *al-Musnad*, 4:118 §17106.
113. Ibn Mājah in *al-Sunan:* Bk.: *Iqāma al-ṣalāh wa al-sunna fīhā* [The Second Call to Prayer and the Sunna Regarding It], Ch.: "Whoever

Leads a People in Prayer Should Lighten It," 1:315 §984.
114. al-Dārimī *al-Sunan*, 1:322 §1259.
115. Ibn Ḥibbān *al-Ṣaḥīḥ*, 5:509 §2137.
116. al-Ṭabarānī in *al-Muʿjam al-Kabīr*, 17:207 §557.
117. al-Bukhārī *al-Ṣaḥīḥ:* Bk.: *al-Adhān* [The *Adhān*], Ch.: "When Someone Prays Alone, Let Him Lengthen it as Long as He Likes," 1:248 §671.
118. Muslim *al-Ṣaḥīḥ:* Bk.: *al-Ṣalāh* [The Prayer], Ch.: "On Commanding the Imams to Lighten the Prayer," 1:341 §468.
119. Aḥmad b. Ḥanbal *al-Musnad*, 2:486 §10311.
120. al-Tirmidhī *al-Sunan:* Bk.: *al-Ṣalāh* [The Prayer], Ch.: "On What has been Reported Regarding the Statement that if One of You Leads the People in Prayer, that He Should Lighten It," 1:461 §236.
121. Abū Dāwūd in *al-Sunan:* Bk.: *al-Ṣalāh* [The Prayer], Ch.: "On Lightening the Prayer," 1:211 §794.
122. al-Nasāʾī *al-Sunan al-Kubrā:* Bk.: *al-Imāma* [The Imamate], Ch.: "On the Duty of the Imam to Lighten [the Prayer]," 2:94 §823.
123. Mālik in *al-Muwaṭṭaʾ:* Bk.: *Ṣalāt al-jamāʿa* [The Congregational Prayer], Ch.: "What is Done in the Congregational Prayer," 1:134 §301.
124. Ibn Ḥibbān *al-Ṣaḥīḥ*, 5:56 §1760.
125. al-Bayhaqī *al-Sunan al-Kubrā*, 3:117 §5058.
126. Muslim in *al-Ṣaḥīḥ:* Bk.: *al-Birr wa al-ṣila wa al-adab* [The Piety, Familial Integration, and Good Manners], Ch.: "The Virtue of the Weak and Obscure," 4:2024 §2622, also in *Kitāb al-Janna wa ṣifa naʿīmihā wa ahlihā* [The Paradise and a Description of its Bounties and Inhabitants], Ch.: "The Tyrants Shall Enter the Hellfire and the Weak Shall Enter Paradise," 4:2191 §2854.
127. al-Bayhaqī in *Shuʿab al-Īmān*, 7:331 §10482.
128. Ibn Rajab in *Jāmiʿ al-ʿUlūm wa al-Ḥikam*, 10:105 and al-Mundhirī in *al-Targhīb wa al-Tarhīb*, 4:73 §4849.
129. Aḥmad b. Ḥanbal *al-Musnad*, 3:145 §12502.
130. al-Tirmidhī *al-Sunan:* Bk.: *al-Manāqib* [The Exemplary Qualities], Ch.: "The Exemplary Qualities of al-Barāʾ b. Mālik," 5:692 §3854.
131. Ibn Ḥibbān in *al-Ṣaḥīḥ*, 14:403 §6483.
132. al-Ḥākim in *al-Mustadrak*, 3:331 §5274.
133. al-Ṭabarānī in *al-Muʿjam al-awsaṭ*, 1:264 §861.
134. ʿAbd b. Ḥumayd *al-Musnad*, 1:370 §1236.
135. al-Maqdisī in *al-Aḥādīth al-mukhtāra*, 4:420 §1595.
136. Aḥmad b. Ḥanbal in *al-Musnad*, 2:301 §7988.
137. Abū Dāwūd in *al-Sunan:* Bk.: *al-Adab* [The Good Manners], Ch.: "On Mercy," 4:286 §4942.
138. al-Tirmidhī in *al-Sunan:* Bk.: *al-Birr wa al-ṣila* [The Piety and Familial Integration], Ch.: "On What has been Reported Regarding Mercy Towards People," 4:323 §1923.

139. al-Bukhārī in *al-Adab al-Mufrad*, 136 §374.
140. Ibn Ḥibbān in al-*Ṣaḥīḥ*, 2:213 §466.
141. Abū Yaʿlā in *al-Musnad*, 10:526 §6141.
142. Ibn Abī Shayba in *al-Muṣannaf*, 5:214 §25360.
143. al-Ṭabarānī in *al-Muʿjam al-Awsaṭ*, 3:54 § 2453.
144. al-Ṭayālisī in *al-Musnad*, 1:330 §2529.
145. al-Bayhaqī in *al-Sunan al-Kubrā*, 8:161 §16420, and in •*Shuʿab al-Īmān*, 7:476 §11050.
146. al-Dhahabī in *Mīzān al-Iʿtidāl*, 5:204.
147. Aḥmad b. Ḥanbal in *al-Musnad*, 4:388 §19470.
148. al-Nasāʾī in *al-Sunan:* Bk.: *al-Janāʾiz* [The Funeral Prayers], Ch.: "On Praying Over a Grave," 4:84 §2022.
149. Ibn Mājah in *al-Sunan:* Bk.: *al-Janāʾiz* [The Funerals], Ch.: "On What has been Reported Regarding Prayer Over Graves," 1:489 §1528.
150. Ibn Abī Shayba in *al-Muṣannaf*, 2:475 §11217.
151. al-Ṭabarānī in *al-Muʿjam al-Kabīr*, 22:240 §628.
152. Ibn Abī ʿĀṣim in *al-Āḥād wa al-Mathānī*, 4:27 §1970.
153. al-Bayhaqī in *al-Sunan al-Kubrā*, 4:48 §6809.
154. *al*-Bazzār in *al-Musnad*, 5:308 § 1925.
155. al-Jahḍamī in *Faḍl al-Ṣalāh ʿAlā al-Nabī* ﷺ, 1:38–39 §25–26.
156. Ibn Saʿd in *al-Ṭabaqāt al-Kubrā*, 2:194.
157. al-Shāshī in *al-Musnad*, 2:253 §826.
158. *al*-Daylamī in *Musnad al-Firdaws*, 1:183 §686.

al-Haythamī in *Majmaʿ al-Zawāʾid*, 9:24; and in *Bughyat al-Bāḥith ʿan Zawāʾid Musnad al-Ḥārith*, 2:884 §953.

159. Al-Bayhaqī, *Dalāʾil al-Nubuwwa*, 1:159–160.
160. Ibn ʿAsākir in *Tārīkh Madīnat Dimashq*, 3:20.

6. The Holy Prophet's Mercy and Kindness toward Women

Essential Reading:

1. Dr Tahir-ul-Qadri, Muhammad ﷺ: The Merciful, Ch:6, p.137-156.

Additional Readings for Teachers and Students:

1. al-Bukhārī in *al-Ṣaḥīḥ:* Bk.: *al-Jihād wa al-siyar* [The Striving and Military Expeditions], Ch.: "On Killing Women in War," 3:1098 §2852.

2. Muslim in *al-Ṣaḥīḥ:* Bk.: *al-Jihād wa al-siyar* [The Striving and Military Expeditions], Ch.: "On the Unlawfulness of Killing Women and the Elderly in War," 3:1364 §1744.
3. Aḥmad b. Ḥanbal in *al-Musnad*, 2:22 §4739.
4. al-Tirmidhī in *al-Sunan:* Bk.: *al-Siyar* [The Military Expeditions], Ch.: "On What has been Reported Regarding the Prohibition of Killing Women and Children," 4:136 §1569.
5. Ibn Mājah in *al-Sunan:* Bk.: *al-Jihād* [The Striving], Ch.: "On Indiscriminate Night Attacks and Killing Women and Children," 2:947 §2841.
6. al-Nasāʾī in *al-Sunan al-Kubrā*, 5:185 §8618.
7. al-Dārimī in *al-Sunan*, 2:293 §2462.
8. Ibn Ḥibbān in *al-Ṣaḥīḥ*, 1:344 §135.
9. al-Bukhārī in *al-Ṣaḥīḥ:* Bk.: *al-Adab* [The Good Manners], Ch.: "Giving Misleading Impressions Leads to Lying," 5:2294 §5857.
10. Muslim in *al-Ṣaḥīḥ:* Bk.: *al-Faḍāʾil* [The Virtues], Ch.: "The Mercy of the Prophet ﷺ Toward Women," 4:1811, 1812 §§73, 2323.
11. al-Nasāʾī in *al-Sunan al-Kubrā*, 6:134–135 §§10359, 10363.
12. Aḥmad b. Ḥanbal in *al-Musnad*, 3:227 §13401.
13. Ibn Ḥibbān in *al-Ṣaḥīḥ*, 13:119 §5801.
14. al-Ṭabarānī in *al-Muʿjam al-Kabīr*, 25:121 §294.
15. Abū Yaʿlā in *al-Musnad*, 5:191 §2809, 7:116, 121 §§4064, 4075.
16. al-Ruwayānī in *al-Musnad*, 2:381 §1357.
17. ʿAbd b. Ḥumayd in *al-Musnad*, 1:398 §1342.
18. al-Bayhaqī in *al-Sunan al-Kubrā*, 10:227 §§20820, 20822.
19. Ibn Saʿd in *al-Ṭabaqāt al-Kubrā*, 8:430–431.
20. al-Haythamī in *Majmaʿ al-Zawāʾīd*, 3:214, 4:320, 8:20
21. al-Bukhārī in *al-Ṣaḥīḥ:* Bk.: *al-Adhān* [The *Adhān*], Ch.: "Concerning One who is Helping his Family and Goes out as the Prayer is Established," 1:239 §644, also in *Kitāb al-Nafaqāt* [The Expenditures], Ch.: "The Service of a Man Toward His Family," 5:2052 §5048, also in *Kitāb al-Adab* [The Good Manners], Ch.: "On How a Man Should Treat His Family," 5:2245 §5692.
22. Aḥmad b. Ḥanbal in *al-Musnad*, 6:49 §24272.
23. al-Tirmidhī in *al-Sunan:* Bk.: *Ṣifat al-qiyāma wa al-raqāʾiq wa al-waraʿ* [The Description of the Resurrection, Heart-softening Narrations, and Scrupulousness], Ch.: 45, 4:654 §2489.
24. al-Ṭayālisī in *al-Musnad*, 1:198 §1383.
25. Ibn Rāhawayh in *al-Musnad*, 3:879 §1550.
26. al-Bayhaqī in *al-Sunan al-Kubrā*, 2:215 §2989.
27. al-Bukhārī *al-Ṣaḥīḥ:* Bk.: *al-Nikāḥ* [The Marriage], Ch.: "On Protective Jealousy [*ghayra*]," 5:2003 §4927.

28. Aḥmad b. Ḥanbal in *al-Musnad*, 3:105 §12046.
29. Abū Dāwūd in *al-Sunan:* Bk.: *al-Buyūʿ* [The Selling], Ch.: "Whoever Ruins Something is Liable for Returning the Like Thereof," 3:297 §3568.
30. al-Nasāʾī in *al-Sunan:* Bk.: *ʿIshra al-nisāʾ* [On Living with Women], Ch.: "On Protective Jealousy [*ghayra*]," 7:70 §3955, also in *al-Sunan al-kubrā*, 5:285 §8903.
31. Ibn Mājah in *al-Sunan:* Bk.: *al-Aḥkām* [The Legal Rulings], Ch.: "The Ruling on the one Who Breaks Something," 2:782 §2334.
32. al-Dārimī in *al-Sunan*, 2:343 §2598.
33. Abū Yaʿlā in *al-Musnad*, 6:455 §3849.
34. al-Bukhārī in *al-Ṣaḥīḥ:* Bk.: *al-Adab* [The Good Manners], Ch.: "On Being of Friendly Countenance with People," 5:2270 §5779.
35. Muslim in *al-Ṣaḥīḥ:* Bk.: *Faḍāʾil al-ṣaḥāba* [On the Virtues of the Companions], Ch.: "On the Virtue of ʿĀʾisha ﷺ," 4:1890 §2440.
36. Aḥmad b. Ḥanbal in *al-Musnad*, 6:234 §26010.
37. Abū Dāwūd in *al-Sunan:* Bk.: *al-Adab* [The Good Manners], Ch.: "On Playing with Girls," 4:283 §4931.
38. Ibn Mājah in *al-Sunan:* Bk.: *al-Nikāḥ* [The Marriage], Ch.: "On Living Kindly with Women," 1:637 §1982.
39. al-Nasāʾī in *al-Sunan al-Kubrā*, 5:305 §8946.
40. Ibn Ḥibbān in *al-Ṣaḥīḥ*, 13:173 §5863.
41. al-Bukhārī in *al-Ṣaḥīḥ:* Bk.: *al-Nikāḥ* [The Marriage], Ch.: "On Living Kindly with One's Family," 5:1988 §4894, also in the Ch.: "On a Woman Looking at Abyssinians and Others who are Trustworthy," 5:2006 §4938.
42. Muslim in *al-Ṣaḥīḥ:* Bk.: *Ṣalāt al-ʿīdayn* [The Two Eid Prayers], Ch.: "The Dispensation for Playing on the Days of *ʿĪd* so long as it Doesn't Entail Disobedience," 2:609 §892.
43. Aḥmad b. Ḥanbal in *al-Musnad*, 6:84 §24585.
44. al-Nasāʾī in *al-Sunan:* Bk.: *Ṣalāt al-ʿīdayn* [The Two Eid Prayers], Ch.: "On Playing Inside the Mosque on the Day of Eid and Women Looking at That," 3:195 §1595.
45. Ibn Rāhawayh in *al-Musnad*, 2:273 §781.
46. al-Bukhārī in *al-Ṣaḥīḥ:* Bk.: *al-ʿĪdayn* [The Two Eids], Ch.: "The Sunna of the Two Eids for the People of Islam," 1:324 §909, also in *Kitāb al-Manāqib* [The Exemplary Traits], Ch.: "On the Entry of the Prophet ﷺ and his Companions into Medina," 3:1430 §3716.
47. Muslim in *al-Ṣaḥīḥ:* Bk.: *Ṣalāt al-ʿīdayn* [The Two Eid Prayers], Ch.: "The Allowance to Engage in Play on the Day of Eid as long as it Doesn't Entail Disobedience," 2:607–608 §892.
48. Ibn Mājah in *al-Sunan:* Bk.: *al-Nikāḥ* [The Marriage], Ch.: "On Singing and Using the Leather Drum," 1:612 §1898.
49. Ibn Ḥibbān in *al-Ṣaḥīḥ*, 13:180, 187 §§5871, 5877.

50. al-Bayhaqī in *al-Sunan al-Kubrā*, 10:224 §20801, also in *Shuʿab al-Īmān*, 4:281 §5110.
51. al-Bukhārī in *al-Ṣaḥīḥ:* Bk.: *al-Adab* [The Good Manners], Ch.: "On Pride," 5:2255 §5724.
52. Aḥmad b. Ḥanbal in *al-Musnad*, 3:98 §11960.
53. Abū Nuʿaym in *Ḥilya al-awliyāʾ*, 7:202.
54. al-Nawawī in *Riyāḍ al-ṣāliḥīn*, 171 §171.
55. Muslim in *al-Ṣaḥīḥ:* Bk.: *al-Faḍāʾil* [The Virtues], Ch.: "The Prophet's Closeness with the People and their Seeking of Blessings [*tabarruk*] from Him," 4:1812 §2326.
56. Aḥmad b. Ḥanbal in *al-Musnad*, 3:119 §12218.
57. Abū Dāwūd in *al-Sunan:* Bk.: *al-Adab* [The Good Manners], Ch.: "On Sitting Upon the Pathways," 4:257 §4818.
58. al-Bukhārī in *al-Ṣaḥīḥ:* Bk.: *al-Waṣāyā* [The Bequests], Ch.: "That One Leaves His Heirs Wealthy is Better than Allowing Them to be a Burden on the People," 3:116 §2591, also in *Kitāb Faḍāʾil al-ṣaḥāba* [On the Virtues of the Companions], Ch.: "On the Prophet's Saying, 'O Allāh! Allow My Companion's Migration to Continue On,'" 3:1431 §3721, also §4147, 5039, 5335, 5344, 6012, 6352.
59. Muslim in *al-Ṣaḥīḥ:* Bk.: *al-Waṣiya* [The Bequests], Ch.: "On Bequeathing One Third of Wealth," 3:1250 §1628.
60. Mālik in *al-Muwaṭṭaʾ:* Bk.: *al-Waṣiya* [The Bequests], Ch.: "Bequeathals Should Not Exceed One Third," 2:763 §1456.
61. ʿAbd al-Razzāq in *al-Muṣannaf*, 9:64.
62. al-Ṭabarānī in *al-Muʿjam al-Awsaṭ*, 2:33 §1147.
63. Abū Yaʿlā in *al-Musnad*, 2:145 §834.
64. al-Bayhaqī in *al-Sunan al-Kubrā*, 6:268 §12345.
65. al-Bukhārī in *al-Ṣaḥīḥ:* Bk.: *al-Īmān* [The Faith], Ch.: "What has been Reported Concerning the fact that Actions are According to their Intentions, and that Everyone shall Receive what He Intended," 1:30 §56: Bk.: *al-Janāʾiz* [The Funerals], Ch.: "The Prophet's Eulogy of Saʿd b. Khawla," 1:435 §1233.
66. Muslim in *al-Ṣaḥīḥ:* Bk.: *al-Waṣiya* [The Bequests], Ch.: "Bequeathing One Third," 3:1250 §1628.
67. al-Nasāʾī in *al-Sunan al-Kubrā*, 5:383 §9206.
68. al-Ṭabarānī in *al-Muʿjam al-Kabīr*, 7:292 §7171.
69. al-Mundhirī in *al-Targhīb wa al-Tarhīb*, 3:41 §3000.
70. al-Bukhārī in *al-Ṣaḥīḥ:* Bk.: *al-Adab* [The Good Manners], Ch.: "Who Among the People Have Most Right to Kind Treatment," 5:2227 §5626.
71. Muslim in *al-Ṣaḥīḥ:* Bk.: *al-Birr wa al-ṣila wa al-ādāb* [The Piety, Familial Integration, and Good Manners], Ch.: "On Kindness Toward One's Parents, and that they are the Most Deserving of it," 4:1974 §2548.

72. Aḥmad b. Ḥanbal in *al-Musnad*, 5:5 §20060.
74. Ibn Mājah in *al-Sunan:* Bk.: *al-Adab* [The Good Manners], Ch.: "On Kindness Toward Parents," 2:1207 §6094.
75. Ibn Ḥibbān in *al-Ṣaḥīḥ*, 2:175 §433.
76. al-Ṭabarānī in *al-Muʿjam al-Kabīr*, 19:405 §961.
77. Abū Yaʿlā in *al-Musnad*, 10:482 §6094.
78. Ibn Rāhawayh in *al-Musnad*, 1:216 §172.
79. al-Bayhaqī in *al-Sunan al-kubrā*, 4:179 §7552.
80. Muslim in *al-Ṣaḥīḥ:* Bk.: *al-Ashriba* [The Drinks], Ch.: "What the Guest Should Do if Someone Uninvited Follows Him," 3:1609 §2037.
81. Aḥmad b. Ḥanbal in *al-Musnad*, 3:123 §12265.
82. al-Bukhārī in *al-Ṣaḥīḥ:* Bk.: *al-Hiba wa faḍlihā* [The Giving Gifts and its Virtue], Ch.: "On a Woman Giving a Gift to Someone Other than her Husband and Relinquishing it, 2:916 §2453: Bk.: *al-Shahādāt* [The Witnesses], Ch.: "On Problematic Areas," 2:955 §2542.
83. Aḥmad b. Ḥanbal in *al-Musnad*, 6:117 §24903.
84. Abū Dāwūd in *al-Sunan:* Bk.: *al-Nikāḥ* [The Marriage], Ch.: "On Dividing [Time] Between Wives," 2:243 §2138.
85. Ibn Mājah in *al-Sunan:* Bk.: *al-Aḥkām* [The Legal Rulings], Ch.: "Deciding by Casting Lots," 2:786 §2347.
86. al-Nasāʾī in *al-Sunan al-Kubrā*, 5:292 §8923.
87. al-Dārimī in *al-Sunan*, 2:194 §2208.
88. al-Bukhārī in *al-Ṣaḥīḥ:* Bk.: *al-Nikāḥ* [The Marriage], Ch.: "The Jealousy and Passion of Women," 5:2004 §4930.
89. Muslim in *al-Ṣaḥīḥ:* Bk.: *Faḍāʾil al-ṣaḥāba* [On the Virtues of the Companions], Ch.: "The Virtue of ʿĀʾisha," 4:1890 §2439.
90. Aḥmad b. Ḥanbal in *al-Musnad*, 6:61 §24363.
91. Ibn Ḥibbān in *al-Ṣaḥīḥ*, 16:49 §7112.
92. Abū Yaʿlā in *al-Musnad*, 8:298–299 §§4893, 4894.
93. al-Ṭabarānī in *al-Muʿjam al-kabīr*, 23:46 §122.
94. al-Tirmidhī in *al-Sunan:* Bk.: *al-Manāqib* [The Exemplary Qualities], Ch.: "The Virtue of the Prophet's ﷺ Wives," 5:709 §3895.
95. Ibn Mājah in *al-Sunan:* Bk.: *al-Nikāḥ* [The Marriage], Ch.: "On Living Kindly with Women," 1:636 §1977.
96. Ibn Ḥibbān in *al-Ṣaḥīḥ*, 9:484 §4177.
97. al-Bazzār in *al-Musnad*, 3:240 §1028.
98. al-Daylamī in *Musnad al-firdaws*, 2:170 §2853.
99. al-Haythamī in *Mawārid al-ẓamʾān*, 1:318 §1312.
100. Aḥmad b. Ḥanbal in *al-Musnad*, 4:447 §20027.
101. Abū Dāwūd in *al-Sunan:* Bk.: *al-Nikāḥ* [The Marriage], Ch.: "On the Woman's Right Over Her Husband," 2:244 §2142.
102. Ibn Mājah in *al-Sunan:* Bk.: *al-Nikāḥ* [The Marriage], Ch.: "On the Woman's Right Over Her Husband," 1:593 §1850.

103. al-Nasāʾī in *al-al-Sunan al-Kubrā*, 5:373, 6:323 §§9171, 11104.
104. ʿAbd *al*-Razzāq in *al-Muṣannaf*, 7:148 §12583.
105. Ibn Ḥibbān in *al-Ṣaḥīḥ*, 9:482 §4175.
106. al-Ṭabarānī in *al-Muʿjam al-Kabīr*, 19:427 §1038.
107. al-Bayhaqī in *al-Sunan al-Kubrā*, 7:305 §14556.
108. al-Mundhirī in *al-Targhīb wa al-Tarhīb*, 3:32 §2968.
109. Ibn Kathīr in *Tafsīr al-Qurʾān al-ʿAẓīm*, 1:272.
110. Aḥmad b. Ḥanbal in *al-Musnad*, 6:144 §25154.
111. Abū Dāwūd in *al-Sunan:* Bk.: *al-Nikāḥ* [The Marriage], Ch.: "On Dividing [Time] Between Wives," 2:232 §2134.
112. al-Dārimī in *al-Sunan:* Bk.: *al-Nikāḥ* [The Marriage], Ch.: "On Dividing [Time] Between Wives," 2:193 §2207.
113. Ibn Ḥibbān in *al-Ṣaḥīḥ*, 10:5 §4205.
114. Ibn Abī Shayba in *al-Muṣannaf*, 4:37 §18541.
115. al-Ḥākim in *al-Mustadrak*, 2:204 §2761.
116. al-Bayhaqī in *al-Sunan al-Kubrā*, 7:298 §14521.
117. Aḥmad b. Ḥanbal in *al-Musnad*, 6:39 §24164.
118. Abū Dāwūd in *al-Sunan:* Bk.: *al-Jihād* [The Striving], Ch.: "On Foot-racing," 3:29 §2578.
119. Ibn Mājah in *al-Sunan:* Bk.: *al-Nikāḥ* [The Marriage], Ch.: "On Treating Women Kindly," 1:531 §1979.
120. al-Nasāʾī in *al-al-Sunan al-Kubrā*, 5:304 §8943.
121. Ibn Ḥibbān in *al-Ṣaḥīḥ*, 10:545 §4691.
122. Ibn Abī Shayba in *al-Muṣannaf*, 6:531 §33588.
123. al-Ṭabarānī in *al-Muʿjam al-Kabīr*, 23:47 §125.
124. al-Bayhaqī in *al-Sunan al-Kubrā*, 10:18 §19544.
125. Aḥmad b. Ḥanbal in *al-Musnad*, 4:371–372 §18418.
126. Abū Dāwūd in *al-Sunan:* Bk.: *al-Adab* [The Good Manners], Ch.: "On Joking," 4:300 §4999.
127. al-Nasāʾī in *al-Sunan al-Kubrā*, 5:139, 356 §§8495, 9155.
128. al-Bazzār in *al-Musnad*, 8:223 §3275.
129. al-Haythamī in *Majmaʿ al-Zawāʾid*, 9:126.
130. al-Nasāʾī in *al-Sunan al-Kubrā:* Bk.: *al-Nikāḥ* [The Playing], Ch.: "On a Man Playing with His Wife," 5:302–303 §§8939, 8940.
131. al-Ṭabarānī in *al-Muʿjam al-Awsaṭ*, 8:118–119 §8147.
132. al-Bayhaqī in *al-Sunan al-Kubrā*, 10:15 §19525.
133. al-Haythamī in *Majmaʿ al-Zawāʾid*, 5:269.
134. al-Mundhirī in *al-Targhīb wa al-Tarhīb*, 2:180 §2014.
135. al-Suyūṭī in *al-Durr al-Manthūr*, 4:86.
136. Ibn Ḥibbān in *al-Ṣaḥīḥ*, 2:386 §620.
137. al-Mundhirī in *al-Targhīb wa al-Tarhīb*, 2:243 §2255.
138. al-Haythamī in *Mawārid al-Ẓamʾān*, 1:139 §523.
139. Abū al-Shaykh in *Akhlāq al-Nabī* ﷺ, 153–154.

140. al-Bukhārī in *al-Ṣaḥīḥ*: Bk.: *Tafsīr al-Qurʾān* [The Qurʾānic Exegesis], Ch.: "Regarding Allah's Words, ❴That Allah may forgive his past and future sins❵," 4:1830 §4557, also from al-Mughīra ؓ in *Kitāb al-Riqāq* [The Heart-softening Narrations], Ch.: "On Exhibiting Patience in Abstaining from Allah's Prohibitions," 5:2375.

141. Muslim in *al-Ṣaḥīḥ*: Bk.: *Ṣifa al-qiyāma wa al-janna wa al-nār* [On the Descriptions of the Resurrection, Paradise, and Hell-fire], Ch.: "On Abundant Works and Dedication in Worship," 4:2172 §2820.

142. al-Tirmidhī from al-Mughīra ؓ in *al-Sunan*: Bk.: *al-Ṣalāh* [The Prayer], Ch.: "On Striving in the Prayer," 2:268 §412

7. THE HOLY PROPHET'S MERCY AND KINDNESS TOWARD INFANTS, YOUNG CHILDREN AND YOUTH

ESSENTIAL READING:

1. Dr Tahir-ul-Qadri, Muhammad ؑ: The Merciful, Ch:7, p.157-180.

ADDITIONAL READINGS FOR TEACHERS AND STUDENTS:

1. al-Bukhārī in *al-Ṣaḥīḥ*: Bk.: *al-Adab* [The Good Manners], Ch.: "On Having Mercy toward One's Child, and Kissing and Hugging Him," 5:2235 §5652, also in al-Bukhārī's *al-Adab al-Mufrad*, 48 §98.
2. Muslim in *al-Ṣaḥīḥ*: Bk.: *al-Faḍāʾil* [The Virtues], Ch.: "His Mercy toward Children and Dependents, His Humility, and its Virtue," 4:1808 §2317.
3. Aḥmad b. Ḥanbal in *al-Musnad*, 6:56 §24336.
4. Ibn Mājah in *al-Sunan*: Bk.: *al-Adab* [The Good Manners], Ch.: "A Father's Goodness and Kindness toward Daughters," 2:1209 §3665.
5. al-Bayhaqī in *Shuʿab al-Īmān*, 7:466 §11013.
6. al-Bukhārī in *al-Ṣaḥīḥ*: Bk.: *al-Janāʾiz* [The Funerals], Ch.: "On the Statement of the Prophet ؐ, "Indeed, We Are Saddened Because of You," 1:439 §1241.
7. Muslim in *al-Ṣaḥīḥ*: Bk.: *al-Faḍāʾil* [The Virtues], Ch.: "His Mercy toward Children and Dependents, His Humility, and its Virtue," 4:1808 §2316.
8. Aḥmad b. Ḥanbal in *al-Musnad*, 3:112 §12123.

9. Abū Yaʿlā in *al-Musnad*, 7:205–206 §§4195, 4197.
10. al-Bayhaqī in *Shuʿab al-Īmān*, 7:465 §11011.
11. Ibn Saʿd in *al-Ṭabaqāt al-Kubrā*, 1:136–137.
12. al-Bukhārī in *al-Ṣaḥīḥ:* Bk.: *al-Ṣalāh* [The Prayer], Ch.: "When He Carried a Young Girl Upon His Shoulders in Prayer," 1:193 §494.
13. Muslim in *al-Ṣaḥīḥ:* Bk.: *al-Masājid wa mawāḍiʿ al-ṣalāh* [The Mosques and Prayer-places], Ch.: "The Permissibility of Carrying Children in Prayer,"1:385 §543.
14. Abū Dāwūd in *al-Sunan:* Bk.: *al-Ṣalāh* [The Prayer], Ch.: "Movement During Prayer," 1:241 §917.
15. al-Nasāʾī in *al-Sunan:* Bk.: *al-Ṣalāh* [The Prayer], Ch.: "On Carrying Children in Prayer and Sitting them Down," 3:10 §1204.
16. Mālik in *al-Muwaṭṭaʾ*, 1:170 §410.
17. Ibn Khuzayma in *al-Ṣaḥīḥ*, 1:383 §§783, 784.
18. al-Bukhārī in *al-Ṣaḥīḥ:* Bk.: *al-Manāqib* [The Exemplary Qualities], Ch.: "The Exemplary Qualities of al-Ḥasan and al-Ḥusayn ﷺ," 3:1370 §3539.
19. Muslim in *al-Ṣaḥīḥ:* Bk.: *Faḍāʾil al-ṣaḥāba* [The Virtues of the Companions], Ch.: "The Virtues of al-Ḥasan and al-Ḥusayn ﷺ," 4:1883 §2422.
21. Aḥmad b. Ḥanbal in *Faḍāʾil al-Ṣaḥāba*, 2:768 §1353.
22. al-Tirmidhī in *al-Sunan:* Bk.: *al-Manāqib* [The Exemplary Qualities], Ch.: "The Exemplary Virtues of al-Ḥasan and al-Ḥusayn ﷺ," 5:661 §3783.
24. Ibn Ḥibbān in *al-Ṣaḥīḥ*, 15:416 §6962.
25. Ibn Abī Shayba in *al-Muṣannaf*, 6:380 §32192.
26. al-Ṭabarānī in *al-Muʿjam al-Kabīr*, 3:31 §2582.
27. al-Bukhārī in *al-Ṣaḥīḥ:* Bk.: *al-Ṭahāra* [The Ritual Purification], Ch.: "The Legal Ruling on the Urine of Young Boys," 1:90 §221.
28. Muslim in *al-Ṣaḥīḥ:* Bk.: *al-Ṭahāra* [The Ritual Purity], Ch.: "The Legal Ruling on the Urine of Nursing Boy and How to Wash it," 1:237 §286.
29. Abū Dāwūd in *al-Sunan:* Bk.: *al-Ṭahāra* [The Ritual Purification], Ch.: "When a Boy's Urine gets on a Garment," 1:102 §374.
30. al-Nasāʾī in *al-Sunan:* Bk.: *al-Ṭahāra* [The Ritual Purification], Ch.: "Concerning the Urine of a Baby Boy that has yet to Eat Solids," 1:157 §302.
31. Mālik in *al-Muwaṭṭaʾ:* Bk.: *al-Ṭahāra* [The Ritual Purification], Ch.: "On What has been Reported Concerning the Urine of Young Baby Boys," 1:64 §141.
32. al-Ṭabarānī in *al-Muʿjam al-Kabīr*, 25:178 §437.
33. al-Ṭaḥāwī in *Sharḥ Maʿānī al-Āthār*, 1:92.
34. al-Bukhārī in *al-Ṣaḥīḥ:* Bk.: *al-Daʿawāt* [The Supplications], Ch.: "Praying for Blessings for Children and Wiping their Heads," 5:2338 §5994.

35. Muslim in *al-Ṣaḥīḥ:* Bk.: *al-Ṭahāra* [The Ritual Purification], Ch.: "The Legal Ruling on the Urine of Nursing Boy and How to Wash it, 1:237 §286.
36. Aḥmad b. Ḥanbal in *al-Musnad*, 6:212 §25812.
37. al-Ṭaḥāwī in *Sharḥ Maʿānī al-Āthār*, 1:93.
38. Ibn Rāhawayh in *al-Musnad*, 2:116 §587.
39. al-Ḥumaydī in *al-Musnad*, 1:88 §164.
40. al-Bukhārī in *al-Ṣaḥīḥ:* Bk.: *al-Adab* [The Good Manners], Ch.: "Good character and generosity and miserliness which is disliked," 5:2245 §5691.
41. Muslim in *al-Ṣaḥīḥ:* Bk.: *al-Faḍāʾil* [The Merits], Ch.: "The Prophet ﷺ was most generous of people," 4:1804 §2309.
42. Aḥmad b. anbal in *al-Musnad*, 3:265 §13823.
43. al-Tirmidhī *al-Jāniʿ al-Ṣaḥīḥ:* Bk.: *al-Birr wa al-ṣila* [Piety and familial integration], Ch.: "The Prophet's Morality," 4:368 §2015.
44. Ibn Ḥibbān in *al-Ṣaḥīḥ*, 7:152 §2893.
45. Abū Yaʿlā in *al-Musnad*, 6:104 §3367.
46. al-Bukhārī in *al-Ṣaḥīḥ:* Bk.: *al-Adhān* [The *Adhān*], Ch.: "On the One who Lightens his Prayer when Young Children Cry," 1:250 §677.
47. Muslim in *al-Ṣaḥīḥ:* Bk.: *al-Ṣalāh* [The Prayer], Ch.: "Commanding the Imams to Lighten the Prayer," 1:343 §470.
48. Aḥmad b. Ḥanbal in *al-Musnad*, 3:109 §12086.
49. Ibn Ḥibbān in *al-Ṣaḥīḥ*, 5:510 §2139.
51. Abū Yaʿlā in *al-Musnad*, 5:441 §3144.
52. al-Bayhaqī in *al-Sunan al-Kubrā*, 2:393 §3848, and in •*Shuʿab al-Īmān*, 7:477 §11054.
53. al-Bukhārī in *al-Ṣaḥīḥ:* Bk.: *al-Adab* [The Good Manners], Ch.: "On Having Mercy Toward a Child and Hugging and Kissing Him," 5:2234 §5649, and in Bk.: *al-Zakāt* [The Zakat], Ch.: "Beware of the Hellfire, Even if with Part of a Date and a Small Amount of Charity," 2:514 §1352.
54. Muslim in *al-Ṣaḥīḥ:* Bk.: *al-Birr wa al-ṣila wa al-adab* [On Piety, Familial Integration, and Good Manners], Ch.: "On the Virtue of Kindness Toward Girls, 4:2027 §2629.
55. Aḥmad b. Ḥanbal in *al-Musnad*, 6:87 §24616.
56. al-Tirmidhī in *al-Sunan:* Bk.: *al-Birr wa al-ṣila* [On Piety and the Familial Integration], Ch.: "On what has been Narrated Concerning Expenditures on Daughters and Sisters," 4:319 §1915.
57. Ibn Ḥibbān in *al-Ṣaḥīḥ*, 7:201 §2939.
58. ʿAbd al-Razzāq in *al-Muṣannaf*, 10:457 §19693.
59. Ibn Rāhawayh in *al-Musnad*, 3:976 §1695.
60. ʿAbd b. Ḥumayd in *al-Musnad*, 1:429 §1473.
61. al-Bukhārī in *al-Ṣaḥīḥ:* Bk.: *al-Aṭʿima* [The Foods], Ch.: "On

Mentioning Allah's Name Over Food and Eating with the Right Hand," 5:2056 §§5061, 5063.

62. Muslim in *al-Ṣaḥīḥ:* Bk.: *al-Ashriba* [The Drinks], Ch.: "On the Etiquette of Food and Drink and their Related Rulings," 3:1599 §2022.
63. Aḥmad b. Ḥanbal in *al-Musnad*, 4:26.
64. Ibn Mājah in *al-Sunan:* Bk.: *al-Aṭʿima* [The Foods], Ch.: "On Eating with the Right Hand," 2:1087 §3267.
65. al-Nasāʾī in *al-Sunan al-Kubrā*, 4:175 §6759, and in *ʿAmal al-Yawm wa al-Layla*, 1:259 §274.
66. al-Bayhaqī in *al-Sunan al-Kubrā*, 7:277 §4389.
67. al-Bukhārī in *al-Ṣaḥīḥ:* Bk.: *al-Musāqa wa al-shurb* [The Watering and Drink], Ch.: "On Drinks," 2:829 §2224, and in Ch.: "On the One who Sees that the Owner of a Watering Hole and Irrigation Channel has More Right to His Water," 2:834 §2237, and in Bk.: *al-Maẓālim wa al-ghaṣb* [On Oppression and Wrongful Seizure of Land], Ch.: "If Someone Give him Permission or Allows him without Specifying for How Long," 2:865 §2319, and in Bk.: *al-Hiba wa faḍlihā wa al-taḥrīḍ ʿalayhā* [On Gift-giving and its Virtues and its Encouragement], Ch.: "On Held and Withheld Gifts and Divided and Undivided Gifts," 2:920 §2464, and in Bk.: *al-Ashriba* [The Drinks], Ch.: "Should a Man Seek Permission from the one on his Right Regarding a Drink in order to Give it to the Eldest?" 5:2130 §5297.
68. Muslim in *al-Ṣaḥīḥ:* Bk.: *al-Ashriba* [The Drinks], Ch.: "The Recommendation to pass Water or Milk or its like to the Right side of the One who Starts with it," 3:1604 §2030.
69. Aḥmad b. Ḥanbal in *al-Musnad*, 5:333, 338 §§22875, 22918.
70. Mālik in *al-Muwaṭṭaʾ:* Bk.: *Ṣifa al-nabī* ﷺ [The Description of the Prophet ﷺ], Ch.: "The Sunna of Drinking and Passing it to the Right," 2:926 §1656.
71. Ibn Ḥibbān in *al-Ṣaḥīḥ*, 12:151 §5335.
72. al-Rabīʿ in *al-Musnad*, 1:149 §375.
73. al-Nawawī in *Riyāḍ al-Ṣāliḥīn*, 1:162.
74. al-Bukhārī in *al-Ṣaḥīḥ:* Bk.: *al-Adab* [The Good Manners], Ch.: "On Giving an Agnomen [*kunya*] to a Child and Man without a Child," 5:2291 §5850.
75. Muslim in *al-Ṣaḥīḥ:* Bk.: *al-Ādab* [The Good Manners], Ch.: "The Recommendation to Rub a Newborn's Palate with a Date after his Birth, and Taking him to a Righteous Person to Perform it," 3:1692 §2150.
76. Aḥmad b. Ḥanbal in *al-Musnad*, 3:119, 171 §§12220, 12776.
77. Abū Dāwūd in *al-Sunan:* Bk.: *al-Adab* [The Good Manners], Ch.: "What has been Reported on a Childless Man taking an Agnomen [*kunya*]," 4:293 §4969.
78. al-Tirmidhī in *al-Sunan:* Bk.: *al-Ṣalāh* [The Prayer], Ch.: "What has

been Narrated Concerning Prayer on a Floor-spread, 2:154 §333.
79. Ibn Mājah in *al-Sunan:* Bk.: *al-Adab* [The Good Manners], Ch.: "On Joking," 2:1226 §3720.
80. Ibn Ḥibbān in *al-Ṣaḥīḥ*, 6:82 §2308.
81. al-Bukhārī in *al-Ṣaḥīḥ:* Bk.: *al-Ṣulḥ* [The Peace Treaties], Ch.: "On the Prophet's ﷺ Saying to Ḥasan b. ʿAlī, 'This Son of Mine is a Sayyid [Chief]," 2:962 §2557.
82. al-Nasāʾī *al-Sunan:* Bk.: *al-Jumuʿa* [The Friday Prayer], Ch.: "On the Imam Addressing his Congregation While on the Pulpit," 3:107 §1410.
83. Aḥmad b. Ḥanbal in *al-Musnad*, 5:37 §20408, and *Faḍāʾil al-Ṣaḥāba*, 2:785 §1460.
84. Ibn ʿAsākir in *Tārīkh Dimashq*, 13:232.
85. al-Bukhārī in *al-Ṣaḥīḥ:* Bk.: *al-Adab* [The Good Manners], Ch.: "On Placing a Young Child on One's Thigh," 5:2236 §5657.
86. Aḥmad b. Ḥanbal in *al-Musnad*, 5:205 §21835.
87. al-Nasāʾī in *al-Sunan al-Kubrā*, 5:53 §8184.
88. Ibn Ḥibbān in *al-Ṣaḥīḥ*, 15:415 §6961.
89. Ibn ʿAsākir in *Tārīkh Dimashq*, 8:53.
90. Ibn Saʿd in *al-Ṭabaqāt al-Kubrā*, 4:62.
91. al-Bukhārī in *al-Ṣaḥīḥ:* Bk.: *al-Adhān* [The *Adhān*], Ch.: "On the One who Lightens his Prayer when Young Children Cry," 1:250 §675, and Ch.: "On Women Going to the Mosques at Nighttime and Darkness," 1:296 §830.
92. Aḥmad b. Ḥanbal in *al-Musnad*, 5:305 §22655.
93. Abū Dāwūd in *al-Sunan:* Bk.: *al-Ṣalāh* [The Prayer], Ch.: "On Lightening the Prayer due to an Unforeseen Happening," 1:209 §789.
94. al-Nasāʾī in *al-Sunan:* Bk.: *al-Imāma* [The Imamate], Ch.: "What is due upon the Imam in Lightening the Prayer," 2:95 §825, and in *al-Sunan al-Kubrā*, 1:290 §899.
95. Ibn Abī Shayba in *al-Muṣannaf*, 1:407 §3678.
96. al-Bayhaqī in *al-Sunan al-Kubrā*, 3:118 §5063.
97. Muslim in *al-Ṣaḥīḥ:* Bk.: *al-Ṣalāh* [The Prayer], Ch.: "On Commanding the Imams to Lighten the Prayer," 1:342 §470.
98. Aḥmad b. Ḥanbal in *al-Musnad*, 3:106 §12609.
99. Abū Yaʿlā in *al-Musnad*, 6:109 §3376.
100. Abū ʿAwāna in *al-Musnad*, 1:422 §1563.
101. al-Bayhaqī in *al-Sunan al-Kubrā*, 2:393 §3847.
102. Muslim in *al-Ṣaḥīḥ:* Bk.: *al-Ṣila wa al-ādāb* [On the Familial Integration and Good Manners], Ch.: "The Virtue of Kindness Toward Daughters," 4:2027 §2631.
103. al-Tirmidhī in *al-Sunan:* Bk.: *al-Birr wa al-ṣila* [The Piety and the Familial Integration], Ch.: "On what has been Reported Concerning Expenditures on Daughters and Sisters," 4:319 §1914.

104. al-Bukhārī in *al-Adab al-Mufrad*, 308 §894.
105. Ibn Abī Shayba in *al-Muṣannaf*, 5:222 §25439.
106. al-Ḥākim in *al-Mustadrak*, 4:196 §7350.
107. al-Ṭabarānī in *al-Muʿjam al-awsaṭ*, 1:176 §557.
108. al-Bayhaqī in *Shuʿab al-īmān*, 6:404 §8674.
109. Aḥmad b. Ḥanbal in *al-Musnad*, 5:345.
110. Abū Dāwūd in *al-Sunan:* Bk.: *al-Ṣalāh* [The Prayer], Ch.: "On the Imam Interrupting the Oratory Due to an Unforeseen Happening," 1:290 §1109.
111. al-Tirmidhī in *al-Sunan:* Bk.: *al-Manāqib* [The Exemplary Qualities], Ch.: "The Exemplary Qualities of Ḥasan and Ḥusayn ﷺ," 5:658 §3774.
112. al-Nasāʾī in *al-Sunan:* Bk.: *Ṣalah al-ʿīdayn* [The Two Eid Prayers], Ch.: "On the Imam Descending from the Pulpit Before He Completes His Oratory," 3:192 §1585.
113. Ibn Mājah in *al-Sunan:* Bk.: *al-Libās* [The Clothing], Ch.: "On Men Wearing Red Garments," 2:1190 §3600.
114. Ibn Khuzayma in *al-Ṣaḥīḥ*, 2:355 §1456.
115. Ibn Ḥibbān in *al-Ṣaḥīḥ*, 13:403 §6039.
116. Ibn Abī Shayba in *al-Muṣannaf*, 6:379 §32189.
117. al-Ḥākim in *al-Mustadrak*, 1:424 §1059.
118. al-Bayhaqī in *al-Sunan al-kubrā*, 3:218 §5610.
119. Aḥmad b. Ḥanbal in *al-Musnad*, 2:207 §6935.
120. Abū Dāwūd in *al-Sunan:* Bk.: *al-Sunna* [The Prophetic Practice], Ch.: "On Mercy," 4:286 §4943.
121. al-Tirmidhī in *al-Sunan:* Bk.: *al-Birr wa al-ṣila* [The Piety and the Familial Integration], Ch.: "On what has been Reported Concerning Mercy Toward Young Children," 4:322 §1920.
122. al-Bukhārī in *al-Ādab al-mufrad*, 130 §355.
123. Ibn Abī Shayba in *al-Muṣannaf*, 5:214 §25359.
124. al-Ḥākim in *al-Mustadrak*, 4:197 §7353.
125. al-Ṭabarānī in *al-Muʿjam al-kabīr*, 8:308 §8154.
126. Aḥmad b. Ḥanbal in *al-Musnad*, 1:257 §2329.
127. al-Tirmidhī in *al-Sunan:* Bk.: *al-Birr wa al-ṣila* [The Piety and the Familial Integration], Ch.: "On what has been Reported Concerning Mercy Toward Young Children," 4:322 §1921.
128. Ibn Ḥībbān in *al-Ṣaḥīḥ*, 2:203 §458.
129. al-Bazzār in *al-Musnad*, 7:158 §2718.
130. al-Ṭabarānī in *al-Muʿjam al-awsaṭ*, 5:107 §4812 and in *al-Muʿjam al-kabīr*, 11:449 §12276.
131. al-Tirmidhī in *al-Sunan:* Bk.: *al-Buyūʿ* [The Sales], Ch.: "The Undesirability of Separating two Brothers or a Mother from Her Child in Sales [of Slaves]," 3:580 §1283.
132. al-Dārimī in *al-Sunan*, 2:299 §2479.

133. al-Dāraquṭnī in *al-Sunan*, 3:67 §256.
134. Aḥmad b. Ḥanbal in *al-Musnad*, 3:447 §15740.
135. Abū Dāwūd in *al-Sunan:* Bk.: *al-Adab* [The Good Manners], Ch.: "On the Severe Condemnation of Lying," 4:298 §4991.
136. Ibn Abī Shayba in *al-Muṣannaf*, 5:236 §25609.
135. al-Bayhaqī in *al-Sunan al-Kubrā*, 10:198 §20629, as well as *Shuʿab al-Īmān*, 4:210 §4822.
136. al-Maqdisī in *al-Aḥādīth al-Mukhtāra*, 9:483 §466.
137. al-Mundhirī in *al-Targhīb wa al-Tarhīb*, 3:370 §4467.
138. al-Nasāʾī in *al-Sunan al-Kubrā:* Bk.: *al-Manāqib* [The Exemplary Qualities], Ch.: "The Virtues of Ḥasan and Ḥusayn," 5:50 §8170.
139. Ibn Khuzayma in *al-Ṣaḥīḥ*, 2:48 §887.
140. Ibn Abī Shayba in *al-Muṣannaf*, 6:378 §32174.
141. al-Bazzār in *al-Musnad*, 5:226 §1834.
142. Ibn Ḥibbān in *al-Ṣaḥīḥ*, 15:426 §6970.
143. Abū Yaʿlā in *al-Musnad*, 8:434 §5017.
144. al-Ṭabarānī in *al-Muʿjam al-Kabīr*, 3:47 §2644.
145. al-Haythamī in *Mawārid al-Ẓamʾān*, 1:552 §2233 and *Majmaʿ al-Zawāʾid*, 9:179.
146. Aḥmad b. Ḥanbal in *al-Musnad*, 4:172 §17597.
147. Ibn Mājah in the introduction to *al-Sunan*, section, "The Virtue of Ḥasan and Ḥusayn, the Two Sons of ʿAlī b. Abī Ṭālib ﷺ," 1:51 §144.
148. al-Bukhārī in *al-Adab al-Mufrad*, 133 §364.
149. Ibn Abī Shayba in *al-Muṣannaf*, 6:380 §32196.
150. Ibn Ḥibbān in *al-Ṣaḥīḥ*, 15:427–428 §6971.
151. al-Ḥākim in *al-Mustadrak*, 3:194 §4820.
152. al-Ṭabarānī in *al-Muʿjam al-Kabīr*, 3:33 §2589.
153. al-Haythamī in *Mawārid al-Ẓamʾān*, 1:554 §2240.
154. al-Nasāʾī in *al-Sunan al-Kubrā:* Bk.: *al-Manāqib* [The Exemplary Qualities], Ch.: "The Children of the Anṣār ﷺ," 5:92 §8349.
155. Ibn Ḥibbān in *al-Ṣaḥīḥ*, 2:205–206 §459.
156. Abū Nuʿaym in *Ḥīlya al-Awliyāʾ*, 6:291.
157. al-Baghawī in *Sharḥ al-Sunna*, 12:224.
158. al-Maqdisī in *al-Aḥādīth al-Mukhtāra*, 4:425 §1603.
159. Aḥmad b. Ḥanbal in *al-Musnad*, 3:435 §15626–15627 and 4:24 §16342.
160. al-Nasāʾī in *al-Sunan al-Kubrā:* Bk.: *al-Siyar* [The Military Expeditions], Ch.: "The Prohibition of Killing the Children of the Pagans," 5:184 §8616.
161. al-Dārimī in *al-Sunan*, 2:294 §2463.
162. Ibn Abī Shayba in *al-Muṣannaf*, 6:484 §33131.
163. Ibn Ḥibbān in *al-Ṣaḥīḥ*, 1:341 §132.
164. Ibn Abī ʿĀṣim in *al-Āḥād wa al-Mathānī*, 2:375 §1160.
165. al-Ḥākim in *al-Mustadrak*, 2:133–134 §2566–2567.

166. al-Ṭabarānī in *al-Muʿjam al-Kabīr*, 1:284;5829 al-Bayhaqī in *al-Sunan al-Kubrā*, 9:77 §17868.
167. Abū Nuʿaym in *Ḥilyat al-Awliyā'*, 8:263.
168. al-Ṭaḥāwī in *Sharḥ maʿānī al-Āthār*, 4:89.
169. Tamām al-Rāzī in *al-Fawā'id*, 2:237 §1616.
170. al-Bayhaqī in *Shuʿab al-Īmān*, 6:410 §8700 and 7:468 §11022.
171. Ibn ʿAsākir in *Tārīkh Dimashq*, 13:396.
172. al-Haythamī in *Majmaʿ al-Zawā'id*, 8:156.
173. Ibn Mājah in *al-Sunan:* Bk.: *al-Nikāḥ* [The Marriage], Ch.: "On Singing the Playing the Leather Drum [*daff*]," 1:612 §1899.
174. Abū Yaʿlā in *al-Musnad*, 6:134 §3409.
175. Abū Nuʿaym in *Ḥilya al-Awliyā'*, 3:120.
176. al-Maqdisī in *Aḥādīth al-Shiʿr*, 1:75 §26.
177. al-Haythamī in *Majmaʿ al-Zawā'id*, 10:42.
178. Ibn al-Sunnī in *ʿAmal al-Yawm wa al-Layla*, 190 §229.
179. al-ʿAsqalānī in *Fatḥ al-Bārī*, 7:261.
180. Aḥmad b. Ḥanbal in *al-Musnad*, 5:51, 49, and 44 §§§20535, 20517, 20466.
181. Ibn Ḥibbān in *al-Ṣaḥīḥ*, 15:418–419 §6964.
182. al-Ṭabarānī in *al-Muʿjam al-Kabīr*, 3:34 §2591.
183. al-Bazzār in *al-Musnad*, 9:111 §3657.
184. al-Haythamī in *Majmaʿ al-Zawā'īd*, 9:175.
185. Aḥmad b. Ḥanbal in *al-Musnad*, 3:231 §13442.
186. Ibn Abī ʿĀṣim in *al-Sunna*, 1:157 §355.
187. Ibn ʿAsākir in *Tārīkh Dimashq*, 50:65.
188. Aḥmad b. Ḥanbal in *al-Musnad*, 4:348 §19082.
189. al-Ṭabarānī in *al-Muʿjam al-Kabīr*, 7:77 §6423.
190. al-Haythamī in *Majmaʿ al-Zawā'īd*, 1:284.

8. The Holy Prophet's Mercy and Kindness toward the Weak, the Poor and the Indigent

Essential Reading:

1. Dr Tahir-ul-Qadri, Muhammad ﷺ: The Merciful, Ch:8, p.181-197.

Additional Readings for Teachers and Students:

1. al-Bukhārī in *al-Ṣaḥīḥ:* Bk.: *al-Adhān* [The *Adhān*], Ch.: "When One

Prays Alone Let Him Lengthen it for as Long as He Likes," 1:248 §671.

2. Muslim in *al-Ṣaḥīḥ:* Bk.: *al-Ṣalāh* [The Prayer], Ch.: "On Commanding the Imams to Lighten the Prayer," 1:341 §467.
3. Aḥmad b. Ḥanbal in *al-Musnad*, 2:486 §10311.
4. Abū Dāwūd in *al-Sunan:* Bk.: *al-Ṣalāh* [The Prayer], Ch.: "On Lightening the Prayer," 1:211 §794.
5. al-Tirmidhī in *al-Sunan:* Bk.: *al-Ṣalāh* [The Prayer], Ch.: "On What has been Reported Regarding the Statement that if One of You Leads the People in Prayer, that He Should Lighten It," 1:461 §236.
6. al-Nasā'ī in *al-Sunan:* Bk.: *al-Imāma* [The Imamate], Ch.: "On the Duty of the Imam to Lighten [the Prayer]," 2:94 §823.
7. Mālik in *al-Muwaṭṭa':* Bk.: *Ṣalāt al-jamā'a* [The Congregational Prayer], Ch.: "What is Done in the Congregational Prayer," 1:134 §301.
8. Ibn Ḥibbān in *al-Ṣaḥīḥ*, 5:56 § 1760.
9. al-Bayhaqī in *al-Sunan al-kubrā*, 3:117 §5058.
10. al-Bukhārī in *al-Ṣaḥīḥ:* Bk.: *Tafsīr al-Qur'ān* [The Qur'ānic Exegesis], Ch.: "On the Verse ﴾Utulun bad dhalika zanim﴿," 4:1870 §4634 and in *Kitāb al-Adab* [The Good Manners], Ch.: "On Arrogance," 5:2255 §5723, and in Bk.: *al-Aymān wa al-nudhūr* [The Trusts and Vows], Ch.: "On Allah's Statement, ﴾*They Swore to Allah with Their Fiercest Oaths*﴿," 6:2452 §6281.
11. Muslim in *al-Ṣaḥīḥ:* Bk.: *al-Janna wa ṣifa na'īmihā wa ahlihā* [On the Description of Paradise and its Bounties and Inhabitants], Ch.: "The Haughty Shall Enter Hellfire and the Weak Shall Enter Paradise," 4:2190 §2853.
12. Aḥmad b. Ḥanbal in *al-Musnad*, 4:306 §18750.
13. al-Tirmidhī in *al-Sunan:* Bk.: *Ṣifa jahannam* [On the Description of the Hellfire], chapter thirteen, 4:717 §2605.
14. Ibn Mājah in *al-Sunan:* Bk.: *al-Zuhd* [The Renunciation], Ch.: "Concerning He to Whom No One Shows Concern," 2:1378 §3116.
15. al-Nasā'ī in *al-Sunan al-kubrā*, 6:497 §11615.
16. al-Bukhārī in *al-Ṣaḥīḥ:* Bk.: *al-Tafsīr* [The Qur'ānic Exegesis], Ch.: "On Allah's Statement, ﴾*Are There Any More?*﴿, 4:1836 §4569.
17. Muslim in *al-Ṣaḥīḥ:* Bk.: *al-Janna wa ṣifa na'īmiha wa ahlihā* [On the Description of Paradise and its Bounties and Inhabitants], Ch.: "The Haughty Shall Enter Hellfire and the Weak Shall Enter Paradise," 4:2186 §2846.
18. Aḥmad b. Ḥanbal in *al-Musnad*, 2:450 §9815.
19. al-Tirmidhī in *al-Sunan:* Bk.: *Ṣifa al-janna* [On the Description of Paradise], Ch.: "On what has been Reported Concerning the Dispute Between the Paradise and Hellfire," 4:694 §2561.
20. 'Abd al-Razzāq *al-Muṣannaf*, 11:422 §20893.
21. Abū Ya'lā in *al-Musnad*, 11:179–180 §6290.

22. Abū ʿAwāna in *al-Musnad*, 1:160 §464.
23. al-Bukhārī in *al-Ṣaḥīḥ:* Bk.: *al-Zakāt* [The Zakat], Ch.: "Charity is Due upon Every Muslim," 2:524 §1376.
24. Muslim in *al-Ṣaḥīḥ:* Bk.: *al-Zakāt* [The Zakat], Ch.: "Demonstrating that the Word Charity [*Ṣadaqa*] Includes Every Type of Goodness," 6:699 §1008; •Aḥmad b. Ḥanbal in *al-Musnad*, 4:295 §19549.
25. al-Nasāʾī in *al-Sunan:* Bk.: *al-Zakāt* [The Zakat], Ch.: "On the Charity of a Slave," 5:64 §2538.
26. al-Dārimī in *al-Sunan*, 2:399 §2747.
27. Ibn Abī Shayba in *al-Muṣannaf*, 5:336 §26649.
28. al-Bazzār in *al-Musnad*, 8:102 §3100.
29. al-Ṭayālisī in *al-Musnad*, 1:67 §495.
30. al-Bukhārī in *al-Ṣaḥīḥ:* Bk.: *al-Ṣalāh* [The Prayer], Ch.: "On Sweeping the Mosque," 1:175–176 §§446, 448; in *Kitāb al-Janāʾiz* [The Funeral Prayer], Ch.: "Praying Over the Grave After [the Deceased] is Buried," 1:448 §2172.
31. Muslim in *al-Ṣaḥīḥ:* Bk.: *al-Janāʾiz* [The Funeral Prayers], Ch.: "Praying Over a Grave," 2:659 §956.
32. Aḥmad b. Ḥanbal in *al-Musnad*, 2:388 §9025.
33. Abū Dāwūd in *al-Sunan:* Bk.: *al-Janāʾiz* [The Funerals], Ch.: "Praying Over a Grave," 3:211 §3203.
34. Ibn Mājah in *al-Sunan:* Bk.: *Mā jāʾ fī al-Janāʾiz* [What has been Reported Regarding the Funerals], Ch.: "On What has been Reported Regarding Prayers Over the Graves," 1:489 §1527–1529.
35. al-Nasāʾī in *al-Sunan al-Kubrā*, 1:651 §2149.
36. Ibn Ḥibbān in *al-Ṣaḥīḥ*, 7:355 §3086.
37. al-Bayhaqī in *al-Sunan al-Kubrā*, 4:46–47 §§§2, 68, 6806.
38. al-Nasāʾī in *al-Sunan:* Bk.: *al-Janāʾiz* [The Funerals], Ch.: "On Praying the Funeral Prayer at Night," 4:69 §1969, and in Ch.: "On Calling the *Adhān* Announcing the Funeral Prayer," 4:40 §1907, also in al-Nasāʾī's *al-Sunan al-Kubrā*, 1:623 §2034.
39. Mālik in *al-Muwaṭṭaʾ:* Bk.: *al-Janāʾiz* [The Funeral Prayer], Ch.: "Uttering *Takbīr* [*Allāh akbar*] During the Funeral Prayer," 1:227 §533.
40. al-Shāfiʿī in *al-Musnad*, 1:358.
41. Ibn Abī Shayba in *al-Muṣannaf*, 2:476 §11223.
42. al-Bayhaqī in *al-Sunan al-Kubrā*, 4:35 §6727.
43. al-Ruwayānī in *al-Musnad*, 2:294 §1238.
44. al-Bukhārī in *al-Ṣaḥīḥ:* Bk.: *al-Jihād* [The Striving], Ch.: "Concerning He Who Seeks the Aid of the Weak and Righteous in War, 3:1061 §2739.
45. al-Nasāʾī in *al-Sunan:* Bk.: *al-Jihād* [The Striving], Ch.: "On Seeking Victory by Means of the Weak," 6:45 §3178, and in *al-Sunan al-Kubrā*, 3:30 §4387.

46. al-Shāshī in *al-Musnad*, 1:132 §70.
47. al-Dawraqī in *Musnad Saʿd*, 105 §51.
48. al-Bayhaqī in *al-Sunan al-Kubrā*, 3:345 §6181 and 6:331 §12684.
49. al-Mundhirī in *al-Targhīb wa al-Tarhīb*, 4:71 §4842.
50. al-Nawawī in *Riyāḍ al-Ṣāliḥīn*, 89.
51. Aḥmad b. Ḥanbal in *al-Musnad*, 5:198 §21779.
52. Abū Dāwūd in *al-Sunan:* Bk.: *al-Jihād* [The Striving], Ch.: "Seeking Victory by the Forelocks of Horses and the Weak People," 3:32 §2594.
53. al-Tirmidhī in *al-Sunan:* Bk.: *al-Jihād* [The Striving], Ch.: "On what has been Reported Concerning the Pursuit of Military Victory by Virtue of the Impoverished Muslims," 4:206 §1702.
54. al-Nasāʾī in *al-Sunan:* Bk.: *al-Jihād* [The Striving], Ch.: "On Seeking Victory by Virtue of the Weak," 6:45 §3179, also in *al-Sunan al-Kubrā*, 3:30 §4388.
55. Ibn Ḥibbān in *al-Ṣaḥīḥ*, 11:85 §4767.
56. al-Ḥākim in *al-Mustadrak*, 2:116–117 §§2509, 2641.
57. Muslim in *al-Ṣaḥīḥ:* Bk.: *al- ayḍ* [The Menstruation], Ch.: "The Description of the Male and Female Sexual Fluids," 1:202 §315.
58. Ibn Khuzayma in *al-Ṣaḥīḥ*, 1:116 §232.
59. Ibn Ḥibbān in *al-Ṣaḥīḥ*, 16:440 §7422.
60. al-Ḥākim in *al-Mustadrak*, 3:548 §6039.
61. al-Ṭabarānī in *al-Muʿjam al-Awsaṭ*, 1:149 §467, and in *al-Muʿjam al-Kabīr*, 2:93 §1414.
62. al-Bayhaqī in *al-Sunan al-Kubrā*, 1:169 §769.
63. al-Bukhārī in *al-Ṣaḥīḥ:* Bk.: *al-Riqāq* [The Heart Softening Narrations], Ch.: "The Virtue of Poverty," 5:2369 §6082.
64. Ibn Mājah in *al-Sunan:* Bk.: *al-Zuhd* [The Renunciation], Ch.: "The Virtue of the Poor," 2:1379 §4120; al-Ṭabarānī in *al-Muʿjam al-Kabīr*, 6:169 §5883.
65. al-Ruwayānī in *al-Musnad*, 2:188–189 §1016.
66. al-Bayhaqī in *Shuʿab al-Īmān*, 7:330 §10481.
67. Aḥmad b. Ḥanbal in *al-Musnad*, 2:343 §8502.
68. al-Tirmidhī *al-Sunan:* Bk.: *al-Zuhd* [The Renunciation], Ch.: "On what has been Reported Concerning the Poor Immigrants Entering Paradise Before Their Wealthy Ones," 4:578 §2354.
69. Ibn Mājah in *al-Sunan:* Bk.: *al-Zuhd* [The Renunciation], Ch.: "The Rank of the Poor," 2:1380 §4122.
70. al-Nasāʾī in *al-Sunan al-Kubrā*, 6:412 §11348.
71. Ibn Ḥibbān in *al-Ṣaḥīḥ*, 2:451 §676.
72. Ibn Abī Shayba in *al-Muṣannaf*, 7:86 §34392.
73. Aḥmad b. Ḥanbal in *al-Musnad*, 5:159 §21453.
74. Ibn Ḥibbān in *al-Ṣaḥīḥ:* Bk.: *al-Birr wa al-iḥsān* [The Piety and Excellence], Ch.: "On Preserving Family Ties and Severing Them,

and a Mention of the Command of the Chosen One [al-Muṣṭafā] ﷺ Concerning the Familial Integration, Even if They Are Severed [by others]," 1:194 §449.

75. al-Bazzār in *al-Musnad*, 9:383 §3966.
76. al-Ṭabarānī in *al-Muʿjam al-Ṣaghīr*, 2:48 §758.
77. al-Bayhaqī in *al-Sunan al-Kubrā*, 10:91 §19973, and in *Shuʿab al-Īmān*, 3:240 §3429.
78. al-Mundhirī in *al-Targhīb wa al-Tarhīb*, 3:228–229 §3802.
79. al-Haythamī in *Mawārid al-Zamʾān*, 1:500 §2041.
80. al-Ḥākim in *al-Mustadrak*, 4:268 §7947 and al-Mundhirī in *al-Targhīb wa al-Tarhīb*, 4:67 §3827.
81. Muslim in *al-Ṣaḥīḥ:* Bk.: *al-Zuhd wa al-raqāʾiq* [The Renunciation and Heart Softening Narrations], 4:2285 §2979 and al-Bayhaqī in *Shuʿab al-Īmān*, 7:300–301, 336 §§§10379, 10381, 10493.
82. al-Bukhārī in *al-Ṣaḥīḥ:* Bk.: *al-Nikāḥ* [The Marriage], Ch.: "Whoever Refuses an Invitation [to a Wedding Banquet] Has Disobeyed Allāh and His Messenger ﷺ," 5:1985 §4882.
83. Muslim in *al-Ṣaḥīḥ:* Bk.: *al-Nikāḥ* [The Marriage], Ch.: "On the Command to Accept the Invitation When Given," 2:1054 §1423.
84. Aḥmad b. Ḥanbal in *al-Musnad*, 2:405 §9250.
86. Abū Dāwūd in *al-Sunan:* Bk.: *al-Aṭʿima* [The Foods], Ch.: "On what has been Reported Concerning the Acceptance of Invitations," 3:341 §3742.
87. Ibn Mājah in *al-Sunan:* Bk.: *al-Nikāḥ* [The Marriage], Ch.: "Responding to Someone's Invitation," 1:616 §1913.
88. al-Nasāʾī in *al-Sunan al-Kubrā*, 4:141 §6613.
89. al-Dārimī in *al-Sunan*, 2:143 §2066.
90. Ibn Ḥibbān in *al-Ṣaḥīḥ*, 12:116 §5304.

9. THE HOLY PROPHET'S MERCY AND KINDNESS TOWARD WIDOWS AND ORPHANS

ESSENTIAL READING:

1. Dr Tahir-ul-Qadri, Muhammad ﷺ: The Merciful, Ch:9, p.199-208.

ADDITIONAL READINGS FOR TEACHERS AND STUDENTS:

1. al-Bukhārī in *al-Ṣaḥīḥ:* Bk.: *al-Istisqāʾ* [The Prayer for Seeking Rain],

Ch.: "On the People Asking the Imam for the Prayer of Seeking Rain When They Suffer from a Drought and Famine," 1:342 §963;

2. Aḥmad b. Ḥanbal in *al-Musnad*, 2:93 §§5673, 26.
3. Ibn Mājah in *al-Sunan:* Bk.: *Iqāmat al-ṣalāh wa al-sunna fīhā* [The Establishment of the Prayer and the Sunna Therein], Ch.: "On what has been Reported Concerning the Invocation Said in the Prayer for Rain," 1:405 §1272.
4. al-Bayhaqī in *al-Sunan al-Kubrā*, 3:352 §6218–6219.
5. al-Khaṭīb al-Baghdādī in *Tārīkh Baghdād*, 14:387 §7700.
6. al-ʿAsqalānī in *Taghlīq al-Taʿlīq*, 2:389 §1009.
7. Ibn Kathīr in *al-Bidāya wa al-Nihāya*, 4:2, 471.
8. al-Mizzī in *Tuḥfa al-Ashrāf*, 5:359 §6775.
9. al-Bukhārī in *al-Ṣaḥīḥ:* Bk.: *al-Ṭalāq* [The Divorce], Ch.: "On Public Imprecation," 5:2032 §4998, and in Bk.: *al-Ādab* [The Good Manners], Ch.: "The Virtue of One Who Supports an Orphan," 5:2237 §5659.
10. Aḥmad b. Ḥanbal in *al-Musnad*, 5:333 §22871.
11. Abū Dāwūd in *al-Sunan:* Bk.: *al-Nawm* [The Sleep], Ch.: "Concerning the One Who Embraces an Orphan," 4:338 §5150.
12. al-Tirmidhī in al-Sunan: Bk.: *al-Birr wa al-ṣila* [The Piety and Familial Integration], Ch.: "On what has been Reported Concerning Mercy and Care for an Orphan," 4:321 §1918.
13. Mālik in *al-Muwaṭṭaʾ:* Bk.: *al-Shiʿr* [The Poetry], Ch.: "The Sunna with Regard to Poetry," 2:948 §1700.
14. Ibn Ḥibbān in *al-Ṣaḥīḥ*, 2:207 §460.
15. Abū Yaʿlā in *al-Musnad*, 13:546 §7553.
16. al-Ṭabarānī in *al-Muʿjam al-Kabīr*, 6:173 §5905.
17. Muslim in *al-Ṣaḥīḥ:* Bk.: *al-Zuhd wa al-raqāʾiq* [The Renunciation and Heart Softening Narrations], Ch.: "On Excellence Toward the Widow, the Indigent, and the Orphan," 4:2287 §2983.
18. Aḥmad b. Ḥanbal in *al-Musnad*, 2:375 §8868.
19. al-Bayhaqī in *Shuʿab al-Īmān*, 7:471 §11030.
20. al-Mundhirī in *al-Targhīb wa al-Tarhīb*, 3:235 §3832.
21. al-Ḥumaydī in *al-Musnad*, 2:370 §838.
22. al-Bukhārī in *al-Adab al-Mufrad*, 62 §133.
23. al-Ṭabarānī in *al-Muʿjam al-Kabīr*, 20:320 §759.
24. Aḥmad b. Ḥanbal in *al-Musnad*, 4:344 §19047.
25. al-Tirmidhī in *al-Sunan:* Bk.: *al-Birr wa al-ṣila* [The Piety and Familial Integration], Ch.: "On what has been Reported Concerning Mercy and Care for the Orphan," 4:320 §1917.
26. Abū Yaʿlā in *al-Musnad*, 2:227 §926.
27. al-Ṭayālisī in *al-Musnad*, 1:187 §1322.
28. Ibn Abī al-Dunyā in *al-ʿIyāl*, 2:806 §605.
29. al-Ṭabarānī in *al-Muʿjam al-Kabīr* 19:300 §228.

30. al-Bayhaqī in *Shuʿab al-Īmān*, 6:196 §7886.
31. al-Haythamī in *Majmaʿ al-Zawāʾid*, 8:161.
32. al-Nasāʾī in *al-Sunan:* Bk.: *al-Jumuʿa* [The Friday Prayer], Ch.: "On the Recommendation to Shorten the Oratory," 3:108 §1414, and in *al-Sunan al-Kubrā*, 1:531 §1716.
33. al-Dārimī in *al-Sunan*, 1:48 §74.
34. Ibn Ḥibbān in *al-Ṣaḥīḥ*, 14:333 §6423.
35. al-Ḥākim in *al-Mustadrak*, 2:671 §4225.
36. al-Ṭabarānī in *al-Muʿjam al-Awsaṭ*, 8:135 §8197, *al-Muʿjam al-Kabīr*, 8:287 §8103, and *al-Muʿjam al-Ṣaghīr*, 1:248 §405.
37. al-Bayhaqī in *Shuʿab al-Īmān*, 6:269 §2114.
38. al-Haythamī in *Mawārid al-Ẓamʾān*, 1:523 §2129 and *Majmaʿ al-Zawāʾid*, 9:20.
39. Abū Yaʿlā in *al-Musnad*, 12:8 §6651, al-Daylamī in *Musnad al-Firdaws*, 1:34 §58.
40. al-Mundhirī in *al-Targhīb wa al-Tarhīb*, 3:236 §3542.
41. al-Haythamī in *Majmaʿ al-Zawāʾid*, 8:162.
42. Ibn Mājah in *al-Sunan:* Bk.: *al-Adab* [The Good Manners], Ch.: "The Right of the Orphan," 2:1213 §3679.
43. al-Bukhārī in *al-Adab al-Mufrad*, 61 §138.
44. al-Ṭabarānī in *Muʿjam al-Awsaṭ*, 5:99 §4785.
45. ʿAbd Ibn Ḥumayd in *al-Musnad*, 1:427 §1468.
46. Ibn al-Mubārak in *al-Zuhd*, 230 §654.
48. Ibn Abī al-Dunyā in *al-ʿIyāl*, 2:808 §3840.
49. al-Mundhirī in *al-Targhīb wa al-Tarhīb*, 3:236 §3840.
50. Ibn Kathīr in *Tafsīr al-Qurʾān al-ʿAẓīm*, 4:510.
51. Aḥmad b. Ḥanbal in *al-Musnad*, 2:263, 267 §§7566, 9006.
52. ʿAbd Ibn Ḥumayd in *al-Musnad*, 1:417 §1426.
53. al-Bayhaqī in *al-Sunan al-Kubrā*, 4:60 §6886, and *Shuʿab al-īmān*, 7:472 §11034.
54. al-Mundhirī in *al-Targhīb wa al-Tarhīb*, 3:237 §3845.
55. al-Haythamī in *Majmaʿ al-Zawāʾid*, 8:160.
56. Aḥmad b. Ḥanbal in *al-Musnad*, 5:250, 265 §§ 22207, 22338.
57. al-Ṭabarānī in *al-Muʿjam al-Kabīr*, 8:202 §7821, and in *al-Muʿjam al-Awsaṭ*, 3:285–286 §3166.
58. Ibn Abī al-Dunyā in *al-ʿIyāl*, 2:810 §609.
59. al-Mundhirī in *al-Targhīb wa al-Tarhīb*, 3:236–237 §3843.
60. al-Haythamī in *Majmaʿ al-Zawāʾid*, 8:160.
61. al-Suyūṭī in *al-Durr al-Manthūr*, 2:528.

10. The Holy Prophet's Mercy and Kindness toward Slaves and Servants

Essential Reading:

1. Dr Tahir-ul-Qadri, Muhammad ﷺ: The Merciful, Ch:10, p.209-220.

Additional Readings for Teachers and Students:

1. al-Bukhārī in *al-Ṣaḥīḥ:* Bk.: *al-ʿItq* [The Manumission], Ch.: "What has been Reported Concerning Manumission and its Virtue," 2:891 §2381.
2. Muslim in *al-Ṣaḥīḥ:* Bk.: *al-ʿItq* [The Manumission], Ch.: "The Virtue of Manumission," 2:1147 §1509.
3. al-Tirmidhī in *al-Sunan:* Bk.: *al-Nudhūr wa al-aymān* [The Vows and Oaths], Ch.: "What has been Reported Regarding the Reward for the One who Manumits a Slave," 4:114 §1541.
4. al-Nasāʾī in *al-Sunan al-Kubrā*, 3:420 §9431.
5. Abū ʿAwāna in *al-Musnad*, 3:242 §4823.
6. Ibn Abī Shayba in *al-Muṣannaf*, 3:118 §12633.
7. al-Bayhaqī in *al-Sunan al-Kubrā*, 1:272 §21096.
8. al-Bukhārī in *al-Ṣaḥīḥ:* Bk.: *al-ʿIlm* [The Knowledge], Ch.: "Regarding a Man Teaching His Maidservant and His Family," 1:48 §97.
9. Muslim *al-Ṣaḥīḥ:* Bk.: *al-Īmān* [The Faith], Ch.: "The Obligation to Have Faith that the Messengership of Our Prophet Muhammad ﷺ is to all of Humanity, and that His Religion Abrogates all other Religions," 1:134 §154.
10. Aḥmad b. Ḥanbal in *al-Musnad*, 4:395 §§402, 414.
11. al-Tirmidhī in *al-Sunan:* Bk.: *al-Nikāḥ* [The Marriage], Ch.: "On Virtue in That," 3:423 §1116.
12. al-Nasāʾī in *al-Sunan:* Bk.: *al-Nikāḥ* [The Marriage], Ch.: "On a Man Freeing His Slave girl and then Marrying Her," 6:115 §3344.
13. Ibn Mājah in *al-Sunan:* Bk.: *al-Nikāḥ* [The Marriage], Ch.: "Regarding a Man who Frees His Slave girl and then Marries Her," 1:629 §1956.
14. Ibn Mandah in *al-Īmān*, 1:504 §395.
15. Ibn Ḥibbān in *al-Ṣaḥīḥ*, 9:360 §4053.
16. al-Bukhārī in *al-Adab al-mufrad*, 80 §203.
17. Muslim in *al-Ṣaḥīḥ:* Bk.: *al-Zuhd* [The Renunciation], Ch.: "The Long Hadith of Jābir and the Story of Abū Yusr," 4:2303 §3007.
18. al-Bukhārī in *al-Adab al-Mufrad*, 75 §187.

19. al-Ṭaḥāwī in *Sharḥ Maʿānī al-Āthār*, 4:356.
20. al-Ṭabarānī in *al-Muʿjam al-Kabīr*, 19:169 §379.
21. al-Quḍāʿī in *Musnad al-Shihāb*, 1:283 §462.
22. Muslim in *al-Ṣaḥīḥ:* Bk.: *al-Aymān* [The Oaths], Ch.: "On Keeping the Company of Slaves and the Expiation for Striking One's Slave," 3:1281 §1659.
23. Abū Dāwūd in *al-Sunan:* Bk.: *al-Adab* [The Manners], Ch.: "On the Rights of Slaves," 4:340 §5159.
24. al-Tirmidhī in *al-Sunan:* Bk.: *al-Birr* [The Piety and Familial Integration], Ch.: "The Prohibition of Striking or Insulting a Servant," 4:335 §1948.
25. ʿAbd al-Razzāq in *al-Muṣannaf*, 9:439, 446 §§17933, 17959.
26. al-Ṭabarānī in *al-Muʿjam al-Kabīr*, 17:235 §684.
27. ʿAbd b. Ḥumayd in *al-Musnad*, 1:107 §239.
28. al-Mundhirī in *al-Targhīb wa al-Tarhīb*, 3:147 §2438.
29. al-Bayhaqī in *Shuʿab al-Īmān*, 6:373 §8569.
30. Muslim in *al-Ṣaḥīḥ:* Bk.: *al-Aymān* [The Oaths], Ch.: "On Keeping the Company of Slaves and the Expiation for Striking One's Slave," 3:1279 §1658.
31. Aḥmad b. Ḥanbal in *al-Musnad*, 5:444 §23793.
32. Abū Dāwūd in *al-Sunan:* Bk.: *al-Adab* [The Manners], Ch.: "On the Rights of Slaves," 4:342 §5166.
33. al-Tirmidhī in *al-Sunan:* Bk.: *al-Nudhūr wa al-aymān* [The Books of Vows and Oaths], Ch.: "On what has been Reported Regarding a Man Who Strikes His Servant," 4:114 §1542.
34. al-Nasāʾī in *al-Sunan al-Kubrā*, 3:194 §5013.
35. Ibn Abī Shayba in *al-Muṣannaf*, 3:115 §12514.
36. al-Ḥākim in *al-Mustadrak*, 4:409 §8103.
37. al-Ṭabarānī in *al-Muʿjam al-Kabīr*, 7:86 §6451.
38. Muslim in *al-Ṣaḥīḥ:* Bk.: *al-Faḍāʾil* [The Exemplary Virtues], Ch.: "The Prophet's ﷺ Closeness to the People and Their Seeking of Blessings from Him," 4:1812 §2324.
39. Aḥmad b. Ḥanbal in *al-Musnad*, 3:137 §12424.
40. ʿAbd Ibn Ḥumayd in *al-Musnad*, 1:380 §1274.
41. al-Bayhaqī in *Shuʿab al-Īmān*, 2:154 §1429.
42. al-Bukhārī in *al-Ṣaḥīḥ:* Bk.: *al-Adab* [The Good Manners], Ch.: "On Pride," 5:2255 §5724.
43. Aḥmad b. Ḥanbal in *al-Musnad*, 3:98 §11960.
44. Abū Nuʿaym in *Ḥilyat al-Awliyāʾ*, 7:202.
45. al-Nawawī in *Riyāḍ al-Ṣāliḥīn* §171.
46. Muslim in *al-Ṣaḥīḥ:* Bk.: *al-Ṣalāt* [The Prayer], Ch.: "The Virtue of Prostration and the Encouragement toward it," 1:305 §489
47. Aḥmad b. Ḥanbal in *al-Musnad*, 2:111 §5899.

48. Abū Dāwūd in *al-Sunan:* Bk.: *al-Adab* [The Good Manners], Ch.: "On the Rights of Slaves," 4:341 §5164.
49. al-Tirmidhī in *al-Sunan:* Bk.: *al-Birr wa al-ṣila* [The Piety and Familial Integration], Ch.: "What has been Narrated about Pardoning One's Servant," 4:336 §1949.
50. Abū Yaʿlā in *al-Musnad*, 10:133 §5760.
51. al-Mundhirī in *al-Targhīb wa al-Tarhīb*, 3:151 §3458.
52. Aḥmad b. Ḥanbal in *al-Musnad*, 2:425 §9488.
53. al-Tirmidhī in *al-Sunan:* Bk.: *Faḍāʾil al-jihād* [The Exemplary Virtues of Striving], Ch.: "What has been Reported about the Reward of the Martyrs," 4:1767 §1642.
54. Ibn Khuzayma in *al-Ṣaḥīḥ*, 4:8 §2249.
55. Ibn Abī Shayba in *al-Muṣannaf*, 8:268 §35969.
56. Ibn Ḥibbān in *al-Ṣaḥīḥ*, 10:151 §4312.
57. al-Ṭayālisī in *al-Musnad*, 1:334 §9567.
58. Aḥmad b. Ḥanbal in *al-Musnad*, 5:58, 371 §20600, 23196.
59. al-Bukhārī in *al-Adab al-Mufrad*, 76 §190.
60. Abū Yaʿlā in *al-Musnad*, 2:221 §920.
61. Aḥmad b. Ḥanbal in *al-Musnad*, 2:505 §10754.
62. al-Ṭayālisī in *al-Musnad*, 1:312 §2369.
63. al-Bayhaqī in *Shuʿab al-Īmān*, 6:373 §8567.
64. al-Bazzār in *al-Musnad*, 4:237 §1399.
65. Abū Nuʿaym in *Ḥilyat al-Awliyāʾ*, 4:378.
66. al-Mundhirī in *al-Targhīb wa al-Tarhīb*, 3:148 §3441.
67. al-Haythamī in *Majmaʿ al-Zawāʾid*, 10:353.
68. Ibn Ḥibbān in *al-Ṣaḥīḥ:* Bk.: *al-ʿItq* [The Manumission], Ch.: "On Keeping Company with Slaves," 10:153 §4314.
69. Abū Yaʿlā in *al-Musnad*, 3:50 §1472.
70. ʿAbd Ibn Ḥumayd in *al-Musnad*, 1:119 §284.
71. al-Bayhaqī in *Shuʿab al-Īmān*, 6:378 §8589.
72. al-Haythamī in *Mawārid al-Ẓamʾān*, 1:293 §1204.

11. The Holy Prophet's Mercy and Kindness toward the Sick and the Deceased

Essential Reading:

1. Dr Tahir-ul-Qadri, Muhammad ﷺ: The Merciful, Ch:11, p.221-248.

ADDITIONAL READINGS FOR TEACHERS AND STUDENTS:

1. al-Bukhārī in *al-Ṣaḥīḥ:* Bk.: *al-Marḍā* [The Patients], Ch.: "On the Expiation of Patients," 5:2137 §5317.
2. Muslim in *al-Ṣaḥīḥ:* Bk.: *al-Birr wa al-ṣila wa al-ādāb* [The Piety, Familial Integration, and Manners], Ch.: "The Reward a Believer Receives when Afflicted with Sickness, Grief, or the Like," 4:1991 §2572.
3. al-Nasāʾī in *al-Sunan al-Kubrā*, 4:352, 353 §§7485, 7477.
4. Aḥmad b. Ḥanbal in *al-Musnad*, 6:88, 173 §§23617, 25442.
5. Ibn Ḥibbān in *al-Ṣaḥīḥ*, 7:167, 187–188 §§2906, 2925.
6. ʿAbd al-Razzāq in *al-Muṣannaf*, 11:197 §20312.
7. al-Ṭabarānī in *al-Muʿjam al-Awsaṭ*, 2:363 §2240; al-Daylamī in *Musnad al-Firdaws*, 3:249 §4735.
8. al-Ṭayālisī in *al-Musnad*, 1:197 §1380.
9. al-Bukhārī in *al-Ṣaḥīḥ:* Bk.: *al-Marḍā* [The Patients], Ch.: "The Severest of Trials are Reserved for the Prophets, and then Those Closest to Them, and then Those Closest to Them," 5:2139 §5324, and in Ch.: "On Placing One's Hand on a Patient," 5:2143 §5336, and in Ch.: "On the Patient's Saying, 'I am in Pain,' or, 'My Head Pains Me,' or, 'My Pain is Severe,'" 5:2145 §5343.
10. Muslim in *al-Ṣaḥīḥ:* Bk.: *al-Birr wa al-ṣila wa al-ādāb* [The Piety, Familial Integration, and Good Manners], Ch.: "The Reward a Believer Receives when Afflicted with Sickness, Grief, or the Like," 4:1991 §2571.
11. Aḥmad b. Ḥanbal in *al-Musnad*, 1:455 §4346.
12. al-Dārimī in *al-Sunan*, 2:408 §2771.
13. al-Nasāʾī in *al-Sunan al-Kubrā*, 4:352 §7483.
14. Ibn Abī Shayba in *al-Muṣannaf*, 2:440 §10800.
15. Ibn Ḥibbān in *al-Ṣaḥīḥ*, 7:199 §2937.
16. Abū Yaʿlā in *al-Musnad*, 9:99 §5164.
17. al-Ṭayālisī in *al-Musnad*, 1:49 §370.
18. al-Bukhārī in *al-Ṣaḥīḥ:* Bk.: *al-Janāʾiz* [The Funerals], Ch.: "The Command to Follow the Funeral Procession," 1:418 §1183.
19. Muslim in *al-Ṣaḥīḥ:* Bk.: *al-Salām* [The Salutations], Ch.: "A Right of a Muslim over another Muslim is to Return the Greetings," 4:1704 §2162.
20. Aḥmad b. Ḥanbal in *al-Musnad*, 2:540 §10979.
21. Abū Dāwūd in *al-Sunan:* Bk.: *al-Adab* [The Manners], Ch.: "On Sneezing," 4:307 §5030.
22. Ibn Mājah in *al-Sunan:* Bk.: *al-Janāʾiz* [The Funerals], Ch.: "What has been Reported about Visiting Patients," 1:461 §1435.
23. al-Nasāʾī in *al-Sunan al-Kubrā*, 6:64 §10049.

24. Ibn Ḥibbān in *al-Ṣaḥīḥ*, 1:476 §241.
25. Abū Yaʿlā in *al-Musnad*, 1:340 §5934.
26. al-Ṭayālisī in *al-Musnad*, 1:303 §2299.
27. al-Ḥākim in *al-Mustadrak*, 1:550 §1292.
28. al-Bukhārī in *al-Ṣaḥīḥ:* Bk.: *al-Marḍā* [The Patients], Ch.: "The Supplication of the Visitor for the Patient," 5:2147 §5351.
29. Muslim in *al-Ṣaḥīḥ:* Bk.: *al-Salām* [The Salutations], Ch.: "The Recommendation to Perform an Incantation [*ruqya*] for the Patient," 4:1722 §2191.
30. Aḥmad b. Ḥanbal in *al-Musnad*, 6:278 §26412.
31. al-Tirmidhī in *al-Sunan:* Bk.: *al-Daʿawāt* [The Supplications], Ch.: "The Supplication for the Patient," 5:561 §3565.
33. Ibn Mājah in *al-Sunan:* Bk.: *al-Ṭibb* [The Medicine], Ch.: "The Things from which the Prophet ﷺ and Others Sought Refuge," 2:1163 §3520.
34. al-Nasāʾī in *al-Sunan al-Kubrā*, 4:458 §7508.
35. Abū Yaʿlā in *al-Musnad*, 8:239 §4811.
36. Ibn Ḥibbān in *al-Ṣaḥīḥ*, 7:237 §2971.
37. al-Bukhārī in *al-Ṣaḥīḥ:* Bk.: *al-Wuḍūʾ* [The Ablution], Ch.: "Using the Excess Ablution Water of Others," 1:81 §187, and *Kitāb al-Manāqib* [The Exemplary Virtues], Ch.: "The Prophet's Agnomen [*kunya*]," 3:1301 §3348, and *Kitāb al-Marḍā* [The Patients], Ch.: "Concerning the One who Takes a Sick Child to be Prayed over," 5:2146 §5346, and *Kitāb al-Daʿawāt* [The Supplications], Ch.: "Praying for Children to have Blessings and Rubbing their Heads," 5:2337 §0991.
38. Muslim in *al-Ṣaḥīḥ:* Bk.: *al-Faḍāʾil* [The Virtues], Ch.: "Affirming the Seal of Prophecy and its Features and Place on His Body ﷺ," 4:1823 §2345.
39. al-Nasāʾī in *al-Sunan al-Kubrā*, 4:361 §7518.
40. al-Ṭabarānī in *al-Muʿjam al-Kabīr*, 7:157 §6682.
41. Ibn Abī ʿĀṣim in *al-Āḥād wa al-Mathānī*, 4:379 §§2420, 3430.
42. al-Bukhārī in *al-Ṣaḥīḥ:* Bk.: *al-Marḍā* [The Patients] Ch.: "What has been Narrated regarding the Expiation for the Patient," 5:2138 §5321.
43. Aḥmad b. Ḥanbal in *al-Musnad*, 2:237 §7234.
44. Mālik in *al-Muwaṭṭa*: Bk.: *al-ʿAyn* [The Evil Eye], Ch.: "What has been Reported about the Reward for the Patient," 2:941 §1684.
45. al-Nasāʾī in *al-Sunan al-Kubrā*, 4:351 §7478.
46. Ibn Ḥibbān in *al-Ṣaḥīḥ*, 7:168 §2907.
47. al-Quḍāʿī in *Musnad al-Shihāb*, 1:224 §344.
48. al-Rabīʿ in *al-Musnad*, 255 §651.
49. al-Mundhirī in *al-Targhīb wa al-Tarhīb*, 4:142 §5162.
50. al-Bukhārī in *al-Ṣaḥīḥ:* Bk.: *al-Jihād* [The Striving], Ch.: "The Traveler's Deeds while Resident are Written for Him when He is on a Journey," 3:1902 §2834.

51. Aḥmad b. Ḥanbal in *al-Musnad*, 4:410, 418 §§19694, 19768.
52. Abū Dāwūd in *al-Sunan:* Bk.: *al-Janā'iz* [The Funerals], Ch.: "If a Person is Accustomed to Performing a Particular Righteous Act but is Prevented due to Sickness or Travel," 3:183 §3091.
53. al-Ḥākim in *al-Mustadrak*, 1:491 §1261.
54. ʿAbd Ibn Ḥumayd in *al-Musnad*, 1:189 §534.
55. al-Ṭabarānī in *al-Muʿjam al-Awsaṭ*, 1:82 §236.
55. Abū Nuʿaym in *Ḥilyat al-Awliyā'*, 10:24.
56. al-Bayhaqī in *al-Sunan al-Kubrā*, 3:374 §6339, and in *Shuʿab al-Īmān*, 7:182 §9928.
57. al-Bukhārī in *al-Ṣaḥīḥ:* Bk.: *al-Aṭʿima* [The Foods], Ch.: "On Allah's Statement: ﴾*Eat of the pure things We have provided you*﴿," 5:2055 §5058, also in Bk.: *al-Marḍā* [The Patients], Ch.: "The Obligation of Visiting the Sick," 5:2139 §5325.
58. Aḥmad b. Ḥanbal in *al-Musnad*, 4:394 §19535.
59. Abū Dāwūd in *al-Sunan:* Bk.: *al-Janā'iz* [The Funerals], Ch.: "Praying for a Sick Person's Wellness when Visiting Him," 3:187 §3105.
60. ʿAbd al-Razzāq in *al-Muṣannaf*, 3:593 §6763.
61. Ibn Ḥibbān in *al-Ṣaḥīḥ*, 8:116 §3324.
62. al-Bazzār in *al-Musnad*, 8:35 §3017.
63. Abū Yaʿlā in *al-Musnad*, 13:309–310 §7325.
64. al-Ṭabarānī in *al-Muʿjam al-Awsaṭ*, 3:93 §2592.
65. al-Ṭayālisī in *al-Musnad*, 1:66 §489.
66. ʿAbd Ibn Ḥumayd in *al-*Musnad, 1:195 §554.
67. al-Bukhārī in *al-Ṣaḥīḥ:* Bk.: *al-Manāqib* [The Exemplary virtues], Ch.: "The Signs of Prophecy in Islam," 3:1324 §3420, and in Bk.: *al-Marḍā* [The Patients], Ch.: "On Visiting the Sick," 5:2141 §5332.
68. al-Nasā'ī in *al-Sunan al-Kubrā*, :4:356 §7499.
69. al-Ṭabarānī in *al-Muʿjam al-Kabīr*, 11:342 §11951.
70. al-Bayhaqī in *al-Sunan al-Kubrā*, 3:383 §6388.
71. al-Bukhārī in *al-Ṣaḥīḥ:* Bk.: *al-Marḍā* [The Patients], Ch.: "On Placing One's Hand on a Patient," 5:2142 §5335, and in *al-Adab al-Mufrad*, 176 §499.
72. Aḥmad b. Ḥanbal in *al-Musnad*, 1:171.
73. al-Nasā'ī in *al-Sunan al-Kubrā*, 4:67 §6318.
74. al-Maqdisī in *al-Aḥādīth al-Mukhtāra*, 3:212 §1013.
75. Muslim in *al-Ṣaḥīḥ:* Bk.: *al-Birr wa al-ṣila wa al-ādāb* [The Piety, Familial Integration, and Good Manners], Ch.: "The Reward a Believer Receives when Afflicted with Sickness, Grief, or the Like," 4:1993 §2575.
76. Abū Yaʿlā in *al-Musnad*, 4:64, 125 §§2083, 2173.
77. al-Bayhaqī in *Shuʿab al-Īmān*, 7:159 §9839.
78. al-Mundhirī in *al-Targhīb wa al-Tarhīb*, 4:152 §5216.
79. Muslim in *al-Ṣaḥīḥ:* Bk.: *al-Birr wa al-ṣila wa al-ādāb* [The Piety,

Familial Integration, and Good Manners], Ch.: "On the Virtue of Visiting the Sick," 4:1989 §2568.

80. Aḥmad b. Ḥanbal in *al-Musnad*, 5:283 §22497.
81. al-Tirmidhī in *al-Sunan:* Bk.: *al-Janā'iz* [The Funerals], Ch.: "What has been Narrated Concerning Visiting the Sick," 3:299 §967.
82. Ibn Abī Shayba in *al-Muṣannaf*, 2:443 §10832.
83. al-Ṭabarānī in *al-Muʿjam al-Kabīr*, 2:101 §1446.
84. al-Quḍāʿī in *Musnad al-Shihāb*, 1:242 §384.
85. al-Bayhaqī in *al-Sunan al-Kubrā*, 3:380 §6371,
86. ibid., in *Shuʿab al-Īmān*, 6:530 §9169.
87. Muslim in *al-Ṣaḥīḥ:* Bk.: *al-Birr wa al-ṣila wa al-ādāb* [The Piety, Familial Integration, and Manners], Ch.: "On the Virtue of Visiting the Sick," 4:1990 §2569.
88. al-Bukhārī in *al-Adab al-mufrad*, 182 §517.
89. Ibn Ḥibbān in *al-Ṣaḥīḥ*, 1:503 §269, 3:224 §944.
90. al-Bayhaqī in *Shuʿab al-īmān*, 6:534 §9182.
91. Ibn Rāhawayh in *al-Musnad*, 1:115 §28.
92. al-Daylamī in *Musnad al-firdaws*, 5:235 §8053.
93. al-Mundhirī in *al-Targhīb wa al-tarhīb*, 2:37 §1406.
94. Aḥmad b. Ḥanbal in *al-Musnad*, 1:81, 118 §§612, 955.
95. Abū Dāwūd in *al-Sunan:* Bk.: *al-Janā'iz* [The Funerals], Ch.: "On the Virtue of Visiting [the Sick] while in a State of Ritual Ablution," 3:185 §3098.
96. al-Tirmidhī in *al-Sunan:* Bk.: *al-Janā'iz* [The Funerals], Ch.: "What has been Narrated Concerning Visiting the Sick," 3:300 §969.
97. Ibn Mājah in *al-*Sunan*:* Bk.: *al-Janā'iz* [The Funerals], Ch.: "What has been Narrated Concerning the Reward for the One who Visits a Sick Person," 1:463 §1442.
98. al-Nasā'ī in *al-Sunan al-Kubrā*, 4:354 §7494.
99. Ibn Abī Shayba in *al-Muṣannaf*, 2:443 §10835.
100. al-Bazzār in *al-Musnad*, 3:28 §777.
101. Ibn Ḥibbān in *al-Ṣaḥīḥ*, 7:224 §2958.
102. al-Ḥākim in *al-Mustadrak*, 1:501 §1293.
103. al-Ṭabarānī in *al-Muʿjam al-Awsaṭ*, 7:266 § 7464.
104. al-Bayhaqī in *al-Sunan al-Kubrā*, 3:380 §6376,
105. ibid., *Shuʿab al-Īmān*, 6:531 §9173.
106. al-Maqdisī in *al-Aḥādīth al-Mukhtāra*, 2:319 §698.
107. Aḥmad b. Ḥanbal in *al-Musnad*, 3:304 §14299.
108. al-Bukhārī in *al-Adab al-Mufrad*, 184 §522.
109. Ibn Abī Shayba in *al-Muṣannaf*, 2:443 §18034.
110. Ibn Ḥibbān in *al-Ṣaḥīḥ*, 7:222 §2956.
111. al-Ḥākim in *al-Mustadrak*, 1:501 §1295.
112. al-Mundhirī in *al-Targhīb wa al-Tarhīb*, 4:166 §5276.

113. al-Haythamī in *Mawārid al-Ẓamʾān*, 1:182 §711, and in *Majmaʿ al-Zawāʾid*, 2:297.
114. Aḥmad b. Ḥanbal in *al-Musnad*, 6:126 §2499.
115. Abū Yaʿlā in *al-Musnad*, 7:436 §4459.
116. al-Ṭabarānī in *Kitāb al-Duʿāʾ*, 336 §1102.
117. al-Ṭayālisī in *al-Musnad*, 1:200 §1404.
118. Ibn al-Sunnī in *ʿAmal al-yawm wa al-layla*, 503 §551.
119. al-Bukhārī in *al-Ṣaḥīḥ:* Bk.: *al-Janāʾiz* [The Funerals], Ch.: "If a Child Embraces Islam and then Dies, Should [the Funeral Prayer] be Prayed over Him, and Should a Child be Offered the Chance to Embrace Islam?" 1:455 §1290, and in *al-Adab al-Mufrad*, 185 §524.
120. Aḥmad b. Ḥanbal in *al-Musnad*, 3:227, 280 §§13399, 14009.
121. Abū Dāwūd in *al-Sunan:* Bk.: *al-Janāʾiz* [The Funerals], Ch.: "On Visiting a Non-Muslim Citizen [*Dhimmī*] who is Sick," 3:185 §3095.
122. al-Nasāʾī in *al-Sunan al-Kubrā*, 5:173 §8588.
123. Abū Yaʿlā in *al-Musnad*, 6:93 §335.
124. al-Bayhaqī in *al-Sunan al-Kubrā*, 3:383 §6389.
125. al-Bukhārī in *al-Ṣaḥīḥ:* Bk.: *al-Kafāla* [The Guarantees], Ch.: "On Debt," 2:805 §2176, and in Bk.: *al-Nafaqāt* [The Expenditures], Ch.: "On the Prophet's Statement ﷺ, 'Whoever Leaves behind Dependents I shall Look after Them on His Behalf,'" 5:2054.
126. Muslim in *al-Ṣaḥīḥ:* Bk.: *al-Farāʾiḍ* [The Inheritance], Ch.: "Whoever Leaves behind Wealth it is for His Heirs," 3:1237 §1619.
127. al-Tirmidhī in *al-Sunan:* Bk.: *al-Janāʾiz* [The Funerals], Ch.: "What is Narrated Concerning Prayers over One who Owes Debts," 3:382 §2070.
128. al-Nasāʾī in *al-Sunan:* Bk.: *al-Janāʾiz* [The Funerals], Ch.: "Praying over Those who are in Debt," 4:66 §1963.
129. Ibn Mājah in *al-Sunan:* Bk.: *al-Aḥkām* [The Legal Rulings], Ch.: "Whoever Leaves behind Debt or Dependents then they are the Responsibility of Allāh and His Messenger ﷺ," 2:807 §2415.
130. Ibn Ḥibbān in *al-Ṣaḥīḥ*, 11:192 §4854.
131. al-Bayhaqī in *al-Sunan al-Kubrā*, 7:44 §13076.
132. al-Bukhārī in *al-Ṣaḥīḥ:* Bk.: *al-Janāʾiz* [The Funerals], Ch.: "The Prayer-rows of Children along with the Men during the Funeral Prayers," 1:444 §1258.
133. Muslim in *al-Ṣaḥīḥ:* Bk.: *al-Janāʾiz* [The Funerals], Ch.: "Praying over a Grave," 2:658 §954.
134. al-Tirmidhī in *al-Sunan:* Bk.: *al-Janāʾiz* [The Funerals], Ch.: "What is Narrated Concerning Prayer over a Grave," 3:355 §1037.
135. Ibn Mājah in *al-Sunan:* Bk.: *Mā jāʾ fī al-Janāʾiz* [The Narrations Concerning Funerals], Ch.: "What is Narrated Concerning Prayer over a Grave," 1:490 §1530.
136. al-Bayhaqī in *al-Sunan al-Kubrā*, 4:46 §6800.

137. al-Bukhārī in *al-Ṣaḥīḥ:* Bk.: *al-Ṣalāh* [The Prayer], Ch.: "On Sweeping the Mosque," 1:175–176 §§446, 448, and in Bk.: *al-Janā'iz* [The Funerals], Ch.: "Praying Over the Grave after [the Deceased] is Buried," 1:448 §2172.
138. Muslim in *al-Ṣaḥīḥ:* Bk.: *al-Janā'iz* [The Funerals], Ch.: "Praying Over a Grave," 2:659 §956.
139. Aḥmad b. Ḥanbal in *al-Musnad*, 2:388 §9025.
140. Abū Dāwūd in *al-Sunan:* Bk.: *al-Janā'iz* [The Funerals], Ch.: "Praying Over a Grave," 3:211 §3203.
141. Ibn Mājah in *al-Sunan:* Bk.: *Mā jā' fī al-Janā'iz* [The Narrations Concerning Funerals], Ch.: "On What has been Reported Regarding Prayers Over the Graves,"1:489 §1527–1529.
142. al-Nasā'ī in *al-Sunan al-Kubrā*, 1:651 §2149.
143. Ibn Ḥibbān in *al-Ṣaḥīḥ*, 7:355 §3086.
144. al-Bayhaqī in *al-Sunan al-Kubrā*, 4:46–47 §§268, 6806.
145. al-Bukhārī in *al-Ṣaḥīḥ:* Bk.: *al-Janā'iz* [The Funerals], Ch.: "Regarding the One who Waits until [the Deceased] is Buried," 1:445 §1261.
146. Muslim in *al-Ṣaḥīḥ:* Bk.: *al-Janā'iz* [The Funerals], Ch.: "The Virtue of Praying the Funeral Prayer and Following the Funeral Procession," 2:652–653 §945.
147. Aḥmad b. Ḥanbal in *al-Musnad*, 2:401 §9197.
148. Abū Dāwūd in *al-Sunan:* Bk.: *al-Janā'iz* [The Funerals], Ch.: "The Virtue of Praying the Funeral Prayer and Following the Funeral Procession," 3:202 §3168.
149. *al*-Tirmidhī in *al-Sunan:* Bk.: *al-Janā'iz* [The Funerals], Ch.: "What is Narrated Concerning the Virtue of Praying the Funeral Prayer," 3:358 §1040.
150. al-Nasā'ī in *al-Sunan:* Bk.: *al-Janā'iz* [The Funerals], Ch.: "The Reward for the One who Prays the Funeral Prayer," 4:76 §1995, and in *al-Sunan al-Kubrā*, 1:645 §2122.
151. Ibn Mājah in *al-Sunan:* Bk.: *Mā jā' fī al-Janā'iz* [The Narrations Concerning Funerals], Ch.: "On the Reward for the One who Prays the Funeral Prayer and Waits until the Deceased in Buried," 1:491 §1539.
152. ʿAbd al-Razzāq in *al-Muṣannaf*, 3:449 §6268.
153. Ibn Ḥibbān in *al-Ṣaḥīḥ*, 7:347 §3078.
154. al-Bukhārī in *al-Ṣaḥīḥ:* Bk.: *al-Wuḍū'* [The Ritual Ablution], Ch.: "What is Narrated Concerning Washing away Urine," 1:88 §215, and in Bk.: *al-Janā'iz* [The Funerals], Ch.: "Palm Leaves Placed over the Grave," 1:458 §1295, and in Bk.: *al-Adab* [The Manners], Ch.: "On Backbiting," 5:2249 §5705, and Ch.: "Tale bearing is an Enormity," 5:2250 §570.
155. Muslim in *al-Ṣaḥīḥ:* Bk.: *al-Ṭahāra* [The Purification], Ch.: "The Proof that Urine is Impure and that One Must Cleanse Himself from It," 1:240 §292.

156. Aḥmad b. Ḥanbal in *al-Musnad*, 1:225 §1980; and 5:35 §20389.
157. Abū Dāwūd in *al-Sunan:* Bk.: *al-Ṭahāra* [The Purification], Ch.: "Cleansing One's Self from Urine," 1:6 §20.
158. al-Tirmidhī in *al-Sunan:* Bk.: *al-Ṭahāra* [The Purification], Ch.: "What has been Narrated Concerning the Severe Warning against [Splashing] Urine," 1:102 §70 (al-Tirmidhī said, "This hadith is *ḥasan-ṣaḥīḥ*").
159. al-Nasā'ī in *al-Sunan:* Bk.: *al-Ṭahāra* [The Purification], Ch.: "Cleansing One's Self from Urine," 1:28 §31, and in Bk.: *al-Janā'iz* [The Funerals], Ch.: "Placing Palm Leaves over the Grave," 4:106 §§2068–2069, and in *al-Sunan al-Kubrā*, 1:69 §27.
160. Ibn Mājah in *al-Sunan:* Bk.: *al-Ṭahāra* [The Purification], Ch.: "The Severe Warning against [Splashing] Urine," 1:125 §§247, 349.
161. al-Dārimī in *al-Sunan*, 1:205 §739.
162. Ibn Abī Shayba in *al-Muṣannaf*, 1:115 §1304.
163. Abū Yaʿlā in *al-Musnad*, 4:43 §2050.
164. Ibn Khuzayma in *al-Ṣaḥīḥ*, 1:32 §55.
165. ʿAbd al-Razzāq in *al-Muṣannaf*, 3:588 §§6753, 7654.
166. Ibn Ḥibbān in *al-Ṣaḥīḥ*, 7:398 §3128.
167. Aḥmad b. Ḥanbal in *al-Musnad*, 4:172 §17595.
168. al-Khaṭīb *al*-Baghdādī in *Mūḍiḥ awhām al-jamʿ wa al-tafrīq*, 1:272.
169. al-Haythamī in *Majmāʿ al-Zawā'id*, 1:205, 9:6.
170. Muslim in *al-Ṣaḥīḥ:* Bk.: *al-Janā'iz* [The Funerals], Ch.: "Imparting the Dying with '*Lā ilāha illā Allāh*,'" 2:631 §916.
171. al-Tirmidhī in *al-Sunan:* Bk.: *al-Janā'iz* [The Funerals], Ch.: "What has been Narrated about Imparting the One on His Death Bed [with '*Lā ilāha illā Allāh*'] and Supplicating in His Presence," 3:306 §976.
172. Aḥmad b. Ḥanbal in *al-Musnad*, 3:3 §1006.
173. Abū Dāwūd in *al-Sunan:* Bk.: *al-Janā'iz* [The Funerals], Ch.: "Regarding the Act of Imparting the Dying [with '*Lā ilāha illā Allāh*'], 3:190 §3117.
174. al-Nasā'ī in *al-Sunan:* Bk.: *al-Janā'iz* [The Funerals], Ch.: "On Imparting the Dying," 4:5 §1826, and in *al-Sunan al-kubrā*, 1:601 §1952.
175. Ibn Mājah in *al-Sunan:* Bk.: *al-Janā'iz* [The Funerals], Ch.: "What has been Narrated about Imparting the Dying with '*Lā ilāha illā Allāh*,'" 1:464–465 §§1444, 1446.
176. al-Bazzār in *al-Musnad*, 6:208 §2248.
177. Ibn Ḥibbān in *al-Ṣaḥīḥ:* Bk.: *al-Janā'iz wa mā yataʿallaq bihā muqaddaman aw mu'akhharan, dhikr al-ʿilla allatī min ajlihā umira bi hādha al-amr* [The Funerals and those Matters that are Related to it, Either before it or after it, and Mention of the Reasoning behind this Command], 7:272 §3004.
178. al-Ṭabarānī in *al-Muʿjam al-Ṣaghīr*, 1:241 §393.
179. Abū Nuʿaym in *Ḥilyat al-Awliyā'*, 10:397.

180. al-Haythamī in *Mawārid al-Ẓam'ān*, 1:184 §719, and in *Majmaʿ al-Zawā'id*, 1:17.
181. Aḥmad b. Ḥanbal in *al-Musnad*, 5:247 §22180.
182. Abū Dāwūd in *al-Sunan:* Bk.: *al-Janā'iz* [The Funerals], Ch.: "On Instructing the Dying," 3:190 §3116.
183. al-Bazzār in *al-Musnad*, 7:77 §2626.
184. al-Ḥākim in *al-Mustadrak*, 1:503 §1299.
185. al-Ṭabarānī in *al-Muʿjam al-Kabīr*, 20:112 §221.
186. Ibn Mandah in *al-Īmān*, 1:248.
187. al-Bayhaqī in *Shuʿab al-Īmān*, 1:108 §94.
188. al-Nawawī in *Sharḥ Ṣaḥīḥ Muslim*, 6:219.
189. Muslim in *al-Ṣaḥīḥ:* Bk.: *al-Janā'iz* [The Funerals], Ch.: "He Who has Forty People Pray over Him will Receive Their Intercession," 2:600 §948.
190. Aḥmad b. Ḥanbal in *al-Musnad*, 1:277 §2509.
191. Abū Dāwūd in *al-Sunan:* Bk.: *al-Janā'iz* [The Funerals], Ch.: "The Virtue of Praying the Funeral Prayer and Following the Funeral Procession," 3:203 §3170.
192. Ibn Ḥibbān in *al-Ṣaḥīḥ*, 7:351 §3082.
193. al-Ṭabarānī in *al-Muʿjam al-Awsaṭ*, 8:369–370 §8898.
194. al-Bayhaqī in *al-Sunan al-Kubrā*, 3:180 §5411.
195. al-Mundhirī in *al-Targhīb wa al-Tarhīb*, 4:178 §5324.
196. Muslim in *al-Ṣaḥīḥ:* Bk.: *al-Janā'iz* [The Funerals], Ch.: "He Who has One Hundred People Pray over Him will Receive Their Intercession," 2:654 §947.
197. al-Tirmidhī in *al-Sunan:* Bk.: *al-Janā'iz* [The Funerals], Ch.: "What has been Narrated Concerning the Funeral Prayer and Intercession for the Deceased," 3:348 §1029.
198. al-Nasā'ī in *al-Sunan:* Bk.: *al-Janā'iz* [The Funerals], Ch.: "The Virtue of the Deceased over Whom One Hundred People Pray," 4:75–76 §§1991, 1992, also in *al-Sunan al-Kubrā*, 1:644 §2118.
199. Ibn Ḥibbān in *al-Ṣaḥīḥ*, 7:351 §3081.
200. Abū Yaʿlā in *al-Musnad*, 7:364 §4398.
201. al-Ṭabarānī in *al-Muʿjam al-Awsaṭ*, 6:145 §6039.
202. al-Bayhaqī in *al-Sunan al-Kubrā*, 4:30 §6694,
203. and in *Shuʿab al-Īmān*, 7:4 §9248.
204. al-Mundhirī in *al-Targhīb wa al-Tarhīb*, 4:178 §5323.
205. al-Tirmidhī in *al-Sunan:* Bk.: *al-Janā'iz* [The Funerals], chapter 11, 3:311 §983.
206. Ibn Mājah in *al-Sunan:* Bk.: *al-Zuhd* [The Renunciation], Ch.: "Mention of Death and Preparation for It," 2:1423 §4261.
207. al-Bayhaqī in *Shuʿab al-Īmān*, 2:4 §1001.
208. al-Mundhirī in *al-Targhīb wa al-Tarhīb*, 4:135 §5125.

209. Abū Dāwūd in *al-Sunan:* Bk.: *al-Janāʾiz* [The Funerals], Ch.: "Seeking Forgiveness for the Deceased at the Graveside at the Time of Departing," 3:215 §3221.
210. al-Bazzār in *al-Musnad*, 2:91 §445.
211. al-Ḥākim in *al-Mustadrak*, 1:526 §1372.
212. Ibn al-Sunnī in *ʿAmal al-yawm wa al-layla*, 537 §585.
213. al-Maqdisī in *al-Aḥādīth al-Mukhtāra*, 1:522 §378, who said, "Its chain is good."
214. Aḥmad b. Ḥanbal in *al-Musnad*, 4:388 §19470.
215. al-Nasāʾī *al-Sunan:* Bk.: *al-Janāʾiz* [The Funerals], Ch.: "On Praying Over a Grave," 4:84 §2022.
216. Ibn Mājah in *Sunan:* Bk.: *al-Janāʾiz* [The Funerals], Ch.: "On What has been Reported Regarding Prayer Over Graves," 1:489 §1528.
217. Ibn Abī Shayba in *al-Muṣannaf*, 2:475 §11317.
218. al-Ṭabarānī in *al-Muʿjam al-Kabīr*, 22:240 §628.
220. Ibn Abī ʿĀṣim in *al-Āḥād wa al-Mathānī*, 4:27 §1980.
221. al-Bayhaqī in *al-Sunan al-Kubrā*, 4:48 §6809.
222. al-Ḥākim in *al-Mustadrak:* Bk.: *al-Janāʾiz* [The Funerals], 1:505–506 §§1308, 1340.
223. al-Ṭabarānī in *al-Muʿjam al-Kabīr*, 1:315 §929.
224. al-Bayhaqī in *Shuʿab al-Īmān*, 7:9 §9265.
225. al-Mundhirī in *al-Targhīb wa al-Tarhīb*, 4:174 §5305.
226. al-Haythamī in *Majmaʿ al-Zawāʾid*, 3:21.

12. The Holy Prophet's Mercy and Kindness toward the Bedouin Arabs, the Ignorant and the Beggars

Essential Reading:

1. Dr Tahir-ul-Qadri, Muhammad ﷺ: The Merciful, Ch:12, p.249-256.

Additional Readings for Teachers and Students:

1. Muslim in *al-Ṣaḥīḥ:* Bk.: *al-Jumuʿa* [The Friday Prayer], Ch.: "The Hadith about Teaching During the Sermon," 2:597 §876.
2. Aḥmad b. Ḥanbal in *al-Musnad*, 5:80 §20772.

3. al-Nasā'ī in *al-Sunan:* Bk.: *al-Zīna* [The Adornment], Ch.: "Sitting on a Chair," 8:220 §5377, and in *al-Sunan al-Kubrā*, 5:510 §9826.
4. al-Bukhārī in *al-Adab al-Mufrad*, 399 §1163.
5. Ibn Khuzayma in *al-Ṣaḥīḥ*, 3:151 §1800.
6. al-Ṭabarānī in *al-Muʿjam al-Kabīr*, 2:59 §1284
7. al-Quḍāʿī in *Musnad al-Shihāb*, 2:179 §1138.
8. al-Bayhaqī in *al-Sunan al-Kubrā*, 3:218 §5608.
9. Aḥmad b. Ḥanbal in *al-Musnad*, 4:240 §18120.
10. al-Tirmidhī in *al-Sunan:* Bk.: *al-Daʿawāt* [The Supplications], Ch.: "The Virtue of Repentance and Seeking Forgiveness," 5:546 §3535.
11. ʿAbd al-Razzāq in *al-Muṣannaf*, 1:205 §206.
12. Ibn Ḥibbān in *al-Ṣaḥīḥ*, 2:322 §562.
13. al-Ṭayālisī in *al-Musnad*, 1:160 §1167.
14. al-Ṭabarānī in *al-Muʿjam al-Kabīr*, 8:61 §7366.
16. al-Maqdisī in *al-Aḥādīth al-Mukhtāra*, 8:33–34 §26.
17. al-Haythamī in *Mawārid al-Ẓam'ān*, 1:73 §186.
18. al-Bukhārī in *al-Ṣaḥīḥ:* Bk.: *al-Istisqā'* [The Prayer for Rain], Ch.: "Concerning the One Who Recieves Rain until it Soaks His Beard," 1:349 §986, and in Bk.: *al-Manāqib* [The Exemplary Traits], Ch.: "The Signs of Prophethood in Islam," 3:1313 §3389, and in Bk.: *al-Ādab* [The Manners], Ch.: "On Smiling and Laughing," 5:2261 §5742, and in Bk.: *al-Daʿawāt* [The Supplications], Ch.: "Supplicating away from the Direction of the *Qibla*," 5:2335 §5982.
19. Muslim in *al-Ṣaḥīḥ:* Bk.: *Ṣalāt al-istisqā'* [The Prayer for Rain], Ch.: "The Supplication Said While Praying for Rain," 2:614 §897.
20. Aḥmad b. Ḥanbal in *al-Musnad*, 3:104 §12038.
21. Abū Dāwūd in *al-Sunan:* Bk.: *Ṣalāt al-istisqā'* [The Prayer for Rain], Ch.: "Raising the Hands During the Prayer for Rain," 1:304 §1174.
22. al-Nasā'ī in *al-Sunan:* Bk.: *al-Istisqā'* [The Prayer for Rain], Ch.: "How [the Hands] are Raised," 3:159–166 §§§ 1515, 1517, 1527–1528.
23. Ibn Mājah in *al-Sunan:* Bk.: *Iqāmat al-ṣalāt wa al-sunna fīhā* [On the Establishment of the Prayer and the Sunna Therein], Ch.: "What has been Narrated Concerning the Supplication Said during the Prayer for Rain," 1:404 §1269.
24. Ibn Khuzayma in *al-Ṣaḥīḥ*, 3:272 §992.
25. ʿAbd al-Razzāq in *al-Muṣannaf*, 3:92 §4911.
26. Ibn Jārūd in *al-Muntaqā*, 1:75 §257.
27. al-Bayhaqī in *al-Sunan al-Kubrā*, 3:221 §563.
28. Aḥmad b. Ḥanbal in *al-Musnad*, 2:288 §7856.
29. Abū Dāwūd in *al-Sunan:* Bk.: *al-Ādab* [The Manners], Ch.: "On the Forbearance and Good Character of the Prophet ﷺ," 4:247 §4775.
30. al-Nasā'ī in *al-Sunan:* Bk.: *al-Qasāma* [The Portioning], Ch.: "*al*-Qaud min *al*-Jabdha," 8:33 §4776, and in *al-Sunan al-Kubrā*, 4:227 §6978.

31. al-Bayhaqī in *Shuʿab al-Īmān*, 6:350 §8473.

13. THE HOLY PROPHET'S MERCY AND KINDNESS TOWARD DISOBEDIENT AND SINFUL

ESSENTIAL READING:

1. Dr Tahir-ul-Qadri, Muhammad ﷺ: The Merciful, Ch:13, p.257-270.

ADDITIONAL READINGS FOR TEACHERS AND STUDENTS:

1. al-Bukhārī in *al-Ṣaḥīḥ:* Bk.: *al-Ṣawm* [The Fasting], Ch.: "If Someone has Sexual Intercourse during Ramaḍān and has Nothing [to Pay as an Expiation] and Someone Pays it as Charity on His Behalf, he Should Expiate," 2:684 §1834, and in Bk.: *Kaffārāt al-aymān* [The Expiation of Oaths], Ch.: "When is Expiation Obligatory upon the Wealthy and the Poor," 6:2467 §6331, and in Ch.: "The Expiation Should be Given to Ten Poor People, whether Close or Distant," 6:2468 §6333.
2. al-Bukhārī in *al-Ṣaḥīḥ:* Bk.: *al-Wuḍūʾ* [The Ritual Ablution], Ch.: "On Pouring Water over Urine in the Mosque," 1:89 §219.
3. Muslim in *al-Ṣaḥīḥ:* Bk.: *al-Ṭahāra* [The Purification], Ch.: "The Obligation to Wash Away Urine," 1:236 §284.
4. Muslim in *al-Ṣaḥīḥ:* Bk.: *al- udūd* [The Prescribed Punishments], Ch.: "Concerning the One Who Confesses to Adultery," 3:1321–1322 §1690.
5. al-Nasāʾī in *al-Sunan al-Kubrā*, 4:286 §7163.
6. al-Dāraquṭnī in *al-Sunan*, 3:91 §49.
7. Abū ʿAwāna in *al-Musnad*, 4:134–135 §6292.
8. al-Ṭabarānī in *al-Muʿjam al-Awsaṭ*, 5:118 §4843.
9. al-Bayhaqī in *al-Sunan al-Kubrā*, 6:83 §11231.
10. Muslim in al-Ṣaḥīḥ: Bk.: *al- udūd* [The Prescribed Punishments], Ch.: "Concerning the One Who Confesses to Adultery," 3:1323 §1695 (2).
11. Aḥmad b. Ḥanbal in *al-Musnad*, 5:348 §22999.
12. Abū Dāwūd in *al-Sunan:* Bk.: *al- udūd* [The Books of Prescribed Punishments], Ch.: "The Woman of Juhayna whom the Prophet ﷺ Ordered to be Stoned," 4:152 §4440.
13. al-Nasāʾī in *al-Sunan al-Kubrā*, 4:304 §7271.
14. al-Dārimī in *al-Sunan*, 2:234 §2324.
15. Ibn Abī Shayba in *al-Muṣannaf* 5:543 §288 (9).

16. Abū ʿAwāna in *al-Musnad*, 4:136–137 §6295.
17. al-Bayhaqī in *al-Sunan al-Kubrā*, 8:221 §16743.
18. Aḥmad b. Ḥanbal in *al-Musnad*, 3:479 §15976.
19. Abū Dāwūd in *al-Sunan:* Bk.: *al- udūd* [The Prescribed Punishments], Ch.: "The Stoning of Māʿiz b. Mālik ؓ," 4:150 §4435.
20. al-Nasāʾī in *al-Sunan*, 4:282 §7184.
21. al-Ṭabarānī in *al-Muʿjam al-Kabīr*, 19:219 §488.
22. al-Bayhaqī in *al-Sunan al-Kubrā* 8:218 §16731.
23. Ibn ʿAsākir in *Tārīkh Dimashq*, 50:293.
24. Aḥmad b. Ḥanbal in *al-Musnad*, 5:216 §21940.
25. Abū Dāwūd in *al-Sunan:* Bk.: *al- udūd* [The Prescribed Punishments], Ch.: "The Stoning of Māʿiz b. Mālik ؓ," 4:145 §4419.
26. al-Nasāʾī in *al-Sunan al-Kubrā*, 4:290 §7205.
27. Ibn Abī Shayba in *al-Muṣannaf*, 5:538 §28767.
28. al-Ḥākim in *al-Mustadrak*, 4:404 §8082.
29. al-Ṭabarānī in *al-Muʿjam al-Kabīr*, 22:201 §530.
30. al-Bayhaqī in *al-Sunan al-Kubrā*, 8:219 §16735.
31. Aḥmad b. Ḥanbal in *al-Musnad*, 5:216 §21940.
32. Abū Dāwūd in *al-Sunan:* Bk.: *al- udūd* [The Prescribed Punishments], Ch.: "Concealing the Offenses of Those Subject to Prescribed Punishments," 4:134 §4377.
33. al-Nasāʾī in *al-Sunan al-Kubrā*, 4:305 §7274.
34. ʿAbd al-Razzāq in *al-Muṣannaf*, 7:323 §13342.
35. Ibn Abī Shayba in *al-Muṣannaf*, 5:540 §28784.
36. al-Ḥākim in *al-Mustadrak*, 4:403 §8080.
37. Aḥmad b. Ḥanbal in *al-Musnad*, 2:70 §5384.
38. Abū Dāwūd in *al-*Sunan*:* Bk.: *al-Jihād* [The Striving], Ch.: "On Fleeing during Battle," 3:46 §2647.
39. al-Bukhārī in *al-Adab al-Mufrad*, 338 §972.
40. Ibn Abī Shayba in *al-Muṣannaf*, 6:541 §33686.
41. al-Ḥusaynī in *al-Bayān wa al-Taʿrīf*, 1:295 §786.
42. Abū Dāwūd in *al-Sunan:* Bk.: *al-Sunna* [The Sunna], Ch.: "On Intercession," 4:236 §4739.
43. al-Tirmidhī in *al-Sunan:* Bk.: *Ṣifat al-qiyāma wa al-raqāʾiq wa al-waraʿ* [On the Description of the Day of Judgment, Heart-melting narrations, and Scrupulousness], Ch.: "What has been Narrated Concerning Intercession," 4:625 §2435.
44. Ibn Mājah (from Jābir ؓ) in *al-Sunan:* Bk.: *al-Zuhd* [The Renunciation], Ch.: "Mention of Intercession," 2:1441 §4310.
45. Abū Yaʿlā in *al-Musnad*, 6:40 §3284.
46. al-Ḥākim in *al-Mustadrak*, 1:139 §228.
47. al-Ṭabarānī in *al-Muʿjam al-ṣaghīr*, 1:272 §448.
48. al-Ṭayālisī in *al-Musnad*, 1:233 §1669.

49. Aḥmad b. Ḥanbal (from Ibn ʿUmar ﷺ) in *al-Musnad*, 2:75 §5452.
50. Ibn Mājah in *al-Sunan:* Bk.: *al-Zuhd* [The Renunciation], Ch.: "Mention of Intercession," 2:1441 §4311.
51. al-Haythamī in *Majmaʿ al-zawāʾid*, 10:378.
52. al-Bayhaqī in *al-Iʿtiqād*, 1:202.

14. The Holy Prophet's Mercy and Kindness toward the Hypocrites

Essential Reading:

1. Dr Tahir-ul-Qadri, Muhammad ﷺ: The Merciful, Ch:14, p.271-286.

Additional Readings for Teachers and Students:

1. al-Bukhārī in *al-Ṣaḥīḥ:* Bk.: *al-Ādab* [The Manners], Ch.: "What has been Narrated Concerning a Man Who Says, 'Woe unto You,'" 5:2281 §5811.
2. Muslim in *al-Ṣaḥīḥ:* Bk.: *al-Zakāt* [The Zakat], Ch.: "On the Kharijites and their Qualities," 2:744 §1064.
3. Aḥmad b. Ḥanbal in *al-Musnad*, 3:65 §11639.
4. al-Nasāʾī in *al-Sunan al-Kubrā*, 5:159 §§8560–8561 and 6:355 §11220.
5. Ibn Ḥibbān in *al-Ṣaḥīḥ*, 15:140 §6741.
6. ʿAbd al-Razzāq in *al-Muṣannaf*, 10:146.
7. al-Bayhaqī in *al-Sunan al-Kubrā*, 8:171.
8. al-Bukhārī in *al-Ṣaḥīḥ:* Bk.: *al-Maghāzī* [The Military Expeditions], Ch.: "The Mission of ʿAlī b. Abī Ṭālib and Khālid b. al-Walīd ﷺ before the Farewell Pilgrimage," 4:1581 §4094.
9. Muslim in *al-Ṣaḥīḥ:* Bk.: *al-Zakāt* [The Zakat], Ch.: "On the Kharijites and their Qualities,"2:742 §1064.
10. Aḥmad b. Ḥanbal in *al-Musnad*, 3:4 §11021.
11. Ibn Khuzayma in *al-Ṣaḥīḥ*, 4:81 §2373.
13. Ibn Ḥībbān in *al-Ṣaḥīḥ*, 1:205 §25.
14. Abū Yaʿlā in *al-Musnad*, 2:390 §1163.
15. Abū Nuʿaym in *al-Musnad al-Mustakhraj*, 3:128 §3275, and in *Ḥilyat al-Awliyāʾ*, 5:81.
16. al-ʿAsqalānī in *Fatḥ al-Bārī*, 8:68 §4094.
17. Ibn al-Qayyim *al-Ḥāshiya*, 13:16.

18. al-Suyūṭī in *al-Dībāj*, 3:160 §1064.
19. Ibn Taymiya in *al-Ṣārim al-Maslūl*, 1:188, 192.
20. Aḥmad b. Ḥanbal in *al-Musnad*, 4:421.
21. al-Nasāʾī in *al-Sunan:* Bk.: *Taḥrīm al-dam* [The Prohibition of Bloodshed], Ch.: "Regarding the One Who Unsheathes His Sword and Wields it among People," 7:119 §4103, and in *al-Sunan al-Kubrā*, 2:312 §3566.
22. Ibn Abī Shayba in *al-Muṣannaf*, 7:559 §37917.
23. al-Bazzār in *al-Musnad*, 9:294, 305 §3846.
24. al-Ḥākim in *al-Mustadrak*, 2:160 §2647.
25. Ibn Abī ʿĀṣim in *al-Sunna*, 2:452 §927.
26. al-Ṭayālisī in *al-Musnad*, 1:124 §923.
27. al-ʿAsqalānī in *Fatḥ al-Bārī*, 12:292.
28. al-Qaysarānī in *Tadhkirat al- uffāẓ*, 3:1101.
29. Ibn Taymiya in *al-Ṣārim al-Maslūl*, 1:188.
30. Aḥmad in *al-Musnad*, 3:354 §1461.
31. Abū Nuʿaym in *al-Musnad al-Mustakhraj*, 3:127 §2372.
32. al-Bukhārī in *al-Ṣaḥīḥ:* Bk.: *Tafsīr al-Qurʾān* [The Qurʾānic Exegesis], Ch.: "On Allah's Statement: ﴾*It is the same whether you sought forgiveness for them or didn't seek forgiveness for them—Allah will never forgive them. Indeed, Allah does not guide the wrongdoing folk*﴿," 4:1861 §3622, and in Ch.: "On Allah's Statement: ﴾*They say, 'When we return to Medina the most honourable shall expel the most abased. To Allah and His Messenger belongs all honour, but the hypocrites know not*﴿," 4:1863 §3624.
33. Muslim in *al-Ṣaḥīḥ:* Bk.: *al-Birr wa al-ṣila wa al-ādāb* [The Piety, Familial Integration, and Manners], Ch.: "Helping One's Brother, whether an Oppressor or Oppressed," 4:1998 §2584.
34. Aḥmad b. Ḥanbal in *al-Musnad*, 3:392 §15260.
35. al-Tirmidhī in *al-Sunan:* Bk.: *al-Tafsīr* [The Qurʾānic Exegesis], Ch.: "Concerning Sūra al-Munāfiqīn," 5:417 §3315.
36. al-Nasāʾī in *al-Sunan al-Kubrā*, 5:271 §8863.
37. Ibn Ḥibbān in *al-Ṣaḥīḥ*, 14:544 §6582.
38. ʿAbd al-Razzāq in *al-Muṣannaf*, 9:468–469 §18041.
39. Abū Yaʿlā in *al-Musnad*, 3:458 §1957.
40. al-Bayhaqī in *al-Sunan al-Kubrā*, 9:32 §17644.
41. ʿAbd al-Razzāq in *al-Muṣannaf*, 3:538 §6627.
42. al-Ḥākim in *al-Mustadrak*, 3:679 §6490–6491.
43. Ibn Abī ʿĀṣim in *al-Āḥād wa al-Mathānī*, 4:23 §1967.
44. Ibn Qāniʿ in *Muʿjam al-Ṣaḥāba*,1:203.
45. al-Haythamī in *Majmaʿ al-Zawāʾid*, 9:318.
46. Qāḍī ʿIyāḍ in *al-Shifā*, 1:503.
47. al-ʿAsqalānī in *Fatḥ al-Bārī*, 8:650, and in *al-Iṣāba*, 4:155.

48. Ibn Jarīr al-Ṭabarī in *Jāmiʿ al-Bayān*, 28:113.
49. Ibn al-Jawzī in *Ṣifat al-Ṣafwa*, 1:608.
50. al-Bukhārī in *al-Ṣaḥīḥ*: Bk.: *al-Janāʾiz* [The Funerals], Ch.: "Using a Shirt as Burial Shroud, whether it Covers Completely or Not, and Regarding the One Who is Not Enshrouded by a Shirt," 1:427 §1210, and in Bk.: *Tafsīr al-Qurʾān* [The Qurʾānic Exegesis], Ch.: "On Allah's Statement: ❴*Seek forgiveness for them or do not seek forgiveness for them—if you sought forgiveness for them seventy times, still, Allah will not forgive them*❵," 4:1715 §4383.
51. Muslim in *al-Ṣaḥīḥ*: Bk.: *Ṣifāt al-munāfiqīn wa aḥkāmuhum* [On the Traits of the Hypocrites and the Rulings that Pertain to Them], 4:2141 §2774, and in Bk.: *Faḍāʾil al-ṣaḥāba* [The Virtues of the Companions], Ch.: "From the Virtues of ʿUmar 🙵," 4:1865 §2400.
52. Aḥmad b. Ḥanbal in *al-Musnad*, 2:18 §468.
53. Abū Dāwūd in *al-Sunan*: Bk.: *al-Janāʾiz* [The Funerals], Ch.: "On Worship," 3:184 §3094.
54. al-Tirmidhī in *al-Sunan*: Bk.: *Tafsīr al-Qurʾān* [The Qurʾānic Exegesis], Ch.: "Concerning Sūra al-Tawba," 5:279 §3098 (al-Tirmidhī said, "This is a fine authentic tradition").
55. al-Nasāʾī in *al-Sunan*: Bk.: *al-Janāʾiz* [The Funerals], Ch.: "On Having a Shirt in the Burial Shroud," 4:36 §1900.
56. Ibn Mājah in *al-Sunan*: Bk.: *Mā jāʾ fī al-Janāʾiz* [What has been Narrated Concerning Funerals], Ch.: "Praying for the People of the Qibla," 1:487 §1523.
57. Ibn Ḥibbān in *al-Ṣaḥīḥ*, 7:447 §3175.
58. al-Bukhārī in *al-Ṣaḥīḥ*: Bk.: *al-Janāʾiz* [The Funerals], Ch.: "Should the Deceased be Removed from the Grave and Burial Niche for Reason?" 1:453 §1285, and in *Kitāb al-Libās* [The Clothing], Ch.: "On Wearing an Over-garment," 5:2184 §5459.
59. Muslim in *al-Ṣaḥīḥ*: Bk.: *Ṣifāt al-munāfiqīn wa aḥkāmuhum* [On the Traits of the Hypocrites and the Rulings that Pertain to Them], 4:2140 §2773.
60. al-Nasāʾī in *al-Sunan*: Bk.: *al-Janāʾiz* [The Funerals], Ch.: "Disinterring the Deceased after He is Placed in the Burial Niche," 4:84 §2019.
61. Abū Yaʿlā in *al-Musnad*, 3:458 §1958.
62. Ibn Kathīr in *Tafsīr al-Qurʾān al-ʿaẓīm*, 2:380, and al-ʿAynī in *ʿUmdat al-qārī*, 8:164, 21–310.
63. al-Bukhārī in *al-Ṣaḥīḥ*: Bk.: *al-Jihād wa al-siyar* [The Striving and Military Expeditions], Ch.: "On Praying for the Guidance of the Idolaters in order to Reconcile Their Hearts," 3:1073 §2779.
64. Muslim in *al-Ṣaḥīḥ*: Bk.: *Faḍāʾil al-ṣaḥāba* [The Virtues of the Companions], Ch.: "From the Virtues of Ghifār, Aslam, Juhayna, Ashjaʿ, Muzina, Daws, and Ṭayʾ," 4:1957 §2524.

65. al-Ṭabarānī in *al-Muʿjam al-Kabīr*, 8:326 §8219, and in *Musnad al-Shāmiyyīn*, 4:296 §3352.
66. al-Bukhārī in *al-Ṣaḥīḥ:* Bk.: *al-Jihād wa al-siyar* [The Striving and Military Expeditions], Ch.: "On Praying for the Guidance of the Idolaters in order to Reconcile Their Hearts," 3:1073 §2779.
67. Muslim in *al-Ṣaḥīḥ:* Bk.: *Faḍāʾil al-ṣaḥāba* [The Virtues of the Companions], Ch.: "From the Virtues of Ghifār, Aslam, Juhayna, Ashjaʿ, Muzina, Daws, and Ṭayʾ," 4:1957 §2524.
68. al-Ṭabarānī in *al-Muʿjam al-kabīr*, 8:326 §8219, and in *Musnad al-Shāmiyyīn*, 4:296 §3352.

15. THE HOLY PROPHET'S MERCY AND KINDNESS TOWARD ENEMIES, DISBELIEVERS AND IDOLATERS

ESSENTIAL READING:

1. Dr Tahir-ul-Qadri, Muhammad ﷺ: The Merciful, Ch:15, p.286-313.

ADDITIONAL READINGS FOR TEACHERS AND STUDENTS:

1. al-Bukhārī in *al-Ṣaḥīḥ:* Bk.: *al-ʿIlm* [The Knowledge], Ch.: "Let the Present Convey the Knowledge to the Absent," 1:51 §104, and in *Kitāb al- ajj* [The Pilgrimage], Ch.: "The Trees of The Sacred Precinct Must Not Be Cut," 2:651 §1735.
2. Muslim in *al-Ṣaḥīḥ:* Bk.: *al- ajj* [The Pilgrimage], Ch.: "The Sanctification of Mecca Along With Its Game, Herbage and Trees," 2:987 §1354.
3. Aḥmad b. Ḥanbal in *al-Musnad*, 4:31 §16420.
4. al-Tirmidhī in *al-Sunan:* Bk.: *al- ajj* [The Pilgrimage], Ch.: "What Has Been Narrated Concerning the Sanctified Nature of Mecca," 3:173 §809.
5. al-Nasāʾī in *al-Sunan:* Bk.: *Manāsik al-ḥajj* [The Rituals of Pilgrimage], Ch.: "The Forbiddance of Fighting During It," 5:205 §2876.
6. al-Ṭabarānī in *al-Muʿjam al-Kabīr*, 22:185 §484.
7. al-Bukhārī in *al-Ṣaḥīḥ:* Bk.: *al-Maghāzī* [The Military Expeditions], Ch.: "Where Did the Prophet Fix the Flag on the Day Mecca Was Conquered?" 4:1559 §4030.
8. al-Bayhaqī in *al-Sunan al-Kubrā*, 9:119 §18058.

9. al-ʿAsqalānī in *Fatḥ al-Bārī*, 8:9.
10. Ibn ʿAsākir in *Tārīkh Dimashq*, 23:454.
11. Ibn ʿAbd al-Barr in *al-Istīʿāb*, 2:597.
12. al-Bukhārī in *al-Ṣaḥīḥ:* Bk.: *al-Hiba wa faḍlihā wa al-taḥrīḍ ʿalaihā* [The Giving Gifts and Its Virtue, and How That is Encouraged], Ch.: "Accepting Gifts from the Polytheists," 2:923 §2474.
13. Muslim in *al-Ṣaḥīḥ:* Bk.: *al-Salām* [The Greeting With Salam], Ch.: "Poison" 4:1721 §2190.
14. Aḥmad b. Ḥanbal in *al-Musnad*, 3:218 §13309.
15. Abū Dāwūd in *al-Sunan:* Bk.: *al-Diyāt* [The Blood Money], Ch.: "Is Retaliation Performed on a Person Who Gives Somebody Poison to Drink or Eat and Kills Him by That," 4:173 §4508.
16. al-Ṭabarānī in *al-Muʿjam al-Ausaṭ*, 3:43 §2417.
17. al-Bayhaqī in *al-Sunan al-Kubrā*, 10:11 §19500.
18. al-Bukhārī in *al-Ṣaḥīḥ:* Bk.: *al-Jihād wa al-siyar* [The Striving and Military Expeditions], Ch.: "Hanging One's Sword on a Tree at Forenoon on a Journey," 3:1065–1066 §2753–2756, and also in *Kitāb al-Maghāzī* [The Military Expeditions], Ch.: "The Battle of Dhāt al-Riqāʿ," 4:515 §3905.
19. Muslim in *al-Ṣaḥīḥ:* Bk.: *al-Faḍāʾil* [The Virtuous Deeds], Ch.: "His reliance on God Most High and How God Most High Protected Him from the People," 4:1786 §843.
20. Aḥmad b. Ḥanbal in *al-Musnad*, 3:311 §14374.
21. al-Nasāʾī in *al-Sunan al-Kubrā*, 5:236, 267 §8772, 8852.
22. al-Bayhaqī in *al-Sunan al-Kubrā*, 6:319 §12613.
23. al-Ṭabarānī in *Musnad al-Shāmiyyīn*, 3:66 §1815.
24. al-Bukhārī in *al-Ṣaḥīḥ:* Bk.: *al-Hiba wa faḍlihā wa al-taḥrīḍ ʿalayhā* [The Giving Gifts and Its Virtue, and How That is Encouraged], Ch.: "Giving Gifts to Polytheists," 2:924 §2477, and also in *Kitāb al-Jizya* [The *Jizya*], Ch.: "The Sinfulness of He Who Makes a Contract and Then Betrays the Trust," 3:1162 §3012.
25. Muslim in *al-Ṣaḥīḥ:* Bk.: *al-Zakāt* [The Zakat], Ch.: "The Virtue of Spending and Giving Alms to One's Close Relatives, Wives, Children and Parents Even If They are Polytheists," 2:696 §1003.
26. Aḥmad b. Ḥanbal in *al-Musnad*, 6:347 §26985.
27. Abū Dāwūd in *al-Sunan:* Bk.: *al-Zakāt* [The Zakat], Ch.: "Giving Charity to Non-Muslim Citizens," 2:127 §1668.
28. ʿAbd al-Razzāq in *al-Muṣannaf*, 6:38 §9932.
29. al-Ṭabarānī in *al-Muʿjam al-Kabīr*, 24:78 §203.
30. al-Bukhārī in *al-Ṣaḥīḥ:* Bk.: *al-Hiba wa faḍlihā wa al-taḥrīḍ ʿalayhā* [The Giving Gifts and Its Virtue, and How That is Encouraged], Ch.: "Giving Gifts to Polytheists," 2:924 §2476, and also in Ch.: "Giving Someone Else a Gift of Clothing That is Offensive to Wear," 2:921

§2470, also in *Kitāb al-Jumuʿa* [The Friday Prayer], Ch.: "On Wearing One's Best Garments," 1:302 §74.

31. Muslim in *al-Ṣaḥīḥ:* Bk.: *al-Libās wa al-zīna* [The Clothing and Adornment], Ch.: "The Prohibtion of Men and Women Using Gold and Silver Instruments, the Prohibition of Men Wearing Gold Rings and Silk and its Allowance for Women, and the Permisiblity of [Silk] Brocade for a Man as long as it does not Exeed Four Fingers in Length," 3:1638 §2068.
32. Aḥmad b. Ḥanbal in *al-Musnad*, 2:103 §5797.
33. Abū Dāwūd in *al-Sunan:* Bk.: *al-Ṣalāh* [The Prayer], Ch.: "What is Worn on Friday," 1:282 §1086.
34. al-Nasāʾī in *al-Sunan:* Bk.: *al-Jumuʿa* [The Friday Prayer], Ch.: "Preparing for the Friday Prayer," 3:96 §1382, and also in *al-Sunan al-Kubrā*, 1:523 §1686.
35. Mālik in *al-Muwaṭṭāʾ:* Bk.: *al-Libās* [The Clothing], Ch.: "What has been Narrating Regarding Garments," 2:918 §1637.
36. al-Shāfiʿī in *al-Musnad*, 62.
37. Ibn Ḥibbān in *al-Ṣaḥīḥ*, 12:255 §5439.
38. al-Bukhārī in *al-Ṣaḥīḥ:* Bk.: *al-Jihād wa al-siyar* [The Struggle and Military Expedition], Ch.: "On Killing Women in War," 3:1098 §2852.
39. Muslim in *al-Ṣaḥīḥ:* Bk.: *al-Jihād wa al-siyar* [The Struggle and Military Expedition], Ch.: "On the Unlawfulness of Killing Women and the Elderly in War," 3:1364 §1744; Aḥmad b. Ḥanbal in *al-Musnad*, 2:22 §4739.
40. al-Tirmidhī in *al-Sunan:* Bk.: *al-Siyar* [The Military Expeditions], Ch.: "On What has been Reported Regarding the Prohibition of Killing Women and Children," 4:136 §1569.
41. Ibn Mājah in *al-Sunan:* Bk.: *al-Jihād* [The Struggle], Ch.: "On Indiscriminate Night Attacks and Killing Women and Children," 2:947 §2841.
42. al-Nasāʾī in *al-Sunan al-Kubrā*, 5:185 §8618.
43. al-Dārimī in *al-Sunan*, 2:293 §2462.
44. Ibn Ḥibbān in *al-Ṣaḥīḥ*, 1:344 §135.
45. ʿAbd al-Razzāq in *al-Muṣannaf:* Bk.: *al-Jihād* [The Striving], Ch.: "Raiding Houses at Night," 5:202 §9385.
46. al-Shafiʿī in *al-Musnad*, 238.
47. al-Bayhaqī in *al-Sunan al-Kubrā*, 9:77 §17865.
48. al-Ṭaḥāwī in *Sharḥ Maʿānī al-Āthār*, 3:221.
49. Ibn Ḥibbān: Bk.: *al-Siyar* [The Military Expeditions], Ch.: "Going Out for Battle and How to Fight, and the Narration That Indicates That Children Who Fight Are to be Fought," 11:109 §4788.
50. ʿAbd al-Razzāq in *al-Muṣannaf*, 10:179 §18742.
51. al-Ṭabarānī in *al-Muʿjam al-Kabīr*, 17:164 §434.

52. al-Bayhaqī in *al-Sunan al-Kubrā*, 6:166 §11098.
53. Aḥmad b. Ḥanbal in his *Musnad*, 3:435 §15626–15627 and 4:24 §16342.
54. al-Nasā'ī in his *al-Sunan al-Kubrā:* Bk.: *al-Siyar* [The Military Expeditions], chapter, "*The Prohibition of Killing the Children of the Pagans*," 5:184 §8616.
55. al-Dārimī in his *Sunan*, 2:294 §2463.
56. Ibn Abī Shayba in his *Muṣannaf*, 6:484 §331231.
57. Ibn Ḥibbān in his *Ṣaḥīḥ* collection, 1:341 §132.
58. Ibn Abī ʿĀṣim in *al-Āḥād wa al-Mathānī*, 2:375 §1160.
59. al-Ḥākim in *al-Mustadrak*, 2:133–134 §§2566–2567.
60. al-Ṭabarānī in *al-Muʿjam al-kabīr*, 1:284.
61. al-Bayhaqī in his *al-Sunan al-kubrā*, 9:77 §17868.
62. Abū Nuʿaym in *Ḥilya al-awliyā'*, 8:263.
63. Aḥmad b. Ḥanbal in *al-Musnad*, 3:488 §16035.
64. Abu Dāwūd in *al-Sunan:* Bk.: *al-Jihād* [The Striving], Ch.: "On Killing Women," 3:53 §2669.
65. Ibn Mājah in *al-Sunan:* Bk.: *al-Jihād* [The Striving], Ch.: "Attacking and Raiding Houses at Night, and Killing Women and Children," 2:948 §2842; al-Nasā'ī in *al-Sunan al-Kubrā*, 5:186–187 §§8625, 8627.
66. Ibn Ḥibbān in *al-Ṣaḥīḥ*, 11:110 §4789.
67. Ibn Abī Shayba in *al-Muṣannaf*, 6:482 §33117.
68. Abū Yaʿlā in *al-Musnad*, 3:115–116 §1546.
69. al-Ḥākim in *al-Mustadrak*, 2:133 §2565.
70. al-Ṭabarānī in *al-Muʿjam al-Kabīr*, 4:10 §3489.
71. al-Bayhaqī in *al-Sunan al-Kubrā*, 9:82 §17883.
72. al-Bukhārī in *al-Ṣaḥīḥ:* Bk.: *al-Maghāzī* [The Military Expeditions], Ch.: "The Arrival of Banū Ḥanīfa and the Narration of Thumāma b. Athāl," 4:1589 §4114.
73. Muslim in *al-Ṣaḥīḥ:* Bk.: *al-Jihād wa al-siyar* [The Martial Arts and Siyar], Ch.: "Tying and Imprisoning Captives, and the Permissibility of Freeing Them," 3:1386 §1764.
74. Aḥmad b. Ḥanbal in *al-Musnad*, 2:246 §7355; •Abū Dāwūd in *al-Sunan:* Bk.: *al-Jihād* [The Striving], Ch.: "On Tying Captives," 3:57 §2679.
75. Ibn Ḥibbān in *al-Ṣaḥīḥ*, 4:42–43.
76. Abū ʿAwāna in *al-Musnad*, 4:257 §6696.
77. al-Bayhaqī in *al-Sunan al-Kubrā*, 6:419.
78. al-Bukhārī in *al-Ṣaḥīḥ:* Bk.: *Istitāba al-murtaddīn wa al-muʿānidīn wa qitālihim* [Demanding the Repentance of the Apostates and Reprobates and Fighting Them], Ch.: "When a Non-Muslim Citizen Insults the Prophet ﷺ Indirectly and Is Not Explicit About It, Such As Saying, '*Al-sāmu ʿalaikum*,'" 6:2538 §6527.

79. Muslim in *al-Ṣaḥīḥ:* Bk.: *al-Salām* [The Salutations], Ch.: "The Prohibition of Greeting the People of the Book Before Them and How to Return Their Greetings," 4:1705 §2163.
80. Aḥmad b. Ḥanbal in *al-Musnad*, 3:218 §13308.
81. Abū Yaʿlā in *al-Musnad*, 5:445 §3153.
82. al-Haythamī in *Majmaʿ al-Zawāʾid*, 8:42.
83. Ibn Ḥazm in *al-Muḥallā*, 11:415.
84. al-Bukhārī in *al-Ṣaḥīḥ:* Bk.: *Istitāba al-murtaddīn wa al-muʿānidīn wa qitālihim* [Demanding the Repentance of the Apostates and Reprobates and Fighting Them], Ch.: When a Non-Muslim Citizen Insults the Prophet ﷺ Indirectly and Is Not Explicit About It, Such As Saying, '*Al-sāmu ʿalaikum*,'"6:2539 §6528.
85. Muslim in *al-Ṣaḥīḥ:* Bk.: *al-Birr wa al-ṣila wa al-ādāb* [The Piety,Fillial Duty and Manners], chapter,: "The Virtue of Gentleness," 4:2003 §2593.
86. Aḥmad b. Ḥanbal in *al-Musnad*, 1:112.
87. Abū Dāwūd in *al-Sunan:* Bk.: *al-Adab* [The Manners], Ch.: "Gentleness," 4:254 §4807.
88. Ibn Mājah in *al-Sunan:* Bk.: *al-Adab* [The Manners], Ch.: "Gentleness," 2:1216 §3688.
89. al-Bukhārī in *al-Ṣaḥīḥ:* Bk.: *al-Janāiz* [The Funerals], Ch.: "Witnessing the Funeral of a Jew," 1:441 §1250.
90. Muslim in *al-Ṣaḥīḥ:* Bk.: *al-Janā'iz* [The Funerals], Ch.: "Witnessing Funerals," 2:661 §961.
91. Aḥmad b. Ḥanbal in *al-Musnad*, 6:6 §23893.
92. al-Nasā'ī in *al-Sunan:* Bk.: *al-Janā'iz* [The Funerals], Ch.: "Witnessing the Funerals of Polytheists," 4:45 §1921 and in *al-Sunan al-Kubrā*, 1:626 §2048.
93. al-Ṭabarānī in *al-Muʿjam al-Kabīr*, 6:90 §5606.
94. Ibn Abī Shayba in *al-Muṣannaf*, 3:39 §11918.
95. Ibn al-Jaʿd in *al-Musnad*, 27 §70.
96. al-Bayhaqī in *al-Sunan al-Kubrā*, 4:27
97. Muslim in *al-Ṣaḥīḥ:* Bk.: *al-Birr wa al-ṣila wa al-ādāb* [The Piety, Familial Integration, and Manners], Ch.: "The Prohibition of Cursing Animals and Others," 4:2006 §2599.
99. al-Bukhārī in *al-Adab al-Mufrad*, 119 §321.
100. Abū Yaʿlā in *al-Musnad*, 11:35 §6174.
101. Abū Nuʿaym in *Dalāʾil al-Nubuwwa*, 1:40 §2.
102. al-Bayhaqī in *Shuʿab al-Īmān*, 2:144 §1403.
103. Ibn ʿAsākir in *Tārīkh Dimashq*, 4:92.
104. al-Ḥusaynī in *al-Bayān wa al-Taʿrīf*, 1:283 §754.
105. Ibn Kathīr in *Tafsīr al-Qurʾān al-ʿAẓīm*, 3:202.
106. Muslim in his *Ṣaḥīḥ* collection in *Kitāb al-Birr wa ṣila wa al-ādāb* [On

Piety, Familial Integration, and Manners], chapter, "The Prohibition of Invoking Curses Against Creatures and Other Things," 4:2006 §2599.

107. al-Bukhārī in *al-Adab al-Mufrad*, 119 §321.
108. Abū Yaʿlā in *al-Musnad*, 11:35 §6174.
109. Abū Nuʿaym in *Dalāʾil al-Nubuwwa*, 1:40 §2.
110. al-Bayhaqī in *Shuʿab al-Īmān*, 2:144 §403.
111. Ibn ʿAsākir in *Tārīkh Dimashq*, 4:92.
112. al- usaynī in *al-Bayān wa al-Taʿrīf*, 1:283 §854.
113. Ibn Ḥibbān in *al-Ṣaḥīḥ:* Bk.: *al-Raqāʾiq* [The Heart Softeners], Ch.: "It Is Not Obligatory to Call God Against One's Enemies Due to What It Entails of Leaving One's Share of Reward," 3:254 §973.
114. Ibn Abī ʿĀṣim in *al-Āḥād al-Maʿānī*, 4:123 §2096.
115. al-Ṭabarānī in *al-Muʿjam al-Kabīr*, 6:120 §5694.
116. al-Daylamī in *Musnad al-Firdaws*, 1:500 §2042.
117. al-Bayhaqī in *Shuʿab al-Īmān*, 2:164 §1448.
118. al-Haythamī in *Majmaʿ al-Zawāʾid*, 6:117.
119. Muslim in *al-Ṣaḥīḥ:* Bk.: *al-Jihād wa al-siyar* [The Striving and Military Expeditions], Ch.: "The Saying of Allah Most High: ﴾*And it is He who restrained their hands from you*﴿ 3:1442 §180.
120. Aḥmad b. Ḥanbal in *al-Musnad*, 3:124, 290 §§12276, 14122.
121. Abū Dāwūd in *al-Sunan:* Bk.: *al-Jihād* [The Striving], Ch.: "Freeing Captives Without Ransom," 3:61 §2688.
122. al-Tirmidhī in *al-Sunan:* Bk.: *Tafsīr al-Qurʾān* [The Qurʾānic Exegesis], Ch.: "From the Sūra al-Fatḥ," 5:386 §3264.
123. al-Nasāʾī in *al-Sunan al-Kubrā*, 5:202, 6:464 §§8667, 11510; •Ibn Abī Shayba in *al-Muṣannaf*, 7:405 §36916.
124. Abū ʿAwāna in *al-Musnad*, 4:291 §§6782, 6783.
125. ʿAbd b. Ḥumayd in *al-Musnad*, 1:363 §1208.
126. Muslim in *al-Ṣaḥīḥ:* Bk.: *al-Jihād wa al-siyar* [The Martial Military Expeditions], Ch.: "The Conquest of Mecca," 3:1407 §1780.
127. Abū Dāwūd in *al-Sunan:* Bk.: *al-Kharāj wa al-imāra wa al-faiʾ* [The Land Tax, Appointing Leaders and War Booty That Is Taken Without Fighting], Ch.: "What Has Been Narrated About Mecca," 3:162 §3021.
128. al-Bazzār in *al-Musnad*, 4:122 §1292.
129. al-Dāraquṭnī in *al-Sunan*, 3:60 §233.
130. Abū ʿAwāna in *al-Musnad*, 4:290 §6780.
131. Ibn Rāhawayh in *al-Musnad*, 1:300 §278.
132. al-Shāfiʿī in *al-Umm*, 7:361.
133. Ibn Ḥibbān in *al-Thiqāt*, 2:56.
134. al-Rabīʿ in *al-Musnad*, 170 §419.
135. al-Bayhaqī in *al-Sunan al-Kubrā*, 9:117 §18055.
136. al-Bukhārī in *al-Ṣaḥīḥ:* Bk.: *Tafsīr al-Qurʾān* [The Qurʾānic Exegesis], Ch.: ﴾*Covering the people, "This is a painful punishment."*﴿ 4:1823

§4544.

137. Muslim in *al-Ṣaḥīḥ:* Bk.: *Ṣifa al-qiyāma wa al-janna wa al-nār* [The Description of the Resurrection, Paradise, and Fire], Ch.: "The Smoke," 4:2156 §2798.
138. Aḥmad b. Ḥanbal in *al-Musnad*, 1:380 §3613.
139. Ibn Kathīr in *Tafsīr al-Qur'ān al-'Aẓīm*, 4:139.
140. al-Bukhārī in *al-Ṣaḥīḥ:* Bk.: *al-Istisqā'* [The Prayer for Rain], Ch.: "When the Polytheists Intercede With the Muslims in Times of Drought," 1:342 §974, and also in *Kitāb Tafsīr al-Qur'ān*, [The Qur'ānic Exegesis], Ch.: ﴾*And she in whose house he was attempted seducing him, closing all the doors, saying:* "Haita lak."﴿ 4:1730 §4416, and also Ch.: "The meaning of Sūra: ﴾*Alif Lām Mīm. The Romans have been defeated*﴿ 4:1791 §449.
141. Muslim in *al-Ṣaḥīḥ:* Bk.: *Ṣifa al-qiyāma wa al-janna wa al-nar* [The Description of the Resurrection, Paradise, and Fire], Ch.: "The Smoke," 4:2155 §2798; Aḥmad b. Ḥanbal in *al-Musnad*, 1:431, 441 §§4140, 4206.
142. al-Tirmidhī in *al-Sunan:* Bk.: *Tafsīr al-Qur'ān* [The Qur'ānic Exegesis], Ch.: "From the Sūra of Smoke," 5:297 §3254.
143. al-Nasā'ī in *al-Sunan al-Kubrā*, 6:456 §11483; al-Ḥumaydī in *al-Musnad*, 1:63 §116.
144. Ibn Ḥibbān in *al-Ṣaḥīḥ*, 11:80 §4764.
145. Abū Ya'lā in *al-Musnad*, 9:78 §5145.
146. al-Ṭabarānī in *al-Mu'jam al-Kabīr*, 9:214 §9046–9048.
147. al-Bayhaqī in *al-Sunan al-Kubrā*, 3:352 §6221.
148. al-Bukhārī in *al-Ṣaḥīḥ:* Bk.: *Bad' al-khalq* [The Beginning of Creation], Ch.: "The Description of Iblīs and His Army," 3:1192 §3095, and also in *Kitāb al-Ṭibb* [The Medicine], Ch.: "Magic," 5:2174 §5430.
149. Muslim on *al-Ṣaḥīḥ:* Bk.: *al-Salām* [The Salutation], Ch.: "Magic," 4:1719–1720 §2189.
150. Aḥmad b. Ḥanbal in *al-Musnad*, 6:57 §24345.
151. Ibn Mājah in *al-Sunan:* Bk.: *al-Ṭibb* [The Medicine], Ch.: "Magic," 2:1173 §3545.
152. al-Nasā'ī in *al-Sunan al-Kubrā*, 4:380 §7615.
153. al-Shāfi'ī in *al-Musnad*, 382.
154. Ibn Abī Shayba in *al-Muṣannaf*, 5:41 §23519.
155. Abū Ya'lā in *al-Musnad*, 8:290–291 §4882.
156. Aḥmad b. Ḥanbal in *al-Musnad*, 3:409 §15417.
157. Ibn Mājah in *al-Sunan:* Bk.: *al-Adhān wa al-sunna fīhā* [The Call to Prayer and its Sunnahs], Ch.: "Pronouncing phrases of *Adhān* twice," 2:234 §708.
158. al-Nasā'ī in *al-Sunan al-Kubrā*, 1:393 §1714.
159. Ibn Abī 'Āṣim in *al-Āḥād wa al-mathānī*, 2:92 §790.

160. al-Dāraquṭnī in *al-Sunan*, 1:233 §1.

16. THE HOLY PROPHET'S MERCY AND KINDNESS TOWARD THE NON-MUSLIM CITIZENS AND THOSE UNDER AN AGREEMENT OF PROTECTION

ESSENTIAL READING:

1. Dr Tahir-ul-Qadri, Muhammad ﷺ: The Merciful, Ch:16, p.315-325.

ADDITIONAL READINGS FOR TEACHERS AND STUDENTS:

1. Muslim in *al-Ṣaḥīḥ:* Bk.: *Faḍā'il al-ṣaḥāba* [The Virtues of the Companions], Ch.: "The Orders of the Prophet ﷺ Regarding the People of Egypt," 4:1970 §2543.
2. Aḥmad b. Ḥanbal in *al-Musnad*, 5:173 §21560.
3. Ibn Ḥibbān in *al-Ṣaḥīḥ*, 15:68 §6676.
4. al-Ṭabarānī in *al-Mu'jam al-Awsaṭ*, 8:303 §8701.
5. al-Tirmidhī in *al-Sunan:* Bk.: *al-Diyāt* [The Blood Money], Ch.: "What Has Been Narrated Concerning He Who Kills Somebody Who Is Under Protection," 4:20 §1403.
6. Ibn Mājah in *al-Sunan:* Bk.: *al-Diyāt* [The Blood Money], Ch.: "Killing Someone Under Protection," 2:896 §2687.
7. Abū Ya'lā in *al-Musnad*, 11:335 §6452.
8. al-Ḥākim in *al-Mustadrak*, 2:138 §2581.
10. al-Bayhaqī in *al-Sunan al-Kubrā*, 9:205 §18511.
11. Abū Dāwūd in *al-Sunan:* Bk.: *al-Kharāj, al-fai' wa al-imāra* [The Land Tax, War Booty That Is Taken Without Fighting, and Appointing Leaders], Ch.: "Taking One Tenth from Non-Muslim Citizens When They Do Business," 3:170 §3052.
12. al-Bayhaqī in *al-Sunan al-Kubrā*, 9:205 §18511.
13. al-Mundhirī in *al-Targhīb wa al-tarhīb*, 4:7 §4558.
14. al-'Ajlūnī in *Kashf al-khafā'*, 2:342.
15. Abū Dāwūd in *al-Sunan:* Bk.: *al-Jihād* [The Striving], Ch.: "Fulling the Rights of The One Under Guarantee of the Protection and His Inviolability," 3:83 §276.
16. al-Dārimī in *al-Sunan*, 2:308 §2504.

17. al-Nasāʾī in *al-Sunan:* Bk.: *al-Qasāma* [The Partitioning], Ch.: "The Gravity of Killing Someone Who is Under Protection," 8:24 §4747, and also in *al-Sunan al-Kubrā*, 4:221 §6949.
18. al-Bazzār in *al-Musnad*, 9:129 §3679.
19. al-Ḥākim in *al-Mustadrak*, 2:154 §2631.
21. al-Ṭabarānī in *al-Muʿjam al-Awsaṭ*, 8:76 §8011.
22. Ibn al-Jārūd in *al-Muntaqā*, 1:213 §835.
23. al-Ṭayālisī in *al-Musnad*, 1:118 §879.
24. al-Bayhaqī in *al-Sunan al-Kubrā*, 9:321 §18629.
25. Aḥmad b. Ḥanbal in *al-Musnad*, 2:186 §6745.
26. al-Nasāʾī in *al-Sunan:* Bk.: *al-Qasāma* [The Partitioning], Ch.: "The Gravity of Killing Someone Who Is Under Protection," 8:24 §4750, and also in *al-Sunan al-Kubrā*, 4:221 §6952.
27. al-Bazzār in *al-Musnad*, 6:631 §2373.
28. al-Ḥākim in *al-Mustadrak*, 2:137 §258.
29. Ibn al-Jārūd in *al-Muntaqā*, 1:212 §834.
30. al-Bayhaqī in *al-Sunan al-Kubrā*, 8:133 §16260.
31. al-Mundhirī in *al-Targhīb wa al-Tarhīb*, 3:204 §3693.
32. Aḥmad b. Ḥanbal in *al-Musnad*, 4, 237, 5, 369 §§ 18097, 23177.
33. al-Nasāʾī in *al-Sunan:* Bk.: *al-Qasāma* [The Partitioning], chapter, "The Gravity of Killing Someone who is under Treaty," 8:25 §4749, and in *al-Sunan al-Kubrā*, 4:221 §7951.
34. al-Mundhirī in *al-Targhīb wa al-Tarhīb*, 3:204 §3695.
35. Abū Nuʿaym in *Musnad Abī Ḥanīfa*, p.104.
36. al-Bayhaqī in *al-Sunan al-Kubrā*, 8:30 §15696.
37. al-Shāfiʿī in *al-Musnad*, p. 343.
38. al-Shaybānī in *al-Mabsūṭ*, 4:488.
39. ibid., *al-Ḥujja* 4:342–344.
40. al-Qurashī in *al-Kharāj*, 82 §238.
41. al-Bayhaqī in *Shuʿab al-Īmān*, 6:517 §9125.
42. al-Ṣaydāwī in *Muʿjam al-Shuyūkh*, 1:97.
43. al-Bukhārī in *al-Ṣaḥīḥ:* Bk.: *al-Jihād wa al-siyar* [The Striving and Expeditions], chapter, "Non-Muslim Citizens are to be Defended and They can not be Taken Captive," 3:1111 §2887, and in *Kitāb al-Janāʾiz* [The Funerals], chapter, "What is Reported Concerning the Grave of the Prophet ﷺ and the Graves of Abū Bakr and ʿUmar," 1:469 1328.
44. Ibn Abī Shayba in *al-Muṣannaf*, 8:436 §37059.
45. Ibn Ḥibbān in *al-Ṣaḥīḥ*, 15:354 §6917.
46. al-Qurashī in *al-Kharāj*, 80 §232.
47. al-Shāfiʿī in *al-Umm*, 7:321.
48. al-Bayhaqi in *al-Sunan al-Kubrā*, 8:32 §15706.
49. al-Shaybānī in *al-Ḥujja*, 4:335.
50. al-Zaylaʿī in *Naṣb al-Rāya*, 4:337.

51. al-Shāfiʿī in *al-Musnad*, 344.
52. Abū Yūsuf in *Kitāb al-Kharāj*, p.187.
53. al-Bayhaqī in *al Sunan al-Kubrā*, 8:34 §15712.
54. al-ʿAsqalānī in *al-Dirāya fī Takhrīj Aḥādīth al-Hidāya*, 2:263.
55. al-Zaylaʿī in *Naṣb al-Rāya*, 4:336.
56. Abū ʿUbayd in *al-Amwāl*, 54 §114.
57. Ibn Qudāma al-Maqdisī in *al-Mughnī*, 9, 290.

17. The Holy Prophet's Mercy and Kindness toward Animals and Birds

Essential Reading:

1. Dr Tahir-ul-Qadri, Muhammad ﷺ: The Merciful, Ch:17, p.326-367.

Additional Readings for Teachers and Students:

1. al-Bukhārī in *al-Ṣaḥīḥ:* Bk.: *Badʾu al-khalq* [On the Beginning of Creation], chapter, "There are Five Injurious Animals that may be Killed in the Sacred Precint," 2:1205 §3140.
2. Muslim in *al-Ṣaḥīḥ:* Bk.: *al-Birr wa al-ṣila wa al-ādab* [The Piety, Fillial Duty, and Good Manners], chapter, "The Unlawfulness of Tormenting Cats and other Non-injurious Animals," 4:2110 §2619.
3. Aḥmad b. Ḥanbal in *al-Musnad*, 2:269 §7635.
4. Ibn Mājah in *al-Sunan:* Bk.: *al-Zuhd* [The Renunciation], chapter, "On Repentance," 2:1421 §4256.
5. ʿAbd al-Razzāq in *al-Muṣannaf*, 11:284 §20549.
6. Abū Yaʿlā in *al-Musnad*, 1:432 §6044.
7. Ibn Rāhawayh in *al-Musnad*, 1:147 §83.
8. al-Daylamī in *Musnad al-Firdaws*, 2:217 §3058.
9. al-Bukhārī in *al-Ṣaḥīḥ:* Bk.: *Ahādīth al-anbiyāʾ* [Narrations of the Prophets], chapter, "On the Narration of the Cave," 3:1279 §328.
10. Muslim in *al-Ṣaḥīḥ:* Bk.: *al-Salām* [The Salutations], chapter, "On Giving Food and Water to Honoured Animals," 4:1761 §2245.
11. Aḥmad b. Ḥanbal in *al-Musnad*, 2:510 §10629.
12. al-Bayhaqī in *al-Sunan al-Kubrā*, 8:14 §15597.
13. al-Daylamī in *Musnad al-Firdaws*, 2:19 §2126.
14. al-Bukhārī in *al-Ṣaḥīḥ:* Bk.: *al-Musāqāt* [The Watering], chapter,

"The Virtue of Providing Water," 2:833 §2234, and in *Kitāb al-Maẓālim wa al-ghaṣb* [On Oppression and Wrongful Seizure of Land], chapter, "Allowing Wells on Pathways as long as They Do not Cause Inconveniance," 2:870 §2334.

15. Muslim in *al-Ṣaḥīḥ:* Bk.: *al-Salām* [The Salutations], chapter, "On Giving Food and Water to Honoured Animals," 4:1761 §2244.
16. Aḥmad b. Ḥanbal in *al-Musnad*, 2:517 §1071.
17. Abū Dāwūd in *al-Sunan:* Bk.: *al-Jihād* [The Striving], chapter, "The Commands Pertaining to the Riding of Animals and Beasts of Burden," 3:24 §255.
18. Mālik in *al-Muwaṭṭā'*, 2:929 §1661.
19. Aḥmad b. Ḥanbal in *al-Musnad*, 1:205 §1754.
20. Abū Dāwūd in *al-Sunan:* Bk.: *al-Jihād* [The Striving], chapter, "The Commands Pertaining to the Riding of Animals and Beasts of Burden," 3:23 §2549.
21. Ibn Abī Shayba in *al-Muṣannaf*, 6, 322 §31756.
22. Abū Yaʿlā in *al-Musnad*, 12:108–109 §6787.
23. Abū ʿAwāna in *al-Musnad*, 1:168 §497.
24. al-Ḍiyā' al-Maqdisī in *al-Aḥādīth al-Mukhtāra*, 9:159 §135.
25. Ibn ʿAbd al-Barr in *al-Tamhīd*, 22:9.
26. Abū al-Maḥāsin in *Muʿtasar al-Mukhtaṣar*, 2:19.
27. al-Mizzī in *Tahdhīb al-Kamāl*, 6:165 §1232.
28. Abū Dāwūd in *al-Sunan:* Bk.: *al-Jihād* [The Striving], chapter, "The Commands Pertaining to the Riding of Animals and Beasts of Burden," 3:23 §2547.
29. Ibn Khuzayma in *al-Ṣaḥīḥ*, 4:143 §2545.
30. al-Mundhirī in *al-Targhīb wa al-Tarhīb*, 3:146 §3433.
31. al-Nawawī in *Riyāḍ al-Ṣāliḥīn*, §242.
32. al-Haythamī in *Majmaʿ al-Zawā'id*, 8:196–197.
33. Muslim in *al-Ṣaḥīḥ:* Bk.: *al-Ṣayd wa al-dhabā'iḥ* [The Game and Slaughtered Animals], Ch.: "The Command to Slaughter and Kill Well and to Sharpen the Blade," 3:1548 §1955.
34. Aḥmad b. Ḥanbal in *al-Musnad*, 4:123, 125 §§17154, 17179.
35. Abū Dāwūd in *al-Sunan:* Bk.: *al-Ḍaḥāyā* [The Sacrificial Animals], Ch.: "The Prohibition of Seizing Animals for Targeting and the Order to Slaughter Gently," 3:100 §2815.
36. al-Tirmidhī in *al-Sunan:* Bk.: *al-Diyāt* [The Blood-Money], Ch.: "The Prohibition of Equal Retribution," 4:23 §1409.
37. al-Nasā'ī in *al-Sunan:* Bk.: *al-Ḍaḥāyā* [The Sacrificial Animals], Ch.: "The Order to Sharpen the Blade," 7:227 §4405, and in Ch.: "Slaughtering Well," 7:229 §4412.
38. Ibn Mājah in *al-Sunan:* Bk.: *al-Dhabā'iḥ* [The Slaughtered Animals], Ch.: "When You Slaughter, Slaughter Well," 2:1058 §3170.

39. Ibn Ḥibbān in *al-Ṣaḥīḥ*, 13:199 §5883.
40. Aḥmad b. Ḥanbal in *al-Musnad*, 3:436, and 5:34 §§15630, 20379.
41. al-Bukhārī in *al-Adab al-Mufrad*, 136 §373.
42. Ibn Abī Shayba in *al-Muṣannaf*, 5:214 §25361.
43. al-Bazzār in *al-Musnad*, 8:257 §3322.
44. al-Ḥākim in *al-Mustadrak*, 4:257 §7562.
46. al-Ṭabarānī in *al-Muʿjam al-Kabīr*, 19:23 §45.
48. al-Haythamī in *Majmaʿ al-Zawāʾid*, 4:33.
49. al-Ṭabarānī in *al-Muʿjam al-Kabīr*, 8:234 §7915.
50. al-Bayhaqī in *Shuʿab al-Īmān*, 7:482 §11070.
51. al-Bukhārī in *al-Adab al-Mufrad*, 138 §181.
52. al-Haythamī in *Majmaʿ al-Zawāʾid*.
53. al-Ṭabarānī in *al-Muʿjam al-Awsaṭ*, 1:271 §885.
54. Abū Nuʿaym in *Ḥilya al-Awliyāʾ*, 8:176.
55. al-Haythamī in *Majmaʿ al-Zawāʾid*, 8:196.
56. al-Bukhārī in *al-Ṣaḥīḥ:* Bk.: *al-Dhabāʾiḥ wa al-ṣayd* [The Slaughtered Animals and Game], Ch.: "The Hatefulness of Cutting Parts of Living Animals or Seizing Them for Targeting," 5:2100 §5196.
57. al-Nasāʾī in *al-Sunan:* Bk.: *al-Ḍaḥāyā* [The Sacrificial Animals], Ch.: "The Prohibition of Seizing Animals for Targeting," 7:238 §4442.
58. al-Dārimī in *al-Sunan*, 2:113 §1973.
59. Ibn Ḥibbān in *al-Ṣaḥīḥ*, 12:434 §5617.
60. al-Bukhārī in *al-Ṣaḥīḥ:* Bk.: *al-Dhabāʾiḥ wa al-ṣayd* [The Slaughtered Animals and Game], Ch.: "The Offensiveness of Cutting Parts of Living Animals or Seizing Them for Targeting," 5:2100 §5197.
61. Aḥmad b. Ḥanbal in *al-Musnad*, 4:307 §§18762, 18764.
62. Ibn Abī Shayba in *al-Muṣannaf*, 4:481 §22321.
63. Ibn al-Jaʿd in *al-Musnad*, 1:85 §476.
64. Ibn Abī ʿĀṣim in *al-Āḥād wa al-Mathānī*, 4:137 §2117.
65. al-Ṭabarānī in *al-Muʿjam al-Kabīr*, 4:124 §3872.
66. al-Nasāʾī in *al-Sunan:* Bk.: *al-Ḍaḥāyā* [The Sacrificial Animals], Ch.: "The Prohibition of Seizing Animals for Targeting," 7:238 §4440, and in *al-Sunan al-Kubrā*, 3:72 §4529.
67. Abū Yaʿlā in *al-Musnad*, 12:162 §679.
68. al-Maqdisī in *al-Aḥādīth al-Mukhtāra*, 9:198–199 §185.
69. Ibn ʿAsākir in *Tārīkh Dimashq*, 59:244.
70. al-ʿAynī in *ʿUmdat al-Qārī*, 21:125.
71. Aḥmad b. Ḥanbal in *al-Musnad*, 2:92, 115 §§5661, 5956.
72. Ibn al-Jaʿd in *al-Musnad*, 330 §2264.
73. al-Mundhirī in *al-Targhīb wa al-Tarhīb*, 2:102 §1676.
74. al-Haythamī in *Majmaʿ al-Zawāʾid*, 4:32.
74. Ibn Rajab al-Ḥanbalī in *Jāmiʿ al-ʿUlūm wa al- ikam*, 1:153.
75. al-ʿAsqalānī in *Fatḥ al-Bārī*, 9:644.

76. al-Bukhārī in *al-Ṣaḥīḥ:* Bk.: *al-Dhabā'iḥ wa al-ṣayd* [The Sacrificial Animals and Game], Ch.: "The Offensiveness of Cutting Parts of Living Animals or Seizing Them for Targeting," 5:2100 §5194.
77. Muslim in *al-Ṣaḥīḥ:* Bk.: *al-Ṣayd wa al-dhabā'iḥ* [The Game and Slaughtered Animals], Ch.: "The Prohibition of Seizing Animals for Targeting," 3:1549 §1956.
78. Aḥmad b. Ḥanbal in *al-Musnad*, 3:171 §12769.
79. Abū Dāwūd in *al-Sunan:* Bk.: *al-Ḍaḥāyā* [The Sacrificial Animals], Ch.: "The Prohibition of Seizing Animals for Targeting and the Order to Slaughter Gently," 3:100 §2816.
80. Abū ʿAwāna in *al-Musnad*, 5:51 §7756.
81. al-Bayhaqī in *al-Sunan al-Kubrā*, 9:86 §17908.
82. Muslim in *al-Ṣaḥīḥ:* Bk.: *al-Ṣayd wa al-dhabā'iḥ* [The Game and Slaughtered Animals], Ch.: "The Prohibition of Seizing Animals for Targeting," 3:1549 §1957.
83. Aḥmad b. Ḥanbal in *al-Musnad*, 1:280, 285, 340 §§§2532, 2586, 3155.
84. al-Tirmidhī in *al-Sunan:* Bk.: *al-Ṣayd* [The Game], Ch.: "The Offensiveness of Eating an Animal That Has Died through Being Seized and Targeted," 4:72 §1475, al-Tirmidhī said, "This is a *ḥasan-ṣaḥīḥ* narration".
85. al-Nasā'ī in *al-Sunan:* Bk.: *al-Ḍaḥāyā* [The Sacrificial Animals], Ch.: "The Prohibition of Seizing Animals for Targeting," 7:238 §4443.
86. Ibn Mājah in *al-Sunan:* Bk.: *al-Dhabā'iḥ* [The Slaughtered Animals], Ch.: "The Prohibition of Seizing Animals for Targeting and Cutting Parts of Living Animals," 2:1063 §3187.
87. Ibn Ḥibbān in *al-Ṣaḥīḥ*, 12:422 §5608.
88. Abū ʿAwāna in *al-Musnad*, 5:52 §7759.
89. al-Ṭaḥāwī in *Sharḥ Maʿānī al-Āthār*, 3:181.
90. al-Bukhārī in *al-Ṣaḥīḥ:* Bk.: *al-Dhabā'iḥ wa al-ṣayd* [The Slaughtered Animals and Game], Ch.: "The Offensiveness of Cutting Parts of Living Animals or Seizing Animals for Targeting," 5:2100 §5196.
91. Ibn al-Sarāyā in *Silāḥ al-Mu'min fī al-Duʿā'*, 1:229 §412.
92. al-Ḥusaynī in *al-Bayān wa al-Taʿrīf*, 2:162 §1367.
93. al-ʿAsqalānī in *al-Wuqūf ʿAlā al-Mawqūf*, 1:105 §134.
94. Muslim in *al-Ṣaḥīḥ:* Bk.: *al-Ṣayd wa al-dhabā'iḥ wa mā yu'kal min al-ḥayawān* [The Game and Slaughtered Animals and Edible Animals], Ch.: "The Prohibition of Seizing Animals for Targeting," 3:1550 §1958.
95. al-Tirmidhī in *al-Sunan:* Bk.: *al-Ṣayd* [The Game], Ch.: "The Offensiveness of Eating an Animal That Has Died through Being Seized and Targeted," 4:72 §1475, al-Tirmidhī said, "This is a *ḥasan-ṣaḥīḥ* narration." al-Nasā'ī in *al-Sunan:* Bk.: *al-Ḍaḥāyā* [The Sacrificial Animals], Ch.: "The Prohibition of Seizing Animals for Targeting," 7:239 §4444.

96. Ibn Mājah in *al-Sunan:* Bk.: *al-Dhabāʾiḥ* [The Slaughtered Animals], Ch.: "The Prohibition of Seizing Animals for Targeting and Cutting Parts of Living Animals," 2:63 §3187.
97. al-Dārimī in *al-Sunan*, 2:113 §1973.
98. al-Ḥākim in *al-Mustadrak*, 4:261 §7575.
99. Abū Nuʿaym in *Ḥilya al-Awliyāʾ*, 4:296.
100. al-Munāwī in *Fayḍ al-Qadīr*, 6:388.
101. Aḥmad b. Ḥanbal in *al-Musnad*, 2:13 §4622.
102. al-Bukhārī in *al-Ṣaḥīḥ:* Bk.: *al-Dhabāʾiḥ wa al-ṣayd* [The Slaughtered Animals and Game], Ch.: "The Offensiveness of Cutting Parts of Living Animals and Seizing Animals for Targeting," 5:2100 §5195.
103. Aḥmad b. Ḥanbal in *al-Musnad*, 2:94 §5682.
104. Abū ʿAwāna in *al-Musnad*, 5:53 §7765.
105. al-Bayhaqī in *al-Sunan al-Kubrā*, 9:334 §19268.
106. Muslim in *al-Ṣaḥīḥ:* Bk.: *al-Ṣayd wa al-dhabāʾiḥ wa mā yuʾkal min al-ḥayawān* [The Game, Slaughtered Animals and Edible Animals], Ch.: "The Prohibition of Seizing Animals and Targeting Them till They Die," 3:1550 §1959.
107. Aḥmad b. Ḥanbal in *al-Musnad*, 3:318, 321 §§14463, 14488.
108. Ibn Mājah in *al-Sunan:* Bk.: *al-Dhabāʾiḥ* [The Slaughtered Animals], Ch.: "The Prohibition of Seizing Animals and Targeting Them till They Die and Cutting Parts of Living Animals," 2:1064 §3188.
109. Abū Yaʿlā in *al-Musnad*, 3:163 §2231.
110. Abū ʿAwāna in *al-Musnad*, 5:54 §7768.
111. al-Bayhaqī in *al-Sunan al-Kubrā*, 9:334 §19269.
112. Aḥmad b. Ḥanbal in *al-Musnad*, 4:389 §19488.
113. al-Nasāʾī in *al-Sunan:* Bk.: *al-Ḍaḥāyā* [The Sacrificial Animals], Ch.: "Killing a Sparrow Without Right," 7:239 §4446, and in *al-Sunan al-Kubrā*, 3:73 §4535.
114. Ibn Ḥibbān in *al-Ṣaḥīḥ*, 13:214 §5894.
115. al-Ṭabarānī in *al-Muʿjam al-Kabīr*, 7:317 §7245.
116. al-Bayhaqī in *Shuʿab al-Īmān*, 7:483 §11076.
117. al-Haythamī in *Mawārid al-Ẓamʾān*, 1:263 §1071.
118. al-Nasāʾī in *al-Sunan:* Bk.: *al-Ṣayd wa al-dhabāiʾḥ* [The Quarries and Sacrificial Animals], Ch.: "Permissibility of Eating Sparrows," 7:206 §4349; and in *al-Sunan al-Kubrā*, 3:163 §4860.
119. al-Shāfiʿī in *al-Sunan al-Maʾthūra*, p. 413 §606; and in *al-Umm*, 4:287.
120. al-Ḥākim in *al-Mustadrak*, 4:261 §7574.
121. al-Ṭayālisī in *al-Musnad*, 1:301 §2279.
122. al-Mundhirī in *al-Targhī wa al-Tarhīb*, 2:101 §1672.
123. Aḥmad b. Ḥanbal in *al-Musnad*, 3:440, 4:234 §§15677, 18081.
124. al-Dārimī in *al-Sunan:* Bk.: *al-Istiʾdhān* [The Seeking Permission], Ch.: "The Prohibition of Using Animals as Seats," 2:371 §2668.

125. Ibn Khuzayma in *al-Ṣaḥīḥ*, 4:142 §2544.
126. Ibn Ḥibban in *al-Ṣaḥīḥ*, 12:437 §5619.
127. al-Ḥākim in *al-Mustadrak*, 1:612, 2:109 §§1625, 2486.
128. al-Bayhaqī in *al-Sunan al-kubrā*, 5:255 §10116.
129. al-Haythamī in *Mawārid al-Ẓamʾān*, 1:491 §2002.
130. Abu Dāwūd in *al-Sunan:* Bk.: *al-Jihād* [The Striving], Ch.: "Standing on Animals," 3:27 §2567.
131. al-Ṭabarānī in *Musnad al-Shāmiyyīn*, 2:34 §867.
132. al-Bayhaqī in *al-Sunan al-Kubrā*, 5:255 §10115, and in *Shuʿab al-Īmān*, 7:485 §11083.
133. al-Baghawī in *Sharḥ al-Sunna*, 11:32.
134. Ibn ʿAsākir in *Tārīkh Dimashq*, 67:212.
135. Muslim in *al-Ṣaḥīḥ:* Bk.: *al-Imāra* [The Appointing Commanders], Ch.: "Considering the Rights of Animals when Riding and the Prohibition of Resting on a Pathway when Journeying," 3:1525 §1926.
136. Aḥmad b. Ḥanbal in *al-Musnad*, 2:378 §8905.
137. Abū Dāwūd in *al-Sunan:* Bk.: *al-Jihād* [The Striving], Ch.: "Moving Swiftly and the Prohibition of Resting on a Pathway when Journeying," 3:28 §2569.
138. al-Tirmidhī in *al-Sunan:* Bk.: *al-Ādab* [The Good Manners], Ch.: "Eloquence and Fluency," 5:143 §2858.
139. al-Nasāʾī in *al-Sunan al-Kubrā*, 5:252 §8814.
140. Ibn Ḥibbān in *al-Ṣaḥīḥ*, 6:422 §2705.
141. Ibn Khuzayma in *al-Ṣaḥīḥ*, 4:145 §2550.
142. Abū ʿAwāna in *al-Musnad*, 4:510 §7516.
143. al-Bayhaqī in *al-Sunan al-Kubrā*, 5:256 §10120.
144. Abū Yaʿlā in *al-Musnad*, 6:301 §3618.
145. al-Ṭaḥāwī in *Mushkil al-āthār*, 1:106 §94.
146. al-Bayhaqī in *al-Sunan al-kubrā*, 5:256 §10123.
147. al-Maqdisī in *al-Aḥādīth al-Mukhtāra*, 7:195 §2630.
148. Aḥmad b. Ḥanbal in *al-Musnad* 3:305 §14316.
149. Ibn al-Sunnī in *ʿAmal al-Yawm wa al-Layla*, 468–470 §532.
150. al-Munāwī in *Fayḍ al-Qadīr*, 1:374.
151. al-Haythamī in *Bughyat al-Bāḥith ʿan Zawāʾid Musnad al-Ḥārith*, 2:838 §885.
152. Muslim in *al-Ṣaḥīḥ:* Bk.: *al-Zuhd wa al-raqāʾiq* [The Renunciation and Heart Softeners], Ch.: "The Long Narration of Jābir and the Story of Abū al-Yusr," 4:2304 §3009.
153. al-Mundhirī in *al-Targhīb wa al-Tarhīb*, 2:322 §2555.
154. Ibn Rajab al-Ḥanbalī in *Jāmiʿ al-ʿUlūm wa al- ikam*, 1:149.
155. al-ʿAsqalānī in *Fatḥ al-Bārī*, 8:347.
156. al-Nawawī in *Riyāḍ al-Ṣāliḥīn*, 335.
157. Aḥmad b. Ḥanbal in *al-Musnad*, 2:428 §9518.

158. al-Nasā'ī in *al-Sunan al-Kubrā*, 5:252 §8815.
159. al-Mundhirī in *al-Targhīb wa al-Tarhīb*, 3:314 §4223.
160. al-Haythamī in *Majma' al-Zawā'id*, 8:77.
161. al-Ṭaḥāwī in *Mushkil al-Āthār*, 9:171.
162. Aḥmad b. Ḥanbal in *al-Musnad*, 1:396 §3763.
163. al-Ṭayālisī in *al-Musnad*, 1:46 §345.
164. al-Fākihī in *Akhbār Makka*, 5:141.
165. al-Haythamī in *Majma' al-Zawā'id*, 4:41.
166. Aḥmad b. Ḥanbal in *al-Musnad*, 1:423 §4018.
167. Abū Dāwūd in *al-Sunan:* Bk.: *al-Jihād* [The Striving], Ch.: "The Offensiveness of Burning the Enemy with Fire," 3:55 §2675, and in *Kitāb al-Ādab* [The Good Manners], Ch.: "Killing Small Ants" 4:367 §5268.
168. al-Nasā'ī in *al-Sunan al-Kubrā*, 5:183 §8614.
169. 'Abd al-Razzāq in *al-Muṣannaf*, 5:213 §9414.
170. al-Haythamī in *Majma' al-Zawā'id*, 4:41.
171. al-Bayhaqī in *Dalā'il al-Nubuwwa*, 6:32–33.
172. Muslim in *al-Ṣaḥīḥ:* Bk.: *al-Libās wa al-zīna* [The Clothing and Adornment], Ch.: "The Prohibition of Striking and Branding the Faces of Animals," 3:1673 §2118.
173. Ibn Ḥibbān in *al-Ṣaḥīḥ*, 12:441 §5624.
174. al-Ṭabarānī in *al-Mu'jam al-Kabīr*, 10:332 §10822.
175. al-Nawawī in *Riyāḍ al-Ṣāliḥīn*, 367.
176. al-Zayla'ī in *Takhrīj al-Aḥādīth wa al-Āthār*, 4:78.
178. Muslim in *al-Ṣaḥīḥ:* Bk.: *al-Libās wa al-zīna* [The Clothing and Adornment], Ch.: "The Prohibition of Striking and Branding the Faces of Animals," 3:1673 §2117.
179. Aḥmad b. Ḥanbal in *al-Musnad*, 3:323 §14499.
180. 'Abd al-Razzāq in *al-Musnad*, 9:444 §17949.
181. Ibn Ḥibbān in *al-Ṣaḥīḥ*, 12:432 §5627.
182. Abū Ya'lā in *al-Musnad*, 4:76 §2099.
183. al-Bukhārī in *al-Adab al-Mufrad*, 72 §175.
184. al-Bayhaqī in *al-Sunan al-Kubrā*, 7:35 §13037.
185. al-Mundhirī in *al-Targhīb wa al-Tarhīb*, 3:153 §3464.
186. al-Nawawī in *Riyāḍ al-Ṣāliḥīn*, 367.
187. al-'Aynī in *'Umdat al-Qārī*, 21:139.
188. Ibn Ḥibbān in *al-Ṣaḥīḥ*, 12:432 §5627.
189. Abū Ya'lā in *al-Musnad*, 4:76 §2099.
190. Aḥmad b. Ḥanbal in *al-Musnad*, 3:323 §14499.
191. 'Abd al-Razzāq in *al-Muṣannaf*, 9:444 §17949.
192. al-Bukhārī in *al-Adab al-Mufrad*, 72 §175.
193. Muslim in *al-Ṣaḥīḥ:* Bk.: *al-Libās wa al-zīna* [The Clothing and Adornment], Ch.: "The Prohibition of Striking and Branding the Faces of Animals," 4:1673 §2118.

194. Ibn Ḥibbān in *al-Ṣaḥīḥ*, 12:441 §5624.
195. al-Ṭabarānī in *al-Muʿjam al-Kabīr*, 10:332 §10822.
196. al-Nawawī in *Riyāḍ al-Ṣāliḥīn*, 367.
197. al-Zaylaʿī in *Takhrīj al-Aḥādīth wa al-Āthār*, 4:78.
198. Ibn Ḥibbān in *al-Ṣaḥīḥ*, 12:440 §5623.
199. al-Bayhaqī in *al-Sunan al-Kubrā*, 7:36 §13041.
200. al-Zaylaʿī in *Takhrīj al-Aḥādīth wa al-Āthār*, 4:78.
201. Between Animals," 3:26 §2562.
202. al-Tirmidhī in *al-Sunan:* Bk.: *al-Jihād* [The Striving], Ch.: "Sowing Discord Between Animals and Striking and Branding Faces," 4:210 §1708.
203. Abu Yaʿlā in *al-Musnad*, 4:389 §2509.
204. al-Ṭabarānī in *al-Muʿjam al-Kabīr*, 11:85 §11123.
205. al-Bayhaqī in *al-Sunan al-Kubrā*, 10:22 §19567, and in *Shuʿab al-Īmān*, 5:246 §6539.
206. al-Mundhirī in *al-Targhīb wa al-Tarhīb*, 3:147 §3437.
207. Muslim in *al-Ṣaḥīḥ:* Bk.: *al-Birr wa al-ṣila wa al-ādāb* [The Piety, Familial Integration, and Good Manners], Ch.: "The Prohibition of Oppression," 41997 §2582.
208. Aḥmad b. Ḥanbal in *al-Musnad*, 2:301, 411 §§7983, 9322.
209. al-Tirmidhī in *al-Sunan:* Bk.: *Ṣifat al-qiyāma wa al-raqāʾiq* [The Description of the Resurrection and Heart Softeners], Ch.: "The Issue of Reckoning and Retribution," 4:614 §2420.
210. Abū Yaʿlā in *al-Musnad*, 11:395 §6513.
211. al-Bayhaqī in *al-Sunan al-Kubrā*, 6:93 §11285.
212. al-Mundhirī in *al-Targhīb wa al-Tarhīb*, 4:217 §5455.
213. Ibn Ḥazm in *al-Muḥallā*, 1:15.
214. al-Nawawī in *Riyāḍ al-Ṣāliḥīn*, 74.
215. al-Ṭabarānī in al *al-Muʿjam al-Awsaṭ*, 7:92 §§6951, 2724.
216. al-Bayhaqī in *al-Sunan al-Kubrā*, 5:255 §10118.
217. Abū Nuʿaym in *Ḥilyat al-Awliyāʾ*, 8:180.
218. al-Maqdisī in *al-Aḥādīth al-Mukhtāra*, 7:271.
219. al-Haythamī in *Majmaʿ al-Zawāʾid*, 3:215.
220. Mālik in *al-Muwaṭṭaʾ:* Bk.: *al-Jihād* [The Striving], Ch.: "Horses, Racing, and Spending on Military Expeditions," 2:468 §1002.
221. Saʿīd b. Manṣūr in *al-Sunan*, 2:203 §2438.
222. al-Haythamī in *Bughyat al-Bāḥith ʿan Zawāʾid Musnad al-Ḥārith*, 2:675 §651.
223. Ibn ʿAbd al-Barr in *al-Tamhīd*, 24:101.
224. al-Bukhārī in *al-Ṣaḥīḥ:* Bk.: *Faḍāʾil aṣḥāb al-nabī* ﷺ [The Virtues of the Prophetic companions], Ch.: "The Virtues of Abū Bakr al-Ṣiddīq ؓ," 3:1339 §3463.
225. Muslim in *al-Ṣaḥīḥ:* Bk.: *Faḍāil al-ṣaḥāba* ؓ [The Virtues of the

Companions ؓ], Ch.: "The Virtues of Abū Bakr ؓ," 4:1858 §2388.
226. al-Tirmidhī in *al-Sunan:* Bk.: *al-Manāqib ʿan Rasūl Allāh* ﷺ [The Exemplary Traits Mentioned by Allāh's Messenger ﷺ], Ch.: "The Exemplary Traits of Abū Bakr and ʿUmar ؓ," 5:615 §3677.
227. al-Ṭabarānī in *al-Muʿjam al-Kabīr*, 11:332 §11916, and in *al-Muʿjam al-Awsaṭ*, 4:53 §3590.
228. al-Ḥākim in *al-Mustadrak*, 4:260 §7570.
229. al-Bayhaqī in *al-Sunan al-Kubrā*, 90:280 §18922.
230. al-Mundhirī in *al-Targhīb wa al-Tarhīb*, 3:142 §3422.
231. al-Haythamī in *Majmaʿ al-Zawāʾid*, 4:33.
232. Aḥmad b. Ḥanbal in *al-Musnad*, 2:108 §5864.
233. Ibn Mājah in *al-Sunan:* Bk.: *al-Dhabāʾiḥ* [The Slaughtered Animals], Ch.: "When You Slaughter, Slaughter Well," 2:1059 §3172.
234. al-Bayhaqī in *al-Sunan al-Kubrā*, 9:280 §18920, and in *Shuʿab al-Īmān*, 7:483 §11074.
235. al-Mundhirī in *al-Targhīb wa al-Tarhīb*, 2:101 §1671.
236. Abū Dāwūd in *al-Sunan:* Bk.: *al-Ṣayd* [The Hunting], Ch.: "When Something is Cut Off from Game," 3:111 §2858.
237. al-Tirmidhī in *al-Sunan:* Bk.: *al-Ṣayd* [The Hunting], Ch.: "That Which is Cut Off from a Living Animal Takes the Ruling of an Animal that Has Died Without Lawful Slaughtering," 4:74 §1480.
238. al-Dārimī in *al-Sunan*, 2:128 §2018.
239. ʿAbd al-Razzāq in *al-Muṣannaf*, 4:494 §8612.
240. al-Dāraquṭnī in *al-Sunan*, 4:292 §83.
241. Abū Yaʿlā in *al-Musnad*, 3:36 §1450.
242. al-Ṭabarānī in *al-Muʿjam al-Kabīr*, 3:248 §3304.
243. Ibn al-Jaʿd in *al-Musnad*, 1:434 §2952.
244. al-Bayhaqī in *al-Sunan al-Kubrā*, 9:245 §18703.
245. Abū Dāwūd in *al-Sunan:* Bk.: *al-Jihād* [The Striving], Ch.: " The Offensiveness of Burning the Enemy with Fire," 3:55 §2675, and in *Kitāb al-Ādab* [The Good Manners], Ch.: "Killing Small Ants," 4:367 §5268.
246. al-Dhahabī in *al-Kabāʾir*, 1:206.
247. al-Zaylaʿī in *Naṣb al-Rāya*, 3:407.
248. al-Nawawī in *Riyāḍ al-Ṣāliḥīn*, 367 §367.
249. al-Bayhaqī in *Dalāʾil al-Nubuwwa*, 6:32–33.
250. Ibn Kathīr in *Shamāʾil al-Rasūl* ﷺ, 289.
251. al-Ḥākim in *al-Mustadrak:* Bk.: *al-Dhabāʾiḥ* [The Slaughtered Animals], Ch.: "4:267 §7599.
252. al-Bayhaqī in *Dalāʾil al-Nubuwwa*, 1:321.
253. al-Hannād in *al-Zuhd*, 2:620 §1337.
254. al-Jazarī in *al-Nihāya*, 4:121.
255. Aḥmad b. Ḥanbal in *al-Musnad*, 4:172 §17595.
256. al-Khaṭīb *al-*Baghdādī in *Mūḍiḥ Awhām al-Jamʿ wa al-Tafrīq*, 1:272.

257. al-Haythamī in *Majmāʿ al-Zawāʾid*, 1:205, 9:6.
258. al-Ṭabarānī in *al-Muʿjam al-Kabīr*, 23:331 §763.
259. al-Mundhirī in *al-Targhīb wa al-Tarhīb*, 1:321 §1176.
260. Ibn ʿAsākir in *Tārīkh Dimashq*, 4:380.
261. al-ʿAsqalānī in *Lisān al-Mīzān*, 6:311 §1124.
262. Ibn Kathīr in *Tuḥfat al-Ṭālib*, 1:186 §80.
263. al-Haythamī in *Majmaʿ al-Zawāʾid*, 8:295.
264. al-Dārimī in *al-Sunan, al-Muqaddima* [The Introduction], Ch.: "How Allāh honoured His Prophet ﷺ by Making the Trees, Animals and Jinn Believe in Him," 1:25 §22.
265. Ibn ʿAsākir in *Tārīkh Dimashq*, 4:376.
266. al-Bayhaqī in *Dalāʾil al-Nubuwwa*, 6:40.
267. Ibn Kathīr in *al-Bidāya wa al-Nihāya*, 6:146, and in *Shamāʾil al-Rasūl* ﷺ, 343, 344.
268. al-Suyūṭī in *al-Khaṣāʾiṣ al-Kubrā*, 2:62.
269. Aḥmad b. Ḥanbal in *al-Musnad*, 4:170, 173.
270. Abū Nuʿaym in *Dalāʾil al-Nubuwwa*, 1:158 §184.
271. ʿAbd b. Ḥumayd in *al-Musnad*, 1:154 §405.
272. al-Mundhirī in *al-Targhīb wa al-Tarhīb*, 3:144 §3430.
273. Ibn ʿAsākir in *Tārīkh Dimashq*, 4:368.
274. al-Haythamī in *Majmaʿ al-Zawāʾid*, 9:5.
275. al-Mundhirī in *al-Targhīb wa al-Tarhīb*, 3:144, 145 §3431.

18. The Holy Prophet's Mercy and Kindness toward Plants and Inanimate Objects

Essential Reading:

1. Dr Tahir-ul-Qadri, Muhammad ﷺ: The Merciful, Ch:18, p.369-385.

Additional Readings for Teachers and Students:

1. al-Bukhārī in *al-Ṣaḥīḥ:* Bk.: *al-Manāqib* [The Exemplary Traits], Ch.: "The Signs of Prophethood in Islām," 3:1313 §3390.
2. Ibn Ḥibbān in *al-Ṣaḥīḥ*, 14:435 §6506.
3. al-Lālikāʾī in *Iʿtiqād Ahl al-Sunna*, 4:797 §1469.
4. al-Tirmidhī in *al-Sunan:* Bk.: *al-Manāqib* [The Exemplary Traits], Ch.: "The Qurʾanic Verses That Affirm the Prophethood of Muhammad ﷺ

and That which Allāh Gave Exclusively to him," 5:594 §3627.
5. Ibn Mājah in *al-Sunan*: Bk.: *Iqāmat al-ṣalāh wa al-sunna fīhā* [The Establishing the Prayer and the Sunna Therein], Ch.: "How the Pulpit Came to Be," 1:454 §1415.
6. al-Bukhārī in *al-Tārīkh al-Kabīr*, 7:26 §108.
7. Abū Yaʿlā in *al-Musnad*, 6:114 §3384.
8. ʿAbd b. Ḥumayd in *al-Musnad*, 1:396 §1336.
9. al-Maqdisī in *al-Aḥādīth al-Mukhtāra*, 5:37 §1643.
10. Aḥmad b. Ḥanbal in *al-Musnad*, 5:137–138 §§21285, 21289.
11. Ibn Mājah in *al-Sunan*: Bk.: *Iqāmat al-ṣalah wa al-sunna fīhā* [The Establishing the Prayer and the Sunna Therein], Ch.: "How the Pulpit Came to Be," 1:454 §1414.
12. al-Dārimī in *al-Sunan*, 1:30 §36.
13. al-Shāfiʿī in *al-Musnad*, 1:65.
15. Ibn Saʿd in *al-Ṭabaqāt al-Kubrā*, 1:252.
16. al-Maqdisī in *al-Aḥādīth al-Mukhtāra*, 1:393 §1192.
17. Ibn ʿAsākir in *Tārīkh Dimashq*, 4:392.
18. al-ʿAsqalānī in *Fatḥ al-Bārī*, 6:603 §3390.
19. Abū al-Maḥāsin in *Muʿtaṣar al-Mukhtaṣar*, 1:9.
20. al-ʿAynī in *ʿUmdat al-Qārī*, 6:215.
21. al-Kinānī in *Miṣbāḥ al-Zujāja*, 2:16 §504.
22. Aḥmad b. Ḥanbal from Ibn ʿAbbās ؓ in *al-Musnad*, 1:249, 363 §§2236, 3430.
23. Ibn Mājah in *al-Sunan*: Bk.: *Iqāmat al-ṣalah wa al-sunna fīhā* [The Establishing the Prayer and the Sunna Therein], Ch.: "How the Pulpit Came to Be," 1:454 §1415.
24. al-Dārimī in *al-Sunan*, 1:31, 442 §39, 1563.
25. al-Bukhārī in *al-Tārīkh al-kabīr*, 7:26 §108.
26. Ibn Abī Shayba from Ibn ʿAbbās ؓ in *al-Muṣannaf*, 6:319 §31746.
27. Abū Yaʿlā in *al-Musnad*, 6:114 §3384.
28. al-Ṭabarānī in *al-Muʿjam al-Kabīr*, 12:187 §12841.
29. ʿAbd b. Ḥumayd in *al-Musnad*, 1:396 §1336.
30. al-Maqdisī in *al-Aḥādīth al-Mukhtāra*, 5:37–38 §1643–1645.
31. Ibn Saʿd in *al-Ṭabaqāt al-Kubrā*, 1:252.
32. al-ʿAsqalānī in *Fatḥ al-Bārī*, 6:602 §3390.
33. al-Kinānī in *Miṣbāḥ al-Zujāja*, 2:16 §505.
34. al-Dārimī in *al-Sunan, al-Muqaddima* [The Introduction], Ch.: "How the Prophet ﷺ Was Honoured by the Longing of the Pulpit," 1:32, 442 §§40, 1565.
35. Ibn Abī Shayba in *al-Muṣannaf*, 6:319 §31747.
36. Abū Yaʿlā in *al-Musnad*, 2:328 §1067, and 4:128 §2177, and 5:142 §2756.
37. Ibn Khuzayma in *al-Ṣaḥīḥ*, 3:139 §1776.

38. Ibn Ḥibbān in *al-Ṣaḥīḥ*, 14:436 §6507.
39. al-Ṭabarānī in *al-Muʿjam al-Awsaṭ*, 2:108 §1408.
40. Ibn al-Jaʿd in *al-Musnad*, 1:466 §3219.
41. al-Haythamī in *Majmaʿ al-Zawāʾid*, 2:180–181.
42. al-Dārimī in *al-Sunan*, *al-Muqaddima* [The Introduction], Ch.: "How the Prophet ﷺ Was Honoured by the Longing of the Pulpit," 1:31 §37.
43. Ibn Abī Shayba in *al-Muṣannaf*, 6:319 §31749.
44. al-ʿAsqalānī in *al-Maṭālib al-ʿĀliya*, 4:698 §2, and in *Fatḥ al-Bārī*, 6:602 §3390.
45. al-ʿAynī in *ʿUmdat al-Qārī*, 16:128.
46. al-Dārimī in *al-Sunan*, *al-Muqaddima* [The Introduction], Ch.: "How the Prophet ﷺ Was Honoured by the Longing of the Pulpit," 1:32 §41.
47. Ibn Khuzayma in *al-Ṣaḥīḥ*, 3:104 §1777.
48. al-Lālikāʾī in *Iʿtiqād ahl al-Sunna*, 4:798 §1472.
49. al-Maqdisī in *al-Aḥādīth al-Mukhtāra*, 4:356–357 §1519–1520.
50. al-ʿAsqalānī in *Fatḥ al-Bārī*, 2:399.
51. al-Dārimī in *al-Sunan*, *al-Muqaddima* [The Introduction], Ch.: "How the Prophet ﷺ Was Honoured by the Longing of the Pulpit," 1:29 §32.
52. Abū Nuʿaym in *Ḥilyat al-Awliyāʾ*, 9:116.
53. al-Bayhaqī in *al-Iʿtiqād*, 1:271, and in *Dalāʾil al-Nubuwwa*, 6:68.
54. Ibn ʿAsākir in *Tārīkh Dimashq*, 4:391.
55. al-ʿAsqalānī in *Fatḥ al-Bārī*, 6:603 §3393.
56. Ibn Kathīr in *Shamāʾil al-Rasūl* ﷺ, 251.
57. al-ʿAynī in *ʿUmdat al-Qārī*, 16:129 §5853.
58. Abū Yaʿlā in *al-Musnad*, 4:128 §2177, 2:328 §1067.
59. Ibn Khuzayma in *al-Ṣaḥīḥ*, 3:139 §1776.
60. al-Haythamī in *Majmaʿ al-Zawāʾid*, 2:181.
61. Ibn Ḥibbān in *al-Ṣaḥīḥ*, Ch.: "The Aforementioned Tree Trunk Stopped Its Longing Only After al-Muṣṭafā ﷺ Had Embraced It," 14:436 §6507.
62. Abū Yaʿlā in *al-Musnad*, 5:142 §2756.
63. al-Ṭabarānī in *al-Muʿjam al-Awsaṭ*, 2:108 §1409.
64. Ibn al-Jaʿd in *al-Musnad*, 1:466 §3219.
65. al-Maqdisī in *al-Aḥādīth al-Mukhtāra*, 5:289 §6507.
66. al-Haythamī in *Mawārid al-Ẓamʾān*, 1:151 §574.
67. al-ʿAsqalānī in *Fatḥ al-Bārī*, 6:602.
68. Ibn Kathīr in *Shamāʾil al-Rasūl* ﷺ, 240.
69. al-Bukhārī in *al-Ṣaḥīḥ:* Bk.: *al-Maghāzī* [The Military Expeditions], Ch.: "The Prophet's Arrival to Hajar ﷺ," 4:1610 §4160, and in *Kitāb al-Zakāt* [The Zakat], Ch.: "Estimating Dates," 2:539 §1411.
70. Muslim in *al-Ṣaḥīḥ:* Bk.: *al-Faḍāʾil* [The Virtues], Ch.: "The Miracles of the Prophet ﷺ," 4:1785 §1392, and in *Kitāb al- ajj* [The Pilgrimage], Ch.: "Uḥud Is a Mountain That Loves Us and Which We Love," 2:1011 §1392.

71. Aḥmad b. Ḥanbal in *al-Musnad*, 5:424 §23652.
72. Ibn Ḥibbān in *al-Ṣaḥīḥ*, 10:355.
73. Ibn Abī Shayba in *al-Muṣannaf*, 7:423 §37006.
74. al-Bayhaqī in *al-Sunan al-Kubrā*, 6:372 §12889.
75. Abū Nuʿaym in *Dalāʾil al-Nubuwwa*, 171 §212.
76. al-Bukhārī in *al-Ṣaḥīḥ:* Bk.: *al-Manāqib* [The Exemplary Traits], Ch.: "The Exemplary Traits of ʿUmar b. al-Khaṭṭāb, " 3:1348 §3483, and in Ch.: "Were I to Choose an Intimate Friend," 3:1344 §3472.
77. Abū Dāwūd in *al-Sunan:* Bk.: *al-Sunna* [The Prophetic Tradition], Ch.: "The Caliphs," 4:212 §4651.
78. al-Tirmidhī in *al-Sunan:* Bk.: *al-Manāqib* [The Exemplary Traits], Ch.: "The Exemplary Traits of ʿUthmān," 5:624 §3697.
79. Ibn Ḥibbān in *al-Ṣaḥīḥ*, 15:280 §6865.
80. al-Nasāʾī in *al-Sunan al-Kubrā*, 5:43 §8135.
81. Muslim in *al-Ṣaḥīḥ:* Bk.: *Faḍāʾil al-ṣaḥāba* [The Virtues of the Companions], Ch.: "The Virtues of Ṭalḥa and al-Zubayr," 4:1880 §2417.
82. Aḥmad b. Ḥanbal in *al-Musnad*, 2:419 §9420.
83. al-Tirmidhī in *al-Sunan:* Bk.: *al-Manāqib* [The Exemplary Traits], Ch.: "The Virtues of ʿUthmān b. ʿAffān," 5:624 §3696.
84. al-Nasāʾī in *al-Sunan al-Kubrā*, 5:59 §8207.
85. Ibn Ḥibbān in *al-Ṣaḥīḥ*, 15:441 §6983.
86. Ibn Abī ʿĀṣim in *al-Sunna*, 2:621 §1441.

SECTION VII

Muhammad ﷺ: The Peacemaker

1. The Prophet's ﷺ Universal Message of Peace and Harmony

1.1 Preliminary Statement

Essential Reading:

1. Dr Tahir-ul-Qadri, Muhammad ﷺ: The Peacemaker, Ch:1.

Additional Readings for Teachers and Students:

1. al-Rāzī in *al-Tafsīr al-Kabīr*, 7:60, 9:53 & 16:81.
2. The Secrets of the Self (*Asrār-e Khudī*)—translated by Reynold A. Nicholson pp.xvi–xx.
3. Qur'ān 2:143.
4. Ibid., 3:103.
5. Ibid., 95:4–6.

1.2 Faith in Allah and His Messenger ﷺ—The Foundation Stone of Peace and Security

Essential Reading:

1. Dr Tahir-ul-Qadri, Muhammad ﷺ: The Peacemaker, Ch:1.

Additional Readings for Teachers and Students:

1. Qur'ān 112:1–4.
2. Ibid., 94: 1–3.

1.3 Prophet Muhammad ﷺ—Conjunction of all Divine Faiths

Essential Reading:

1. Dr Tahir-ul-Qadri, Muhammad ﷺ: The Peacemaker, Ch:1.

1.3.1 The Prophet's ﷺ Stopover at Medina, Mount Sinai and Bethlehem during His Ascension Journey

Essential Reading:

1. Dr Tahir-ul-Qadri, Muhammad ﷺ: The Peacemaker, Ch:1.

1.3.2 The Prophet's ﷺ Address in *al-Aqṣā* Mosque, Jerusalem

Essential Reading:

1. Dr Tahir-ul-Qadri, Muhammad ﷺ: The Peacemaker, Ch:1.

Additional Readings for Teachers and Students:

1. Qur'ān 21:107.

1.3.3 Universality of the Prophetic Message

Essential Reading:

1. Dr Tahir-ul-Qadri, Muhammad ﷺ: The Peacemaker, Ch:1.

Additional Readings for Teachers and Students:

1. Qur'ān 7:158.
2. Ibid., 4:1.
3. Ibid., 21:30.

1.3.4 Declaration of the Moderate Character of Islamic Community

Essential Reading:

1. Dr Tahir-ul-Qadri, Muhammad ﷺ: The Peacemaker, Ch:1.

ADDITIONAL READINGS FOR TEACHERS AND STUDENTS:

1. Qur'ān 2:143.
2. Narrated by al-Bazzār in *al-Baḥr al-Zakhkhār*, 17:8.
3. al-Bayhaqī in *Dalā'il al-nubuwwa*, 2:401.
4. Ibn Abī ātim al-Rāzī in *Tafsīr al-Qur'ān al-ʿaẓīm*, 7:2311.
5. Ibn Jarīr al-Ṭābarī in *Tahdhīb al-āthār*, 1:437 & in *Jāmiʿ al-bayān fī tafsīr al-Qur'ān*, 17:337.
6. Qāḍī ʿIyāḍ in *al-Shifā bi taʿrīf ḥuqūq al-Muṣṭafā*, p.182.
7. al-Thaʿlabī in *al-Kashf wa al-bayān*, 6:59.
8. al-Haythamī in *Majmaʿ al-zawā'id*, 1:236.
9. Ibn Kathīr in *Tafsīr al-Qur'ān al-ʿaẓīm*, 3:19.
10. al-Buqāʿī in *Naẓm al-durar fī tanasub al-āyāt wa al-suwar*, 11:296.
11. al-Suyūṭī in *al-Durr al-Manthūr*, 5:201.
12. ibid., *al-Khaṣā'ṣ al-kubrā*, 2:338.

1.4 THE PEACE-LOVING NATURE OF ISLAMIC FAITH

ESSENTIAL READING:

1. Dr Tahir-ul-Qadri, Muhammad ﷺ: The Peacemaker, Ch:1.

2. PEACE BUILDING CHARACTER OF THE HOLY PROPHET ﷺ

ESSENTIAL READING:

1. Dr Tahir-ul-Qadri, Muhammad ﷺ: The Peacemaker, Ch:2.

2.1 Preliminary Statement

Essential Reading:

1. Dr Tahir-ul-Qadri, Muhammad ﷺ: The Peacemaker, Ch:2.

2.2 Peacebuilding in the Holy Prophet's Young Life

Essential Reading:

1. Dr Tahir-ul-Qadri, Muhammad ﷺ: The Peacemaker, Ch:2.

2.3 Statement of Khadija ؓ, his First Wife, on the Peace Loving Character of the Holy Prophet ﷺ

Essential Reading:

1. Dr Tahir-ul-Qadri, Muhammad ﷺ: The Peacemaker, Ch:2.

2.4 Statement of Jaʿfar in Abyssinian Royal Court on the Humanistic Character of the Holy Prophet ﷺ

Essential Reading:

1. Dr Tahir-ul-Qadri, Muhammad ﷺ: The Peacemaker, Ch:2.

2.5 The Prophet's Commandment of Peace to the Medinan Delegates at al-ʿAqaba

Essential Reading:

1. Dr Tahir-ul-Qadri, Muhammad ﷺ: The Peacemaker, Ch:2.

2.6 The Prophet's Message of Peace to Medinans at His Arrival in Medina

Essential Reading:

1. Dr Tahir-ul-Qadri, Muhammad ﷺ: The Peacemaker, Ch:2.

2.7 The Prophet's Instructions of Peace to the People of Khaybar

Essential Reading:

1. Dr Tahir-ul-Qadri, Muhammad ﷺ: The Peacemaker, Ch:2.

2.8 Declaration of Peace and Security for non-Muslim Inhabitants of Mecca at its Conquest

Essential Reading:

1. Dr Tahir-ul-Qadri, Muhammad ﷺ: The Peacemaker, Ch:2.

2.9 The Prophet's Address on Peace and Security at Tabūk

Essential Reading:

1. Dr Tahir-ul-Qadri, Muhammad ﷺ: The Peacemaker, Ch:2.

2.10 Proclamation of the Charter of Peace & Human Rights at his Last Hajj

Essential Reading:

1. Dr Tahir-ul-Qadri, Muhammad ﷺ: The Peacemaker, Ch:2.

2.11 General Policy Statements of the Holy Prophet ﷺ for Peacemaking

Essential Reading:

1. Dr Tahir-ul-Qadri, Muhammad ﷺ: The Peacemaker, Ch:2.

2.12 Continuity of Prophetic Policies for Peacemaking in the Caliphate Period

Essential Reading:

1. Dr Tahir-ul-Qadri, Muhammad ﷺ: The Peacemaker, Ch:2.

3. Seeking Inner and Outer Peace through Self Purification and Spiritual Transformation

3.1 Preliminary Statement

Essential Reading:

1. Dr Tahir-ul-Qadri, Muhammad ﷺ: The Peacemaker, Ch:3.

3.2 The Ideal of Allah's Pleasure Leads to Inner and Outer Peace

Essential Reading:

1. Dr Tahir-ul-Qadri, Muhammad ﷺ: The Peacemaker, Ch:3.

Additional Readings for Teachers and Students:

1. Qur'ān, 9:20–21.
2. Ibid., 59:8.
3. Ibid., 2:207.
4. Ibid., 4:114.
5. Ibid., 3:174.
6. Ibid., 5:119.

3.3 Each Act of the Believer is for Allah's Pleasure

Essential Reading:

1. Dr Tahir-ul-Qadri, Muhammad ﷺ: The Peacemaker, Ch:3.

Additional Readings for Teachers and Students:

1. Qur'ān 27:19.

3.4 The Ideal of Allah's Pleasure Leads to the Righteous Character

Essential Reading:

1. Dr Tahir-ul-Qadri, Muhammad ﷺ: The Peacemaker, Ch:3.

Additional Readings for Teachers and Students:

1. Qur'ān, 24:37.
2. Ibid., 21:90.
3. Ibid., 32:16.
4. Ibid., 18:28.
5. Ibid., 6:52.
6. Ibid., 5:15–16.
7. Ibid., 9:111.

3.5 The Love of Faith: A Fountainhead of Peace and Tranquillity

Essential Reading:

1. Dr Tahir-ul-Qadri, Muhammad ﷺ: The Peacemaker, Ch:3.

Additional Readings for Teachers and Students:

1. Qur᾿ān, 47:19.
2. Qur᾿ān, 48:29.
3. Jalā᾿ al-Khāṭir ("Purification of the Mind"), translated by Prof. Shetha al-Dargazelli and Dr Luay Fathi, pp.22–23.
4. Ibid., p.24.
5. Ibid., p.27 (Qur᾿ān 32:16).
6. Narrated by al-Ṭabarānī in *al-Muᶜjam*.

3.6 The Anatomy of Divine Pursuit

Essential Reading:

1. Dr Tahir-ul-Qadri, Muhammad ﷺ: The Peacemaker, Ch:3.

Additional Readings for Teachers and Students:

1. Qur᾿ān, 91:10.
2. Ibid., 25:70.
3. Ibid., 2:151.
4. Ibid., 62:2.
5. Ibid., 20:75–76.
6. Ibid., 87:14.
7. Ibid., 3:14.
8. Aḥmad b. Ḥanbal in *al-Musnad*, 3:198 §13071.
9. al-Bayhaqī in *Shuᶜab al-Īmān*, 1:41 §8.
10. al-Quḍāᶜī in *Musnad al-Shihāb*, 2:62 §887;
11. al-Mundhirī in *al-Targhīb wa al-Tarhīb*, 3:240 §3860;
12. Ibn Rajab in *Jāmiᶜ al-ᶜUlūm wa al-Ḥikam*, 1:75.
13. al-Haythamī in *Majmaᶜ al-Zawā᾿id*, 1:53.

3.7 THE GENETICS OF PEACEFUL AND RIGHTEOUS CHARACTER

ESSENTIAL READING:

1. Dr Tahir-ul-Qadri, Muhammad ﷺ: The Peacemaker, Ch:3.

ADDITIONAL READINGS FOR TEACHERS AND STUDENTS:

1. Qur'ān, 91:10.
2. Ibid., 25:70.
3. Ibid., 2:151.
4. Ibid., 62:2.

4. ESTABLISHING PEACE THROUGH MERCY, FORGIVENESS AND MODERATION

4.1 PRELIMINARY STATEMENT

ESSENTIAL READING:

1. Dr Tahir-ul-Qadri, Muhammad ﷺ: The Peacemaker, Ch:4.

4.2 ISLAM LIGHTENS THE BURDEN OF OBLIGATIONS

ESSENTIAL READING:

1. Dr Tahir-ul-Qadri, Muhammad ﷺ: The Peacemaker, Ch:4.

Additional Readings for Teachers and Students:

1. Qur'ān, 4:28.
2. Ibid., 8:66.
3. Ibid., 3:159.
4. Ibid., 33:45.
5. al-Bukhārī in al-Ṣaḥīḥ: Bk.: al-Buyūʿ [Transactions], Ch.: "The Prohibition of Being Loud and Boisterous in the Marketplace," 2:747 §201
6. Qur'ān 9:61.
7. Ibid., 21:107.
8. Ibid., 9:128.
9. Ibid., 7:157.

4.3 Islam Teaches Easiness and does not Approve of Harshness

Essential Reading:

1. Dr Tahir-ul-Qadri, Muhammad ﷺ: The Peacemaker, Ch:4.

Additional Readings for Teachers and Students:

1. Muslim in al-Ṣaḥīḥ: Bk.: al-Ṭalāq [The Divorce], Ch.: "Merely Giving a Woman the Option of Divorce Does not Make the Divorce Effective, But Only When it is Actually Intended," 2:1104 §1478.
2. al-Bukhārī in al-Ṣaḥīḥ: Bk.: al-ʿAmal fī al-ṣalāt [On Extraneous Actions Performed in the Prayer], Ch.: "When One's Animal Runs Away During the Prayer," 1:405 §1153.
3. Ibid., Bk.: Mawāqīt al-ṣalāt [The Timing of the Prayers], Ch.: "On the Missed Prayers that Can Be Prayed After the ʿAṣr Prayer," 1:213 §565.

4.4 The Holy Prophet ﷺ Chose the Easier of the Two Options

Essential Reading:

1. Dr Tahir-ul-Qadri, Muhammad ﷺ: The Peacemaker, Ch:4.

Additional Readings for Teachers and Students:

1. Ibid., Bk.: al-Manāqib [The Exemplary Virtues], Ch.: "The Qualities of the Prophet a," 3:1306 §3367.
2. Muslim in al-Ṣaḥīḥ: Bk.: al-Faḍā'il [Virtues], Ch.: "The Prophet's Distance Away from Sins," 4:1813 §2327.

4.5 The Best of Islamic Religion is the Middle Course and Moderation

Essential Reading:

1. Dr Tahir-ul-Qadri, Muhammad ﷺ: The Peacemaker, Ch:4.

Additional Readings for Teachers and Students:

1. Ibid., Bk.: al-Īmān [The Faith], Ch.: "The Religion is Ease," 1:23 §39.
2. Aḥmad b. Ḥanbal in al-Musnad, 3:479.
3. al-Haythamī in Majmaʿ al-zawā'id, 1:61.
4. Ibn Ḥajar in Fatḥ al-Bārī, 1:94; while al-Ṭabarānī in al-Muʿjam al-kabīr, 18:230 §573.
5. Ibn Abī ʿĀṣim in al-Āḥād wa al-mathānī, 4:349 §2383.
6. al-Quḍāʿī in Musnad al-Shihāb, 2:219–220 §1224–1225.
7. al-Maqdisī in al-Aḥādīth al-mukhtāra (7:132 §2565).

4.6 Prohibition of Extremism and Commandment of Moderation

Essential Reading:

1. Dr Tahir-ul-Qadri, Muhammad ﷺ: The Peacemaker, Ch:3.

Additional Readings for Teachers and Students:

1. al-Nasāʾī, *al-Sunan*, 5:268 §3058.
2. Ibn Mājah, *al-Sunan*, 2:1008 §3029.
3. Ibn Ḥibbān, *al-Ṣaḥīḥ*, 9:183–184 §3871.
4. Abū Yaʿlā, *al-Musnad*, 4:316 §2427.
5. al-Ṭabarānī, *al-Muʿjam al-kabīr*, 12:156 §12747.
6. al-Bayhaqī, *al-Sunan al-kubrā*, 5:127.
7. Aḥmad b. Ḥanbal, *al-Musnad*, 5:350, 361.
8. al-Ṭayālisī, *al-Musnad*, p. 109 §809.
9. Ibn Abī ʿĀṣim, *al-Sunna*, 1:46 §95.
10. Ibn Khuzayma, *al-Ṣaḥīḥ*, 2:199 §1179.
11. al-Ḥākim, *al-Mustadrak*, 1:457 §1176.
12. al-Bayhaqī, *al-Sunan al-kubrā*, 3:18.
13. Aḥmad b. Ḥanbal, *al-Musnad*, 1:236.
14. ʿAbd b. Ḥumayd, *al-Musnad*, p. 199 §569.
15. al-Bukhārī, *al-Adab al-mufrad*, p. 108 §287.
16. Aḥmad b. Ḥanbal, *al-Musnad*, 6:116, 233.
17. al-Ḥumaydī, *al-Musnad*, 1:123 §254.
18. Ibn Ḥajar, *Fatḥ al-bārī*, 2:444.
19. al-Bukhārī, *al-Ṣaḥīḥ*, 1:173 §443 and 3:1063 §2745.
20. Muslim, *al-Ṣaḥīḥ*, 2:608–610 §892–893.

4.7 No Soul should be Burdened beyond its Ability

Essential Reading:

1. Dr Tahir-ul-Qadri, Muhammad ﷺ: The Peacemaker, Ch:4.

ADDITIONAL READINGS FOR TEACHERS AND STUDENTS:

1. Qur'ān 6:152.
2. Ibid., 2:286.
3. Ibid., 94:5–6.
4. al-Bukhārī in *al-Ṣaḥīḥ:* Bk.: *al-Iʿtiṣām* [The Holding Fast to the Qur'ān and Sunna], Ch.: "Emulating the Sunnas of Allah's Messenger ﷺ," 6:2658 §6858.
5. Muslim in *al-Ṣaḥīḥ:* Bk.: *al-Faḍā'il* [The Virtues], Ch.: "Respect for the Prophet ﷺ and Avoiding Frequent Questions Posed to Him as Long as There is No Harm," 4:1832 §2359.
6. Ibid., Bk.: *al-Aḥkām* [The Legal Rulings], Ch.: "How the Imam is to Take the Pledge of Fealty from the People," 6:2633 §6776.
7. Muslim in *al-Ṣaḥīḥ:* Bk.: *al-Imāra* [The Leadership], Ch.: "Swearing fealty for listening to and obeying the orders of the leader as far as possible," 3:1490 §1867.
8. Ibid., 6:2633 §6778;
9. Muslim in *al-Ṣaḥīḥ:* Bk.: *al-Īmān* [The Faith], Ch.: "Explanation that the Religion is Sincere Counsel," 1:75 §56.
10. Aḥmad b. Ḥanbal in *al-Musnad*, 6:357, 365.
11. Mālik in *al-Muwaṭṭa'*, 2:982 §1775.

4.8 THINGS BE MADE EASY SO THAT PEOPLE MAY NOT FEEL AVERSION

ESSENTIAL READING:

1. Dr Tahir-ul-Qadri, Muhammad ﷺ: The Peacemaker, Ch:4.

ADDITIONAL READINGS FOR TEACHERS AND STUDENTS:

1. al-Bukhārī in al-Ṣaḥīḥ: Bk.: al-ʿIlm [Knowledge], Ch.: "On the Prophet a Being Careful about Giving People Admonition and Knowledge Lest They Feel Aversion to It," 1:38 §69;
2. Muslim in al-Ṣaḥīḥ: Bk.: al-Jihād wa al-siyar [The Striving and Military Expeditions], Ch.: "The Command to Make Things Easy and Not

Making Others Feel Aversion," 3:1359 §1734.
3. Ibid., Bk.: al-Maghāzī [The Expeditions], Ch.: "Abū Mūsā al-Ashʿarī and Muʿādh's Mission to Yemen before the Farewell Pilgrimage," 3:1104 §2873.
4. Muslim in al-Ṣaḥīḥ, ibid., 3:1359 §1733.
5. Muslim in al-Ṣaḥīḥ, ibid., 3:1358 §1732.
6. Abū Dāwūd in al-Sunan, 4:260 §4835.
7. al-Bukhārī in al-Ṣaḥīḥ: Bk.: al-Wuḍūʾ [The Ablution], Ch.: "Pouring Water Over Urine in the Mosque," 1:89 §217.
8. Muslim in al-Ṣaḥīḥ: Bk.: al-Ṭahāra [The Purification], Ch.: "The Obligation to Wash Away Urine and Other Impurities," 1:236 §§284–285.
9. Muslim in al-Ṣaḥīḥ: Bk.: al-Dhikr wa al-duʿā [The Remembrance and Supplication], Ch.: "The Virtue of Congregating to Recite the Qurʾān and Invoke,' 4:1996 §2580.

4.9 Prescription of a Balanced and Moderate Way of Life

Essential Reading:

1. Dr Tahir-ul-Qadri, Muhammad ﷺ: The Peacemaker, Ch:4.

Additional Readings for Teachers and Students:

1. al-Bukhārī in al-Ṣaḥīḥ: Bk.: al-Īmān [The Faith], Ch.: "The Most Beloved Element of the Religion in the Sight of Allah is the Most Consistent of It," 1:24 §43.
2. Muslim in al-Ṣaḥīḥ: Bk.: Ṣalāt al-musāfirīn [The Travelers' Prayer], Ch.: "The Virtue of Consistent Actions Such as Night Vigil Prayer and the Like,' 1:540 §782.
3. Ibid., Bk.: al-Ṣawm [The Fasting], Ch.: "The Body's Right When Fasting," 2:697 §1874.
4. Muslim in al-Ṣaḥīḥ: Bk.: al-Ṣiyām [The Fasting], Ch.: "The Prohibition of Perpetual Fasts for Those Who are Harmed by Them," 2:812–817 §1159.
5. al-Bukhārī in al-Ṣaḥīḥ: Bk.: al-Nikāḥ [Marriage], Ch.: "The Prohibition

celibacy and castration," 5:1952 §4786; •Muslim in al-Ṣaḥīḥ: Bk.: al-Nikāḥ [Marriage], Ch.: "Fasting of that who is unable to support and marry," 2:1020 §1402.
6. Ibid., Bk.: al-Nikāḥ [The Marriage], Ch.: "The Encouragement to Marry," 5:1949 §4776.
7. Muslim in al-Ṣaḥīḥ: Bk.: al-Nikāḥ [Marriage], Ch.: "The Recommendation of Marriage for Those who are Able," 2:1020 §1401.
8. Muslim in al-Ṣaḥīḥ: Bk.: Ṣalāt al-musāfirīn [The Travelers' Prayer], Ch.: "The Command for the One who is Drowsy while Praying, or Who Mixes up The Qur'ān or Remembrance, to Take Rest," 1:541 §784.
9. Aḥmad b. anbal in al-Musnad, 3:101.

4.10 EXTREMISM DESTROYS COMMUNITIES

ESSENTIAL READING:

1. Dr Tahir-ul-Qadri, Muhammad ﷺ: The Peacemaker, Ch:4.

ADDITIONAL READINGS FOR TEACHERS AND STUDENTS:

1. Aḥmad b. Ḥanbal, *al-Musnad*, 6:198.
2. al-Maqdisī, *al-Aḥādīth al-mukhtāra*, 6:120 §2115.
3. al-Nasā'ī, *al-Sunan*, 5:268 §3058.
4. Ibn Mājah, *al-Sunan*, 2:1008 §3029.
5. Ibn Ḥibbān, *al-Ṣaḥīḥ*, 9:183–184 §3871.
6. Abū Yaʿlā, *al-Musnad*, 4:316 §2427.
7. al-Ṭabarānī, *al-Muʿjam al-kabīr*, 12:156 §12747.
8. al-Bayhaqī, *al-Sunan al-kubrā*, 5:127.
9. al-Bukhārī in *al-Ṣaḥīḥ:* Bk.: *al-Wuḍū'* [The Ablution], Ch.: "On Performing Ablution after Sleep," 1:87 §209.
10. Muslim in *al-Ṣaḥīḥ:* Bk.: *Ṣalāt al-musāfirīn* [The Travelers' Prayer], Ch.: "The Command for the One who is Drowsy while Praying, or Who Mixes up The Qur'ān or Remembrance, to Take Rest," 1:542 §786.
11. al-Bukhārī in *al-Ṣaḥīḥ:* Bk.: *al-Wuḍū'* [The Ablution], Ch.: "On Performing Ablution after Sleep," 1:87 §209.
12. Muslim in *al-Ṣaḥīḥ:* Bk.: *Ṣalāt al-musāfirīn* [The Travelers' Prayer], Ch.: "The Command for the One who is Drowsy while Praying, or Who

Mixes up The Qur'ān or Remembrance, to Take Rest," 1:542 §786.
13. al-Bukhārī in *al-Ṣaḥīḥ:* Bk.: *al-Wuḍū'* [The Ablution], Ch.: "On Performing Ablution after Sleep," 1:87 §209.
14. Muslim in *al-Ṣaḥīḥ:* Bk.: *Ṣalāt al-musāfirīn* [The Travelers' Prayer], Ch.: "The Command for the One who is Drowsy while Praying, or Who Mixes up The Qur'ān or Remembrance, to Take Rest," 1:542 §786.
15. Muslim in *al-Ṣaḥīḥ:* Bk.: *al-ʿIlm* [The Knowledge], Ch.: "The Extremists Have Perished," 4:2055 §2670.
16. al-Bukhārī in *al-Ṣaḥīḥ:* Bk.: *al-ʿIlm* [The Knowledge], Ch.: "Delivering Fatwas While Stationary upon an Animal," 1:43 §83.
17. Muslim in *al-Ṣaḥīḥ:* Bk.: *al-Ḥajj* [The Hajj], Ch.: "Regarding the One Who Shaves His Head before Sacrificing or Sacrifices before Casting Stones," 2:948 §1306.
18. Muslim in *al-Ṣaḥīḥ:* Bk.: *Ṣalāt al-musāfirīn* [The Travelers' Prayer], Ch.: "On Combining between Two Prayers while Resident," 1:489 §705.

4.11 Recommendation of Lenience and Tolerance

Essential Reading:

1. Dr Tahir-ul-Qadri, Muhammad ﷺ: The Peacemaker, Ch:4.

Additional Readings for Teachers and Students:

1. al-Bukhārī in al-Ṣaḥīḥ: Bk.: al-Ṣawm [The Fasting], Ch.: "On Perpetual Fasts," 2:694 §1865; •Muslim in al-Ṣaḥīḥ: Bk.: al-Ṣiyām [The Fasting], Ch.: "The Prohibition of Engaging in a Perpetual Fast," 2:774 §1103.
2. Ibid., Bk.: al-Istiqrāḍ [The Loans], Ch.: "Easyness in Sale and Purchase," 2:730 §1970.
3. Ibid., Bk.: al-Istiqrāḍ [The Loans], Ch.: "Seeking Loans for Camels," 2:842 §2260.
4. Muslim in al-Ṣaḥīḥ: Bk.: al-Musāqāt [The Sharecropping], Ch.: "On the One Whose Property is Damaged and Receives Something Better than It," 3:1225 §1601.
5. Ibid., Bk.: al-Istiqrāḍ [The Loans], Ch.: "Seeking Loans for Camels," 2:842 §2260.
6. Muslim in al-Ṣaḥīḥ: Bk.: al-Musāqāt [The Sharecropping], Ch.: "On the

One Whose Property is Damaged and Receives Something Better than It," 3:1225 §1601.
7. Ibid., Bk.: al-Istiqrāḍ [The Loans], Ch.: "Seeking Loans for Camels," 2:842 §2260.
8. Muslim in al-Ṣaḥīḥ: Bk.: al-Musāqāt [The Sharecropping], Ch.: "On the One Whose Property is Damaged and Receives Something Better than It," 3:1225 §1601.
9. Muslim in al-Ṣaḥīḥ: Bk.: al-Zuhd [Renunciation], Ch.: "The Long Hadith of Jābir and the Story of Abū al-Yasar," 4:2302 §3006.

4.12 Allah's Pleasure Lies in Helping and Forgiving Behaviour

Essential Reading:

1. Dr Tahir-ul-Qadri, Muhammad ﷺ: The Peacemaker, Ch:4.

Additional Readings for Teachers and Students:

1. Aḥmad b. Ḥanbal in al-Musnad, 2:361 §8715.
2. al-Nasā'ī in al-Sunan: Bk.: al-Buyūʿ [The Sales], Ch.: "On Dealing with Others Well and Being Kind in Seeking Repayment of Loans," 7:381 §3696.
3. Ibn Ḥibbān in al-Ṣaḥīḥ, 11:422 §5403.
4. al-Ḥākim in al-Mustadrak, 2:33 §2223.

4.13 Social and Economic Empowerment of the neglected segments of society

Essential Reading:

1. Dr Tahir-ul-Qadri, Muhammad ﷺ: The Peacemaker, Ch:4.

4.13.1 Providing what is Desired for People

Essential Reading:

1. Dr Tahir-ul-Qadri, Muhammad ﷺ: The Peacemaker, Ch:4.

4.13.2 Charity Encompasses the Whole of Society

Essential Reading:

1. Dr Tahir-ul-Qadri, Muhammad ﷺ: The Peacemaker, Ch:4.

4.13.3 Charity to Relatives

Essential Reading:

1. Dr Tahir-ul-Qadri, Muhammad ﷺ: The Peacemaker, Ch:4.

4.13.4 Helping the Poor and Freeing the Captives

Essential Reading:

1. Dr Tahir-ul-Qadri, Muhammad ﷺ: The Peacemaker, Ch:4.

4.13.5 Facilitating the Deprived

Essential Reading:

1. Dr Tahir-ul-Qadri, Muhammad ﷺ: The Peacemaker, Ch:4.

4.13.6 The Reward of Someone who Helps Peo-ple in Difficulties

Essential Reading:

1. Dr Tahir-ul-Qadri, Muhammad ﷺ: The Peacemaker, Ch:4.

4.14 Everything is Permissible unless Expressly Prohibited

Essential Reading:

1. Dr Tahir-ul-Qadri, Muhammad ﷺ: The Peacemaker, Ch:4.

Additional Readings for Teachers and Students:

1. Qur'ān 2:29.
2. Al-Nasafī, Madārik al-tanzīl, 1:35.
3. Al-Zamakhsharī, al-Kashshāf ʿan ḥaqāʾiq ghawāmiḍ al-tanzīl, 1:152.
4. Qur'ān 7:32.
5. Al-Ṭabarī, Jāmiʿ al-bayān fī tafsīr al-Qur'ān, 8:163.
6. Abū al-Saʿūd, Irshād al-ʿaql al-salīm ilā mazāyā al-Qur'ān al-karīm, 3:224.
7. Qur'ān 7:31.
8. Al-Ṭabarī, Jāmiʿ al-bayān fī tafsīr al-Qur'ān, 8:159.
9. Qur'ān 4:24.
10. Ibid., 5:3.
11. Ibid., 6:119.
12. Ibid., 5:101.
13. Ibid., 16:116.
14. Ibid., 10:59.
15. al-Tirmidhī in al-Sunan: Bk.: al-Libās [The Dresses], Ch.: "What is said about furry clothes?" 4:220 §1726; and Ibn Mājah in al-Sunan: Bk.: al-Aṭʿima [The Foods], Ch.: "Eating of ghee and cheese," 2:1117 §3367.
16. al-Bukhārī in al-Ṣaḥīḥ: Bk.: al-Iʿtiṣām bi al-Kitāb wa al-Sunna [Holding Fast to the Book and the Sunna], Ch.: "What is disliked of asking too

many questions and burdening oneself with that which does not concern one," 6:2658 §6859.

17. Muslim in al-Ṣaḥīḥ: Bk.: al-Faḍā'il [The Virtues and Merits], Ch.: "The Prophet's veneration and leaving aside the questions which are not required," 4:1831 §2358.
18. Ibn ajar al-ʿAsqalānī, Fatḥ al-bārī, 13:268.
19. al-Sarakhsī in al-Mabṣūṭ, 24:77; and al-Suyūṭī in al-Ashbāh wa al-naẓā'ir, p. 60.

4.15 Legal Dispensations under Pressing Needs

Essential Reading:

1. Dr Tahir-ul-Qadri, Muhammad ﷺ: The Peacemaker, Ch:4.

Additional Readings for Teachers and Students:

1. Qur'ān 2:173.
2. Ibid., 5:3.
3. Ibid., 16:115.
4. Ibid., 4:43.
5. Ibid., 5:6.
6. al-Bukhārī in al-Ṣaḥīḥ: Bk.: al-Jihād wa al-siyar [Jihad and Military Expeditions], Ch.: "Silk during war," 3:169 §2763.
7. Aḥmad b. anbal in al-Musnad, 5:218 §21948, 21951.
8. al-Bayhaqī in al-Sunan al-kubrā, 9:356.
9. al-Nawawī in al-Majmūʿ, 1:576 & 8:16, 204; and al-Suyūṭī in al-Ashbāh wa al-naẓā'ir, p. 83.

4.16 Summary with Some Examples

Essential Reading:

1. Dr Tahir-ul-Qadri, Muhammad ﷺ: The Peacemaker, Ch:3.

4.16.1 Obligatory Prayer

Essential Reading:

1. Dr Tahir-ul-Qadri, Muhammad ﷺ: The Peacemaker, Ch:4.

4.16.2 Obligatory Fasting

Essential Reading:

1. Dr Tahir-ul-Qadri, Muhammad ﷺ: The Peacemaker, Ch:4.

4.16.3 Obligatory Charity

Essential Reading:

1. Dr Tahir-ul-Qadri, Muhammad ﷺ: The Peacemaker, Ch:4.

4.16.4 Performance of Hajj

Essential Reading:

1. Dr Tahir-ul-Qadri, Muhammad ﷺ: The Peacemaker, Ch:4.

4.16.5 Tenets of Faith

Essential Reading:

1. Dr Tahir-ul-Qadri, Muhammad ﷺ: The Peacemaker, Ch:4.

4.16.6 Acts of Worship

Essential Reading:

1. Dr Tahir-ul-Qadri, Muhammad ﷺ: The Peacemaker, Ch:4.

4.16.7 Manner of Invitation

Essential Reading:

1. Dr Tahir-ul-Qadri, Muhammad ﷺ: The Peacemaker, Ch:4.

4.16.8 Human Interactions

Essential Reading:

1. Dr Tahir-ul-Qadri, Muhammad ﷺ: The Peacemaker, Ch:4.

4.16.9 Marriage

Essential Reading:

1. Dr Tahir-ul-Qadri, Muhammad ﷺ: The Peacemaker, Ch:4.

4.16.10 Family Relations

Essential Reading:

1. Dr Tahir-ul-Qadri, Muhammad ﷺ: The Peacemaker, Ch:4.

4.16.11 International Relations

Essential Reading:

1. Dr Tahir-ul-Qadri, Muhammad ﷺ: The Peacemaker, Ch:4.

4.16.12 Sins and Punishments

Essential Reading:

1. Dr Tahir-ul-Qadri, Muhammad ﷺ: The Peacemaker, Ch:4.

5. Establishing Peace Through Human Rights

5.1 Preliminary Statement

Essential Reading:

1. Dr Tahir-ul-Qadri, Muhammad ﷺ: The Peacemaker, Ch:5.

Additional Readings for Teachers and Students:

1. Ibid., 71:7.
2. Ibid., 89:6–13.
3. Ibid., 2:49–50.
4. Ibid., 81:8–9.
5. Ibid., 5:32.

5.2 THE RIGHT TO PROTECTION OF LIFE

ESSENTIAL READING:

1. Dr Tahir-ul-Qadri, Muhammad ﷺ: The Peacemaker, Ch:5.

5.3 THE RIGHT TO FREEDOM FROM SLAVERY

ESSENTIAL READING:

1. Dr Tahir-ul-Qadri, Muhammad ﷺ: The Peacemaker, Ch:5.

ADDITIONAL READINGS FOR TEACHERS AND STUDENTS:

1. Qur'ān 58:3.
2. Ibid., 4:92.
3. al-Dimyāṭī in Iʿāna al-ṭālibīn, 4:322–323.
4. al-Ṣanʿānī in Subul al-salām, 4:139.
5. al-Ḥākim in al-Mustadrak, 3:349 §5348.
6. Ibn ajar al-ʿAsqalānī in al-Iṣāba, 4:349.
7. al-Ḥākim in al-Mustadrak, 3:351 §5357.

5.4 THE RIGHT TO LIBERTY AND SECURITY OF PERSON

ESSENTIAL READING:

1. Dr Tahir-ul-Qadri, Muhammad ﷺ: The Peacemaker, Ch:5.

Additional Readings for Teachers and Students:

1. Abū ʿUbayd al-Qāsim b. al-Sallām in Kitāb al-Amwāl, 1:183.
2. umayd b. Zanjawayh in Kitāb al-Amwāl, p. 206.
3. al-Bayhaqī in al-Sunan al-kubrā, 8:106.
4. Ibn Hishām in al-Sīra al-Nabawiyya, 2/271.
5. al-Suhaylī in al-Rawḍ al-unuf, 2:349.
6. Ibn Sayyid al-Nās in ʿUyūn al-athar, 1:227.
7. Ibn Taymiyya in al-Ṣārim al-maslūl, p. 54.
8. Ibn al-Qayyim al-Jawziyya in Aḥkām Ahl al-Dhimma, p. 543.
9. Ibn Kathīr in al-Bidāya wa al-Nihāya, 3:236.
10. al-Ṣāliḥī in Subul al-hudā wa al-rishād, 3:382.
11. Aḥmad b. Ḥanbal in al-Musnad, 3/498 §16108.
12. al-Tirmidhī in al-Sunan: al-Fitan [Tribulations], chapter: What has come to us that your blood and your property are inviolable for you, 4:461 §2159, & Bk.: al-Tafsīr [Interpretation], Ch.: From Sūra al-Tawba, 5/273 §3087.
13. Ibn Mājah in al-Sunan: Bk.: al-Diyyāt [Blood Money], Ch.: Concerning intermediation, 2/890 §2669, & Bk.: al-Manāsik [Pilgrimage Rites], Ch.: Sermon, 2/1015 §3055.
14. Ibn Hishām in al-Sīra al-Nabawiyya, 6/10.
15. Ibn al-Sarrī in al-Zuhd, 1:281 §493.
16. al-Ṭabarī in Tārīkh al-Umam wa al-Mulūk, 2/206.
17. Ibn ʿAbd al- akam in Futūḥ Miṣr wa akhbāruhā, p. 114-115.
18. al-Hindī in Kanz al-ʿUmmāl, 12/294 §36010.

5.5 The Right to Justice

Essential Reading:

1. Dr Tahir-ul-Qadri, Muhammad ﷺ: The Peacemaker, Ch:5.

Additional Readings for Teachers and Students:

1. Qurʾān 5:8.
2. Aḥmad b. Ḥanbal in al-Musnad, 5/411 §23536.
3. al-Bayhaqī in Shuʿab al-Īmān, 4/289 §5137.

4. al-Quḍāʿī in Musnad al-Shihāb, 1/145 §195.
5. Ibn Hishām in al-Sīra al-Nabawiyya, 6/82.
6. Ibn Ḥibbān in al-Thiqāt, 2/157.
7. al-Bayhaqī in al-Sunan al-Kubrā, 6/353 §12788.
8. Ibn al-Athīr in al-Kāmil fī al-Tārīkh, 195/2.
9. al-Ṭabarī in Tārīkh al-Umam wa al-Mulūk, 2/238.
10. al-Kalaʿī in al-Iktifa, 2:446.
11. Abū Jaʿfar al-Ṭabarī in al-Riyāḍ al-Naḍra, 2/213.
12. Ibn Kathīr in al-Bidāya wa al-Nihāya, 6/301.
13. al-Muḥibb al-Ṭabarī in al-Riyāḍ al-naḍra fī manāqib al-ʿashra, 2:389.
14. Qurʾān, 2:256

5.6 The Right to Religious Freedom

Essential Reading:

1. Dr Tahir-ul-Qadri, Muhammad ﷺ: The Peacemaker, Ch:5.

Additional Readings for Teachers and Students:

1. Qurʾān 10:99.
2. bid., 109:1–6.
3. Ibid., 5:99.
4. Ibid., 6:107.
5. Ibid., 88:21–22.

5.7 The Right to Equality and Rule of Law

Essential Reading:

1. Dr Tahir-ul-Qadri, Muhammad ﷺ: The Peacemaker, Ch:5.

5.7.1 Ensuring Human Dignity and Equality

Essential Reading:

1. Dr Tahir-ul-Qadri, Muhammad ﷺ: The Peacemaker, Ch:5.

5.7.2 Sacredness of Human Life

Essential Reading:

1. Dr Tahir-ul-Qadri, Muhammad ﷺ: The Peacemaker, Ch:5.

5.8 The Right to be Heard

Essential Reading:

1. Dr Tahir-ul-Qadri, Muhammad ﷺ: The Peacemaker, Ch:5.

5.9 The Protection of the Rights of non-Muslims

Essential Reading:

1. Dr Tahir-ul-Qadri, Muhammad ﷺ: The Peacemaker, Ch:5.

5.10 The Protection of Women's Rights

Essential Reading:

1. Dr Tahir-ul-Qadri, Muhammad ﷺ: The Peacemaker, Ch:5.

5.10.1 The Prohibition of Domestic Violence and Forced Marriage

Essential Reading:

1. Dr Tahir-ul-Qadri, Muhammad ﷺ: The Peacemaker, Ch:5.

Additional Readings for Teachers and Students:

1. al-Bukhārī in al-Ṣaḥīḥ: Bk.: al-Ikrāh [The Coercion], Ch.: "A marriage of someone who is coerced is not valid", 6:2547 §6546.
2. Abū Dāwūd in al-Sunan: Bk.: al-Nikāḥ [Wedlock], Ch.: "The married woman", 2:233 §2101.
3. al-Dārimī in al-Sunan, 2:187 §2192.
4. Aḥmad b. anbal in al-Musnad, 1:273 §2469.
5. Abū Dāwūd in al-Sunan: Bk.: al-Nikāḥ [Wedlock], Ch.: "A father marries his virgin daughter without asking her consent", 2:232 §2096.
6. Ibn Mājah in al-Sunan: Bk.: al-Nikāḥ [Wedlock], Ch.: "If someone marries his daughter when she dislikes", 1:603 §1875.
7. Aḥmad b. anbal in al-Musnad, 6:136 §25087.
8. al-Nasā' in al-Sunan: Bk.: al-Nikāḥ [Wedlock], Ch.: "A father marries his virgin daughter against his willingness", 6:86 §3269.
9. Ibn Mājah in al-Sunan: Bk.: al-Nikāḥ [Wedlock], Ch.: "Is someone marries his daughter while she dislikes", 1:602 §1874.
10. al-Dāraquṭnī in al-Sunan: Bk.: al-Nikāḥ [Wedlock], 3:232 §45.
11. Ibn al-Athīr in al-Nihāya, 3:106.

12. Ibn ajar al-ʿAsqalānī in Talkhīṣ al-ḥabīr, 3:146.
13. al-Ghazālī in Iḥyā ʿulūm al-Dīn, 2:41.
14. al-Subkī in Ṭabaqāt al-Shāfiʿiyya al-kubrā, 6:310.
15. al-Daynawirī in Mujālasa wa jawāhir al-ʿulūm, pp. 249, 566 §1437, 3354.
16. al-Hindī in Kanz al-ʿummāl, 16:208 §45626.
17. Ibn ajar al-ʿAsqalānī in Talkhīṣ al-ḥabīr, 3:146.
18. Ibn ʿAbd al-Barr in al-Intiqāʾ fī faḍāʾil al-thalātha al-aʾimma al-fuqahāʾ, p. 98.
19. Abū Nuʿaym in ilya al-awliyāʾ, 9:125.
20. al-Quḍāʿī in Musnad al-Shihāb, 1:102

5.10.2 Integration of the Women into the Mainstream of Social Struggle

Essential Reading:

1. Dr Tahir-ul-Qadri, Muhammad ﷺ: The Peacemaker, Ch:5.

5.10.3 Integration of the Women into the Mainstream of Social Struggle

Essential Reading:

1. Dr Tahir-ul-Qadri, Muhammad ﷺ: The Peacemaker, Ch:5.

5.11 The Protection of the Rights of Parents

Essential Reading:

1. Dr Tahir-ul-Qadri, Muhammad ﷺ: The Peacemaker, Ch:5.

Additional Readings for Teachers and Students:

1. Muslim in al-Ṣaḥīḥ: Kitāb al-Birr wa al-ṣila wa al-adab [The Book of Piety, Filial Duty, and Manners], chapter: "The Disgrace of Someone Who Finds His Parents, Or One of Them, in Old Age, but Does Not Care for Them, for He Will Not Enter Paradise," 4:1978 §2551.
2. al-Daylamī in al-Firdaws bi-Ma'thūr al-Khiṭāb, 2:276 §3280.
3. al-Bayhaqī in Shu'ab al-Īmān, 6:195 §7884.
4. al-Tirmidhī in al-Sunan: Kitāb al-Birr wa al-ṣila [The Book Piety and Filial Duty], chapter: "What Has Come to Us Regarding the Good Pleasure of Parents," 4:310 §1899.
5. al-Ḥākim in al-Mustadrak, 4:168 §7249.
6. al-Bukhārī in al-Ṣaḥīḥ, Kitāb al-Adāb [The Book of Propriety], chapter: "A Son Must Not Go to War Unless He Has His Parent's Permission," 5:2227 §5627.
7. Muslim in al-Ṣaḥīḥ, Kitāb al-Birr wa al-Ṣila wa al-Adab [The Book of Piety, Filial Duty, and Manners], chapter: "Filial piety towards One's Parents, and the Fact That They Are Most Deserving of It," 4:1975 §2549.
8. Abū Dāwūd in al-Sunan, Kitāb al-Jihād [The Book of Jihad], chapter: "About a Man Who Goes for Battle Though His Parents Disapprove," 3:17 §2528–2529.
9. al-Nasā'ī in al-Sunan: Kitāb al-Bay'a [The Book on the Pledge of Fealty], chapter: "The Pledge for Migration," 7:143 §4163.

5.12 The Protection of the Rights of Children and Orphans

Essential Reading:

1. Dr Tahir-ul-Qadri, Muhammad ﷺ: The Peacemaker, Ch:5.

ADDITIONAL READINGS FOR TEACHERS AND STUDENTS:

1. al-Ṭabarānī in al-Muʿjam al-Kabīr, 11:354 §11997.
2. al-Bayhaqī in al-Sunan al-Kubrā, 6:177 §11780.
3. al-Ṭaḥāwī in Sharḥ Maʿānī al-Āthār, 4:86.
4. al-Haythamī in Majmaʿ al-Zawāʾid, 4:153; al-Ḥārith in al-Musnad (Zawāʾid al-Haythamī), 1:512 §454.
5. al-Bukhārī in al-Ṣaḥīḥ: Kitāb al-Hiba wa Faḍluhā [The Book of Gifts and Their Excellent Merit], chapter: "The Gift for the Child, and If Someone Gifts Something to His Children, It is Not Permissible Unless He Treats All of Them Fairly and Gives Equally," 2:913.
6. Abū Dāwūd in al-Sunan: Kitāb al-Adab [The Book of Propriety], chapter: "On Changing Names," 4:287 §4948.
7. al-Dārimī in al-Sunan, 2:380 §2694.
8. Aḥmad b. Ḥanbal in al-Musnad, 5:194 §22035.
9. al-Bayhaqī in al-Sunan al-Kubrā, 9:306, and in Shuʿab al-Īmān, 6:393 §8633.
10. Ibn al-Ja'd in al-Musnad 1:360 §2492.
11. al-Haythamī in Mawārid al-ẓamʾān, 1:479 §1944.
12. al-Tirmidhī in al-Sunan: Kitāb al-Birr wa al-ṣila [The Book of Piety and Filial Duty], chapter: "What Has Come to Us Regarding Kind Treatment of Children," 4:322 §1920.
13. Abū Dāwūd in al-Sunan: Kitāb al-Adab [The Book of Propriety], chapter: "On Kindness," 4:286 §4941.
14. Aḥmad b. Ḥanbal in al-Musnad, 2:222 §7073.
15. al-Ḥākim in al-Mustadrak, 1:131 §209.
16. al-Bukhārī in al-Adab al-Mufrad, 1:129 §353.
17. al-Bukhārī in al-Ṣaḥīḥ: Kitāb al-Ṭalāq [The Book of Divorce], chapter: "On Curses," 5:2032 §4998, and Kitāb al-Adab [The Book of Propriety], chapter: "The Excellent Merit of Someone Who Provides for an Orphan," 5:2237 §5659.
18. Muslim in al-Ṣaḥīḥ: Kitāb al-Zuhd wa al-Raqāʾiq [The Book of Renunciation and the Heart-softening Traditions], chapter: "Good Treatment of the Widow, the Pauper, and the Orphan," 4:2287 §2983.
19. al-Tirmidhī in al-Sunan, Kitāb al-Birr wa al-ṣila [The Book of Piety and Filial Duty], chapter: "What Has Come to Us Regarding Kind the Kind Treatment of an Orphan and His Guardianship," 4:321 §1918.
20. Abū Dāwūd in al-Sunan: Bk.: al-Adab [Good Manners], Ch.: "Someone Who Embraces an Orphan," 4:338 §5150.
21. Mālik in al-Muwaṭṭa', 2:948.
22. Aḥmad b. Ḥanbal in al-Musnad, 5:333 §22871.
23. Aḥmad b. Ḥanbal in al-Musnad, 3:435 §§15626–15627, and al-Bayhaqī

in al-Sunan al-kubrā, 9:77 §17868.
24. al-Bukhārī in al-Ṣaḥīḥ: Bk.: al-Ṣalāh [The Prayer], Ch.: "When He Carried a Young Girl Upon His Shoulders in Prayer," 1:193 §494.
25. Muslim in al-Ṣaḥīḥ: Bk.: al-Masājid wa mawāḍiʿ al-ṣalāh [The Mosques and Prayer-places], Ch.: "The Permissibility of Carrying Children in Prayer,"1:385 §543.
26. Abū Dāwūd in al-Sunan: Bk.: al-Ṣalāh [The Prayer], Ch.: "Movement During Prayer," 1:241 §917
27. al-Nasāʾī in al-Sunan: Bk.: al-Ṣalāh [The Prayer], Ch.: "On Carrying Children in Prayer and Sitting them Down," 3:10 §1204
28. Mālik in al-Muwaṭṭaʾ, 1:170 §410
29. Ibn Khuzayma in al-Ṣaḥīḥ, 1:383 §§783–784.
30. Ibn ibbān in al-Ṣaḥīḥ, 15:418 §6964.
31. al-Muḥibb al-Ṭabarī in Dhakhāʾir al-ʿuqbā fī manāqib dhawī al-qurbā, 1:25.
32. al-Bukhārī in al-Ṣaḥīḥ: Bk.: al-Adhān [The Adhān], Ch.: "On the One who Lightens his Prayer when Young Children Cry," 1:250 §677.
33. Muslim in al-Ṣaḥīḥ: Bk.: al-Ṣalāh [The Prayer], Ch.: "Commanding the Imams to Lighten the Prayer," 1:343 §470.
34. Aḥmad b. Ḥanbal in al-Musnad, 3:109 §12086.
35. Ibn Ḥibbān in al-Ṣaḥīḥ, 5:510 §2139.
36. Abū Yaʿlā in al-Musnad, 5:441 §3144.
37. al-Bayhaqī in al-Sunan al-Kubrā, 2:393 §3848, and in Shuʿab al-Īmān, 7:477 §11054.
38. al-Bukhārī in al-Ṣaḥīḥ: Bk.: al-Ashriba [The Drinks], Ch.: "What is disliked of the mutilation of live animals, setting up animals in a cage as a target and tying up live animals as targets," 5:2130 §5297.
39. Muslim in al-Ṣaḥīḥ: Bk.: al-Ashriba [The Drinks], Ch.: "The commendation of circulating milk or water (in an assembly) from the right-hand side," 3:1604 §2030.

5.13 Protection of the Rights of Neighbours

Essential Reading:

1. Dr Tahir-ul-Qadri, Muhammad ﷺ: The Peacemaker, Ch:5.

ADDITIONAL READINGS FOR TEACHERS AND STUDENTS:

1. al-Tirmidhī in al-Sunan: Kitāb al-Birr wa al-Ṣila [The Book of Piety and Filial Duty], chapter: "What Has Come to Us Regarding the Right of the Neighbor," 4:333 §1944.
2. Aḥmad b. Ḥanbal in al-Musnad, 2:167 §6566.
3. al-Dārimī in al-Sunan, 2:284 §2437; al-Ḥākim in al-Mustadrak, 1:610 §1620.
4. Ibn Khuzayma in al-Ṣaḥīḥ, 4:140 §2539.
5. al-Bukhārī in al-Adab al-Mufrad, 1:53 §115.
6. al-Bukhārī in al-Ṣaḥīḥ: Kitāb al-Adab, chapter: "Whosoever Believes in Allah and the Last Day Must Not Harm His Neighbor," 5:2240 §5672, and in chapter: "On Honoring the Guest and Serving Him Personally," and in Kitāb al-Riqāq [The Book of Heart-softening Traditions], chapter: "Safeguarding the Tongue," 5:2376 §6110.
7. Muslim in al-Ṣaḥīḥ: Kitāb al-Īmān [The Book of Faith] chapter: "Urging Piety for the Neighbor and the Guest, and the Necessity of Silence Except When Having something Good to Say," 1:6968 §47–48.
8. al-Tirmidhī in al-Sunan: Kitāb al-Adab wa al-Raqā'iq [The Book of Propriety and Heart-softening Traditions], chapter 50; 4:659 §2500.
9. Abū Dāwūd in al-Sunan: Kitāb al-Adab [The Book of Propriety], chapter: "The Rights Owed to One's Neighbors," 4:339 §5154; Ibn Mājah in al-Sunan: Kitāb al-Adab [The Book of Propriety], chapter: "The Rights Owed to One's Neighbors," 2:1211 §3672.
10. Ibn Ḥibbān in al-Ṣaḥīḥ, 2:273 §516; and al-Dārimī in al-Sunan: 2:134 §2036.

5.14 PROTECTION OF THE RIGHTS OF BIRDS AND ANIMALS

ESSENTIAL READING:

1. Dr Tahir-ul-Qadri, Muhammad ﷺ: The Peacemaker, Ch:5.

5.14.1 Saving a Dog's Life

Essential Reading:

1. Dr Tahir-ul-Qadri, Muhammad ﷺ: The Peacemaker, Ch:5.

Additional Readings for Teachers and Students:

1. al-Bukhārī in al-Ṣaḥīḥ: Bk.: Ahādīth al-anbiyā' [Narrations of the Prophets], chapter, "On the Narration of the Cave," 3:1279 §328.
2. Muslim in al-Ṣaḥīḥ: Bk.: al-Salām [The Salutations], chapter, "On Giving Food and Water to Honoured Animals," 4:1761 §2245.
3. Aḥmad b. Ḥanbal in al-Musnad, 2:510 §10629.
4. al-Bayhaqī in al-Sunan al-Kubrā, 8:14 §15597.
5. al-Daylamī in Musnad al-Firdaws, 2:19 §2126.

5.14.2 The Sin of Taking a Cat's Life

Essential Reading:

1. Dr Tahir-ul-Qadri, Muhammad ﷺ: The Peacemaker, Ch:5.

Additional Readings for Teachers and Students:

1. al-Bukhārī in al-Ṣaḥīḥ: Kitāb Bad'u al-khalq [The Book of the Beginning of Creation], chapter, "There are Five Injurious Animals that may be Killed in the Sacred Precint," 2:1205 §3140.
2. Muslim in al-Ṣaḥīḥ: Kitāb al-Birr wa al-ṣila wa al-ādab [The Book of Piety, Fillial Duty, and Good Manners], chapter, "The Unlawfulness of Tormenting Cats and other Non-injurious Animals," 4:2110 §2619.
3. Aḥmad b. Ḥanbal in al-Musnad, 2:269 §7635.
4. Ibn Mājah in al-Sunan: Kitāb al-Zuhd [The Book of Renunciation],

chapter, "On Repentance," 2:1421 §4256.
5. ʿAbd al-Razzāq in al-Muṣannaf, 11:284 §20549.
6. Abū Yaʿlā in al-Musnad, 1:432 §6044.
7. Ibn Rāhawayh in al-Musnad, 1:147 §83.
8. al-Daylamī in Musnad al-Firdaws, 2:217 §3058.

6. ESTABLISHING PEACE THROUGH CONFLICT RESOLUTION

ESSENTIAL READING:

1. Dr Tahir-ul-Qadri, Muhammad ﷺ: The Peacemaker, Ch:6.

6.1 PEACEMAKING THROUGH BUILDING RELATIONSHIPS AND RESOLVING CONFLICTS

ESSENTIAL READING:

1. Dr Tahir-ul-Qadri, Muhammad ﷺ: The Peacemaker, Ch:6.

6.2 COLLABORATIVE ACTIONS AND SOLIDARITY

ESSENTIAL READING:

1. Dr Tahir-ul-Qadri, Muhammad ﷺ: The Peacemaker, Ch:6.

6.3 Islamic Community (Ummah)

Essential Reading:

1. Dr Tahir-ul-Qadri, Muhammad ﷺ: The Peacemaker, Ch:6.

6.4 Inclusivity and Participatory Process

Essential Reading:

1. Dr Tahir-ul-Qadri, Muhammad ﷺ: The Peacemaker, Ch:6.

6.5 Right to people's participation in collective activities

Essential Reading:

1. Dr Tahir-ul-Qadri, Muhammad ﷺ: The Peacemaker, Ch:6.

7. Establishing Peace Through Charity, Altruism and Benevolence

7.1 Preliminary Statement

Essential Reading:

1. Dr Tahir-ul-Qadri, Muhammad ﷺ: The Peacemaker, Ch:7.

7.2 The Qur'ānic Approach to Charity and Righteousness

Essential Reading:

1. Dr Tahir-ul-Qadri, Muhammad ﷺ: The Peacemaker, Ch:7.

Additional Readings for Teachers and Students:

1. Qur'ān, 2:215.
2. Ibid., 51:19.
3. Ibid., 2:267.

7.3 The Concepts of Ownership, Trust and Charity

Essential Reading:

1. Dr Tahir-ul-Qadri, Muhammad ﷺ: The Peacemaker, Ch:7.

Additional Readings for Teachers and Students:

1. Qur'ān, 63:10.
2. Ibid., 2:267.
3. Ibid., 2:219.
4. al-Tirmidhī in al-Sunan: Kitāb al-Manāqib [The Book of Virtues], chapter: "The Virtues of Abū Bakr and ʿUmar ﷺ," 6:52 §3675.
5. Abū Dāwūd in al-Sunan: Kitāb al-Zakāt [The Book of Zakat], chapter: "License Therein," 2:129 §1678.
6. al-Dārimī in al-Sunan, 1:480 §1660.
7. al-Bazzār in al-Musnad, 1:263 §159.
8. al-Maqdisī in al-Aḥādīth al-Mukhtāra, 1:173 §81.
9. ʿAbd b. Ḥumayd in al-Musnad, 1:33 §14.

10. Ibn Abī ᶜĀṣim in Kitāb al-Sunna, 2:579 §1240.
11. Narrated by al-Bukhārī in al-Ṣaḥīḥ: Kitāb al-Nafaqāt [The Book of Expenditures], chapter: "The Obligation of Supprting One's family and Dependants," 5:2048 §5041.
12. Aḥmad b. Ḥanbal in al-Musnad, 2:278 §7727.
13. Abū Dāwūd in al-Sunan: Kitāb al-Zakāt [The Book of Zakat], chapter: "The Man Spends Out of His Wealth, 2:128 §1673.
14. Muslim in al-Ṣaḥīḥ: Kitāb al-Zakāt [The Book of Zakat], chapter: "Explanation of the Fact that the Upper Hand is Better than the Lower Hand," 2:718 §1036.
15. al-Tirmidhī in al-Sunan: Kitāb al-Zuhd [The Book of Renunciation], chapter: "From It," 4:573 §2343.
16. al-Ṭabarānī in al-Muᶜjam al-Kabīr, 8:139 §7625.

7.4 The Benevolent Character of Allah's Beloved Servants

Essential Reading:

1. Dr Tahir-ul-Qadri, Muhammad ﷺ: The Peacemaker, Ch:7.

7.5 Whether Affluent or Poor, They Give to Charity

Essential Reading:

1. Dr Tahir-ul-Qadri, Muhammad ﷺ: The Peacemaker, Ch:7.

7.6 Act of Altruism and Charity Purifies the Self and Brings Peace

Essential Reading:

1. Dr Tahir-ul-Qadri, Muhammad ﷺ: The Peacemaker, Ch:7.

Additional Readings for Teachers and Students:

1. Qur'ān, 64:16.
2. Ibid., 3:180.

7.7 Charity and Benevolence Affirm the Faith

Essential Reading:

1. Dr Tahir-ul-Qadri, Muhammad ﷺ: The Peacemaker, Ch:7.

Additional Readings for Teachers and Students:

1. Qur'ān, 107:1–3.

7.8 Miserliness is Declared as a Form of Hypocrisy

Essential Reading:

1. Dr Tahir-ul-Qadri, Muhammad ﷺ: The Peacemaker, Ch:7.

7.9 The Altruistic Character of the Companions of the Prophet Muhammad

Essential Reading:

1. Dr Tahir-ul-Qadri, Muhammad ﷺ: The Peacemaker, Ch:7.

Additional Readings for Teachers and Students:

1. Qur'ān, 107:1–3.

7.9 The Altruistic Character of the Companions of the Prophet Muhammad

Essential Reading:

1. Dr Tahir-ul-Qadri, Muhammad ﷺ: The Peacemaker, Ch:7.

Additional Readings for Teachers and Students:

1. Qur'ān 76:7–9.
2. Ibid., 9:100.
3. Ibid., 59:8.
4. al-Bukhārī in al-Ṣaḥīḥ, 2:880 §2354.
5. Muslim in al-Ṣaḥīḥ, 4:1944 §2500.
6. al-Nasā'ī in al-Sunan al-Kubrā, 5:247 §8798.
7. Abū Ya'lā in al-Musnad, 13:293 §7309.
8. al-Bayhaqī in al-Sunan al-Kubrā, 10:132 §20223.
9. Muslim in al-Ṣaḥīḥ, 3:1354 §1728.
10. Aḥmad b. anbal in al-Musnad, 3:34 §11311.
11. Abū Dāwūd in al-Sunan, 2:125 §1663.
12. Ibn ibbān in al-Ṣaḥīḥ, 12:238 §5419.
13. Abū Ya'lā in al-Musnad, 2:326 §1064.
14. al-Bayhaqī in al-Sunan al-Kubrā, 4:182 §7571.
15. al-Bukhārī in al-Ṣaḥīḥ, 1:216 §577; 3:1312 §3388; 5:2274 §5789; 5:2274 §5790.
16. Muslim in al-Ṣaḥīḥ, 3:1627 §2057.
17. Aḥmad b. anbal in al-Musnad, 1:197 §1702, 1712.
18. al-Bazzār in al-Musnad, 6:228 §2263.
19. Abū 'Awāna in al-Musnad, 5:204 §8398.
20. Muslim in al-Ṣaḥīḥ, 3:1630 §2059.
21. Aḥmad b. anbal in al-Musnad, 3:301, 382 §14260, 15144.
22. al-Tirmidhī in al-Sunan, 4:267 §1820.
23. Ibn Mājah in al-Sunan, 2:1084 §3254.

24. al-Bukhārī in al-Ṣaḥīḥ, 5:2061 §5077.
25. Muslim in al-Ṣaḥīḥ, 3:1630 §2058.
26. Aḥmad b. anbal in al-Musnad, 2:407 §9266.
27. al-Tirmidhī in al-Sunan, 4:267 §1820.
28. Muslim in al-Ṣaḥīḥ, 3:1354 §1728.
29. Aḥmad b. anbal in al-Musnad, 3:34 §11311.
30. Abū Dāwūd in al-Sunan, 2:125 §1663.
31. Ibn ibbān in al-Ṣaḥīḥ, 12:238 §5419.
32. Abū Yaʿlā in al-Musnad, 2:326 §1064.
33. al-Bayhaqī in al-Sunan al-Kubrā, 4:182 §7571.

7.10 The Prophet ﷺ Established the Society of Benevolence

Essential Reading:

1. Dr Tahir-ul-Qadri, Muhammad ﷺ: The Peacemaker, Ch:7.

7.11 A Comparison of Justice and Benevolence

Essential Reading:

1. Dr Tahir-ul-Qadri, Muhammad ﷺ: The Peacemaker, Ch:7.

Additional Readings for Teachers and Students:

1. al-Tirmidhī in al-Sunan, Bk.: The virtues according to Allah's Messenger ﷺ, Ch.: The virtues of Abū Bakr and ʿUmar ؓ, 6/52 §3675.
2. Abū Dāwūd in al-Sunan: Bk.: The alms-due, Ch.: Licence therein, 2/129 §1678.
3. al-Dārimī in al-Sunan, 1/480 §1660.
4. al-Bazzār in al-Musnad, 1/263 §159.
5. al-Maqdisī in al-Aḥādīth al-Mukhtāra, 1/173 §81.
6. ʿAbd b. Ḥumayd in al-Musnad, 1/33 §14.

7. Ibn Abū ʿĀṣim in Kitāb al-Sunna, 2/579 §1240.

8. Establishing Peace through Fraternization and Integration

Fraternization

Essential Reading:

1. Dr Tahir-ul-Qadri, Muhammad ﷺ: The Peacemaker, Ch:8.

8.1 The Tribal Set-up of Medina

Essential Reading:

1. Dr Tahir-ul-Qadri, Muhammad ﷺ: The Peacemaker, Ch:8.

8.2 Integration of Meccan Immigrants in Medinan Society through Fraternization

Essential Reading:

1. Dr Tahir-ul-Qadri, Muhammad ﷺ: The Peacemaker, Ch:8.

8.3 Creating a Nation through the Constitution of Medina

Essential Reading:

1. Dr Tahir-ul-Qadri, Muhammad ﷺ: The Peacemaker, Ch:8.

Integration

8.4 The Prophet ﷺ Integrated the Jews and the Muslims into One Community

Essential Reading:

1. Dr Tahir-ul-Qadri, Muhammad ﷺ: The Peacemaker, Ch:8.

8.5 The Prophetic Pronouncement: "The Jews Together with the Muslims are One Nation"

Essential Reading:

1. Dr Tahir-ul-Qadri, Muhammad ﷺ: The Peacemaker, Ch:8.

Essential Reading:

1. Dr Tahir-ul-Qadri, Muhammad ﷺ: The Peacemaker, Ch:8.

8.6 The Implications of the Prophetic Statement "The Jews of Banū ʿAwf together with the Muslims are one Nation"

Essential Reading:

1. Dr Tahir-ul-Qadri, Muhammad ﷺ: The Peacemaker, Ch:8.

8.6.1 Interpretation by Ibn al-Athīr al-Jazarī

Essential Reading:

1. Dr Tahir-ul-Qadri, Muhammad ﷺ: The Peacemaker, Ch:8.

8.6.2 Interpretation by al-Zamakhsharī

Essential Reading:

1. Dr Tahir-ul-Qadri, Muhammad ﷺ: The Peacemaker, Ch:8.

8.6.3 Interpretation by Ibn Abī ʿUbayd al-Harawī

Essential Reading:

1. Dr Tahir-ul-Qadri, Muhammad ﷺ: The Peacemaker, Ch:8.

8.7 Five other Jewish Tribes were also Included in One Community along with Muslims

Essential Reading:

1. Dr Tahir-ul-Qadri, Muhammad ﷺ: The Peacemaker, Ch:8.

9. Establishing Peace through Education

Essential Reading:

1. Dr Tahir-ul-Qadri, Muhammad ﷺ: The Peacemaker, Ch:9.

9.1 Pre-Hijra Emphasis on Literacy, Knowledge and Education

Essential Reading:

1. Dr Tahir-ul-Qadri, Muhammad ﷺ: The Peacemaker, Ch:9.

Essential Reading:

1. Dr Tahir-ul-Qadri, Muhammad ﷺ: The Peacemaker, Ch:9.

9.2 Formulation and Enforcement of Education System

Essential Reading:

1. Dr Tahir-ul-Qadri, Muhammad ﷺ: The Peacemaker, Ch:9.

9.2.1 The Prophet A Himself would Manage Time to Educate the Illiterate Community

Essential Reading:

1. Dr Tahir-ul-Qadri, Muhammad ﷺ: The Peacemaker, Ch:9.

9.2.1.1 POWs Appointed as Teachers

Essential Reading:

1. Dr Tahir-ul-Qadri, Muhammad ﷺ: The Peacemaker, Ch:9.

9.2.1.2 Establishment of Boarding School—al-Ṣuffa—and Appointment of Teachers for Different Faculties of Knowledge

Essential Reading:

1. Dr Tahir-ul-Qadri, Muhammad ﷺ: The Peacemaker, Ch:9.

9.2.1.3 Trained Teachers Dispatched as Trainers of Different Tribes

Essential Reading:

1. Dr Tahir-ul-Qadri, Muhammad ﷺ: The Peacemaker, Ch:9.

9.2.1.4 The Prophetic Policy of Moving People Closer to Medina for Education

Essential Reading:

1. Dr Tahir-ul-Qadri, Muhammad ﷺ: The Peacemaker, Ch:9.

9.2.1.5 70 Teachers Sent to Najd to train Neighbouring Tribes

Essential Reading:

1. Dr Tahir-ul-Qadri, Muhammad ﷺ: The Peacemaker, Ch:9.

9.2.1.6 Healthy Influx of Students

Essential Reading:

1. Dr Tahir-ul-Qadri, Muhammad ﷺ: The Peacemaker, Ch:9.

9.2.1.7 Nine Mosque Schools in Medina

Essential Reading:

1. Dr Tahir-ul-Qadri, Muhammad ﷺ: The Peacemaker, Ch:9.

9.2.1.8 The Study Circles and Worship Circles

Essential Reading:

1. Dr Tahir-ul-Qadri, Muhammad ﷺ: The Peacemaker, Ch:9.

9.2.1.9 The Prophet's Supervision and Control

Essential Reading:

1. Dr Tahir-ul-Qadri, Muhammad ﷺ: The Peacemaker, Ch:9.

9.2.1.10 Sudden Increase in the Literacy Rate

Essential Reading:

1. Dr Tahir-ul-Qadri, Muhammad ﷺ: The Peacemaker, Ch:9.

9.2.2.1 The Qur'ānic Commandment for Written Record of Trade Transactions

Essential Reading:

1. Dr Tahir-ul-Qadri, Muhammad ﷺ: The Peacemaker, Ch:9.

9.2.2.2 Expansion of the Scope of Written Work

Essential Reading:

1. Dr Tahir-ul-Qadri, Muhammad ﷺ: The Peacemaker, Ch:9.

9.2.2.3 Prophetic Letters and Traditions

Essential Reading:

1. Dr Tahir-ul-Qadri, Muhammad ﷺ: The Peacemaker, Ch:9.

9.2.2.4 Introduction of Seals and Stamps

Essential Reading:

1. Dr Tahir-ul-Qadri, Muhammad ﷺ: The Peacemaker, Ch:9.

9.2.2.5 Commencement of Specialization and Research Work

Essential Reading:

1. Dr Tahir-ul-Qadri, Muhammad ﷺ: The Peacemaker, Ch:9.

9.2.2.6 Teachers Disallowed to Accept Gifts from Pupils

Essential Reading:

1. Dr Tahir-ul-Qadri, Muhammad ﷺ: The Peacemaker, Ch:9.

9.2.2.7 Promotion of Foreign Languages and Their Experts

Essential Reading:

1. Dr Tahir-ul-Qadri, Muhammad ﷺ: The Peacemaker, Ch:9.

9.2.2.8 The Curricula and Syllabi Development

Essential Reading:

1. Dr Tahir-ul-Qadri, Muhammad ﷺ: The Peacemaker, Ch:9.

9.2.2.9 Emphasis on Women Education

Essential Reading:

1. Dr Tahir-ul-Qadri, Muhammad ﷺ: The Peacemaker, Ch:9.

10. Establishing Intercommunal Peace through Tolerant and Compassionate Behaviour

10.1 Preliminary Statement

Essential Reading:

1. Dr Tahir-ul-Qadri, Muhammad ﷺ: The Peacemaker, Ch:10.

10.2 Freedom of Faith and Beliefs for Non-Muslims

Essential Reading:

1. Dr Tahir-ul-Qadri, Muhammad ﷺ: The Peacemaker, Ch:10.

Additional Readings for Teachers and Students:

1. Qur'ān 2:256.
2. Ibid., 88:21–22.
3. Ibid., 10:99.
4. Ibid., 18:29.
5. Ibid., 109:6.
6. Ibid., 6:108.
7. Ibid., 3:64.
8. Ibid., 6:164.
9. Abū Dāwūd in al-Sunan: Kitāb al-kharāj wa al-imāra wa al-fay' [The Book on the Land Tax, Leadership and Spoils Acquired without Fighting], chapter: "Taking One Tenth from Non- Muslim Citizens When They Do Business," 3:170 §3052.
10. al-Bayhaqī in al-Sunan al-kubrā, 9:205 §18511.
11. al-Mundhirī in al-Targhīb wa al-tarhīb, 4:7 §4558.

13. al-ʿAjlūnī in Kashf al-khafāʾ, 2:342.
14. al-Bayhaqī in Dalāʾil al-Nubuwwa, 5:382.
15. Ibn Saʿd in al-Ṭabaqāt al-kubrā, 1:357.
16. Ibn Hishām in al-Sīra al-Nabawiyya, 2:239–240.
17. Ibn Kathīr in al-Sīra, 4:108.
18. Ibn Qayyim in Zād al-maʿād, 3:629.
19. al-Bayhaqī in Dalāʾil al-Nubuwwa, 5:359, 389.
20. Ibn Saʿd in al-Ṭabaqāt al-kubrā, 1:288, 358.
21. Abū Yūsuf in Kitāb al-kharāj, p. 78.
22. Abū ʿUbayd al-Qāsim b. Sallām in Kitāb al-amwāl, pp. 244–245 §503.
23. Ibn Zanjawayh in Kitāb al-amwāl, pp. 449–450 §732.
24. al-Bayhaqī in al-Sunan al-kubrā, 9:85 §17904.
25. al-Ṭaḥāwī in Sharḥ Mushkil al-āthār, 3:144.
26. Ibn ʿAsākir in Tārīkh Madina Dimashq, 2:75.
27. al-Hindī in Kanz al-ʿummāl, 4:203 §11408.
28. Ibn Abī Shayba in al-Muṣannaf, 6:467 §32982.
29. al-Bayhaqī in al-Sunan al-kubrā, 9:202 §18496.
30. Ibn Zanjawayh in Kitāb al-amwāl, p. 328.
31. Ibn Qudāma in al-Mughnī, 9:283.
32. al-Maqdisī in al-Furūʿ, 6:250.
33. Ibn al-Qayyim in Aḥkām ahl al-dhimma, 3:1181, 1195, 1235.
34. Ibn Ḍawyān in Manār al-sabīl, 1:283.
35. al-Balādhurī, Futūḥ al-buldān, p. 132.
36. Ibn Kathīr, Tafsīr al-Qurʾān al-ʿAẓīm, 1:310.
37. Ibn Kathīr, Tafsīr al-Qurʾān al-ʿAẓīm, 1:310.
38. Qurʾān 22:40.
39. Abū Bakr al-Jaṣṣāṣ, Aḥkām al-Qurʾān, 5:83.
40. Ibn al-Qayyim, Aḥkām ahl al-dhimma, 3:1169.
41. Ibn al-Qayyim, Aḥkām ahl al-dhimma, 3:1169.
42. Abū Bakr al-Jaṣṣāṣ, Aḥkām al-Qurʾān, 5:83.

10.3 Absolute Justice for Non-Muslims

Essential Reading:

1. Dr Tahir-ul-Qadri, Muhammad ﷺ: The Peacemaker, Ch:10.

Additional Readings for Teachers and Students:

1. Qurʾān 2:194.
2. Ibid., 5:8.
3. Ibid., 60:8.
4. Ibid., 6:164.
5. Ibid., 57:25.
6. al-Shāfiʿī in al-Musnad, p. 343 and in al-Umm, 7:320.
7. Abū Nuʿaym in Musnad Abī Ḥanīfa, p. 104.
8. al-Bayhaqī in al-Sunan al-kubrā, 8:30 §15696.
9. al-Shaybānī in al-Mabsūṭ, 4:488 and in al- ujja, 4:342-344.
10. al-Qurashī in al-Kharāj, p. 82 §238.
11. al-Bayhaqī in al-Sunan al-kubrā, 8:30 §15697 and in Maʿrifa al-sunan wa al-āthār, 6:149 §4814.
12. al-Daraquṭunī in al-Sunan, 3:135 §167.
13. al-Shāfiʿī in al-Musnad, 1:443.
14. Abū Dāwūd in al-Sunan: Kitāb al-diyāt [The Book of Blood Money], chapter: "The Leader Should Urge Forgiveness in the Matter of Shedding Blood," 4:169 §4496.
15. ʿAbd al-Razzāq in al-Muṣannaf, 10:86 §18454.
16. al-Shāfiʿī in al-Umm, 7:320. •al-Shaybānī in Kitāb al-ḥujja ʿalā ahl al-Madīna, 4:347.
17. Ibn Abī Shayba in al-Muṣannaf, 5:406 §27444.
18. ʿAbd al-Razzāq in al-Muṣannaf, 10:97 §18494.
19. al-Tirmidhī in al-Sunan: Kitāb al-diyāt [The Book of Blood Money], chapter: "What Has Come To Us Concerning The Blood Money Of Non-Muslims," 4:25 §1413.
20. ʿAbd al-Razzāq in al-Muṣannaf, 10:95 §18491.
21. al-Shāfiʿī in al-Umm, 7:321.
22. al-Shaybānī in al-Ḥujja, 4:351.
23. al-Bukhārī in al-Ṣaḥīḥ: Kitāb al-ʿilm [The Book of Knowledge [illegible] r: "On Writing Down Knowledge," 1:53 §111.
24. al-Shāfiʿī in al-Umm, 7:321.
25. al-Bayhaqī in al-Sunan al-kubrā, 8:32 §15706.
26. al-Shaybānī in al- ujja, 4:335.
27. al-Zaylaʿī in Naṣb al-rāya, 4:337.
28. Ibn ʿAbd al- akam in Futūḥ Miṣr wa akhbaru-hā, p. 114–115.
29. al-Hindī in Kanz al-ʿummāl, 12:294 §36010.

10.4 Treating Non-Muslims with Piety and Excellence

Essential Reading:

1. Dr Tahir-ul-Qadri, Muhammad ﷺ: The Peacemaker, Ch:10.

10.5 Non-Revengeful, Forbearing and Tolerant Behaviour towards Non-Muslims

Essential Reading:

1. Dr Tahir-ul-Qadri, Muhammad ﷺ: The Peacemaker, Ch:10.

10.6 The Fulfilment of Agreements and Covenants with Non-Muslims

Essential Reading:

1. Dr Tahir-ul-Qadri, Muhammad ﷺ: The Peacemaker, Ch:10.

10.7 Financial Support for the Elderly, Infirm and Feeble amongst the Non-Muslims

Essential Reading:

1. Dr Tahir-ul-Qadri, Muhammad ﷺ: The Peacemaker, Ch:10.

11. Prophetic Reconciliatory Efforts and Peace Treaties with Different Nations, Tribes and Communities

Essential Reading:

1. Dr Tahir-ul-Qadri, Muhammad ﷺ: The Peacemaker, Ch:11.

11.1 Peace Treaty with the People of Ḍamra (Safar 2 AH)

Essential Reading:

1. Dr Tahir-ul-Qadri, Muhammad ﷺ: The Peacemaker, Ch:11.

11.2 Peace Treaty with the People of Zurʿa and Rabʿa

Essential Reading:

1. Dr Tahir-ul-Qadri, Muhammad ﷺ: The Peacemaker, Ch:11.

11.3 Peace Treaty of Hudaybia (6 AH)

Essential Reading:

1. Dr Tahir-ul-Qadri, Muhammad ﷺ: The Peacemaker, Ch:11.

11.3.1 The Terms of the Hudaybia Treaty

Essential Reading:

1. Dr Tahir-ul-Qadri, Muhammad ﷺ: The Peacemaker, Ch:11.

11.3.2 Allah Declared the Treaty of Hudaybia 'A Clear Victory'

Essential Reading:

1. Dr Tahir-ul-Qadri, Muhammad ﷺ: The Peacemaker, Ch:11.

11.4 Peace Treaty of St. Catherine (Sinai, Egypt)

Essential Reading:

1. Dr Tahir-ul-Qadri, Muhammad ﷺ: The Peacemaker, Ch:11.

11.5 Peace Treaty with the Jews of Khaybar (7 AH)

Essential Reading:

1. Dr Tahir-ul-Qadri, Muhammad ﷺ: The Peacemaker, Ch:11.

11.6 Peace Treaty with the People of Ṭāʾif and Thaqīf (8—9 ah)

Essential Reading:

1. Dr Tahir-ul-Qadri, Muhammad ﷺ: The Peacemaker, Ch:11.

11.7 Peace Treaty with the Christians of Najran (8 ah)

Essential Reading:

1. Dr Tahir-ul-Qadri, Muhammad ﷺ: The Peacemaker, Ch:11.

11.8 The Prophet's Letter to the Christians of Najran (8 ah)

Essential Reading:

1. Dr Tahir-ul-Qadri, Muhammad ﷺ: The Peacemaker, Ch:11.

11.9 Peace Treaty with the Jews of Tayma (9 ah)

Essential Reading:

1. Dr Tahir-ul-Qadri, Muhammad ﷺ: The Peacemaker, Ch:11.

11.10 Peace Treaties with the Peoples of Banu Janba, Hayna, Maqnaᶜ, Ayla, Jarbā and Adhruh (9 AH)

Essential Reading:

1. Dr Tahir-ul-Qadri, Muhammad ﷺ: The Peacemaker, Ch:11.

11.11 Peace Treaty with the Jews of South and East of Arabia (9 AH)

Essential Reading:

1. Dr Tahir-ul-Qadri, Muhammad ﷺ: The Peacemaker, Ch:11.

11.12 The Prophet's Letters to the Different Tribes Granting them Peace and Security

Essential Reading:

1. Dr Tahir-ul-Qadri, Muhammad ﷺ: The Peacemaker, Ch:11.

11.12.1 Letter to Banū al-Khashkhāsh

Essential Reading:

1. Dr Tahir-ul-Qadri, Muhammad ﷺ: The Peacemaker, Ch:11.

11.12.2 Letter to the People of Jabl Ti āma

Essential Reading:

1. Dr Tahir-ul-Qadri, Muhammad ﷺ: The Peacemaker, Ch:11.

11.12.3 Letter to Different Tribes of the Jews

Essential Reading:

1. Dr Tahir-ul-Qadri, Muhammad ﷺ: The Peacemaker, Ch:11.

11.13 Peace Treaty with the People of Ghifār (2 AH)

12. *Al-Qitāl* (Defensive Warfare) and Qur᾿ānic Peacemaking Mechanism

Essential Reading:

1. Dr Tahir-ul-Qadri, Muhammad ﷺ: The Peacemaker, Ch:12.

12.1 Peacemaking Struggle in Meccan Period

Essential Reading:

1. Dr Tahir-ul-Qadri, Muhammad ﷺ: The Peacemaker, Ch:12.

12.2 Permission of Defensive War for Maintaining Peace during the Medinan Period

Essential Reading:

1. Dr Tahir-ul-Qadri, Muhammad ﷺ: The Peacemaker, Ch:12.

12.3 The Prophet A Preferred Diplomacy over War for the Sake of Peace

Essential Reading:

1. Dr Tahir-ul-Qadri, Muhammad ﷺ: The Peacemaker, Ch:12.

12.4 Historical Background of the Permission for Defensive War

Essential Reading:

1. Dr Tahir-ul-Qadri, Muhammad ﷺ: The Peacemaker, Ch:12.

12.5 The Prophet A Imposed further Conditions and Limits on a Lawful War in Repulsion of Aggression and Prevention of Tyranny

Essential Reading:

1. Dr Tahir-ul-Qadri, Muhammad ﷺ: The Peacemaker, Ch:12.

Recommended Books for Further Study and Teaching

The complete references for all the subjects have been detailed above. Given below are the books and English lectures by Shaykh-ul-Islam Dr. Muhammad Tahir-ul-Qadri that provide complete material on all the subjects that have been covered:

1. Fatwa: Dehshat Gardī aur Fitna-e Khawārij (comprehensive historic fatwa)
2. Islām mein Insānī Ḥuqūq
3. Islāmi Riyāsat mein Ghayr Muslim ke Jān o Māl kā Taḥaffuẓ
4. Islām mein Aqaliyaton ke Ḥuqūq
5. Islām mein ʿUmar Rasīda aur Maʿzur Afrād ke Ḥuqūq
6. Islām aur Ahl-e Kitāb (Taʿlīmāt-e Qurʾān o Sunnat aur Taṣrīḥāt-e Aʾimma)
7. Khūn-e Muslim kī Ḥurmat
8. Lā Ikrāha fī al-Dīn kā Qurʾānī Falsafa
9. Jihād aur Bilād-i ʿĀlam
10. al-Jihād al-Akbar
11. Islām mein Muḥabbat aur ʿAdm-e Tashaddud
12. Muqadimma Sīrāt al-Rasūl (Ḥiṣṣa Avval)
13. Muqadimma Sīrāt al-Rasūl (Ḥiṣṣa Duvvum)
14. Muqadimma Sīrāt al-Rasūl (Ḥiṣṣa Haftam: Falsafa Jang o Amn)
15. Iqtiṣādiyāt-e Islām
16. Islām aur Kafālat-e ʿĀmma
17. al-Bayān fī Raḥma al-Mannān (Raḥmat-i Ilāhī par Īmān Afroz Aḥādīth kā Majmūʿa)
18. al-Wafā fī Raḥma al-Nabī al-Muṣṭafā (Jāmiʿ Khalq par Ḥazūr Nabī Akram ki Raḥmat aur Shafqat)
19. Silsila Arbaʿīnāt: al-ʿAṭāʾ al-ʿAmīm fī Raḥma al-Nabī al-ʿAẓīm ﷺ (Raḥmat-e Muṣṭafā)
20. al-Aḥkām al-Sharʿī fī Kawn al-Islām Dīn Li Khidma al-Insāniyya [Islām aur Khidmat-e Insāniyyat]
21. Maʿārij al-Sunan li al-Najāt min al-Ḍalāl wa al-Fitan, Bāb: Ḥuqūq ʿĀmma al-Muslimīn wa al-ʿAlaqa baynahum.
22. Maʿārij al-Sunan li al-Najāt min al-Ḍalāl wa al-Fitan, Bāb: Ḥuqūq Ghayr al-Muslimīn wa al-ʿAlaqa maʿahum.

23. Maʿārij al-Sunan li al-Najāt min al-Ḍalāl wa al-Fitan, Bāb: Ḥuqūq al-Ḍuʿafā wa al-Masākīn
24. Maʿārij al-Sunan li al-Najāt min al-Ḍalāl wa al-Fitan, Bāb: Faḍl Ādāb al-Ḥasana
25. Maʿārij al-Sunan li al-Najāt min al-Ḍalāl wa al-Fitan, Bāb: Faḍl at-Taʿāwun ʿalā al-Birr wa al-Ṣalāḥ
26. Maʿārij al-Sunan li al-Najāt min al-Ḍalāl wa al-Fitan, Bāb: Kathra Ṭuruq al-Khayr.
27. Maʿārij al-Sunan li al-Najāt min al-Ḍalāl wa al-Fitan, al-Juzʾ: al-Akhlāq al-Ḥasana wa Faḍluhā
28. Maʿārij al-Sunan li al-Najāt min al-Ḍalāl wa al-Fitan, al-Juzʾ: Ḥuqūq wa Wājibāt al-Wulāt wa al-Muwātinīn
29. al-Lubāb fī al-Ḥuqūq wa al-Ādāb (Insānī Ḥuqūq o Adab – Aḥādīth-e Nabawī ki Raushnī Mai
30. Minhāj al-Salāma fī al-Daʿwā ilā al-Iqāma
31. Tuḥfa an-Nuqabāʾ fī Faḍīla al-ʿIlm wa al-ʿUlamāʾ (Faraugh-e ʿIlm o Shaʿūr kī Ahmiyyat o Fazīlat)
32. Silsila Arbaʿīnāt: Nūr al-Mishkā fī Faḍl al-Zakāh (Fazāʾil-e Zakāh)
33. Silsila Arbaʿīnāt: al-Thamarāt fī Faḍāʾil al-Ṣadaqāt (Fazāʾil-e Ṣadaqāt o Khayrāt)
34. Silsila Arbaʿīnāt: al-Idrāk fī Faḍl al-Infāq wa Dham al-Imsāk (Allāh kī Rāh mein Kharch Karnay kī Fazīlat)
35. Silsila Arbaʿīnāt: al-Raḥamāt fī Iṣāl al-Thawāb ilā al-Amwāt (Iṣāl-e Thawāb)
36. Silsila Arbaʿīnāt: Jalāʾ al-Ṣudūr fī Ziyāra al-Qubūr (Fazīlat-e Ziyārat-e Qubūr)
37. al-Intibāh li al-Khawārij wa al-Harūraʾ
38. Taḥrīk-e Minhāj al-Qurʾān kā Taṣavvur-e Dīn
39. Firqa Parastī kā Khātima Kyūnkar Mumkin hai
40. ʿAsr-e Ḥāzir aur Ijmāʿ-e Ummat
41. Mīthāq-e Madīna kā Aʾīnī Tajziya
42. New World Order aur ʿĀlam-e Islām
43. Fitna-e Khawārij (Tārīkhī, Nafsiyātī, ʿIlmī aur Sharʿī Jāʾiza)
44. Ḥuqūq-e Vālidayn
45. Islām kā Tasavvur-e ʿIlm
46. ʿIlm-Taujīhī Yā Takhlīqī
47. Mazhabī aur Ghayr Mazhabī ʿUlūm ke Iṣlāḥ Ṭalab Pehlū

48. Baydārī-e Shuʿūr: Zarūrat o Ahmiyyat
49. Silsila Taʿlīmāt-i Islām 2: Islām
50. Silsila Taʿlīmāt-i Islām 3: Īmān
51. Silsila Taʿlīmāt-i Islām 4: Iḥsān
52. Silsila Taʿlīmāt-i Islām 8: Zakāt aur Ṣadaqāt

Taṣawwuf kā Paighām-e Amn

53. Ḥusn-e Aʿmāl
54. Ḥusn-e Aḥvāl
55. Ḥusn-e Akhlāq
56. Salūk o Taṣawwuf kā ʿAmlī Dastūr
57. Iṭāʿat-e Ilāhī
58. Zikr-e Ilāhī
59. Maḥabbat-e Ilāhī
60. Khashiyat-e Ilāhī aur Uss ke Taqāẓe
61. Tazkare aur Ṣuḥbatain
62. Akhlāq al-Anbiyāʾ
63. Ṣafā-yi Qalb o Bāṭin
64. Fasād-e Qalb aur Uss kā ʿIlāj
65. Zindagī Nekī aur Badī kī Jang hai
66. Har Shakhṣ Apne Nashah-yi ʿAmal mein Gariftār hai
67. Hamāra Aṣlī Vaṭan
68. Jurm, Tauba aur Iṣlāḥ-e Aḥvāl
69. Ṭabaqāt al-ʿIbād (Allah Taʿālā ke Maḥbūb Bandon kā Bayān)
70. Fiṭrat kā Qurʾānī Taṣavvur
71. Tarbiyat kā Qurʾānī Minhāj

English Books:

72. Fatwa on Terrorism and Suicide Bombings
73. Islam on Mercy & Compassion
74. Muhammad ﷺ: The Merciful
75. Muhammad ﷺ: The Peacemaker
76. Islamic Means of Peace
77. Islam on Serving Humanity

78. Islam on Love & Non-Violence
79. The Constitution of Medina (63 Constitutional Articles with English and Urdu Translations along with References)
80. The Supreme Jihad
81. Relations of Muslims and Non-Muslims
82. Peace, Integration and Human Rights
83. Righteous Character & Social Interactions (*al-Minhāj al-Sawī* [Part II])
84. Divine Pleasure (The Ultimate Ideal)
85. Qur'ānic Philosophy of Benevolence (*Iḥsān*)
86. Islamic Spirituality & Modern Science (The Scientific Bases of Sufism)
87. Teachings of Islam Series: Peace and Submission
88. Teachings of Islam Series: Faith
89. Teachings of Islam Series: Spiritual & Moral Excellence
90. Teachings of Islam Series: Zakah and Charity

Recommended Lectures for Further Study and Teaching

There are thousands of lectures and speeches delivered on several hundreds of topics by Shaykh-ul-Islam Dr Muhammad Tahir-ul-Qadri in the areas such as peace and security, mercy and love for humanity and eradication of extremism.

Due to their great number, the following is a selected list of Urdu and English lectures which provide material for the topics under discussion. (The list of lectures by Shaykh-ul-Islam can be viewed online at www.deenislam.com)

Urdu Lectures

1. Peace, Love and Mercy

	Lecture no.	Title	Venue	Date
1	Er-1	uzūr ﷺ Baḥaysiyyat Raḥma li al-ʿĀlamīn	Lahore	28th Jan 1983
2	Er-2	uzūr ﷺ ka Raḥma li al-ʿĀlamīn Haunā Takmīl-e Dīn ke Hawāley se	Nankana	20th Apr 1986
3	Er-3	Maḥbūb ye Terey Rabb kī Raḥmat kā Bayān Hai	Lahore	5th Dec 1991
4	Er-4	Sārī Kāʾināt Raḥmat-e Muṣṭafā ﷺ kī Muḥtāj hai	Lahore	13th Dec 1991
5	Fm-36	Insānī Shakhṣiyat kā Rūḥānī aur Akhlāqī Pehlū (Raḥmat)	Lahore	1st Mar 2002
6	Fm-37	Raḥmat, Dil kā Ghanī Hounā hai	Lahore	10th May 2002
7	Fm-41	Taṣavvur-e Muḥabbat		29th Jan 1999

8	Eu-67	Muḥabbat (Mīlād-e Muṣṭafā ﷺ Conference)	New Jersey	29th May 2011
9	Fq-2	Irāda, Raḥmat aur Muḥabbat (Qur'ān aur Taṣavvur-e Muḥabbat)	Lahore	5th Jun 1987
10	Fq-3	Ma'nā-ye Muḥabbat (Qur'ān aur Taṣavvur-e Muḥabbat)	Lahore	12th Jun 1987
11	Fq-4	Muḥabbat-e Ilāhī, Allāh ke Bandai se Muḥabbat (Qur'ān aur Taṣavvur-e Muḥabbat)	Lahore	19th Jun 1987
12	Fq-5	Qur'ān aur Taṣavvur-e Muḥabbat (Muḥabbat-e Ilāhī, Bandai ki Allāh ﷻ se Muḥabbat)	Lahore	26th Jun 1987
13	Fq-6	Dhikr-e Ilāhī (Qur'ān aur Taṣavvur-e Muḥabbat)	Lahore	3rd Jul 1987
14	Fq-9	Itā'at-e Ilāhī ('Alāmāt-e Muḥabbat)	Lahore	24th Jul 1987
15	Fq-10	ukm-e Ilāhī aur Aḥwāl-e Muḥabbat (Maqām-e Tafriqa o Jama')	Lahore	17th Sep 1993
16	Fq-11	Taṣavvur-e Muḥabbat [Qur'ān aur adīth kī Raushanī mein (Volume 1)]	Lahore	5th Mar 1999
17	Fq-12	Taṣavvur-e Muḥabbat [Qur'ān aur adīth kī Raushanī mein (Volume 2)]		12th Mar 1999
18	Fq-19	Islām Dīn-e Muḥabbat Hai	Regent Plaza, Karachi	28th Feb 2009
19	Ha-39	Bunyād Parastī (Maghrib kī Tanqīd aur aqīqat-e āl)	Awari Hotel	30th Nov 1995
20	Ha-44	Islām Dīn-e Āsān o Raḥmat Hai (Islām mein Insānī uqūq aur Taṣavvur-e Amn—Nashist Avval)		23rd Sep 2008

21	Ha-51	Allāh Taʿālā kī Shān-e Rabūbiyyat o Raḥmat (Islām Dīn-e Amn o Raḥmat Hai—Episode 1)		2009
22	Ha-52	Allāh Taʿālā kī Shān-e Rabūbiyyat o Raḥmat (Islām Dīn-e Amn o Raḥmat Hai—Episode 2)		2009
23	Ha-53	Allāh Taʿālā kī Shān-e Rabūbiyyat o Raḥmat (Islām Dīn-e Amn o Raḥmat Hai—Episode 3)		2009
24	Ha-54	Allāh Taʿālā kī Shān-e Rabūbiyyat o Raḥmat (Islām Dīn-e Amn o Raḥmat Hai—Episode 4)		2009
25	Ha-55	Wusʿat-e Raḥmat-e Ilāhī (Islām Dīn-e Amn o Raḥmat Hai—Episode 5)		2009
26	Ha-56	Wusʿat-e Raḥmat-e Ilāhī (Islām Dīn-e Amn o Raḥmat Hai—Episode 6)		2009
27	Ha-57	Wusʿat-e Raḥmat-e Ilāhī (Islām Dīn-e Amn o Raḥmat Hai—Episode 7)		2009
28	Ha-58	Islāmī Qawānīn kā Falsafa Yusr (Islām Dīn-e Amn o Raḥmat Hai—Episode 8)		2009
29	Ha-59	Islāmī Qawānīn kā Falsafa Yusr (Islām Dīn-e Amn o Raḥmat Hai—Episode 9)		2009
30	Ha-60	Islāmī Qawānīn kā Falsafa Yusr (Islām Dīn-e Amn o Raḥmat Hai—Episode 10)		2009
31	Ha-61	Wusʿat-e Raḥmat-e Ilāhī (Islām Dīn-e Amn o Raḥmat Hai—Episode 11)		2009

32	Ha-62	Wusʿat Raḥmat-e Muṣṭafā ﷺ (Islām Dīn-e Amn o Raḥmat Hai—Episode 12)		2009
33	Ha-63	Wusʿat Raḥmat-e Muṣṭafā ﷺ (Islām Dīn-e Amn o Raḥmat Hai—Episode 13)		2009
34	Ha-64	Wusʿat Raḥmat-e Muṣṭafā ﷺ (Islām Dīn-e Amn o Raḥmat Hai—Episode 14)		2009
35	Ha-65	Wusʿat Raḥmat-e Muṣṭafā ﷺ (Islām Dīn-e Amn o Raḥmat Hai—Episode 15)		2009
36	Ha-66	Wusʿat Raḥmat-e Muṣṭafā ﷺ (Islām Dīn-e Amn o Raḥmat Hai—Episode 16)		2009
37	Ha-67	Wusʿat Raḥmat-e Muṣṭafā ﷺ (Islām Dīn-e Amn o Raḥmat Hai—Episode 17)		2009
38	Ha-68	uzūr ﷺ kī Ṣaḥāba Kirām Par Raḥmat o Shafqat (Islām Dīn-e Amn o Raḥmat Hai—Episode 18)		2009
39	Ha-69	uzūr ﷺ kī Ghunahgāron aur Nāfarmānon Par Raḥmat o Shafqat (Islām Dīn-e Amn o Raḥmat Hai—Episode 19)		2009
40	Ha-70	uzūr ﷺ kī Ghunahgāron aur Nāfarmānon Par Raḥmat o Shafqat (Islām Dīn-e Amn o Raḥmat Hai—Episode 20)		2009
41	Ha-71	uzūr ﷺ kī Dīhātiyon aur Anparhon Par Raḥmat o Shafqat (Islām Dīn-e Amn o Raḥmat Hai—Episode 21)		2009

42	Ha-72	uzūr ﷺ kī Kamzauron, Fuqarā', Masākīn Par Raḥmat o Shafqat (Islām Dīn-e Amn o Raḥmat Hai—Episode 22)		2009
43	Ha-73	uzūr ﷺ kī Khawātīn Par Raḥmat o Shafqat (Islām Dīn-e Amn o Raḥmat Hai—Episode 23)		2009
44	Ha-74	uzūr ﷺ kī Bachchon Par Raḥmat o Shafqat (Islām Dīn-e Amn o Raḥmat Hai—Episode 24)		2009
45	Ha-75	uzūr ﷺ kī Bachchon Par Raḥmat o Shafqat (Islām Dīn-e Amn o Raḥmat Hai—Episode 25)		2009
46	Ha-76	uzūr ﷺ kī Bachchon Par Raḥmat o Shafqat (Islām Dīn-e Amn o Raḥmat Hai—Episode 26)		2009
47	Ha-77	uzūr ﷺ kī Yatīmon, Baiwāon aur Khādimon Par Raḥmat o Shafqat (Islām Dīn-e Amn o Raḥmat Hai—Episode 27)		2009
48	Ha-78	uzūr ﷺ kī Kamzauron, Fuqarā', Masākīn Par Raḥmat o Shafqat (Islām Dīn-e Amn o Raḥmat Hai—Episode 28)		2009
49	Ha-79	uzūr ﷺ Kuffār o Mushrikīn Par Raḥmat (Islām Dīn-e Amn o Raḥmat Hai—Episode 29)		2009
50	Ha-80	uzūr ﷺ Kuffār o Mushrikīn Par Raḥmat (Islām Dīn-e Amn o Raḥmat Hai—Episode 30)		2009

51	Ha-81	uzūr ﷺ Kuffār o Mushrikīn Par Raḥmat (Islām Dīn-e Amn o Raḥmat Hai—Episode 31)		2009
52	Ha-82	uzūr ﷺ Kuffār o Mushrikīn Par Raḥmat (Islām Dīn-e Amn o Raḥmat Hai—Episode 32)		2009
53	Ha-83	uzūr ﷺ kī Jānwaru Par Raḥmat wa Shafqat (Islām Dīn-e Amn o Raḥmat Hai—Episode 33)		2009
54	Ha-84	Salām kā Mafhūm aur Islām kā Paighām Amn o Salāmatī	London	27th June 2009
55	Ha-86	Islām Dīn-e Amn Hai	Oman	16TH Jan 2004
56	Ha-44	Islām Dīn-e Āsān o Raḥmat Hai (Islām mein Insānī uqūq aur Taṣavvur-e Amn—Nishist Avval)	Shehr-e Iʿtikāf, Lahore	23rd Sep 2003
57	Ha-87	Islām kā Paighām-e Amn wa Bayn al-Madhāhib Rāwadārī	Tennis Pavilion, Bangalore	10th Mar 2012
58	Ha-89	Islām Dīn-e Amn o Salāmtī Hai (European Peace Conference 2012)	Denmark	9th Sep 2012
59	Ha-90	uzūr ﷺ kī Amn Pasandī o Insāniyyat Nawāzī	PC Hotel, Lahore	7th Feb 2013
60	Ha-95	Muḥabbat-e Insāniyyat aur ʿAdm-e Tashaddud (31st ʿĀlmī Mīlād Conference)	Mīnār-e Pākistān Lahore	3rd Jan 2015
61	Hb-74	Dehshat Gardī aur Fitna-e Khawārij ke Bārey mein Fatwā	Markaz Secteriate, Minhaj-ul-Quran	5th Dec 2009

62	Hb-75	Dehshat Gard Maujūda Daur ke Khawārij Hein	Markaz Secteriate, Minhaj-ul-Quran	10th Dec 2009
63	Hb-76	Dehshat Gardī aur Fitna-e Khawārij Par Fatwā	New Delhi, India	22nd Feb 2012
64	Hc-6/2	uzūr ﷺ ko Apnī Ummat Se Kitnā Piyār Hai	Al-Hamra, Arts Council, Lahore	18th Dec 1987
65	Ie-15	Dīn mein Amn kī Ahmiyyat	Engineering University, Lahore	19th Nov 1997

2. Unity of the *Umma*

	Lecture No.	Title	Venue	Date
66	Ie-1	Islām aur Firqa Parastī	Lahore	25th Mar 1983
67	Ie-2	Islām aur Firqa Parastī	Lahore	1st Apr 1983
68	Ie-3	Islām aur Firqa Parastī	Lahore	8th Apr 1983
69	Ie-4	Islām aur Firqa Parastī	Lahore	15th Apr 1983
70	Ka-4	Ittiḥād Bayn al-Muslimīn	PTV, Lahore	1986
71	Ie-5	Ummat-e Muslima kā Ittihād aur Tafriqa o Intishār kā Anjām	Lahore	26th Sep 1986
72	Ie-6	Rabṭ-e Tawḥīd o Risālat aur Ittiḥād-e Ummat (Pehla ʿĀm Urdū Khiṭāb)	Khayṭān Jadīd Madrasa, Kuwait	23rd Apr 1987

73	Eu-13	Ittiḥād-e Ummat ke Liye Muḥabbat-e Rasūl ﷺ kā Luzūm	Dīwān Rifāʿī, Kuwait	24th Apr 1987
74	Et-1	Ittiḥād-e Ummat aur Nisbat-e Risālat ke Taqāẓe: Muḥabbat, Adab, Itāʿat aur Nuṣrat	Madrasa Maʿhad al-Īmān Sharʿī, Kuwait	25th Apr 1987
75	Ie-7	Minhaj-ul-Quran International Islamic Conference	Wembley, London	19th Jun 1988
76	Ia 34	Teḥrīk-e Minhaj-ul-Quran ke ʿAnāṣir Arbaʿa (Taṣawwuf, ʿIshq-i Rasūl ﷺ, Ittiḥād-e Ummat, Inqilāb)	Fath Jang, Atakk	5th Aug 1989
77	Ie-9	Ittiḥād Bayn al-Muslimīn Hamārī Pehchān Hai (Minhaj-ul-Qurān Conference)	Tindhwala Yaar	2nd Oct 1989
78	Ie-10	Ummat-e Muḥammadiyya ke uqūq aur Ittiḥād-e Ummat kī Zarūrat	Lahore	22nd Feb 1990
79	Ie-11	Firqa Parastī kā Khātima Kiyunkar Mumkin Hai	Jang Forum	15th Oct 1991
80	Ie-12	Ittiḥād-e Ummat aur Hamārī Zimmadāriyān (Minhaj-ul-Quran Conference)	Rawal-pindi	19th Apr 1992
81	Hl-25	Iḥyā-e Islām, Ittiḥād-e Ummat aur Teḥrīk-e Minhaj-ul-Quran		8th Oct 1992
82	Ia-44	Ittiḥād-e Ummat aur ʿUlamāʾ Ahl-e Sunnat kī Dhimma Dāriyān (Seynkro ʿUlamāʾ kī Shamūliyat)	Lahore	14th Aug 1994
83	Ie-13	Firqa Wāriyat ke Khilāf Jihād aur Hamārī Dhimma Dāriyān	Lahore	1995

84	Ic-14	Ittiḥād-e Ummat Conference	Lahore	Mar 1995
85	Ib-27	Ittiḥād-e Ummat mein āil Mushkilāt aur Unkā āl	Shehr-e Iʿtikāf	3rd Feb 1997
86	Ie-17	Pākistān mein Firqa Wāriyat ke Asbāb	Lahore	12th Jan 2001
87	Ie-18	Masājid ke Nām Par Tafriqa o Takhrīb ke Marākiz (Sūra al-Tawba)	Lahore	11th Jan 2002
88	Ie-19	Ittiḥād-e Ummat Kiyun Kar Mumkin Hai?	Hong Kong	6th Feb 2000
89	Ie-20	Ittiḥād-e Ummat aur ʿUlamāʾ Ahl-e Sunnat kī Dhimma Dāriyān	Taj Mahal Shadi Hall, Lahore	6th Mar 1995
90	Ie-22	Ittiḥād-e Ummat aur Sīrat-e Nabawī	Hey-drabad Dakkan, India	2nd Mar 2012
91	Ie-21	ʿAṣr-e āẓir aur Ijmāʿ-e Ummat (Mashāʾikh Conference)	Birming-ham	11th Aug 2009

3. STATE AND NATION BUILDING

	LECTURE NO.	TITLE	VENUE	DATE
92	Ha-28	Islām aur Samājī Behbūd	Kotli, Azad Kashmir	
93	Ha-35	Riyāsat-e Madīna ke Hawāle Se Sīrat Conference	France	30th July 2000
94	Hc-1	Taʿmīr-e Millat aur Naujawāno kā Akhlāqī Kirdār (Shām Hamdard)	Fletize Hotel, Lahore	3rd Nov 1983

95	Hc-2	Taqrīb Āwāz-e Akhlāq	Karachi	10th Nov 1983
96	Hc-3	Qiyām-e Pākistān kī Fikrī aur Naẓaryātī Asās	Engineering University, Lahore	11th Mar 1984
97	Hc-4	Āo Har Zarra Khāk o Waṭan se Muḥabbat Karain	Fletize Hotel, Lahore	4th Jul 1985
98	Hc-6/1	Akhlāqiyāt-e Asātiza o Tilāmiza (Shām Hamdard)	Fletize Hotel, Lahore	2nd Sept 1987
99	Hc-8	ʿAllāma Iqbāl Kā Khawāb aur Āj kā Pākistān	Al-Hamra Hall, Lahore	8th Nov 1994
100	Hc-9	Badalte Rehte hain Chehre Yahān Niẓām Nahīn	Al-Hamra Hall, Lahore	13th Aug 1995
101	Hc-12	Jamhūrī Muʿāshara aur Wusʿat-e Ẓarf kī Taʿlīm (Sūra ujurāt Āyat 7)	Baghdad Town, Lahore	26th May 2000
102	Hc-13	Niẓām Jamhūriyat aur Mashawarat Key Qurʾānī Uṣūl (Sūra ujurāt Āyat 7)	Baghdad Town, Lahore	9th Jun 2000
103	Hc-14	Pākistān kī Taraqqī mein Ṭulabāʾ kā Jumhūrī Kirdār	Lahore	5th May 2002
104	Hc-16	Qāʾid-e Aʿẓam ke Afkār aur Āj Kā Pākistān (Rauznāmā Jang ke Zeyr-e Ihtimām	PC Hotel, Lahore	24th Dec 2004
105	Hc-19	Iqbāl kā Pākistān aur Āj kā Naujavān	Markazi Secreteriate, Lahore	30th Nov 2006
106	Hc-20	Qaumī Waḥdat kī Ẓarūrat (Sawāt kī Sūrat āl ke Tanāẓur mein)	Markazi Secreteriate, Lahore	4th Jun 2009

4. State and Nation Building

	Lecture No.	Title	Venue	Date
107	Ha-9	Islām aur Hamārī Zindagī (uqūq-e Vālidayn— iṣṣa Avval)	Ittifaq Masjid, Lahore	9th Sep 1988
108	Ha-10	Islām aur Hamārī Zindagī (uqūq-e Vālidayn— iṣṣa Duvvum)	Ittifaq Masjid, Lahore	16th Sep 1988
109	Ha-11	Islām aur Hamārī Zindagī (Vālida ke uqūq)	Ittifaq Masjid, Lahore	23rd Sep 1988
110	Ha-14	Islām aur Hamārī Zindagī (Aulād ke uqūq)	Ittifaq Masjid, Lahore	27th Jan 1989
111	Fm-12	uqūq-e Zaujayn: Mardon ke Awraton par uqūq	Markazi Secreteriate, Lahore	27th Mar 1998
112	Fm-13	uqūq al-ʿIbād aur usn-e Muʿāmalāt (Vol 5)	Markazi Secreteriate, Lahore	24th Apr 1998
113	Ha-2	Musalmāno ke Aik Dusre par uqūq (Khuṭba-e Jumʿa)		28th Jun 1985
114	Ha-24	ʿIlm, Amn aur Insānī uqūq (Panchawa Yaum-e Taʾsīs MSM)	International Islamic University, Islamabad	6th Oct 1999
115	Ha-13	Islām aur Hamārī Zindagī (uqūq wa Farāʾiḍ me Tawāzun)	Ittifaq Masjid, Lahore	20th Jan 1989
116	Ha-45	Vālidayn aur Zaujayn ke uqūq (Islām mein Insānī uqūq aur Taṣavvur-e Amn—Nashist Duvvum)	Shehr-e Iʿtikāf, Lahore	24th Sep 2008

117	Ha-46	Yatāmā, Masākīn aur ayāwānāt ke uqūq (Islam mein Insānī uqūq aur Taṣavvur-e Amn—Nashist Savvum)	Shehr-e Iʿtikāf, Lahore	25th Sep 2008
118	Ha-47	Ghayr Muslimon ke uqūq (Islam mein Insānī uqūq aur Taṣavvur-e Amn—Nashist Chāram)	Shehr-e Iʿtikāf, Lahore	26th Sep 2008
119	Ha-92	Vālidayn aur Qarībī Rishte Dāron ke uqūq	Shehr-e Iʿtikāf, Lahore	4th Aug 2013
120	Ha-93	ʿAurton aur Bīvīyon ke uqūq	Shehr-e Iʿtikāf, Lahore	6th Aug 2013
121	Ha-94	Shohar aur Awlād ke uqūq	Shehr-e Iʿtikāf, Lahore	7th Aug 2013

5. Morals and Etiquettes

	Lecture no.	Title	Venue	Date
122	Fm-9	usn-e Akhlāq aur usn-e Muʿāmalāt (Vol 1)	Lahore	6th Mar 1998
123	Fm-10	usn-e Akhlāq aur usn-e Muʿāmalāt (Vol 2)	Lahore	13th Mar 1998
124	Fm-11	usn-e Akhlāq aur usn-e Muʿāmalāt (Vol 3)	Lahore	20th Mar 1998
125	Fm-18	Ḍarūrāt-e Tarbiyat aur Akhlāq-e asana kī Ahmiyyat (Tarbiyati Camp)	Holland	17th Jul 1998
126	Fm-19	Akhlāq kī Do Shākhey: Tawāḍuʿ aur Akhuwwat (Tarbiyati Camp)	Holland	17th Jul 1998

127	Fm-20	Tawāḍuᶜ, Akhuwwat aur Ulfat kā Bayān (Tarbiyati Camp)	Holland	18th Jul 1998
128	Fm-21	Taḥammul aur Burdabārī [usn-e Akhlāq aur usn-e Muᶜāmalāt (Vol 9)]	Lahore	21st Aug 1998
129	Fm-22	Guṣṣa [usn-e Akhlāq aur usn-e Muᶜāmalāt (Vol 10)]	Lahore	30th Oct 1998
130	Fm-23	Badgumānī aur Gībat [usn-e Akhlāq aur usn-e Muᶜāmalāt (Vol 11)]	Lahore	6th Nov 1998
131	Fm-24	asad [usn-e Akhlāq aur usn-e Muᶜāmalāt (Vol 12)]	Lahore	11th Dec 1998
132	Fm-26	usn-e Akhlāq (Sūra ujarāt kī Roshnī me)	Lahore	25th Feb 2000
133	Fm-27	usn-e Akhlāq (Sūra ujarāt kī Roshnī me)	Lahore	10th Mar 2000
134	Fm-28	Badgumānī se Bachne kā Qurʾānī Nuskha (Sūra ujarāt, Āyāt 6)	Lahore	31st Mar 2000
135	Fm-29	Akhlāq aur Khuluq-e Muḥammadī kī aqīqat	Shehr-e Iᶜtikāf, Lahore	18th Dec 2000
136	Fm-30	usn-e Akhlāq	Shehr-e Iᶜtikāf, Lahore	19th Dec 2000
137	Fm-31	Tawāḍuᶜ, ᶜĀjizī aur Inkisārī	Shehr-e Iᶜtikāf, Lahore	20th Dec 2000
138	Fm-32	usn-e Akhlāq, Akhuwwat wa Muḥabbat	Shehr-e Iᶜtikāf, Lahore	21st Dec 2000
139	Fm-33	Adab kyā he? (Sehrī Programme)	Shehr-e Iᶜtikāf, Lahore	10th Dec 2000

140	Fm-35	Insānī Shakhsiyyat kā Rūḥānī aur Akhlāqī Pehlū (usn-e Akhlāq)	Lahore	15th Feb 2002
141	Fm-38	usn-e Akhlāq wa Ādāb	Shehr-e Iʿtikāf, Lahore	3rd Oct 2005
142	Fm-42	usn-e Akhlāq	New York	12th Feb 1999
143	Fm-43	usn-e Akhlāq (Sūra ujarāt kī Roshnī me)	Lahore	3rd Mar 2000
144	Fm-45	Insānī Shakhsiyyat me Ṣifat-e ʿAdl kī Ahmiyyat (Dars al- ikam al-ʿAṭāʾiyya)	Lahore	2nd Apr 2009
145	Fm-46	usn-e Naẓm ke Ẓāhirī wa Bāṭinī Maʿārif	Canada	26th Mar 2011
146	Fm-47	uẓūr ke Akhlāq-e asana	Minar-e Pakistan, Lahore	24th Jan 2013
147	Ha-7	Islām aur Hamārī Zindagī: Dīn me Iʿtidāl aur Miyāna Rawī	Lahore	26th Aug 1988
148	Ha-8	Islām aur Hamārī Zindagī: Dīn me Iʿtidāl aur Miyāna Rawī	Lahore	2nd Sep 1988
149	Hc-7	Rifʿat-e Insāniyyat (Shām-e Hamdard)	Sirina Hotel, Faisalabad	22nd Feb 1988
150	Hc-10	usn-e Ijtimāʿiyyat aur uss ke Taqāẓe wa Atharāt	France	13th Jul 1997
151	Hc-11	Insānī Kamzoriyān aur aqīqat-e ʿAẓmat	Lahore	6th Feb 1998
152	Hc-18	Taʿmīr-e Shakhṣiyyat me Shuʿūr kī Kār Farmaʾī	Lahore	23rd Aug 1996

6. Asceticism and Sufism

	Lecture no.	Title	Venue	Date
153	Fc-1	Taṣawwuf kyā he? (Taʿlīmāt aur Maqāṣid ke avāley se)	Lahore	16th May 1983
154	Fc-2	Taṣawwuf Sunnat-e Nabawī ke Roshnī me (Vol 1)	Lahore	23rd May 1983
155	Fc-3	Taṣawwuf Sunnat-e Nabawī ke Roshnī me (Vol 2)	Lahore	30th May 1983
156	Fc-4	Taṣawwuf Ṣaḥāba Kirām kī Zindagī ke Muʿāmalāt kī Roshnī me	Lahore	6th Jun 1983
157	Fc-5	Taṣawwuf kī aqīqat (Mukhtalif Shubuhāt aur un kī Vaẓāḥat)	Lahore	5th Jul 1987
158	Fc-6	Taṣawwuf kī aqīqat	Hatala Colony	
159	Fc-7	Taṣawwuf kī Bunyād ʿIlm He (Dars-e Taṣawwuf)	Baghdad Town, Lahore	19th Nov 1991
160	Fc-8	Taṣawwuf (Qurʾān wa adīth kī Roshnī mein)	Lahore	9th Oct 1992
161	Fc-15	Ṣūfī kon he?	Lahore	3rd Apr 2004
162	Fc-16	Taṣawwuf aur ʿIlm-e Rūḥānniyat (Minhajians se Khiṭāb)	Lahore	6th Aug 2004
163	Fc-25	aqīqat-e Īmān hī Taṣawwuf He	Karachi	25th Mar 2005
164	Fc-28	Taṣawwuf aur Wilāyat Kyā He?	Birmingham	28th Jul 2008

165	Fc-29	Taʿārifī Guftugū [Taṣawwuf aur Taʿlīmāt-e Ṣūfiyāʾ (Qurʾān aur Sunnat kī Roshnī mein)—Episode No. 1)]		2009
166	Fc-30	Tārīkh-e Taṣawwuf [Taṣawwuf aur Taʿlīmāt-e Ṣūfiyāʾ (Qurʾān aur Sunnat kī Roshnī mein)—Episode No. 2)]		2009
167	Fc-31	Tārīkh-e Taṣawwuf [Taṣawwuf aur Taʿlīmāt-e Ṣūfiyāʾ (Qurʾān aur Sunnat kī Roshnī mein)—Episode No. 3)]		2009
168	Fc-32	Taṣawwuf kā Lughvī Istiḥqāq aur Maʿnavī Istiḥqāq [Taṣawwuf aur Taʿlīmāt-e Ṣūfiyāʾ (Qurʾān aur Sunnat kī Roshnī mein)—Episode No. 4)]		2009
169	Fc-33	Taṣawwuf kā Lughvī Istiḥqāq aur Maʿnavī Istiḥqāq [Taṣawwuf aur Taʿlīmāt-e Ṣūfiyāʾ (Qurʾān aur Sunnat kī Roshnī mein)—Episode No. 5)]		2009
170	Fc-34	Taṣawwuf kā Lughvī Istiḥqāq aur Maʿnavī Istiḥqāq [Taṣawwuf aur Taʿlīmāt-e Ṣūfiyāʾ (Qurʾān aur Sunnat kī Roshnī mein)—Episode No. 6)]		2009
171	Fc-35	Taṣawwuf kā Lughvī Istiḥqāq aur Maʿnavī Istiḥqāq [Taṣawwuf aur Taʿlīmāt-e Ṣūfiyāʾ (Qurʾān aur Sunnat kī Roshnī mein)—Episode No. 7)]		2009

172	Fc-36	Taṣawwuf kā Lughvī Istiḥqāq aur Maʿnavī Istiḥqāq [Taṣawwuf aur Taʿlīmāt-e Ṣūfiyāʾ (Qurʾān aur Sunnat kī Roshnī mein)—Episode No. 8)]		2009
173	Fc-37	Taṣawwuf kā Lughvī Istiḥqāq aur Maʿnavī Istiḥqāq [Taṣawwuf aur Taʿlīmāt-e Ṣūfiyāʾ (Qurʾān aur Sunnat kī Roshnī mein)—Episode No. 9)]		2009
174	Fc-38	Taṣawwuf kā Lughvī Istiḥqāq aur Maʿnavī Istiḥqāq [Taṣawwuf aur Taʿlīmāt-e Ṣūfiyāʾ (Qurʾān aur Sunnat kī Roshnī mein)—Episode No. 10)]		2009
175	Fc-39	Taṣawwuf kā Lughvī Istiḥqāq aur Maʿnavī Istiḥqāq [Taṣawwuf aur Taʿlīmāt-e Ṣūfiyāʾ (Qurʾān aur Sunnat kī Roshnī mein)—Episode No. 11)]		2009
176	Fc-40	Taṣawwuf kā Lughvī Istiḥqāq aur Maʿnavī Istiḥqāq [Taṣawwuf aur Taʿlīmāt-e Ṣūfiyāʾ (Qurʾān aur Sunnat kī Roshnī mein)—Episode No. 12)]		2009
177	Fc-41	Taṣawwuf kā Lughvī Istiḥqāq aur Maʿnavī Istiḥqāq [Taṣawwuf aur Taʿlīmāt-e Ṣūfiyāʾ (Qurʾān aur Sunnat kī Roshnī mein)—Episode No. 13)]		[illegible]

178	Fc-42	Taṣawwuf kā Lughvī Istiḥqāq aur Maʿnavī Istiḥqāq [Taṣawwuf aur Taʿlīmāt-e Ṣūfiyāʾ (Qurʾān aur Sunnat kī Roshnī mein)—Episode No. 14)]		2009
179	Fc-43	Taṣawwuf kā Lughvī Istiḥqāq aur Maʿnavī Istiḥqāq [Taṣawwuf aur Taʿlīmāt-e Ṣūfiyāʾ (Qurʾān aur Sunnat kī Roshnī mein)—Episode No. 15)]		2009
180	Fc-44	Taṣawwuf kī aqīqat aur Ibtidāʾ (Qurʾān-e akīm kī Roshnī mein) [Taṣawwuf aur Taʿlīmāt-e Ṣūfiyāʾ (Qurʾān aur Sunnat kī Roshnī mein)—Episode No. 16)]		2009
181	Fc-45	Taṣawwuf kī aqīqat aur Ibtidāʾ (Qurʾān-e akīm kī Roshnī mein) [Taṣawwuf aur Taʿlīmāt-e Ṣūfiyāʾ (Qurʾān aur Sunnat kī Roshnī mein)—Episode No. 17)]		2009
182	Fc-46	Taṣawwuf kī aqīqat aur Ibtidāʾ (Qurʾān-e akīm kī Roshnī mein) [Taṣawwuf aur Taʿlīmāt-e Ṣūfiyāʾ (Qurʾān aur Sunnat kī Roshnī mein)—Episode No. 18)]		2009
183	Fc-47	Taṣawwuf kī aqīqat aur Ibtidāʾ (Qurʾān-e akīm kī Roshnī mein) [Taṣawwuf aur Taʿlīmāt-e Ṣūfiyāʾ (Qurʾān aur Sunnat kī Roshnī mein)—Episode No. 19)]		2009

184	Fc-48	Taṣawwuf kī aqīqat aur Ibtidā᾿ (Qur᾿ān-e akīm kī Roshnī mein) [Taṣawwuf aur Taʿlīmāt-e Ṣūfiyā᾿ (Qur᾿ān aur Sunnat kī Roshnī mein)—Episode No. 20)]		2009
185	Fc-49	Taṣawwuf kī aqīqat wa Māhiyat [Taṣawwuf aur Taʿlīmāt-e Ṣūfiyā᾿ (Qur᾿ān aur Sunnat kī Roshnī mein)—Episode No. 21)]		2009
186	Fc-50	Taṣawwuf kī aqīqat wa Māhiyat [Taṣawwuf aur Taʿlīmāt-e Ṣūfiyā᾿ (Qur᾿ān aur Sunnat kī Roshnī mein)—Episode No. 22)]		2009
187	Fc-51	Taṣawwuf kī aqīqat wa Māhiyat [Taṣawwuf aur Taʿlīmāt-e Ṣūfiyā᾿ (Qur᾿ān aur Sunnat kī Roshnī mein)—Episode No. 23)]		2009
188	Fc-52	Taṣawwuf kī aqīqat wa Māhiyat [Taṣawwuf aur Taʿlīmāt-e Ṣūfiyā᾿ (Qur᾿ān aur Sunnat kī Roshnī mein)—Episode No. 24)]		2009
189	Fc-53	Taṣawwuf kī aqīqat wa Māhiyat [Taṣawwuf aur Taʿlīmāt-e Ṣūfiyā᾿ (Qur᾿ān aur Sunnat kī Roshnī mein)—Episode No. 25)]		2009
190	Fc-54	Taṣawwuf kī aqīqat wa Māhiyat [Taṣawwuf aur Taʿlīmāt-e Ṣūfiyā᾿ (Qur᾿ān aur Sunnat kī Roshnī mein)—Episode No. 26)]		2009

191	Fc-55	Taṣawwuf kī aqīqat wa Māhiyat [Taṣawwuf aur Ta'līmāt-e Ṣūfiyā' (Qur'ān aur Sunnat kī Roshnī mein)—Episode No. 27)]		2009
192	Fc-56	Taṣawwuf kī aqīqat wa Māhiyat [Taṣawwuf aur Ta'līmāt-e Ṣūfiyā' (Qur'ān aur Sunnat kī Roshnī mein)—Episode No. 28)]		2009
193	Fc-57	Taṣawwuf kī aqīqat wa Māhiyat [Taṣawwuf aur Ta'līmāt-e Ṣūfiyā' (Qur'ān aur Sunnat kī Roshnī mein)—Episode No. 29)]		2009
194	Fc-58	Taṣawwuf kī aqīqat wa Māhiyat [Taṣawwuf aur Ta'līmāt-e Ṣūfiyā' (Qur'ān aur Sunnat kī Roshnī mein)—Episode No. 30)]		2009
195	Fc-59	Taṣawwuf kī aqīqat wa Māhiyat [Taṣawwuf aur Ta'līmāt-e Ṣūfiyā' (Qur'ān aur Sunnat kī Roshnī mein)—Episode No. 31)]		2009
196	Fc-60	Taṣawwuf kī aqīqat wa Māhiyat [Taṣawwuf aur Ta'līmāt-e Ṣūfiyā' (Qur'ān aur Sunnat kī Roshnī mein)—Episode No. 32)]		2009
197	Fc-61	Taṣawwuf kī aqīqat wa Māhiyat [Taṣawwuf aur Ta'līmāt-e Ṣūfiyā' (Qur'ān aur Sunnat kī Roshnī mein)—Episode No. 33)]		2009

198	Fc-62	Taṣawwuf kī aqīqat wa Māhiyat [Taṣawwuf aur Taʿlīmāt-e Ṣūfiyāʾ (Qurʾān aur Sunnat kī Roshnī mein)—Episode No. 34)]		2009
199	Fc-63	Taṣawwuf aur Luzūm Qurʾān wa Sunnat [Taṣawwuf aur Taʿlīmāt-e Ṣūfiyāʾ (Qurʾān aur Sunnat kī Roshnī mein)—Episode No. 35)]		2009
200	Fc-64	Taṣawwuf aur Luzūm Qurʾān wa Sunnat [Taṣawwuf aur Taʿlīmāt-e Ṣūfiyāʾ (Qurʾān aur Sunnat kī Roshnī mein)—Episode No. 36)]		2009
201	Fc-65	Taṣawwuf aur Luzūm Qurʾān wa Sunnat [Taṣawwuf aur Taʿlīmāt-e Ṣūfiyāʾ (Qurʾān aur Sunnat kī Roshnī mein)—Episode No. 37)]		2009
202	Fc-66	Taṣawwuf aur Luzūm Qurʾān wa Sunnat [Taṣawwuf aur Taʿlīmāt-e Ṣūfiyāʾ (Qurʾān aur Sunnat kī Roshnī mein)—Episode No. 38)]		2009
203	Fc-67	Taṣawwuf aur Luzūm Qurʾān wa Sunnat [Taṣawwuf aur Taʿlīmāt-e Ṣūfiyāʾ (Qurʾān aur Sunnat kī Roshnī mein)—Episode No. 39)]		2009
204	Fc-68	Taṣawwuf aur Luzūm Qurʾān wa Sunnat [Taṣawwuf aur Taʿlīmāt-e Ṣūfiyāʾ (Qurʾān aur Sunnat kī Roshnī mein)—Episode No. 40)]		2009

205	Fc-77	Taṣawwuf aur Luzūm Qur'ān wa Sunnat [Taṣawwuf aur Ta'līmāt-e Ṣūfiyā' (Qur'ān aur Sunnat kī Roshnī mein)—Episode No. 41)]		2009
206	Fc-78	Taṣawwuf aur Luzūm Qur'ān wa Sunnat [Taṣawwuf aur Ta'līmāt-e Ṣūfiyā' (Qur'ān aur Sunnat kī Roshnī mein)—Episode No. 42)]		2009
207	Fc-79	Taṣawwuf par Uthai Jāney Wāley I'tirāzāt [Taṣawwuf aur Ta'līmāt-e Ṣūfiyā' (Qur'ān aur Sunnat kī Roshnī mein)—Episode No. 43)]		2009
208	Fc-80	Taṣawwuf par Uthai Jāney Wāley I'tirāzāt [Taṣawwuf aur Ta'līmāt-e Ṣūfiyā' (Qur'ān aur Sunnat kī Roshnī mein)—Episode No. 44)]		2009
209	Fc-81	'Allāma Iqbāl aur Taṣawwuf [Taṣawwuf aur Ta'līmāt-e Ṣūfiyā' (Qur'ān aur Sunnat kī Roshnī mein)—Episode No. 45)]		2009
210	Fc-82	'Allāma Iqbāl aur Taṣawwuf [Taṣawwuf aur Ta'līmāt-e Ṣūfiyā' (Qur'ān aur Sunnat kī Roshnī mein)—Episode No. 46)]		2009
211	Fc-83	Taṣawwuf aur Mustashriqīn [Taṣawwuf aur Ta'līmāt-e Ṣūfiyā' (Qur'ān aur Sunnat kī Roshnī mein)—Episode No. 47)]		2009

212	Fc-84	Taṣawwuf aur Mustashriqīn [Taṣawwuf aur Taʿlīmāt-e Ṣūfiyāʾ (Qurʾān aur Sunnat kī Roshnī mein)—Episode No. 48)]		2009
213	Fc-85	Taṣawwuf aur Mustashriqīn [Taṣawwuf aur Taʿlīmāt-e Ṣūfiyāʾ (Qurʾān aur Sunnat kī Roshnī mein)—Episode No. 49)]		2009
214	Fc-86	Taṣawwuf aur Mustashriqīn [Taṣawwuf aur Taʿlīmāt-e Ṣūfiyāʾ (Qurʾān aur Sunnat kī Roshnī mein)—Episode No. 50)]		2009
215	Fc-87	Taṣawwuf aur Mustashriqīn [Taṣawwuf aur Taʿlīmāt-e Ṣūfiyāʾ (Qurʾān aur Sunnat kī Roshnī mein)—Episode No. 51)]		2009
216	Fc-88	Taṣawwuf aur Mustashriqīn [Taṣawwuf aur Taʿlīmāt-e Ṣūfiyāʾ (Qurʾān aur Sunnat kī Roshnī mein)—Episode No. 52)]		2009
217	Fc-89	Taṣawwuf aur Mustashriqīn [Taṣawwuf aur Taʿlīmāt-e Ṣūfiyāʾ (Qurʾān aur Sunnat kī Roshnī mein)—Episode No. 53)]		2009
218	Fc-90	Taṣawwuf aur Mustashriqīn [Taṣawwuf aur Taʿlīmāt-e Ṣūfiyāʾ (Qurʾān aur Sunnat kī Roshnī mein)—Episode No. 54)]		2009

219	Fc-91	Taṣawwuf aur Mustashriqīn [Taṣawwuf aur Taʿlīmāt-e Ṣūfiyāʾ (Qurʾān aur Sunnat kī Roshnī mein)—Episode No. 55)]		2009
220	Fc-92	Taṣawwuf aur Mustashriqīn [Taṣawwuf aur Taʿlīmāt-e Ṣūfiyāʾ (Qurʾān aur Sunnat kī Roshnī mein)—Episode No. 56)]		2009
221	Fc-93	aqāʾiq-e Taṣawwuf aur Ṭarāʾiq-e Maʿrifat: iṣṣa Avval	Lahore	22nd Aug 2011
222	Fc-94	aqāʾiq-e Taṣawwuf aur Ṭarāʾiq-e Maʿrifat: iṣṣa Duvvum	Lahore	23rd Aug 2011
223	Fc-95	aqāʾiq-e Taṣawwuf aur Ṭarāʾiq-e Maʿrifat: iṣṣa Savvum	Lahore	24th Aug 2011
224	Fc-96	aqāʾiq-e Taṣawwuf aur Ṭarāʾiq-e Maʿrifat: iṣṣa Chāram	Lahore	25th Aug 2011
225	Fc-97	aqāʾiq-e Taṣawwuf aur Ṭarāʾiq-e Maʿrifat: iṣṣa Panjam	Lahore	27th Aug 2011
226	Fc-98	aqāʾiq-e Taṣawwuf aur Ṭarāʾiq-e Maʿrifat: iṣṣa Shasham	Lahore	27th Aug 2011
227	Fc-99	aqāʾiq Taṣawwuf aur Ṭarāʾiq-e Maʿrifat: iṣṣa Haftam	Lahore	29th Aug 2011
228	Fc-100	aqāʾiq-e Taṣawwuf aur Ṭarāʾiq-e Maʿrifat: iṣṣa Hashtam	Lahore	30th Aug 2011
229	Fc-69	Muslim aur Muʾmin mein Farq (Dars-e Taṣawwuf: Nashist Avval)		1st Sep 2009

230	Fc-70	Mu'min aur Muḥsin: adīth Jibrā'īl kī Roshnī mein (Dars Taṣawwuf: Nashist Duvvum)	London	2nd Sep 2009
231	Fc-71	Roz-e Maḥshar aur Shān-e Mu'minīn wa Muḥsinīn (Dars-e Taṣawwuf: Nashist Suvvum)	London	3rd Sep 2009
232	Fc-72	Taṣawwuf, Iḥsān aur Mushāhida aqq (Dars-e Taṣawwuf: Nashist Chāram)	London	4th Sep 2009
233	Fc-73	Ta'līmāt-e Taṣawwuf aur ayāt-e Qalbī (Dars-e Taṣawwuf: Nashist Panjam)	London	5th Sep 2009
234	Fc-74	Zuhd aur Ta'līmāt-e Ṣūfiyā' (Dars-e Taṣawwuf: Nashist Shasham)	London	6th Sep 2009

English Lectures

	Lecture No.	Title	Venue	Date
235	N-6	What is Islam? A Comparative Study	US	Apr 1986
236	N-7	Basic Features of an Islamic Society	US	11th Apr 1986
237	N-9	What is Islam? Lecture to Danish Non-Muslims	Denmark	13th Apr 1987
238	N-12	Reality of Islam	US	3rd Sep 1987
239	N-14	Love for Allah	New York, US	3rd Sep 1987
240	N-16	Two Levels of Islamic Justice and Benevolence	Canada	6th Sep 1987
241	N-18	How Should Islam Be Presented? (Friday Sermon)	Washington DC, US	11th Sep 1987

242	N-48	Meaning of Islam (Welcome Reception)	Durban, SA	10th Jun 1994
243	N-56	Interfaith Dialogue (Discussion with Dr. John G. Lemond)	Kowloon, Hong Kong	23rd Oct 1994
244	N-64	Human Rights Interfaith Dialogue Jews, Christians & Islamic Scholars	Toronto, Canada	26th Jul 1997
245	N-65	Interfaith Dialogue Discussion with Rev, Bishop David Smith	Lahore	21st Oct 1997
246	N-67	Interfaith Dialogue	Hong Kong	
247	N-69	International Peace Conference	Oslo, Norway	13th Aug 1999
248	N-72	Peace Symposium		13th Jul 2000
249	N-73	Human Rights in Islam	Denmark	4th Jul 1992
250	N-76	Does Islam Teach Terrorism?	Canada	30th Apr 2003
251	N-78	*Taṣawwuf* is the Remembrance of the Righteous	ICIS, MUL	2nd Nov 2003
252	N-79	*Taṣawwuf* is the Remembrance of the Righteous	ICIS, MUL	7th Dec 2003
253	N-95	Practical Explanation and Implementation of *Taṣawwuf*	Scotland	20th Aug 2004
254	N-99	Renouncing Terror, Regaining Peace	UK	30th Jul 2003
255	N-114	Various Aspects of Human Personality	UK	26th Aug 1994
256	N-116	Question & Answers Session (The Myth of Islam)	Denmark	8th Sep 1994
257	N-118	What Islam is (in the Light of its Origin)	Japan	Oct 1994

258	N-122	*Taṣawwuf* is the Path of Righteous	ICIS, MUL	7th Dec 2003
259	N-123	Remembrance of the Righteous is Allah's *Sunna*	Lahore	20th Dec 2003
260	N-124	The Doctrine of *Khawārij*	ICIS, MUL	11th Jan 2004
261	N-132	The Islamic State (Terminology & Gradualism)	ICIS, MUL	10th May 2004
262	N-133	The Islamic State (*al-Sawād al-Aʿẓam* & Deviant Groups)	ICIS, MUL	11th May 2004
263	N-135	*Dars-e Taṣawwuf*	UK	20th Aug 2004
264	N-142	Four Supreme Categories of Blessed People (Part 1)	Lahore	17th Feb 2005
265	N-143	Four Supreme Categories of Blessed People (Part 2)	Lahore	17th Feb 2005
266	N-152	Internal Conflict Between the *Nafs* & *Rūḥ*	UK	24th Aug 2007
267	N-154	Further Aspects of the *Nafs* & *Rūḥ*	UK	25th Aug 2007
268	N-159	Piety and Self Purification	UK	27th Aug 2007
269	N-161	Peace Integration and Human Rights (in the Light of Qur'ān)	UK	30th Aug 2008
270	N-163	Islam: An Ideology of Openness and Authenticity		30th Nov 2008
271	N-164	An Introduction to Islamic Legal Theory (Session 1)	Warwick University UK	8th Aug 2009
272	N-165	An Introduction to Islamic Legal Theory (Session 2)	Warwick University UK	8th Aug 2009
273	N-166	Turning Back to Allah (Session 3)	Warwick University UK	8th Aug 2009

274	N-167	The Messenger of Mercy (Session 3)	Warwick University UK	9th Aug 2009
275	N-168	A Constitution for Humanity (Session 4)	Warwick University UK	9th Aug 2009
276	N-169	The Sacred Struggle (Session 6)	Warwick University UK	9th Aug 2009
277	N-170	The Sublime Status of the Prophet ﷺ (Session 6)	Warwick University UK	9th Aug 2009
278	N-171	Exemplars of Piety (Session 7)	Warwick University UK	10th Aug 2009
279	N0172	Fatwa on Suicide Bombings and Terrorism	London	2nd Mar 2010
280	N-180	Restoring Balance: Faith, Law and Courage to Love	Toronto, Canada	2nd May 2010
281	N-181	Questions & Answers Session	Toronto, Canada	2nd May 2010
282	N-182	Jihad: Perception and Reality [Global Peace and Unity Conference 2010, UK]	London, UK	24th Oct 2010
283	N-183	Struggle Against Radicalism in Islam (with Question-Answer Session)	USIP, Washing-ton DC	10th Nov 2010
284	N-185	Islam is a Religion of Peace and Equality	Westville, South Africa	10th Jun 1994
285	N-186	Islam Today, Challenging Misconceptions	Warwick University UK	7th Aug 2010
286	N-187	Loving God: the True Meaning	Warwick University UK	7th Aug 2010

287	N-188	Companionship of the *Awliya*: The Etiquettes and Benefits (Part-1)	Warwick University UK	8th Aug 2010
288	N-189	Companionship of the *Awliya*: The Etiquettes and Benefits (Part-2)	Warwick University UK	8th Aug 2010
289	N-190	Living Islam: Question and Answer Session at Al-Hidayah 2010	Warwick University UK	9th Aug 2010
290	N-192	Extremism & Terrorism: Past, Present & Future (with Question-Answer Session)	George-town University, Washing-ton DC	8th Nov 2010
291	N-195	Islam's Message of Peace		27th Mar 2011
292	N-196	What is Traditional Islam?	London	24th Oct 2010
293	N-198	Muhammad ﷺ: the Merciful [Peace for Humanity Conference]	Wembley Arena	24th Sep 2011
294	N-201	Terrorism and Integration (with Question-Answer Session)	NSW Legislative Council Sydney	11th Jul 2011
295	N-202	Islam is a Religion of Universality and Humanism	Dar-ul-Fatwa, NSW, Australia	Jul 2011
296	N-205	Islam and Peace Today	Elmhurst College, Chicago	9th Sep 2011
297	N-206	Islam: A Religion of Love & Peace	Sydney	16th Jul 2011
298	N-207	Islam: Peace for Humanity	Mel-bourne, Australia	23rd Jul 2011

299	N-208	Peace for Humanity & *Mawlid al-Nabī* ﷺ Conference	Nassau Coliseum, US	3rd Jun 2012
300	N-209	European Launch of Fatwa on Terrorism & Suicide Bombings	Copenhagen, Denmark	6th Sep 2012
301	N-210	Political and Religious Radicalism (Conference Organised by the Danish Ethnic Youth Council)	Copenhagen, Denmark	11th Sep 2012
302	N-211	Islam & Peace (with Question-Answer Session)	University of South Carolina School of Law, US	14th Apr 2012
303	N-212	The Status of the Prophet Muhammad ﷺ (in Light of the Holy Qur'ān)	South Carolina, US	15th Apr 2012
304	N-213	Islam: A Blend of Moderation and Modernism	University of Utah, NY	16th Jun 2012
305	N-214	Launching of Fatwa on Terrorism & Suicide Bombings Question—Answer Session Press Conference [Urdu]	Long Island City, NY	28th May 2011
306	N-216	Struggle for Peace in Afghanistan	Istanbul, Turkey	2nd Dec 2011

Bibliography

al-Qur'ān

Exegesis of the Qur'ān

Ālūsī, Abū al-Fiḍā' Shihāb al-Dīn al-Sayyid Maḥmūd al- (1270 AH/1854 CE), *Rūḥ al-Maʿānī fī Tafsīr al-Qur'ān al-ʿAẓīm wa al-Sabʿ al-Mathānī*. Beirut, Lebanon: Dār Iḥyā' al-Turāth.

Ismāʿīl aqqī, Barūswī or Iskūdārī (1063-1137 AH/1652-1724 CE), *Rūḥ al-Bayān*. Beirut, Lebanon: Dār al-Fikr.

Anbaytawī, Mullā Aḥmad Jīwan, *Tafsīrāt Aḥmadiyya*. Lahore, Pakistan: Quran Company Ltd.

Baghawī, Abū Muḥammad usayn b. Masʿūd b. Muḥammad al-Farrā' al- (436-516 AH/1044-1122 CE), *Maʿālim al-Tanzīl*. Beirut, Lebanon: Dār al-Maʿrifah, 1407 AH/1987 CE.

Bayḍāwī, Nāṣir al-Dīn Abū Saʿīd ʿAbd Allāh b. ʿUmar b. Muḥammad al-Shīrāzī al- (791 AH). *Anwār al-Tanzīl*, Beirut, Lebanon: Dār al-Fikr, 1416 AH/1006 CE.

Thaʿlabī, Abū Isḥāq Aḥmad b. Muḥammad b. Ibrāhīm al- (427 AH), *al-Kashf wa al-Bayān ʿan Tafsīr al-Qur'ān*. Beirut, Lebanon: Dār al-Iḥyā' al-Turāth al-ʿArabī, 1422 AH/2002 CE.

Jaṣṣāṣ, Abū Bakr Aḥmad b. ʿAlī al-Rāzī al- (305-370 AH), *Aḥkām al-Qur'ān*. Beirut, Lebanon: Dār Iḥyā' al-Turāth, 1405 AH & Pakistan: Suhayl Academy.

Ibn al-Jawzī, Abū al-Faraj ʿAbd al-Raḥmān b. ʿAlī b. Muḥammad b. ʿAlī b. ʿUbayd Allāh (510-579 AH/1116-1201 CE), *Zād al-Masīr fī ʿIlm al-Tafsīr*. Beirut, Lebanon: al-Maktab al-Islamī, 1404 AH/1984 CE.

Ibn Abī ātim, ʿAbd al-Raḥmān b. Abī ātim Muḥammad b. Idrīs Abū Muḥammad al-Rāzī al-Tamīmī (240-327 AH/854-938 CE), *Tafsīr al-Qur'ān al-ʿAẓīm*. Saudi Arabia: Maktaba Nizār Muṣṭafā al-Bāz, 1419 AH/1999 CE & Lebanon: al-Maktaba al-ʿAṣariyya.

Abū Hafṣ al- anbalī, Sirāj al-Dīn ʿUmar b. ʿAlī b. ʿĀdil al-Dimashqī, *al-Lubāb fī ʿUmm al-Kitāb*. Beirut, Lebanon: Dār al-Kutub al-ʿIlmiyyah, 1419 AH/1998 CE.

Abū ayyān Muḥammad b. Yūsuf (654–745 AH), *al-Baḥr al-Muḥīṭ*. Beirut, Lebanon: Dār al-Kutub al-ʿIlmiyyah, 1422 AH/2001 CE.

Khāzin, ʿAlī b. Muḥammad b. Ibrāhīm b. ʿUmar b. Khalīl (678-741 AH/1279-1340 CE) al-, *Lubāb al-Taʾwīl fī Maʿānī al-Tanzīl*. Beirut, Lebanon: Dār al-Maʿrifa.

Rāzī, Fakhr al-Dīn Muḥammad b. ʿUmar b. asan b. usayn b. ʿAlī al-Tamīmī al-Shāfiʿī al-, (544-606), *Mafātīḥ al-Ghayb (al-Tafsīr al-Kabīr)*. 1421 AH & Tehran, Iran: Dār al-Kutub al-ʿIlmiyya.

Zamakhsharī, Jār Allāh Abū al-Qāsim Maḥmūd b. ʿUmar b. Muḥammad al-Khawārizmī al- (467-538 AH), *al-Kashshāf ʿan aqāʾiq Ghawāmiḍ al-Tanzīl*. Beirut, Lebanon: Dār Iḥyāʾ al-Turāth & Cairo, Egypt: 1373 AH/1953 CE.

Abū Saʿūd, Muḥammad b. ʿImādī (898-982 AH/1493-1575 CE), *Irshād al-ʿAql al-Salīm ilā Mazāyā al-Qurʾān al-Karīm (Tafsīr Abī al-Saʾūd)*. Beirut, Lebanon: Dār Iḥyāʾ al-Turāth al-ʿArabī.

Sulamī, Abū ʿAbd al-Raḥmān Muḥammad b. usayn b. Muḥammad al-Azdī al-Nīshāpūrī al- (325-412 AH/936-1021 CE), *aqāʾiq al-Tafsīr (Tafsīr al-Sulamī)*. Beirut, Lebanon: Dār al-Kutub al-ʿIlmiyya, 1421 AH/2001 CE.

Samarqandī, Abū al-Layth Naṣr b. Muḥammad b. Ibrāhīm al-anafī al- (333-373 AH), *Baḥr al-ʿUlūm (Tafsīr al-Samarqandī)*. Beirut, Lebanon: Dār al-Fikr & Beirut, Lebanon: Dār al-Kutub al-ʿIlmiyya.

Samʿānī, Abū al-Muẓaffar Manṣūr b. Muḥammad b. ʿAbd al-Jabbār al-Samʿānī (426-489 AH), *Tafsīr al-Qurʾān*. Riyadh, Saudi Arabia: Dār al-Waṭan, 1418 AH/1997 CE.

Suyūṭī, Jalāl al-Dīn Muḥammad b. Aḥmad al-Maḥallī (864 AH) & Jalāl al-Dīn Abū al-Faḍl ʿAbd al-Raḥmān b. Abī Bakr b. Muḥammad al-Suyūṭī (849-911 AH/1445-1505 CE), *Tafsīr al-Jalālayn*. Beirut, Lebanon: Dār Ibn Kathīr, 1419 AH/1998 ce.

Suyūṭī, Jalāl al-Dīn Abū al-Faḍl ʿAbd al-Raḥmān b. Abī Bakr b. Muḥammad al-Suyūṭī (849-911 AH/1445-1505 CE), *al-Durr al-*

Manthūr fī al-Tafsīr bi al-Maʾthūr. Beirut, Lebanon: Dār al-Fikr, 1993 & Beirut, Lebanon: Dār al-Maʾrifa.

Ṭabarī, Abū Jaʿfar Muḥammad b. Jarīr b. Yazīd b. Khālid (224-310 AH/839-923 CE), *Jāmiʿ al-Bayān fī Tafsīr al-Qurʾān*. Beirut, Lebanon: Dār al-Fikr, 1405 AH.

Ibn al-ʿArabī, Abū Bakr Muḥammad ʿAbd Allāh al-Maʿāfirī al-Andalusī al-Ishbilī (468-543 AH/1076-1148 CE), *Aḥkām al-Qurʾān*. Lebanon: Dār al-Fikr li al-Ṭabaʿa wa al-Nashr.

Ibn ʿAṭiyya al-Andalusī, Abū Muḥammad ʿAbd al- aqq b. Ghālib b. ʿAṭiyya (d. 546 AH), *al-Muḥarrar al-Wajīz fī Tafsīr al-Kitāb al-ʿAzīz*. Beirut, Lebanon: Dār al-Kutub al-ʿIlmiyya, 1413 AH/1993 CE.

Fayrūz Ābādī, Abū Ṭāhir Muḥammad b. Yaʿqūb b. Muḥammad b. Ibrāhīm b. ʿUmar b. Abī Bakr b. Aḥmad b. Maḥmūd (729-817 AH/1329-1414 CE), *Baṣāʾir Dhawī al-Tamyīz fī Laṭāʾif al-Kitāb al-ʿAzīz*. Cairo, Egypt: al-Majlis al-Aʿlā li al-Shuʾūn al-Islāmiyya.

Qāḍī Thanā Allāh Pānī Patī (1225 AH), *al-Tafsīr al-Maẓharī*. Beirut, Lebanon: Dār Iḥyāʾ al-Turāth al-ʿArabī & Baluchistan Book Depot Quetta, Pakistan: Baluchistan Book Depot.

Qurṭubī, Abū ʿAbd Allāh Muḥammad b. Aḥmad b. Muḥammad b. Yaḥyā b. Mufarraj al-Umawī al- (671 AH), *al-Jāmiʿ li Aḥkām al-Qurʾān*. Beirut, Lebanon: Dār Iḥyāʾ al-Turāth al-ʿArabī & Cairo, Egypt: Dār al-Shaʿb, 1372 AH.

Ibn Kathīr, Abū al-Fiḍāʾ Ismāʿīl b. ʿUmar b. Kathīr b. Ḍawʾ b. Kathīr b. Zaraʿ al-Barṣawī (701-774 AH/1301-1373 CE), *Tafsīr al-Qurʾān al-ʿAẓim*. Beirut, Lebanon: Dār al-Fikr, 1401 AH & Dār al-Maʿrifa 1400 AH/1980 CE.

Māturīdī, Abū Manṣūr Muḥammad b. Muḥammad b. Maḥmūd al- (333 AH), *Tafsīr al-Qurʾān al-ʿAẓīm (Taʾwīlāt Ahl al-Sunna)*. Beirut, Lebanon: Muʾassasa al-Risāla, 1425 AH/2004 CE.

Muḥammad Aḥmad Ismāʿīl al-Muqaddam, *Tafsīr al-Qurʾān al-Karīm*.

Muqātil b. Sulaymān, Abū al- asan Muqātil b. Sulaymān b. Bashīr al-Azdī al-Balkhī (150 AH), *Tafsīr al-Qurʾān*. Beirut, Lebanon: Dār al-Kutub al-ʿIlmiyya, 1424 AH/2003 CE.

Naḥḥās, Abū Jaʿfar Aḥmad b. Muḥammad b. Ismāʿīl al- (338 AH), *Maʿānī al-Qurʾān al-Karīm*. Makka al-Mukarrama, Saudi Arabia: Umm al-Qurā University, 1409 AH.

Nasafī, ʿAbd Allāh b. Maḥmūd b. Aḥmad al- (710 AH), *Madārik al-Tanzīl wa aqāʾiq al-Taʿwīl*. Beirut, Lebanon: Dār Iḥyāʾ al-Turāth al-ʿArabī.

Nīshāpūrī, Niẓām al-Dīn asan b. Muḥammad b. usayn al-Qummī al-, *Tafsīr Gharāʾib al-Qurʾān wa Raghāʾib al-Qurʾān*. Egypt: Maṭbaʿa al-Kubrā al-Amīriyya, 1323 AH.

Wāḥidī, Abū al- asan ʿAlī b. Aḥmad al-Wāḥidī al-Nīshāpūrī al- (468 AH), *al-Wajīz fī Tafsīr al-Kitāb al-ʿAzīz*. Beirut, Lebanon & Damascus, Syria: Dār al-Qalam, 1415 AH.

—. *al-Wasīṭ fī Tafsīr al-Qurʾān al-Majīd*. Beirut, Lebanon: Dār al-Kutub al-ʿIlmiyya, 1415 AH/1994 CE.

Hadith Collections

Aḥmad b. anbal, Abū ʿAbd Allāh b. Muḥammad (164-241 AH/780-855 CE), *al-Musnad*. Beirut, Lebanon: al-Maktab al-Islāmī, 1398 AH/1978 CE & Dār al-Kutub al-ʿIlmiyya, 1986 CE & Muʾassasa al-Risālah, 1420 AH/1999 CE & 1403 AH/1983 CE.

Azdī, Rabīʿ b. abīb b. ʿUmar al-Baṣrī al-, *al-Jāmiʿ al-Ṣaḥiḥ Musnad al-Imām al-Rabīʿ b. abīb*. Beirut, Lebanon: Dār al-ikma, 1415 AH & al-Maktab al-Islāmī, 1403 AH.

Albānī, Nāṣir al-Dīn al- (1333-1420 AH/1914-1999 CE), *Silsila al-Aḥādīth al-Ṣaḥīḥa*. Beirut, Lebanon: al-Maktab al-Islāmī, 1405 AH/1985 CE & Riyadh, Saudi Arabia: Maktaba al-Maʿārif li al-Nashr wa al-Tawzīʿ.

Bukhārī, Abū ʿAbd Allāh Muḥammad b. Ismāʿīl b. Ibrāhīm b. Mughīra al- (194-256 AH/810-870 CE), *al-Adab al-Mufrad*. Beirut: Dār al-Bashāʾir al-Islāmiyya, 1409 AH/1989 CE & Dār Ibn Kathīr, al-Yamāma, 1407 AH/1987 CE & Damascus, Syria: Dār al-Qalam, 1401 AH/1981 CE.

Bazzār, Abū Bakr Aḥmad b. ʿAmr b. ʿAbd al-Khāliq al-Baṣrī al- (215-292 AH/830-905 CE), *al-Musnad (al-Baḥr al-Zukhkhār)*. Beirut, Lebanon: Muʾassasa ʿUlūm al-Qurʾān, 1409 AH.

Baghawī, Abū Muḥammad b. Farrā' usayn b. Mas'ūd b. Muḥammad al- (436-516 AH/1044-1122 CE), *Sharḥ al-Sunna*. Beirut, Lebanon: al-Maktab al-Islāmī, 1403 AH/1983 CE.

Bayhaqī, Abū Bakr Aḥmad b. usayn b. 'Alī b. 'Abd Allāh b. Mūsā al- (384-458 AH/994-1066 CE), *al-Sunan al-Kubrā*. Madina, Saudi Arabia: Maktaba al-Dār, 1410 AH/1983 CE & 1414 AH/1994 CE & Maktaba Dār al-Bāz, 1414 AH/1994 CE.

—. *Shu'ab al-Īmān*. Beirut, Lebanon: Dār al-Kutub al-'Ilmiyya, 1410 AH/1983 CE.

—. *Ma'rifa al-Sunan wa al-Āthār*. Beirut, Lebanon: Dār al-Kutub al-'Ilmiyya.

Tirmidhī, Abū 'Īsā Muḥammad b. 'Īsā b. Sawra b. Mūsā b. Ḍaḥḥāk al-Sulamī al- (210-279 AH/825-892 CE), *al-Sunan*. Beirut, Lebanon: Dār al-Iḥyā' al-Turāth al-'Arabī & Dār al-Gharb al-Islāmī, 1998.

Ibn Jārūd, Abū Muḥammad 'Abd Allāh b. 'Alī b. Jārūd al-Nīshāpūrī (307 AH), *al-Muntaqā min al-Sunan al-Musnada*. Beirut, Lebanon: Mu'assasa al-Kitāb al-Thaqāfiyya, 1418 AH/1988 CE.

Ibn Ja'd, Abū al- asan 'Alī b. Ja'd b. 'Ubayd al-Hāshimī (133-230 AH/750-845 CE), *al-Musnad*. Beirut, Lebanon: Mu'assasa Nādir, 1410 AH/1990 CE.

ākim, Abū 'Abd Allāh Muḥammad b. 'Abd Allāh b. Muḥammad (321-405 AH/933-1014 CE), *al-Muṣtadrak 'alā al-Ṣaḥīḥayn*. Beirut, Lebanon: Dār al-Kutub al-'Ilmiyya, 1411 AH/1990 CE & Maktaba Islāmī, 1398 AH & Makkah, Saudi Arabia: Dār al-Bāz.

Ibn ibbān, Abū ātim Muḥammad b. ibbān b. Aḥmad b. ibbān (270-354 AH/884-965 CE), *al-Ṣaḥīḥ*. Beirut, Lebanon: Mu'assasa al-Risāla, 1414 AH/1993 CE.

Ibn ajar al-'Asqalānī, Aḥmad b. 'Alī b. Muḥammad b. 'Alī b. Aḥmad al-Kinānī (773-852 AH/1372-1449 CE), *Talkhīṣ al- abīr fī Aḥādīth al-Rāfi'ī al-Kabīr*. Medina, Saudi Arabia: 1384 AH/1964 CE.

—. *al-Dirāya fī Takhrīj Aḥādīth al-Hidāya*. Beirut, Lebanon: Dār al-Ma'rifa.

—. *al-Maṭālib al-ʿĀliya*. Beirut, Lebanon: Dār al-Maʿrifa, 1407 AH/1978 CE.

Hindī, ʿAlī ʿAlāʾ al-Dīn b. ʿAbd al-Malik isām al-Dīn Muttaqī al- (975 AH), *Kanz al-ʿUmmāl fī Sunan al-Aqwāl wa al-Afʿāl*. Beirut, Lebanon: Muʾassasa al-Risālah, 1399 AH/1999 CE.

akīm al-Tirmidhī, Abū ʿAbd Allāh Muḥammad b. ʿAlī b. asan b. Bashīr al- (320 AH), *Nawādir al-Uṣūl fī Aḥādīth al-Rasūl*. Beirut, Lebanon: Dār al-Jīl, 1992 CE.

umaydī, Abū Bakr ʿAbd Allāh b. Zubayr (219 AH/834 CE), *al-Musnad*. Beirut, Lebanon: Dār al-Kutub al-ʿIlmiyya & Cairo, Egypt: Maktaba al-Muntahā.

Ibn Khuzayma, Abū Bakr Muḥammad b. Isḥāq b. Khuzayma al-Sulamī al-Nīshāpūrī (223-311 AH/838-924 CE), *al-Ṣaḥīḥ*. Beirut, Lebanon: al-Maktab al-Islāmī, 1390 AH/1970 CE.

Khaṭīb al-Tabrīzī, Walī al-Dīn Abū ʿAbd Allāh Muḥammad b. ʿAbd Allāh al- (741 AH), *Mishkāt al-Maṣābīḥ*. Beirut, Lebanon: Dār al-Kutub al-ʿIlmiyya, 1424 AH/2003 CE.

Khallāl, Abū Bakr Aḥmad b. Muḥammad b. Hārūn b. Yazīd (234-311 AH), *al-Sunna*. Riyadh, Saudi Arabia: Dār al-Rāyah, 1410 AH.

Dārquṭnī, Abū al- asan ʿAlī b. ʿUmar b. Aḥmad b. Mahdī b. Masʿūd b. Nuʿmān al- (306–385 AH/918-995 CE), *al-Sunan*. Beirut, Lebanon: Dār al-Maʿrifa, 1386 AH/1966 CE.

Dārimī, Abū Muḥammad ʿAbd Allāh b. ʿAbd al-Raḥmān al- (181-255 AH), *al-Sunan*. Beirut, Lebanon: Dār al-Kitāb al-ʿArabī.

Abū Dāwūd, Sulaymān b. Ashʿath b. Isḥāq b. Bashīr b. Shaddād al-Azdī al-Sijistānī (202-275 AH/817-889 CE), *al-Sunan*. Beirut, Lebanon: Dār al-Fikr, 1414 AH/1994 CE.

Daylamī, Abū Shujāʿ Shayrwayh b. Shahradār b. Shayrwayh b. Fanākhusrū al-Hamadānī al- (445-509 AH/1053-1115 CE), *Musnad al-Firdaws*. Beirut, Lebanon: Dār al-Kutub al-ʿIlmiyya, 1986 CE.

Dhahabī, Abū ʿAbd Allāh Shams al-Dīn Muḥammad b. Aḥmad b. ʿUthmān al- (673-748 AH/1274-1348 CE), *al-Kabāʾir*. Beirut, Lebanon: Dār al-Nadwa al-Jadīda.

Ibn Rāhawayh, Abū Yaʿqūb Isḥāq b. Ibrāhīm b. Mukhallad b. Ibrāhīm b. ʿAbd Allāh (161-237 AH/778-851 CE), *al-Musnad*.

Medina, Saudi Arabia: Maktaba al-Īmān, 1412 AH/1991 CE.
Rabīʿ b. abīb b. ʿUmar al-Azdī al-Baṣrī, *al-Jāmiʿ al-Ṣaḥiḥ Musnad al-Imām al-Rabīʿ b. abīb*. Beirut, Lebanon: Dār al-ikma, 1415 AH.
Ibn Rajab al- anbalī, Abū al-Faraj ʿAbd al-Raḥmān b. Aḥmad (736-795 AH), *Jāmiʿ al-ʿUlūm wa al- ikam fī Sharḥ Khamsīn adīthan min Jawāmiʿ al-Kalim*. Beirut, Lebanon: Dār al-Maʿrifa, 1408 ce.
Rūyānī, Abū Bakr Muḥammad b. Hārūn al- (307 AH), *al-Musnad*. Cairo, Egypt: Muʾassasa al-Qurtuba, 1416 AH.
Zaylaʿī, Abū Muḥammad ʿAbd Allāh b. Yūsuf al- anafī al- (762 AH), *Naṣb al-Rāya li Aḥādīth al-Hidāya*. Egypt: Dār al- adīth, 1357 AH.
Sakhāwī, Shams al-Dīn Abū ʿAbd Allāh Muḥammad b. ʿAbd al-Raḥmān b. Muḥammad b. Abī Bakr b. ʿUthmān b. Muḥammad al- (831-902 AH/1428-1497 CE), *al-Maqāṣid al- asana*. Beirut, Lebanon: Dār al-Kitāb al-ʿArabī, 1405 AH/1985 CE.
Saʿīd b. Manṣūr, Abū ʿUthmān b. al-Khurāsānī (d. 225 AH), *al-Sunan*. India: al-Dār al-Salafiyya, 1982 CE & Riyadh: Dār al-ʿAṣīmī, 1414 AH.
Ibn Sulaymān, Khaythama b. Sulaymān al-Qurashī al-Ṭarābulusī, (250-343 AH), *Min adīth Khaythama b. Sulaymān al-Qurashī al-Ṭarābulusī*. Beirut: Dār al-Kitāb al-ʿArabī, 1400 AH/1980 CE.
Suyūṭī, Jalāl al-Dīn Abū al-Faḍl al- (849-911 AH/1445-1505 CE), *Jamʿ al-Jawāmiʿ (al-Maʿrūf al-Jāmiʿ al-Kabīr)*.
—. *Jāmiʿ al-Aḥādīth*.
Shāfiʿī, Abū ʿAbd Allāh Muḥammad b. Idrīs (150-204 AH/767-819 CE), *al-Sunan al-Maʾthūra*. Beirut: Dār al-Maʿrifa, 1406 AH.
—. *al-Musnad*. Beirut: Dār al-Kutub al-ʿIlmiyya.
Shaybānī, Abū Bakr Aḥmad b. ʿAmr b. Ḍaḥḥāk b. Mukhlid (206-287 AH/822-900 CE), *al-Āḥād wa al-Mathānī*. Riyadh: Dār al-Rāya, 1411 AH/1991 CE.
Ibn Abī Shayba, Abū Bakr ʿAbd Allāh b. Muḥammad (159-235 AH/776-849 CE), *al-Muṣannaf*. Riyadh: Maktaba al-Rushd, 1409 AH & Karachi: Idāra al-Qurʾān wa ʿUlūm al-Islāmiyya.
Ṣaydāwī, Muḥammad b. Aḥmad b. Jāmiʿ Abū al- usayn, (305-402 AH), *Muʿjam al-Shuyūkh*. Beirut: Muʾassasa al-Risāla,

1405 AH.

Ṭabarānī, Sulaymān b. Aḥmad al- (260-360 AH/873-971 CE), *Musnad al-Shāmiyyīn*. Beirut: Mu'assasa al-Risālah, 1405 AH/1984 CE.

—. *al-Mu'jam al-Awsaṭ*. Riyadh: Maktaba al-Ma'ārif, 1405 AH/1948 CE & Cairo: Dār al- aramayn, 1415 AH.

—. *al-Mu'jam al-Saghīr*. Beirut: al-Maktab al-Islāmī, 1405 AH/1985 CE.

—. *al-Mu'jam al-Kabīr*. Cairo: Maktaba Ibn Taymiyya & Mosul: Maktaba al-'Ulūm wa al- ikam, 1973 CE & Maṭba'a al-Zahrā' al- adītha.

Ṭaḥāwī, Abū Ja'far Aḥmad b. Muḥammad al- (229-321 AH/853-933 CE), *Sharḥ Mushkil al-Āthār*. Beirut: Mu'assasa al-Risāla, 1408 AH/1987 CE & Dār al-Kutub al-'Ilmiyya, 1399 AH.

—. *Mukhtaṣar Ikhtilāf al-'Ulamā'*. Beirut: Dār al-Bashā'ir al-Islāmiyya, 1418 AH.

Ṭayālisī, Abū Dāwūd Sulaymān b. Dāwūd Jārūd al- (133-204 AH/751-819 CE), *al-Musnad*. Beirut: Dār al-Ma'rifa.

Ibn Abī 'Āṣim, Abū Bakr Aḥmad b. 'Amr (206-287 AH/822-900 CE), *al-Āḥād wa al-Mathānī*. Riyadh: Dār al-Rāya, 1411 AH/1991 CE.

—. al-Sunna. Beirut: al-Maktab al-Islāmī, 1400 AH.

'Abd b. umayd, Abū Muḥammad 'Abd Allāh b. umayd (249 AH/863 CE), *al-Musnad*. Cairo: Maktaba al-Sunna, 1408 AH/1988 CE.

'Abd al- aqq Muḥaddith al-Dahlawī (958-1052 AH/1551-1642 CE), *Ash'at al-Lam'āt Sharḥ Mishkāt al-Maṣābīḥ*. Sukkur, Pakistan: Maktaba Nūriyya Riḍwiyya, 1976 CE.

'Abd al-Razzāq al-San'ānī, Abū Bakr 'Abd al-Razzāq b. Hammām (126-211 AH/744-826 CE), *al-Muṣannaf*. Beirut: al-Maktab al-Islāmī, 1403 AH.

'Abd Allāh b. Aḥmad, Ibn Muḥammad b. anbal al-Shaybānī (213-290 AH), *al-Sunna*. Dammam: Dār Ibn al-Qayyim, 1406 AH.

'Ajlūnī, Abū al-Fiḍā' Ismā'īl b. Muḥammad al-Jarāḥī al- (1087-1162 AH/1676-1749 CE), *Kashf al-Khifā'*. Beirut: Mu'assasa al-Risāla, 1405 AH/1985 CE.

Abū ʿAwāna, Yaʿqūb b. Isḥāq Ibrāhīm b. Zayd Nisāpūrī (230-316 AH/845-928 CE), *al-Musnad*. Beirut: Dār al-Maʿrifa, 1998 CE.

Quḍāʿī, Abū ʿAbd Allāh Muḥammad b. Salama (454 AH/1062 CE), *Musnad al-Shihāb*. Beirut: Muʾassasa al-Risāla, 1407 AH/1986 CE.

Kinānī, Aḥmad b. Abī Bakr b. Ismāʿīl al- (762-840 AH), *Miṣbāḥ al-Zujāja fī Zawāʾid Ibn Mājah*. Beirut: Dār al-ʿArabiyya, 1403 AH.

Ibn Mājah, Abū ʿAbd Allāh Muḥammad b. Yazīd al-Qazwīnī (209-273 AH/824-887 CE), *al-Sunan*. Beirut: Dār al-Fikr & Dār Iḥyāʾ al-Turāth al-ʿArabī, 1395 AH/1975 CE & Dār al-Kutub al-ʿIlmiyya, 1419 AH/1998 CE.

Mālik, Ibn Anas b. Mālik (93-179 AH/716-795 CE), *al-Muwaṭṭaʾ*. Beirut: Dār Iḥyāʾ al-Turāth al-ʿArabī, 1406 AH/1985 CE.

Ibn Mubārak, Abū ʿAbd Allāh ʿAbd al-Raḥmān ʿAbd Allāh b. Wāḍ iḥ al-Marwazī (118-181 AH/736-798 CE), *al-Musnad*. Riyadh: Maktaba al-Maʿārif, 1408 AH.

Marwazī, Abū Bakr Aḥmad b. ʿAlī b. Saʿīd Umawī, (202-296 AH). *Musnad Abī Bakr al-Ṣiddīq*. Beirut: al-Maktab al-Islāmī.

Muslim, Abū al- usayn Ibn al- ajjāj b. Muslim al-Qushayrī Nisāpūrī (206-261 AH/821-875 CE), *al-Ṣaḥīḥ*, Beirut: Dār Iḥyāʾ al-Turāth al-ʿArabī.

Maqdisī, Abū ʿAbd Allāh Muḥammad b. ʿAbd Allāh (569-643 AH/1173-1245 CE), *al-Aḥādīth al-Mukhtāra*. Mecca: Maktaba al-Nahḍa al- adītha, 1410 AH/1990 CE.

Mundhirī, Abū Muḥammad ʿAbd al-ʿAzīz ʿAbd al-Qawī al- (581-658 AH/1185-1258 CE), *al-Targhīb wa al-Tarhīb*. Beirut: Dār al-Kutub al-ʿIlmiyya, 1417 AH.

Nasāʾī, Abū ʿAbd al-Raḥmān Aḥmad b. Shuʿayb b. ʿAlī (215-303 AH/830-915 CE), *al-Sunan*. Beirut Lebanon: Dār al-Kutub al-ʿIlmiyya, 1416 AH/1995 CE & 1411 AH/1991 CE & alab, Syria: Maktab al-Maṭbūʿāt al-Islāmiyyah, 1406 AH/1986 CE & Karachi, Pakistan: Qadīmī Kutab Khāna & Beirut: Dār al-Kutub al-ʿIlmiyya., 1411 AH/1991 CE.

Abū Nuʿaym, Aḥmad b. ʿAbd Allāh b. Aḥmad b. Isḥāq (336-430 AH/948-1038 CE), *Musnad Imām Abī anīfa*. Riyadh: Maktaba al-Kawthar, 1415 AH.

—. *al-Musnad al-Mustakhraj ʿalā Ṣaḥīḥ Muslim*. Beirut: Dār a Kutub al-ʿIlmiyyah, 1996 CE.

Nuʿaym b. ammād, Abū ʿAbd Allāh al-Marwazī (288 AH) *a Fitan*. Cairo: Muʾassasa al-Kutub al-Thaqāfiyya, 1408 AH.

Haythamī, Nūr al-Dīn Abū al- asan b. Abī Bakr b. Sulaymā (735-807 AH/1335-1405 CE), *Majmaʿ al-Zawāʾid wa Manbaʿ a Fawāʾid*. Cairo: Dār al-Rayyān li al-Turāth & Beirut: Dār a Kitāb al-ʿArabī, 1407 AH/1987 CE.

—. *Mawārid al-Ẓamān ilā Zawāʾid Ibn ibbān*. Beirut & Damascus: Dār al-Thaqāfa li ʿArabiyya, 1411 AH/1990 C

Abū Yaʿlā, Aḥmad b. ʿAlī b. Muthannā b. Yaḥyā (210-307 AH/82 919 CE), *al-Musnad*. Damascus: Dār al-Maʾmūn li Turāth, 140 AH/1984 CE.

—. *al-Muʿjam*. Faisalabad, Pakistan: Idāra al-ʿUlūm al-Athariyy 1408 AH.

Hadith Commentaries

Ibn Athīr, Abū al-Saʿādāt Mubārak b. Muḥammad b. Muḥamma b. ʿAbd al-Karīm (544-606 AH/1149-1210 CE), *Manāl al-Ṭāl fī Sharḥ Ṭiwāl al-Gharāʾib*. Beirut, Damascus: Dār al-Maʾmū li al-Turāth.

Anwar Shāh Kashmīrī, Muḥammad Anwar b. Muḥamma Muʿaẓẓam Shāh Kashmīrī (1292-1352 AH), *Fayḍ al-Bārī ʿa Ṣaḥīḥ al-Bukhārī*. Beirut: Dār al-Fikr, 1399 AH/1979 CE.

Ibn Baṭṭāl, Abū asan ʿAlī b. Khalaf b. ʿAbd al-Malik al-Qurṭub (449 AH), *Sharḥ Ṣaḥīḥ al-Bukhārī*. Riyadh: Maktaba al-Rush 1423 AH/2003 CE.

—. *Takmila al-Majmūʿ Sharḥ al-Muhadhdhab li al-Imām Yūs al-Shīrāzī*. Beirut: Dār al-Kutub al-ʿIlmiyya.

Ibn ajar al-ʿAsqalānī, Abū al-Faḍl Aḥmad b. ʿAlī b. ajar a Kinānī al-Shāfiʿī (773-852 AH/1372-1449 CE), *Fatḥ al-Bārī Shar Ṣaḥīḥ al-Bukhārī*. Beirut: Dār al-Maʿrifa, 1379 CE & Lahor Pakistan: Dār Nashr al-Kutub al-Islāmiyya, 1401 AH/1981 C

—. *Hādī al-Sārī Muqaddima Fatḥ al-Bārī*. Beirut: Dār al-Maʿrif

Ibn Rajab al- anbalī, Abū al-Faraj ʿAbd al-Raḥmān b. Aḥma

(736-795 AH), *Sharḥ adīth Labbayk*. Mecca: Dār ʿĀlam al-Fawāʾid, 1417 AH.

Shabbīr Aḥmad ʿUthmānī, Shabbīr Aḥmad b. Faḍl al-Raḥmān al-Hindī (1305-1369 AH/1889-1949 CE). *Fatḥ al-Mulhim bi Sharḥ Ṣaḥīḥ al-Imām al-Muslim*. Damascus: Dār al-Qalam, 1427 AH/2002 CE.

Shawkānī, Muḥammad b. ʿAlī b. Muḥammad (1173-1250 AH/1760-1834 CE), *Nayl al-Awṭār Sharḥ Muntaqā al-Akhbār*. Beirut: Dār al-Fikr, 1402 AH/1982 CE.

Abū al-ʿAbbās al-Qurṭubī, Abū al-ʿAbbās Aḥmad b. ʿUmar b. Ibrāhīm (578-656 AH). *al-Mufham li mā Ashkala min Talkhīṣ Kitāb Muslim*. Beirut, Damascus: Dār Ibn Kathīr, 1420 AH/1999 CE.

Ibn ʿAbd al-Barr, Abū ʿUmar Yūsuf b. ʿAbd Allāh b. Muḥammad (368-463 AH/979-1071 CE), *al-Istidhkār*. Beirut: Dār al-Kutub al-ʿIlmiyya, 2000 CE.

—. *al-Tamhīd*. Morocco: Wizārāt ʿUmūm al-Awqāf wa al-Shuʾūn al-Islāmiyya, 1387 AH.

ʿAynī, Badr al-Dīn Abū Muḥammad Maḥmūd al- (762-855 AH/1361-1451 CE), *ʿUmda al-Qārī Sharḥ Ṣaḥīḥ al-Bukhārī*. Beirut: Dār al-Fikr, 1399 AH/1979 CE & Dār Iḥyāʾ al-Turāth al-ʿArabī.

Qāḍī ʿIyāḍ, Abū al-Faḍl ʿIyāḍ b. Mūsā b. ʿIyāḍ (476-544 AH/1083-1149 CE), *Ikmāl al-Muʿlim bi Fawāʾid Muslim*. Beirut: Dār al-Wafā li Ṭabāʿa wa al-Nashr wa al-Tawzīʿ, 1419 AH/1998 CE.

Qastalānī, Abū al-ʿAbbās Aḥmad b. Muḥammad b. Abī Bakr al- (851-923 AH/1448-1517 CE), *Irshād al-Sārī li Sharḥ Ṣaḥīḥ al-Bukhārī*. Beirut: Dār al-Fikr.

Mubārakpūrī, Abū al-ʿAlā Muḥammad Abd al-Raḥmān b. ʿAbd al-Raḥīm al- (1283-1353 AH), *Tuḥfa al-Aḥwadhī fī Sharḥ Jāmiʿ al-Tirmidhī*. Beirut: Dār al-Kutub al-ʿIlmiyya.

Mullā ʿAlī al-Qārī, Nūr al-Dīn b. Sulṭān Muḥammad al-Harawī al- anafī (1014 AH/1606 CE), *Mirqāt al-Mafātīḥ Sharḥ Mishkāt al-Maṣābīḥ*. Beirut: Dār al-Kutub al-ʿIlmiyya, 1422 AH/2001 CE & Multān, Pakistan: Maktaba Imdādiyya.

Manāwī, ʿAbd al-Raʾūf b. Tāj al-ʿĀrifīn b. ʿAlī b. Zayn al-ʿĀbidīn al- (952-1031 AH/1545-1621 CE), *al-Taysīr bi Sharḥ al-Jāmiʿ al-Saghīr*. Riyadh: Maktaba al-Imām Shāfiʿī, 1408 AH/1988 CE.

—. *Fayḍ al-Qadīr Sharḥ al-Jāmiʿ al-Saghīr*. Egypt: Maktaba Tijāriyya Kubrā, 1356 AH.

Nawawī, Abū Zakariyyā Yaḥyā b. Sharaf al- (631-677 AH/1233-1278 CE), *Sharḥ al-Nawawī ʿalā Ṣaḥīḥ Muslim*. Beirut: Dār Iḥyāʾ al-Turāth, 1392 AH & Karachi, Pakistan: Qadīmī Kutub Khāna, 1378 AH/1956 CE.

Biography of Hadith Narrators

Bukhārī, Abū ʿAbd Allāh Muḥammad b. Ismāʿīl al- (194-256 AH/810-870 CE), *al-Tārīkh al-Kabīr*. Beirut: Dār al-Kutub al-ʿIlmiyya, 1422 AH/2001 CE.

Ibn ibbān, Abū Hātim Muḥammad b. ibbān b. Aḥmad b. ibbān (270-354 AH/884-965 CE), *al-Thiqāt*. Beruit: Dār al-Fikr, 1395 AH/1975 CE.

Ibn ajar al-ʿAsqalānī, Aḥmad b. ʿAlī b. Muḥammad (773-852 AH/1372-1449 CE), *al-Iṣāba fī Tamyīz al-Ṣaḥāba*. Beirut: Dār al-Jīl, 1412 AH.

—. *Tahdhīb al-Tahdhīb*, Beirut: Dār al-Fikr, 1404 AH.

—. *Lisān al-Mīzān*, Beirut: Muʾassasa al-ʿIlmī al-Maṭbūʿāt, 1406 AH/1986 CE.

Khaṭīb al-Baghdādī, Abū Bakr Aḥmad b. ʿAlī (392-463 AH/1002-1071 CE), *al-Muttafiq wa al-Muftariq*. Damascus: Dār al-Qādrī li Ṭabāʿa wa al-Nashr wa al-Tawzīʿ, 1417 AH/1997 CE.

Dhahabī, Shams al-Dīn Muḥammad b. Aḥmad b. ʿUthmān al- (673-748 AH/1274-1348 CE), *Tārīkh al-Islām wa Wafayāt al-Mashāhir wa al-Aʿlām*. Beirut: Dār al-Kitāb al-ʿArabī, 1407 AH/1987 CE.

—. *Siyar Aʿlām al-Nubalāʾ*, Beirut: Muʾassāsa al-Risāla, 1413 AH.

Shaʿrānī, ʿAbd al-Wahhāb b. Aḥmad b. ʿAlī al- (898-973 AH/1493-1665 CE), *al-Ṭabaqāt al-Kubrā*. Beirut: al-Maʿrifa, 1426 AH/2005 CE.

Ibn ʿAdī, ʿAbd Allāh b. ʿAdī b. ʿAbd Allāh (277-365 AH), *al-Kāmil fī Ḍuʿafāʾ al-Rijāl*. Beirut: Dār al-Fikr, 1409 AH/1988 CE.

Mizzī, Abū Hajjāj Yūsuf b. Zakī, (654-742 AH/1256-1341 CE), *Tahdhīb al-Kamāl*. Beirut: Mu'assasa al-Risāla, 1400 AH/ 1980 CE.

Ibn Abī Ya'lā, Abū al- usayn Muḥammad b. Muḥammad (521 AH). *Ṭabaqāt al- anābila*. Beirut: Dār al-Ma'rifa.

Science of Hadith

Sam'ānī, Abū Sa'īd 'Abd al-Karīm b. Muḥammad b. Manṣūr Tamīmī al- (562 AH), *Adab al-Imlā' wa al-Istimlā'*. Beirut: Dār al-Kutub al-'Ilmiyya, 1401 AH/1981 CE.

Suyūṭī, Jalāl al-Dīn Abū al-Faḍl 'Abd al-Raḥmān al- (849-911 AH/1445-1505 CE), *Tadrīb al-Rāwī fī Sharḥ Taqrīb al-Nawāwī*. Riyadh: Maktaba al-Riyāḍ al- adītha.

—. *Miftāḥ al-Janna*. Medina: al-Jāmi'a al-Islāmiyya, 1399 CE.

Jurisprudence

Aḥmad Riḍā, Muḥaddith al-Hind Ibn Naqī 'Alī Khān al-Qādrī (1272-1340 AH/1852-1921 CE), *al-'Aṭāyā al-Nabawiyya fī al-Fatāwā al-Riḍawiyya*. Lahore, Pakistan: Razā Foundation, Jāmi'a Niẓāmiyya Riḍawiyya, 1991 CE.

I'zāz 'Alī. *āshiya 'alā Kanz al-Daqā'iq*.

Bujayrimī, Sulaymān b. 'Umar b. Muḥammad al- (1221 AH). *āshiya al-Bujayrimī 'alā Sharḥ Minhāj al-Ṭullāb*. Diyarbakir, Turkey: al-Maktaba al-Islāmiyya.

Ibn Bazzāz, Muḥammad b. Muḥammad b. Shihāb al-Kurdarī (827 AH), *al-Fatāwā al-Bazzāziyya 'alā Hāmish al-Fatāwā al-'Ālamkīriyya*. Beirut: 1393 AH/1973 CE.

Bahūtī, Manṣūr b. Yūnus b. Idrīs al- (1051 AH). *Kashshāf al-Qinā' 'an Matn al-Iqnā'*. Beirut: Dār al-Fikr, 1402 AH & Cairo.

Ibn Taymiyya, Abū al-'Abbās Aḥmad b. 'Abd al- alīm (661-728 AH/1263-1328 CE), *al-Muḥarrar fī al-Fiqh 'alā Madhhab al-Imām Aḥmad b. anbal*. Riyadh: Maktaba al-Ma'ārif, 1404 AH.

—. *Majmūʿ al-Fatāwā*. Beirut: Dār al-Fikr, 1406 AH & Maktaba Ibn Taymiyya.

Ibn Juzay, Muḥammad b. Aḥmad b. Jazay al-Kalbī al-Gharnāṭī (693-741 AH). *al-Qawānīn al-Fiqhiyya*.

Ibn azm, Abū Muḥammad ʿAlī b. Aḥmad (383-456 AH/993-1064 CE). *al-Muḥallā*. Beirut: Dār al-Āfāq al-Jadīda.

aṣkafī, ʿAlāʾ al-Dīn Muḥammad b. ʿAlī b. Muḥammad anafī al- (1088 AH/1677 CE). *al-Durr al-Mukhtār ʿalā Hāmish al-Radd al-Muḥtār*. Beirut: Dār al-Fikr, 1385 AH.

Khiraqī, Abū al-Qāsim ʿUmar b. usayn (334 AH). *Mukhtaṣar al-Khiraqī min Masāʾil al-Imām Aḥmad b. anbal*. Beirut: al-Maktab al-Islāmī, 1403 AH.

Dārdīr, Abū al-Barakāt Aḥmad al-, *al-Sharḥ al-Kabīr*. Beirut: Dār al-Fikr.

Dasūqī, Muḥammad b. Aḥmad b. ʿUrfa al-Mālikī al- (1230 AH/1815 CE), *āshiya ʿalā al-Sharḥ al-Kabīr*. Beirut: Dār al-Fikr.

Ibn Rushd, Abū Walīd Muḥammad b. Aḥmad (595 AH), *Bidāya al-Mujtahid*. Beirut: Dār al-Fikr.

Zakariyyā al-Anṣārī, Abū Yaḥyā Zakariyyā b. Muḥammad b. Aḥmad (823-926 AH), *Minhāj al-Ṭullāb*. Beirut: Dār al-Kutub al-ʿIlmiyya, 1418 AH.

Ibn Zanjawayh, amīd (251 AH), *Kitāb al-Amwāl*. Riyadh: Markaz al-Malak Fayṣal li Buhūth wa al-Dirāsāt al-Islāmiyya, 1406 AH/1986 CE.

Zaylaʿī, Fakhr al-Dīn ʿUthmān b. ʿAlī (743 AH). *Tabyīn al- aqāʾiq Sharḥ Kanz al-Daqāʾiq*. Cairo: Dār al-Kutub al-Islāmī, 1313 AH.

Sarakhsī, Shams al-Aʾimma Muḥammad b. Aḥmad b. Abī Sahl al- (483 AH). *Sharḥ Kitāb al-Siyar al-Kabīr*. Beirut: Dār al-Kutub al-ʿIlmiyya, 1417 AH/1997 CE.

—. *Kitāb al-Mabsūṭ*. Beirut: Dār al-Maʿrifa, 1398 AH/1978 CE.

Shāṭibī, Abū Isḥāq Ibrāhīm b. Mūsā (790 AH), al-Iʿtiṣām. Egypt: al-Maktaba al-Tijāriyya.

—. *al-Muwāfaqāt fī Uṣūl al-Sharīʿa*. Beirut: Dār al-Maʿrifa, 1393 AH.

hāfiʿī, Abū ʿAbd Allāh Muḥammad b. Idrīs al- (150-204 AH/767-819 CE), *al-Umm*. Beirut: Dār al-Maʿrifa, 1393 AH.

hirbīnī, Muḥammad Khaṭīb al- (977 AH), *al-Iqnāʿ fī al Alfāẓ Abī Shujāʿ*. Beirut: Dār al-Fikr, 1415AH.

—. *Mughnī al-Muḥtāj ilā Maʿrifa Maʿānī Alfāẓ al-Minhāj*. Beirut: Dār Iḥyāʾ al-Turāth al-ʿArabī, 1402 AH/1982 CE.

hawkānī, Muḥammad b. ʿAlī b. Muḥammad al- (1173-1250 AH/1760-1834 CE), *al-Sayl al-Jarrār*. Beirut: Dār al-Kutub al-ʿIlmiyya, 1405 AH.

—. *Fatḥ al-Qadīr*. Beirut: Dār al-Fikr, 1402 AH/1982 CE.

—. *Nayl al-Awṭār Sharḥ Muntaqā al-Akhbār*. Beirut: Dār al-Jīl, 1973 CE.

haybānī, Abū ʿAbd Allāh Muḥammad b. asan b. Farqad al- (132-189 AH), *Kitāb al- ujja ʿalā Ahl al-Madīna*. Beirut: ʿĀlam al-Kutub, 1403 CE.

—. *al-Mabsūṭ*. Karachi, Pakistan: Idāra al-Qurʾān wa ʿUlūm al-Islāmiyya.

bn Dawyān, Ibrāhīm b. Muḥammad b. Sālim (1275-1353 AH), *Manār al-Sabīl*. Riyadh: Maktaba al-Maʿārif, 1405 AH.

Ṭabrasī, Abū ʿAlī Faḍl b. asan al- (548 AH), *al-Muʿtalif min al-Mukhtalif bayna Aʾimma al-Salaf*. Iran: Maṭbaʿa Sayyid al-Shuhadā, 1410 AH.

Ibn ʿĀbidīn al-Shāmī, Muḥammad b. Muḥammad Amīn (1244-1306 AH), *Radd al-Muḥtār ʿalā al-Durr al-Mukhtār*. Beirut: Dār al-Fikr, 1412 AH/1992 ce & Quetta, Pakistan: Maktaba Mājidiyya, 1399 AH.

Ibn Abī ʿĀṣim, Abū Bakr ʿAmr b. ʿĀṣim Ḍaḥḥāk al-Shaybānī (206-287 AH/822-900 CE), *al-Diyāt*. Karachi, Pakistan: Idāra al-Qurʾān wa al-ʿUlūm, 1407 AH.

Ibn ʿAbd al-Barr, Abū ʿUmar Yūsuf b. ʿAbd Allāh (368-463 AH/979-1071 CE), *al-Kāfī fī Fiqh Ahl al-Madīna*. Beirut: Dār al-Kutub al-ʿIlmiyya, 1407 AH.

ʿArūsī, Dr. Muḥammad Tāj Shaykh ʿAbd al-Raḥmān, *Fiqh al-Jihād wa al-ʿAlāqāt al-Dawliyya fī al-Islām*. Islamabad, Pakistan: Instant Print System, 1999 CE.

Ibn ʿAlāʾ, ʿĀlim b. al-ʿUlāʾ al-Anṣārī al-Dahlawī al- anafī (78
AH), *al-Fatāwā al-Tātārkhāniyya fī al-Fiqh al- anafī*. Beirut
Dār al-Kutub al-ʿIlmiyya, 2005 CE.

ʿAbd al-Raḥmān al-Jazīrī, *al-Fiqh ʿalā al-Madhāhib al-Arbaʿa*
Beirut: Dār Iḥyāʾ al-Turāth al-ʿArabī.

Abū ʿUbayd, Qāsim b. Salām (224 AH), *Kitāb al-Amwāl*. Beirut
Dār al-Fikr, 1408 AH.

ʿAlī Aḥmad al-Jarjāwī, *ikma al-Tashrīʿ wa Falsafatuhu*.

ʿAynī, Badr al-Dīn Abū Muḥammad Maḥmūd (762-855 AH/1361-1451 CE), *al-Bināya Sharḥ al-Hidāya*. Beirut: Dār al-Kutub al-ʿIlmiyya, 1420 AH/2000 CE.

—. *al-Fatāwā al-Hindiyya*. Beirut: Dār al-Fikr, 1411 AH/1991 CE & Dār al-Maʿrifa, 1393 AH/1973 CE.

Fawzān, Ṣāliḥ b. Fawzān b. ʿAbd Allāh, *al-Jihād wa Ḍawābiṭa al-Sharʿiyya*.

Fahd al- uṣayn, *al-Fatāwā al-Sharʿiyya fī al-Qaḍāyā al-ʿAṣariyya*.

Qāḍī Khān, Fakhr al-Dīn Abū al-Maḥāsin asan b. Manṣūr (592 AH). *Fatāwā Qāḍī Khān fī Madhhab al-Imām al-ʿAzam Abī anīfa al-Nuʿmān*. Beirut: Dār al-Kutub al-ʿIlmiyya.

Ibn Qudāma, Abū Muḥammad ʿAbd Allāh b. Aḥmad (541-620 AH), *al-Kāfī fī Fiqh Ibn anbal*. Beirut: al-Maktab al-Islāmī.

—. *al-Mughnī fī Fiqh al-Imām Aḥmad b. anbal al-Shaybānī*. Beirut: Dār al-Fikr.

—. *al-Mughnī ʿalā Mukhtaṣar al-Khiraqī*. Beirut: Dār al-Kutub al-ʿIlmiyya.

Ibn Qudāma, ʿAbd al-Raḥmān b. Muḥammad b. Aḥmad al-Maqdisī al- anbalī (682 AH), *al-Sharḥ al-Kabīr ʿala Matn al-Muqnaʿ*. Beirut: Dār al-Kutub al-ʿIlmiyya.

Qarāfī, Abū al-ʿAbbās Shihāb al-Dīn Aḥmad b. Idrīs al-Mālikī al-, (684 AH), *al-Dhakhīra fī Fiqh al-Mālikī,* Beirut: Dār al-Gharb, 1994 CE.

—. *Anwār al-Burūq fī Anwāʿ al-Furūq*. Beirut: Dār al-Kutub al-ʿIlmiyya, 1418 AH/1998 CE.

Ibn al-Qayyim, Abū ʿAbd Allāh Muḥammad b. Abī Bakr Ayyūb al-Zarʿī (691-751 AH), *Aḥkām Ahl al-Dhimma*. Beirut: Dār Ibn azm, 1418 AH/1997 CE.

Kāsānī, ʿAlāʾ al-Dīn al- (587 AH), *Badāʾiʿ al-Ṣanāʾiʿ fī Tartīb al-Sharāʾiʿ*. Beirut: Dār al-Kitāb al-ʿArabī, 1982 CE.

Mālik, Ibn Anas b. Mālik b. Abī ʿĀmir (93-179 AH/712-795 CE), *al-Mudawwana al-Kubrā*. Cairo: Dār Ṣādir & Cairo: Dār al-adīth.

Māwardī, Abū al- asan ʿAlāʾ al-Dīn ʿAlī b. Sulaymān al- (817-885 AH), *al-Aḥkām al-Sulṭāniyya*. Beirut: Dār al-Kutub al-ʿIlmiyya, 1398 AH/1978 CE.

—. *al-Iqnāʿ fī al-Fiqh al-Shāfiʿī*.

Marʿī, Ibn Yūsuf b. Abī Bakr b. Aḥmad Kirmī al-Maqdisī al-anbalī al- (1033 AH). *Ghāya al-Muntahā*.

Murghīnānī, Burhān al-Dīn Abū al- asan ʿAlī b. Abī Bakr, *al-Hidāya Sharḥ Bidāya al-Mubtadi*. Beirut: Dār Arqam, 1997 CE & al-Maktaba al-Islāmiyya & Karachi, Pakistan: Muḥammad ʿAlī Kārkhāna Islāmī Kutub.

Marwazī, Abū ʿAbd Allāh Muḥammad b. Naṣr b. al- ajjāj al- (202-294 AH). *Taʿẓīm Qadr al-Ṣalāh*. Medina: Maktaba al-Dār, 1406 AH.

Muṣṭafā b. Saʿd, al-Suyūṭī al-Ruhaybānī, *Maṭālib Ūlī al-Nuhā fī Sharḥ Ghāya al-Muntahā*. Damascus: al-Maktab al-Islāmī, 1961 CE.

Ibn Mufliḥ, Shams al-Dīn Muḥammad Abū ʿAbd Allāh Maqdisī al- anbalī (717-762 AH). *al-Furūʿ*. Beirut: Dār al-Kutub al-ʿIlmiyya, 1418 AH.

Ibn Mufliḥ, Abū Isḥāq Ibrāhīm b. Muḥammad b. ʿAbd Allāh al-anbalī (816-884 AH), *al-Mabdaʿ fī Sharḥ al-Maqnaʿ*. Beirut: al-Maktab al-Islāmī.

Makkī b. Abī Ṭālib al-Muqrī, Abū Muḥammad (437 AH), *al-Hidāya ilā Bulūgh al-Nihāya*. Shārja, UAE: University of Shārja.

Mullā ʿAlī al-Qārī, ʿAlī b. Sulṭān Muḥammad Nūr al-Dīn al-anafī (1014 AH/1606 CE), *Fatḥ Bāb al-ʿInāya*. Beirut: Dār Arqam, 1997 CE.

Nadhīr usayn, Sayyīd al-Dahlawī (1800-1903 CE), *Fatāwā Nadhīriyya*. Gujrānwāla, Pakistan: Maktaba al-Maʿārif al-Islāmiyya, 1409 AH/1988 CE.

Nasafī, Abū al-Barakāt ʿAbd Allāh b. Aḥmad b. Maḥmūd al- (710 AH). *Kanz al-Daqāʾiq*. Karachi: Idāra al-Qurʾān wa al-ʿUlūm

al-Islāmiyya.
Nafrāwī, Aḥmad b. Ghunaym b. Sālim al- (1126 AH), *al-Fawākih al-Dawānī*. Beirut: Dār al-Fikr, 1415 AH.
Ibn Nujaym, Zayn b. Ibrāhīm b. Muḥammad (926-970 AH), *al-Baḥr al-Rā'iq Sharḥ Kanz al-Daqā'iq*. Beirut: Dār al-Ma'rifa.
Nawawī, Abū Zakariyyā Muḥī al-Dīn Yaḥyā b. Sharaf al- (676 AH). *Rawḍa al-Ṭālibīn wa 'Umda al-Muftiyīn*. Beirut: al-Maktab al-Islāmī, 1405 AH.
—. *al-Majmū' Sharḥ al-Muhadhdhab li al-Imām Abū Isḥāq Ibrāhīm b. 'Alī b. Yūsuf al-Shīrāzī*. Beirut: Dār al-Kutub al-'Ilmiyya.
Ibn Hubayra, Wazīr Abū al-Muẓaffar 'Awn al-Dīn Yaḥyā al- anbalī (560 AH), *al-Ifṣāḥ 'an Ma'ānī al-Ṣiḥāḥ fī al-Fiqh 'alā al-Madhāhib al-Arb'a*.
Ibn Hummām, Kamāl al-Dīn Muḥammad b. 'Abd al-Wāḥid Sīwāsī al-Iskandarī (790-861 AH), *Fatḥ al-Qadīr Sharḥ al-Hidāya*. Quetta, Pakistan: Maktaba Rashīdiyya.
Yaḥyā b. Ādam, Abū Zakariyyā b. Sulaymān al-Qurashī (203 AH), *Kitāb al-Khirāj*. Lahore: al-Maktaba al-Islāmiyya, 1974 CE.
Abū Ya'lā al- anbalī, Muḥammad b. usayn b. Muḥammad b. Khalaf b. Aḥmad b. al-Farrā' (458 AH/1066 CE), *al-Mu'tamad fī Uṣūl al-Dīn*. Beirut: Dār al-Mashriq, 1974 CE.
Abū Yūsuf, Ya'qūb b. Ibrāhīm (182 AH), *Kitāb al-Khirāj*. Beirut: Dār al-Ma'rifa.

Prophetic Biography

Ibn Isḥāq, Muḥammad b. Isḥāq b. Yassār (85-151 AH), *al-Sīra al-Nabawiyya*. Ma'had al-Dirāsāt wa al-Abhāth li Ta'rīf.
Bayhaqī, Abū Bakr Aḥmad b. usayn al- (384-458 AH/994-1066 CE), *Dalā'il al-Nubuwwa*. Beirut: Dār al-Kutub al-'Ilmiyya, 1423 AH/2002 CE.
alabī, 'Alī b. Burhān al-Dīn al- (1404 AH), *al-Sīra al- alabiyya*. Beirut: Dār al-Ma'rifa, 1400 AH.
Zurqānī, Abū 'Abd Allāh Muḥammad b. 'Abd al-Bāqī al- (1055-1122 AH/1645-1710 CE), *Sharḥ Mawāhib al-Ladunniya*. Beirut:

Dār al-Kutub al-ʿIlmiyya, 1417 AH/1996 CE.

Ibn Saʿd, Abū ʿAbd Allāh Muḥammad (168-230 AH/784-845 CE), *al-Ṭabaqāt al-Kubrā*. Beirut: Dār Bayrūt li al-Ṭabāʿa wa al-Nashr, 1398 AH/1978 CE & Dār Ṣādir.

Suyūṭī, Jalāl al-Dīn Abū al-Faḍl b. Abī Bakr al- (849-911 AH/1445-1505 CE), *al-Shamāʾil al-Sharīfa*. Dār Ṭāʾir al-ʿIlm li al-Nashr wa al-Tawzīʿ.

Ṣāliḥī, Abū ʿAbd Allāh Muḥammad b. Yūsuf al- (942 AH/1534 CE), *Subul al-Hudā wa al-Rashād*. Beirut: Dār al-Kutub al-ʿIlmiyya, 1414 AH/1993 CE.

Ṭabarī, Abū Jaʿfar Aḥmad b. ʿAbd Allāh al- (615-694 AH/1218-1295 CE), *al-Riyāḍ al-Naḍira fī Manāqib al-ʿAshra*. Beirut: Dār al-Gharb al-Islāmī, 1996 CE.

Qāḍī ʿIyāḍ, Abū al-Faḍl ʿIyāḍ b. Mūsā b. ʿIyāḍ (476-544 AH/1083-1149 CE), *al-Shifā bi Taʿrīf uqūq al-Muṣṭafā* ﷺ. Beirut: Dār al-Kitāb al-ʿArabī & Multan, Pakistan: ʿ Abd al-Tawwāb Academy.

Qasṭalānī, Abū al-ʿAbbās Aḥmad b. Muḥammad al- (851-923 AH/1448-1517 CE), *al-Mawāhib al-Ladunniya bi al-Minaḥ al-Muḥammadiyya*. Beirut: al-Maktab al-Islāmī, 1412 AH/1991 CE.

Ibn Qayyim, Abū ʿAbd Allāh Muḥammad b. Abī Bakr Ayyūb al-Zarʿī, (691-751 AH), *Zād al-Maʿād fī Hadya Khayr al-ʿIbād*. Beirut: Muʾassasa al-Risāla, 1407 CE/1986 CE & Kuwait, Maktaba al-Manār al-Islāmiyya, 1986 CE.

Ibn Kathīr, Abū al-Fiḍāʾ Ismāʿīl b. ʿUmar b. Kathīr (701-774 AH/1301-1376 CE), *al-Sīra al-Nabawiyya*. Beirut: Dār al-Maʿrifa.

Kalāʿī, Abū al-Rabīʿ Sulaymān b. Mūsā al-Andalūsī al- (565-634 AH), *al-Iktifāʾ fī Maghāzī Rasūl Allāh* ﷺ *wa al-Thalātha al-Khulafāʾ*. Beirut: Maktaba al-Hilāl, 1387 AH/1968 CE.

Abū Nuʿaym, Aḥmad b. ʿAbd Allāh b. Aḥmad (336-430 AH/948-1038 CE), *Dalāʾil al-Nubuwwa*. Hyderabad, India: Majlis Dāʾira Maʿārif ʿUthmāniyya, 1369 AH/1950 CE.

Ibn Hishām, Abū Muḥammad ʿAbd al-Malik Hishām al- imyarī (213 AH/828 CE), *al-Sīra al-Nabawiyya*. Beirut: Dār Ibn Kathīr, 1423 AH/2003 CE & Beirut: Dār al-Jīl, 1411 AH.

Theology

Ājurrī, Abū Bakr Muḥammad b. usayn b. ʿAbd Allāh al- (360 AH). *al-Sharīʿa.* Riyadh: Dār al-Waṭan, 1420 AH/1999 CE.

Bayhaqī, Abū Bakr Aḥmad b. usayn b. ʿAlī b. ʿAbd Allāh b. Mūsā (384-458 AH/994-1066 CE), *al-Iʿtiqād.* Beirut: Dār al-Āfāq, 1401 AH.

Ibn Taymiyya, Abū al-ʿAbbās Aḥmad b. ʿAbd al- alīm (661-728 AH/1263-1328 CE), *al-Sunna al-Nabawiyya.* Cairo: Muʾassasa Qurṭuba, 1406 AH & Beirut: Dār al-Kitāb al-ʿArabī, 1405 AH/1985 CE.

Abū anīfa, Nuʿmān b. Thābit (80-150 AH), *al-Fiqh al-Absaṭ (Majmūʿa al-ʿAqīda wa ʿIlm al-Kalām li Shaykh Zāhid al-Kawtharī).* Beirut: Dār al-Kutub al-ʿIlmiyya, 1425 AH/2004 CE.

Dhahabī, Abū ʿAbd Allāh Shams al-Dīn Muḥammad b. Aḥmad b. ʿUthmān (673-748 AH/1274-1348 CE), *al-Muntaqā min Minhāj al-Iʿtidāl.*

Ṭaḥāwī, Abū Jaʿfar Aḥmad b. Muḥammad al- (229-321 AH/853-933 CE), *al-ʿAqīda al-Ṭaḥāwiyya.* Beirut: Dār al-Kutub al-ʿIlmiyya, 1399 CE.

Ibn Abī al-ʿIzz, Ṣadr al-Dīn Muḥammad b. ʿAlāʾ al-Dīn (731-792 AH), *Sharḥ al-ʿAqīda al-Ṭaḥāwiyya.* Beirut: al-Maktab al-Islāmī, 1408 AH/1988 CE.

ʿAbd al-ʿAzīz, Muḥaddith al-Dahlawī (1229 AH). *Tuḥfa Ithnā ʿAshariyya.* Istanbul, Turkey: Maktaba al- aqīqa, 1408 AH/1988 CE.

ʿAbd al-Qādir al-Baghdādī, Abū Manṣūr b. Ṭāhir b. Muḥammad (429 AH/1037 CE), *al-Farq bayna al-Firāq wa Bayān al-Firqa al-Nājiya.* Beirut: Dār al-Āfāq al-Jadīda, 1977 CE.

Ibn Minda, Abū ʿAbd Allāh Muḥammad b. Isḥāq b. Yaḥyā (310-395 AH/922-1005 CE), *al-Īmān.* Beirut: Muʾassasa al-Risāla, 1406 AH.

Abū Manṣūr al-Maturīdī, Muḥammad b. Muḥammad b. Manṣūr al- anafī (333 AH). *Taʾwilāt Ahl al-Sunna.* Beirut: Dār al-Kutub al-ʿIlmiyya.

Sufism

Bayhaqī, Abū Bakr Aḥmad b. usayn b. ʿAlī b. ʿAbd Allāh b. Mūsā al- (384-458 AH/994–1066 CE), *al-Zuhd al-Kabīr*. Beirut: Muʾassasa al-Kutub al-Thaqāfiyya, 1996 CE.

Tamām al-Rāzī, Abū Qāsim Tamām b. Muḥammad al-Rāzī (330-414 AH), *al-Fawāʾid*. Riyadh: Maktaba al-Rashīd, 1412 AH.

Ibn al-Jawzī, Abū al-Faraj ʿAbd al-Raḥmān b. ʿAlī b. Muḥammad b. ʿAlī b. ʿUbayd Allāh (510-579 AH/1116-1201 CE), *Ṣifa al-Ṣafwa*. Beirut: Dār al-Kutub al-ʿIlmiyya, 1409 AH/1989 CE.

—. *Dhamm al-Hawā*.

Ibn ajar al-Haytamī, Abū al-ʿAbbās Aḥmad b. Muḥammad (909-973 AH/1503-1566 CE), *al-Zawājir*. Lebanon: al-Maktaba al-ʿAṣariyya, 1420 AH/1999 CE.

Ibn ayyān, Abū Muḥammad ʿAbd Allāh b. Muḥammad b. Jaʿfar b. ibbān al-Aṣbahānī (274-369 AH). *al-Tawbīkh wa al-Tanbīh*. Cairo: Maktaba al-Furqān.

Ibn Abī al-Dunyā, Abū Bakr ʿAbd Allāh b. Muḥammad b. ʿUbayd b. Sufyān Qays al-Qurashī (208-281 AH), *al-Ishrāf fī Manāzil al-Ashrāf*. Riyadh: Maktaba al-Rashīd, 1411 AH/1990 CE.

—. *al-Ahwāl*. Egypt: Maktaba Āl Yāsir, 1413 AH/1993 CE.

—. *al-Marḍ wa al-Kaffārāt*. Bombay, India. Dār al-Salafiyya, 1411 AH/1991 CE.

Dhahabī, Shams al-Dīn Muḥammad b. Aḥmad b. ʿUthmān al- (673-748 AH/1274-1348 CE), *al-Kabāʾir*. Beirut: Dār al-Nadwa al-Jadīda.

Rifāʿī, Aḥmad al-Rifāʿī al- usaynī al- (512-578 AH), *al-Burhān al-Muʾayyid*. Lebanon: Dār al-Kutub al-Nafīs, 1408 AH.

Ibn Surāyā, Muḥammad b. Muḥammad ʿAlī b. Hammām b. Rājī Allāh b. Dāwūd (677-745 AH), *Salāḥ al-Muʾmin fī al-Duʿāʾ*. Beirut: Dār Ibn Kathīr, 1414 AH/1993 CE.

Ibn Sirrī, Hinād b. Sirrī al-Kūfī (152-243 AH), *al-Zuhd*. Kuwait: Dār al-Khulafāʾ li al-Kitāb al-Islāmī, 1406 AH.

Ibn al-Sunnī, Aḥmad b. Muḥammad Dīnawrī (284-364 AH). *ʿAmal al-Yawm wa al-Layla*. Beirut: Dār Ibn azm, 1425 AH/2004 CE.

Abū al-Shaykh, Muḥammad b. usayn al-Birjānī (238 AH), *al-Karam wa al-Jūd wa Sakhā' al-Nafūs*. Beirut: Dār Ibn azm, 1412 AH.

Ṭabarānī, Abū al-Qāsim Sulaymān b. Aḥmad al- (260-360 AH/873-971 CE), *Kitāb al-Du'ā'*. Beirut: Dār al-Kutub al-'Ilmiyya, 1421 AH/2001 CE.

Qushayrī, Abū al-Qāsim 'Abd al-Karīm b. Hawāzan al-Nīshāpūrī al-, (376-476 AH/986-1073 CE), *al-Risāla*. Beirut: Dār al-Jīl & Dār al-Kutub al-'Ilmiyya, 1426 AH/2005 CE.

Ibn al-Qayyim, Abū 'Abd Allāh Muḥammad b. Abī Bakr Ayyūb al-Zar'ī (691-751 AH), *Miftāḥ Dār al-Sa'āda*. Beirut: Dār al-Kutub al-'Ilmiyya.

Ibn Mubārak, Abū 'Abd al-Raḥmān 'Abd Allāh b. Waḍiḥ al-Marwazī (118-181 AH/736-798 CE), *Kitāb al-Zuhd*. Beirut: Dār al-Kutub al-'Ilmiyya, 1425 AH/2004 CE.

Marwazī, Abū 'Abd Allāh usayn b. asan b. al- arb al- (202-294 AH), *al-Birr wa al-Ṣila*. Riyadh: Dār al-Waṭan, 1419 AH.

Maqdisī, Abū 'Abd Allāh Muḥammad b. 'Abd Allāh al- (569-643 AH/1173-1245 CE), *Faḍā'il al-A'māl*. Cairo: Dār al-Ghad al-'Arabī.

Abū Nu'aym, Aḥmad b. 'Abd Allāh b. Aḥmad b. Isḥāq (336-430 AH/948-1038 CE), *ilya al-Awliyā' wa al-Ṭabaqāt al-Aṣfiyā'*. Beirut: Dār al-Kitāb al-'Arabī, 1405 AH/1985 CE & 1400 AH/1980 CE & Dār al-Kutub al-'Ilmiyya, 1423 AH/2002 CE.

—. *Kitāb al-Arba'īn 'alā Madhhab al-Mutaḥaqqiqīn min al-Ṣūfiyya*. Beirut: Ibn azm, 1414 AH/1993 CE.

Nawawī, Abū Zakariyyā Yaḥyā b. Sharaf al- (631-677 AH/1233-1278 CE), *al-Adhkār min Kalām Sayyid al-Abrār*. Beirut: al-Maktaba al-'Aṣariyya, 1423 AH/2003 CE.

—. *Riyāḍ al-Ṣāliḥīn min Kalām Sayyid al-Mursalīn*. Beirut: Dār al-Khayr, 1412 AH/1991 CE.

Hinād, Ibn Sirrī al-Kūfī (152-243 AH), *al-Zuhd*. Kuwait: Dār al-Khulafā' li al-Kitāb al-Islāmī, 1406 AH.

ISLAMIC ETHICS AND ETIQUETTES

Ibn al- ājj, Abū ʿAbd Allāh Muḥammad b. Muḥamamd b. Muḥammad ʿAbdārī al-Fāsī al-Mālikī (737 AH), *al-Madkhal*. Beirut: Dār al-Fikr, 1401 AH/1981 CE.

Kharāʾiṭī, Abū Bakr Muḥammad b. Jaʿfar b. Sahl (327 AH), *Makārim al-Akhlāq wa Maʿālīhā*. Damascus: Dār al-Fikr, 1986 CE.

Ibn Abī al-Dunyā, Abū Bakr ʿAbd Allāh b. Muḥammad b. ʿUbayd b. Sufyān Qays al-Qurashī (208-281 AH), *al-Ikwān*. Beirut: Dār al-Kutub al-ʿIlmiyya, 1409 AH/1988 CE.

—. *al- ilm*. Beirut: Muʾassasa al-Kutub al-Thaqāfiyya, 1413 AH.

—. *al-Ṣamt*. Beirut: Dār al-Kitāb al-ʿArabī, 1410 AH.

—. *al-ʿAql wa Faḍluhu*. Riyadh: Dār al-Rāba, 1409 AH.

—. *al-ʿAyyāl*. Saudi Arabia: Dār Ibn al-Qayyim, 1410 AH/1990 CE.

—. *Qaḍāʾ al- awāʾij*. Cairo: Maktaba al-Qurʾān.

—. *Madārāt al-Nās*. Beirut: Dār Ibn azm, 1412 AH/1990 CE.

—. *Makārim al-Akhlāq*. Cairo: Maktaba al-Qurʾān, 1411 AH/1990 CE.

Ibn Rajab al- anbalī, Abū al-Faraj ʿAbd al-Raḥmān b. Aḥmad (736-795 AH), *Jāmiʿ al-ʿUlūm wa al- ikam fī Sharḥ Khamsīn adīthan min Jawāmiʿ al-Kalim*. Beirut, Lebanon: Dār al-Maʾrifa, 1408 AH.

Sulamī, Abū ʿAbd al-Raḥmān Muḥammad b. usayn b. Muḥammad al-Azdī al-Nīshāpūrī al- (325-412 AH/936-1021 CE), *Ādāb al-Ṣuḥba wa usn al-ʿAshīra*. Tanta: Dār al-Ṣaḥāba li al-Turāth, 1410 AH/1990 CE.

Ibn Shāhīn, Abū Hafṣ ʿUmar b. Aḥmad b. ʿUthmān (297-385 AH), *al-Targhīb fī Faḍāʾil al-Aʿmāl wa Thawāb Dhālik*. Beirut: Dār al-Kutub al-ʿIlmiyya, 1424 AH/2004 CE.

Ibn ʿAbd al-Barr, Abū ʿUmar Yūsuf b. ʿAbd Allāh b. Muḥammad (368-463 AH/979-1071 CE), *Jāmiʿ Bayān al-ʿIlm wa Faḍlihi*. Beirut: Dār al-Kutub al-ʿIlmiyya, 1398 AH/1975 CE.

Ghazālī, Abū āmid Muḥammad b. Muḥammad (450-505 AH), *Iḥyāʾ ʿUlūm al-Dīn*. Beirut: Dār al-Maʿrifa.

Ibn Qudāma, Abū Muḥammad ʿAbd Allāh b. Aḥmad (541-620 AH), *al-Mutaḥābīn fī Allāh*. Damascus: Dār al-Ṭabaʿ, 1411 AH/1991 CE.
Ibn al-Qayyim, Abū ʿAbd Allāh Muḥammad b. Abī Bakr Ayyūb al-Jawziyya (691-751 AH), *al-Wābil al-Ṣayyib*. Beirut: Dār al-Kitāb al-ʿArabī, 1405 AH/1985 CE.
Māwardī, Abū al- usayn ʿAlī b. Muḥammad b. abīb al- (364-450 AH), *Adab al-Dunyā wa al-Dīn*. Cairo: Dār al-Miṣriyya al-Lubnāniyya, 1408 AH/1988 CE.
Maqdisī, Shams al-Dīn Abū ʿAbd Allāh Muḥammad b. Mufliḥ b. Muḥammad b. Mafraj al-Dimashqī al-, (763 AH), *al-Ādāb al-Sharʿiyya*. Beirut: Muʾassasa al-Risāla, 1417 AH/1996 CE.

History

Ibn Athīr, Abū al- asan ʿAlī b. Muḥammad b. ʿAbd al-Karīm al-Shaybānī al-Jazarī (555-630 AH/1160-1233 CE), *al-Kāmil fī al-Tārīkh*. Beirut: Dār Ṣādir, 1399 AH/1979 CE.
Abū Zahra, Muḥammad. *al-ʿAlāqāt al-Dawliyya fī al-Islam*. Cairo: Dār al-Fikr al-ʿArabī, 1995 CE.
Balādhurī, Aḥmad b. Yaḥyā b. Jābir al- (279 AH). *Futuḥ al-Buldān*. Beirut: Dār al-Kutub al-ʿIlmiyya, 1403 AH/1983 CE.
Ibn azm, ʿAlī b. Aḥmad b. Saʿīd al-Andalusī (384-456 AH/994-1064 CE), *al-Faṣl fī al-Milal wa al-Niḥal*. Beirut: Dār al-Jīl, 1416 AH/1996 CE & Cairo: Maktaba al-Khānjī.
Khaṭīb al-Baghdādī, Abū Bakr Aḥmad b. ʿAlī (392-463 AH/1002-1071 CE), *Tārīkh Baghdād*. Beirut: Dār al-Kutub al-ʿIlmiyya.
Ibn Khallāl, Aḥmad b. Muḥammad b. Hārūn b. Yazīd Abū Bakr (311-334 AH), *Aḥkām Ahl al-Milal min al-Jāmiʿ li Masāʾil al-Imām Aḥmad b. anbal*. Beirut: Dār al-Kutub al-ʿIlmiyya, 1414 AH/1994 CE.
Ibn Khaldūn, ʿAbd al-Raḥmān b. Muḥammad al-Haḍramī (732-808 AH), *Muqaddima*. Beirut: Dār al-Qalam, 1984 CE.
Shahrastānī, Abū al-Fatḥ Muḥammad b. ʿAbd al-Karīm b. Abī Bakr Aḥmad al- (479-548 AH), *al-Milal wa al-Niḥal*. Beirut: Dār al-Maʿrifa, 2001 CE.

Ṭabarī, Abū Jaʿfar Muḥammad b. Jarīr b. Yazīd b. Khālid (224-310 AH/839-923 CE), *Tārīkh al-Umam wa al-Mulūk*. Beirut: Dār al-Kutub al-ʿIlmiyya, 1407 AH.

Ṭūsī, Abū Jaʿfar Muḥammad b. asan al- (385-460 AH), *al-Iqtiṣād al-Hādī ilā Ṭarīq al-Rashād*. Tehran, Iran: Maktaba Jāmiʿ Chalstūn.

Ibn ʿAbd al- ikam, Abū al-Qāsim ʿAbd al-Raḥmān b. ʿAbd Allāh ʿAbd al- ikam (187-257 AH/803-871 CE), *Futūḥ Miṣr wa Akhbāruhā*. Beirut: Dār al-Fikr, 1416 AH/1996 CE.

Ibn ʿAsākir, Abū Qāsim ʿAlī b. asan b. Hiba Allāh (499-571 AH/1105-1167 CE), *Tārīkh Dimashq al-Kabīr (Tārīkh Ibn ʿAsākir)*. Beirut: Dār Iḥyāʾ al-Turāth al-ʿArabī, 1421 AH/2001 CE.

—. *Tārīkh Madīna Dimashq*. Beirut: Dār al-Fikr, 1995 CE.

Fākihī, Abū ʿAbd Allāh Muḥammad b. Isḥāq b. ʿAbbās al-Makkī al-, *Akhbār Makka fī Qadīm al-Dahr wa adītha*. Beirut: Dār Khiḍr, 1414 AH.

Qazwīnī, ʿAbd al-Karīm b. Muḥammad al-Rāfiʿī, *al-Tadwīn fī Akhbār Qazwīn*. Beirut: Dār al-Kutub al-ʿIlmiyya, 1987 CE.

Ibn Kathīr, Abū al-Fiḍāʾ Ismāʿīl b. ʿUmar b. Kathīr b. Ḍawʾ b. Kathīr b. Zarʿ Baṣrawī (701–774 AH/1301-1373 CE), *al-Bidāya wa al-Nihāya*. Beirut: Dār al-Fikr, 1419 AH/1998 CE & Maktaba al-Maʿārif.

Nimyarī, Abū Zayd ʿUmar b. Shayba al-Baṣrī al- (262 AH), *Akhbār al-Madīna*. Beirut: Dār al-Kutub al-ʿIlmiyya, 1417 AH/1996 CE.

Yaʿqūbī, Aḥmad b. Abī Yaʿqūb b. Jaʿfar al- (287 AH/897 CE), *Tārīkh al-Yaʿqūbī*. Beirut: Dār Ṣādir.

Linguistics

Ibn Athīr, Abū al-Saʿādāt Mubārak b. Muḥammad b. Muḥammad b. ʿAbd al-Karīm (544-606 AH/1149-1210 CE), *al-Nihāya fī Gharīb al- adīth wa al-Athar*. Qum, Iran: Muʾassasa Maṭbūʿātī Ismāʿīliyān, 1364 CE.

Azharī, Abū Manṣūr Muḥammad b. Aḥmad al- (282-370 AH), *Tahdhīb al-Lugha*. al-Dār al-Miṣriyya li al-Taʾlīf wa al-Tarjuma.

Thānwī, Muḥammad b. ʿAlī b. al-Qāḍī Muḥammad āmid b. Muḥammad Ṣābir al-Fārūqī al- anafī al- (1158 CE). *Kashshāf Iṣṭilāḥāt al-Funūn wa al-ʿUlūm*. Beirut: Maktaba Lubnān Nāshirūn, 1996 CE.

ājī Khalīfa, Muṣṭafā b. ʿAbd Allāh al- anafī (1017-1067 AH), *Kashf al-Ẓunūn*. Baghdad: al-Maktaba al-Muthannā, 1947 CE.

usaynī, Ibrāhīm b. Muḥammad (1054-1120 AH), *al-Bayān wa al-Taʿrīf*. Beirut: Dār al-Kitāb al-ʿArabī, 1401 CE.

Jurjānī, ʿAlī b. Muḥammad b. ʿAlī (740-816 AH), *al-Taʿrīfāt*. Beirut: ʿĀlam al-Kutub, 1416 AH/1996 CE.

Jazarī, Abū al-Saʿādāt Mubārak b. Muḥammad al- (544-606 AH). *al-Nihāya fī Gharīb al-Athar*. Beirut: al-Maktaba al-ʿIlmiyya, 1399 AH.

Daynūrī, Abū Bakr Aḥmad b. Marwān b. Muḥammad al-Qāḍī al-Mālikī al- (333 AH). *al-Majālisa wa al-Jawāhir al-ʿIlm*. Beirut: Dār Ibn azm, 1419 AH.

Rāghib al-Aṣfahānī, Abū Qāsim usayn b. Muḥammad b. Mafḍal (502 AH/1108 CE), *Muḥāḍarāt al-Adbāʾ wa Muḥāwarāt al-Shuʿarāʾ wa al-Bulaghāʾ*. Beirut: Dār al-Qalam, 1420 AH/1999 CE.

—. *al-Mufradāt fī Gharīb al-Qurʾān*. Beirut: Dār al-Maʿrifa.

Zamakhsharī, Jār Allāh Abū al-Qāsim Maḥmūd b. ʿUmar b. Muḥammad al-Khawārizmī al- (467–538 AH). *al-Fāʾiq fī Gharīb al- adīth*. Beirut: Dār al-Maʿrifa.

Saʿdī, Abū abīb, *al-Qāmūs al-Fiqhī*. Karachi, Pakistan: Idāra al-Qurʾān wa al-ʿUlūm al-Islāmiyya.

Shāfiʿī, Abū ʿAbd Allāh Muḥammad b. Idrīs (150-204 AH/767-819 CE), *Dīwān al-Shāfiʿī*. Cairo: Maktaba Ibn Sīnā.

Ibn Fāris, Abū al- usayn Aḥmad b. Fāris b. Zakariyyā al-Qazwīnī al-Rāzī (395 CE). *Muʿjam Maqāyīs al-Lugha*. Damascus: Ittiḥād al-Kitāb al-ʿArab, 1423 AH/2002 CE.

Qanūjī, Abū al-Ṭayyib Ṣiddīq b. asan al- (1248-1307 AH), *Abjad al-ʿUlūm al-Washī al-Marqūm fī Bayān Aḥwāl al-ʿUlūm*. Beirut: Dār al-Kutub al-ʿIlmiyya, 1978 CE.

Ibn Manẓūr, Muḥammad b. Mukrim b. ʿAlī b. Aḥmad b. Abī Qāsim b. Habqa al-Ifrīqī (630-711 AH/1232-1311 CE), *Lisān al-ʿArab*. Beirut: Dār al-Ṣādir.

Harawī, Abū ʿUbayd Aḥmad b. Muḥammad (410 AH). *al-Gharībīn fī al-Qurʾān wa al- adīth*. Beirut: Maktaba ʿAṣariyya, 1999 CE.

Miscellaneous

amīdullāh, Dr. Muḥammad, *Majmūʿa al-Wathāʾiq al-Siyāsiyya*. Beirut: Dār al-Irshād.

Muḥammad Abduhu, (1268-1323 AH/1849-1905 CE). *al-Muslimūn wa al-Islām*.

Ismāʿīl Muḥammad Mīqā, *Mabādī al-Islām wa Minhājuhu*.

Taʿlīm-e-Amn aur Islām, Darsī Kitāb Barāʾey Aʿla Thānwī Darajāt. Islamabad, Pakistan: Idāra Amn aur Taʿlīm, 1435 AH/2014 CE.

www.binbaz.org.sa/mat/1934

Books in English

Hitti, Phillip K, *History of the Arabs*. Macmillan Education Ltd., 1991.

John Laffin, *Holy War: Islam Fights*. London, Graffton Books, 1988.

Karen Armstrong, *Holy War: The Crusades and their Impact on Today's World*. New York: Anchor Books, 2001.

Reuven Firestone, *Jihad: The Origin of Holy War in Islam*. New York: Oxford University Press, 1999.

Suhas Majumdar, *JIHAD: The Islamic doctrine of Permanent War*. New Delhi: The Voice of India, 1994.

Watt, William Montgomery, *Islamic Political Thought: The Basic Concepts*. Edinburgh University Press, 1980.